FLUENCY 6

With Information Technology

SKILLS, CONCEPTS, & CAPABILITIES

LAWRENCE SNYDER
UNIVERSITY OF WASHINGTON

Pearson
Boston Columbus Indianapolis New York San Francisco Upper Saddle River
Amsterdam Cape Town Dubai London Madrid Milan Munich Paris Montreal Toronto
Delhi Mexico City Sao Paulo Sydney Hong Kong Seoul Singapore Taipei Tokyo

Editorial Director, ECS: Marcia Horton
Acquisitions Editor: Matt Goldstein
Director of Marketing: Christy Lesko
Marketing Manager: Yezan Alayan
Marketing Assistant: Jon Bryant
Director of Production: Erin Gregg
Managing Editor: Jeff Holcomb
Senior Project Manager: Marilyn Lloyd
Manufacturing Buyer: Linda Sager
Cover Designer: Joyce Cosentino Wells
Text Designer: Gillian Hall
Manager, Text Permissions: Tim Nicholls
Text Permission Project Manager: Jenell Forschler
Manager, Image Permissions: Karen Sanatar
Cover Image: © Fotolia
Media Project Manager: Renata Butera
Full-Service Project Management: Gillian Hall
Composition: Laserwords
Printer/Binder: Courier Kendallville
Cover Printer: Lehigh-Phoenix Color

Credits and acknowledgments borrowed from other sources and reproduced, with permission, appear on the Credits page in the endmatter of this textbook.

Library of Congress Cataloging-in-Publication Data
Snyder, Lawrence.
Fluency with information technology: skills, concepts, & capabilities/Lawrence Snyder—6th ed.
p. cm.
Includes bibliographical references and index.
ISBN 978-0-13-357739-6
1. Information technology. 2. Computer literacy. I. Title.
T58.5.S645 2014
004--dc23 2014000850

10 9 8 7 6 5 4 3 2 1

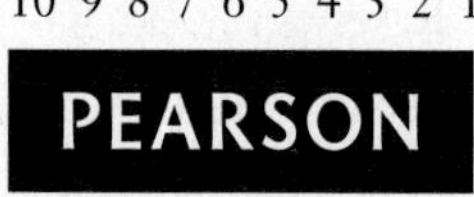

www.pearsonhighered.com

ISBN 10: 0-13-357739-2
ISBN 13: 978-0-13-357739-6

PREFACE

WELCOME to the Sixth Edition of *Fluency with Information Technology: Skills, Concepts, & Capabilities*. This book teaches the foundational ideas of computing. Today's students, having grown up in a world in which computers are ubiquitous, know how to use them, intuitively. But *use* is not understanding. Today's students belong to a world that requires them to be "computational thinkers," able to conceptualize how computation can be used effectively. Few students will work as programmers, but most will decide how to apply computation. And many will imagine new ways for computers to serve humanity. To be effective at these tasks, they must understand the fundamental ideas of computing. This is their book.

What's New in This Edition?

More than any previous edition, this sixth edition illustrates a fundamental point about *Fluency*: Though the concepts are constant, their practical manifestations change at warp speed. Concept-wise, the sixth edition retains all of the fundamental ideas that underlie the Fluency vision. In practice, however, much of the text has been rewritten to accommodate how students encounter computation: advances in smartphones, HTML5, CSS3, new browser support for JavaScript programming, cloud technology, and on and on. These affect how students use and perceive the fundamentals. Topics like crowd sourcing, privacy, security, phishing, AI, netiquette, copyright, and so forth evolve, and so they must be explained in contemporary terms consistent with student experience. And "ambient knowledge" changes, too. For example, unlike the past today's students have at least heard a term like *algorithm*. But, awareness is not understanding, and so the sixth edition has been revised to explain the concept with a new, more intuitive approach. Other newly familiar terms have been similarly treated.

Readers familiar with earlier versions of *Fluency* should take a close look at this sixth edition. It maintains the core "fluency vision," while positioning the presentation squarely in the second decade of the 21st century.

Briefly, the four parts of Fluency have been updated as follows:

- Part 1 has undergone a complete makeover. Chapter 1 "Defining IT," Chapter 3 "Networking," and Chapter 5 "Web" are (again) new. Chapter 4 "HTML" is redeveloped to teach HTML5 and CSS3. Chapter 2 "Human-Computer Interface" and Chapter 6 "Debugging" have been substantially revised.
- In Part 2, the "bits part" of Chapter 7 "Digital Information" has been redeveloped, Chapter 9 "Computer Organization" has been completely rewritten to be more intuitive, and Chapter 10 "Algorithms" is new and much simplified.

- In Part 3, Chapter 11 "Social Implications" is mostly new, and Chapter 12 "Privacy and Security" is completely revised to deal with recently revealed privacy threats (NSA) and ongoing security attacks. The "Spreadsheets" chapters (13 and 14) have been revised to increase compatibility with different implementations, including various Excel versions. Chapter 15 "Database Concepts" has a complete reformulation of the relational model. Chapter 16 the "iDiary Database" received a wholesale revision.
- Finally, in Part 4, the "JavaScript" chapters (17–21) have been redeveloped to use the Firefox Scratchpad sandbox for code development, a definite pedagogical advance. Chapter 22, the artificial intelligence chapter, has had its Watson discussion augmented by a new interview with David Ferrucci, the Watson project leader.

A number of "Try It" exercises and the end-of-chapter Review Questions have been heavily revised; new exercises have been added. Further resources are listed below.

Fluency—a Text for Computer Science Principles

The vision of *Being Fluent with Information Technology* (see below) is to introduce fundamental computational concepts to college students; implementing that vision was the original purpose of this book. The Computer Science Principles vision is virtually identical, but for high school students. Think of a college Fluency course as the class that successful AP CS Principles students get credit for. It follows that *Fluency* is a suitable text for CS Principles.

Depending on specific choices of the instructor, the two curricula overlap about 85–90 percent in terms of concepts and ideas. Both cover algorithms, digital data and metadata, programming, Internet fundamentals, security and privacy, AI, and so on. The difference is more on emphasis than with content. The courses have been described as

> "Fluency introduces computing ideas to enhance students' ability to apply computation" and
>
> "CS Principles introduces computing ideas for their scientific richness."

Both are important (and not mutually exclusive) goals; I have ensured that *Fluency* fulfills both.

To illustrate, recall that the Computer Science Principles curriculum is guided by the Seven Big Ideas [www.csprinciples.org]. The content of *Fluency*'s chapters (sections or possibly the entire chapter) aligns with the big ideas as follows:

- Creativity—4, 5, 6, 10, 16, 18, 19, 20, 21
- Abstraction—1, 4, 10, 17, 18, 19, 20, 21
- Data—7, 8, 13, 14, 15, 16, 17, 22
- Algorithms—1, 2, 7, 8, 9, 10, 22
- Programming—4, 6, 9, 10, 16, 17, 18, 19, 20, 21, 22
- Internet—3, 4, 5, 8, 11, 12, 16, 19, 20, 21
- Global Impacts—1, 2, 3, 4, 5, 9, 11, 12, 22

The alignment is explained in finer grain detail in the Instructor's Resources.

What Is Fluency with Information Technology?

This book is inspired by a report from the National Research Council (NRC), *Being Fluent with Information Technology*. In that study, commissioned by the National Science Foundation, the committee asserted that traditional computer literacy does not have the "staying power" students need to keep pace with the rapid changes in IT. The study concluded that the educational "bar needs to be raised" if students' knowledge is to evolve and adapt to that change. The recommended alternative, dubbed *fluency with information technology*, or *FIT*, was a package of skills, concepts, and capabilities wrapped in a project-oriented learning approach that ensures that the content is fully integrated. The goal is to help people become effective IT users immediately and to prepare them for lifelong learning.

The Vision

This textbook largely implements the vision of the NRC committee in which they proposed a three-part content and recommended integrating that content by using projects.

Three-Part Content

To make students immediately effective and launch them on the path of lifelong learning, they need to learn three types of knowledge: Skills, Concepts, and Capabilities.

- **Skills** refers to proficiency with contemporary computer applications such as email, word processing, Web searches, and so forth. This knowledge, originally described as "literacy," is now generally known to students on arrival at college; it need not be taught. Only "advanced skills"—essentially spreadsheets and database queries—remain in *Fluency*.
- **Concepts** refers to the fundamental knowledge underpinning IT, such as computer functionality, digital representation of information, assessment of information authenticity, and so forth. Concepts provide the principles on which students will build new understanding as IT evolves.
- **Capabilities** refers to higher-level thinking processes such as problem solving, reasoning, complexity management, and troubleshooting. Creativity is a key capability. Capabilities embody modes of thinking that are essential to exploiting IT, but they apply broadly. Reasoning, problem solving, and so forth are standard components of education; their significance in IT makes them topics of emphasis in the *Fluency* approach.

For each component, the NRC report lists 10 recommended items, which are covered as needed in this book.

Audience

This book is designed for freshmen "nontechies," students who will not be majoring in science, engineering, or math. ("Techies" benefit too, but because "hot shots" can intimidate others, they should be discouraged from taking the class, or better, encouraged to join an accelerated track or honors section.) No mathematical skills are required beyond arithmetic. There are no prerequisites.

Chapter Dependencies

Fluency with Information Technology is organized so that it can be taught in a variety of ways. In addition to the preliminary material in Chapters 1 and 2, social issues in Chapters 11 and 12, and the wrap-up in Chapter 23, the overall structure of the book includes stand-alone chapters with few dependencies, as well as small chapter sequences devoted to a sustained topic. The sequences are as follows:

- Chapters 3, 4, and 5—networking, HTML, and information
- Chapters 7, 8, 9, and 10—data representations, computers, and algorithms
- Chapters 13, 14, 15, and 16—spreadsheets and database principles
- Chapters 17, 18, 19, 20, and 21—programming in JavaScript

One effective way to use this design is to present one of the chapter sequences as the basis for a project assignment. Then, while the students are working on the project—projects may span two or more weeks—material from stand-alone chapters is covered.

There are many sequences, but three stand out as especially effective to present the material:

- **Networking cycle.** The linear sequence of chapters is designed to begin with information and networking and progressively advance through computation and databases to JavaScript, where it returns to the networking theme. This is the basic Chapters 1 to 23 sequence, adjusted by local reordering to accommodate the timing of projects as needed.
- **Internet forward.** I teach *Fluency* in the 1–10, 17–21, 11–16, 22–23 order. This approach begins with information and HTML, progresses through to algorithms, then jumps to JavaScript to continue the Web page building theme, and finally wraps up with databases. The strategy is dictated largely by the logistics of teaching the class in a quarter (10 weeks) and is recommended for that situation.
- **Traditional.** In this approach, the material is taught to parallel the time sequence of its creation. So, information representation and computers come well before networking. In this case, the order is 1–2, (22), 7–16, 3–6, 17–23. Chapter 22, which contains more philosophical content like the Turing test, Kasparov/Deep Blue chess tournament, and Watson, might optionally be presented early for its foundational content.

Each of these strategies has a compelling pedagogical justification. The one chosen depends more on the instructor's taste and class logistics than on a need to present material in a specific order.

Pedagogical Features

- **Learning Objectives:** Each chapter opens with a list of the key concepts that readers should master after reading the chapter.

There are several boxed features that appear throughout the text to aid in students' understanding of the material:

- FLUENCY TIP Practical hints and suggestions for everyday computer use

- 

and FLUENCY BYTE Interesting facts and statistics
- FLUENCY ALERT Warnings and explanations of common mistakes
- 

Short, in-chapter exercises with provided solutions

Throughout the text, notable material is distinguished by the following features:

- FLUENCY BACK STORY A historical look at some of the major people and milestones in computing
- **Glossary:** Important words and phrases are bold throughout the text, and a glossary of terms is included at the end of the book; glossary terms are bold in the book's index
- **Answers:** Solutions are provided to selected questions for the multiple-choice and short-answer sections
- **Appendix A:** XHTML reference including a chart of Web-safe colors
- **Appendix B:** RSA public key cryptosystem
- **Appendix C:** The XML database and the XSL template style information for iDiary in Chapter 16
- **Appendix D:** JavaScript programming rules
- **Appendix E:** Bean Counter Program: A complete JavaScript and HTML example
- **Appendix F:** Memory Bank Page: A complete JavaScript and HTML example
- **Appendix G:** Smooth Motion Application: A complete JavaScript and HTML example

Supplements

The Companion Web site for *Fluency with Information Technology* is located at:

www.pearsonhighered.com/snyder

The following student supplements are available at the Web site:

- **23 online labs (1 for each chapter in the book).** The labs are designed to more fully explore (and test) students' understanding of concepts in the book and how those issues or concepts apply to their lives. For example, in Chapter 1 the lab explores the conflicting interests of searchable, interconnected information and privacy. It directs students to a variety of Web-based resources that can help them understand what kinds of information they (and their devices) are sharing, which can be surprisingly personal and sometimes can even uniquely identify the user. Understanding the scope and type of information sharing that is happening helps reinforce the overall theme of understanding how things work "under the hood." See the listing of labs at the end of the preface or see the complete set of labs at www.pearsonhighered.com/snyder.

- **Computer Skills Workbook by Sharon Scollard.** This book covers the basics of Microsoft Office suite and includes 14 comprehensive labs on Excel, Word, PowerPoint, and other topics.
- **VideoNotes.** VideoNotes are short, tutorial videos that enhance concepts presented in the textbook.
- **HTML sources, database designs, and JavaScript programs used in the textbook examples**
- **JavaScript reference card**
- **Glossary flashcards**
- **A downloadable workbook (PDF) on Alice and the Alice development environment**

The following instructor supplements are available to qualified instructors only. Please contact your local Pearson Education representative for information on how to access them (you can find your rep at www.pearsonhighered.com).

- **PowerPoint slides**
- **Instructor's Solutions Manual**
- **Test Bank**
- **Test Generator** (available for use with Blackboard Learn, Blackboard CE/Vista, Moodle, Angel, Sakai, and D2L platforms)

Note to Students

Fluency is a somewhat unusual topic, making this a somewhat unusual book. I have one bit of advice to make it easier to learn this material.

- **Study *Fluency* steadily.** If this book is successful, it will change the way you think, making you better at problem solving, better at reasoning, better at debugging, and so forth. These Capabilities are useful in IT and elsewhere in life, so they make learning *Fluency* worthwhile. But changing how you think won't happen by putting the book under your pillow. It'll take some studying. To learn *Fluency* you must apply good study habits: read the book, do the end-of-chapter exercises (answers to selected questions appear at the back of the book), begin your assignments early, ask questions, and so on. I think it's a good idea if you spend some time online studying *Fluency* (instead of surfing) every day, because it takes time for the ideas to sink in. Students with good study habits tend to do well in *Fluency* class, and because it improves their problem-solving abilities, and more, they become even better students! It takes some discipline but it pays.

Finally, reading this book is enhanced by having a computer handy so you can try the examples. The files used are available at pearsonhighered.com/snyder. Good luck! Writing this book has truly been a pleasure. I hope reading it is equally enjoyable.

Acknowledgments

It is a pleasure to thank my collaborators in the creation of the *Fluency* concept, the NRC Committee on Computer Literacy—Al Aho, Marcia Linn, Arnie Packer, Allen Tucker, Jeff Ullman, and Andy van Dam. Special thanks go to Herb Lin of the NRC staff who assisted throughout the *Fluency* effort, tirelessly and in his usual great good humor. Two enthusiastic supporters of *Fluency*—Bill Wulf of the National Academy of Engineering and John Cherniavski of the National Science Foundation—have continually supported this effort in more ways than I am aware. It has been a pleasure to know and work with this team.

I am particularly grateful for the keen insights and valuable feedback from the reviewers of this book. For this edition, my thanks go to the following: Deborah Noonan (College of William & Mary), Jie Meichsner (Saint Cloud State University), Melissa Wiggins (Mississippi College), Lynn Thibodeau (University of Hartford), Paolina Centonze (Iona College), Timothy Highley (La Salle University), Thomas Bennet (Mississippi College).

Thank you to Susan Evans for contributing to the end-of-chapter Review Questions.

Thanks to Rebecca Greenberg, whose editing has improved the content and presentation significantly; as always it is a great pleasure to work with Gillian Hall. And, once again it is my pleasure to thank Matt Goldstein and the whole Pearson team, especially Jeff Holcomb and Marilyn Lloyd.

Finally, my wife, Julie, has been patient, encouraging, and, most important, a continual source of good humor throughout this effort. It is with my deepest appreciation that I thank her for everything.

—Larry Snyder, January 2014

For Julie

CONTENTS

PART 3 Data and Information

Location of VideoNotes in the Text

Online Labs

This series of labs is designed to help students understand different perspectives on technology, to get hands-on experience with tools, and to think about what it means to live in a world where more and more of what they do on a daily basis involves using technology.

Each lab has an introduction, a "To Consider" section, a set of exercises, and a "Moving On" summary. Once students become familiar with one lab, they'll know what to expect in the others.

Labs can be accessed at www.pearsonhighered.com/snyder

Lab 00	Introduction and Resources
Lab 01	Information on the Web
Lab 02	Human Computer Interfaces
Lab 03	How the Internet Is Connected
Lab 04	HTML Introduction
Lab 05	Search
Lab 06	Debugging
Lab 07	Digital Encoding
Lab 08	Digital Media
Lab 09	The Fetch/Execute Cycle
Lab 10	Algorithmic Thinking
Lab 11	Collaboration over the Web
Lab 12	Privacy
Lab 13	Introduction to Spreadsheets
Lab 14	Data and Information Visualizations
Lab 15	Introduction to Databases
Lab 16	Adding an RSS Feed to the iDiary
Lab 17	Introduction to JavaScript
Lab 18	Extending the Bean Counter Program

The Master said: "To learn something and then put it into practice at the right time. Is this not a joy?"

—THE ANALECTS OF CONFUCIUS

PART 1

Becoming Skilled at Computing

CHAPTER

INTRODUCTION

OUR STUDY of computing assumes that you have used computers your whole life. Being an accomplished computer user means that you have a general idea of how to make computing systems work for you, so there is no need to teach you to be a user. Instead, we will explain "what's happening" under the glitzy graphics and "how it works" behind the magic. Most of us wonder from time to time what makes the technology click, and that is reason enough to study this material. But what you learn in this class will almost certainly make you a better and more knowledgeable user. So whether it's curiosity or knowhow that drives your interest, learning computing more fully will pay off.

Part 1 focuses on setting a firm foundation for the future. The Internet is everywhere and consumes our lives. We need to know more about it, how it works, and how to use it effectively. We begin by setting the context for further study, and explaining why you do what you do intuitively. We study how networking works, try our hand at HTML, tune-up our searching skills, and practice debugging. These topics will get us off to a fast start.

CHAPTER 1

Defining Information Technology

Terms of Endearment

learning objectives

- Explain what was the "big idea" of computing inventions
- Explain why it's important to know the right word
- Define basic hardware and software terms
- Define and give examples of "idea" terms

CHAPTER 1

I have always wished for my computer to be as easy to use as my telephone; my wish has come true because I can no longer figure out how to use my telephone.

—BJARNE STROUSTRUP, 2011, INVENTOR OF C++

It would appear that we have [as a society] reached the limits of what it is possible to achieve with computer technology, although one should be careful with such statements as they tend to sound pretty silly in five years.

—JOHN VON NEUMANN, 1947, COMPUTER PIONEER

PROCESSING DIGITAL information is a technology that is more than 120 years old; that is, it was developed before any of us was born. For college students, that's true for most of the other technologies computation relies on, too. It seems as if computing has always been here, created by wizards in the distant past. So, as you start to become "Fluent" in information technology (IT), it makes sense to step back and look briefly at how digital computation has developed, and "what was so great" about the key inventions over the years.

This chapter begins with a short overview of "computing's greatest hits," the most significant ideas that are responsible for what we see and use today. Most of us could list some of the important technologies—computers, microchips, the Internet—but we are less familiar with what it is about those technologies that makes them so important. What was the big idea? So that will be our emphasis: To explain what the problem was that the idea solved, and how it was implemented to advance our usage.

The other goal of this chapter is to introduce a few conceptual words such as "algorithm" that are important in computing. Like algorithm, you've probably heard them used, so the task is simply to be sure we agree on what they mean, because we will be using them throughout the remainder of the book.

Computation's Greatest Hits

In this section we take a fast tour of the eight most important developments that make digital computation what it is today:

- Digitizing information
- Stored-program computers
- Transistors
- Integrated circuits
- "Personal" computers
- The Internet
- World Wide Web
- Layered software

The list is by no means exhaustive—there are other extremely important technical ideas. This list includes only items that "changed everything" and thus justify our close attention. Figure 1.1 shows a timeline for computer-related milestones.

Digitizing Information

The dictionary definition of "digital information" says it is "data represented using numbers." For example, this book is represented by its ISBN number, 10: 0-13-282893-6, which is actually several numbers encoding different aspects of it. Archaeologists and

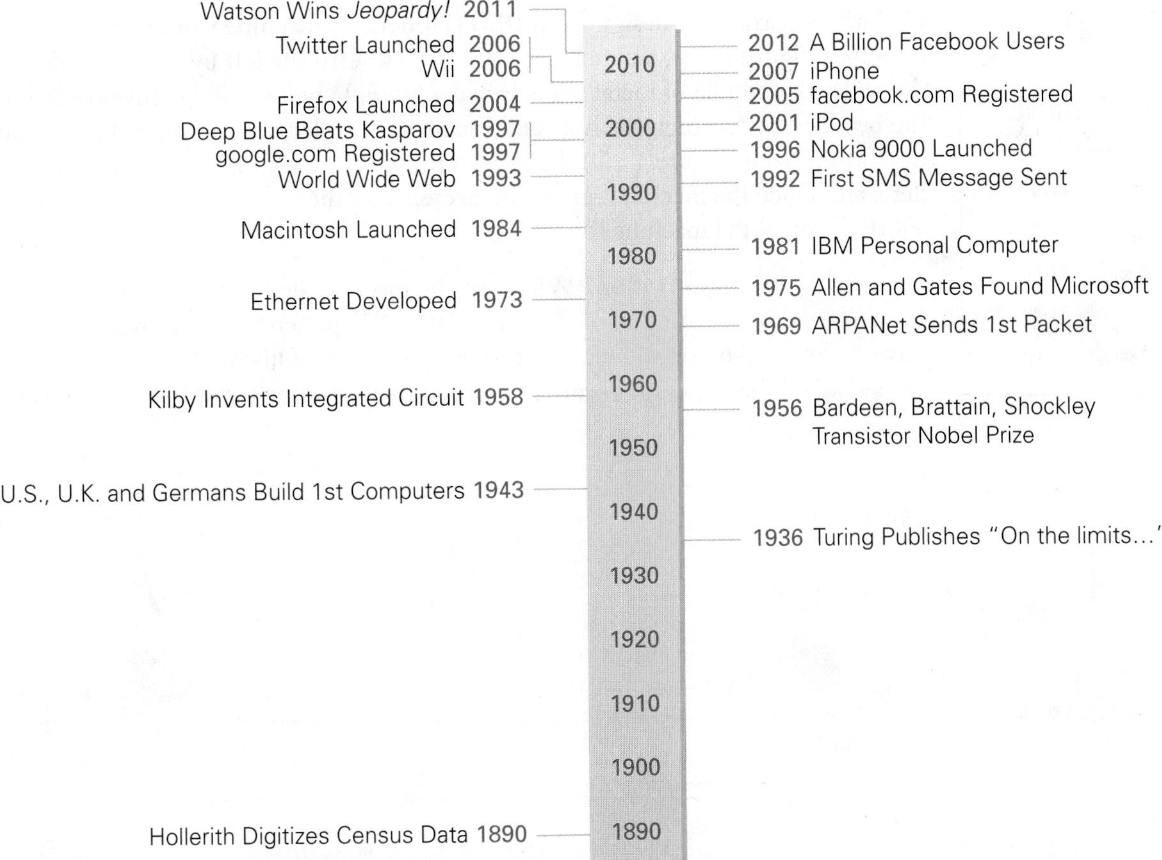

Figure 1.1 Selected Events In Computing: More than 90 years passed between the first automated use of digital information and the announcement of the PC.

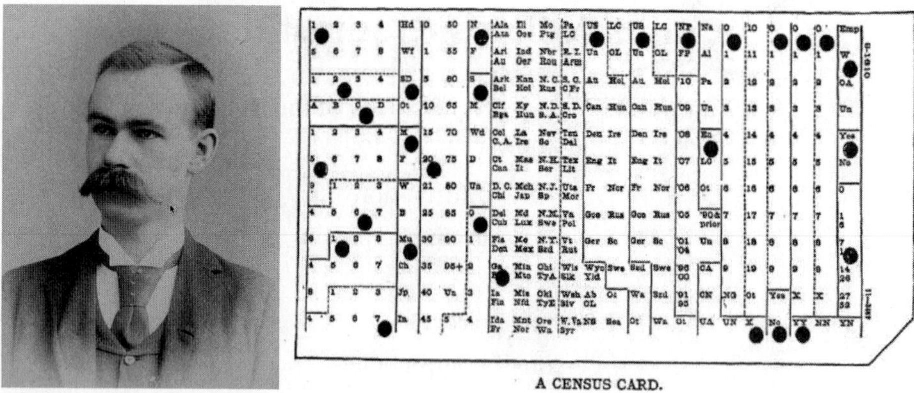

Figure 1.2 Digital pioneers: Herman Hollerith and the punch card he invented.

historians tell us that people have probably used data represented as numbers since earliest times. Representing information as numbers was not the big breakthrough. Getting a machine to read digital information was the breakthrough.

Herman Hollerith is generally credited with the first "production" application of digital information. Hollerith was a statistician employed by the U.S. Census Bureau in the nineteenth century. He knew that processing census data by hand was slow—the 1880 census took eight years to complete. So, Hollerith invented a machine to tabulate data based on holes punched in cards (see Figure 1.2(b)). It was used for the 1890 census, allowing its analysis to be completed in one year.

How to Digitize a Punch Card. To describe how to digitize a punch card, we use two diagrams illustrating a design from IBM (Hollerith's machine worked slightly differently). In Figure 1.3(a), a punch card is moved toward the left by a metal roller. Above the roller is a bundle of metal wires called a *brush*. When the hole moves over the roller, the brush pokes through the hole and touches the roller, making an electrical connection, as shown in Figure 1.3(b). In the figure, the electrical signal indicates that a "2" was detected. Once the machine senses the presence of the hole, it passes the signal on to another part of the machine for further processing.

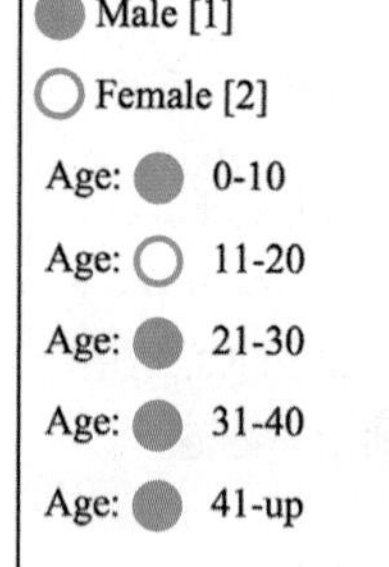

Processing the Information. What can the machine do in response to detecting a "2"? It can, for example, place all of the cards with a "2" punch into a separate stack. If the cards had the encoding shown at left, then the stack would contain all input cards encoding females. The stack of "1" cards would contain all input cards for males. The machine

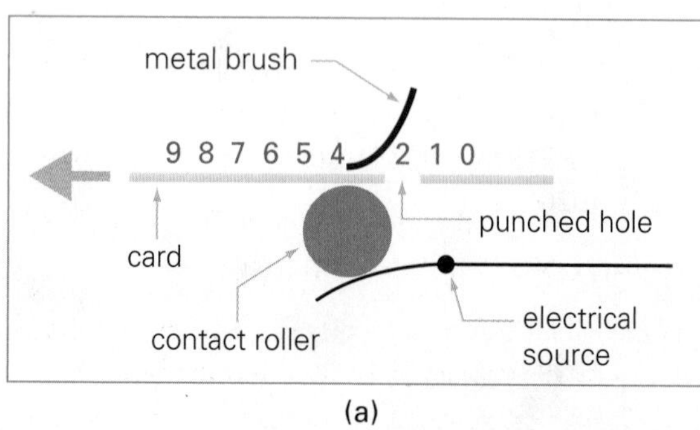

(a)

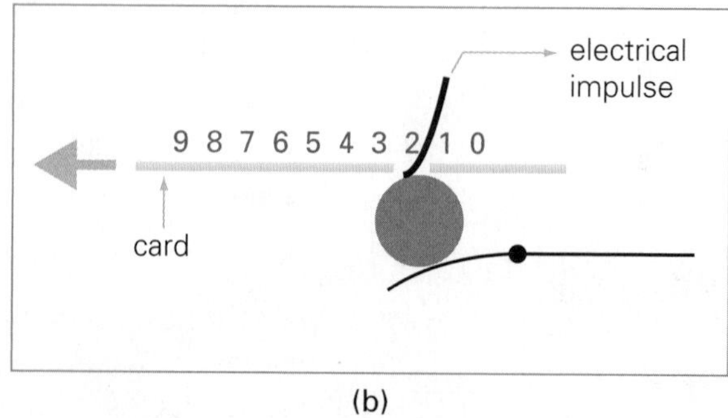

(b)

Figure 1.3 Operation of a punch card reader: (a) the card is moved leftward by a metal roller, and (b) when the hole passes over the roller, the metal brush makes an electrical connection.

can count the cards using its odometer, which counts cards like a car counts miles. By first separating the input into the two stacks, and then running each stack through the machine again to count them, the number of males and females in the input can be determined mechanically.

No Computer Needed. Notice that this device is not a computer. It is a card reader and stacker, detecting the presence or absence of a hole in a card. But, by careful application, it can perform information-processing activies such as determining how many men and women are in the population.

1.1 Counting Boys. Imagine a large stack of cards encoded as shown above. Suppose that when the machine reads the right column, it places the cards in one of five stacks based on the holes in the cards. Explain how to use the card reader/stacker to determine how many males in the input are under 21 years of age.

Stored-Program Computers

Hollerith's idea was a huge hit. Punch cards and tabulating machines were immediately adopted by other governments and by businesses. Punch cards were the primary digital technology for roughly 75 years. But, they weren't perfect.

All Hardware All the Time. Tabulating machines were electro-mechanical devices. They were all *hardware*—built out of wires, rollers, and motors. Thus, to change the operations that the machine performed required it to be rewired. To be more versatile, machines evolved to have plugboards to help "programmers" rewire them, but it was neither fast nor glamorous. Its main problem, however, was that only very simple operations were possible when the "program" was expressed using wires.

Put the Program in Memory. The electronic computer solved the "rewiring" problem by using a special device, the *central processing unit* (explained in Chapter 9), which performs instructions stored in the computer's memory. This effectively changed instructions from "hard," that is, wires, to "soft," that is, memory bits. Thus, the name *software*.

Compared to hard instructions, the advantages of soft instructions are huge:

- Programs can be changed rapidly, simply by loading new instructions into the memory; it's a feature you use every time you double-click or tap on an app.
- Programs can be much more complex, being limited only by the size of the memory—a limitation easily overcome—and the ingenuity of programmers.
- Computations are autonomous, meaning that they can run on their own without a person attending to them to, say, feed in punch cards.

Creating the central processing unit (CPU) to interpret instructions was a tremendous advancement, and it is a defining property of a "digital computer."

Big and Expensive. The main problem with early computers, and especially the CPU part, was their complexity: It is a difficult technical problem to build a hardware device that can read, decode, and perform instructions. It takes many parts, and at the beginning none of them had undergone any miniaturization. So, the original computers were enormous, filling entire rooms. The photos of ENIAC (Figures 1.4 and 1.5), the

Figure 1.4 ENIAC. The Electronic Numerical Integrator and Calculator, started in 1943 and finished in 1946, shown in its formal portrait.

first electronic computer, show its huge cabinets and a half dozen people working on it. Built at the University of Pennsylvania, it weighed 30 tons, contained more than 17,000 vacuum tubes, and reportedly dimmed the streetlights in Philadelphia when it was powered up.

Burned Out. Reliability—or the lack of it—was another major headache for early computer developers. Electonic circuits were built from vacuum tubes (see Figure 1.4(a)), which were reasonably reliable for most applications. But the complexity of an instruction-executing CPU required tens of thousands of them to work all at once (see Figure 1.4(b)), and that takes a lot better reliability. The chances were good that one or more tubes would fail at power-up or after sustained computation, causing the computer to crash.

For all of its initial challenges, the electronic computer became a powerful, "game changing" tool within a decade. The main reason: transistors.

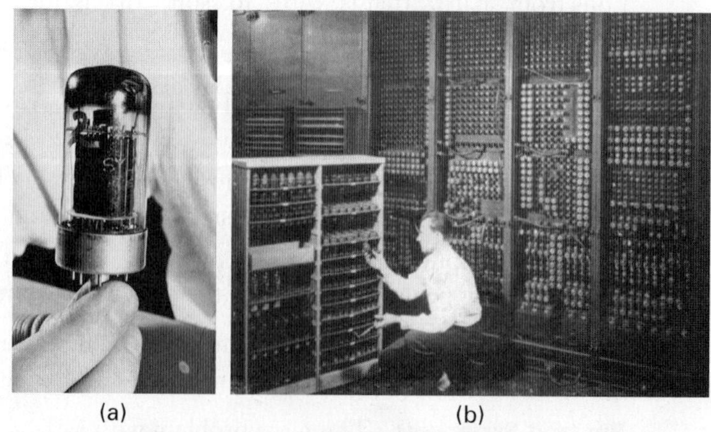

Figure 1.5 Vacuum tubes for ENIAC: (a) ENIAC-era vacuum tube; (b) technician inspecting ENIAC's vacuum tube racks, most of which are to his right.

The Beginning of Computer Science. So, did the computer science (CS) field start with the invention of the computer? No. Most people mark the start of CS as 1936—before any computer in our present sense of the word existed. That year Alan M. Turing wrote a landmark paper on the (theortical) limits to computation: *On Computable Numbers with an Application to the Entscheidungs Problem*; see Chapter 22 for more about Turing's ideas. The name "computer science" was adopted in the 1960s.

The Switch to Transistors

In 1956, three Bell Labs scientists—John Bardeen, Walter Brattain, and William Shockley—received the Nobel Prize for their 1947 invention of the semiconductor transistor, shown in Figure 1.6(a).

Transistors solved many of the toughest problems facing computer engineers. Transistors are

- low power, meaning less heat (and streetlight dimming),
- extremely reliable, and
- small in size and weight.

Though there are other advantages compared to vacuum tubes, these features of transistors changed electronics dramatically. Computers got much, much smaller, extremely reliable, and very cheap compared to their predecessors. This made computers affordable (to corporations), but it mainy allowed them to have much more complex CPUs.

Much Assembly Required. Building a computer or any large electronic system in the 1950s and 60s—even with transistors—was a tedious and time-consuming activity, because the tens of thousands of separate parts had to be assembled. Each transistor (three wires), each capacitor (two wires), and each resistor (two wires) had to be soldered on to circuit boards (see Figure 1.6(c)). Though the boards were preprinted with connecting wires, they still had to be populated with parts. Memory was made by stringing tiny magnetic "donuts" onto a grid of wire threads. It was expensive, tedious, and often unreliable, though not as unreliable as vacuum tube computers.

If computers were still built this way, they would still be rare.

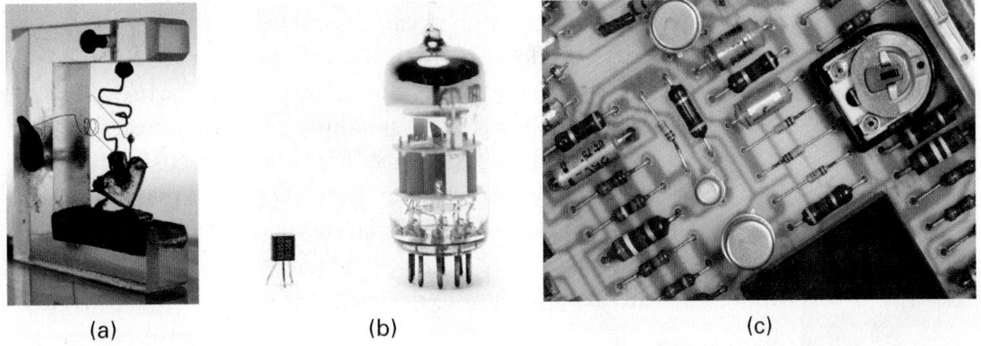

(a) (b) (c)

Figure 1.6 Transistors: (a) the first transistor made by Bardeen, Brattain, and Shockley; (b) a size comparison of a packaged transistor compared to a vacuum tube; and (c) a circuit board with electronic components mounted.

Making a Machine. Building electronic equipement with discrete components is nicely presented in a beautifully produced AT&T Archives video called *The Hello Machine* (www.youtube.com/watch?v=8uMbpaFp3i4). The equipment is an electronic switching system for telephones, which isn't a computer in the sense we're discussing, but the scale, components and assembly techniques are the same as for computers of the day. In addition to funky 1970s music, there are several points to notice: circuit board populating [1:18], the many manual steps in assembly [2:10–4:20], and the suspicious "please start" command [9:47]. Computers were built by the same process.

The Hello Machine

Integrated Circuits

The problem of efficiently assembling computers out of trasistors, resistors, capacitors, and wires was solved by integration. It is the "silicon technology" that gave Silicon Valley its name.

5 B Boron 10.811	6 C Carbon 12.011	7 N Nitrogen 14.00674
13 Al Aluminum 26.981539	14 Si Silicon 28.0855	15 P Phosphorus 30.973762
31 Ga Gallium 69.732	32 Ge Germanium 72.64	33 As Arsenic 74.92159

Integration. Integrated circuits (ICs) are monolithic blocks (chips) made of silicon and closely related elements in which both active parts like transistors and connective parts like wires are fabricated together in a multistep process. For example, wires and contacts are made of aluminum, and transistors are made of silicon that has been doped—yes, that's the technical term for contaminating pure silicon—with boron or phosphorous. With ICs, parts are connected together before they are even fully formed; this is dramatically different than manufacturing the components first and later connecting them.

Photolithography. The technique that makes ICs so spectacularly successful is *photolithography*. In photolithography, chip makers "print" the wires (and all the other parts) onto the chip. (Chapter 9 has diagrams of how this works.) Beginning with a wafer of pure silicon, a series of layers is printed, each contributing to one part of the overall circuit. For example, in the finished chip at left we see the last (top) layer of aluminum wires. The layer below it is a transparent layer of insulator (glass) separating the top layer of wires from another layer of wires below, which we see the outlines of. Notice that the glass layer has been printed to have holes in it called *contact cuts* (squares at the end of the wire) so the top layer of wires can connect at the right places to lower layers.

Top View

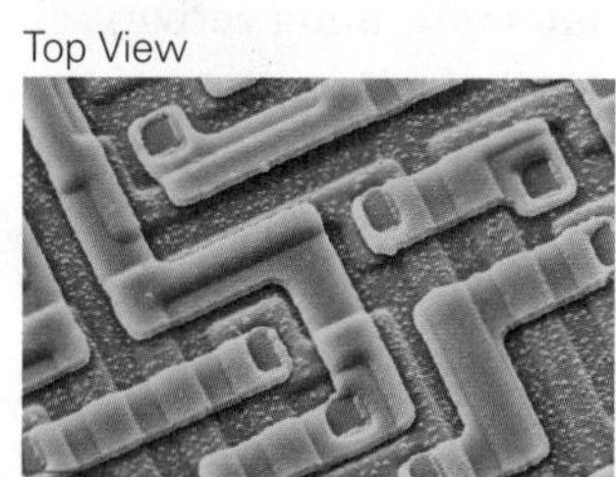

Cross Section

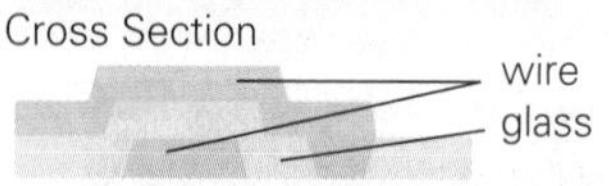

The Genius of Printing. To print on a chip, the photolithography process requires a mask to specify the shapes of a layer—it's like a photographic negative used before digital cameras. Because the printing uses light passing through the mask, it doesn't matter how complex or simple the mask is. Like printing a newspaper, which costs the same to print 5 words on a page or 5,000 words, silicon chip layers can be as simple or as complicated as needed. It costs the same to print the layer either way. This is a spectacular advantage, because when ICs became available computer engineers could make circuits as complicated as necessary. The problem of the tabulating machines, ENIAC, and discrete component computers—complexity is expensive—was now solved. Complexity is cheap to manufacture, though it remains expensive to design.

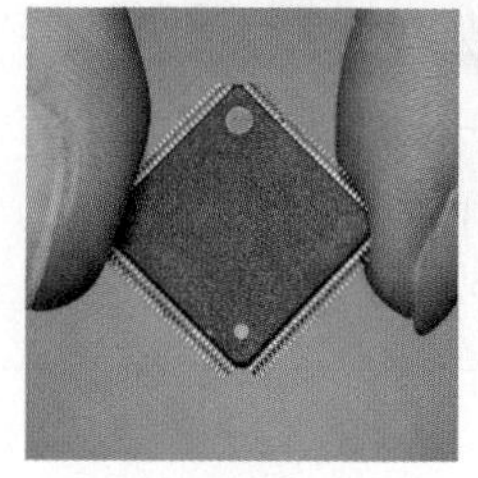

Progress? The payoff from transistors assembled as integrated circuits fabricated using photolithography has been monumental. Computers that are almost immeasureably more powerful than the ENIAC, shown in Figure 1.4, are fabricated as chips that can be held between two fingers. (And the chips often contain multiple computers.)

"Personal" Computers

Not only did ICs vanquish the complexity issue, but the "silicon foundries"—the companies that manufactured chips—kept improving their process, fitting more transistors on each chip. This steady improvement, known as "Moore's Law" for Gordon Moore, the Intel chairman, meant that a computer of a given capacity needed fewer and fewer chips as the years went by, and therefore became cheaper and cheaper. So inexpensive, in fact, that everyone could afford one. The personal computer had arrived.

A Personal Computer? It seems obvious today that people want—in fact, need—computation. (How many computers do you carry with you all the time, counting your phone, music player, and, possibly, a tablet or laptop?) But the first decade and a half were rocky for personal computers. Invented in 1973 at Xerox's Palo Alto Research Center, the Alto was the first serious attempt to make a personal machine, albeit for an office worker. It introduced the concepts of a graphical user interface and the mouse. The $40,000 price tag was cheap compared to similar computers of the day, but it was too expensive even for companies, and was never sold.

The personal computer overcame formidible barriers before it was widely accepted. First, people didn't see why anyone would need one. In 1977, Ken Olsen, president of Digital Equipment Corporation, a manufacturer of small computers, famously said, "There is no reason for any individual to have a computer in their home." And given how difficult they were to use, and how few and feeble the applications were, people had a point. However, games, primitive word processing, and, eventually, email attracted enough users to push the development forward.

Serious Resistance. Perhaps the greatest problem was the inherent fear of most adults of computers. Knowing nothing about computation, and hesitant to be seen as clueless, most adults stayed away from them. IBM confronted the issue directly, introducing its PC with a humble "every man" strategy. For some, this worked, but for most people it would take the World Wide Web before PCs attracted serious interest. Parents did have the idea that their children's schoolwork would benefit from a personal computer. Since most kids are fearless, personal computers were most succesful with younger users, beginning a generational gap that continues to this day.

The Internet

The forerunner of the Internet—the ARPANet—sent its first packet in 1969. Though originally used only by research and academic communities, networking developed continuously throughout the 1970s and 80s. The value of connecting computers together became so clear that networks sprang up everywhere. The key idea (1973) was to allow these separate networks to connect together only if they both used a common communication protocol called TCP/IP, explained in Chapter 3. Thus, the Internet—a network of networks—was born.

Initially, most users connected to the Internet by acoustic modem, the so-called "dial-up connection," which was slow and fussy. Today, broadband is widely available, though many people access the Internet most frequently via their smartphones.

The main uses of the Internet were originally email and some transferring of files. There weren't that many other things networking could do for the general population. But, then, Tim Berners-Lee and his team had an idea!

HTTP and the World Wide Web

The idea was to create an online center—later dubbed a "home page"—where everyone could access the documents, images, and other resources of CERN, the agency for whom Berners-Lee worked (see Figure 1.7); if other organizations did the same, they could all enjoy rapid dissemination of information. A few other efforts at the time had similar goals, but this one quickly swamped the competition to become the universal tool it is today.

Notice that the key idea here is that the familiar HTTP protocol is universal; see Chapter 4. That is, when you access a page using the HTTP protocol, your browser (the client) and the host (the Web server) know exactly how to interact: what's requested and what will be returned, and how, and in what format. Such standards—TCP/IP is another—are essential when many people are developing software and content independently.

Mosaic, the first widely used Web browser, got its name because it handled several of the protocols competing at the start. The Firefox browser—required for this book—is a grandchild (or possibly great-great-. . . -grandchild) of Mosaic.

CERN has recently reposted their original home page at its original address, **http://info.cern.ch/hypertext/WWW/TheProject.html**. It is extremely basic, but the usual features, such has blue hyperlinks, are there.

First Web Page

Layered Software Development

The last of the "greatest hits" wasn't the creation of a single person or team, nor did it happen in a single moment in time. Rather, it is the collective accomplishment of many computer scientists, chiefly programmers, software developers, their companies, and the academics who study software development. Without these advances the spectacular features of computing—social media, to pick one—could not have happened.

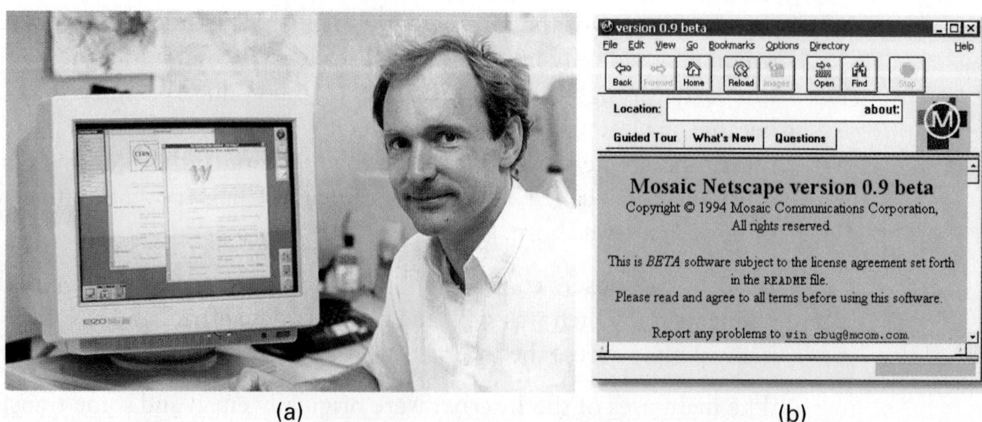

(a) (b)

Figure 1.7 Pioneers: (a) Sir Tim Berners-Lee (1994) at CERN showing a Web page, and (b) splash page of the "0.9 Beta" version of Mosaic, the first widely used graphical Web browser.

Layered Software Development. Until the 1980s programs tended to be monolithic, with little structure; they were difficult to write and impossible to maintain. Terms like "spaghetti code" referred to programs whose logic was incomprehensibly knotted like a pile of spaghetti. Some still write programs like this; however, professionals do not. Software development has steadily matured, becoming more disciplined and sophisticated.

Software development applies a layered approach in which programs at one level apply code for the more primitive operations from lower levels, and provide more advanced facilities for higher levels. For example, the program stack for the Android smartphone is shown in Figure 1.8. This is a logical description of the resources available to anyone who is writing code for the phone. Each layer above the blue level represents hundreds or possibly thousands of programs that collectively support the kind of activity that labels the box. For example, SQLite in the green area is database software; OpenGL/ES provides graphics facilities.

An Accumulation of Knowledge. The two key points about layered software development are:

- Programmers can use the software in these boxes without ever understanding how those programs work, beyond knowing the proper way to use them. They are building on the work of thousands of other programmers, who have contributed to these layers.
- As technology advances, more boxes will be included (this figure is not exhaustive) and more layers will be added. For example, before the creation of the Android smartphone much of this software—the database code, for example—already existed. Other parts were created for this product, maybe the telephony manager. Over time, the stack grows, both in terms of components and layers.

The take-home message from these two points is that software gets more and more complex, and more and more sophisticated based on the combined efforts of many programmers. We build on what we can already do.

Applications	Home	Contacts	Phone	Browser	Other
Android Frameworks	Activity Manager	Window Manager	Content Providers	View System	Notification Manager
	Package Manager	Telephony Manager	Resource Manager	Location Manager	XMPP Service
Libraries & Runtime	Surface Manager	Media Framework	SQLite	Core Libraries	
	OpenGL/ES	FreeType	WebKit	Dalvik Virtual Machine (DVM)	
	SGL	SSL	libc		
Linux Kernel	Display Driver	Camera Driver	Bluetooth Driver	Flash Memory Driver	Binder (IPC) Driver
	USB Driver	Keypad Driver	WiFi Driver	Audio Drivers	Power Management
	Hardware				

Complexity ↑

Figure 1.8 The software stack for the Android smartphone; the hardware is on the bottom, the apps are on top.

The Great Part of the Greatest Hits

Our tour of this series of awesome ideas has demonstrated that many very clever people have been captivated by computation and motivated to make it better. But because each idea has been so significant, the fact that there is a theme running through many of these accomplishments can be easily missed.

Notice that reducing the impact of complexity has often been a key result of these discoveries.

- The CPU and soft instructions allowed a machine to do more complex computations, and to accomplish them autonomously.
- Integration and photolithography all but eliminated the complexity of building electronic devices.
- Layered software development allows programmers to build on the work of thousands of others without the need to understand the operation of their computations—only how to use them. And then others will build on their work.

Others of the ideas reduced complexity less directly; indeed, digitization—the core property of all of these hits—reduced the complexity of analyzing the census from 8 years to 1. It was an auspicious start.

Terms of Endearment

There is a French phrase that we have adopted in English, although it may not be familiar: *le mot juste* (luh·MO·joost). It means "the right phrase or word." This odd term is mentioned here to emphasize that as we learn computing it will be necessary to learn *le mot juste*, the right phrase or word for the phenomenon being discussed. Not only should you learn the right computing terms, but you should also understand how to use them to benefit completely from the technology. There are two practical reasons for this.

Tech Support

Everyone needs and uses tech support. It is very rare for the tech person to be standing at your side, watching you recreate the problem at hand. Usually, you must look up the answer yourself using the so-called *Help* feature, or you must phone, email, or use some chat technology to communicate with a tech support staffer. In all cases, you will need to explain what is wrong. If you call it "that flashing thingy" rather than a *cursor*, the technician might guess what you mean, but probably will not; the search algorithm of the *Help* facility definitely won't know what you mean.

Help! I Need Help? Before window-based operating systems, computers and software were packaged with printed manuals. People actually looked up stuff in them, and because it's easy to skim a book—its table of contents, its index, its illustrations, and so forth—it was easy to find an answer to a question even if they were not quite sure of the right term. With online manuals and search commands, the skimming advantages disappeared. Now *Help* doesn't help much, so it's appropriate that the icon for help is a question mark. The "helper" often seems clueless, too!

Describing your problem using the right words is amazingly effective. Usually you get a speedy and helpful answer from tech support. It is so helpful, in fact, that in rare cases when a knowledgeable techie doesn't know the right term, he or she will look it up first. It pays to learn *le mot juste* even if only to remove frustration when you need tech support.

Anchoring Knowledge

It makes sense that to learn a new subject, we must learn its terminology. The main advantage is that our brains seem to be organized so that when we name a thing or idea, we remember it. For example, in ice hockey, *icing* is the term for hitting the puck across the blue lines and the opponent's goal line. We might not even notice this amid all the passing and slap shots. By knowing this new definition for the familiar word *icing*, we start watching for it, increasing our understanding and enjoyment of the game. Eventually the word stops sounding weird and becomes a part of our vocabulary. At that point, we use the right word without even thinking about it.

The Right Way to Say IT

You can learn vocabulary by reading a computer dictionary, of course, but that's *waaay* too boring. Instead, we introduce most of the basic terminology as we encounter it in the text, and summarize it in the glossary at the end of the book. A few words are so common to our study, that we simply discuss them in a few sections below.

Learning New Words. Since many of us are online all the time, the easiest way to learn the meaning of a new word (if it isn't in this book's glossary) is to ask a search engine to define it. Both Google and Bing accept queries of the form **define** *term*.

Computers, Software, Algorithms

In this section we define a few of the terms we have already used above, making sure we define and explain them in the way they are being used today.

Find the Computer

Historically, computers have steadily become smaller and cheaper, primarily because of amazing advancements of electronics—the Moore's Law effect, mentioned above—and secondarily, because they are so useful; the market is huge, motivating innovation. It's not that nearly everyone wants a computer, it's that most people already own many computers. Not all of them have a big video display and sit on a desk. Where else are they?

Processors. Today, computers are everywhere. Mostly the computers you use are embedded as components of phones, the Wii, microwave ovens, music players, brakes, and so forth. These are all computers in the technical sense, but they are packaged with other components, and are typically more specialized to a given task than, say, a laptop. Because it doesn't really matter if the computer is attached to a printer or an accelerometer (so it knows when it's moving), we will refer to computers by their more technical name, **processors**. A processor (Chapter 9) includes the CPU, a small amount of memory usually called a **cache**, and is connected to some input and/or output devices. The main variation comes with the devices the computer is connected to, and, of course, the software.

The "Smart" Part(s). In "tech speak," *processor* is a synonym for *computer*. The words are used interchangeably in conversation and in this book. We refer to "the" computer, although technically most general-use computer systems—desktops, laptops, tablets, smartphones, game consoles, and so on—contain more than a single processor.

Figure 1.9(a) shows the inside of an iPhone 5 as revealed by a "teardown" by Fixit.com. (Androids and other smartphones are similar, as are tablets and iPods.) Notice in Figure 1.9(a) that the battery appears to take up approximately half of the space. The circuit board, which takes up the other half of the package, shows the A6 processor chip (green) that performs general operations, like running apps. Other chips provide the flash memory, telephony, and other specialized services. Figure 1.9(c) shows the inside of the A6, with regions marked indicating where circuits for the processors are: notice

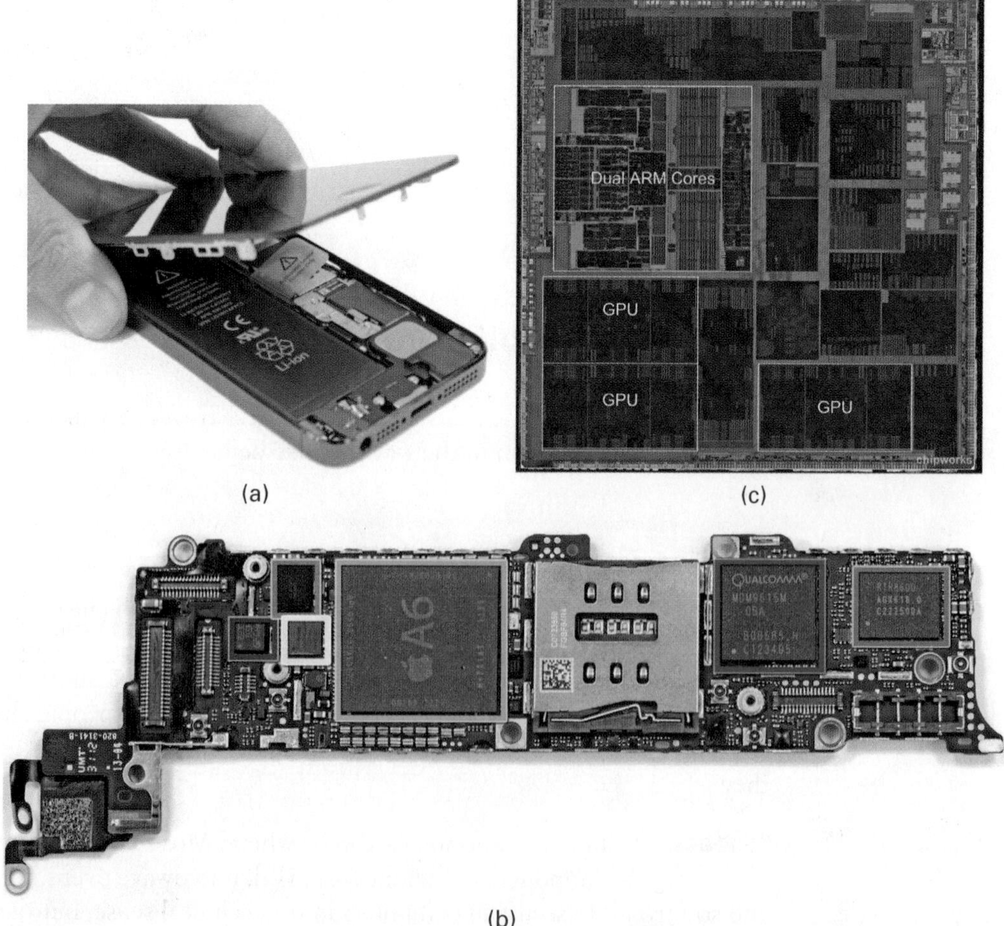

Figure 1.9 "Teardown" of the iPhone 5: (a) the open case showing that more than half of the volume seems to be a lithium-ion battery, (b) the circuit board, which contains all the electronics including the A6 main processor chip (green), and is opposite the battery, and (c) detail of the A6 chip showing two ARM processors plus three graphics processing units—all are computers.

two ARM processors and three GPUs, graphics processing units. That is, this phone contains at least five computers, and maybe more, depending on how some of the other parts are designed.

ARMs Race. The ARM is a processor specialized to be part of other systems, though it's found everywhere these days. ARM is an acronym for Advanced RISC Machine, and RISC is an acronym for Reduced Instruction-Set Computer. (Notice that acronym ARM contains the acronym RISC, an instance of "name layering," perhaps?) The value in using a computer as an embedded part of some other consumer product is that it's much easier to write code for a computer to manage the operations of, say, a microwave oven or other task, than it is to design specific electonics for the functions. That is, designers choose software over hardware. Again.

Disarming Information. Cellular phones and other mobile devices use multiple computers to perform their functions. The iPhone 5 has at least five. The average cell phone has 2.4 ARMs; that is, more than the person holding it.

Software

Although computer hardware and chip technology are fascinating, the greatest interest in computing is in software. **Software** is a collective term for **programs**, the instructions computers perform to implement applications. Software "instructs" the computer hardware by providing the steps needed to perform a task, say, to display a Web page or play a game. The computer, using the CPU, follows the program and carries out the instructions extremely rapidly and with great accuracy. So, specifying what to do is the point of greatest leverage.

Terminology. A *program* is a collection of computer instructions that implement a function or action. *Software* is one or more programs. So, the commonly heard phrase "software programs" is redundant. Either word says it all.

Writing software—the job of programmers and software developers—is a difficult and challenging engineering profession. **Programming** is "instructing an agent to perform some function or action" by giving a step-by-step process. The **agent** is anything that can follow the instructions. For software professionals, the agent is a computer. Sometimes the agent is a person, as when we give driving directions. We program a person to navigate to a specific place. Writing a recipe is programming. Or when we explain to a friend how to get some "rockin" effect in video editing, we give a step-by-step process. That's programming, too. And we instruct computers all the time, as when we perform a Web search, use a spreadsheet, edit images, and so on. Therefore, learning a little more about software can make us better users.

1.2 Acronyms Are Important, LOL. Acronyms are important in computing terminology. Using online search, find out what the three-letter acronym TLA stands for, and give an example.

Algorithms

An **algorithm** is a precise and systematic method for producing a specified result. We discuss them fully in Chapter 10, but for now we'll treat algorithm and program as synonyms—they're different in a way that doesn't matter at the moment.

We are taught some algorithms, such as the process to add a column of numbers, beginning in elementary school. But people think up algorithms all the time as the processes that solve their problems. All of the programming examples given above—driving directions, recipes, video editing tricks—are processes, and if they fulfill a few important requirements, they're algorithms as well.

Input specified
Output specified
Definite
Effective
Finite

For a process to be an algorithm, it must have the five properties shown at left. *Specifying input and output* means to say what the computation is given as data, and what it will produce as a result. *Definite* means the whole process is spelled out unambiguously, and *effective* means it is within the "abilities" of the agent following the instructions. *Finite* means the agent will eventually finish the computation, giving the right answer, or stop and report that none is possible.

Let's illustrate these terms using the familiar algorithm of finding if an item *e* is in a list, such as finding a student's name in a class list. The process has five steps:

Input: A list containing one or more items, and an item *e*

Output: A report that will be either "Yes, *e* Found" or "*e* Not Found"

1. place a marker—a cursor or a finger or a coin—by the first item in the list
2. if there is no item by the marker, stop and report "*e* Not Found"
3. if the item by the marker is *e*, stop and report "Yes, *e* Found"
4. advance the marker to the next position
5. continue with Step 2

Does this process meet the test for being an algorithm? Its inputs—a list of items and an item to be found—are specified. The output, one of two reports, is given. The process has five clear steps, some of which are direct operations—advance the marker—and some of which are tests. The tests may or may not apply, but if they do apply, we're told what to do; if they don't apply we just continue on. For these reasons, our process is *definite*. It is also *effective*, because people can read, understand, and perform all of the instructions used. Operations like "place a marker" and "if the item by the marker is *e*" are within the capabilities of people. (The process has not been specified well enough for a computer, however, so the agent must be a person.) Finally, the process is *finite*. This is not obvious, because some instructions are repeated. But, if we notice that the repeated instructions (a) stop when there are no more items left, and (b) each repetition considers a new list item—the marker has been advanced—so for any finite list the items will eventually be "used up," and the process will stop. And, we should note, (c) the process gets the right answer. So, this process *is* an algorithm, known as the *linear search algorithm*.

1.3 Watching an Algorithm. For a list with three items, the last of which is the desired item *e*, how many times is the whole sequence of instructions 2–5 performed?

To Boot. **Booting** means to start a computer and **rebooting** means to restart it. Because rebooting most often happens after a catastrophic error or crash, you might guess that the term is motivated by frustration—we want to kick the computer like a football. Actually, the term *booting* comes from *bootstrap.*

Computers were originally started by an operator who entered a few instructions into the computer's empty memory using console push buttons. Those instructions told the computer to read in a few more instructions—a very simple operating system—from punch cards. This tiny operating system could then read in the instructions of the real operating system from magnetic tape, similar to a VCR tape. Finally, the computer was able to start doing useful work. This incremental process was called *bootstrapping,* from the phrase "pulling yourself up by your bootstraps," because the computer basically started itself.

Today, the instructions to start a computer are part of the Basic Input/Output System (BIOS) and are stored on a microchip called the Boot ROM.

The Words for Ideas

Although understanding the physical parts of computing—the processor, software stack, and memory—seems very important, we are not too concerned with them here. Instead, we will focus on *concept* words, such as those discussed in this section.

"Abstract"

One of the most important "idea" words used in this book is the verb *abstract.* It has several meanings. In British mysteries, *to abstract* means *to remove*, as in *to steal*: "The thief abstracted the pearl necklace while the jeweler looked at the diamond ring." In computing, *to abstract* also means to remove, but the thing being removed is not physical. Rather it's an idea or a process, and it is extracted from some form of information.

To **abstract** is to remove the basic concept, idea, or process from a situation. The removed concept is usually expressed in another, more succinct and usually more general form, called an **abstraction**.

We are familiar with abstraction in this sense. Parables and fables, which teach lessons in the form of stories, require us to abstract the essential point of the story. When we read about a fox that can't reach a bunch of grapes and therefore calls them sour, we abstract the idea from the story: When people fail to get what they want, they often decide that they didn't want it after all.

Notice two key points. First, many but not all of the details of the story are irrelevant to the concept. When abstracting, we must decide which details are relevant and which are irrelevant. The "grapes" and the "fox" are unimportant in the parable, but "failure" is important. Being able to tell the difference between important and unimportant details is essential to understanding the point of a story, and to abstracting in general. Second, the idea—the abstraction—has meaning beyond the story. The point of repeating the parable, of course, is to convey an idea that applies to many situations.

In computing, separating the relevant from the irrelevant, and applying the abstraction to other cases, are both essential.

1.4 Abstract Idea. Read the parable below and say which of "chirping," "corn," and "preparation" are relevant to the abstract idea being presented.

The Ant and the Grasshopper

In a field one summer's day a Grasshopper was hopping about, chirping and singing. An Ant passed by carrying corn to its nest.
"Why not come and chat with me," said the Grasshopper, "instead of working so hard?"
"I am helping to store food for the winter," said the Ant, "and I recommend you to do the same."
"Why bother?" said the Grasshopper. "There is plenty of food."
But the Ant went on its way and continued to save corn.
When winter came the Grasshopper had no food and was dying of hunger. The ants, he saw, ate corn every day from the supply they had collected in the summer. Then the Grasshopper knew:

It is wise to prepare for the future.

"Generalize"

A process similar to abstraction is to recognize the common idea in two or more situations. Recognizing how different situations have something basic in common is why we create parables, rules, and so on.

To **generalize** is to express an idea, concept, or process that applies to many situations. The statement that sums up that idea is called a **generalization**.

For example, most of us notice that twisting a faucet handle left turns water on and twisting it right turns it off. But not always—some water taps have only a single "joy stick" handle, and others have horizontal bars that pull forward. However, since it's true most of the time, we generalize that "on" is to the left and "off" is to the right. Perhaps we also notice that twisting lids, caps, screws, and nuts to the left usually loosens them, and turning them to the right usually tightens them. Again, we generalize that left means loosen and right means tighten. We probably also generalize that both situations are examples of the same thing: a generalization of generalizations!

Noticing patterns and generalizing about them is a very valuable habit. Although generalizations do not always apply, recognizing them gives us a way to begin in a new, but similar, situation.

"Operationally Attuned"

Another term related to extracting concepts and processes refers to being aware of how a gadget works. To be **operationally attuned** is to apply what we know about how a device or system works to simplify its use.

For example, we generalized that with few exceptions, all caps, lids, screws, and nuts loosen by turning left and tighten by turning right. We might know this intuitively, but knowing it *explicitly* makes us operationally attuned. Knowing this fact as a rule means that when a lid or nut is stuck, we can twist it very hard, certain that we are forcing it to loosen rather than tighten. Being operationally attuned makes us more effective.

The term "operationally attuned" is introduced here to emphasize that thinking about how computation works makes it simpler to use. We don't expect to be experts on all of the technology—few are. But by asking ourselves, "How does this work?" and using what we learn by thinking about the answer, we will be more successful at applying IT. Our Fluency study focuses on learning enough to answer many of the "How does this work?" questions well enough to succeed.

Tuning In to Everyday Explanations. Explaining to ourselves how things work makes using them easier. This is true even if the explanation isn't really correct—just as long as the explanation matches the operation, it will work. For example, if we have a deadbolt lock on our door, we may check it often to see if it's locked. But, if we think about its operation, we can tell at a distance and save time. How does a deadbolt work? If we don't know we formulate an explanation that matches the facts.

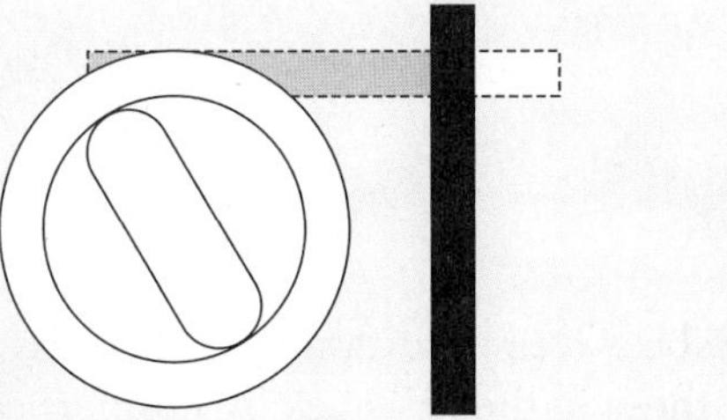

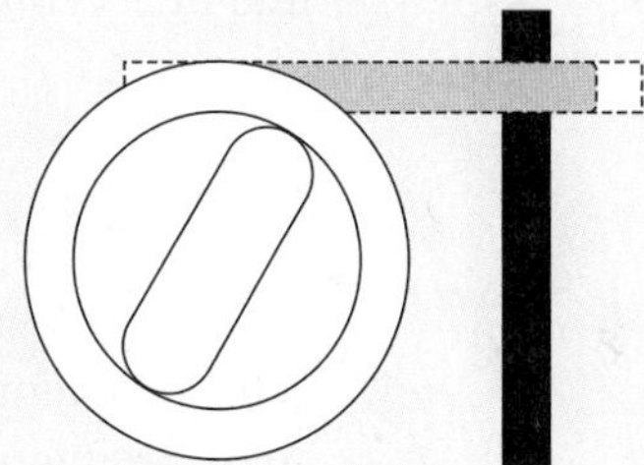

Because the knob is turned to the 11:00 position when the lock is open, we imagine that the bolt, which is inside the door and not visible, is attached to the top of the knob. Turning it right to 1:00 moves the bolt into the locked position. This simple explanation, which is probably not very accurate and possibly wrong, lets us see from a distance whether the door is locked: Knob at 11:00 means not locked, knob at 1:00 means locked. Our imagined explanation reminds us which is which. (Of course, there are many other kinds of deadbolts, and even this kind can be installed differently.)

"Mnemonic"

Mnemonic is a rather unusual term that we use in IT and in other fields as well. The silent *m* implies that it's a word with an unusual past, which happens to be Greek.

A mnemonic (ni·MÄ·nik) is an aid for remembering something. The reminder can take many forms, such as pronounceable words or phrases. We remember the five Great Lakes between the United States and Canada with the acronym HOMES—Huron, Ontario, Michigan, Erie, and Superior. The order for the colors in the rainbow is: Roy G. Biv, for red, orange, yellow, green, blue, indigo and violet. When Pluto was downgraded from planetary status, we had to change our mnemonic for the planets from *My Very Educated Mother Just Served Us Nine Pickles*, to *Mary's Violet Eyes Make John Stay Up Nights*. Acronyms often start out as mnemonics and end up becoming the names for things.

There are many IT details that we need to know only occasionally. They're not worth memorizing, but they're inconvenient to look up. Therefore, thinking of a mnemonic that helps us remember the details when we need them makes using technology simpler.

SUMMARY

In this chapter we have set the context for our future study. We learned how to do the following:

- Know what is important about the major computing inventions of the past one hundred years or so.
- Know and use the right word because as we learn words, we learn ideas; knowing the right words helps us to communicate clearly.
- Give informed definitions for common computer terms.
- Consider a brief list of "idea" words, such as abstract and generalize.

The remainder of the book elaborates on the content of this chapter. You will continue to recognize and learn more about Fluency in information technology, a topic we hope you find interesting.

TRY IT SOLUTIONS

1.1 This problem can be solved in several ways: Process the whole input on the left column. Using only those in the "1" stack (males), process on the right column. This produces five stacks. Combine the two stacks corresponding to 0–10 and 11–20. Run the combined stack back through the machine counting them: They are the boys under 21. (Equivalently, the right column can be processed first; combining the first two stacks gives all children; separating male and female and then counting the males produces the same result.)

1.2 TLA stands for "three-letter acronym" in computing, and it is its own example.

1.3 The 2–5 sequence is performed once when the marker is on the first item, and once when the marker is on the second item, but when the marker is on the third item, the process ends on Step 3.

1.4 "Chirping" and "corn" are irrelevant features of the story; "preparation" is a part of the abstract idea.

REVIEW QUESTIONS

Multiple Choice

1. In order for something to be considered a computer it must have a keyboard attached.
   a. true
   b. false
   c. only certain computers
2. What was used to make analyzing results faster for the 1890 census?
   a. integrated circuits
   b. processors
   c. punch cards and punch card readers
   d. ENIAC

3. When using Google or Bing, what keyword can be used to provide you with a definition of a certain term?
   a. look-up
   b. define
   c. dictionary
   d. definition
4. What word is interchangeable with computer?
   a. processor
   b. desktop
   c. personal
   d. integrated circuit
5. What educational background is required to write algorithms?
   a. BS in computer science or computer engineering
   b. MS in computer science or computer engineering
   c. a high school diploma
   d. no educational background is required
6. An agent could be a
   a. computer
   b. human
   c. program
   d. all of the above

Short Answer

1. _______ was the name of the first electronic computer, and it was located in _______.
2. The instructions written in software are followed or executed by _______.
3. _______ made computers more affordable and allowed them to have more complex CPUs.
4. _______, _______, and _______ were three technologies that increased ones' desire to own a personal computer.
5. Complexity is _______ to manufacture, though it remains _______ to design.
6. Software is a collective term for _______.
7. Abstracting requires you to separate information into two categories: _______ and _______.
8. A program acts on _______ and results in _______.

Exercises

1. How many computers do you have? List them.
2. Explain in detail why the phrase "software program" is redundant.
3. What is the difference between hard and soft instructions?
4. Similar to video production, which is now accessible to many nonprofessionals, name two other things that over time have been made more accessible because of computer software.

5. Explain why it is important to use the right words when describing your problem to tech support.
6. Explain in detail the difference between booting and rebooting.
7. Write an algorithm that provides someone with clear directions on how to make your favorite snack.

CHAPTER 2

Exploring the Human-Computer Interface

Face It, It's a Computer

learning objectives

- Give names to computing features that you know intuitively
- Explain placeholders and the placeholder technique
- Explain how "metaphor" is used in computing
- Describe the desktop metaphor, giving examples of appropriate icons
- Describe the touch metaphor, giving sample motions
- Explain how the desktop and touch metaphors differ

CHAPTER 2

Don't anthropomorphize computers, they hate it.

—ANONYMOUS

HAVING USED COMPUTERS your whole life, there are many things that you "know" about them that make using them easy. You probably don't know these things explicitly; it's intuitive knowledge built from experience. Occasionally, when something goes wrong, or you encounter a totally new application, what seems intuitive doesn't work. Then, you need to know what you know—that is, what is the rule your intuition is based on? That's the topic of this chapter, and it should be very easy to learn . . . almost intuitively.

The chapter begins by making explicit a few concepts that you know intuitively, including feedback, consistent interfaces, the *New* command, and others. Next, a fundamental property of digital information—perfect reproduction—is discussed, and applied in a series of practical settings, including the placeholder technique. Then, technological metaphors are introduced. After a brief review of the origin of the desktop metaphor, the more recent touch metaphor is introduced. Finally, the two metaphors are compared, indicating that they constitute different ways of thinking about how users interact with computers.

A Few Useful Concepts

There are some aspects of everyday computer usage you know intuitively, but which you should understand explicitly.

Feedback

A computer is our assistant, ready to do whatever we tell it to do. It is natural that when any assistant performs an operation, he, she, or it must report to the person who made the request, describing the progress. This is especially true when the assistant is a computer, because the user needs to know that the task was done and when to give the next command. So, computer systems will always give the user feedback about "what's happenin'."

Feedback is any indication that either the computer is still working or has completed the request. Feedback takes many forms, depending on what operation a user has commanded. If the operation can be performed instantaneously—that is, so fast that a user doesn't have to wait for it to complete—the user interface (UI) simply indicates that the operation is complete. When the operation is an editing change, for example, the proof that it is done is that the revision is visible and the app is ready for another command. When the effect of the command is not discernible—say, when one clicks a button—then there is some other indication provided; for example, highlighting, shading, graying, underlining, color changing, or an audible click.

The most obvious forms of feedback are the indications that the computer is continuing to perform a time-consuming operation. As the operation is carried out in desktop computing, the cursor is replaced with an icon such as an hourglass, a rainbow spinner, or another form like a little dog running. Applications can also give the user custom feedback. A common indicator is the busy spinner, a revolving circle of a dozen radial bars. When the completion time can be predicted, applications show a meter, called a *progress bar*.

Finally, when an operation is processing a series of inputs, the "completion count" gives the tally of the completed instances, or equivalently, the number remaining.

Always expect feedback and notice it.

Consistent Interface

Have you noticed that applications, especially from the same vendor like Microsoft, Google, or Apple, are consistent? Start up MS Word and MS PowerPoint and you notice that they have a lot in common—icons to menus—even though Word is for making documents that are mostly textual, and PowerPoint is for creating presentations that are mostly visual. "App store" applications have similar characteristics, too.

Fundamental Similarities. You have doubtless noticed that older desktop applications, regardless of vendor, have a *File* menu and an *Edit* menu. Newer applications without explicit *File* and *Edit* menus may use a ribbon (Microsoft), a collection of icons, or action (double tap on a smartphone) to display available operations. No matter how they are shown, many, many applications support these operations:

File: *New*, *Open*, *Close*, *Save*, *Save As*, *Page Setup*, *Print*, *Exit*, and others
Edit: *Cut*, *Copy*, *Paste*, *Undo*, *Redo*, *Select All*, *Find*, *Replace*, and others

These familiar operations are frequently available for a fundamental reason.

2.1 Clearing Italics. Suppose in your term paper you used *italics* often to *emphasize* your meaning, but now you find that your grumpy professor hates this use of italics. Describe how to remove all italics in your term paper.

You might guess that the reason for this similarity is that software companies reuse the same code in each application. That's true, but it doesn't fully explain it. Another partial answer to explaining the similarity is that if operations you use in one application are needed in a different application, making them look and work the same helps you learn and use the second application. And that's true, too. The main reason for consistency across computer applications, however, is that certain operations are fundamental to processing information no matter what the application. The vendors didn't think them up as cool features to add on; the applications require them. Vendors must include them, and once they are there, making them behave consistently is easier for them and more convenient for you.

Command and Control. Sometimes it's necessary to refer to an operation like *Copy* without limiting to a single operating system. In such cases we write ^C to indicate that the shortcut requires either the *Command* (⌘) (for Mac OS) or *Control* (Ctrl) (for Windows) key or something else, depending on the operating system.

Clicking and Blazing. The consistency we have discussed provides a strong sense of familiarity when we see a new application. As a result, when we install a new app we immediately and intuitively perform two important activities:

- "Clicking around" is exploring the application to see what features are available. This makes sense because you know intuitively—and from experience—that you will recognize many features from other applications.
- "Blazing away" is "going boldly where you've never gone before"—that is, trying the application assertively. This makes sense too, because what you know intuitively is that you cannot break anything. It's software. The only thing happening is that electrons are moving around inside a few silicon chips. Sure, you may have to restart the app, or even reboot, but nothing will go "clunk" or catch fire.

These are standard activities that you routinely follow with any new application. Clicking around is justified by the consistent interface, and blazing away is justified because running software can't break the computer.

Getting Out and Getting Back In. Exiting and relaunching an application after making a mistake is so common in computing—it's called *getting out and getting back in*—that it has become the subject of some geek humor. A mechanical engineer, an electrical engineer, and a computer engineer are camped at Mt. Rainier. In the morning, they pack up to leave and get into their car, but it doesn't start. The ME says, "The starter motor is broken, but I can fix it," and he gets out of the car. The EE says, "No way. It's the battery, but I know what to do," and she gets out of the car. The CE, after getting out of the car says, "Now, let's get back in."

New Instance

When you use a computer you usually find the familiar *New* command as a button, icon, or entry under the *File* menu. It creates a "blank" instance of the kind of information or files the application creates. What is "blank information"?

Figure 2.1 A visual form of a blank instance of contact information from an electronic address book; the instance has structure inside the computer with empty fields, as shown.

To understand this fundamental idea, notice that all information is grouped into **types**, based on its properties. Digital photographs are a type of information; among the properties of every image is its height and width in pixels. Monthly calendars are a type of information, with properties such as the number of days, day of the week on which the first day falls, and year. Text documents are another type of information; the length of a document in characters is one property. Any specific piece of information—an image, a month, or a document—is an **instance** of its type. Your term paper is an instance of the document type of information; July 2014 is an instance of the calendar type of information.

To store or process information of a given type, the computer sets up a structure to record all of the properties and store its content. A "new" or "blank" instance is simply the structure without any properties or content filled in. For example, imagine an empty form for contact information in an electronic address book, as shown in Figure 2.1. That's a new instance, ready to receive its content.

When *New* is available on certain devices such as phones, it it may not create a file. More likely it creates a blank entry in a database.

Perfect Reproduction

Next, we consider another fundamental idea and let it lead us to its everyday applications.

As you know, computers encode information as a sequence of binary digits, 0's and 1's. (But no one seems to know why graphic designers always make binary blue or green!) Because of the two digits, we call it **digital information**. Relying only on 0 and 1 means that digital information has many great advantages. For one thing, it can be perfectly reproduced or replicated.

An Exact Duplicate

By representing information as a sequence of 0's and 1's, we can make another copy simply by duplicating the sequence. Furthermore, because it is digital, we can directly check to make sure the two sequences are identical, verifying that no mistakes were made; computer systems make such checks continually.

c	o	p	y
0110 0100	0110 1111	0111 0000	0111 1001
⇓ ⇓	⇓ ⇓	⇓ ⇓	⇓ ⇓
0110 0100	0110 1111	0111 0000	0111 1001
c	**o**	**p**	**y**

The fact that the digital copy is identical to the original is obvious, but it's one way digital improves on analog information.

Perfect reproduction is not a property of analog information, such as vinyl records, or paper documents, such as newspapers. **Analog** information comes from or is stored on a continuously variable medium. So, a newspaper can print any color of gray they need just by varying the color and amount of ink used. With digital encoding, there are only a limited number of choices of gray—or any color. So, if you want to reproduce that great picture of yourself from a paper document, the reproduction won't be the same. The following problems could apply:

- Wrong paper, although it might be possible to get very similar paper
- Wrong ink, although it might be possible to get very similar ink
- Wrong amount of ink, which cannot be recovered

For copying a newspaper clipping, details such as too light or too dark don't matter; for audio, video, photography, art, and so on, they do.

Because this feature of digital information is so important, let's call it the **perfect reproduction** property. You probably think, correctly, that it's pretty obvious. It is, but its consequences changed the world.

His Master's Voice. In the pre-digital days of audio, still photography, TV, movies, and similar media, the analog encoding of information required that all original work had to be kept as a "master" from which copies were made for the public. Every copy differed (perhaps only slightly) from the original; copies made from copies differed from them (perhaps only slightly); and so they differed further from the original by more, and so forth. The reproducibility of a medium depended on limiting these errors as much as possible. Eventually, the master's physical medium—tape or film, for example—would age or wear out, limiting the lifetime of high-quality forms of the work. Much of that great work has been lost, or is known only in "grainy" duplicate-of-a-duplicate form. The move to digital encoding eliminated the problem and brought a new and valuable benefit.

Micrograph of vinyl record grooves, an analog technology difficult to reproduce exactly.

Copying

Perfect reproduction is a property you use everyday. Let's check out some ways of copying and see how you might benefit even more from it.

The Ethics of Copying. In most situations "copying" is penalized or at least discouraged. In school you learn little when copying someone else's work; in fashion you want your own style, not a copy of someone else's. It's against the law to copy copyrighted material. But those prohibitions all apply to copying *other people's work.* With computers, copying is a terrific idea, and there are many benefits from copying *your own work.*

Copy/Paste/Edit. The *Copy* and *Paste* operations are widely available and they are our friends. When editing, we have the option to create identical content directly by retyping or redrawing, or to use *Copy/Paste* to reproduce it from another location. Most people correctly pick *Copy/Paste* (**C/P**) because of its advantages:

- It is generally faster (depending on the length) than entering content, and the copy is perfect!
- All instances have the *exact* same form, so if the content is searched—perhaps to be modified by *Find and Replace All*—it will always "hit," including spacing; entered text may not match exactly.
- And for advanced applications—spreadsheets, drafting and design tools, for example—that can be very fussy about the content *and* the form of the input they get, C/P introduces no tiny mistakes that the app doesn't like.

C/P reproduces the content *and* other characteristics of the source value, minimizing formatting mistakes.

Make a Note. Clicking *Copy* causes the computer to duplicate the binary sequence and save it in memory. Each time you *Paste*, a copy is made of that saved version. So, both *Copy* and *Paste* copy.

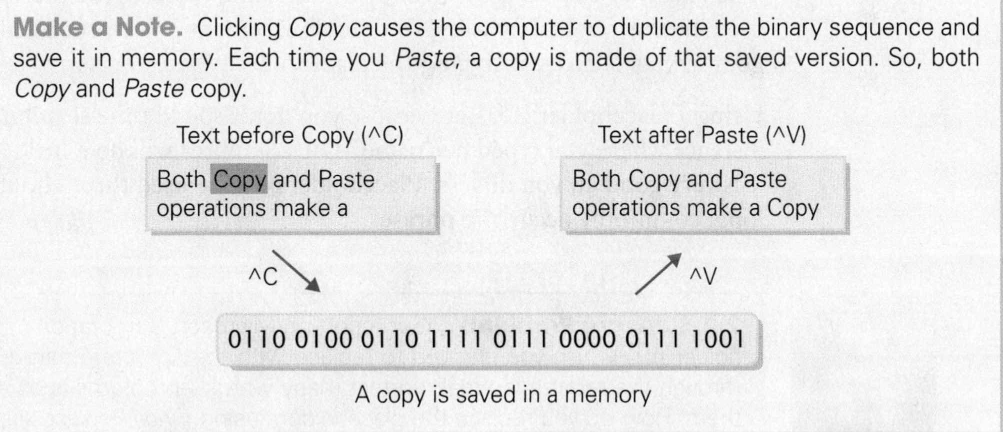

Find and Replace All. Another way to benefit from digital copies is using *Find* and *Replace*. Recall that in *Find/Replace* (**F/R**) editing operations—available in many applications—we give the source content to *Find* in the document, and the target content to *Replace* it with. *Find/Replace All* (**F/RA**) is an "applied in all cases" version of *Copy/Paste*, and our main interest here.

Save Typing with a Placeholder. One opportunity to use F/RA effectively is when you need to enter complex information again and again. For example, imagine you are writing a paper on 1991 Nobel Prize winner Aung San Suu Kyi (pronounced

Aung San Suu Kyi

Figure 2.2 Aung San Suu Kyi, winner of the 1991 Nobel Peace Prize "for her nonviolent struggle for democracy and human rights."

approximately as OUN SUN ZOOT CHEE). She won for her nonviolent opposition to the government of Burma (see Figure 2.2). She has a long, difficult to spell (and pronounce!) name, but it will occur in many places in your paper. (Be happy you don't have to spell it in Burmese!)

You could use C/P by carefully typing her name into your report the first time, and then every time you use it again, find it, copy it, and paste it. It's probably faster and more accurate than typing it each time, but there is a better way.

While writing your paper, adopt a **placeholder** for her name, perhaps *assk*. It doesn't matter what the placeholder is. Any short letter sequence that is easy to type works as long as you can remember it and *it is not used anywhere else in your report*. Whenever you refer to her by name, just use the placeholder.

> Because she was under house arrest, assk could not go to
> Oslo to accept the prize.

Then, just before proofreading your paper, do a *Find* on the placeholder and a *Replace All* with her name spelled out exactly.

The result, of course, is that a copy of her name replaces the placeholder wherever it's used in your paper. It's wise to do the replacement *before* proofreading in case something goes wrong, such as mistyping the placeholder.

Using a placeholder is faster because you don't spend time searching for an earlier instance where you typed her name. The computer will do a little more work of the kind it is very good at; you do less. Placeholders can be used throughout your work for all long, commonly occurring phrases.

2.2 Software Problems. Your report on Microsoft Corporation used the obvious placeholder *ms*, which you planned to replace with the corporate name. Then about half way through the report, you realized that many words—proble*ms* is an example—have *ms* in them. How do you replace the placeholders using *Find / Replace All* in this case, and also avoid ruining words containing *ms*?

Placeholders Gone Wrong

Placeholder Technique. The *Find/Replace All* operations are very powerful, but they require some thought to use effectively. For example, suppose you have written your report using *etc* throughout, and then you realize that the proper form is *etc.* with a period.

First, you think you will replace all cases of *etc* with *etc.*, but then you realize that often *etc* falls at the end of a sentence. They are followed by a period already. In those cases, your direct use of F/RA would cause a double period. Not to worry, you think. You will

Original	Correct text hidden	Correction made	Correct text restored
Et cetera is abbreviated etc. An alternative to using etc is to say "and so forth," "and others," etc. Remember that before etc an "and" is unnecessary.	Et cetera is abbreviated # An alternative to using etc is to say "and so forth," "and others," # Remember that before etc an "and" is unnecessary.	Et cetera is abbreviated # An alternative to using etc. is to say "and so forth," "and others," # Remember that before etc. an "and" is unnecessary.	Et cetera is abbreviated etc. An alternative to using etc. is to say "and so forth," "and others," etc. Remember that before etc. an "and" is unnecessary.

Figure 2.3 Illustration of the placeholder technique changing *etc* to *etc.* without inserting double periods.

do another F/RA to change double periods to a single period. Then you remember that you've used two (or more) periods for other purposes in your paper. (An ellipsis (. . .) is an example, but there are many others.) So, converting two periods to one will mess up those cases. Will you make the corrections manually? Of course not.

The clever **placeholder technique** is used to "hide" part of the text that shouldn't be tampered with when using F/RA. In this example, we hide the cases of *etc.* that happen to be correct because they are at the end of the sentence. We don't want to change them. Figure 2.3 shows how it works.

Begin with a *Find/Replace All* to change every *etc.* into a placeholder, such as # or some other character not used in the text. All of the remaining *etc* instances need a period. We use F/RA to change those to *etc.* everywhere. Of course, the # symbols are not affected. Finally, change all placeholder characters back into their original text, that is, change the # characters back to *etc.*, restoring them to their original form. Every *etc* is now followed by a single period.

2.3 Number Punctuation. Suppose your document contains data that is to be imported into a spreadsheet, but the large numbers are punctuated: 1,048,576. Of course, the rest of the document contains commas in their normal English usage. Use the placeholder technique to remove commas from the numbers.

Summarizing, the placeholder technique is a three-step process—hide, edit, restore—as this summary shows:

- *Hide* correct items — *Replace all correct text sequences with a placeholder (#)*
- *Edit* as needed — *Make corrections to remaining text sequences with F/RA*
- *Restore* correct items — *Replace the placeholder (#) with the original text*

This simple algorithm comes in very handy.

2.4 Abstracting an Algorithm. In Chapter 1, we discussed that *abstraction* is "removing" the essentials of an idea or process and ignoring everything else. Abstracting is how we create algorithms. The description of changing etc to etc. above was abstracted to get the three-step hide-edit-restore *Placeholder* algorithm. Referring to the etc. description, give two nonessential and two essential words or ideas that were involved in the abstraction activity.

What We See and What We Think

When many of us encounter a new technology—a device or application—for the first time, its purpose and operation seem obvious. True, using certain technologies, such as driving a car or playing a piano, require explicit instructions; others, like riding a bicycle, benefit from an experienced person showing us how; and still others, like using a chain saw or food processor, require at least that we read the directions in the manual. Even excusing those cases, much of the technology we use we figure out on our own without help. Even if we've never seen it before, we know intuitively what to do. That impression is no accident.

Metaphors

Are we geniuses? Yes, of course. But, we also get tremendous assistance from product developers who create technologies that minimize learning time. For example, if a device has controls that perform a standard operation such as increasing/decreasing something, and the new product presents that control in a form that looks like a volume control from a media player, we know immediately what to do: turn or slide the control. When it causes an increase or decrease in whatever it is controlling, we know we understand it. We probably aren't even aware of it. Designers presented that control purposely. Notice that matching our expectations is often (and correctly) carried to an extreme: For example, in increase/decrease situations, low is usually left (slider) or counterclockwise (dial) and high is the opposite. When designers make the technology work this way, it reinforces this convention and fulfills our expectations more completely.

A **metaphor**—you probably learned this once in English class as a "figure of speech," but we use it much more generally—is an icon or image or a concept used as a representative of or symbolic of a computation. The controlling volume example is a metaphor for the operation of increasing or decreasing something else that may not be volume. When designers create a technology, they use metaphors to help users know how to operate their devices without reading a manual. (No one wants to read the manual!) Metaphors are a terrific solution, and it's worth it for us to pay attention to them.

Though the metaphor idea applies in many situations, it is most widely used and most apparent in software, which is why we brought the whole subject up.

The Desktop

Now that we've introduced the idea of a technological metaphor, it's time to discuss a bit of history.

When the Alto, the first personal computer, was created at the Xerox Palo Alto Research Center (PARC), the designers introduced a graphical user interface (GUI) to replace the prevailing command line interface (CLI), which only a techie could love (see Figure 2.4). The CLI's metaphor—as the name suggests—is a rather militaristic one of a sequence of commands.

The PARC designers were building a personal computer for an office worker, so they adopted the desktop metaphor: What the users see on the screen is a virtual desktop. The designers invented the now-familiar idea of displaying documents in overlapping windows as though they were papers on a desktop; users control the position of the window over the document with scroll bars as if changing focus on the page. There were buttons, an email icon, and window clipping. A key part of the Alto user interface was the mouse, invented by Douglas Engelbart in 1967, which let users reposition their focus on the screen by pointing (see Figure 2.5).

Macintosh was introduced in 1984, the first successful personal computer with a graphical user interface. Famously, it used and extended ideas from the Alto, adding

Figure 2.4 The command line interface: The top line is a user request for a command list of the file transfer program; the response is the available commands. After that, the user asks for an explanation of "get" and gets a two-word answer. In the last line, the computer waits for the user to type the next command.

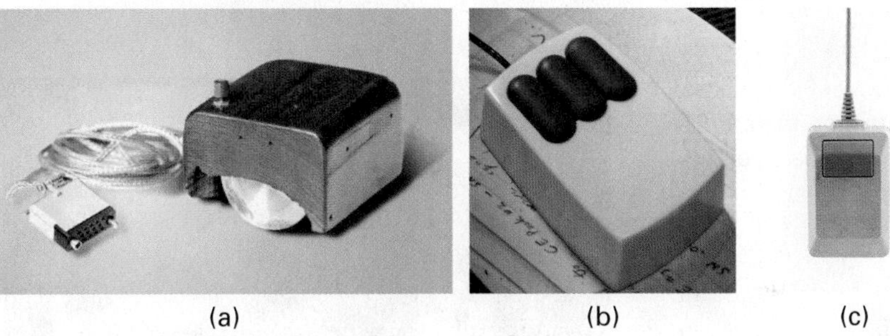

(a) (b) (c)

Figure 2.5 Evolution of the mouse: (a) prototype of Engelbart's 1967 invention, (b) Alto's three-button mouse, and (c) original Macintosh one-button mouse.

to the desktop metaphor with new icons and mechanisms. It showcased the mouse for painting and drawing applications.

Did You See That Mouse? The mouse was invented by Douglas Engelbart in 1967, and first shown publicly in 1968 at a demo so epic in its new ideas and technical sophistication (for its time) it's now known as "The Mother of All Demos." He demonstrated now-familiar software and hardware for human-computer interaction. In the B/W video of the event (www.youtube.com/watch?v=hRYnloqYKGY), he demonstrates the mouse and chord keys (which never caught on), and explains why it's called a mouse. See also SRI's video www.youtube.com/watch?v=TPuC2dqdd_8

SRI Mouse

A year and a half later Microsoft introduced their Windows operating system, adding even more icons and more desktop-motivated features. Today, the desktop remains the interface of choice for much conventional computing. Other devices need a different metaphor.

The Touch Metaphor

When computers went mobile, the mouse, which had been so powerful on the desktop—literally, *on* a desktop—was now a problem: how does a mouse fit with a

"1984 Won't Be Like *1984*." The Apple Macintosh was launched in January 1984 by a one-minute commerical shown only once, after the third quarter of the Super Bowl. The commercial has become nearly as famous as the computer, as a quick check of Wikipedia confirms. View it at https://www.youtube.com/watch?v=8UZV7PDt8Lw

hand-held device? The stylus is one solution, but its use has always been limited. With no mouse, and the desktop's best uses of little interest—editing documents, for example—it made sense to change to a *touch* metaphor.

A familiar example of the **touch** metaphor is the Cover Flow mechanism for scanning through a list, especially of graphical items such as album covers or movie posters: A sweeping motion of the pointer (usually, a finger) across a sequence of items causes them to stream by with continuous, physical motion that slows to a stop; as the items move by, one item is identified as the selected one (see Figure 2.6).

Other gestures supporting the touch metaphor are available, though not yet standardized. A list of frequently recognized gestures is shown in Table 2.1.

Figure 2.6 Cover Flow, part of the touch metaphor; the item in the center (face on) is selected.

Table 2.1 Gestures supporting the touch metaphor

Gesture	Description	Typical Use	Typical Result
Sweep or Swipe	Move finger across surface	Scan through a list	Items sweep by, with one selected
Tap	Light one-finger tap on surface	Select or choose	Item identified
Double Tap	Light two-finger tap on surface	Launch	Selected item starts
Drag	Move selected item by pulling	Move item	Item in new position
Pinch Fingers/Pull Fingers Apart	Contract/expand separation between fingers	Shrink/zoom	Image is resized
Two-Finger Scroll	Move fingers across surface	Navigation	Move around a clipped image
Flick	Quick sweep, finger leaves surface	Express acceleration	Sustained sweep

Why So Metaphoric? Computing uses metaphors so extensively because all user interaction is created. Returning to volume controls, analog systems like record players use dials for volume control because the electronic device being controlled revolves to change its electrical properties. Using a dial for volume in that case is basically required. In computing, the entire UI is created; nothing is required, so controls can have any form. Using metaphors leverages intuition and experience.

Relationship Between Metaphors

Touch is new, but is it a new *metaphor*? Isn't it just a cool way to eliminate the mouse and use a touch-sensitive screen? That might seem true, because we are so focused on the gestures. However, touch is a basic change in how users are to think about interacting with the computer, and that makes it a new metaphor. Consider an example.

In a long list or other content that cannot all be displayed on the screen at once—a hundred album covers, for example—the desktop metaphor dictates that scroll bars should be introduced on the bottom (and/or the side) of the display, so users can navigate to where their interest lies. Using drag or other mouse motions, users can move the slider to see later items in the list move past the screen *as if viewed through a window* (see Figure 2.7). Contrast that action with the touch metaphor.

The Touch Metaphor. With the touch metaphor, there is no change to the display; scroll bars are not introduced, although in some cases there is positional feedback. (Eliminating scroll bars better uses the small screen real estate of mobile devices.) The user simply uses a swipe of a finger across the items *to move them out of the way* to navigate. If that were the end of it, then touch would simply be an alternative to the mouse. In fact, multitouch trackpads give users the touch motions just described in a desktop or laptop context.

The navigation motion illustrates that the metaphor changed:

> *Navigation motion*: In the touch metaphor you sweep your finger *left* to go later in the list; using the scroll bars of the desktop metaphor you pull the slider *right* to go later in the list. The direction of motion is the opposite between the touch and the desktop metaphors.

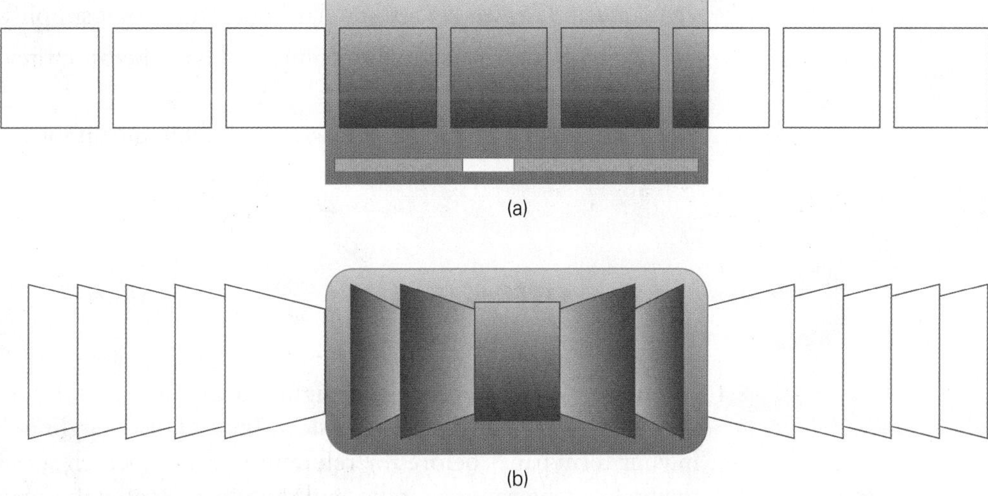

Figure 2.7 Schematic of two metaphors: (a) desktop metaphor window with scroll bar, and (b) touch metaphor with Cover Flow. To navigate to the last item on the right end, move the scroll bar *right*, or swipe the covers *left*.

The navigation action is different in the two metaphors because how you think about what you see—how the metaphor represents the screen content—is different. With the touch metaphor you "have your hands on the content." You push it around to locate your point of interest. In the desktop metaphor you "slide a window over the content"; you're not touching it. They are different actions because they support different metaphors.

Summary of Metaphors

We use technical metaphors daily, on our phones, tablets, iPods, and computers. They are 100 percent synthetic, created to simplify our use of the devices. The desktop metaphor is classic; the touch metaphor is serving users in places where file cabinets and wastebaskets have no place. The two will co-exist, and we will use both daily, being largely unaware of them, and how extensively they determine our thinking and behavior.

2.5 Know Your Metaphor. Referring to Table 2.1 and using your experience with computing, explain how to zoom in (say, on an image) in the two metaphors.

SUMMARY

This chapter began by exploring how we learn to use technology. We concluded the following:

- We can figure out software because designers use consistent interfaces, suggestive metaphors, and standard functionality.
- We should explore a new application by "clicking around" and "blazing away."
- Making exact copies is a fundamental property of digital information that we use daily.
- *Find* and *Replace All* are standard operations that simplify our computer use.
- Metaphors are essential to computer usage because they guide us in learning and using software.
- The desktop metaphor is classic; the touch metaphor is newer; they will co-exist.

TRY IT SOLUTIONS

2.1 Although your word processor might allow you to search for italicized words, changing each occurrence is too slow. Instead, use toggling: Select all of the text in your term paper before the references section, which should have italics, make the body of the paper all italic, and then make it all italic again—that is, toggle it. When you change the text to italics, the positions of all of the previous italics are lost; when it is italicized again—that is, changed back—all of the italics will be removed.

2.2 The *ms*, meaning Microsoft, will appear with a blank space in front of it; using F/RA with *space*ms solves the problem.

2.3 The commas that should stay will be followed by a space or possibly a closed quote ("). Hide them with two placeholders, remove the remaining commas, and restore the hidden text.

2.4 The specific sample text (etc.) and the placeholder (#) are nonessential; any text and any placeholder character meeting the "not used elsewhere" requirement works. The use of F/RA and the order of operations are essential to the abstraction.

2.5 In the desktop metaphor, zooming is usually done by moving a slider bar in the direction of + or –; in the touch metaphor, zooming is done by expanding or contracting two fingers. This is another example that the metaphors are different.

REVIEW QUESTIONS

Multiple Choice

1. What is a UI?
   a. update identification
   b. user identification
   c. user interface
   d. update interface
2. Which of the following is not a common computer metaphor?
   a. buttons
   b. door handles
   c. menus
   d. sliders
3. Which of the following is not an instance?
   a. image
   b. song file
   c. word processing document
   d. menu
4. Computers do
   a. exactly what you tell them to do
   b. only what other computers tell them to do
   c. instructions at random
   d. everything
5. A good way to learn how to use a new application or piece of software is to
   a. read the entire manual
   b. skim through the manual
   c. call tech support
   d. click around
6. Each time you paste, what is made of that saved version?
   a. file
   b. copy
   c. type
   d. replace

7. What key sequence does ^C indicate to the user
   a. Ctrl+C or Command+C
   b. c
   c. C
   d. Caps Lock + C
8. When computers went mobile, this popular device was now a problem.
   a. printer
   b. keyboard
   c. power cord
   d. mouse
9. What company introduced the mouse?
   a. Microsoft
   b. Apple
   c. IBM
   d. Xerox

Short Answer

1. Digital is better than analog encoding of information because with digital it is possible to have a(n) ________.
2. Software designers help users understand their software through the use of ________.
3. *Open*, *New*, *Close*, and *Save* can usually be found in the ________ menu.
4. Perfect reproduction is a property of ________ information.
5. In an application with menus, *Undo*, *Cut*, *Copy*, and *Paste* can usually be found in the ________ menu.
6. ________, ________, and ________ are the three steps of the placeholder technique.
7. ________ and ________ are important to keep in mind when using a placeholder.
8. ________ is any indication that the computer is still processing a task or has already completed it.
9. Overlapping windows were first used in the user interface of the ________.
10. Usually applications from the same vendor are ________.

Exercises

1. Explain the desktop metaphor.
2. Discuss the advantages of a consistent interface from both the consumer's and developer's point of view.
3. What is the purpose of computers displaying progress bars when items are loading?
4. Create a new document with the following text: "******". Then find "***" and replace it with "**". How many times did it find and replace? Explain in detail how the process worked.
5. Explain why feedback is important for the user.
6. State the perfect reproduction property of digital information and explain its power.
7. Explain why both copy and paste are considered copying information.

8. Angel decided to use the placeholder “the” to stand for Theodore Hertzsprung Englebert. Why was this a bad placeholder for Angel to use? Explain your answer in detail.
9. Explain the touch metaphor in detail, and explain what changed about computing to bring about the touch metaphor.
10. Explain why the touch metaphor has not replaced the desktop metaphor.
11. Why is it useful to “blaze away” when using a new piece of software?

CHAPTER 3

The Basics of Networking

Making the Connection

learning objectives

- Tell whether a communication technology (Internet, radio, LAN, etc.) is synchronous or asynchronous; broadcast or point-to-point
- Explain the roles of Internet addresses, domain names, and DNS servers in networking
- Distinguish between types of protocols (TCP/IP and Ethernet)
- Describe how computers are interconnected by an ISP and by a LAN
- Distinguish between the Internet and the World Wide Web
- Explain file structure, and how to navigate up and down the hierarchy

CHAPTER 3

We've all heard that a million monkeys banging on a million typewriters will eventually reproduce the entire work of Shakespeare. Now, thanks to the Internet, we know this is not true.

—ROBERT WILENSKY

Describing the Internet as the Network of Networks is like calling the Space Shuttle a thing that flies.

—JOHN LESTER

While modern technology has given people powerful new communications tools, it apparently can do nothing to alter the fact that many people have nothing useful to say.

—LEE GOMES, *SAN JOSE MERCURY NEWS*

COMPUTERS ALONE ARE USEFUL. Computers connected together are even more useful. Dramatic proof of this occurred in the mid-1990s when the Internet, long available to researchers, became generally available to the public. The Internet is the totality of all wires, fibers, switches, routers, satellite links, and other hardware for transporting information between addressed computers. For the first time, many people could conveniently and inexpensively connect their computers to the Internet and thereby connect to all other computers attached to the Internet. They could send email and surf the Web from home. This convenient access to volumes of information, eCommerce, blogs, and other capabilities greatly expanded the benefits people derived from computers. And the power and convenience of networking has improved dramatically every year since!

We begin this chapter by defining fundamental communication terms. These will help you compare the Internet with other forms of communication. Some topics are designed to give you a sense of how the Internet works without the technical details: naming computers, packets, the TCP/IP and Ethernet protocols, and connecting your computer to the Internet. Finally, the World Wide Web and file structures are explained in preparation for our discussion of HTML in Chapter 4.

Comparing Communication Types

To understand the Internet, which is a network of networks, it is necessary to explain some basic communication vocabulary.

General Communication

Communication between two entities, whether they are people or computers, can be separated into two broad classes: synchronous and asynchronous. **Synchronous communication** requires that both the sender and the receiver are active at the same time. A telephone conversation is an example of synchronous communication because both people in the conversation must perform one of the two parts of the communication—sending (talking) or receiving (listening)—simultaneously. In **asynchronous communication**, the sending and receiving occur at different times. Postcards and text messages are examples of asynchronous communication because they are written at one time and read at another. Answering machines and voice mail make synchronous telephones asynchronous because the caller leaves a message and the receiver listens to it later. Email is asynchronous; applications like Skype are synchronous computer communication.

Another property of communication concerns the number of receivers. **Broadcast communication** involves a single sender and many receivers. Radio and television are examples of broadcast communication. The term **multicast** is used when there are many receivers, but the intended recipients are not the whole population. Magazines, often covering specialized topics, are an example of multicast communication. The opposite of broadcasting and multicasting is **point-to-point communication**. Telephone communication and text messages are point-to-point because there is one specific sender and one specific receiver. The property of broadcast *versus* point-to-point communication is separate from the property of synchronous *versus* asynchronous communication.

Network of Networks. The Internet is a network built of networks. It is huge. In March 2013 it was estimated that 640 TB (trillion bytes) of data were transferred every minute. It was also estimated that in the course of 1 minute, 30 hours of video was uploaded to YouTube.

The Internet's Communication Properties

The Internet supports point-to-point asynchronous communication. A fundamental feature of the Internet is that it provides a general communication "fabric" linking all computers connected to it (see Figure 3.1). That is, the computers and the network become a single medium that can be applied in many ways to produce alternatives to established forms of communication. For example, the Internet can act like the postal system, but at electronic speed. In fact, the Internet is fast enough to mimic synchronous communication, which is why we can Skype: Two or more people can have a conversation by the rapid exchange of asynchronous messages, allowing the Internet to be used like a phone. Also, multicasting is possible, enabling small- to modest-size groups to communicate via blogs or discussion boards. Finally, because it is possible to post a Web page or YouTube video that can be accessed by anyone, the Internet offers a form of broadcasting that compares with radio or television. The Internet is truly a universal communications medium.

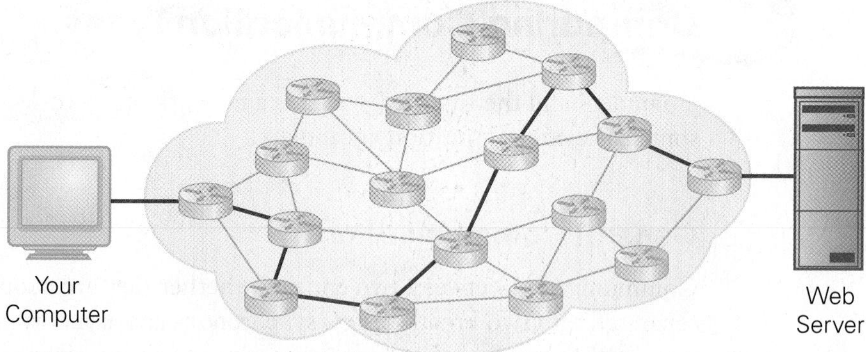

Figure 3.1 A schematic diagram of the Internet.

The Internet also becomes more effective with each additional computer added to it. That is, if x computers are already attached to the Internet, adding one more computer results in x potential new connections—that computer with each of the original machines.

Internet. The present-day Internet is the commercial descendant of the ARPANet, developed for the U.S. Department of Defense Advanced Research Projects Agency (DARPA). The ARPANet sent its first messages in 1969 at UCLA, and that fact—surprisingly—was mentioned in the campus paper *Daily Bruin* of July 19th.

Country's computers linked here first

A computer facility here will become the first station in a nation-wide network which, for the first time, will link together computers of different makes and using different machine languages.

Creation of the system "represents a new area of what computers might be like in the future . . . it will serve the faculty," according to the public information office here.

The project is supported by the Defense Department's Advanced Research Project Agency (ARPA).

The Client/Server Structure

Most interactions over the Internet use a protocol known as **client/server interaction**. This simple idea is illustrated by following what happens when you browse the Web.

A Brief Encounter. When you click a Web link, your computer begins the process of accessing the page for you. At that moment, your computer enters into a client/server interaction. Yours is the client computer and the computer on which the Web page is stored is the server computer, which is why it's called a **Web server** (see Figure 3.2). The term "client" refers to any situation where one computer, the *client*, gets services from another computer, the *server*. As a result of your client request, the server sends the page back over the Internet, fulfilling the request. That completes the operation started when you clicked on the link, and it ends that client/server relationship.

Moving in the Right Direction. When we get files like Web pages from a server, we are **downloading** them; when we put files on a server like posting videos to YouTube, we are **uploading** them. Think of the client as "below" the server.

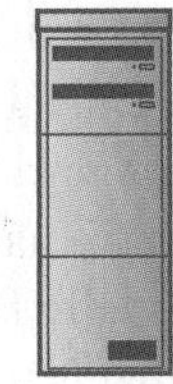

Server Computer
Provides services
(Returns the Web page file)

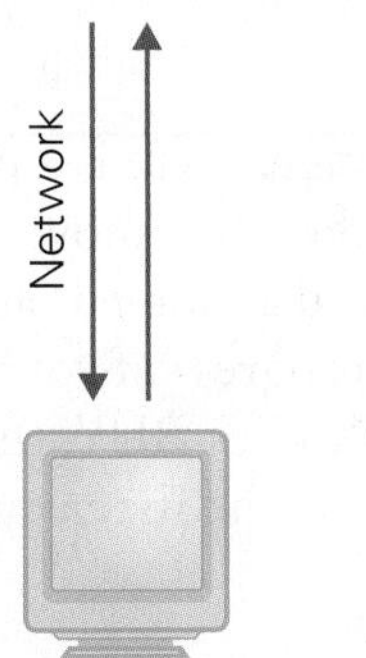

Client Computer
Requests services
(Sends URL for a Web page)

Figure 3.2 The basic client/server interaction, as illustrated by the browser (client) requesting Web pages provided by the Web server.

The client/server structure is fundamental to Internet interactions. A key aspect of the idea is that, as shown in Figure 3.2, only a single service request and response are involved. It is a very brief relationship, lasting from the moment the request is sent to the moment the service is received. Unlike a landline telephone call, in which a connection is made and *held* for as long as the call lasts, and during which there are many alternating exchanges, the client/server relationship is very short. It only entails the client's single request for a service and the server's reply in response.

Many Brief Relationships. An important advantage of this approach is that the server can handle many clients at a time. Typically between two consecutive client requests from your browser—between getting a Web page and asking for the next Web page from the same site—that server could have serviced hundreds or perhaps thousands of other clients. This is a very efficient system, because the server is busy with you only for as long as it takes to perform your single request. Once it's fulfilled, the relationship is over from the server's viewpoint. But the relationship is over from the client's (your) viewpoint, too. Your next click could be on a link for a different server. Between that click and the next time you visit the site, if ever, you and your browser could be clients to hundreds or perhaps thousands of other Web servers. Figure 3.3 shows the client/server relationship over an interval of time.

Getting More Connected. Although at its most basic level the Internet is a point-to-point asynchronous communication system, software has been built on it to implement the many forms of communication we use. For example, instant messaging and voice and video chat applications use client software—that is, software on the computers of the people communicating—to manage

Staying Connected. With wired telephones, callers stay connected even if no one is talking. In a client/server interaction, there is no connection. There is a client-to-server transmission for requests and a server-to-client transmission for replies. But doesn't your computer stay connected to the Internet? Yes, but only to your ISP—that is, to the Internet—not to a Web server.

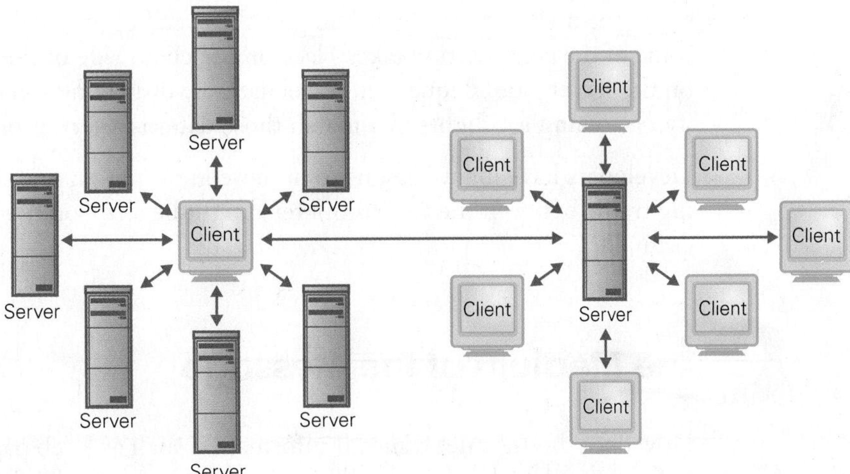

Figure 3.3 Client/server relationships as they might evolve over time.

the interaction. The client software "slices up" the signals coming from the computer's microphone and video camera into packet-size blocks (explained in a moment). The content is transferred to the other party, whose client reassembles the sound and image to display to you. The whole process depends on fast, reliable transmission to make it seem like a direct connection. As we shall see, the Internet Protocol is usually fast and generally reliable enough to make this work, but neither property is guaranteed. Nevertheless, the process works very well.

Appearing to Stay Connected

Because the client/server protocol is built around one quick exchange, there is a problem for sites that want to "stay connected" with users. How does the bank know your "Check Balance" request applies to the account number you entered a moment ago? Or, how does an airline that is selling tickets online keep track of the progress of your ticket purchase? During the time from which you started until you finally click BUY, the site may have sent itineraries to hundreds of people since it first sent you the itinerary you requested.

Two Solutions. Web sites use two basic solutions to give the illusion of a continuous connection using the client/server protocol.

- **Cookies** are small files stored on the client computer by the server, and returned to the server with each page request. The file contains enough data from the server, such as a unique identifier, that it can connect you to earlier interactions.
- **URL Parameters** are information added by a client to a URL when it connects to the server. You notice this information, for example, when you're buying airline tickets: flybynite.com/buytix.php?trip=round&leg1=ORDtoLAX&dep=041114&ret=. . . It's the information following the question mark.

Both techniques allow your client to send enough data to the server for it to figure out which of its recent interactions was yours, and to give you the illusion of having stayed connected. Both techniques are common; cookies are both convenient and dangerous, and they are discussed further in the Security Chapter 12.

Client Side/Server Side. One more aspect of the client/server interaction is worth knowing about. The question is, "Who does the work?" For example, when an airline sends you a Web page so you can give the specifics of a flight you want to purchase, some of the computation takes place on the client side of the communication, and some on the server side. Requesting travel dates by displaying a calendar is a client-side activity. Searching for flights that match those dates is a server-side activity.

Developers have many reasons to prefer computing on one side or the other. Reducing traffic between the two computers might be a reason to shift work to the client, for example.

The Medium of the Message

How does the Internet transmit information such as Web pages and email messages? Complex and sophisticated technologies are used to make the Internet work well, but the basic idea is extremely simple.

The Name Game of Computer Addresses

To begin, recall that the Internet uses point-to-point communication. When anything is sent point-to-point—a phone conversation, a letter, or furniture—the destination address is required.

IP Addresses. Each computer connected to the Internet is given a unique address called its **IP address**, short for **Internet Protocol address**. An IP address is a sequence of four numbers separated by dots. For example, the machine I am typing on has the IP address 128.208.3.136, and the machine where I receive email is 128.95.1.4. Although the range of each of the four numbers (0–255) allows for billions of Internet addresses, IP addresses are actually in short supply.

Change of Address. Since the 1970s we have used Internet Protocol Version 4 (IPv4). IPv4 specifies that IP addresses consist of four one-byte numbers. Four was plenty for the days when only about 200 computers were networked. Now most of the 1.5 billion computer users have a personal computer, motivating the development of Internet Protocol Version 6 (IPv6). IPv6 specifies IP addresses to be sixteen numbers long, solving the IP address problem for good.

IP Packet

#: 1 Tech Bits: 11001001
Sender: 128.208.3.136
Receiver: 192.33.92.189
Payload: Hello! Blah-blah-blah-blah-blah-blab-blah-

IP Packet. A computer communicates with another computer by sending an **IP packet** to its IP address. The packet is like a postcard: It has the IP address of the computer being contacted and the return IP address; it also has a sequence number (more about that later), a few bits used for technical purposes, and a payload. The **payload** is what's being sent—it may be one byte, or thousands.

The Size of an IP Packet. An IP packet starts with a header of 12 bytes containing the bits needed for technical purposes, including sequencing; after that, there are 4 bytes for the sender's IP address and 4 bytes for the destination's IP address, giving a total of 20. After the header comes the actual data, or payload, of up to 65,528 bytes. The grand total is 20 + 65,528 = 65,548 bytes.

Routing and Switching. As suggested by Figure 3.1, the Internet is many switches and routers connected by copper wires, fiber optic cable, microwave links, radios, and other technologies. When an IP packet arrives at a switch, the switch reads the destination IP address, decides which of the routers that it's connected to will take the packet closer to its destination, and forwards the packet on. The transition from one router to the next is called a **hop**.

Many Paths. All routers and switches are connected to several others. They can send packets to any of their neighbor routers. If a router's neighbor is not responding—possibly, because it has failed, is busy, has been taken offline for maintenance, or for another reason—the router simply uses some other neighbor. As a result, IP packets headed to the same place can take different routes to their destination.

Trace Route. Because two packets can take different routes to one destination, networking engineers record (and analyze) the routes packets take. They use a tool called *Trace Route*. Figure 3.4 shows the route a packet took from my office at the University of Washington in Seattle to the Swiss National Technical University in Zurich (ETHZ). It required 20 hops.

Traceroute

Tracing route to 192.33.92.189

Hop	Time	Host	IP	Locations
1	0.692	10.0.0.1	10.0.0.1	Local (CSE)
2	3.074	10.20.62.254	10.20.62.254	Local (UW?)
3	5.035	r2-l3tca-cr2.nextweb.net	216.237.3.33	Irvine, CA
4	10.195	ge-6-15.car2.Tustin1.Level3.net	4.79.142.41	Tustin, CA
5	159.713	vl-3202-ve-134.ebr2.Tustin1.Level3.net	4.69.160.17	Tustin, CA
6	167.65	ae-7-7.ebr3.LosAngeles1.Level3.net	4.69.153.225	Los Angeles
7	190.5	ae-12-12.ebr3.LosAngeles1.Level3.net	4.69.132.82	Los Angeles
8	185.48	ae-81-81.csw3.Washington1.Level3.net	4.69.134.138	Washington, DC
9	170.699	ae-72-72.ebr2.Washington1.Level3.net	4.69.134.149	Washington, DC
10	170.967	ae-42-42.ebr2.Paris1.Level3.net	4.69.137.53	Paris, FR
11	166.41	ae-9-9.car1.Lyon1.Level3.net	4.69.134.49	Lyon, FR
12	162.49	ae-5-5.car1.Geneva1.Level3.net	4.69.137.81	Geneva, CH
13	171.875	DANTE.car1.Geneva1.Level3.net	213.242.73.74	Geneva, CH
14	170.299	swiLS2-10GE-1-3.switch.ch	130.59.37.2	Zurich, CH
15	184.92	swiEZ2-10GE-1-1.switch.ch	130.59.36.206	Zurich, CH
16	170.094	rou-gw-rz-tengig-to-switch.ethz.ch	192.33.92.1	ETH
17	190.544	rou-fw-rz-rz-gw.ethz.ch	192.33.92.169	Local (ETH)
21	N/A	192.33.92.189	192.33.92.189	

Figure 3.4 A packet's route from the University of Washington, Seattle, to ethz.ch, the Swiss National Technical University in Zurich (note that the figure doesn't show the local hops 18–20). Try it: whatismyipaddress.com/traceroute-tool.

The packet started its route at my computer in the CSE Department and had to make its way through local networks to reach the Internet gateway; IP addresses starting with 10 are reserved for such local routing purposes. From the gateway it went directly to Irvine, California, and took several hops around Los Angeles—both Irvine and Tustin are near Los Angeles. It then crossed the United States in one hop to Washington, D.C., took a local hop in D.C., and then crossed the Atlantic in one more hop. It toured Western Europe, visiting Paris, Lyon, and Geneva. From Geneva it hopped to Zurich, then to ETH, and routed locally (not listed) to the destination computer. Notice that most of the hops can be classified as a local (physically nearby) hop or a very long-distance hop.

Following Protocol

Having figured out how a computer addresses other computers to send them information, we still need to describe how the information is actually sent. The sending process uses **Transmission Control Protocol/Internet Protocol (TCP/IP)**. It sounds technical—and is—but the concept is easy to understand.

TCP/IP Postcard Analogy. To explain how TCP/IP works, we repeat an analogy used by Vinton Cerf, one of the pioneers of IP: Sending information over the Internet is like sending your novel from your home in Tahiti to your publisher in New York City using only postcards. How could you do that? You begin by breaking up the novel into small units, only a few sentences long, so that each unit fits on a postcard. Then, you number each postcard to indicate where in the sequence of your novel the sentences belong, and write the publisher's address on each. As you complete the postcards, you drop them into a mailbox. The postal service in Tahiti sends them to the publisher (eventually), but the cards are not kept together, nor do they all take the same route. Some postcards may go west, via

#1
Chapter 1:
It was a dark
and stormy night.
Rain pelted the
glass as Sir
Bulwer-Lytton
dozed restlessly.
Great Books
1830 1st Ave
New York, NY
USA

Hong Kong; others may go east, via Los Angeles. From Hong Kong and Los Angeles, there are multiple routes to New York City. Eventually the postcards arrive at the publisher, who uses the numbers to put the postcards in order and reconstruct the novel.

Cerf's postcard analogy makes the concept of TCP/IP clear. Sending any amount of information, including a whole novel, is possible by breaking it into a sequence of small fixed-size units. An IP packet, like the postcard, has space for one unit of information, a destination and return IP address, and a sequence number. IP packets are filled in order and assigned sequence numbers. The packets are sent over the Internet one at a time, independently, using whatever route is available. At the destination, they are reordered by sequence number to assemble the information.

3.1 Too Wordy! The novel *Atlas Shrugged* by Ayn Rand is estimated to be 645,000 words long. If a word is five letters (on average) followed by a space, there is one punctuation symbol every four words (on average, because dialog needs so many), and all letters and symbols use one byte, how many IP packets would it take to transmit *Atlas Shrugged* over the Internet?

Packets Are Independent. Consider the advantages of TCP/IP. For example, it is natural to assume that IP packets would take a single path to their destinations, like wired telephone calls do, but they do not. Because each packet can take a different route, congestion and service interruptions do not delay transmissions. If sending the first postcard via Hong Kong meant that all following postcards had to be sent via Hong Kong, then a typhoon preventing aircraft from flying between Tahiti and Hong Kong would delay the novel's transmission. But if the postcards can take any available route, the transmission can continue via Los Angeles. As a result, all of the novel might be delivered via Los Angeles before airline service is restored between Tahiti and Hong Kong. This concept motivated engineers to decide to make TCP/IP packets independent.

The TCP/IP protocol is robust, meaning that it continues to work under adverse conditions. For example, when traffic gets heavy and the progress of a packet slows down, the protocol allows the packet to be thrown away. It's okay to kill packets for congestion relief or other reasons, because when they don't show up at the destination quickly, the recipient server will request a resend. Also, because packets take different routes, they can arrive out of order. Both of these characteristics are discovered during packet assembly, allowing the system to recover from unusual circumstances.

Netting a Prize. Vint Cerf and Bob Kahn received the 2004 Turing Award from the Association of Computing Machinery (ACM), computing's Nobel Prize, for the development of TCP/IP.

Far and Near: WAN and LAN

The Internet is a collection of **wide area networks (WANs)**, meaning networks designed to send information between two locations widely separated and not directly connected. In our postcard analogy, Tahiti and New York City are not directly connected; that is, we don't expect there to be a single airline flight between Tahiti and the Big Apple. So, each postcard takes a sequence of connecting flights, just as the IP packet takes a sequence of hops.

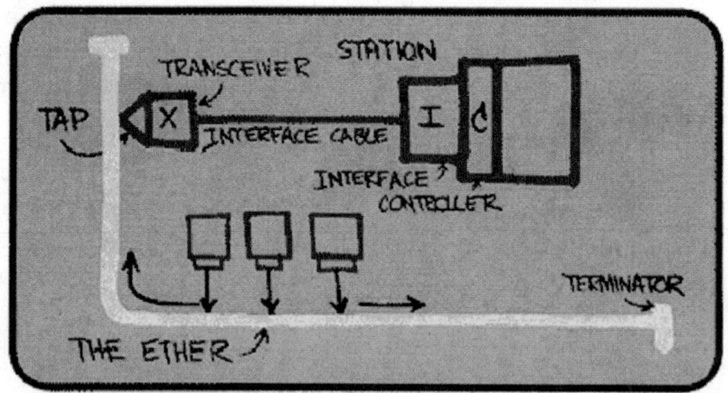

Figure 3.5 Robert Metcalfe's original drawing of the Ethernet design; the unlabeled boxes (computers) "tap" into the wire (yellow) that Metcalfe labeled "The Ether." He described the Ethernet (in 1973) as a "multipoint data communication channel with collision detection."

When computers are close enough to be linked by a single cable or pair of wires, the interconnection is referred to as a **local area network (LAN)**. Ethernet is the main technology for local area networks, and is appropriate for connecting all the computers in a lab or building. An Ethernet network is radically different from the Internet, but it's equally easy to understand.

Ethernet, the Setup. Depending on the technology, the physical setup for an Ethernet network is a wire, wire pair, or optical fiber, called the **channel**, that winds past a set of computers. (Robert Metcalfe, the inventor of the Ethernet design, described the channel as the "The Ether," giving the technology its name; see Figure 3.5.) Engineers "tap" the channel to connect a computer, allowing it to send a signal (that is, drive an electronic pulse or light flash onto the channel). All computers connected to the channel can detect the signal, including the sender. Thus, the channel supports broadcast communication.

Ethernet, Party Analogy. To understand how an Ethernet network works, consider another analogy. A group of friends is standing around at a party telling stories. While someone is telling a story, everyone is listening. The speaker is broadcasting to the group. When the story is over, how do the friends decide who tells the next story? Since there is no plan or agreement as to who should speak next, someone typically just begins talking. If no one else begins talking, that speaker continues telling the story to completion. At the end of the story, the same situation arises. There is a pause, and then someone else starts talking.

If two or more people begin talking after the pause, they will notice that someone else is speaking and immediately stop. There is a pause while everyone waits for someone to go ahead. Assuming speakers tend to wait a random length of time, someone will begin talking. It's possible that two or more speakers will again start at the same time, notice the situation, stop, and wait a random length of time. Eventually one person will begin telling another story.

In this analogy, we have assumed all the friends are equal; that is, there is no difference in status, nor does anyone have an especially loud or soft voice. Even so, the system isn't fair, because it favors the person who waits the shortest length of time at the end of a story. Of course, we all know such people!

Ethernet, the Protocol. Ethernet communication works like the party protocol. When a computer is sending signals on the channel, as when someone is telling a story, all of the computers listen to it. (Unlike storytelling, however, only one computer typically keeps the transmitted information; that is, this broadcast medium is being used for point-to-point communication.) A pause indicates the end of the transmission when no computer is sending signals and the channel is quiet. A computer wanting to transmit starts sending signals and, at the same time, starts listening to the channel to detect what is being transmitted. If it is exactly the information the computer sent, the computer knows it's the only one sending, and it completes its transmission. If the computer's signals are mixed in with signals from one or more other computers, it notices the garbled message and stops transmitting immediately. The other computer(s) stop, too. Each machine pauses for a random length of time. The computer that waits the shortest length of time begins sending, and if there are no conflicting computers, it continues. If not, the colliders repeat the process.

Many Versus One. There is an important difference between the Internet's TCP/IP protocol and Ethernet's party protocol. The Internet uses a point-to-point network to implement point-to-point communication. An Ethernet uses a broadcast network for point-to-point communication. The difference is that with the Internet, multiple communications can take place at once over different wires, but with the Ethernet, only one communication can take place at a time because there is just one wire. This limitation is usually not a problem, because Ethernets usually carry much less traffic.

Notice that the Ethernet scheme is completely decentralized and requires no schedule or plan. Each computer listens to the channel, and if it's quiet, it's free. The computer transmits unless some other computer starts at the same moment. When that happens, both computers back off for a brief (random) amount of time and then try again.

The Size of an Ethernet Packet. An Ethernet packet is limited to 1500 bytes, and because many of us use an Ethernet to access the Internet, the effective size of an IP packet is reduced to 1480 bytes plus the 20 header bytes required when the packet gets to the Internet.

Connecting Your Computer to the Internet

Much of the time when we want to connect to the Internet, it's just there. At school. At the espresso shop. Someone has already established a connection. How? Today there are two basic methods:

- Connection via an Internet service provider (ISP)
- Connection provided by a campus or enterprise network

Transportation Networks

Most of us use both kinds of connections daily, depending on where we study or work. Let's look at each approach, illustrated in Figure 3.6.

Connections by ISP. As the name implies, Internet service providers sell connections to the Internet. Examples of ISPs are phone companies and cable companies, but there are thousands of providers. Most home users connect to the Internet by ISPs. Here's how an ISP connection usually works.

Your ISP company gives you a modem for your house. Modems convert the bits a computer outputs into a form (the orange line in the figure) that is compatible with the carrier. These signals are sent to the carrier's business where they are converted (via another modem) into a form suitable for the server that connects to the Internet

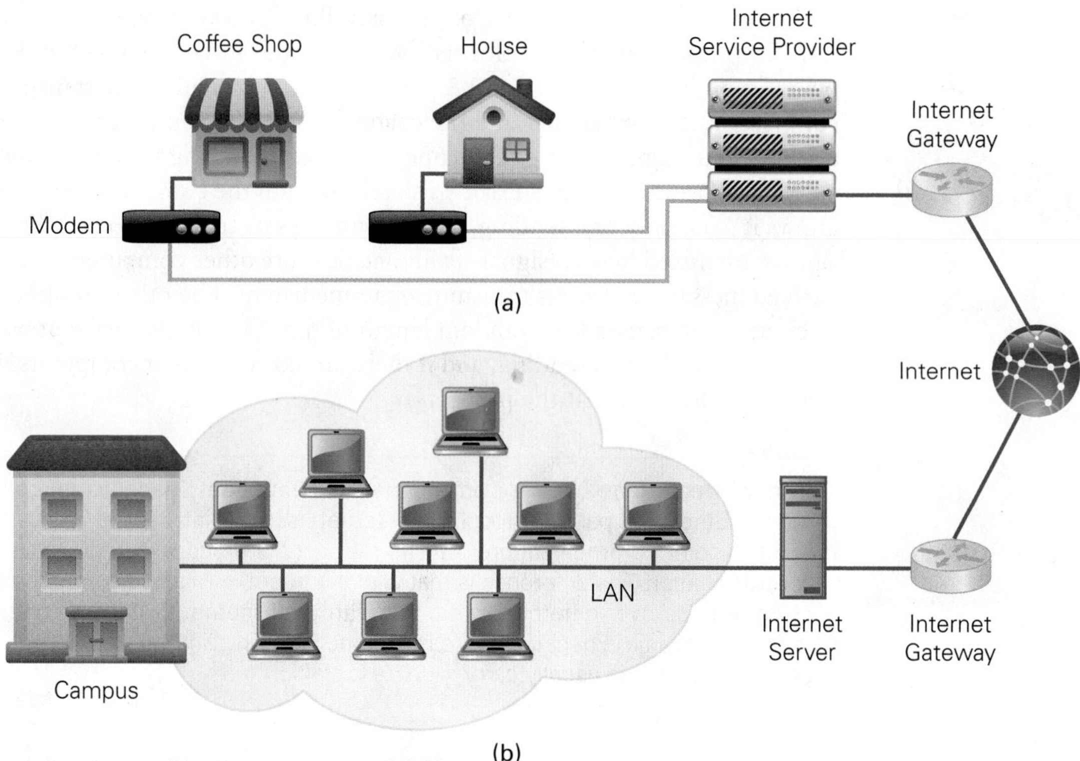

Figure 3.6 Schematic diagram of connecting to the Internet. (a) An ISP's modem converts the computer's bits to signals the carrier's technology (phone lines, cable, microwave, etc.) can use; their servers connect to the Internet gateway. (b) On campus (or at another enterprise), the local network's server connects directly to the Internet gateway.

via the Internet gateway. The digital subscriber line (DSL or ADSL, for asymmetric DSL) and cable (the same folks that bring you TV) are two very common service providers. When you use your smartphone, it has a modem for connecting to the so-called "wireless broadband" network such as the 4G network provided by phone carriers; its radio signals behave just like the orange line to connect you to the Internet.

Enterprise Network Connections (LAN). The other way to connect to the Internet is as a user of a larger networked organization such as a school, business, or governmental unit. In this case, the organization's system administrators connect the computers to form a local area network (LAN) or interconnected LANs using Ethernet. These local networks, collectively known as an **intranet**, support communication within the organization, but they also connect to the Internet by a gateway.

With either method, ISP or LAN, you usually send and receive information across the Internet transparently—that is, without knowing or caring which method is used.

Wireless Networks. **Wireless networking** is a variation on the LAN connection and is often referred to by its protocol name, **802.11**, pronounced *eight-oh-two-eleven* (see Figure 3.7). It is the technology used inside coffee shops and homes. The **router** is physically connected to an ISP's modem connected to the Internet and is capable of broadcasting and receiving radio frequency (RF) signals. The router and any computers within signal range (with their wireless communication turned on) participate in a network based on the Ethernet principles described earlier. The router relays Internet requests for the participating computers.

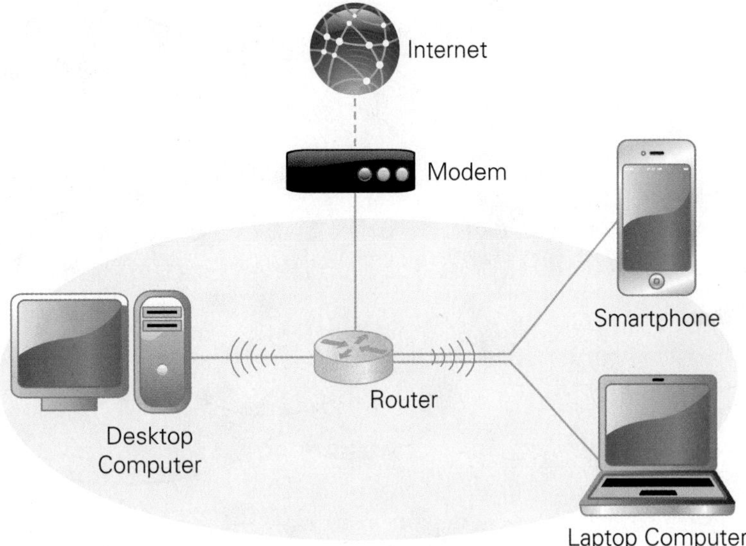

Figure 3.7 Standard Wi-Fi network configuration. A wireless router is connected via the modem to the ISP's Internet modem; laptops and other wireless-enabled devices connect by radio signals to the router.

Should I Know My Computer's IP Address? No. If you connect to the Internet via an ISP, your computer is assigned a temporary IP address when you initially access the ISP; you keep it until you break the connection. If you access the Internet via an intranet, one of two cases applies. Your network administrator may have permanently assigned your computer an IP address when it was set up. Alternatively, if no permanent address was assigned, you get a temporary address when you boot your machine. Temporary addresses are assigned using the **Dynamic Host Configuration Protocol (DHCP)**. Wireless uses DHCP, too. In all cases, the IP address is nothing you have to worry about.

Domains and the DNS

We have focused on IP addresses, the numbers computers use to refer to each other on the Internet, but *we* don't use IP addresses. You don't call it 107.22.185.79, you call it kickstarter.com. You use **domain names** to refer to computers, rather than their IP addresses. This is as it should be, because who wants to type in long numbers?

Hierarchy Is Handy. The **domain name system (DNS)** is the hierarchical structure we use to name computers. The domain name for the computer I'm typing on (128.208.3.136) is spiff.cs.washington.edu. This computer name has a structure.

The edu portion of the name, as you probably know, implies that the computer is part of an educational organization; edu is a top-level domain name used by accredited educational organizations. One such institution is the University of Washington, and all of the computers at the university are part of the washington domain, within the edu domain. Among the departments at UW is the computer science department, and all of its computers are part of the cs domain, within the washington domain, within the edu domain. And spiff is one of those computers in the cs domain. We know all of this simply by breaking the domain name into its parts.

One benefit of a hierarchical organization is that it is easy to remember computer names.

Peers. Domains at the same level in the hierarchy are *peers* of each other (see Figure 3.8). Other computers used by members of the CS Department are peers of spiff. For example,

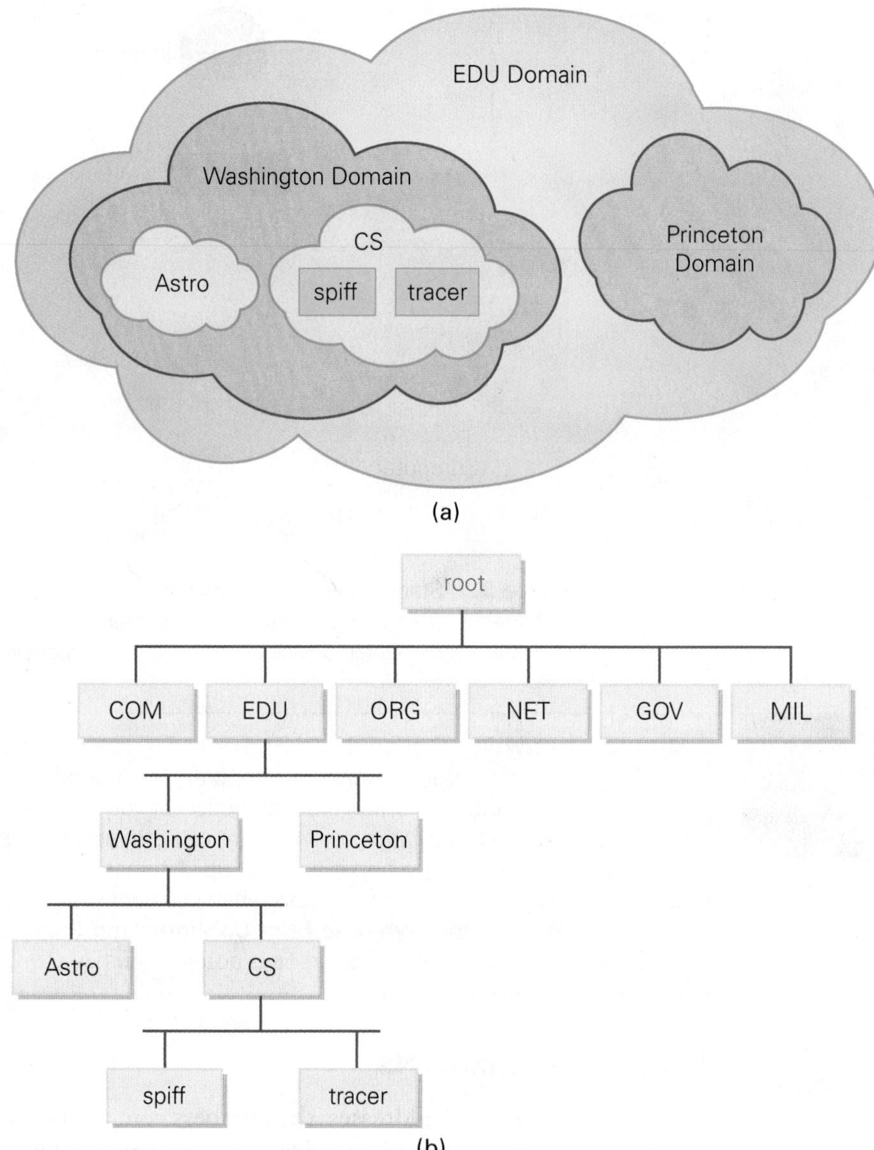

Figure 3.8 Two ways to think of the Internet domain hierarchy.

tracer.cs.washington.edu is a peer, because it is a member of the exact same domains. Other departments at UW are peers in the washington.edu domain; astro.washington.edu, for example, is a peer of cs.washington.edu. The other universities in the edu domain are peers of each other; for example, princeton.edu. And the edu domain is a peer of other top-level domains, such as com or org.

Top-Level Domains. When the Domain Name Systems was first set up in 1985, it recognized only seven **top-level domain names**: com, edu, gov, int, mil, net, and org; int is for international organizations like NATO and the United Nations, and mil is for the U.S. military.

The original top-level domains, except int, apply to organizations in the United States. Additionally, a set of mnemonic two-letter country domains were chosen, such as **ca** (Canada), **uk** (United Kingdom), **de** (Germany, as in Deutschland), **es** (Spain, as in España), **ch** (Switzerland, as in Confoederatio Helvetica, its Latin name), and so on. (See Table 3.1 for a complete list.) These allow domain names to be grouped by their country of origin. The top-level domains were expanded in 2000 to include biz, info, name, travel, and others; more have been added since. The full list can be found at www.icann.org.

Table 3.1 Top-level country domain names.

Code	Country Name	Code	Country Name	Code	Country Name	Code	Country Name
AF	Afghanistan	DK	Denmark	LS	Lesotho	LC	Saint Lucia
AL	Albania	DJ	Djibouti	LR	Liberia	WS	Samoa
DZ	Algeria	DM	Dominica	LY	Libya	SM	San Marino
AS	American Samoa	DO	Dominican Republic	LI	Liechtenstein	ST	Sao Tome and Principe
AD	Andorra	EC	Ecuador	LT	Lithuania	SA	Saudi Arabia
AO	Angola	EG	Egypt	LU	Luxembourg	SN	Senegal
AI	Anguilla	SV	El Salvador	MO	Macao	RS	Serbia
AQ	Antarctica	GQ	Equatorial Guinea	MK	Macedonia	SC	Seychelles
AG	Antigua and Barbuda	ER	Eritrea	MG	Madagascar	SL	Sierra Leone
AR	Argentina	EE	Estonia	MW	Malawi	SG	Singapore
AM	Armenia	ET	Ethiopia	MY	Malaysia	SX	Sint Maarten (Dutch Part)
AW	Aruba	FK	Falkland Islands	MV	Maldives	SK	Slovakia
AU	Australia	FO	Faroe Islands	ML	Mali	SI	Slovenia
AT	Austria	FJ	Fiji	MT	Malta	SB	Solomon Islands
AZ	Azerbaijan	FI	Finland	MH	Marshall Islands	SO	Somalia
BS	Bahamas	FR	France	MQ	Martinique	ZA	South Africa
BH	Bahrain	GF	French Guiana	MR	Mauritania	GS	S Georgia S Sandwich Islands
BD	Bangladesh	PF	French Polynesia	MU	Mauritius	SS	South Sudan
BB	Barbados	GA	Gabon	MX	Mexico	ES	Spain
BY	Belarus	GM	Gambia	FM	Micronesia	LK	Sri Lanka
BE	Belgium	GE	Georgia	MD	Moldova	SD	Sudan
BZ	Belize	DE	Germany	MC	Monaco	SR	Suriname
BJ	Benin	GH	Ghana	MN	Mongolia	SZ	Swaziland
BM	Bermuda	GI	Gibraltar	ME	Montenegro	SE	Sweden
BT	Bhutan	GR	Greece	MS	Montserrat	CH	Switzerland
BO	Bolivia	GL	Greenland	MA	Morocco	SY	Syria
BA	Bosnia and Herzegovina	GD	Grenada	MZ	Mozambique	TW	Taiwan
BW	Botswana	GP	Guadeloupe	MM	Myanmar	TJ	Tajikistan
BV	Bouvet Island	GU	Guam	NA	Namibia	TZ	Tanzania
BR	Brazil	GT	Guatemala	NR	Nauru	TH	Thailand
BN	Brunei Darussalam	GG	Guernsey	NP	Nepal	TG	Togo
BG	Bulgaria	GN	Guinea	NL	Netherlands	TK	Tokelau
BF	Burkina Faso	GW	Guinea-Bissau	NC	New Caledonia	TO	Tonga
BI	Burundi	GY	Guyana	NZ	New Zealand	TT	Trinidad and Tobago
KH	Cambodia	HT	Haiti	NI	Nicaragua	TN	Tunisia
CM	Cameroon	HN	Honduras	NE	Niger	TR	Turkey
CA	Canada	HK	Hong Kong	NG	Nigeria	TM	Turkmenistan
CV	Cape Verde	HU	Hungary	NU	Niue	TC	Turks and Caicos Islands
KY	Cayman Islands	IS	Iceland	NF	Norfolk Island	TV	Tuvalu
CF	Central African Republic	IN	India	MP	Mariana Islands	UG	Uganda
TD	Chad	ID	Indonesia	NO	Norway	UA	Ukraine
CL	Chile	IR	Iran	OM	Oman	AE	United Arab Emirates
CN	China	IQ	Iraq	PK	Pakistan	GB	United Kingdom
CX	Christmas Island	IE	Ireland	PW	Palau	US	United States
CC	Cocos (Keeling) Islands	IM	Isle of Man	PS	Palestine	UY	Uruguay
CO	Colombia	IL	Israel	PA	Panama	UZ	Uzbekistan
KM	Comoros	IT	Italy	PG	Papua New Guinea	VU	Vanuatu
CG	Congo	JM	Jamaica	PY	Paraguay	VE	Venezuela
CD	Congo, Drc	JP	Japan	PE	Peru	VN	Viet Nam
CK	Cook Islands	JE	Jersey	PH	Philippines	VG	Virgin Islands, British
CR	Costa Rica	JO	Jordan	PN	Pitcairn	VI	Virgin Islands, U.S.
CI	CÔTE D'Ivoire	KZ	Kazakhstan	PL	Poland	EH	Western Sahara
HR	Croatia	KE	Kenya	PT	Portugal	YE	Yemen
CU	Cuba	KI	Kiribati	PR	Puerto Rico	ZM	Zambia
CW	Curaçao	KP	Korea, DPR	QA	Qatar	ZW	Zimbabwe
CY	Cyprus	KR	Korea	RE	Réunion		
CZ	Czech Republic	KW	Kuwait	RO	Romania		
		KG	Kyrgyzstan	RU	Russia		
		LA	Lao	RW	Rwanda		
		LV	Latvia	SH	Saint Helena		
		LB	Lebanon	KN	Saint Kitts and Nevis		

3.2 Where in the World? You have probably used **bit.ly**, the URL shortening service, whose top-level domain is Libya. The *New York Times* newspaper has a URL shortening service, too: **nyti.ms**. Where is their top-level domain registered? Could they have chosen a better country?

A Problem. People use hierarchical domain names. Computers use IP addresses. For you to visit facebook.com, the computer needs to know that you mean 31.13.69.128. Figuring that out is the task for the Domain Name System (DNS) servers.

All Internet-connected computers, when they are first set up to connect to the Internet, are given the IP address of one or more DNS servers (see Figure 3.9). These machines look up domain names you use and find the corresponding IP addresses. They just have a list of [*domain name* : IP *address*] pairs. Given a domain name, the DNS server returns the address to your computer, which continues with connecting you to the site. Nothing could be easier.

Wait! How does the DNS server get the list? *There is no master list of all domains on the Internet*. None. To solve this problem, suppose you want to visit the Web site of the National Air & Space Museum in Washington, D.C. Its domain name is airandspace.si.edu. Your computer asks its DNS server for the IP address, but it's not in the list. "Houston, we have a problem."

Authoritative Name Server. Although your DNS server never heard of airandspace.si.edu, some computer knows its IP address. That computer is the **authoritative name server** for the domain that airandspace is in, which is the si domain. Every domain on the Internet has one: a single computer that knows the IP address of all of the computers in its domain. This computer—let's abbreviate it ANS—is the *authority*; if a computer isn't on its list, it's not in the domain; if it is, it knows its IP address. So, all your DNS server needs to do is ask the si-ANS for the IP address of airandspace, get the answer back, and add the pair [airandspace.si.edu : 160.111.252.58] to its list.

Unfortunately, your DNS server probably doesn't have the IP address of si-ANS, either. Are we making any progress? Yes. The authoritative name server idea can fix it.

Start at the Top. We just said that every domain on the Internet has an ANS. It knows all. So, we need to start at the top of the hierarchy, not at the bottom like we just did. That is, begin by finding the IP address for the edu-ANS. It knows the IP addresses for the ANS machines for all of its domain. Ask it for the IP address of si-ANS. That machine knows the IP addresses of all of the computers in its domain. Ask it for the IP address of airandspace.

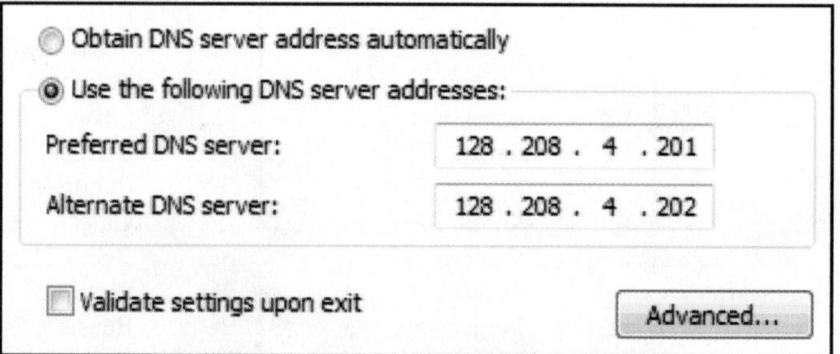

Figure 3.9 The DNS servers displayed for a computer running the Windows 7 OS.

This is a solution that will always work: move along the domain name in the URL (right to left) asking the authoritative name server at each level what the IP address is for the ANS in the next level down. When you get to the last ANS, presto, it knows the answer. It works, but we need to know the ANS machines for the top-level domains.

The computers that know the IP addresses for the top-level domain, for example, edu-ANS, are the 13 **root name servers**. Think of root as the domain *above* all of the top-level domains; it's a virtual domain. In this view, every domain name ends with .root, as in airandspace.si.edu.root.

Root Name Servers. These 13 computers scattered around the world are the authoritative name servers for all of the top-level domains (TLDs). They have a complete list of TLD authoritative name servers, but only for the TLDs. From them, your DNS can find edu-ANS; from it, your DNS can find si-ANS; from it, your DNS can find the IP address for airandspace. It's a clever solution.

Where does your DNS server get the IP addresses of the 13 root name servers? The IP addresses are preloaded when the machine boots. How does your DNS choose which one to ask? They are all the same so it doesn't matter; ask the closest one. The list of 13 [*domain name* : IP *address*] pairs is not much information considering it is enough to start to find any IP address of the billions of computers connected to the Internet.

Where do the root name servers get the list of IP addresses they keep of the TLDs? They are just loaded when the machine boots, too. If a new TLD is added, they are all reloaded.

3.3 Asking for Help. The Web server for the Astronomy Picture of the Day (APOD) has the domain name **apod.nasa.gov** and the IP address **204.202.20.2**. In principle, what authoritative name servers will your computer's DNS server ask to find this IP address for you?

Caching. The process as described is how DNS works *in principle*, but there are a lot of shortcuts. For example, it seems as if the root name servers would get a lot of traffic, and they do. But, once a DNS server finds out the IP address for, say edu-ANS, it saves it for future reference. It doesn't have to ask again right away. This reduces the traffic enormously. The act of saving information for possible reuse soon is called **caching**. Caching is a big idea in computing, and it helps DNS servers a lot. If anyone that the DNS serves has referenced a site recently, it will have the [*domain name* : IP *address*] in its list. It doesn't have to look it up again; it just uses it. That's a big win.

Redundancy. There are 13 root name servers to help share the load, but also to make sure that some machines will always be running. The use of multiple copies of information—the TLD list in this case—is called **redundancy**.

In fact, there are many more copies of the TLD list than 13. As shown in Figure 3.10, there are "mirror" sites duplicating each of the 13 original roots. Check the site www.root-servers.org to find the 13 machines (A through M) and their mirrors around the world. Can you figure out which "mirror" is closest to your home?

DNS Summary

The Doman Name System is amazing. It is a completely decentralized system—no one is in charge, though the Internet Assigned Names Authority (IANA) takes care of the root

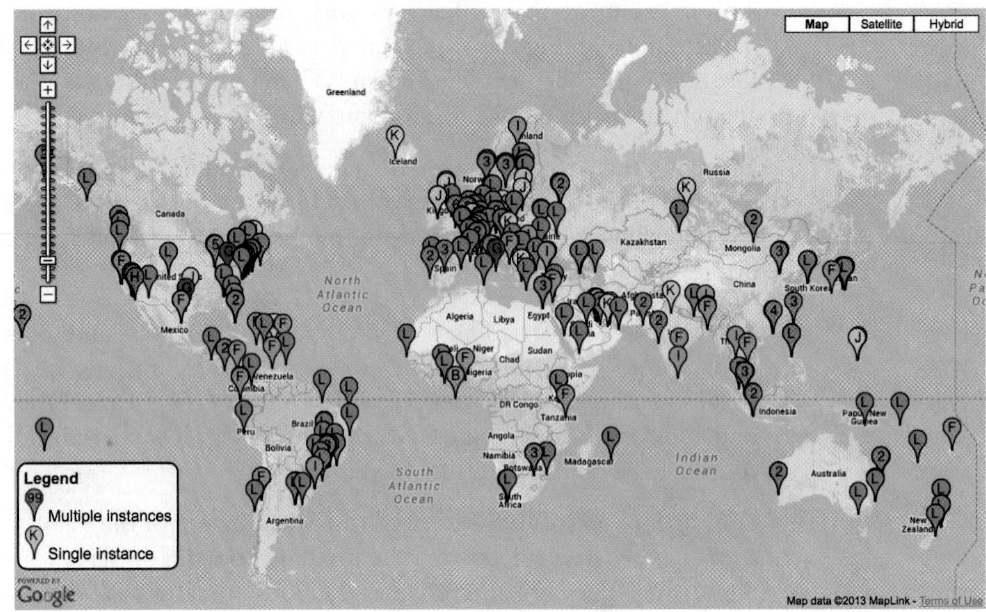

Figure 3.10 The map of root name servers and their "mirrors;" for example, there is a copy of Root K in Reykjavik, Iceland.

name servers. Operating autonomously, the DNS translates billions of domain names into IP addresses every minute. Counting the DNS servers and the authoritative name servers, it involves millions of computers. When machines fail, some of the Internet is temporarily unavailable, but the rest of it works just fine, which is the beauty of decentralization.

To add a new computer to the Internet, the administrator of the domain puts its name and address on "the list" of the authoritative name server for that domain. At that point, the new computer is connected, although no other computer in the world will know its IP address yet. When someone uses the domain name, their DNS will track down the ANS, find the IP address, and begin communicating with the new machine. The DNS is a remarkable worldwide service.

The World Wide Web

Some of the computers connected to the Internet are **Web servers**. They accept HTTP requests from browsers running on other (client) computers, and return files that the browsers can display. Together these Web servers and their files define the **World Wide Web (WWW)**. In addition to Web pages, Web servers store, process, and send many other kinds of files, and they provide a huge variety of services from email to entertainment.

When described in these terms, the Web doesn't seem like much. And technically, it's not. What makes the World Wide Web significant is the information contained in the files and the ability of the client and server computers to process it.

No Confusion. The World Wide Web and the Internet are different. The Internet is all of the wires and routers connecting named computers, that is, the hardware. The World Wide Web is a subset of those computers (Web servers), their files, and their services.

VideoNote

Internet Traffic Signals

Requesting a Web Page

As noted earlier, Web requests are processed in a client/server interaction. When you request a page, such as the really geeky T-shirt design at http://blogs.ucls.uchicago.edu/cstsc/files/2007/07/0_new_1_csci.gif, your browser is a client asking for a file from a Web server computer using the familiar **URL (Universal Resource Locator)**. The URL has three main parts.

- **Protocol:** The http:// part, which stands for **Hypertext Transfer Protocol**, tells the computers how to handle the file. There are other ways to send files, such as ftp, **File Transfer Protocol**.
- **Server computer's domain name:** The blogs.ucls.uchicago.edu part, which gives the name or the server in the domain hierarchy.
- **Page's pathname:** The /cstsc/files/2007/07/0_new_1_csci.gif part, which gives the pathname saying where to find the page or other file.

All URLs have this structure, although you may not think so, because in some cases, you can leave parts out and the software fills in the missing parts. (This is further explained in the next section.) However, it is never a mistake to use the full form.

Summarizing, Web browsers and Web servers both "speak" HTTP. When you specify a URL in your browser's location window, you say where the information is to be found (the server's name), what information you want (the pathname), and what protocol the two computers will use to exchange the information (e.g., HTTP).

3.4 Take It to the Bank. Classify each part of this URL according to the three parts just described: https://accts.lastbank.com/newdeposits/welcome/toaster.html.

The Internet and the Web

We use the Internet to access Web pages, of course. To refer to a Web server, you *must* give its name exactly, because your computer will ask the DNS server for the Web server's IP address using that name. If the name is wrong, either you will access the wrong IP address or, more typically, the DNS lookup will fail. Your browser will give you an error message (e.g., "404 Not Found") advising you to check the address. So, there is no option: You must give the name exactly.

404 Page Not Found Although error messages are nearly always boring, the 404 message has invited considerable creativity. This one from www.magntize.com/404 reports the error and uses a Venn diagram to propose two possible explanations; a Web search will locate hundreds of other creative 404s.

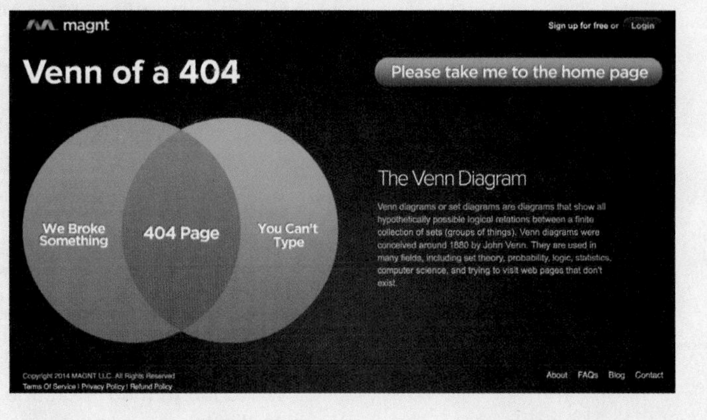

No organization taking the trouble to put a Web server on the Internet wants visitors to fail to reach them, so their Web administrators try to save users from mistakes. For example, Web sites change form regularly, and links no longer in use would normally cause a 404. But Web masters redirect from the old address to its new location; that's why you often see the URL change from what you typed. Another trick is to register misspellings of their domain name, and if someone arrives at the misspelled site, they are redirected to the true site.

Describing a Web Page

As you might know, servers do not store Web pages in the form seen on our screens. Instead, the pages are stored as a *description* of how they should appear on the screen. When the Web browser receives the description (**source**) file, it then creates the Web page image that it displays. There are at least two advantages to storing and sending the source rather than the image itself:

- A description file usually requires less information.
- The browser can adapt the source image to your computer more easily than a literal pixel-by-pixel description. For example, the description is easier to shrink or expand in response to changes in the size of the browser window, than is the image itself.

Figure 3.11 shows a simple Web page and its source. In Chapter 4 we study HTML, the main language for specifying a Web page, to learn how Web pages are created and processed. In Chapter 5 we explore the content of the WWW.

```
<!doctype html>
<html>
<head> <title> Alto Computer </title>
  <meta charset="UTF-8" />
  <style>
   body {background-color : white; font-family:Helvetica}
  </style>
</head>
<body>
  <img style="float:right" src="alto.jpg" alt="Alto Personal Computer"
       height="300"/>
  <h1>Alto, <br/>A Computer of Note</h1>
   <p>The Alto was the first networked personal computer. It was invented
   at the Xerox Palo Alto Research Center (PARC) by the team of Ed McCreight,
   Chuck Thacker, Butler Lampson, Bob Sproull and Dave Boggs to explore
   office automation. Altos were the first production computers to have a
   bit-mapped display, windows and a mouse. Ethernet technology, also
   invented at PARC, was first used to connect Altos.</p>
   <p>Though Xerox was unable to market the Alto -- they cost $32,000
   in 1979 -- the computer impressed many others who did push the technologies.
   For example, Apple Computer co-founder Steve Jobs was so impressed when
   he saw the Alto, he created the revolutionary Apple Macintosh in its image.</p>
  </body>
</html>
```

Alto Computer

Alto,
A Computer of Note

The Alto was the first networked personal computer. It was invented at the Xerox Palo Alto Research Center (PARC) by the team of Ed McCreight, Chuck Thacker, Butler Lampson, Bob Sproull and Dave Boggs to explore office automation. Altos were the first production computers to have a bit-mapped display, windows and a mouse. Ethernet technology, also invented at PARC, was first used to connect Altos.

Though Xerox was unable to market the Alto -- they cost $32,000 in 1979 -- the computer impressed many others who did push the technologies. For example, Apple Computer co-founder Steve Jobs was so impressed when he saw the Alto, he created the revolutionary Apple Macintosh in its image.

Figure 3.11 A Web page and the HTML source that produced it. Notice that an additional image file, alto.jpg, is also required to display the page.

Stated Briefly. Tiny URLs, popular with SMS, Twitter, and other space-constrained users, are not actually URLs at all, but simply short names for the true URL. For example, TinyURL.com returned kpjf6xb for https://www.youtube.com/watch?feature=player_embedded&v=ohQzHz9gy6c, a NASA video on noctilucent clouds. Sites supporting tiny URLs are simply Web applications that keep a list of the short names and corresponding URLs; when we use the short name (for example, tinyurl.com/kpjf6xb), they look it up in their list and open the page.

Hypertext. To describe how a Web page should look, most pages use **Hypertext Markup Language (HTML)**. Markup languages, traditionally used in publishing and graphic design, describe the layout of a document, including margin width, font, text style, image placement, and such. Hypertext began as an experiment to break away from the straight sequence of normal text: first paragraph, second paragraph, third paragraph, and so on. As you know, with hypertext it's possible to jump from one point in the text to somewhere else in the text or to some other document and then return. This familiar feature, which breaks a document's linear sequence, gives it a more complex structure. The (usually blue) highlighted words—the **hyperlinks**—provide the point from which we can (optionally) jump and return. The term *hypertext* was coined in the late 1960s by Theodore Nelson, although in his book *Literary Machines* he credits the original idea to computer pioneer Vannevar Bush. Combining the two ideas—markup languages and hypertext—was the contribution of Tim Berners-Lee. It lets us build nonlinear documents, which are ideal for the dynamic and highly interconnected Internet. The World Wide Web was born! The first Web page is here: http://info.cern.ch/hypertext/WWW/TheProject.html.

Web servers don't have to be named www. It's just what people usually name their Web servers. Web servers are named www because when the Web got started, many domains added a separate computer as their Web server. The server needed a name that people could remember. Because the first groups named their servers www, later groups did, too. Now it seems like a requirement, but it is only a tradition.

File Structure

To use networks well, we need to understand file structures, although the topic is not technically part of networking. Recall from your experience using a personal computer that a **folder**—also known as a **directory**—is a named collection of files or other folders or both.

3.5 Web Server Name. When we study computer security in Chapter 12 you will learn about phishing scams. They try to fool you into trusting a site. Determine the trustworthiness of this site for a credit card transaction by figuring out the domain name: http://www.leon.com/wallet.secure.chase.com/update/params=eJwlyL0O.

Directory Hierarchy

Because folders can contain folders, which can contain files and other folders, and on and on, the whole scheme—called the **file structure** of the computer—forms the **directory hierarchy**. Think of any **hierarchy** as a tree; in the case of file structures,

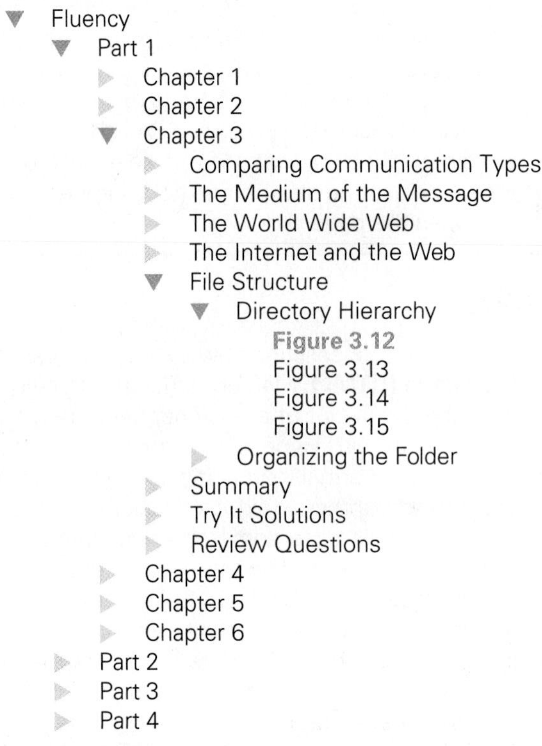

Figure 3.12 The hierarchy of this book highlighting the path to this figure; downward-pointing triangles are expanded; right-pointing triangles are not.

folders are the branch points and files are the leaves. Hierarchy trees are often drawn in odd ways, such as sideways or upside down, but in all cases, two terms are standard:

- *Down* or *lower* in the hierarchy means into subfolders; that is, toward the leaves.
- *Up* or *higher* in the hierarchy means into enclosing folders; that is, toward the root.

To illustrate these terms, Figure 3.12 shows part of the hierarchy of this book formed from its parts, chapters, sections and figures; the parts, chapters and sections are branch points and the figures are leaves. The "tree" of Figure 3.12 is drawn with the root, Fluency, at the top. The path from the root (the whole book) to the leaf (the figure) is highlighted. We move *up* or *higher* in the hierarchy when we move, say, from Chapter 3 to Part 1, since it is more inclusive. We move *down* or *lower* in the hierarchy when we move, say, from Chapter 3 to the "Directory Hierarchy" section, since it is more specific.

Learning the "directionality" of hierarchical references makes navigating the Web simpler.

Pulling Rank. An easy way to remember the directions of "higher" and "lower" in a hierarchy is to think of the military hierarchy: general, colonel, major, captain, lieutenant, sergeant, corporal, and private. Moving up or down in the hierarchy corresponds to moving up or down the chain of command, or to higher or lower rank.

Generally, the path in a URL tells the server computer how to navigate to the requested file in the server's directory hierarchy. For example, to access the live Webcam of Old Faithful Geyser in Yellowstone National Park, hosted by the National Park Service (NPS), see Figure 3.13, we click the URL http://www.nps.gov/yell/photosmultimedia/webcams.htm.

Figure 3.13 Yellowstone National Park's Old Faithful Geyser Webcam.

Old Faithful Webcam

The path to the Webcam page from the URL is /yell/photosmultimedia/webcams.htm and is illustrated in Figure 3.14.

The top-level folder is yell, and we can guess that because the NPS manages many parks and probably has Web pages for each one, this is the folder specifically for Yellowstone Park. (The assumption is confirmed because the top-level folder for Olympic National Park is olym.)

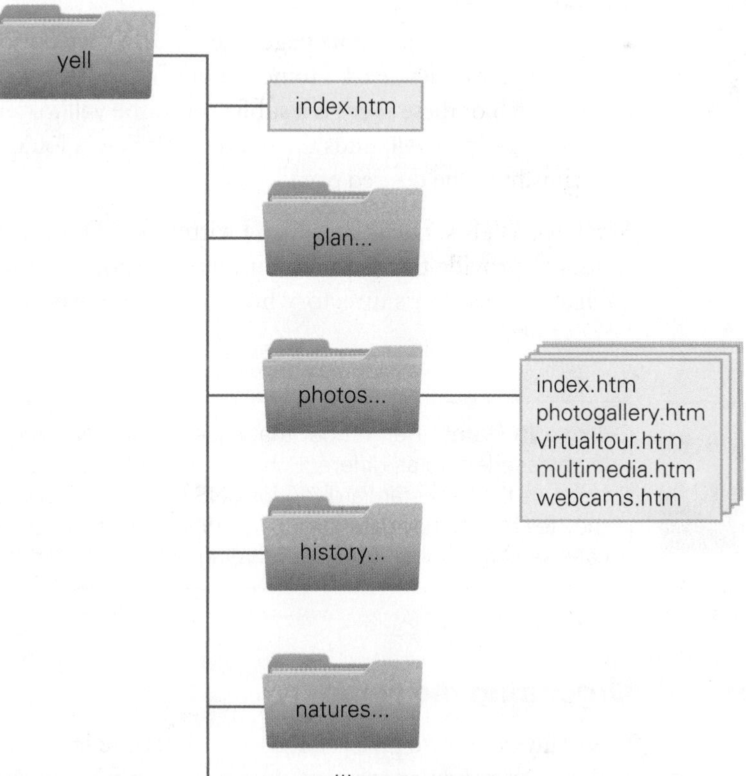

Figure 3.14 Top-level structure of the Yellowstone folder for the NPS Web server.

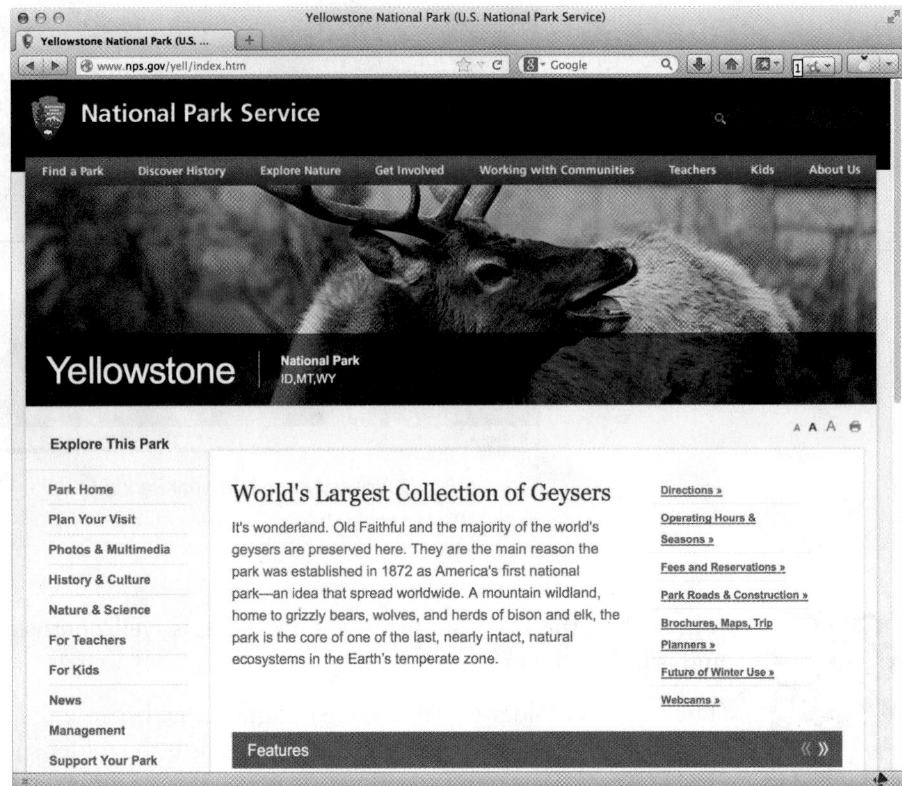

Figure 3.15 Yellowstone National Park home page (www.nps.gov/yell/index.htm).

From the Yellowstone home page (Figure 3.15), we notice (on the left side of the page) that the site covers topics "Park Home" (index.htm), "Plan Your Visit," "Photos & Multimedia," etc. For each of these there is a subfolder in the yell folder for its content. The path we requested looks in yell, finds the photosmultimedia folder and inside of it, finds the file webcams.htm, the desired page.

For huge Web-services sites like Twitter and Tumblr, the servers use different techniques to provide the content you want, but for most sites, the path portion of a URL navigates the server's directory hierarchy to your desired page.

Case in Point. Remember that case sensitivity means computers treat uppercase and lowercase letters as different characters. In URLs, domain names are not case sensitive, because they are standardized for DNS lookup. Pathnames can be case sensitive, because they tell how to navigate through the Web server's file structure, which may or may not be case sensitive. Be careful when typing pathnames, and when in doubt, try lowercase first.

Organizing the Folder

Normally, when we give a URL, we expect the last item in the sequence to be a file name, such as homepage.html, but it is not always necessary. Other technologies besides HTML are used to produce Web pages. Also, when a URL ends in a slash (which means the last item on the path is a folder rather than a file name), the browser automatically looks in that folder for a file called index.html or index.htm. So, a request for the URL www.nps.gov/yell/index.htm to Yellowstone's home page is the same as www.nps.gov/yell/ because a browser that finds the folder named yell will automatically look for a file called index.htm in it. Of course, the index.html file will exist only if the person who set up the Web pages and built the file hierarchy decided to organize it that way and provide the index pages. Some people do and some people don't, but the browser will look when necessary.

Why build a hierarchy at all? Why not dump all the files into one huge folder and save typing? Most people build hierarchies to organize their own thinking and work. Because directories cost nothing, there is no reason not to use them, and it is highly recommended.

Universal Language. Most people are amazed at the Web's ability to provide access to information around the world. Few have observed, however, that it is the universal HTTP language that makes this communication possible. Every computer—regardless of who manufactured it, how it's configured, its operating system type and version, the applications it runs, the (native) language of its user, and so on—can communicate because the computers "speak" this common language. Imagine the benefits if every *person* on the planet spoke a common language!

SUMMARY

In this chapter we discussed the basics of networking, including the following:

- Basic types of communication: point-to-point, multicast, broadcast, synchronous, and asynchronous.
- Networking, including IP addresses, domains, IP packets, IP protocol, WANs and LANs, Ethernet protocol, ISPs, enterprise networks, and wireless networks.
- The difference between the Internet and the World Wide Web.
- File hierarchies in preparation for our further study of HTML.

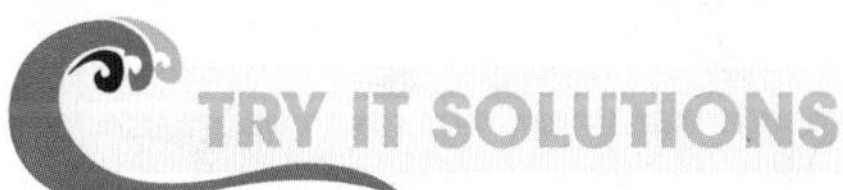

TRY IT SOLUTIONS

3.1 645,000 × 6 + 645,000/4 = 3,870,000 + 161,250 = 4,031,250
4,031,250/65,528 = 61.52, or 62 packets

3.2 Montserrat has the top-level domain .ms. They might have registered nytim.es in Spain.

3.3 It begins by asking one of the 13 root name servers for gov-ANS; getting that, it asks for nasa-ANS, and getting that, it asks for the IP address of apod—so it asks three.

3.4 The parts of the URL are its protocol, https://, which is the secure form of HTTP, the server computer's domain name, accts.lastbank.com, and the page's pathname, /newdeposits/welcome/toaster.html.

3.5 The domain is leon.com; wallet.secure.chase.com looks like the domain name of a bank but it is a folder name.

REVIEW QUESTIONS

Multiple Choice

1. Saving information for possible reuse is called
   a. caching
   b. hopping
   c. DNS lookup
   d. serving
2. If the Internet consisted of four computers, there would be six possible connections. If it consisted of five computers, there would be ten possible connections. How many connections are possible with ten computers?
   a. 10
   b. 30
   c. 45
   d. infinite
3. What is the *potential* number of IPv4 addresses available?
   a. 65,536
   b. 16,777,216
   c. 4,294,967,296
   d. infinite
4. Root name servers
   a. maintain a list of all computer users
   b. manage all emails sent
   c. maintain the relationship between IP addresses and symbolic computer names
   d. maintain a list of all Web pages
5. This type of communication results in the sending and receiving of information at different times.
   a. synchronous
   b. asynchronous
   c. slow
   d. DNS
6. The Internet is fast enough to mimic _______ communication.
   a. synchronous
   b. asynchronous
   c. special
   d. LAN
7. The Internet and the World Wide Web are different names for the same thing.
   a. true
   b. it depends
   c. the Internet is what we used to call the World Wide Web
   d. false
8. What can folders contain?
   a. files
   b. folders
   c. neither files nor folders
   d. both files and folders

Short Answer

1. All IP addresses of authoritative name servers for TLDs are maintained and managed by 13 ________ servers.
2. A communication that goes out to many people within a specific target audience is called a(n) ________
3. A hierarchy of related computers on a network is called a(n) ________.
4. Computers on an Ethernet network "tap" into a cable called the ________.
5. ________ is the main technology for local area networks.
6. Local networks that support communications wholly within an organization are called ________.
7. Special computers that send files to Web browsers elsewhere on the Internet are known as ________.
8. In a Web address, the http:// is the ________.
9. Files are often sent over the Internet via a process known by the acronym ________.
10. The source file for a Web page contains the ________ of the page, not the actual image of the page.
11. In the client/server structure, the customer's computer is the ________ and the business's computer is the ________.
12. When we get files from a server we are ________ them. When we put files on a server we are ________ them.
13. Instead of typing in the IP address, we use symbolic names, which are also called ________.
14. In URLs, ________ are not case sensitive, but ________ may be case sensitive.
15. When moving inside of a directory hierarchy, moving up is the same as moving ________, and moving down is the same as moving ________.

Exercises

1. Explain how "Imagine the benefits if every person on the planet spoke a common language!" relates to the Internet.
2. Label the following with an *S* to indicate synchronous communication or an *A* to indicate asynchronous communication.
   a. ________ movie
   b. ________ chat session
   c. ________ email
   d. ________ video conference
   e. ________ Web page
   f. ________ book
   g. ________ concert
   h. ________ text messaging
   i. ________ Web board
   j. ________ blog
3. If you have previously visited a Web page, the DNS server usually knows the translation because it has processed and saved it. Explain what happens if it does not know the translation.

4. Go to internettrafficreport.com/namerica.htm and check out the Internet traffic for North America. How does the time of day affect the traffic? How does the time of day affect overseas Internet traffic?
5. What is the file name of the Web address in Question 4? Now, try the Web address without the file name. What do you get? Explain.
6. In this chapter, the author wrote: "The Internet is truly a universal communications medium." What is meant by this? Explain your answer in detail.
7. What industries have prospered and which ones might have suffered because of the growth of the Internet? Why?
8. Are there more client computers or more server computers on the Internet? Explain.
9. Explain how it is possible for the server to handle many clients at a time.
10. Identify each part of the following URL: http://airandspace.si.edu/exhibitions/gal100/pioneer.html
    a. protocol _______
    b. domain _______
    c. top-level domain _______
    d. pathname _______
    e. Web page _______
11. State what the following acronyms stand for, and briefly explain each.
    a. TCP/IP
    b. LAN
    c. WAN
    d. DSL
    e. WWW
    f. URL
    g. HTML
    h. ISP
12. Explain in detail how telephone companies are now using the Internet.
13. What motivated engineers to make TCP/IP packets more independent?
14. Why do Web masters sometimes register misspellings of their domains?

CHAPTER 4

A Hypertext Markup Language Primer

Marking Up with HTML

learning objectives

- Know the meaning of and use hypertext terms
- Use HTML tags to structure a document
- Use HTML tag attributes
- Use Cascading Style Sheets to style a Web page
- Use HTML tags to link to other files
- Explain the differences between absolute and relative pathnames
- Use HTML lists and tables to structure a Web page

CHAPTER 4

Computers are like Old Testament gods; lots of rules and no mercy.

—JOSEPH CAMPBELL

Good judgment comes from experience, and experience comes from bad judgment.

—FREDERICK P BROOKS, JR.

WEB PAGES ARE CREATED, stored, and sent in encoded form; a browser converts them to the image we see on the screen. The Hypertext Markup Language (HTML) is the main language used to define how a Web page should look. Features like background color, font, and layout are specified in HTML. Learning to "speak" HTML is easy. So easy, in fact, that most Web pages are not created by people writing HTML directly, but by people using Web authoring software; that is, using programs to write the HTML for them automatically. Learning basic HTML, however, helps you to understand the World Wide Web, gives you experience directing a computer to do your work, and prepares you for studying other *Fluency* topics. When you are finished, you will speak a new "foreign" language!

This chapter begins by introducing the dozen most basic HTML tags. Next comes document structuring, including details such as headings and alignment. After discussing special characters, we create an example of a text-only Web page. We decide that the page should have an image and hyperlinks, so we discuss styling Web pages with Cascading Style Sheets (CSS). Placing images and links and connecting them to files comes next. With this knowledge, we improve our sample page. After completing our discussion of the ingenious way CSS helps us make Web pages attractive, we turn to the basics of lists and tables. Finally, we create our own horizontal and vertical navigation bars.

Marking Up with HTML

HTML is straightforward: In addition to the words and pictures on a Web page, hidden formatting tags in the file describe how the page should look. We use HTML5, the **Hypertext Markup Language** version 5, which is the newest and best WWW standard language. If you learned some HTML in the past, then you'll be happy to meet new tags like <audio> and <video>. And, what's better, virtually all of what you learned in the past still applies. If you haven't learned HTML yet, then you'll be learning the state-of-the-art version. Also, HTML5 is more fun than earlier versions.

Formatting with Tags

Tags are words or abbreviations enclosed in angle brackets, < and >, like <title>, that come in pairs, the second with a slash (/), like </title>. It's the same slash used in division. In HTML5, the tags *must* be lowercase, making <TITLE>, <Title>, and <tITle> illegal. The tag pair surrounds the text to be formatted like parentheses. So a title, which every HTML Web page has, is written as

```
<title>Willem-Alexander, King of NL</title>
```

These tags can be read as "this is where the title starts" and "this is where the title ends." They are referred to as the **start tag** and the **end tag**, and also as the *open tag* and *close tag*, emphasizing that they are like parentheses. The title appears on the title bar of the browser (the very top of the window where the Close button is) when the page is displayed.

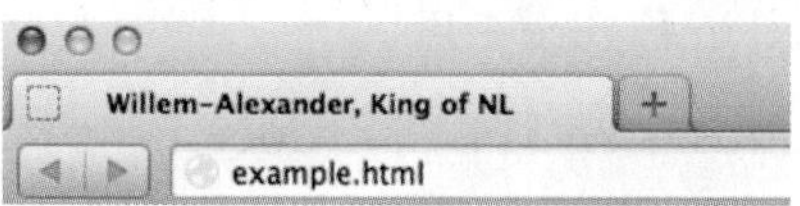

Say Less. The proper term for / is *slash*; it's used in division, URLs, end tags, and other places. Its opposite, \, is a *backslash*. The opposite of a backslash is a slash, not a "forward slash."

Tags for Bold and Italic

HTML has tags for bold text, <b> and </b>; for italic text, <i> and </i>; and for paragraphs, <p> and </p>. <p>Bronze, <b>Silver,</b> <i>Gold!</i></p> produces

Bronze, **Silver**, *Gold!*

You can use more than one kind of formatting at a time, such as bold italic text, by properly "nesting" the tags, as in

```
<p><b><i>Bronze, Silver, Gold!</i></b></p>
```

which produces

Bronze, Silver, Gold!

It doesn't matter whether italic follows bold, or vice versa. You get the same result if you put the italic before the bold:

```
<p><i><b>Bronze, Silver, Gold!</b></i></p>
```

The rule is to make sure the tags nest correctly. All the tags between a starting tag and its ending tag should be matched. So, in the ***Bronze, Silver, Gold!*** example, between the starting paragraph tag <p> and its ending tag </p>, all other starting tags are properly nested with their matching ending tags. That's true for the tags inside, too.

Singleton Tags. A few tags are not paired and so do not have a matching ending tag beginning with a /. In those cases, the closing angle bracket > of the **singleton tag** is replaced by />. One example is the *horizontal rule* <hr/> tag, which displays a horizontal line after a paragraph. Another example is the *break*
 tag, which continues the text on the next line and is useful for inserting blank lines within a paragraph. These tags do not surround anything, so they don't need to be paired with a closing tag. (Technically, HTML5 doesn't require />, but it is legal; it is required in the other important markup language, XHTML, which we use in Chapter 16. By always including the slash, our code works everywhere.)

Although most tags come in pairs, we will refer to the pair by the first tag only, as in the <title> tag. You will know that the reference is to a singleton tag, because it has the slash at the end, as in the <br/> tag.

Required Tags

When we create a Web page, we make a text file of the tags and the content. A few tags are required for every HTML5 Web page, as illustrated in Figure 4.1.

```
<!doctype html>
<html>
  <head>
    <meta charset="UTF-8"/>
    <title>Required Tags</title>
  </head>
  <body>
    <p>Content</p>
  </body>
</html>
```

Figure 4.1 Required tags for HTML5.

The first tag, <!doctype html>, says that this is an HTML5 document file. It's there so the browser knows what is coming next, and *must be given exactly as shown* as the first line. What's coming next is HTML, so not surprisingly, the remainder of the file is enclosed in <html> tags. Everything inside the <html> tags is divided into two parts, a **head** and a **body**.

The head is surrounded by <head> tags; the body is surrounded by <body> tags. It's straightforward.

Mostly the head is the place to describe characteristics of the whole page. It doesn't typically contain content, unless we consider <title> as content, which it probably is. One feature that applies to the whole page is what character set it's written in—the alphabet, basically—and specifying that is what the <meta/> tag does:

```
<meta charset="UTF-8"/>
```

Notice that <meta/> is a singleton tag. It must be given exactly as shown, and its contents, charset="UTF-8", will be explained in a moment; the meaning of UTF-8 will be explained in Chapter 7.

The content of the Web page is all contained in the body section surrounded by <body> tags. By the way, the content need not be a paragraph (as shown in the figure), because the page's content might be something else, like a photograph. *This form must always be followed, and all of these tags are required.*

There's not very much to HTML. By the end of the next section, you will have produced your first Web page!

What's Up, Doc? The <!doctype html> tag is strange in so many ways. It is a standalone tag, but doesn't get a closing slash. There's an exclamation point following the angle bracket <. It has just the word **html** inside, which as we'll see in a moment, is not how stuff inside of tags goes. And, it's actually okay to capitalize it, as in <!DOCTYPE HTML>. No other tag has these features. Strange!

Lab Practice I

Fluency is a hands-on study. You have to do it to learn it. That means *Fluency* has a reading component and a lab component. But to become fluent you don't need to go to a special lab. Any "suitably configured" computer will do; even a smartphone, but it's not recommended. So, to help you write HTML in this and future chapters, we "suitably configure" your computer. That just means that you will check that two programs are installed, and if not, install them.

The two programs are a browser and a text editor, and both are free. The browser is Firefox, and the text editor—either Notepad++ for Windows or TextWrangler for Macs—depends on which operating system your computer is running. Your computer already has one or more browsers and one or more text editors installed, so you might think there is no reason to change. However, these programs are preferred for technical reasons, which we won't go into, and for educational reasons: They are friendly and helpful to learners; they guide you away from trouble, and when you make a mistake, they help you get back on track. That's why we will use them.

Trying Your Best Works! You might think that the clean look of Google's home page was chosen for its minimalist design style. Legend has it, however, that when they started, founders Larry Page and Sergey Brin just didn't know HTML very well; it was the best they could do. Obviously, trying your best with HTML pays off!

Google

Google Search I'm Feeling Lucky

Firefox

Firefox is a free **open source** browser distributed by the Mozilla Foundation. Open source means that the program code is publicly available, and any programmer can contribute improvements to it (thousands have). Firefox is an outstanding browser, and it is the browser referenced throughout this book. Firefox is available at www.mozilla.com/en-US/firefox/all.html. Follow the installation instructions for your operating system.

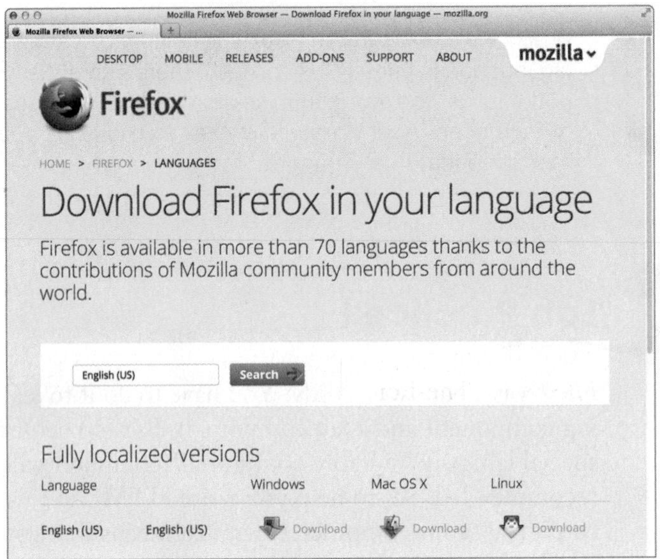

Firefox Browser. Firefox is a browser from the Mozilla Project, and it is very popular because of its great features. When Firefox 4.0 was released in March 2011, 8.75 million copies were downloaded in 24 hours—breaking the Firefox 3.0 Guinness World Record for downloads in a day.

Text Editor

A **text editor** is a more basic way to process text than our familiar what-you-see-is-what-you-get (WYSIWYG) word processors such as Word and WordPerfect. Word processors include many application-specific tags and other information in their files along with the normal characters that you type. This information confuses browsers, and so must not be part of an HTML Web page. Because text editors do not include this extra information, they produce the sort of files that browsers like.

```
helloWorld.html
<!doctype html>
<html>
  <head>
    <meta charset="UTF-8">
    <title>My First Page</title>
  </head>
  <body>
    <p>Hello, World!</p>
  </body>
</html>
```

HTML Highlighted in NotePad++

You *must* use a text editor to write HTML, because browsers want Web pages written in ASCII characters only. We will discuss ASCII in Chapter 7, but for now think of ASCII as the normal keyboard characters with "nothing strange." Also, when a text editor figures out what language you are writing in, it will color code your HTML to make it easier to read. As mentioned earlier, if you use a Mac, then TextWrangler is your recommended text editor. If you use Windows, then Notepad++ is recommended. Get the appropriate programs at the following sites and follow the installation instructions:

TextWrangler:
www.barebones.com/products/TextWrangler/download.html

Notepad++:
notepad-plus-plus.org/download

Hello, World!

Assuming you have now installed Firefox and your text editor, it's time to write your first HTML page. When programmers write a program in a new language, typically

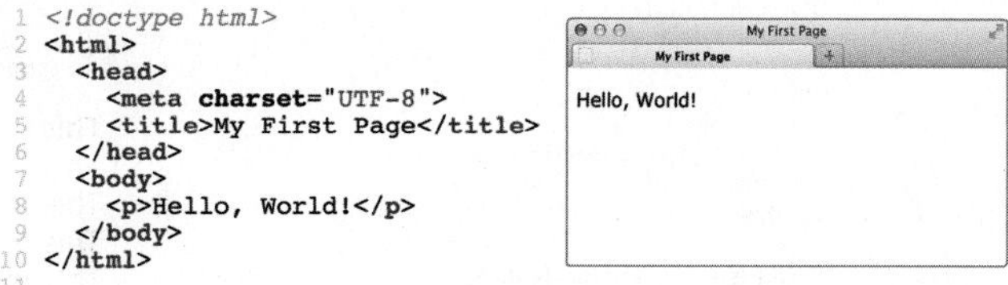

Figure 4.2 Text for a simple HTML5 Web page displayed as Page Source, and its display in Firefox.

they begin with a program that prints out *Hello, World!*, and does nothing else. We will follow this time-honored tradition.

To produce your first HTML page, follow these instructions:

1. In your text editor, open a *New* document instance.
2. Carefully type in the text shown in Figure 4.1, making these replacements:
    - Change the title to something personal, like <*your name*>'s First Page.
    - Replace the paragraph content with, <p>Hello, World!</p>
3. Save the file as starterPage.html.
4. Open the file with the Firefox browser.

The result is a very simple Web page, as shown in Figure 4.2.

The Computer's View. A browser's job is to display a Web page that has been written in HTML. Usually, we only see the finished page. But, to see what the browser is working with, check out the Page Source, the actual HTML the browser was given. Every browser shows you the source. In Firefox, find it at *Tools* > *Web Developer* > *Page Source* or just type ^U. Figure 4.2 shows the Page Source form for Firefox; notice how it is colored.

Save This Page

Although your first HTML page is very simple, it will also be very useful. Because all HTML files have the same structure as your starterPage.html file, you can use it as a template for *all* of your future HTML coding. This is a timesaving way to get started on your next page *without forgetting any required tags.*

Set up a new folder, perhaps called HTMLFiles, where you will keep your HTML files. Place the starterPage.html file in the new folder. Then, when you start working on a new HTML project, make a copy of this file and rename it. Edit the title—your new page will want a better title—and replace the *Hello, World!* text with the new content of your page. That way, you are sure that your future pages will always have the correct form.

Practicing in the Lab

In keeping with the idea of the last paragraph to save a starter file and build new pages from it, let's make a practice page. Our purpose is to learn some new formatting tags by example. (Much of HTML programming is learned by example.) The page shown in Figure 4.3 is a good place to start.

```
<!doctype html>
<html>
 <head>
  <meta charset="UTF-8">
  <title>Formatting Practice</title>
 </head>
 <body>
  <p>
   This is <b>bold</b> text.                              <br>
   This is <i>italic</i> text.                            <br>
   This is <strong>strong</strong> text.                  <br>
   This is <em>emphasized</em> text.                      <br>
   This is <small>small</small> text.                     <br>
   This is <u>underlined</u> text.                        <br>
   This is <sub>subscripted</sub> text.                   <br>
   This is <sup>superscripted</sup> text.                 <br>
   This is <q>A short quote </q> text.                    <br>
   This is <s>no longer correct</s> text.                 <br>
   This is <ins>text inserted</ins> into the doc.<br>
   This is
  </p>
  <blockquote>
      a blockquote, for quotations longer than a line.
      The blockquote tag doesn't go inside of a
      paragraph tag. It is separate and should be
      considered an "equal" of a paragraph. It is
      capable of handling a lot of text!
  </blockquote>
  <p>And those are some pretty handy tags.</p>
 </body>
</html>
```

Formatting Practice

This is **bold** text.
This is *italic* text.
This is **strong** text.
This is *emphasized* text.
This is small text.
This is underlined text.
This is subscripted text.
This is superscripted text.
This is "A short quote " text.
This is ~~no longer correct~~ text.
This is text inserted into the doc.
This is

> a blockquote, for quotations longer than a line. The blockquote tag doesn't go inside of a paragraph tag. It is separate and should be considered an "equal" of a paragraph. It is capable of handling a lot of text!

And those are some pretty handy tags.

Figure 4.3 A practice Web page for various formatting tags, and its display. Experiment with resizing the browser window to see how the <blockquote> text changes.

Edit your saved starterPage.html to include the text shown in Figure 4.3. This HTML demonstrates how various tags look when a browser displays them, and it is a good way to get familiar with them. (All browsers should look pretty much identical.) As you type in this code, remember that copy/paste/edit are your friends!

Formatting Tags. Documents can be formatted in many ways, as Figure 4.3 shows. And each formatting feature requires its own tag, meaning that HTML has many tags. But we don't have to memorize them all. Programmers and Web designers remember how to use a few common tags, and then when they need one they do not use often, they just look it up; it's easier than memorizing long lists of uncommon tags. Whenever we need to be reminded which tag to use to achieve a specific effect, we check a list like www.w3schools.com/tags/default.asp.

Structuring Documents

The point of a markup language is to describe how a document's parts fit together. Because those parts are mostly paragraphs, headings, and text styles like italic and bold, document tags and the formatting section are the most common and most useful.

Headings in HTML

Documents tend to have headings, subheadings, and such, so HTML gives us several levels of *heading* tags to choose from: from level one (the highest) headings, <h1> and </h1>, to level two, <h2> and </h2>, all the way to level six, <h6> and </h6>. The headings display their content in larger letters on a new line. For example,

```
<h1>Country: USA</h1> <h2>State: Hawaii</h2> <h3>County: Hawai'i</h3> <h4>City:
Hilo</h4> <h5>Neighborhood: Waiakea</h5> <h6>Street: Ululani</h6> Standard text size
```

Country: USA

State: Hawaii

County: Hawai'i

City: Hilo

Neighborhood: Waiakea

Street: Ululani

Standard text size

appears as shown at left. As you can see, the headings are bold and get less "strong" (smaller and perhaps not so bold) as the level number increases.

HTML Format Versus Display Format

Notice in the last example that although the HTML text was run together on a line, it was displayed formatted on separate lines. This illustrates an important point: The HTML source code tells the browser how to produce the formatted page based on the *meanings* of the tags, not on how the source instructions look. Heading tags always begin on a new line. Although the source's form is unimportant, we usually write HTML in a structured way to make it easier for people to understand. There is no agreed upon form, but the example might have been written with indenting to emphasize the levels:

```
<h1>Country: USA</h1>
  <h2>State: Hawaii</h2>
    <h3>County: Hawai'i</h3>
      .
```

White Space

The two HTML forms produce the same result. Computer experts call spaces that have been inserted for readability **white space**. We create white space with spaces, tabs, and new lines (return or enter). HTML ignores white space. The browser turns any sequence of white space characters into a single space before it begins processing the HTML, and then it inserts white space as needed to make the page look the way the HTML tells it. The only exception is **preformatted** information contained within <pre> and </pre> tags, which is displayed as it appears.

The fact that white space is ignored is important when the browser formats paragraphs. All text within *paragraph* tags, <p>, is treated as a paragraph, and any sequence of white space characters is converted to a single space. So

```
<p> <b>Xeno's Paradox: </b>
Achilles and a turtle were to run a race. Achilles could
run twice as fast as the turtle. The turtle,
being a slower runner,
got a 10 meter head start, whereupon
Achilles started and ran the 10 meter distance. At that
moment the turtle was 5 meters farther.
When Achilles had run
that distance the turtle had gone another 2.5 meters,
and so forth. Paradoxically, the turtle always remained
ahead. </p>
```

appears as

Xeno's Paradox

Xeno's Paradox: Achilles and a turtle were to run a race. Achilles could run twice as fast as the turtle. The turtle, being a slower runner, got a 10 meter head start, whereupon Achilles started and ran the 10 meter distance. At that moment the turtle was 5 meters farther. When Achilles had run that distance the turtle had gone another 2.5 meters, and so forth. Paradoxically, the turtle always remained ahead.

The width of a line of text is determined by the width of the browser window. Of course, a narrower or wider browser window makes the lines break in different places, which is why HTML ignores white space and changes the paragraph's formatting to fit the space available. Table 4.1 summarizes some basic HTML tags.

TRY
IT

4.1 Doing the Wave. Write the HTML code that produces:

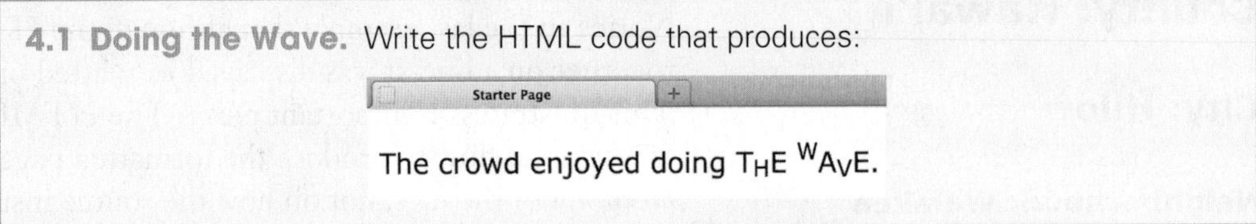
Starter Page
The crowd enjoyed doing THE WAVE.

Attributes

One final feature of HTML tagging concerns the idea of attributes. Recall the tag

```
<meta charset="UTF-8"/>
```

which is one of the standard tags every HTML file needs. This tag has an **attribute**, defined to be an additional input specification for the tag. Because attributes are inputs, they are always listed as name/value pairs. In this case the name of this attribute is charset, short for "character set", and its value, that is, the input, is the letter sequence "UTF-8", short for Unicode Transformation Format, 8-bit version. Attributes are placed inside of the tag's brackets and have the form

attribute_name = "*value*"

Table 4.1 Basic tags for HTML

Start Tag	End Tag	Meaning	Required
<!doctype html>		First tag in an HTML5 file	✓
<html>	</html>	Tag enclosing all HTML text	✓
<title>	</title>	Title bar text; describes page	✓
<head>	</head>	Preliminary material; e.g., title at start of page	✓
<body>	</body>	The main, content part of the page	✓
<p>	</p>	Paragraph	
<hr/>		Line (horizontal rule)	
<h1>...<h6>	</h1>...</h6>	Headings, six levels	
<b>	</b>	Bold	
<i>	</i>	Italic	
<pre>	</pre>	Preformatted text in which white space matters	
<a href="*fn*">	</a>	Anchor reference, *fn* must be a pathname to an HTML file	
<img src="*fn*"/>		Image source reference, *fn* must be a pathname to a .jpg, png, or .gif file	
 		Break, continue text on the next line	

The attribute name comes first, the equal sign is next, and quotation marks enclose the value. These items are all required. If there are several attributes inside a tag, they must be separated from each other by at least one space.

Some attributes are mandatory. For example, in the image tag (discussed a little later in this chapter), the source attribute (`src`) gives the name of the file to be displayed. Where to find the image is obviously a required input. But, image tags also have `width` and `height` attributes. They are optional, because they are not needed if the image's natural width and height are to be used. If you want to change either width or height, say, to make the image smaller than its natural size, use a `width` or `height` attribute.

To learn which attributes apply to a specific tag, check the tag list reference page (www.w3schools.com/tags/default.asp), find the tag in the list, and on its page, find its attributes.

Width Before Height. In some applications the width and height of an image are often specified without saying which is which; for example, as 500 × 400. As a rule, width will always be given first.

Brackets in HTML: The Escape Symbol

Notice that there would be a problem if our Web page had to show a math relationship such as *0<p>r*, because the browser might misinterpret *<p>* as a paragraph tag and not display it. Using angle brackets as text is prohibited. So to show angle brackets on the page, we use an **escape symbol**—the ampersand (&)—followed by an abbreviation, followed by a semicolon. For example:

< displays as <
> displays as >
& displays as &

If we think of < as "less than" and > as "greater than," the abbreviations are pretty easy to remember. Notice that the escape symbol, the ampersand, needs an escape, too! So, our math problem would be written in HTML as

```
<i>0&lt;p&gt;r</i>
```

Accent Marks in HTML

Letters with accent marks also require the escape symbol. The general form is an ampersand, followed by the letter (and whether it is uppercase or lowercase matters), followed by the name of the accent mark, followed by a semicolon. So, for example, `é` displays as é, `È` displays as È, `ñ` displays as ñ, and `Ö` displays as Ö. Table 4.2 lists a few useful special characters for some Western European languages.

Although names like *tilde* help Spanish speakers and others to remember the escape, each special symbol can be specified by a number, too. Write # followed by its

Table 4.2 Specifying accent marks for Western European languages

Symbol	Text	Number	Symbol	Text	Number	Symbol	Text	Number
à	à	à	ê	ê	ê	ô	ô	ô
ä	ä	ä	î	î	î	ù	ù	ù
é	é	é	ó	ó	ó	ã	ã	ã
í	í	í	ø	ø	ø	è	è	è
ò	ò	ò	ü	ü	ü	ì	ì	ì
ö	ö	ö	â	â	â	ñ	ñ	ñ
û	û	û	ç	ç	ç	õ	õ	õ
á	á	á	ë	ë	ë	ú	ú	ú
å	å	å	ï	ï	ï			

Note: For an accent mark on an uppercase letter, make the letter following the & uppercase or find the number for the uppercase letter at www.w3schools.com/tags/ref_entities.asp.

Unicode number; we discuss Unicode in Chapter 7. For example, ñ and ñ are the same letter. Where do you find the number? You can find a complete list at www.w3schools.com/tags/ref_entities.asp.

Although we have introduced only a few HTML tags so far, we can already create Web pages, as shown in Figure 4.4.

Study the HTML and notice the following points:

- The title is shown on the title bar of the browser pane.
- The statement of Russell's Paradox is in bold, because it's an H2 heading.
- The line between the two paragraphs crosses the width of the browser window.

```
<!doctype html>
<html>
 <head>
  <meta charset="UTF-8">
  <title> Twentieth Century Paradoxes </title>
 </head>
 <body>
  <h1>Paradoxes</h1>
  <h2>Russell's Paradox</h2>
   <p>The Twentieth Century logician Bertrand Russell
   introduced a curious paradox: <b>This statement is
   false.</b> The statement can't be true, because it
   claims the converse. However, if it is not true, then it's
   false, just as it says. That makes it true. Paradoxically,
   it seems to be neither true nor false, or perhaps both
   true and false.</p>
  <hr/>
  <h2>Magritte's Paradox</h2>
   <p> The famous Belgian artist Ren&eacute; Magritte
   rendered the idea of Russell's Paradox visually in his
   famous painting <i>Ceci n'est pas une pipe</i>. The
   title translates from French, This Is Not A Pipe. The
   painting shows a pipe with the text <i>Ceci n'est pas
   une pipe</i> below it. Superficially, the painting looks
   like a true statement, since it is a <i>picture</i> of
   the pipe, not an actual pipe. However, the assertion is
   also part of the picture, which seems to make it false,
   because it is clearly a painting of a pipe. Paradoxically,
   the truth seems to depend on whether the statement is
   an assertion about the painting or a part of it. But, it's
   both. </p>
 </body>
</html>
```

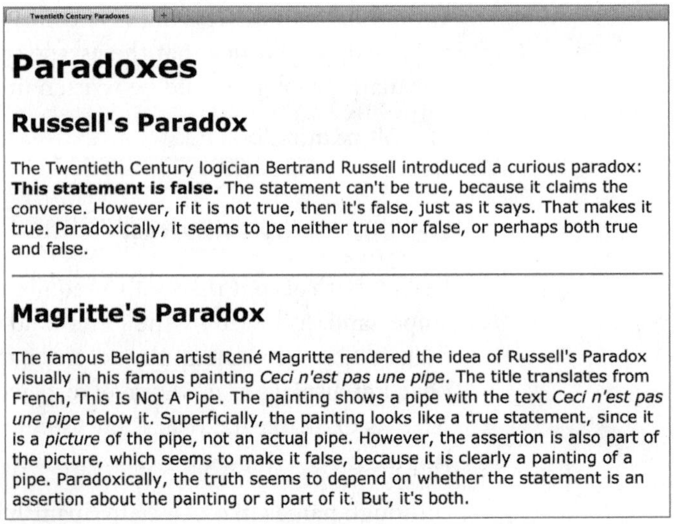

Figure 4.4 The HTML for a simple page and the result (inset).

4.2 Further Explanation. Write HTML to produce the content of this page:

- An acute accent is used in Magritte's first name.
- The French phrase from the painting is in italics.
- The word *picture* is in italics for emphasis.

It's a simple page and it was simple to produce. The tags tell how everything is formatted.

Lab Practice II

Programmers develop habits that help them produce correct, error-free programs easily; Web developers do the same. Our starterPage.html is an example. It is a saved template containing all of the *required* tags for a Web page. It saves us from having to type them fresh every time, and therefore helps avoid mistakes. In this section, we discuss two more "tricks of the trade" that will make learning HTML much easier.

Compose and Check

Most often Web pages are created all at once—both content and form. It can be complicated because we must concentrate on two things at once: what it says *and* what it looks like. As a result, it is smart to check your typing and your tagging very often, perhaps after writing only a few tags. The reason is simple. Assume a page is okay up to a given point, and then after adding a few more tags it is wrong. It must be that the last tags added are the place to find the error. This approach greatly limits the search for errors. The process is called **compose and check**.

A productive way to work while using the compose and check process is to keep two windows open: your text editor for composing, and your browser for checking (see Figure 4.5). Both of them are processing the same file. After writing a few HTML formatting tags in the editor, *Save* (^S) your file. Then check the result in Firefox by a *Reload* (^R) of the source. The refresh will display the updated (newly saved) page. After seeing the result, return to the editor, make a few more changes, and then repeat the *Save*, followed by the *Reload*. With this method, development can proceed very fast.

Markup Validation Service

Another way to limit the mistakes you make and ensure that your Web page "works" for all Web surfers is to have it automatically *validated*. This service checks to make sure your HTML does not violate any HTML5 rules. If it is wrong, the service tells you where the mistakes are and what's not proper.

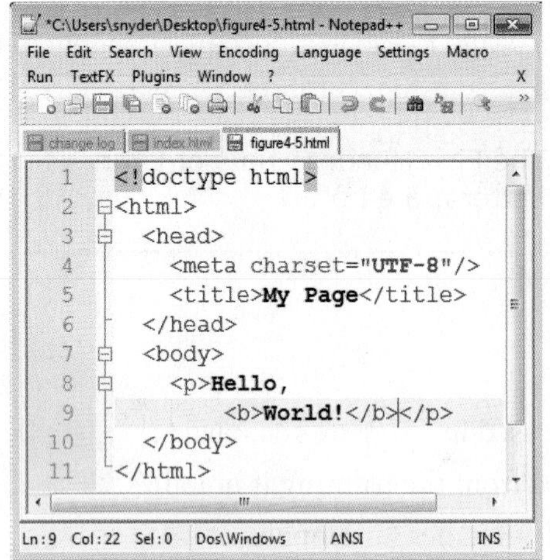

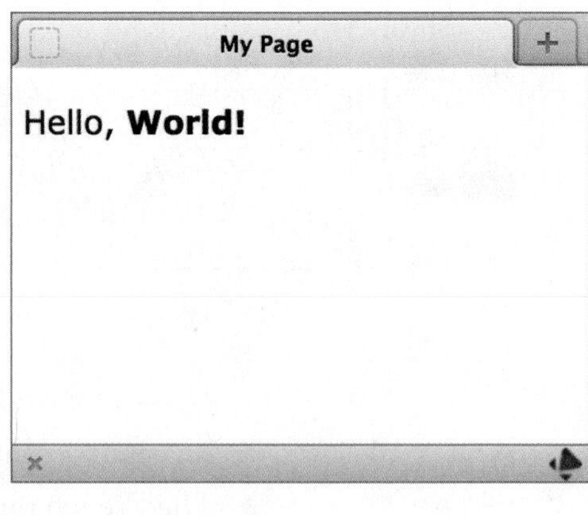

Figure 4.5 The compose and check process: With both the browser and text editor open, alternate between composing HTML and checking it. To check, save (^S) in the editor, and refresh (^R) Firefox's display of your HTML. If it displays correctly, go back to composing.

Check My Work. Normally, we don't validate tags with each compose/check cycle. We wait until the HTML file is stable. (Of course, it's okay to validate all of the time, but waiting for a good "stopping place" is more convenient.) To validate a file, go to the W3C Markup Validation Service at validator.w3.org/#validate_by_upload. The page that displays is shown in Figure 4.6. Simply browse for your HTML file and then click *Check*.

What comes back is either a green banner telling you your HTML5 checks out, or a red banner and a list of errors together with an explanation of what's wrong. Don't panic if you get many errors. It's very common to get a lot of errors at the start, because we all make mistakes. And very often one mistaken character can lead to many, many error messages.

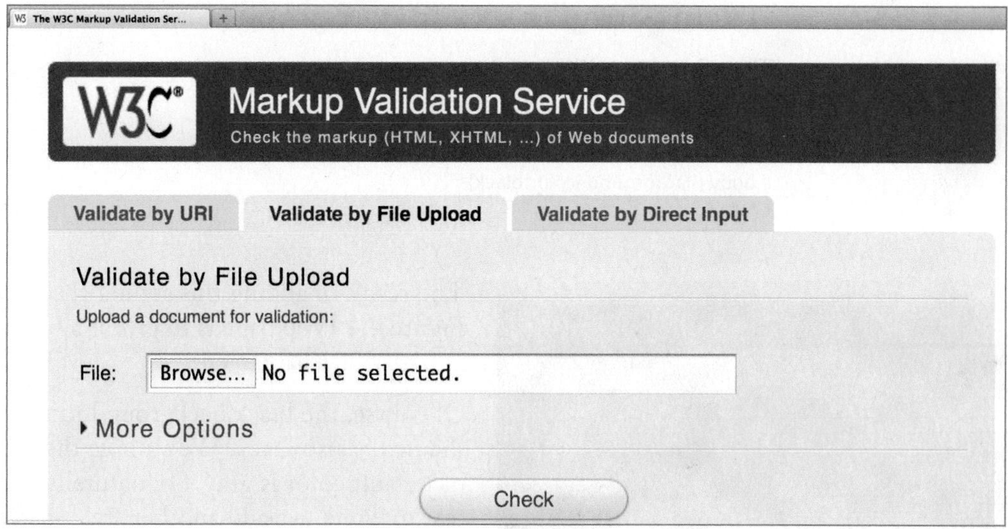

Figure 4.6 The W3C Markup Validation Service page; browse for your HTML file and then click *Check*.

4.3 Validate Yourself. Validate your starterPage.html file. It should be perfect. Now type into your paragraph some non-HTML tags, like <bold>Find This Mistake!</bold>, and validate it. Did it find your error?

Get Into Style with CSS

The Paradoxes page (Figure 4.4) may be interesting, but it is plain and uninviting. Knowing how "rockin'" Web pages can be, you can guess that it's easy to add some style to this page. The secret is **CSS**: Cascading Style Sheets.

A Place for Style

To add style to a Web page with CSS, you place <style> tags in the head section of the page. Typically, the <style> tags come after the <title> tags. So, referring to Figure 4.4, we place the <style> tags just after the </title> tag,

```
<title>Twentieth Century Paradoxes</title>
<style>
    CSS style specifications go here
</style>
```

We will refer to this as the *style section* of the page.

Styling Background and Paragraph

The idea with CSS is that for each tag, such as <body>, you give a property, such as background-color, and its value, such as black, as in

```
<style>
  body {background-color:black}
</style>
```

The result of adding this styling specification on the Figure 4.4 Web page is to give it a black background, shown at left. What happened?

Of course, the black background ruined our page, because the text is also black. We still see the horizontal rule because its default color is gray. So, naturally, to change the color of text to white, we add another style specification

```
<style>
  body {background-color:black; color:white}
</style>
```

And now the text shows up; the page displays the opposite of Figure 4.4—white letters on black. So, that's the idea: Specify for each tag how you would like it styled.

Twentieth Century Paradoxes

Paradoxes

Russell's Paradox

The Twentieth Century logician Bertrand Russell introduced a curious paradox: **This statement is false.** The statement can't be true, because it claims the converse. However, if it is not true, then it's false, just as it says. That makes it true. Paradoxically, it seems to be neither true nor false, or perhaps both true and false.

Magritte's Paradox

The famous Belgian artist René Magritte rendered the idea of Russell's Paradox visually in his famous painting *Ceci n'est pas une pipe*. The title translates from French, This Is Not A Pipe. The painting shows a pipe with the text *Ceci n'est pas une pipe* below it. Superficially, the painting looks like a true statement, since it is a *picture* of the pipe, not an actual pipe. However, the assertion is also part of the picture, which seems to make it false, because it is clearly a painting of a pipe. Paradoxically, the truth seems to depend on whether the statement is an assertion about the painting or a part of it. But, it's both.

CSS Styling

Notice the form of the styling information just discussed. The entry begins with a word (body) that is really a tag, but without its < and >. The word is called the tag's **element**. The specification of the style follows the element and is enclosed in braces. The entries are called **property/value** pairs. The property is the styling feature to change; the value is what to change it to. Notice how they are written. If there are several styling properties—as is typical—*they are separated by semicolons.*

elem_name { *prop*1 : *val*1 ; . . . ; *prop*N : *val*N}

This means that all occurrences of this tag will be styled by this specification.

How do we know that to specify the background color we use background-color? We *do not* memorize all of the styling specifications of CSS! Rather, we refer to www.w3schools.com/css/default.asp for lists of all of the styling possibilities. This site has many examples, which may be the easiest way to find out, because you see the "styling in action." And, there are also tutorials to teach you more. Eventually, through use, you may learn a few of them, but most people look them up if they don't use HTML and CSS every day.

Designing the Paradoxes Page

To further illustrate how to use the power of the style section, we will style the Paradoxes page. Our goal is to create the page shown in Figure 4.7.

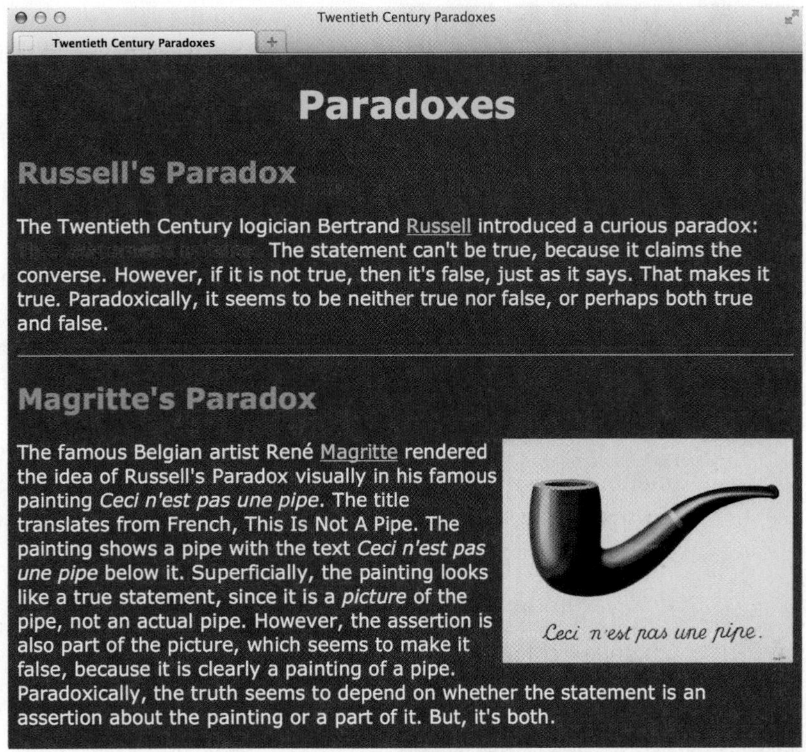

Figure 4.7 Styled Paradoxes page.

Global Styling. The first thing we notice about the page is that it uses a combination of colors to draw attention to different parts of the content. Also, the colors "work together—some are compatible with each other, and others are chosen for contrast. For example, the background is darkslategray and the paragraph text is lightyellow, a more pleasant combination than the black/white we used above. Although millions of colors are possible, about 130 commonly used colors have been given names; check www.w3schools.com/cssref/css_colornames.asp. In general, we want a page where the colors and design help the user understand the content.

To match Figure 4.7, we need to change our earlier style section to

```
<style>
  body {background-color:darkslategray}
  p {color:lightyellow}
</style>
```

This defines the page's background color and the color of the paragraph text. Unlike the black-and-white version above, this styling doesn't change the color of the heading text. So, we need other specifications for them.

Continuing the colorizing, we choose gold to color the <h1> heading at the top. The two <h2> headings are colored darkorange. That requires the specifications

```
h1 {color:gold}
h2 {color:darkorange}
```

be added *inside* the <style> tags, giving us four styling tags, total so far.

One additional adjustment that we want for the <h1> tag is to center its text. We check the CSS reference to find out what property we need to center text. It's the text-align

Paradoxes

Russell's Paradox

The Twentieth Century logician Bertrand Russell introduced a curious paradox: **This statement is false.** The statement can't be true, because it claims the converse. However, if it is not true, then it's false, just as it says. That makes it true. Paradoxically, it seems to be neither true nor false, or perhaps both true and false.

Magritte's Paradox

The famous Belgian artist René Magritte rendered the idea of Russell's Paradox visually in his famous painting *Ceci n'est pas une pipe*. The title translates from French, This Is Not A Pipe. The painting shows a pipe with the text *Ceci n'est pas une pipe* below it. Superficially, the painting looks like a true statement, since it is a *picture* of the pipe, not an actual pipe. However, the assertion is also part of the picture, which seems to make it false, because it is clearly a painting of a pipe. Paradoxically, the truth seems to depend on whether the statement is an assertion about the painting or a part of it. But, it's both.

property with the value of center. (The options are left, center, and right.) So, we add an additional property to the <h1> tag, as in

```
h1 {color:gold; text-align:center}
```

Notice the required semicolon between the two property/value pairs.

The style specifications given in the head section apply to all of the tags on the page. There are two <h2> tags, for example, and the one styling specification will apply to both. But, it's also possible to make one-time style specifications.

Inline Styling. Checking Figure 4.7, we see that the statement of Russell's paradox is formatted in bold, red text. The bold letters are achieved by enclosing the sentence in <b> tags. What we want to do is also make them red.

To make a styling specification that applies to a tag in only one place, we use the style *attribute* in the tag, as in

```
<b style="color:red">
```

Paradoxes

Russell's Paradox

The Twentieth Century logician Bertrand Russell introduced a curious paradox: This statement is false. The statement can't be true, because it claims the converse. However, if it is not true, then it's false, just as it says. That makes it true. Paradoxically, it seems to be neither true nor false, or perhaps both true and false.

Magritte's Paradox

The famous Belgian artist René Magritte rendered the idea of Russell's Paradox visually in his famous painting *Ceci n'est pas une pipe*. The title translates from French, This Is Not A Pipe. The painting shows a pipe with the text *Ceci n'est pas une pipe* below it. Superficially, the painting looks like a true statement, since it is a *picture* of the pipe, not an actual pipe. However, the assertion is also part of the picture, which seems to make it false, because it is clearly a painting of a pipe. Paradoxically, the truth seems to depend on whether the statement is an assertion about the painting or a part of it. But, it's both.

which makes all text between <b> and </b> both bold and red. This style applies only to this one location.

Notice that the style attribute is unusual. First, it's an *attribute*, meaning it is placed inside a tag. (We've also seen <style> as a *tag*, earlier, defining the style section at the top of the page.) Second, its value is *any* property/value pair styling that might appear in the style section. It's like being able to extend the style section for one specific tag only. And finally, because the value incorporates the ideas of the style section, a semicolon must separate the property/value pairs if there's more than one. The style attribute may be unusual, but it's extremely useful, as we shall see.

Misquotes. Quotation marks are the cause of many HTML errors. Of course, quotes must match, and it is easy to forget one of the pair. But there are also different kinds of quotes: Simple quotes (" and ') are the kind HTML likes; the fancy, curved quotes, called "smart quotes" (“” and ‘’) are the kind HTML doesn't like. Check *carefully* for messed-up quotes if your HTML produces an incorrect result. Notice that your text editor should never give you smart quotes.

Marking Links and Images

We are making progress on marking up our Web page, but we need to add links to biographies for Russell and Magritte, and the painting of the pipe.

Two Sides of a Hyperlink

In this section we explain how to make **hyperlinks**. As you know, when a user clicks a hyperlink, the browser loads a new Web page. This means there must be two parts to a hyperlink: the text in the current document that the user sees, which is highlighted and is called the **anchor text**; and the URL of the Web page that the computer links to, which is called the **hyperlink reference**.

Both parts of the hyperlink are specified in the **anchor tag** using attributes. It is constructed as follows:

- Begin with <a and make sure there's a space after the a but not before it. The a is for anchor.
- Give the hyperlink reference using the href attribute href="filename", making sure to include the double quotes.
- Close the anchor tag with the > symbol.
- Give the anchor text, which will be highlighted when it is displayed by the browser.
- End the hyperlink with the </a> tag.

For example, suppose http://www.biyo.com/bios/sci/russell.html is the URL for a Web biography of Bertrand Russell. We would anchor it to his last name on our Web page with the anchor tag

This hyperlink would be displayed with Russell's last name highlighted as follows:

Bertrand Russell

When the browser displays the page and the user clicks Russell, the browser downloads the biographical page given in the href. As another example, if Magritte's biography is at the same site, the text

<a href="http://www.biyo.com/bios/art/magritte.html">Magritte</a>

would give the reference and anchor for his hyperlink.

4.4 Popular Culture. Give the HTML needed to allow surfers to click on Mr. Graffiti and link to the page http://www.biyo.com/bios/art/haring.html.

Paradoxes

Russell's Paradox

The Twentieth Century logician Bertrand Russell introduced a curious paradox: This statement is false. The statement can't be true, because it claims the converse. However, if it is not true, then it's false, just as it says. That makes it true. Paradoxically, it seems to be neither true nor false, or perhaps both true and false.

Magritte's Paradox

The famous Belgian artist René Magritte rendered the idea of Russell's Paradox visually in his famous painting *Ceci n'est pas une pipe*. The title translates from French, This Is Not A Pipe. The painting shows a pipe with the text *Ceci n'est pas une pipe* below it. Superficially, the painting looks like a true statement, since it is a *picture* of the pipe, not an actual pipe. However, the assertion is also part of the picture, which seems to make it false, because it is clearly a painting of a pipe. Paradoxically, the truth seems to depend on whether the statement is an assertion about the painting or a part of it. But, it's both.

We make those two modifications to our Paradoxes Web page. To get the links to show in bright green we add a styling specification to our style section for the anchor element,

```
a     {color:greenyellow}
```

The links will show brightly.

Structure of the Image Tag

An **image tag**, which is analogous to an anchor tag, specifies a file that contains an image. The image tag format is

<img src="*filename*" alt="*description*"/>

where src is the required attribute for the image "source," and *filename* is the name of the image file. Notice that <img /> is a standalone tag. The file name needs to have the correct file extension, and we typically use .gif, .png, or .jpg. The alt attribute's value specifies an alternative form for the image, usually a textual description. It was introduced to assist people who are visually impaired. For example, screen readers, which speak Web pages to blind people, don't know what the image is a picture of, but they can say the description of the alt tag. HTML *requires* alt tags, and they benefit all of us, because when an image is not available or is slow to load, browsers can display the alt information.

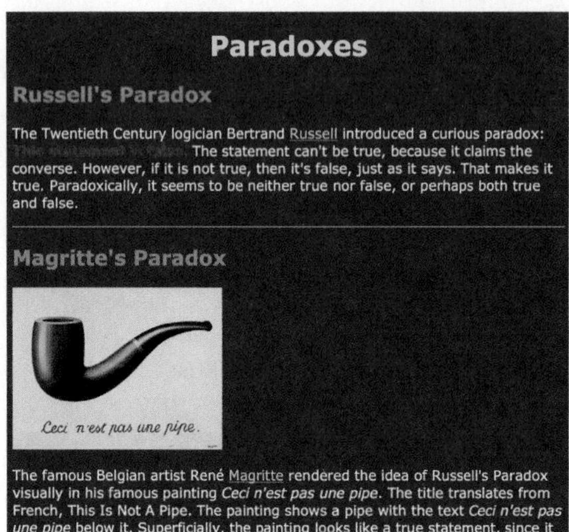

Including the Pipe Photo. If the image of Magritte's painting is stored in a file pipe.jpg, in the same folder as the Paradoxes page, we can include the image by giving its name

```
<img src="pipe.jpg" alt="Magritte's pipe art" width="250"/>
```

which finds the image and places it in the document. Notice the third attribute giving the width of the image. Its natural size is too large, so the width specification tells the browser to shrink it until its 250 pixels wide before placing it on the page.

Change Either Width OR Height. As noted earlier, the width and height attributes are optional for <img/> tags. If you want to change an image's size, specify either the new width *or* the new height, but not both. When the browser knows one of them, it will figure out the other based on the aspect ratio—that is, the shape—of the image.

Styling Position for Images. The pipe image didn't quite turn out as we wanted. It is all by itself following the <h2> heading. This is consistent with the image placement rule: *Images are inserted in the page at the point in the HTML text where the* <img/> *tag is specified, and the text lines up with the* bottom *of the image*. To get the text to "flow" around the image, as we want, we need to see how this rule applies.

If the image is the same size or smaller than the surrounding text, it is placed in line ■ just like a letter. This is convenient for icons or smilies. If the image is larger than the letters ■, it appears in the text, following the rule, but the line spacing is increased to separate it from the previous line.

What we want is for the text to flow around the image, either by positioning the image on the left with the text to its right, or vice versa. To make the text flow around the image, we use the style attribute again; this time in the image tag. Its value is "float:left" (shown here) or "float:right" (what we need for the page). This forces the image to the left or right of the browser window:

```
<img src="pipe.jpg" alt="Magritte's pipe art" width="250" style="float:right"/>
```

The text will continue from left to right, and from top to bottom, in the remaining space, flowing around the image.

Finally, to display an image by itself, centered, without any text around it, simply put it inside paragraph tags. That will separate it from the paragraphs above and below. Styling the paragraph to center the image

is accomplished by centering the text using the text-align property again,

```
<p style="text-align : center"><img src = ... /></p>
```

even though the only "text" is the image.

The result of our Paradoxes styling project is a complete page, which now exactly matches Figure 4.7.

Making an Image a Link. As you have noticed while surfing the Web, not all anchors are *text*. Sometimes you click on an image (gif or jpg) to follow a hyperlink. To use an image as the anchor, place it inside of the anchor tags. For example, imagine that we have a small GIF, say this small red square, ■, called red.gif. Then we can use it as a button to link to a document, say, history_red_square.html, simply by placing the image where the anchor text would normally go:

```
<a href="history_red_square.html"><img src="red.gif" alt="Red Box"/></a>
```

When the page displays, the usual highlighting that links receive will be used to mark the .gif as a link. Suppose the highlight is blue decoration. Then the box ■ has a blue frame around it, and clicking it will load the history_red_square.html page.

Referring to Files

We have been successful creating a basic page and styling it. Much of the mystery is gone. But there are still a few things that we need to know about how to refer properly to files.

Referring to Pages and Images

When we link to pages on the Web using the anchor tag, as in

```
<a href="http://apod.nasa.gov/apod/astropix.html">Astronomy Picture of the Day</a>
```

the hypertext reference, href, attribute has a full URL as its value. This is the correct way to make references to Web pages on *other* sites. Such references using a full URL are called **absolute references**.

Local Page Reference. Often a Web site is made up of many pages that are all stored on the same server, and link to each other. For these pages—local pages—it is wrong to use a full URL in the href attribute. In this case, we simply name the file we want to link to. Such references are called **relative references**.

For example, suppose your main page is in a folder called myCat, which includes the HTML code index.html and its photos, and there are other folders in it for related pages, as illustrated in Figure 4.8.

Then to link from the main page (index.html) in myCat to the

a. aGift.html page, write <a href="aGift.html">how I got my cat</a>, because the two files are in the same folder.

b. fun.html page, write <a href="lolcat/fun.html">see my cat being hilarious</a> because it is in the folder lolcat.

c. tabby.html page, write <a href="lolcat/friend/tabby.html">the neighbor's cat</a>, because it is in the folder friend in the folder lolcat.

The rule is that to refer to pages deeper in the file hierarchy, give the navigation paths to them. The path begins in the folder where the reference is being made—myCat in these cases, because the reference is from index.html—and refers to the contents of a folder with a slash /. For example, lolcat is in the folder where index.html is, so to refer to a page stored in lolcat, we use lolcat/fun.html. Similarly, two hops—lolcat/friend/tabby.html—take us to tabby.html.

Images. Referencing image files in <img/> tags works exactly the same. So, index.html can reference fatcat.jpg directly, as in

```
<img src="fatcat.jpg" alt="Overweight cat"/>the kitten got bigger</a>
```

because it is in the same folder. As you can guess, to reference deeper pictures from index.html requires either one step, lolcat/yarn1.jpg, or two, lolcat/friend/aVisitor.jpg.

Notice that it is better to reference the pictures where they are located in the Web site's hierarchy rather than duplicating them. We explain the hazards of duplication in a later chapter.

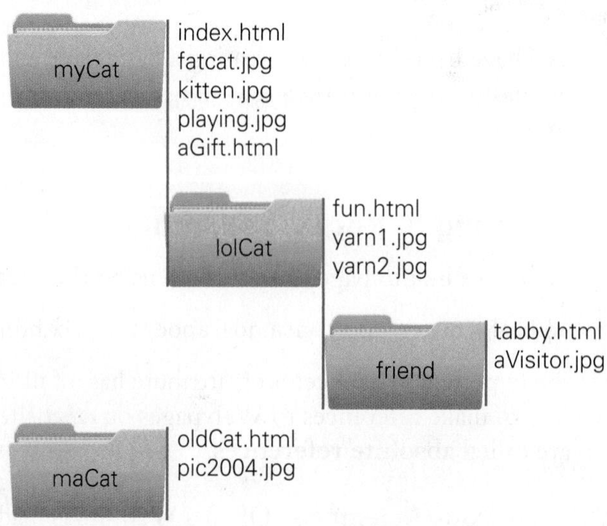

Figure 4.8 Sample directory (folder) structure for a Web site.

Going Up in the World Using the rule "make a path that refers to the contents of a folder with a /" works for files deeper in the hierarchy. But how can we refer to files higher up? To create a path that goes up into an enclosing folder use ../—called **dot-dot-slash**. This notation from the UNIX operating system allows us to navigate the whole file hierarchy.

For example, think of the tabby.html Web page, deep in the hierarchy of Figure 4.8, and see how it references photos elsewhere on the site. The tabby.html page can refer to pictures in its own folder directly, aVisitor.jpg. To refer to photos in the enclosing folder (lolcat), it "moves up" using dot-dot-slash with the reference ../yarn2.jpg. To refer to a photo in the main (myCat) folder, it needs two moves up, and so uses ../../kitten.jpg.

Finally, it is possible to go up and then come back down. Continuing with the tabby.html page perspective, suppose we want to refer to the photo pic2004.jpg. We must go up three levels—to the folder that contains myCat and maCat—and then enter the maCat folder to get the file. The reference (from tabby.html) is

```
<img src="../../../maCat/pic2004.jpg" alt="1st cat"/>
```

Following the path, the first step is *into* lolcat, the second is *into* myCat, the third is *into* its containing folder (not named here), then into maCat to find the file.

4.5 Mother May I? Give the reference from the oldCat.html Web page to the photo yarn2.jpg.

We all make programming mistakes. Every one of us. Even Google's programmers fail HTML5 Validation on their home page. Still, browsers manage to display Web pages right. Thanks, browser developers, for saving us from our own mistakes!

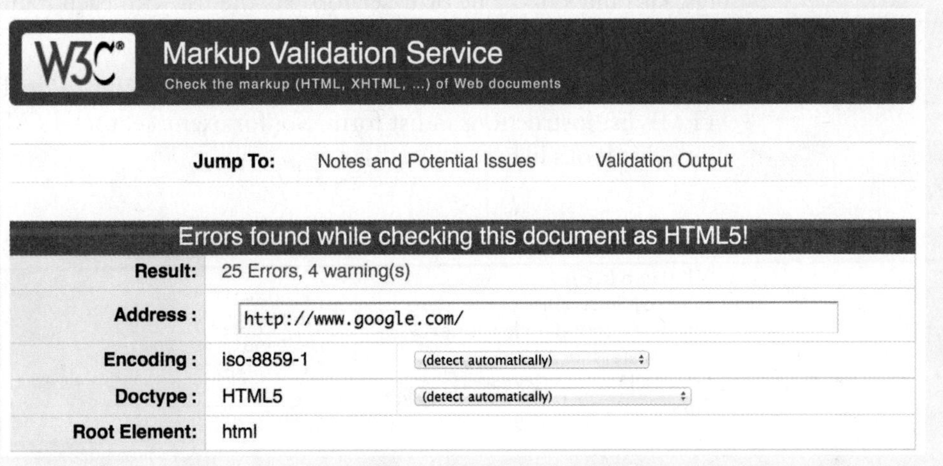

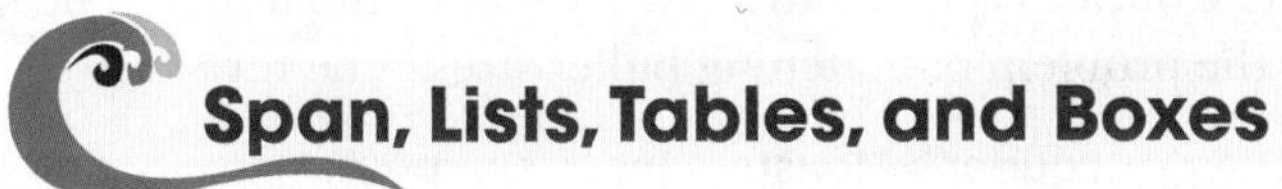

Span, Lists, Tables, and Boxes

This section introduces some very common features in HTML Web pages. All concepts give Web designers tight control of what is presented on the screen.

Span

In developing the Paradox styling, we colored Russell's Paradox red by adding a style attribute to the <b> tag. The text that was to be bold was also exactly the text that should be red. So everything worked out well. We just added a style attribute to the <b> tag. But, how can we color text that is not enclosed in a convenient tag? Meet <span>!

The <span> tag simply surrounds content that we want to style in a certain way. We enclose the content in <span> tags, and then include the styling attribute. Nothing could be easier. So, writing

```
<span style="color:darkturquoise">Eeny</span>
<span style="color:blue">Meeny</span>
<span style="color:violet">Miny</span>
<span style="color:darkmagenta">Mo</span>
```

results in

Span is an extremely useful tag.

Lists Tags

There are many kinds of lists in HTML, and each has its special properties. We give the highlights. The full story is explained at www.w3schools.com/html/html_lists.asp.

Unordered Lists. Perhaps the easiest list is an unordered list. The unordered list tags, <ul> and </ul>, surround the items of the list, which are themselves enclosed in list item tags, <li> and </li>. The browser formats the list with each item bulleted, indented, and starting on its own line.

As usual, though the form of the HTML doesn't matter to the browser, we write the HTML list instructions in list form. So, for example, the HTML for a favorite animated movie list looks like

```
<ul>
  <li>Luxo Jr.</li>
  <li>Toy Story</li>
  <li style="font-family:courier">
     Monsters Inc.</li>
  <li>Wall&#8226;E</li>
</ul>
```

Favorite Animations

- Luxo Jr.
- Toy Story
- Monsters Inc.
- Wall•E

Notice that the bullets take their size information from the font in use. So, for Monsters Inc., the change to the Courier typeface affected the size of the bullet. The <span> tag, just discussed, solves the problem of matching bullet sizes. The text

```
<li><span style="font-family:courier">Monsters Inc.</span></li>
```

changes the font inside of the "already formatted" list item, producing a bullet that is the same size as the others.

Also, notice that Wall•E needs a special character, which we present using Unicode, just as we would with accent marks.

Ordered Lists. Another kind of list is an ordered list, which uses the tags <ol> and </ol> and replaces the bullets with numbers. Otherwise, the ordered list behaves just like an unnumbered list. Thus, the HTML for a ranking of the world's largest reefs looks like

```
<ol>
  <li>Great Barrier Reef: 2500 km</li>
  <li>Red Sea Coral Reef: 1900 km</li>
  <li>New Caledonia Barrier Reef: 1500 km</li>
  <li>Mesoamerican Barrier Reef: 943 km</li>
</ol>
```

Coral Reef Rankings

1. Great Barrier Reef: 2500 km
2. Red Sea Coral Reef: 1900 km
3. New Caledonia Barrier Reef: 1500 km
4. Mesoamerican Barrier Reef: 943 km

Although we use normal Arabic numerals to number the items, Roman numerals and all sorts of other counting marks are possible (see www.w3schools.com/cssref/pr_list-style-type.asp).

Sublists. We can also have a list within a list, simply by making items the sublist of the main list. Applying this idea in HTML looks like

```
<ul>
  <li>Speedo</li>
  <li>Bikini
      <ul>
        <li>Top</li>
        <li>Bottom</li>
      </ul>
  </li>
  <li>Boardies</li>
</ul>
```

At The Beach

- Speedo
- Bikini
    - Top
    - Bottom
- Boardies

Notice that sublists use a different bullet symbol, which can be changed, of course.

Definitional Lists. Finally, there is a handy list form called the **definitional list**, indicated by the tags <dl> and </dl>. A definitional list is usually made up of a sequence of **definitional terms**, surrounded by the tags <dt> and </dt>, and **definitional data**, surrounded by the tags <dd> and </dd>. So, for example, a definitional list is formatted by browsers as

```
<dl>
  <dt> Man </dt>
   <dd><i>Homo sapiens</i>, the greatest
        achievement of evolution. </dd>
  <dt> Woman </dt>
   <dd><i>Homo sapiens</i>, a greater
        achievement of evolution, and clever
        enough not to mention it to man. </dd>
</dl>
```

List Example

Man

Homo sapiens, the greatest achievement of evolution.

Woman

Homo sapiens, a greater achievement of evolution, and clever enough not to mention it to man.

Of course, other formatting commands such as italics and bold can be used within any line items.

Handling Tables

A table is a good way to present certain types of information. Creating a table in HTML is straightforward. It's like defining a list of lists, where each of the main list items, called *rows*, has one or more items, called *cells*. The browser aligns cells to form columns.

A Basic Table. A table is enclosed in table tags, <table> and </table>. Each row is enclosed in table row tags, <tr> and </tr>. The cells of each row are enclosed in table data tags, <td> and </td>. So, a table with four rows, each with three cells is defined by

```
<table border="1">
  <tr><td>1</td><td>2</td><td>3</td></tr>
  <tr><td>4</td><td>5</td><td>6</td></tr>
  <tr><td>7</td><td>8</td><td>9</td></tr>
  <tr><td>*</td><td>0</td><td>#</td></tr>
</table>
```

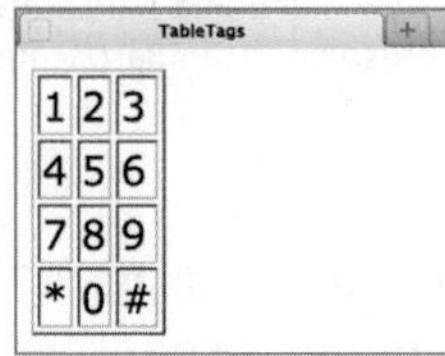

1	2	3
4	5	6
7	8	9
*	0	#

Notice the border attribute; leave it out or set it to "0" to eliminate the border.

The standard table is often quite unappealing. To improve its look, styling commands are needed, mostly for the <td> tag. For example, the preceding table can be styled into a telephone keypad by removing the border attribute

and adding these property/value pairs to a td element in the style section:

```
td {
      border-style:solid;
      border-width:4px;
      border-color:mediumblue;
      padding:5px;
      width:20px;
      text-align:center;
      font-family:optima;
      font-size:large;
      background-color:midnightblue;
      color:lavender;
   }
```

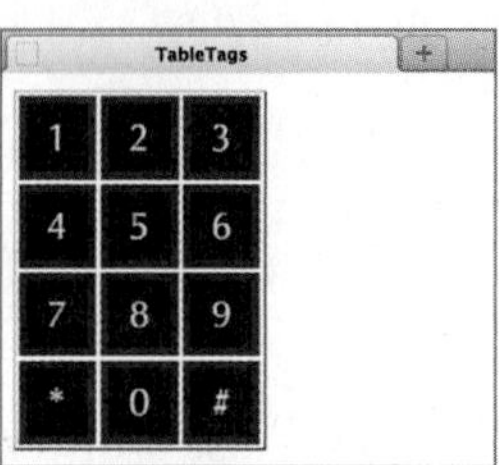

1	2	3
4	5	6
7	8	9
*	0	#

Always expect to style tables. (Padding is explained in the next section.)

Embellishing Tables. Tables can be given captions and column headings. Captions are enclosed in <caption> tags. Place them inside of the table tags, usually before the first row. By default, the caption is centered at the top of the table. Place the column headings as the first table row. In the heading row, replace the table data tags with table heading tags, <th> and</th>, and keep the table row tags <tr> as usual. The table headings are automatically displayed in bold. Illustrating these ideas, we have:

```
<table border="1">
   <caption>Bilingual Countries</caption>
   <tr><th>Country</th><th colspan="2">Languages</th></tr>
   <tr><td>Belgium</td><td>Dutch</td><td>French</td></tr>
   <tr><td>Canada</td><td>English</td><td>French</td></tr>
   <tr><td>Cyprus</td><td>Greek</td><td>Turkish</td></tr>
   <tr><td>Philippines</td><td>English</td><td>Filipino</td></tr>
</table>
```

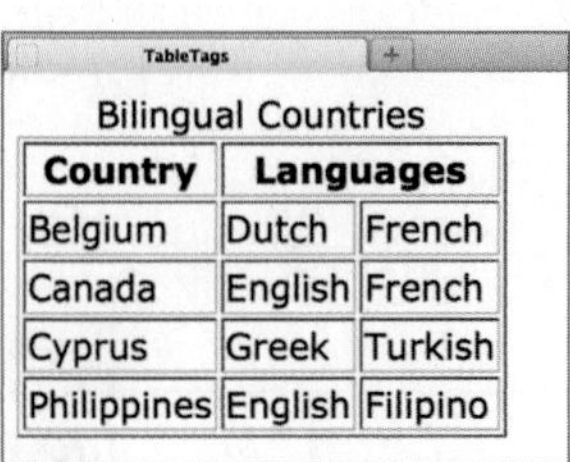

Bilingual Countries

Country	Languages	
Belgium	Dutch	French
Canada	English	French
Cyprus	Greek	Turkish
Philippines	English	Filipino

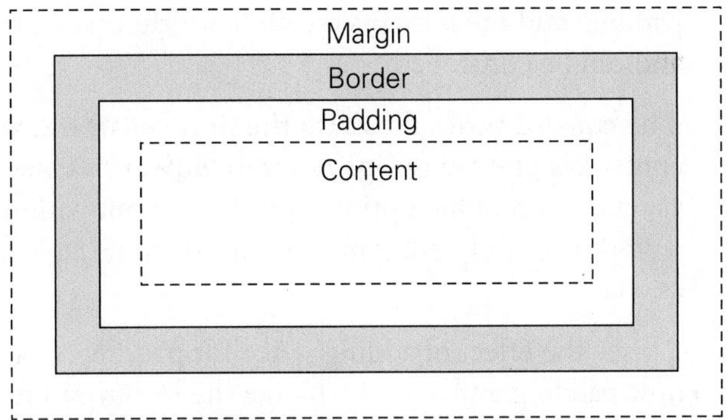

Figure 4.9 The boxes of the Box Model: Content is enclosed in padding, which is enclosed in a border, which is enclosed by a margin. All of these can be controlled.

Notice that the first row uses the <th> tag rather than the <td> tag to specify the column headings. If instead row headings are required, place the <th> as the first cell in each row.

This example illustrates one other tool for designing tables. The heading "Languages" spans two columns. See how this is achieved: the cell tag (<th> in this case) uses the attribute colspan="2" to tell the browser to have this cell be a doublewide. (There is also a rowspan attribute.) Of course, when spanning more than one column, the row will have fewer cells than completely filled rows.

The "Box Model"

For styling purposes, CSS considers nearly every HTML5 element to be enclosed in a "box." The boxes are not visible unless we purposely make them visible, or use them with other elements that reveal that they're there. This concept of HTML5 elements being treated as if in boxes is called the **Box Model of CSS**. It's very handy, because the boxes are our key to styling HTML5 well.

The virtual box around HTML5 elements is shown in Figure 4.9. Notice the four parts to the figure: In the center is the content, and padding separates the content from the border. The border can be explicitly displayed. And finally around the border is the margin separating this element from other elements.

To emphasize this idea, Figure 4.10 shows a small page with a heading and a definitional list. All of the elements have been given a colored border. Notice that in the figure the

```
  <style>
    h2 {border-style:solid; border-color:red}
    dl  {border-style:solid; border-color:gold}
    dt  {border-style:solid; border-color:blue}
    dd  {border-style:solid; border-color:magenta}
  </style>
</head>
<body>
  <h2>Comments on the Universe</h2>
    <dl>
      <dt>Albert Einstein </dt>
      <dd>Only two things are infinite, the
           universe and human stupidity, and
           I'm not sure about the former.</dd>
    </dl>
```

Comments on the Universe

Albert Einstein

Only two things are infinite, the universe and human stupidity, and I'm not sure about the former.

Figure 4.10 The boxes around definitional list elements with 0-width padding and margin.

padding and the margins are all 0-width; that is, they are not visible. But they are there and can be controlled.

The colored boxes illustrate the purpose of the model. We notice that the <dt> tag's content is pressed up against the <dd> tag's content. Perhaps we would like some spacing there. One option would be to put padding around "Albert Einstein"; another would be to put a margin around the <dd> tag's quotation. And there are other choices.

To see the effect of adding space for padding and margins, see Figure 4.11, which shows how padding and margin change the layout of Figure 4.10.

There is one additional way to control padding, borders, and margins: *They can be specified for each side of the box separately*. So, it is possible to add a margin at the top of an element only. The importance of this can be seen by comparing Figure 4.11(b) and (c). When we added the 10px margin to the purple box of (b) to get (c), we lost the indenting of the quotation. That's because the default for a <dd> tag is to have a left-side-only margin; when we changed the margin to apply to all sides, we lost it. The lesson: To separate the blue and purple boxes, use margin-top:10px as in Figure 4.11(d). That leaves the left margin alone, and it will be indented again.

Check the CSS reference section on the Box Model for more information: www.w3schools.com/css/css_boxmodel.asp.

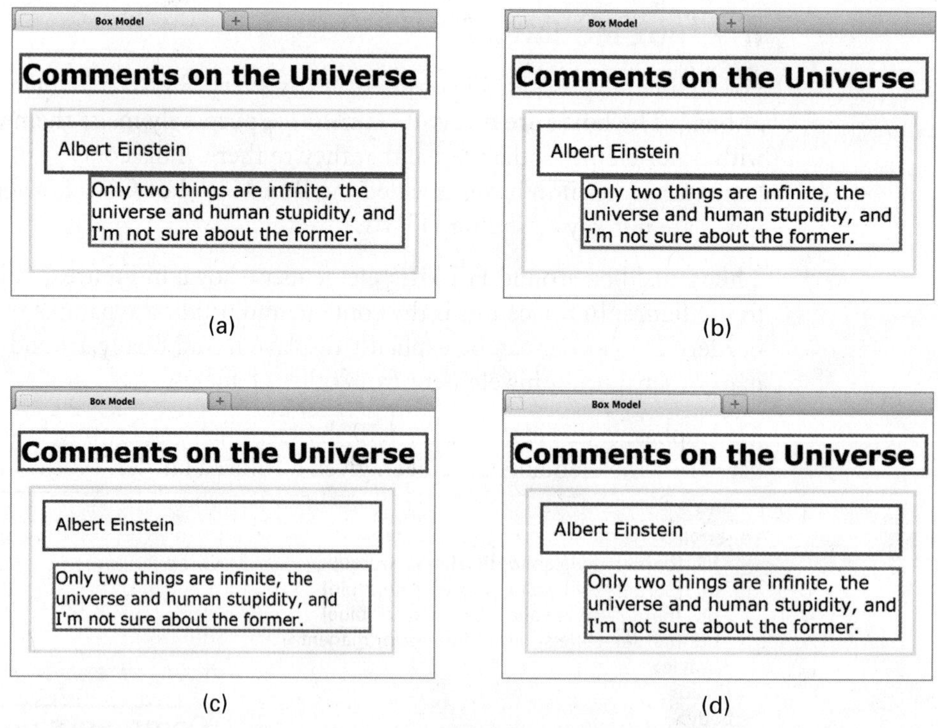

Figure 4.11 Padding and margins of 10 pixels (px): (a) yellow, both padding and margin; (b) blue, padding only; (c) purple, margin only; (d) purple, only top margin styled.

4.6 Thinking Outside the Box. Give the change(s) to Figure 4.10 needed to produce this layout.

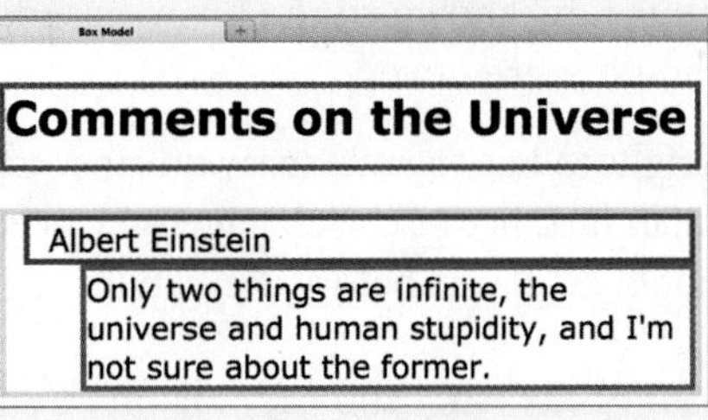

Cascading Style Sheets

It is clear why the word "style" is in the name Cascading Style Sheets. And perhaps all of the text inside the <style> tags at the top of our Web page could be called a "style sheet." But why is it *cascading*? In this section we find out.

Style in Many Places

We have placed styling information in several places. For example, <span> tags, such as

```
<span style="font-family:courier">
```

allowed us to style specific places in the Web page that are not associated with any tag. We also added style information to tags we were using, as in

```
<b style="color:red">
```

Both cases used the style attribute to produce very localized styling.

Globally Speaking

Thinking about style that applies to the whole page, we defined the style section in the page's head using <style> tags. Styling in this section applies to all occurrences of a tag.

That information could be used to style other pages, too. For example, if each page in a site used it, they would have a consistent "look and feel." To apply one set of styling specifications to multiple pages, we could Copy/Paste them into other HTML files (bad idea), or we can place them in a file by themselves, and simply reference the style file from each of the pages (excellent idea). Here's how.

Style File. Transfer the style section of a page to a *text file* (using your trusty text editor). Do *not* include the <style> tags, just the actual styling for the elements. Save the file with a name like myFaveStyle.css. The extension is important.

Once the file is created, place a reference to it in the head section of the page using a <link/> tag, as in

```
<link rel="stylesheet" type="text/css" href="myFaveStyle.css" />
```

This tag tells the browser that styling information, written in CSS, is to be found in the file. (Notice our friend href.) The browser gets the specifications and includes them in the HTML file as if they were explicitly written. The information formerly in the style section is now known to the browser, and so it is no longer needed in the style section and should be removed.

It is alright to have a style section using <style> tags in addition to the external file. (It is typical, in fact, because each page may need its own customization.) In such cases the <link/> tag should be placed before the <style> tags, so they take precedence over the file.

Inherently Stylish. And there is one more case of global styling. We can figure it out if we recall: It's possible to display a Web page without giving any style information at all. That's what we did in Figure 4.4. The browser already knew what font to use, and how much space to put between the headings and a paragraph. Where did that come from? Answer: The browser has a built-in set of default style specifications allowing it to display pages without any additional styling. Generally, this is the styling your styling choices hide.

The Cascade

Summarizing, we have the following sources for style information:

- Default—comes with the browser
- External—styling in a file
- Style Section—defined inside of <style> tags
- Inherited—properties set by enclosing tag
- Tagged—defined with the style attribute

(We explain inherited formatting in the next section.) Here is how the sources relate to each other: Each level's style specifications for an element take precedence over—that is, hide—the specification for that element given by the levels above it.

For example, there is a default styling for <dd> tags, which we saw earlier in the *Homo sapiens* example; the text color was black. Any style specifications in the external file, like changing the text to green,

```
dd {color:green}
```

takes precedence over the default black. If the <style> section further redefines text color to be seagreen,

```
dd {color:seagreen}
```

that takes precedence over the green. But, inside the <dd> tag itself, there could be a style attribute that changes the color again to mediumseagreen

```
<dd style="color:mediumseagreen">
```

taking precedence over seagreen. The text color will be mediumseagreen. It is this cascade of styling options that "hide" or take precedence over "higher up" styling that gives CSS its name.

The rule: *For any property, the closest specification wins.*

This rule allows us to make more and more customized styling choices as we get "closer and closer" to the item being styled.

Styling with Class

With our understanding of CSS, a Web page as is shown in Figure 4.12 is completely understandable. The <h2> tag has been formatted to have a background with white letters. The definitional terms have a large font, and the <dt> specifies some space above them to separate items. Also, <dd> tags receive a border along the bottom of the box to visually separate them from the entry below.

After considering the page's design, we decide that it mixes comments about the universe from a scientist with comments about the universe from cartoonists. These are separate groups that the formatting should emphasize. So, we decide to make the scientist names red text, and the cartoonist names blue text.

A class Attribute

We could use local styling, adding a style attribute to each <dt> tag, giving the right color for the speaker, but that would be time-consuming and annoying, especially if we had hundreds of people in each category. And, we would probably change our mind on the color scheme after it was done, requiring many changes. The CSS class concept is the solution.

A class is just a group of related things that need a specific styling. We will invent the scientist class and the cartoonist class. To use class, we append the class name to the element, and give them styling, as in

```
dt.scientist {color:red}
```

We have a separate styling for the cartoonist class, and keep the previous styling for the <dt> tag. This gives us three different styling specifications for this element:

```
dt {padding-top:8px; font-size : large;}
dt.scientist   {color:red}
dt.cartoonist {color:royalblue; }
```

```
<style>
  h2 {background-color : rosybrown; color : white;}
  dt {padding-top:8px; font-size : large;}
  dd {font-style : italic; border-bottom-style:solid;
      border-bottom-color:rosybrown;
      border-bottom-width:3px;}
</style>
</head>
<body><h2>Comments on the Universe</h2>
  <dl><dt>Albert Einstein </dt>
      <dd>Only two things are infinite, the universe
         and human stupidity, and I'm not sure about
         the former.</dd>
      <dt>Bill Waterson </dt>
      <dd>The surest sign that intelligent life exists
        elsewhere in the universe is that it has never
        tried to contact us.</dd>
      <dt>Charles Schultz </dt>
      <dd>Don't worry about the world coming to an end
        today. It is already tomorrow in Australia.</dd>
      <dt>Randall Munroe</dt>
      <dd>The universe started in 1970. Anyone claiming
         to be over 38 is lying about their age.</dd>
  </dl>
```

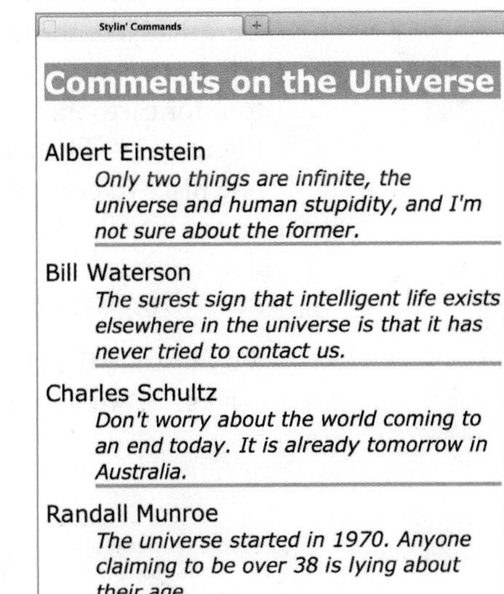

Figure 4.12 Styling for a page with a definitional list. (Munroe's joke from 2008 is explained in the Fluency Byte on pages 560 and 561.)

```
<style>
  h2 {background-color : rosybrown; color : white;}
  dt {padding-top:8px; font-size : large;
       text-align:right}
  dt.scientist   {color:red}
  dt.cartoonist {color:royalblue;
       font-family:comic sans MS}
  dd {font-style : italic; border-bottom-style:solid;
       border-bottom-color:rosybrown;
       border-bottom-width:3px;}
 </style>
</head>
<body><h2>Comments on the Universe</h2>
    <dl><dt class="scientist">Albert Einstein </dt>
          <dd>Only two things are infinite, the universe
             and human stupidity, and I'm not sure about
             the former.</dd>
          <dt class="cartoonist">Bill Waterson </dt>
          <dd>The surest sign that intelligent life exists
            elsewhere in the universe is that it has never
            tried to contact us.</dd>
```

Stylin' Commands

Comments on the Universe

Albert Einstein

Only two things are infinite, the universe and human stupidity, and I'm not sure about the former.

Bill Waterson

The surest sign that intelligent life exists elsewhere in the universe is that it has never tried to contact us.

Charles Schultz

Don't worry about the world coming to an end today. It is already tomorrow in Australia.

Randall Munroe

The universe started in 1970. Anyone claiming to be over 38 is lying about their age.

Figure 4.13 The definitional list exploiting the class feature to style scientists and cartoonists differently.

These cascade. All <dt> tags will have padding and large font. In addition, scientists will be colored red and cartoonists colored blue. Of course, the browser has no idea which is which, so we include the class attribute in the <dt> tag, as in

```
<dt class="scientist">Albert Einstein </dt>
<dd>Only two things are infinite, the universe
   and human stupidity, and I'm not sure about
   the former.</dd>
<dt class="cartoonist">Bill Waterson </dt>
<dd>The surest sign that intelligent life exists
  elsewhere in the universe is that it has never
  tried to contact us.</dd>
```

Because of the cascading, we can be very selective as to where to make changes. Suppose we would like the person's name to be right justified. Because that change applies to all <dt> terms, we add text-align:right to the dt element. If we also decide to change the font for cartoonists to comic sans, we only change dt.cartoonist. The result is shown in Figure 4.13. Then when friends complain that comic sans is a lame font, we have only one place to correct.

An Alternate Class

To illustrate the class idea further, we return to the Bilingual Countries table developed earlier. As we said then, the form is very plain. Recall that this is the table and its code.

```
<table border="1">
   <caption>Bilingual Countries</caption>
   <tr><th>Country</th><th colspan="2">Languages</th></tr>
   <tr><td>Belgium</td><td>Dutch</td><td>French</td></tr>
   <tr><td>Canada</td><td>English</td><td>French</td></tr>
   <tr><td>Cyprus</td><td>Greek</td><td>Turkish</td></tr>
   <tr><td>Philippines</td><td>English</td><td>Filipino</td></tr>
</table>
```

TableTags

Bilingual Countries

Country	Languages	
Belgium	Dutch	French
Canada	English	French
Cyprus	Greek	Turkish
Philippines	English	Filipino

```
caption {
        font-size:large;
        font-variant:small-caps;
        font-weight:bold}
td, th {
        border-style:solid;
        border-width:1px;
        padding:5px;
        text-align:center;
        background-color:cornsilk;
        color:saddlebrown;
    }
```

TableTags

BILINGUAL COUNTRIES

Country	Languages	
Belgium	Dutch	French
Canada	English	French
Cyprus	Greek	Turkish
Philippines	English	Filipino

Figure 4.14 The Bilingual Countries table, styled to enhance the caption and make the cells easier to read.

So we add more styling for the caption, the headings, and the cells. Our main interest will be the rows. And we begin by eliminating the border="1" attribute.

Initial Styling. Figure 4.14 shows the results of our first pass at styling the table, together with the properties that implement it.

Several features are illustrated here. In the caption, the properties font-variant and font-weight are both used. The font-variant transforms the text in the file to a different form. These are part of a long list of font-controlling properties.

More importantly, notice that the td element and the th element are styled together. They should have the similar features for the table to look consistent, but they could have been styled separately. It's better to do them together: If multiple elements have a common set of property/value entries, it is good practice to style them together. It tells anyone reading the CSS that the elements match.

Alternating Rows. Large tables—both long and wide—are often difficult to read, especially if the cells are packed together tightly. "Zebra" tables—tables with rows of alternating color—seem to improve readability. To achieve this effect we use the class concept again, illustrated in Figure 4.15.

TableTags

BILINGUAL COUNTRIES

Country	Languages	
Belgium	Dutch	French
Canada	English	French
Cyprus	Greek	Turkish
Philippines	English	Filipino

```
td, th {
        border-style:solid;
        border-width:1px;
        padding:5px;
        text-align:center;
        background-color:cornsilk;
        color:saddlebrown;
    }
tr.alt td {
        background-color:blanchedalmond;
    }
```

```
<table>
  <caption>Bilingual Countries</caption>
  <tr><th>Country</th><th colspan="2">Languages</th></tr>
  <tr><td>Belgium</td><td>Dutch</td><td>French</td></tr>
  <tr class="alt"><td>Canada</td><td>English</td><td>French</td></tr>
  <tr><td>Cyprus</td><td>Greek</td><td>Turkish</td></tr>
  <tr class="alt"><td>Philippines</td><td>English</td><td>Filipino</td></tr>
</table>
```

Figure 4.15 Table with rows of alternating color, and the styling that achieves it.

In Figure 4.15, which shows the table and its styling, notice a tr element with the alt class. This is followed by another td element that defines the colors of the alternate rows. This is the td styling that is to be used in the context of the alt class. So, <tr> tags of alternating rows are specified as being in the class="alt", and the others remain unchanged.

The td inherits all of the properties that normal td elements get, but gets a different background-color from <tr>. By the cascading rule—closest styling wins—the tr color applies for alt rows and hides the original cell background. This is the "inherited" case referred to in the cascading discussion above.

Hovering Above Links

We complete our HTML discussion by explaining some properties used to change the style of links. We are most interested in how to change the anchor text or images as the cursor hovers over them.

Pseudo Classes

Normally, the default is for links to be colored blue and underlined. To change this, we style the anchor tag:

```
<style>
  a          {text-decoration : none}
  a:link     {color : darkviolet }
  a:visited  {color : gray }
  a:hover    {color : red}
</style>
```

The first of these specifications removes the underline typical of a link. The next three, which refer to different states that an anchor tag could be in, are called *pseudo classes*. The pseudo classes recognize, for example, that it's important to a reader whether a link has been visited or not. Pseudo classes are separated from the element a by a colon (:).

The four pseudo class states are

link, styling for an unvisited link (anchor text)
visited, styling for links that have been visited
hover, styling when the cursor hovers over a link
active, styling for links that are in process

Notice this order. One of the stranger requirements of HTML: If hover is styled—that is, you change its styling with pseudo-classes—its style definition must come *after* the styling for link and visited, and *before* active.

Keeping Order in Class The CSS documentation advises that to be interpreted correctly, the order of pseudo class-modified anchor elements must always be defined in the order: link, visited, hover, active. A standard mnemonic: *LoVe, HAte.*

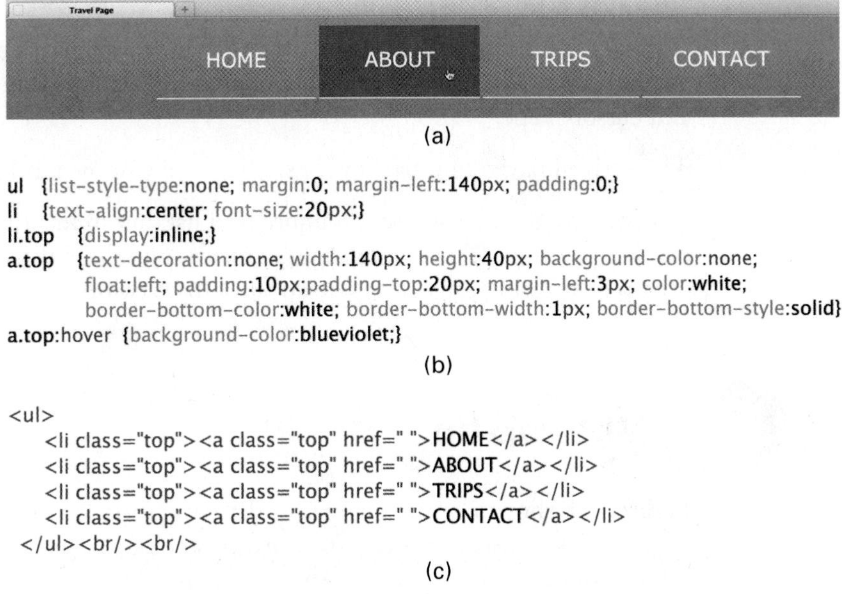

(a)

```
ul  {list-style-type:none; margin:0; margin-left:140px; padding:0;}
li  {text-align:center; font-size:20px;}
li.top   {display:inline;}
a.top   {text-decoration:none; width:140px; height:40px; background-color:none;
         float:left; padding:10px;padding-top:20px; margin-left:3px; color:white;
         border-bottom-color:white; border-bottom-width:1px; border-bottom-style:solid}
a.top:hover {background-color:blueviolet;}
```

(b)

```
<ul>
    <li class="top"><a class="top" href=" ">HOME</a></li>
    <li class="top"><a class="top" href=" ">ABOUT</a></li>
    <li class="top"><a class="top" href=" ">TRIPS</a></li>
    <li class="top"><a class="top" href=" ">CONTACT</a></li>
 </ul><br/><br/>
```

(c)

Figure 4.16 Horizontal navigation bar: (a) hovering, (b) style specification, and (c) usage in the body.

Navigation Bars

A common way to exploit the change-on-hover property of links is in navigation bars. Horizontal navigation bars are common at the top of many of the Web pages we visit. Vertical navigational bars are also extremely common. Figures 4.16 and 4.17 show an example of each. Let's see how these work.

The first thing to notice is that the navigation bar is built using an unordered list of links. Normally, the items of such a list are displayed vertically, but because of the li.top {display:inline} specification, those in the top class are just listed one after another. Additionally, the list items have no bullet marks, because of the list-style-type:none specification. Similarly, the anchors do not have any decoration, either. The first five styling lines layout the image; the last one makes a hovered-over item change its background color.

Past Trips
2014
2013
2012
2011
2010
2009
2008
2007
2006

(a)

```
<ul style="float:left; margin-right:35px; margin-left:25px">
   <li class="side">Past Trips</li>
   <li class="side"><a class="side" href=" ">2014</a></li>
   <li class="side"><a class="side" href=" ">2013</a></li>
   <li class="side"><a class="side" href=" ">2012</a></li>
   <li class="side"><a class="side" href=" ">2011</a></li>
   <li class="side"><a class="side" href=" ">2010</a></li>
   <li class="side"><a class="side" href=" ">2009</a></li>
   <li class="side"><a class="side" href=" ">2008</a></li>
   <li class="side"><a class="side" href=" ">2007</a></li>
   <li class="side"><a class="side" href=" ">2006</a></li>
</ul>
```

(b)

```
ul  {list-style-type:none; margin:0; margin-left:140px; padding:0;}
li  {text-align:center; font-size:20px;}
a.side  {text-decoration:none;display:block; width:100px;
         color:white; background-color:none; }
a.side:hover {background-color:magenta;}
```

(c)

Figure 4.17 Vertical navigation bar: (a) hovering, (b) use in the body, and (c) styling specifications.

When the browser detects that the cursor is over a "box"—as in the Box Model—containing a link, it applies the hover styling, which for this example is to change the background only. Of course, many changes are possible, including changes in color, text size, and cursor shape.

The vertical navigation bar is very similar, and is shown in Figure 4.17.

Vertical navigation also uses an unordered list, but in its normal mode of operation: one item per line. There are no bullet marks, and the links have no decoration. In this example, hovering causes the background to be colored as before.

HTML Wrap-Up

Figure 4.18 shows a small page using the navigation bars just discussed. We use this page to illustrate a couple of handy features not already covered in this chapter. (The full text of this page is given in Appendix A.)

Gradient Background

Notice that the Travel Page uses an orange-to-dark blue gradient. There are various ways to do this in HTML/CSS; we choose the easiest. We first create the gradient image that we want to use, and save it as a jpg. This will typically be quite narrow, but tall to cover a long page. Then we use that image as the background for the page, allowing it to be repeated in the *x*-direction. This is accomplished by the styling

```
body {background-image:url('background1.jpg');
      background-repeat:repeat-x; color:white;
      font-family:Helvetica Neue Light;}
```

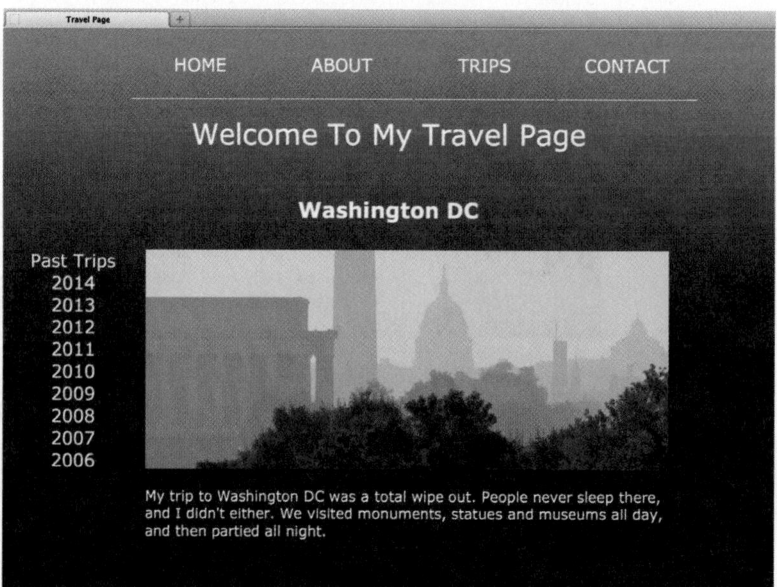

Figure 4.18 A Web page with navigation bars.

We use the property background-image and give it a url( ) for its value. Inside the parentheses of the url( ) operation, we give the pathname to locate the proper image; as discussed previously, standard absolute and relative path references apply. Notice that by repeating the image in the x-direction to fill the space, we create a complete gradient, as we wanted. It is possible not to repeat a background image using the background-repeat:no-repeat property, but we are happy to have the copies here.

Easy Enough for a Computer

In learning HTML, you have seen how a Web page is encoded. Although HTML has a few more exotic features beyond those presented here, and the other Web languages have even more powerful features, they are all variations on a theme: Tags surround all objects that appear on the page, the context is set by specifying properties of the page's tags, and each feature of the format is specified in detail, <i>isn't it?!</i>. It's so easy, even a computer can do it! Indeed, that's what happens most of the time. Web authors usually don't write HTML directly; they use Web authoring tools, such as the free open source editor KompoZer (www.kompozer.net/). They build the page as it should look on the screen using a WYSIWYG (what-you-see-is-what-you-get) Web authoring program, and then the computer generates the HTML to implement it. You may even have used such software . . . now you know exactly what it's doing!

Uploading. Pages are created and tested on a personal computer. To be accessed from other computers on the Internet, the HTML files, the image files, and the directory structure created for them must be uploaded (transmitted) to a Web server, a process known as *publishing*.

SUMMARY

You learned that Web pages are stored and transmitted in an encoded form before a browser turns them into images, and that HTML is the most widely used encoding form. (Table 4.3 lists the references for the specifications that we discussed.) The chapter opened by recalling the idea of using tags for formatting and went on to introduce you to the following:

- A working set of HTML tags, giving you the ability to create a Web page.
- An explanation of how links are marked with anchor tags.
- Absolute and relative pathnames. Relative pathnames refer to files deeper or higher in the directory hierarchy.

Table 4.3 Official W3C Web sites referenced in this chapter

Tags	www.w3schools.com/tags/default.asp
Special characters like Ö	www.w3schools.com/tags/ref_entities.asp
Validation	validator.w3.org/#validate_by_upload
CSS	www.w3schools.com/css/default.asp
Color names	www.w3schools.com/cssref/css_colornames.asp
HTML lists	www.w3schools.com/html/html_lists.asp
List styles	www.w3schools.com/cssref/pr_list-style-type.asp
Box Model	www.w3schools.com/css/css_boxmodel.asp

- The two most popular image formatting schemes—GIF and JPG—and how to place them in a page.
- Cascading Style Sheets, a general system for styling Web documents.
- Lists and tables.
- The precision achievable by using classes.

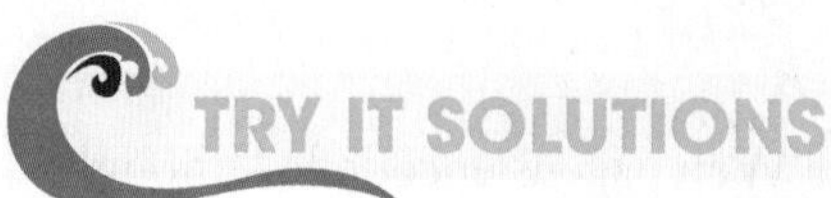

TRY IT SOLUTIONS

4.1 <p>The crowd enjoyed doing T_HE^WA_VE.</p>

4.2 <p>The Five <s>Hundred</s> Hats of Latin Letters: â ê î ô û</p>

4.3 Yes, the validator finds <bold>Find this mistake!</bold>

4.4 <a href="http://www.biyo.com/bios/art/haring.html">Mr. Graffiti</a>

4.5 ../myCat/lolcat/yarn2.jpg

4.6

```
h2 {border-style:solid; border-color:red;padding-bottom:10px}
dl {border-style:solid; border-color:gold}
dt {border-style:solid; border-color:blue;padding-left:10px;margin-left:10px}
dd {border-style:solid; border-color:magenta}
```

REVIEW QUESTIONS

Multiple Choice

1. HTML tags must be
   a. uppercase
   b. lowercase
   c. case does not matter
   d. either all uppercase or all lowercase
2. Space inserted to make a document more readable is called
   a. special space
   b. white space
   c. CSS space
   d. HTML space
3. The <p> </p> tags indicate the beginning and end of a
   a. package
   b. picture
   c. paragraph
   d. preformatted text section
4. The attribute specifying a blue background is
   a. bgcolor = #000000
   b. background = "blue"
   c. style = "background-color:blue"
   d. bgcolor = blue

5. The ../ notation in a relative path of hypertext reference means to
   a. go down a folder
   b. open the parent folder
   c. search a folder
   d. create a folder
6. To place an image on the right side of the window with the text filling the area to the left of the image, the tag would need to look like
   a. <img src = "mountains.jpg" style="float:right" />
   b. <img src align = "mountains.jpg" "right" />
   c. <img = "mountains.jpg" src align = "right" />
   d. <img = "mountains.jpg" align src = "float:right" />
7. The dimensions for an image on a Web page
   a. are set using the x and y attributes
   b. are set using the width and height attributes
   c. must be set to the actual size of the image
   d. are automatically adjusted by the browser to fit in the space allotted
8. Betsy created some nested tags as displayed here: <p><b><i>Rock On!</i></b></p>. Did she nest the tags appropriately?
   a. No, italic tags must always come before bold tags.
   b. No, paragraph tags need to be right before the actual text.
   c. The first part is right, but the second part should be </p></b></i>.
   d. Yes, the tags are nested correctly.
9. What tags are required for an HTML page?
   a. html, head
   b. html, head, body, foot
   c. html, head, body
   d. no tags are required
10. If you want to display an image without any text around it, you should nest it inside of which tag(s)?
   a. <p : img>
   b. <p>
   c. <pa>
   d. <img><p>

Short Answer

1. You have to ______ it to ______ it.
2. The ______ tag is a way to get more than one consecutive space in a line of a Web page.
3. ______ tags are tags between other tags.
4. Specifications inside a tag are called ______.
5. The src in an image tag stands for ______.
6. To put the 10 greatest inventions of all time, in order, on a Web page, you should use a(n) ______.
7. ______ is the main language that defines how a Web page should look.

8. _______ is the tag for the heading that is the largest and the darkest.
9. HTML _______ white space.
10. _______ separates the content from the border.

Exercises

1. Explain why you should learn HTML if authoring tools will do the work for you. Give other examples of where you are expected to learn something when there are tools available that will do the work.
2. How can you check if your HTML and CSS files display correctly? How often should you check? Why?
3. Indicate the hyperlink reference and the anchor text in this anchor tag. Then break down the hyperlink reference into the protocol, domain, path, and file name. `<a href="http://www.nasm.si.edu/museum/"> National Air and Space Museum</a>`
4. Explain in detail what problems Cascading Style Sheets (CSS) solve.
5. What does "the closest specification wins" mean? Give a detailed example in your answer.
6. Create a calendar for the current month using a table. Put the name of the month in a caption at the top. Change the color of the text for Sunday and holidays. Make note of any special days during the month. Add an appropriate graphic to one of the blank cells at the end of the calendar.
7. Why is it a bad idea to write an entire HTML document before loading it in a Web browser?
8. View and then print the source for the author's homepage at www.cs.washington.edu/homes/snyder/index.html. What is the title of the page? Indicate the heading and the body for the page. Find the table. Find the list. Find the email addresses, and say how they are displayed so they are not found by a spam crawler. Find the absolute hyperlinks and the relative hyperlinks. How many graphics are on this page?
9. Create a link tag to your school's Web site. Also create a style section for the link tag. The link should be yellow at the beginning, green after it has been clicked on, and blue when someone is hovering over it.
10. Open a new file in your text editor. Create your own Web page that has the following:
    a. A title that is your name.
    b. At least three paragraphs, two of them displayed in different colors (find the colors at www.w3schools.com/cssref/css_colornames.asp).
    c. A link to a Web site you like.
    d. At least three levels of headings.
    e. A link to the page you made in Exercise 9.
    f. At least one image or picture.
    g. Save this file as *YourInitials* Web2.html.
11. Make a copy of the Web page you made in Exercise 10. (Yes, make a copy; if you edit the original, you will lose it.) Then make the following additions:
    a. Add a paragraph that contains a list of four of your favorite music groups. Before the list, put in this level 2 heading: My favorite musical groups.

b. Add a table at the bottom of the page that has two rows and three columns. In the first row, list three of your favorite restaurants; in the second row, list your favorite food at each of the restaurants in the first row.
c. Set the background color to an attractive pastel color.
d. Add a link to a Web page. For example, you might want to link to your home-page on a social networking site if you have one, or a Web site for one of the restaurants you listed in (b).

CHAPTER 5

Locating Information on the WWW

The Search for Truth

learning objectives

- Explain how a Web search engine works
- Find information by using a search engine
- Use logical operators and filtering to express complex queries
- Recognize and find authoritative information sources
- Decide whether Web information is truth or fiction

CHAPTER 5

With Google I'm starting to burn out on knowing the answer to everything. People in the year 2020 are going to be nostalgic for the sensation of feeling clueless.

—DOUG COUPLAND

BY SOME ESTIMATES, Americans perform more than 300 million Web searches per day. That is, on average, every American searches the Web every day. Do they find what they are looking for? Though many searches are easy, it is often difficult to express to a search engine what you are looking for. Studies show that users are often unsuccessful when trying complex queries. Because most of us search many more times than once a day, it makes sense to learn how to do it right.

The main goal of this chapter is to explain the technology behind Web searches, and to explore strategies for quickly applying that technology to find accurate information. To start, we look at how a search engine works, and explain how it finds answers to our questions so fast. Next, we explore Google's Advanced Search interface and illustrate how to use it effectively. This leads to the main section on Web searching, which explains how to select good search terms, how to understand a hit list, how to skim a hit list for sites that interest you, and finally, how to locate the actual information. Having gotten the information, we next determine if we can rely on it—is it true? Finally, we put the knowledge together to decide if a Web site is believable.

Web Search Fundamentals

A **search engine** is a collection of computer programs that helps us find information on the Web. Though programs for text searching existed long before the Web, the explosion of Web-based digital information and its distribution across the globe made the invention of search engines necessary. No one organizes the information posted on the Web, so these programs look around to find out what's out there and organize what they find. It's a big task. How do search engines do it?

Meeting of the Minds. The Google search engine was created by two Stanford graduate students, Larry Page and Sergey Brin. According to Google lore, they met when Page, a University of Michigan graduate, was visiting Stanford, and Brin was asked to show him around: "According to some accounts, they disagreed about most everything during this first meeting."

Larry Page (left) and Sergey Brin, 1995

How a Search Engine Works

The first step, called *crawling*, visits every Web page that it can find. Where does the **crawler**—the software that does the crawling—get the pages? The crawler has a *To Do list* of URLs that it is given to begin with. Then, whenever it notices a URL while crawling a page, it adds the URL to the To Do list if it hasn't yet been crawled.

Shortsightedness. Search engines crawl only a fraction (probably less than half) of the Web. Because it is growing so fast, there are always new pages to be visited. Librarians call the pages not crawled the "invisible Web." There are other reasons that crawlers miss pages:

- No page points to it, so it never gets on the To Do list.
- The page is synthetic—that is, created on-the-fly by software for each user.
- The encoding is a type the crawler does not recognize, that is, not HTML, PDF, or other common format.

Crawler. The main work of the crawler is to build an index. The **index** is a list of **tokens** (such as words) that are associated with the page. They're called tokens because crawlers recognize text like HTML5 and J-Lo, which aren't actually words. To be associated with a page, the word might be part of the page's title, but there are other ways for a token to be included too. For each token, the crawler creates a list of the URLs associated with that token. For example, referring to Figure 5.1, when page www.fan.cy/beckyR is crawled, its URL is entered in the list for each word in its title. If the page has a link, say pet-home.com/molly, then the words in the anchor text each get the link's URL added to their token lists too.

Three Little Words. The crawler considers almost anything followed by a space or punctuation symbol to be a token, except short words like *a*, *an*, and *the*. But even these words can become tokens by being part of important phrases, like *The New York Times*.

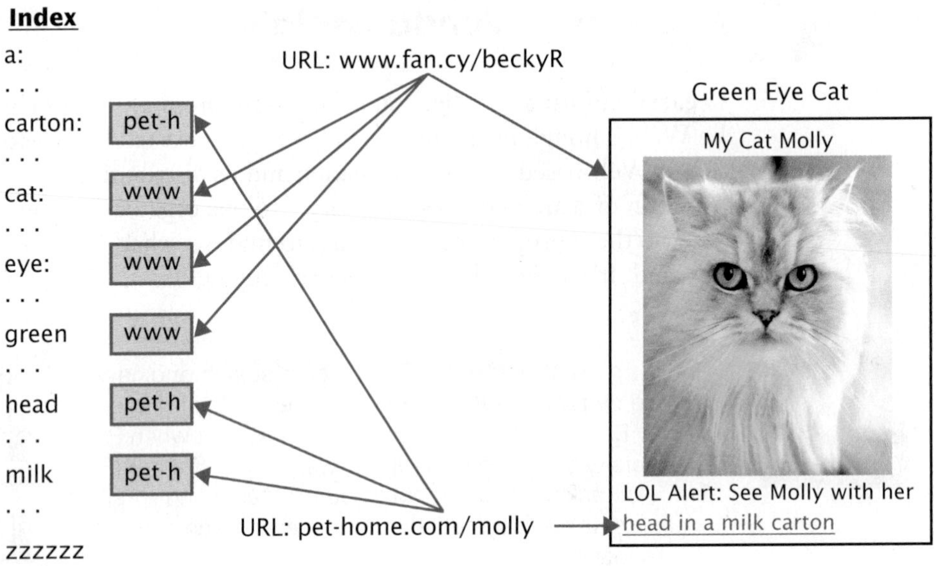

Index
a:
. . .
carton: pet-h
. . .
cat: www
. . .
eye: www
. . .
green www
. . .
head pet-h
. . .
milk pet-h
. . .
zzzzzz

URL: www.fan.cy/beckyR

Green Eye Cat

My Cat Molly

LOL Alert: See Molly with her head in a milk carton

URL: pet-home.com/molly

Figure 5.1 Crawling over the Green Eye Cat page: The crawler adds the page's URL to the lists for each word in its title; for words in the anchor text, the link URL is added to their lists.

Query Processor. The second part of a search engine is *query processing*. The user presents tokens, that is, search terms, to the **query processor**, which looks them up in the index. So, if you type the word cat into your favorite search engine, it looks up the word in the index and returns a hit list of pages associated with "cat." In principle, that is a list of 1.55 billion URLs, because the crawler found all of those URLs to be associated with the search term "cat."

By creating the index ahead of time, search engines are able to answer user queries very quickly, even if the original crawling takes a long time.

Multiword Searches

Generally, when we make a multiple-word query, we want the pages returned by the query processor to be appropriate for all of the words. That is, when we type

human powered flight

we mean that each page returned should be associated with *all* of those words. (This is called an **AND-query** because it instructs the query processor to find pages relevant to the words human *and* powered *and* flight. We will learn more about AND-queries and other forms of queries momentarily.)

The problem for the query processor is that there is no index entry corresponding to a *set* of tokens, only the lists for the individual words. There is no time to crawl the Web to build an index for that set of words. What is a query processor to do?

Intersecting Queries. To locate pages containing multiple words, the query processor simply fetches the index lists for each of the terms, and finds URLs that are in all of the lists. We say the query processor **intersects** the lists. To make the task of intersecting multiple lists easier, the URL lists are alphabetized. This speeds up the processing because it is possible to notice easily when the same URL is on multiple lists. For example, for the index lists of the three tokens, the result of the intersection is www.rs.org, because that URL is on all three lists, meaning it is associated with all three tokens, as requested.

token1	token2	token3
www.ab.com	www.aa.com	www.rs.org
www.rs.org	www.ab.com	www.zz.edu
www.ru.com	www.m.edu	
	www.rs.org	

Rules for Intersecting Alphabetized Lists. To intersect several alphabetized lists, the computer follows four simple rules:

1. Put a marker such as an arrow at the start of each token's list.
2. If all markers point to the same URL, save it, because all tokens are associated with the page.
3. Move the marker(s) to the next position for whichever URL is earliest in the alphabet.
4. Repeat Steps 2–3 until some marker reaches the end of the list, then quit.

The result is a list of the URLs saved in Rule 2. Figure 5.2 illustrates this process.

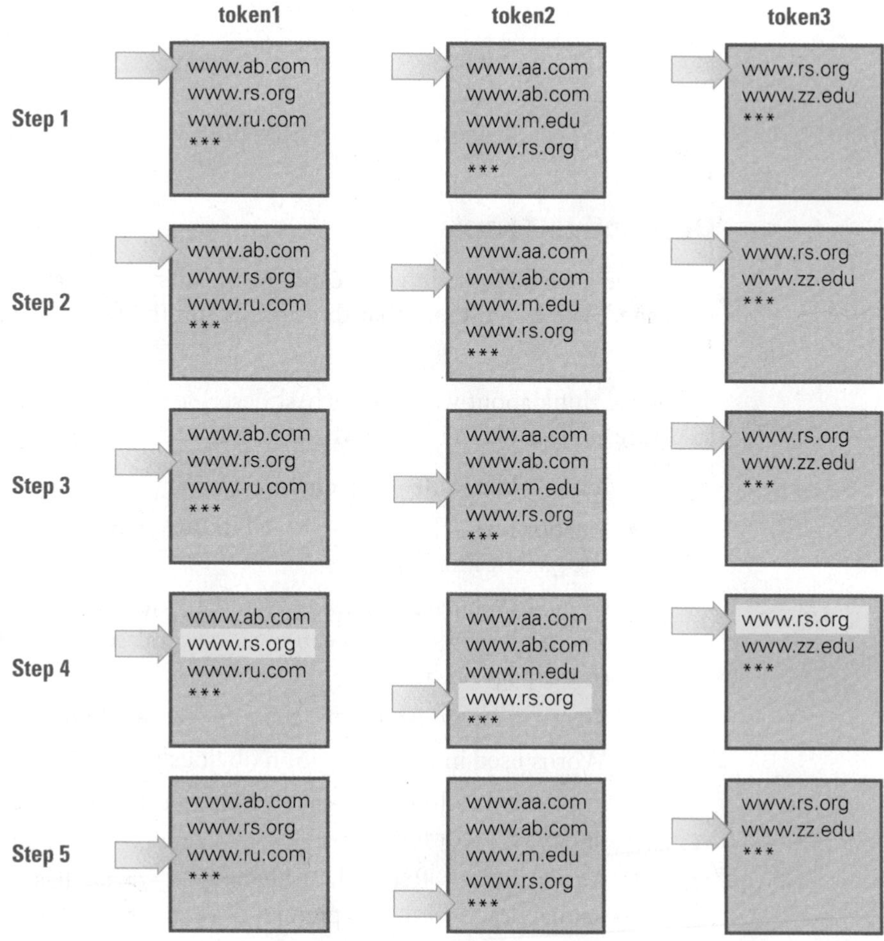

Figure 5.2 Illustrating the Intersecting Alphabetized Lists rules: In each step (row of boxes) one or more arrows advance; notice Step 3 where the arrow has advanced in two lists in the same step because the earliest URL is on both lists.

5.1 Intersecting Index Lists. Find the result of intersecting the following lists using the Intersecting Alphabetized Lists rules. How many steps does it take?

human	powered	flight
en.wikipedia.org/wiki/Human	en.wiktionary.org/wiki/powered	aa.com/reservations
musclepowered.org	musclepowered.org	alaskaair.com
news.discovery.com	www.cmsimple.org	armorgames.com/play/7598/flight
www.hpva.us	www.gaspowered.com	musclepowered.org
www.innerbody.com/htm/body/html	www.hpva.us	www.hpva.us

In summary, indexed search is very powerful because the computer takes the time to crawl the data (Web pages) and build an index first. Then "all" it needs to do is find the index entries for each word and intersect the lists to find the information for an AND-query. This is how a search engine like Google can look at billions of Web pages and return an answer in a quarter of a second.

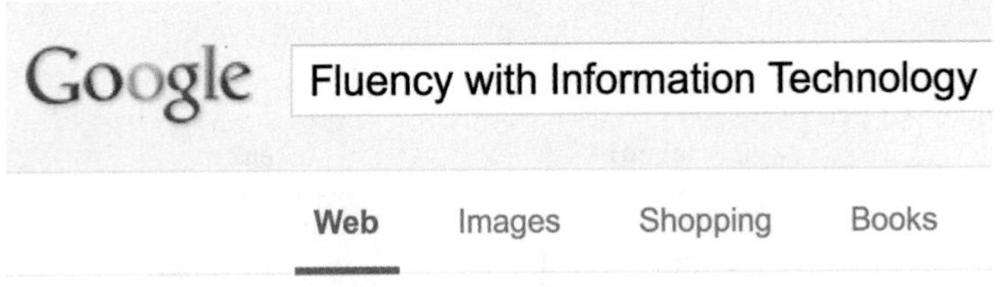

Descriptive Terms

So far, we have discussed that a search term "hits" for a page when it is "associated with the page." We haven't said that the word is "on the page," because it may or may not be. Here's why.

When we think about what words best describe a page, we notice that the Web page structure as revealed in the HTML tags helps a lot to identify *descriptive* text:

- Title—The <title> tags enclose a short phrase describing the whole page.
- Anchor text—The highlighted link text, which is inside <a . . . > tags, describes the page it links to.
- Meta—Web page creators can add a <meta name="description" . . . /> tag in the head section, which can give a several-sentence description of the content of the page, as in

  <meta name="description" content="travel photos; volcanoes of Hawaii"/>

  Words used in the description obviously apply to the page.
- Top-level heading tags, <h1> often give a general description of a section of a document's content.
- Alt attributes—Recall that the <img . . . /> tag has an alt attribute that gives a textual description of a picture, as in

  <img src="volcano.jpg" alt="Lava on Hawaii's Kilauea Volcano"/>.

  Alt tags are a good source of descriptive terms for the image and the page it's on.

Try Natural Language. Google, Bing, and Yahoo! want you to be successful, so they preprocess the search terms before beginning to check the index. This means that sometimes all you have to do is just ask the question directly in normal English. For example,

```
how do you cite films in apa
```

might be sufficient to find the information you need when writing a report that requires American Psychological Association (APA) citation rules. Search engines all return simple "how to" rules from respected universities as the top five hits. It can also do arithmetic, answering 365 / 12, and providing a calculator as the first "hit." So, go ahead . . . just ask!

Crawlers will add the page's URL to the index list of the tokens found inside these tags. That creates a huge index list (see Figure 5.3).

Notice that the anchor text works slightly differently than the other sources of descriptive terms, because it is not on the page it is describing. The anchor text's description applies to the page it is linking to; that is, the page with the URL given in the href. For example, the anchor tag

```
. . . the <a href="hawaiivisitor.org/maunaloa.html>world's largest volcano</a>.
```

would produce

We could see Mauna Loa, the world's largest volcano.

The crawler will add the URL hawaiivisitor.org/maunaloa.html to the index list for volcano, not the URL for the page containing this sentence.

Figure 5.3 In Google's data center, Dalles, Oregon. A search engine's index is huge, because in *principle* it keeps URLs for most of the words used on the Web; Google's index has been reported to be "100 million gigabytes" = 10^{17} bytes. However big it is, they can't store just one copy, because they need a backup in case some of those LEDs go dead.

Page Rank

It is rather miraculous that when the hit list of a search with millions of hits is returned, the page you're looking for is often first on the hit list, and when it's not first, it's usually in the top 10. How is this possible?

The order in which hits are returned to a query is determined—at least in part—by a number Google calls the **PageRank**. Generally, the higher the PageRank, the closer to the top of the list a page will be, but other information—like timeliness—is also considered. Google pioneered the page ranking idea as a way to determine which pages are likely to be most important to you. Of course, the computer has no way of actually knowing what is important to you, but page ranking works pretty well.

Links to Other Pages. Although Google has not revealed the complete information about how PageRank weights sites, we do know that it works like a voting system. If page A, www.shoutOut.net/A.html, links to page B, www.celeb.com/B.html, then in the page ranking system, A's link adds to B's importance, increasing its rank.

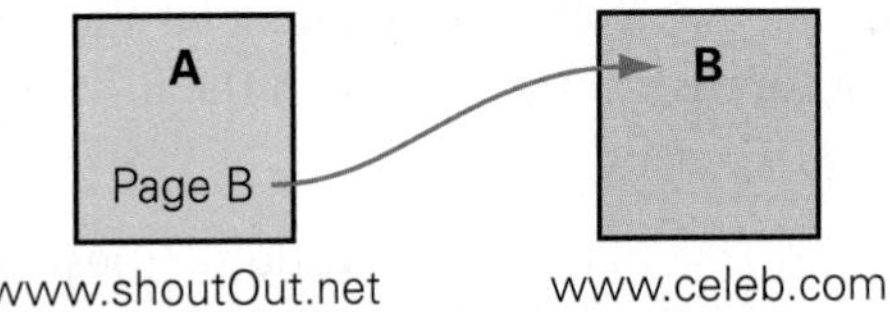

It is as if shoutOut's link is a vote for the celeb page. Pages that are linked to by many pages have a higher page ranking and, therefore, are assumed to be more important. This seems to make sense.

Notice that PageRank's voting information is gathered when the href link is being added to the tokens of the anchor text. That is, in Figure 5.1, while pet-home.com/molly is being added to carton's list, the browser can also record that www.fan.cy/beckyR just voted for pet-home.com/molly. From the point of view of the page getting the vote (pet-home.com or celeb.com), these references are called *back links* in computer science terminology. Since recording this kind of information was a big idea on their first system, Page and Brin called that first search engine BackRub.

A second important property of Google's page ranking system is that links from pages with a high page ranking are viewed as more important than links from pages with a low page ranking. So, if shoutOut has a high page ranking, its link will contribute more to celeb's rank than, say, a link from myLameBlog.org/faveCeleb.html, which we presume has a low page ranking.

The PageRank is computed by the crawler: As the crawler looks at page A, it notices the links to another page B, and scores one for B. Counting the number of links to a page is not sufficient, however. So, after the crawling is completed, the PageRank computation is completed. Finally, as the query processor is putting together the hit list, the URLs

Go to the Library. In the twenty-first century we are focused on digital information, so we don't think of libraries as a research resource. In fact, large public libraries and university libraries contain an enormous amount of reliable *digital* information. They are user-friendly and they link to pre-digital information, which is nearly everything prior to about 1985. Every college student should bookmark useful college libraries (theirs and others they like).

found by the intersecting process are sorted by their page ranking, highest to lowest, and returned to the user in that order.

Advanced Searches

With the index telling the query processor all of the pages containing each word, it makes sense to try to get the most out of the "crawl-then-query" scenario. For this reason, query processors can give us the option for an *advanced search*. Figure 5.4 shows the Web page for Google's Advanced Search.

The Logical Operator AND

Basic queries, including the previous human-powered flight query, are AND-queries: They require that all words given must be associated with the page for it to hit. A good way to think about AND-queries is that the page is a hit if

```
human AND powered AND flight
```

are all associated with the page. When we write the query this way, we are using the word AND as a **logical operator.** A logical operator specifies a logical relationship between the words it connects. Therefore, `human AND powered` says that the two logical tests for "Is *human* associated with the page?" AND "Is *powered* associated with the

Google Advanced Search
Google
Advanced Search
Find pages with...
all these words:
this exact word or phrase:
any of these words:
none of these words:
numbers ranging from: to
Then narrow your results by...
language: any language
region: any region
last update: anytime
site or domain:

Figure 5.4 Google's Advanced Search window. Notice that text panes are provided for AND-words, quote phrases, OR-words, and NOT-words; the combined query is in the text window surrounded by blue.

page?" must both be true. AND-queries are specified using the "all these words" line of the Advanced Search UI shown in Figure 5.4.

Recognize that the noun phrase "human-powered flight" is meaningful to us as one concept, and even though two words are hyphenated, search engines treat it as three independent words. That is, the words can be associated with the page in any way or order, and the page will still be a hit. Because you know how the query processor works (using intersection of index lists), this is not surprising; the lists are independent.

You might think that to have the phrase apply to people trying to fly, you should put quotes around it, as in "human-powered flight". Quotes mean the *exact phrase must appear* as given. Doing this is usually a *bad* idea. It may often be true that the exact phrase as given will be on the page you want; but maybe not. For example, if you are looking for an image that happens to have the caption "First pedal-powered flight achieving the human dream of flying," you'll miss it. All three words are there, but the specific phrase isn't. Treating query terms as independent is almost always what you want to do.

The rare case to use quotes is truly when the terms *only* appear in a specific way. Examples are quotations—they are called *quotes* for a reason—book and movie titles, clichés, and so forth. It is not necessary to give the whole quote or title, only that part you are sure will appear on the page you want. So "all your base" will hit for the famous Web meme, "All your base are belong to us."

Complex Queries

VideoNote

Operators and Search

Besides AND, another logical operator is OR. An **OR-query** such as

```
marshmallow OR strawberry OR chocolate
```

hits on pages that are associated with one (at least, but possibly more) of the words. Using the Advanced Search page shown in Figure 5.4, OR-queries are given in the third text window. The logical operator in marshmallow OR strawberry says that one or the other (or both) of the logical tests—"Is *marshmallow* associated with the page?" OR "Is *strawberry* associated with the page?"—is true.

5.2 Once Is Enough. To answer OR-queries like lisa OR bart OR homer, the query processor could simply combine the index list for each word. One problem is that a page associated with bart may also be associated with homer, so that page will be listed twice. The process for removing such duplicates is very similar to that of creating Intersecting Alphabetized Lists. Revise the four rules for Intersecting Alphabetized Lists on page 117 to create new rules that will create a hit list without duplicates.

The fourth line of the Advanced Search window is for specifying words that are *not* to be associated with the page. In advanced searches that do not use the handy page shown in Figure 5.4, we use the logical operator NOT to specify such words; the construction is a NOT-query. So, for example, we write

```
tigers AND NOT baseball
```

to find pages about the striped animal rather than Detroit's major league baseball team. Notice that the AND is included because we want both requirements to be true: "Is *tigers* associated with the page?" AND NOT "Is *baseball* associated with the page?"

Plus Numbers. Google ignores numbers on queries such as `rocky 3`. However, including a plus sign in front of the number tells Google not to ignore it and to use it as part of the query. Therefore, queries like `apollo +13` finds pages about that specific flight.

Combining Logical Operators

Sometimes the queries we are interested in need AND, OR, *and* NOT operators. Because the logical operators work like arithmetic, we can combine them and group them using parentheses. So, we can write

```
(marshmallow OR strawberry OR chocolate) AND sundae
```

to require that one (or more) of the flavors and the word *sundae* be associated with the page. Write the OR portion of the query in parentheses so that it is clear that the flavors go together.

If the OR-terms did not use the parentheses, as in

```
marshmallow OR strawberry OR chocolate AND sundae
```

the query would be ambiguous, which means that it has two or more meanings. One possible meaning is the one given above with parentheses. Another possible meaning would be parenthesized as

```
marshmallow OR strawberry OR (chocolate AND sundae)
```

which allows hits on pages associated with only the word *marshmallow* or only the word *strawberry*, because *sundae* is required only for *chocolate*.

It is usually acceptable to write queries in the form shown here using uppercase letters for the logical operators and parentheses to make the associations clear. In Google, it is *also* acceptable to leave out the AND, because a space is interpreted to mean AND, making

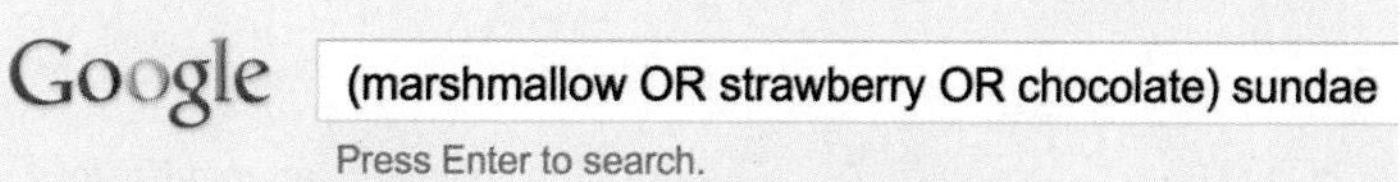

acceptable. Also, if the OR-words are grouped together they don't need to be enclosed in parentheses, assuming that what you're looking for is one of the OR-choices together with whatever the remainder of the query specifies. Thus,

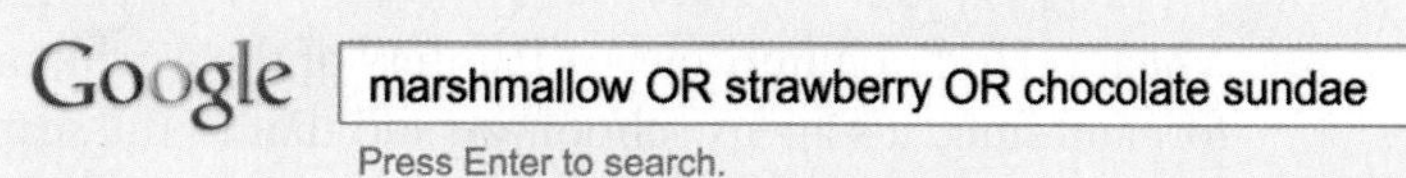

is okay too. But not all advanced search software accepts blanks and ignores parentheses; it is wise to give the formal query—it is rarely a mistake.

Google has other nice features. For example, minus (–) can be used as an abbreviation for NOT; it should be snuggled up right next to the associated word. So we can write

```
simpson bart OR lisa OR maggie –homer –marge
```

to get pages on the Simpson children.

5.3 Sunny Day Driving. Write a query for Google's basic *I'm Feeling Lucky* search window to find pages about convertibles for any of these brands: Corvette, Mazda, and Porsche.

Restricting Global Search

Many sites offer the opportunity to perform a **site search**, which means looking only on their site. The site search is usually offered on the homepage with a search window and a **Go** button. If you know a site has the information you want, it is advisable to perform a site search. This is usually the fastest way to find the right page.

Focused Searches

Often when we need information we don't care where it's found, and we ask a search engine to check the whole Web. The result is frequently many, many hits that take time to look through. So, when we know more about the topic we're searching for, we can direct the search by adding additional constraints; see the bottom half of Google's Advanced Search page in Figure 5.4.

Filtered Searches. The constraints help us pinpoint the pages we want. For example, suppose you remember seeing a video of an art school's arts festival called Manifest. It was a slick name and a great video, but you don't remember much else about it. There must be a Web site for it—can we find it?

Starting out, we search art manifest and get

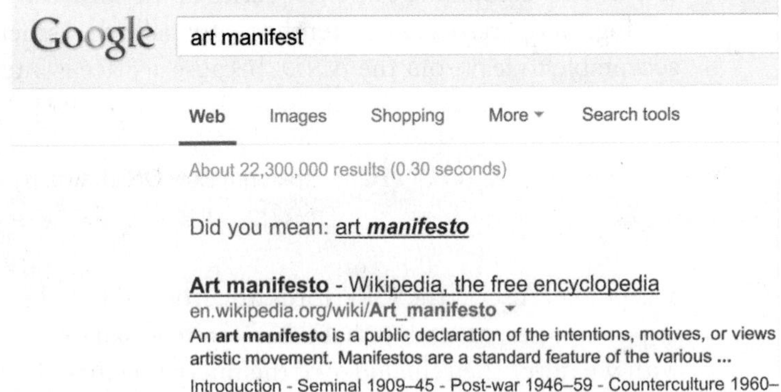

which is kind of humorous—"Painters of the world, unite!" It's not what we're looking for, and since it's an art school, we add that to the search terms and get

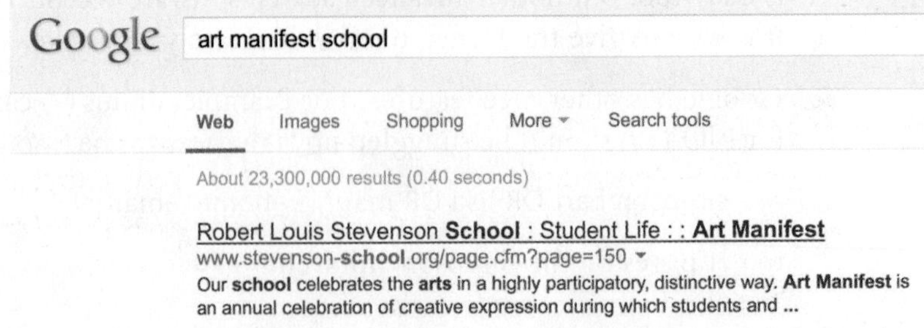

which is at least an art school celebration, but again the page we want isn't in the top 10 hits.

Although we don't remember much else about the festival, it isn't the end of our search.

At the bottom of the Google Advanced Search UI, we are offered filtering options (see Figure 5.4).

Guessing that the school will be in the .edu domain, we limit our search to that. Now, searching only for manifest with that limitation delivers the page we're looking for at the top of the top 10 list.

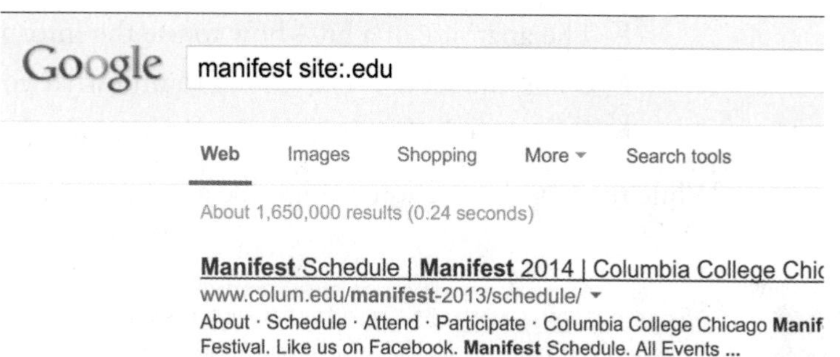

That's impressive, considering the hefty list of hits from the original search. We decide to make greater use of filtering tools in the future, and settle back to watch the video again.

Page Ranking Local Searches. There is one more way that these filtering tools can help. Many large sites like National Public Radio, the Internal Revenue Service, YouTube, and so forth provide a local search through their own documents. Often these searches work well, especially if the search term you're looking for is reasonably rare, and so the number of hits is small. But when it's not, and the hit list is large, the local search is often either unordered—presented in the sequence that the search engine found them—or else in some order that doesn't help you, say chronological.

In such cases, making the same search but in Google and restricting it to that specific domain—for example, www.npr.org—works because the page ranking information orders the hits. The local search doesn't know the page ranking information and so cannot give you the advantages of that ordering. Such searches are usually very, very effective.

Web Searching

For most of us, casual use of a search engine to answer questions on the Web has become a daily activity. We're good at it. Research, however, is a more serious matter. What if you are preparing a report in which the information *must* be correct? This section gives specific guidelines to help you be successful when using Web searches for reports and research projects.

The strategies are organized as follows:

VideoNote
Understanding Search Engines

- Selecting search terms—choosing good words to include in a query
- The anatomy of a hit—how to use the information returned in the hit list
- Using the hit list—skimming to find what you want quickly, or trying again
- Once you find a likely page—locating the desired data on the found page

While reading this section it might be a good idea to try a complicated query.

Search engines process queries before they try to answer them, but the companies don't explain what they do. So, with no guidance from them, we assume they do nothing. The following sections apply standard querying concepts, and they work well.

Selecting Search Terms

Our approach to finding the search terms for the information we want unfolds as a sequence of ever-more precise terms. The following is the order in which we will discuss them:

- Use advanced search
- Begin with a general topic
- Choose descriptive terms
- Refine by adding words
- Avoid overconstraining
- Remove specific words

Although not guaranteed, these heuristics should help to narrow in on useful pages.

Use Advanced Search. Google's Advanced Search (Figure 5.4) gives considerable control over the results returned, allowing you to find what you want faster. It's possible to use the "I'm Feeling Lucky" page or Bing or Yahoo! for complex queries, but Google's Advanced Search is preferred for its control. (Find it at www.google.com/advanced_search and bookmark it in your Firefox browser.)

Begin with the General Topic. Giving the topic seems obvious, but it's easy to forget. The general topic helps because many words have multiple meanings. Giving the topic will usually eliminate most of those conflicting words. So, for example, if you want to know the cubic volume of a boxcar, the query boxcar volume hits on

- The **volume** of alert sounds on the **Boxcar** messaging service
- **Boxcar** Willie's Best Loved Favorites, **Volume** 2

- **Boxcar** Willie's Songbook, a three **volume** set
- **Boxcar** Children's Stories, **Volume** 6
- **Volume** Consultants vs. Quality Consultants at **Boxcar** Marketing
- A math exercise figuring the **volume** of an imaginary **boxcar**
- A review of the DJ's use of the **volume** control at the **Boxcar** Ale House

All of these hits (from the first 10) use one or both terms in a different sense than we intended. All of these hits can be eliminated (or pushed much deeper in the hit list) simply by including the general topic "train," as in

```
train boxcar volume
```

So, giving the general topic is powerful. It is also smart to start with the topic word(s).

Choose Descriptive Words. In casual conversation, most of us are not very picky about the words we use to describe something. But writers are. Because we are often searching text that was thoughtfully written (as opposed to social media chitchat), we will be more successful by selecting more precise terms. So, to find out how many sailors are on a submarine, we don't want to ask

```
submarine sailors
```

because every page that mentions submarines probably also mentions sailors. A better query would be

```
submarine crew
```

Sailors are said to be "assigned" to a sub, and sailors (both men and women) are said to "man" a ship, but both terms have many other meanings, making them less useful. They may be equally descriptive as "crew," but not as precise.

Refine by Adding Words. A handy technique is to make a "first guess" search, like the two just discussed, and then check the results. If the search engine figures out what you want, your lucky feeling was justified! You've got your result.

For more complex queries, however, the answer may be in the list, but you may not be close enough to find it. Checking the initial hit list to see what you've found will often suggest another term to ask. Skimming what you got back might suggest a word that could be definitive. Researchers often go through several rounds of adding a word to the query each time to narrow the number of hits.

5.4 Words of Wisdom. For a research paper on accuracy in famous documents, Tracy needs to find the text of Lincoln's speech on the plaque outside the Visitors Center in Gettysburg, Pennsylvania. Which would be a better search: "four score and seven" or gettysburg visitors center plaque to find images of it? Explain.

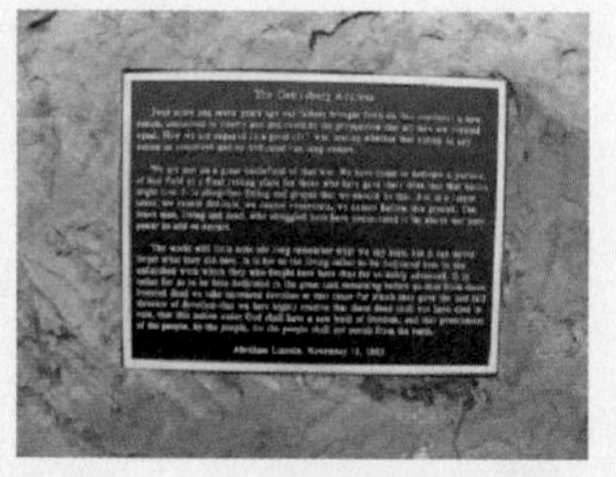

An interesting experiment to illustrate this point is actually to search for the words for several colors. The hit counts from four queries dramatically prove the point that

including more words can greatly reduce the search result because these are all AND queries:

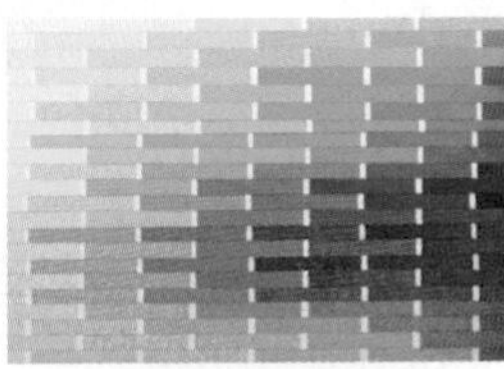

Query Words	Hit Count
red	3.86 Billion
red burgundy	58.3 Million
red burgundy fuchsia	5.30 Million
red burgundy fuchsia rose	3.01 Million

At this point maybe the only hits left show color chips.

Though including more terms helps to eliminate uninteresting pages, it is not perfect.

Avoid Overconstraining. One reason to begin with an inclusive search and then to add more words one at a time is because eagerly adding terms might eliminate interesting pages accidentally. This happens because those pages may not include the particular term, even though other pages do. Care is required in this process: Add a word only if you are sure the pages you want will have it.

Remove Specific Words (Minus or NOT). Although adding terms to narrow the search is typical, it's also useful to consider eliminating pages with certain words. It's the opposite, really. Adding words says, "I know the page I want will have this word"; removing words by including them in the list with a minus sign in front of them (–token) says, "I am sure the pages I want won't have this word." The minus sign is a good way to eliminate wrong interpretations of your words. Referring to the boxcar example, if all of Boxcar Willie's pages included the term "train," we can keep train (to eliminate the other meanings) and remove "Willie" with –willie.

The Anatomy of a Hit

As we work on finding the goldmine of perfect pages using the preceding guidelines, what are we learning from the hit list? Next, we check out the information in a hit (see Figure 5.5).

The standard Google search displays the first 10 hits, according to its *PageRank* algorithm; Bing is very similar. What is displayed with each hit?

- **Title**—This is the text between the page's <title> and </title> tags.
- **Snippet**—This information is a preview of what might be on the page; usually it is a short phrase or two from the page containing one or more of the searched words; searched words are shown in bold. Google may also show as a snippet the page's description, as shown in its meta-description tags, such as

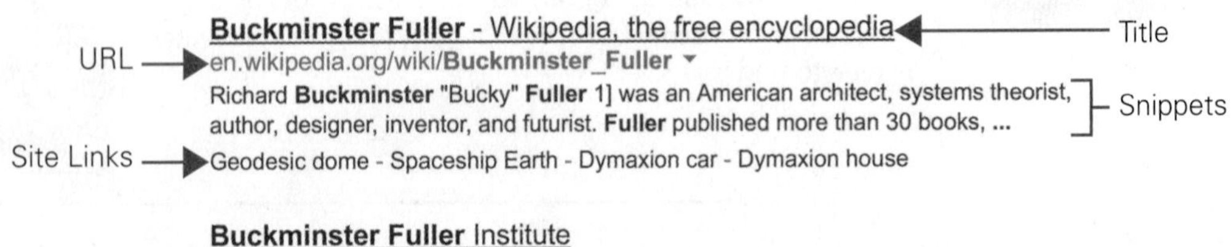

Figure 5.5 The first two hits from a Google search for buckminster fuller.

<meta name="description" content="Your descriptive sentence or two go here" />. Not all pages have a description, but if the page does, Google may use it.

- **URL**—This is the site's URL that is linked from the title line.
- **Site links**—These are useful links from the site, which are basically shortcuts. Google doesn't explain how they are chosen, but they're found algorithmically and are not "sponsored," that is, no one pays to have these pages listed.

A somewhat more technical description of a hit from Google's Matt Cutts can be viewed here: http://www.youtube.com/watch?v=vS1Mw1Adrk0.

5.5 Title Insurance. Sometimes, Google will modify or adjust the title displayed to make it more useful. Check to see if this is true for the Buckminster Fuller Institute page (the second hit in Figure 5.5).

Using the Hit List

Effectively locating information on the Web requires that we use the returned list of hits. It's useful to think of checking the hits as a process of filtering:

Skim the top level of information, and when an item looks promising, look deeper.

> If it fails, return to skimming;
>
> If it continues to look promising, look deeper still.

This is a sensible (and quick) way to zero in on likely pages you want.

The "look deeper" directive causes us to rank the information in a hit as follows:

- **Title**—It's the first source of information about the page; when the title checks out, look at the . . .
- **Snippet**—The search terms are shown in bold and the context around the occurrence is given. This is a good way to see if the site uses the keyword the way you want; your search for harvard can produce a snippet ". . . **Harvard** beets . . . " and ". . . **Harvard** University. . . ," but you probably only want one of them. If the snippet checks out, look at the . . .
- **URL**—It gives the domain of the site hosting the page; remember that the *domain* is the site's name, the part before the .com or .edu. The site name is important because it's the first check of how authoritative the information is; if it's a reputable site, click it; if not, continue skimming. If (as is typical) it's not clear whether it's a reputable site, skip it for the moment, but return to it if something better is not quickly found. If the URL checks out, look at the . . .
- **Page** itself.

At this point, there is some likelihood that the page includes information you care about, and now you need to load it and check it out. The other hit information may still be useful (for example, the date the file was crawled), but for the moment, we are done with the hit list.

Very Uninteresting. It is common in Web searches to get millions of hits—the search of Figure 5.5 got 1.42 million hits. If only one of them is the page you want, you've got very low odds of stumbling on it. Even going through the list in order (possible only in principle) would—statistically—require you to check half the hits. Looking for it intelligently is usually your only way to be successful, which is why we emphasize skimming and refining your search.

Once You Find a Likely Page

We have found a page with a suggestive title, a promising snippet, and a reliable domain. Or at least it is worthy of further checking. Now, we must quickly figure out how close we are to what we want. We expect to do all or some of the following:

- First, "roll through the page" checking out its main features. Is it mostly photos? Is it mostly text? Is it the *kind* of site that you're looking for? For example, if you want a restaurant review but landed at the restaurant's homepage, it's time to leave.
- Next, having found a promising page, look for a date to see how current it is; often we find promising pages, but then we discover they are too old to be useful. Notice first that dates are often in the URL, so for time-sensitive material (a recent sports event, for example), it is often possible to eliminate a page earlier, while studying the domain name, by noting a date in the path.
- Finally, if you are not intending to read the whole page (when seeking facts, we usually are not), then find the location of one of the keywords. You may not find the snippet, but in any case, you'll locate a specific mention of one of your important terms. Keep in mind that your goal is still to determine whether you want to stay on the page. If you've found what you want, you're done; if not, returning to the hit list is probably wise.

Assuming that you've found a site with the information you want, there is still one more thing to do: decide how important it is that the information is perfectly correct.

- If you are out with friends checking on who wins a bet, you're done. Even if the facts are wrong, the bet is settled (until the next morning!).
- If you're working on a report or you're simply learning new things, you should cross-check with another site.
- If you're seeking information with consequences (for example, medical data), you must check out the site and also locate corroborating information.

Obviously, if further checking is necessary, this is a good time to do it; returning to the hit list is a good place to start.

Searching by Pictures. If the information you want is likely to have a characteristic photo or classic picture, skimming images is a fast way to go through a hit list. When the hit list comes back, click Images (tab at upper left of Advanced Search) to display images. A quick "roll through" often finds the page directly. For example, if you can't remember the word "Sneeches" from the Dr. Seuss book, but you'd recognize the cover, search on seuss and skim for the images of the cover.

Searching Strategy Summary

We have provided guidelines for choosing search terms, data on what the parts of a hit mean, and suggestions for skimming the material returned. Searching for "deep information" is a creative activity; you'll be thinking the whole time. Although the Web is mind-bogglingly large, search engines do a phenomenal job at helping us locate information. We should expect to be successful in our search. We may not find it on the first query, but by following the strategy discussed, it should be possible to succeed.

Bing Search

Bing is Microsoft's search engine, developed in collaboration with Yahoo! Its crawler and index builder work as described earlier. The hit list is similar (Bing does not have a specific Advanced Search page, although there are advanced searching properties available at onlinehelp.microsoft.com/en-us/bing/ff808421.aspx). There are a few differences, however. Bing processes the query terms differently, and it orders the returned hits using somewhat different techniques from Google.

So, which search engine is better? Several attempts have been made to compare them with the unsurprising result that they're not that different. They work pretty well most of the time. Unfortunately, it's not easy to determine the advantages of each. Therefore, as users, we must simply try both to see which works best for the questions and searching styles at hand.

Authoritative Information

We have arrived at the page we want! The next question is: "How authoritative is the information?" Authoritative pages are reliable, likely to be true, and correct. In this section, we learn how to figure out if Web-based information is authoritative.

Don't Believe Everything You Read

VideoNote
Books Versus Web Sites

There is no one in charge of the WWW, so no one checks to see that the information given on Web pages is correct. You probably know from personal experience that some information on Facebook and Twitter is inaccurate. They are not the only examples. Most information on the Web should be considered suspect.

In the past, people got their information from books available at the library. First, before printing a book, publishers confirmed that the author was knowledgeable about the subject matter. It is no accident that *author* is part of *authoritative*. Second, reviewers and editors read the manuscript and combed through looking for errors. After it was printed librarians reviewed the book before buying it for their libraries, asking: "Is this a knowledgeable author?" "Does the publisher usually publish reliable books?" "Do other respected libraries stock this book?" After such a process, it was likely—though not guaranteed—that readers received valid information. The Web changed all that.

Today, anyone can post a Web page and make any random statements or claims. The statements may be true and correct, or they may be partly true and partly false, or they may be complete "baloney." Because the page is written, posted, crawled, and stored in the index, it is a hit in your search with the right query. Click the link, and you see the statements and claims as written. You may be the first human to see it besides the author. From the writer direct to the reader with *no one* checking!

Wikipedia

Wikipedia, the online encyclopedia, is an open source document created by knowledgeable and community-minded Internet users. Anyone can contribute to Wikipedia. Because it draws on a wide range of contributors, Wikipedia covers an enormous number of topics, and it contains fascinating information that might not be included in any printed encyclopedia. Its coverage and timeliness make it a valuable resource.

It is both a weakness and a strength that many people contribute to Wikipedia. The weakness is that it's possible for anyone to add any nonsense to an entry. Although there is an editorial process that imposes some quality control, the content is not validated by "domain experts," that is, people who truly know the facts. It's also possible for anyone to edit Wikipedia, which allows anyone to remove the nonsense, too. In this way, the community is also responsible for the quality of Wikipedia.

Wikipedia Disclaimer. It's handy and usually very helpful, but Wikipedia cannot be used alone. The Wikipedia site has explained:

> Wikipedia is not considered a credible source. Wikipedia is increasingly used by people in the academic community, from first-year students to professors, as an easily accessible tertiary source for information about anything and everything. **However, citation of Wikipedia in research papers may not be considered acceptable, because Wikipedia is not considered a credible source.**
>
> This is especially true considering anyone can edit the information given at any time.
>
> Follow two simple rules:
>
> - Do your research properly. Remember that *any* encyclopedia is a starting point for research, not an ending point.
> - Use your judgment. Remember that all sources must be evaluated.

How authoritative is Wikipedia? Generally it is quite good. There is no way to know if the article you reach is authoritative. You might think that because you cannot be sure the information is correct, "why waste time reading the article?" That's the wrong viewpoint. It assumes that there is one perfectly correct article on your topic of interest, and if you read it, you'll know everything you want or need to know. That's not how information works.

Whenever you use the Web, you need to apply good research practices. This short set of rules will ensure that you get highly reliable information:

- Question the information—
  - Does it make sense? Is it believable? Is it consistent?
  - Does the information fit with everything you already know?
- Never rely on a single source; always use multiple sources.
- Assess the site's authoritativeness (see next section).
- Vary the kinds of resources you use, including offline resources.

It is wise to keep these rules in the back of your mind any time you search the Web.

Changing History. Although it doesn't happen often, people do try to change Wikipedia for their own purposes. A documented example occurred in 2011 when former Vice Presidential candidate Sarah Palin visited a historic site in Boston and misremembered her history. The Slate Web site takes up the story:

> Last week, Sarah Palin told a local news station in Boston that Paul Revere "warned the British that they weren't gonna be takin' away our arms." As the news media rushed to point out that Revere was, in fact, warning the American colonists, not the British, Palin's supporters apparently attempted to update the Wikipedia entry on Revere in order to make the facts conform to Palin's version of history.
> According to the revision history on the Wikipedia page, Palin supporters attempted to add the line in italics below:
>
> > Revere did not shout the phrase later attributed to him ("The British are coming!"), largely because the mission depended on secrecy and the countryside was filled with British army patrols; *also, most colonial residents at the time considered themselves British as they were all legally British subjects.*
>
> That revision was deleted with the explanation "content not backed by a reliable sources [sic] (it was sarah palin interview videos)."

From http://www.slate.com/blogs/blogs/weigel/archive/2011/06/06/editing-wikipedia-to-make-palin-right-about-paul-revere.aspx.

What Is Authoritative?

When we search the Web, we want true and correct information. But, what's true? It is a long (and confusing) philosophical discussion to decide what is truth and how we know it. We don't want to spend time on such discussions. So, instead of "truth" we choose to find information that is "authoritative," because that usually means it is true.

By **authoritative**, we mean that it is what experts say. We assume that experts are well informed on the topic, and that what they say is true. Since we usually have no way to verify what they say without becoming an expert on the topic ourselves, we have to accept that it's the best available information. This is what a librarian does when deciding whether to request a book for the library.

Trusting Wikipedia? Although Wikipedia says that it can't be a source for a research paper, it is a very valuable site to check when doing research. It has a tremendous amount of quality information, and the community steadily makes it better. See their more complete statement about their process: en.wikipedia.org/wiki/Wikipedia:Reviewing. By knowing what they put into it, you'll know how to assess what you get out of it.

Respected Sources. An easy way to find authoritative information is to get it from respected organizations. For example, the best possible medical information is likely to come from the World Health Organization, the Centers for Disease Control, or the Mayo Clinic. These organizations are staffed with doctors and researchers who study medical problems. Health care information from their sites is authoritative. Thousands of professional organizations host Web sites that we can trust.

Individuals can also be extremely good sources of information, as long as we have some reason to believe that they know what they are talking about. These are the "credentials" that historians and other scholars, researchers, and writers list. They are not (usually) bragging about what they know, but rather telling about their background. We use that information to assess whether or not to trust what they say on a specific topic.

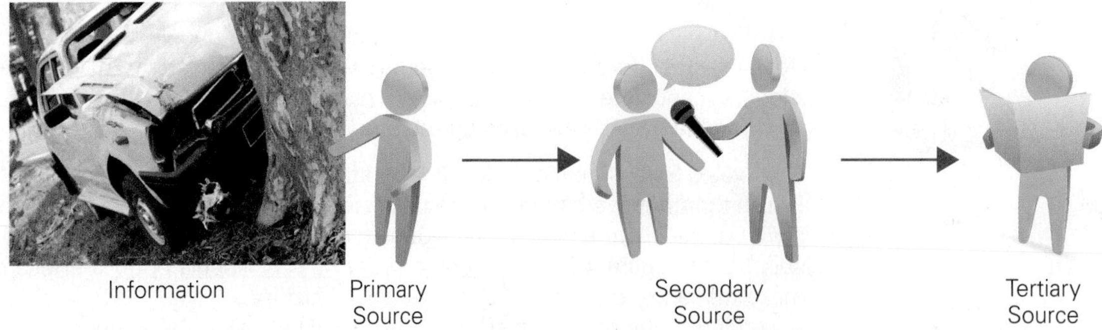

Figure 5.6 A schematic diagram of how sources relate to an original information source.

Primary Sources. A **primary source** is a person who has direct knowledge of the information (see Figure 5.6). For example, participants in an event or witnesses who see it are primary sources. They are generally the best possible sources of information. People who interview primary sources, such as reporters and journalists, are **secondary sources**. They are not as reliable as primary sources because the telling by the primary source and the retelling by the secondary source present opportunities for distortion and mistakes. People who watch journalists on TV or read newspaper reports are **tertiary sources**, meaning they are three levels removed from the person with the direct knowledge of the event; notice that Wikipedia described itself as a "tertiary source." Generally, we want information from sources closest to the action.

Notice that using a secondary source does not mean that the information is likely to be wrong, only that the possibility exists. Historians, who talk to people involved in important events, usually take extreme care to get the information right, and to check thoroughly, but technically they are secondary sources. Many, but not all, biographers also try to get at the truth. Scientists describe many events that they are not a part of—for example, the evolution of man or the origin of the sun—and they devote their whole careers to getting the story straight.

Finally, notice that there is no guarantee that even primary sources tell the truth. People do lie about the things they know. More often, they may leave out relevant content or embellish the basic facts with other information that is incorrect. So, we must even be a little skeptical of information from a primary source. And, of course, there are people with access to correct and undisputed facts—defense attorneys, for example—who "repackage" the truth so it provides their clients a better defense.

Multiple Sources. The best advice for online researchers is always to check multiple sources. Hoaxes, Wikipedia pages that have been tampered with, discussions about fabricated "stories," and junk "information" can be easily discredited by referring to additional sources. The World Wide Web is huge and searching it is simple, so there is really no reason not to have several sources.

Find Different Sources. When picking additional sources, be careful to choose *independent* sources. If each of your sources gets its information from the same place, the sources are not independent.

Authoritative Sources

The easiest way to get authoritative information is to go to a site that you know to be authoritative and look for the information there. So, for example, to find reliable tax information, visit www.irs.gov and search the site, or for information about space, visit www.nasa.gov. Need information on toxins? Try the Environmental Protection Agency (EPA, www.epa.gov). Want information on car crashes? Try the National Transportation Safety Board (NTSB, www.ntsb.gov). The point is that many agencies and organizations publish information you can depend on. The following are some examples:

Topic	Reliable Source
Dietary guidelines	U.S. Department of Agriculture (USDA)
Gas prices in CA	Gasbuddy.com
On-time record for AA flights	American Airlines
Most popular baby girl's name	U.S. Census Bureau
Medical information about MS	National Institutes of Health (NIH)
Blood alcohol level for DUI	State government agency

By going directly to an authoritative source, you are ensured that the information you learn is reliable. It beats determining its reliability *after* you find the information.

Keep Searching. Often times, the right site is obvious, but finding the right page there is tough. Keep in mind that most large sites have site-specific Search facilities on the home page. Or you can limit your Google Advanced Search to that one site. Once you're on the right page, don't forget Find (^F) to locate key terms on the page.

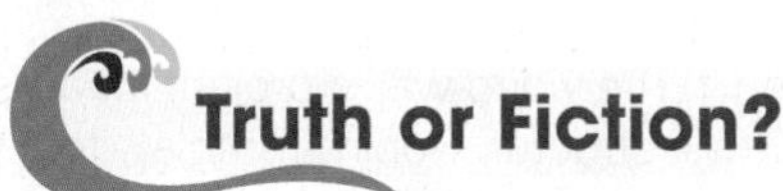

Truth or Fiction?

As the creators of the Dihydrogen Monoxide site well know, no one filters this stuff. (Dihydrogen monoxide is better known as H_2O, and it's a fun page: www.dhmo.org.) The fact that Web posts are **unmediated**—that is, no one limits what people post—is generally good. But sites are not always labeled as parodies or hoaxes or completely-made-up-by-the-author-for-reasons-no-one-understands. If we are not alert, we might believe them. And some sites are very believable.

Site Analysis

How is it possible to recognize bogus Web sites? When surveyed, people say they become skeptical of a site when they find a series of shortcomings on the page, including the following:

- Broken links
- Failure to give contact information
- Failure to have a non-Web identity
- Simplistic design
- No recent updates or blog entries
- Spelling mistakes

Golden Eagle Snatches Kid. In December 2012 the Internet "lit up," as they say, in response to a video showing a golden eagle swooping in, grabbing a small child who was playing near his father in a Montreal park (Figure 5.7), and then dropping him a few moments later (see www.youtube.com/watch?v=CE0Q904gtMI).

Eagle Grabs Kid

Figure 5.7 Frame from the video *Golden Eagle Snatches Kid.*

The movie seems to be an afternoon-in-the-park sort of video one takes with a phone. It was uploaded by MrNuclearCat to YouTube at 7:00 PM. In half an hour it was posted on Reddit; by 8:00 PM. the link had been tweeted. By the next morning, 1.2 million views had been logged.

Comments indicated that people believed the video to show an actual event, though soon a squabble broke out on Reddit over its authenticity. A Portuguese gamer Tiago Duarte (Cyatek) was suspicious, and after analyzing the video frame by frame, he pronounced it "fake" five hours after it was originally posted. After being attacked by commenters, he uploaded his own video showing his analysis of its flaws (at www.youtube.com/watch?v=GjOljUMc-Nc).

It is not real, and the authors quickly admitted it. The video was a project for a visual effects (VFX) class at the University of Montreal. The instructor, Robin Tremblay, told the class if they could create a video that got 100,000 hits, they would get an A. The students (shown) got A's for *Golden Eagle Snatches Kid* after the hundreds of hours they logged learning new software, developing the script, filming the baseline video, creating the eagle and baby models, and so on. The video has had 42 million hits to date. Get the full story at bit.ly/XPDTYy.

Students Loïc Mireault, Antoine Seigle, Félix Marquis-Poulin, and Normand Archambault

Most of us do not have the experience that the VFX students or Duarte have, so it is difficult for us to assess a video's truthfulness. Our only choice is to remain skeptical when we see something "too strange to believe."

Though these are useful *red flags*, keep in mind that a site can meet each of these requirements and still be false.

When we click the link to protect the Pacific Northwest Tree Octopus (zapatopi.net/treeoctopus), a famous hoax, we find that all internal links work, and connect to reputable sites, such as the official site of Olympic National Park and *National Geographic*, and so forth. In fact, the site is "perfect" in that it doesn't have any of the red-flag problems just mentioned.

It does have red flags, however. These appear when you dig deeper. One point of concern is that two of the site's "supporters"—Greenpeas and People for the Ethical Treatment of Pumpkins (P.E.T.PU)—are clearly parodies. Also, there is a citation to a page on the ancient traditions of the sasquatch, the *mythical* "forest ape" of the Northwest rainforests. The link points to a page headed Bureau of Sasquatch Affairs, Republic of Cascadia. What? At this point, we should guess that the endangered octopus might be more entertainment than crusade.

It seems that those who create fake sites for fun often want you to discover it eventually.

Very Credible. The endangered Pacific Northwest Tree Octopus received considerable attention when Professor Don Leu of the University of Connecticut asked 25 seventh graders about the authenticity of the site (zapatopi.net/treeoctopus). All "fell for" it, and 24 gave it a "very credible" rating. After being told it is a hoax, Professor Leu reported "some students still insisted vehemently that the Pacific Northwest Tree Octopus really exists." See advance.uconn.edu/2006/061113/06111308.htm/.

Tough Work

The tree octopus site might be "credible" to junior high kids, but most of us would probably not be taken in for long. Other sites are tougher to figure out. An excellent example is The Manhattan Airport Foundation (manhattanairport.org), a site that burst onto the scene in July 2009 (see Figure 5.8). The site appears to be advocating for an airport to be built smack in the center of New York City in Central Park.

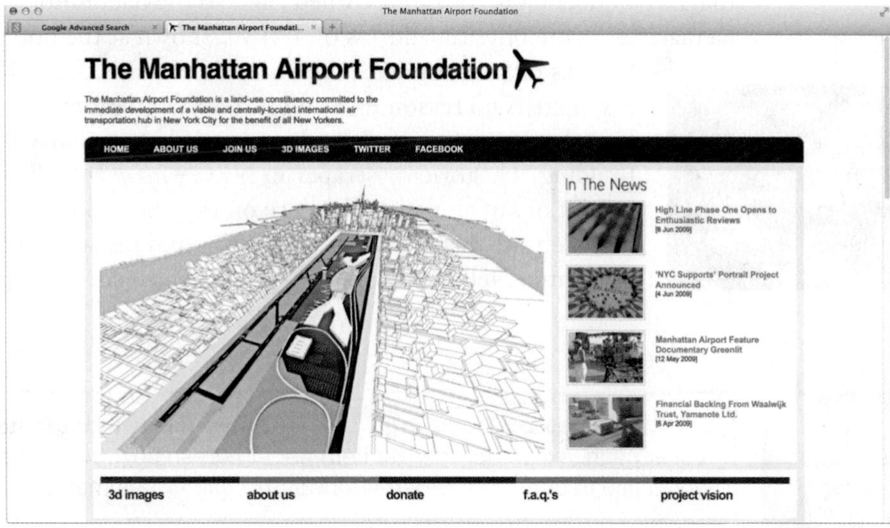

Figure 5.8 The Manhattan Airport Foundation home page.

Is it "fake" or "for real?" It is difficult to figure out. The Huffington Post news aggregation service reported it (briefly) as legitimate news according to Gawker (gawker.com/5319855/huffington-post-serves-up-hoax-on-front-page). It seems inconceivable to think of building an airport in Central Park in Manhattan, but people have strange ideas, and the site is beautifully done:

- It meets all of the red-flag criteria, including physical location.
- It has its own domain name.
- It has a Wikipedia page.
- It's on Facebook and Twitter.

These are characteristics of legitimate sites. So, this one probably is, too, right? (The dates of news items are now stale, but they were current in 2009.)

As with most "entertainment" sites, there are statements that are over the top, which usually imply that the site is a spoof. For example, TMAF writes

> . . . high-density areas the world over have empowered themselves to reclaim disused and blighted urban spaces and infuse them with new life . . .

which implies that Central Park and the area around it is "blighted." In fact, it has some of the most expensive property in the United States. The site also says that the (now closed) 75-year old, world-famous restaurant Tavern on the Green, which is in Central Park, can apply to be part of the airport's food court. These are extreme statements, but they do not mean the people who created the site are not serious about the project, as crazy as it is.

Domain Owner. To find out who owns a Web page, visit www.internic.net/whois.html, fill in the domain name (remember that it is the stuff before the first slash), and submit. You get back the owner, or where to find the owner, or a statement that the site's ownership is not publicly available.

As usual, the way to work out whether a site like this is legitimate is to *check the claimed-to-be-factual content* of the site. For example, we might begin by finding out who owns the domain name by asking the people who monitor the Internet. It's a good idea, but the TMAF domain is "privately owned" and so the data is not available to us. Another factual item is the physical address of TMAF, shown at the bottom of the front page.

contact us
The Manhattan Airport Foundation
233 Broadway, 58th Floor
New York, New York 10007
General Email
info@manhattanairport.org

It looks like a legitimate address, and for those of us who are not New Yorkers, there is no reason to doubt it. But if we search on 233 Broadway New York, Google gives a map, followed by the Wikipedia entry for the Woolworth Building, a historic skyscraper in NYC *with only 57 floors*. The Web site makes a point of saying their offices are on the 58th floor. There are other features of the Web site that are unlikely, but this and the implausibility of an airport in Manhattan, tell us this site is not to be believed.

5.6 Man Flies by Flapping. The site www.ornithopter.org/history.manned.shtml seems real enough, except for the last item about human-powered flight. Give the evidence you would use to determine whether or not this site is legitimate.

SUMMARY

We have studied ways to be effective as Web researchers by understanding how powerful Web tools like search engines work, and how to apply them to our purposes. In this chapter we have learned the following:

- We need software and our own intelligence to search the Internet effectively.
- Search engines are composed of a crawler and a query processor.
- We create complex queries using the logical operators AND, OR, and NOT, and specific terms to pinpoint the information we seek.
- Filtering and "subtracting" search terms removes extraneous hits.
- Once we've found information, we must judge whether it is correct by investigating the organization that publishes the page, and examining the facts claimed on the page.
- We must crosscheck the information with other sources, especially when the information is important.

TRY IT SOLUTIONS

5.1 The two intersections are musclepowered.org and www.hpva.us, which take nine steps.

5.2 The revised rules for removing duplicates in OR-queries would be as follows:

1. Put a marker such as an arrow at the start of each list.
2. Check the URLs pointed to by the markers, and add the alphabetically earliest URL to the result list.
3. Advance the marker one position of the alphabetically earliest URL; if two or more URLs are alphabetically earliest, advance the markers for all of them.
4. Repeat Steps 2–3 until all markets reach the end of the list.

5.3 The query is one of the following:

(corvette OR mazda OR porsche) AND convertible

(corvette OR mazda OR porsche) convertible

convertible corvette OR mazda OR porsche

5.4 gettysburg visitors center plaque, because it says what Tracy wants most directly. The quoted phrase—this is consistent enough to use quotes—will simply find many uses of that text, and encountering the right instance is unlikely.

5.5 By checking the page source of the bfi.org site and locating the <title> tag, we see that Google used only the first half of the title, which actually repeats.

5.6 Check the red-flag tests. Do an independent search for such terms as todd reichert or snowbird to check for other confirming or refuting sources.

REVIEW QUESTIONS

Multiple Choice

1. Some Web pages are "invisible." That is, no search engine will return them in a query. Why do these pages exist?
   a. no other Web page links to them
   b. they are synthetic
   c. they are file types browsers don't understand
   d. all of the above
2. The main responsibility of a crawler is to
   a. find Web pages with false or illegal information
   b. count the number of Web pages
   c. make sure lots of people visit certain pages
   d. build a list of tokens that are associated with each page
3. When picking additional sources you should choose
   a. independent sources
   b. sources created by the same author
   c. sources with the same domain name
   d. additional sources are never needed
4. Enclosing search terms in quotes asks for pages with
   a. the search terms in any order
   b. the search terms in the exact order as written
   c. only the first word in the search terms
   d. only some of the words in the search terms
5. Google usually ignores numbers. What symbol could you add to a query to make sure Google uses the number as part of the query?
   a. –
   b. <>
   c. &
   d. +
6. When searching on Google, this is the same as using the AND keyword.
   a. +
   b. OR
   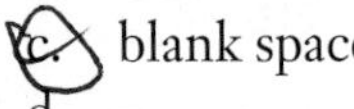
   c. blank space
   d. –
7. A primary source is
   a. something shared by a government
   b. a person with direct knowledge
   c. a teacher or a librarian
   d. the person who created the Web site
8. Who is in charge of the World Wide Web?
   a. Vint Cerf
   b. Larry Page and Sergey Brin
   c. the United States government
   d. no one

9. When should a researcher be skeptical of a primary source?
   a. never; primary sources are always credible
   b. when the primary source is only one person
   c. always; the researcher should verify the information from other sources
   d. about 50 percent of the time; it depends on the situation
10. After finding the Web page you want, what is the next question you should ask yourself?
   a. Is the information authoritative?
   b. When was the Web page first published?
   c. Who owns this Web page?
   d. Could I find this same Web page using a different search engine?

Short Answer

1. The higher the _______ is, the closer to the top of the list a Web page will be in the returned results of a search query.
2. _______ in Google search queries are interpreted as AND.
3. The main work of the _______ is to build an index.
4. If a Web page meets all the authoritative rules given in this chapter, it can still contain _______ information.
5. _______ is the keyboard shortcut for finding certain words on a Web page.
6. Treating query terms as independent is almost _______ what you actually want.
7. Wikipedia is validated by _______.
8. Wikipedia is not considered a _______ source.
9. Crawlers crawl less than _______ of the Web.
10. To find corroborating information on the Web, you should always _______ with another independent Web page.

Exercises

1. Why do we need search engines? What do search engines do? Answer both of these questions in great detail.
2. Explain what a crawler is and what it does.
3. Explain why in the past physical books were trusted much more than Web pages are trusted today.
4. Is the information on journalofpetite**lapgiraffe**science.weebly.com/sokoblovsky-farms.html and www.ovaprima.org/ true and accurate? Explain how you know.
5. Explain the differences between the AND and OR logical operators and when you should use them in Web searches.
6. What is an independent source, and why is it important to use independent sources when researching?
7. Give three examples of when you would want to use quotes around your search query.

8. What is a cached page and how is it useful?
9. Provide at least two concrete examples of when you would want to limit the domain of your Web search.
10. What are the pros and cons of using Wikipedia to find information?
11. Use the search query "HTML quick reference" in your preferred search engine. Then describe each part of the first result found including page title, snippet, URL, cached page, and site links.
12. What are the rules for Intersecting Alphabetized Lists? How are they used to implement search queries?

CHAPTER 6

An Introduction to Debugging

To Err Is Human

learning objectives

- Explain how ordinary precision differs from computing precision
- Describe the six-step strategy for debugging
  - Explain the purpose of each step
  - Give an example of each step
- Apply the six-step strategy for debugging the HTML code for a Web page
- Learn how to approach debugging when you don't understand the system
- Appreciate the problems of making perfectly reliable computing systems

CHAPTER 6

One item could not be deleted because it was missing.

—MAC OS SYSTEM 7.0 ERROR MESSAGE

The most overlooked advantage of owning a computer is that if they foul up there's no law against whacking them around a bit.

—ERIC PORTERFIELD

IT MAY BE TRUE that "To err is human," but to really foul things up takes a computer. One characteristic that makes a computer so useful—and sometimes so frustrating—is that it does exactly what it is told to do, and nothing more. Because it follows each instruction "to the letter" and continually checks itself, it operates almost perfectly. So, in truth, the computer doesn't foul things up at all. We humans—those of us who write the software and those of us who use it—are not perfect, and that combination can really foul things up. So we have to learn how to troubleshoot what's wrong and to get ourselves out of difficulties. Learning debugging techniques—the subject of this chapter—is perhaps the best way to deal successfully with mistakes and errors, and to avoid the foul-ups in the first place.

The first goal of this chapter is to recognize that the greatest, most common source of problems is our lack of care. Computers don't understand what we *mean*, only what we *say*. So we must say exactly what we mean. We introduce the debugging process using a student/parent scenario. This lets us analyze the process as the student/parent interaction unfolds. The next goal is to abstract the debugging principles from the story. These principles do not give a mechanical procedure guaranteeing success, but rather a reliable set of guidelines. We apply the principles to debugging a faulty Web page design. This detective work won't reveal *who*dunit—because we are the obvious "perps"—but rather *what*dunit, our error. Then we show how to approach a seemingly impossible task: debug a system when we have no idea how the system works. Finally, we discuss the possibility of bug-free software.

Precision: The High Standards of Computing

The best way to handle bugs in computing is not to make any mistakes in the first place. This seems like useless advice because humans make mistakes. It's a fact. Furthermore, people don't knowingly do it. So, suggesting that we not make mistakes is like asking us not to be human.

Be Accurate

It's still good advice, however, because there are many cases where we can be alert to the possibility of making mistakes, and be very careful. An important example is when entering information into a computer application:

- Recognizing mistaken substitutions: l for 1, O for 0, \ for /, and so forth
- Knowing that certain fonts can be very confusing: Corbel zero (o) and oh (o)
- Respecting upper- and lowercase in pathnames: www.ex.org/AllMine.html is likely not to be the same as www.ex.org/allmine.html
- Respecting upper- and lowercase in passwords: extra care is required if someone creates a password for you

These are common causes of mistakes, but most popular applications are prone to input errors, and we quickly learn where to pay attention. It's better to enter the input correctly in the first place (even if it takes more time) than to mess up and try to figure out what went wrong.

Be Observant

A principle of computing is that you should expect feedback when interacting with software. This is why "busy icons" tell us that an operation is not yet complete. We rely on this information.

But, there are many, many more subtle forms of feedback. It is important to train ourselves to pay attention to these cues. For example,

- Later in this chapter we will find that the text "caption-align" is wrong, and we know that because the editor has not highlighted it for us in:

```
caption {caption-align:bottom;padding-top:4px}
```

500
500

- Spreadsheets by default align data so that text is left justified and numbers are right justified, as shown; the upper 500 is a number, the lower 500 is text, and most of the time it matters.
- In Chapter 11, when discussing email, we observe that it is embarrassing to click *Reply All* instead of *Reply* when we intend to send a private message, so we ALWAYS want to check the address list before clicking *Send*.

The list is endless. By training ourselves to pay attention to feedback, we can often catch errors when we make them, saving significant effort later to track them down.

Debugging: What's the Problem?

Debugging is a process by which one figures out why an application or system doesn't work properly. Debugging is usually applied to computer or communication systems, especially software, but the techniques are the same whether the systems are mechanical, architectural, business, and so on. Though debugging relies mostly on logical reasoning and is usually "learned from experience," there are general debugging principles and effective strategies that you can learn (see below). Knowing these techniques is important because in computing, a major part of using a system is knowing how to figure out why things are not working properly.

Debugging in Everyday Life

People debug or **troubleshoot** all the time. When their cars don't start, they figure out whether the battery is dead or whether the fuel tank is empty. Faults and failures in everyday life usually involve devices that are correct, working systems with a broken or worn-out part. That is, the system is properly designed and constructed, but some part fails. The car's dead battery keeps it from starting, for example. When the part is replaced, the system works.

Debugging in Information Technology

Debugging a computation is slightly different. In computing, we might have entered wrong data or wrong configuration information in a working system. When it's corrected, the system works. Another possibility is that the system might have a *logical design error*. An analogy in car design is when the backup lights, which should only work when the car is in reverse, also come on when we brake. This is a design or construction error. In software, such logical errors are possible even in commercial software, and users must be aware that they may not be using a correct, working system. Despite this fact, we will always begin by assuming a "correct, working system."

Whose Problem Is It?

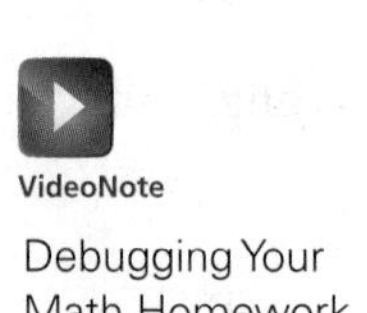
VideoNote

Debugging Your Math Homework

When debugging a computing system, remember that *we* are almost always part of the problem: We command the computer to do tasks and we input the information. When the computer is in an error state despite our thinking that everything should have worked perfectly, two of the three possible problems—wrong data, wrong command, or broken system—involve us personally. And because the hardware and software have been tested thoroughly, the two possibilities that involve us are the two most likely possibilities. Our commands or data probably led to the problem, so we'll have to fix them. Computers cannot debug themselves.

Because people don't knowingly make errors, we think that what we did is right, and that it's the computer's fault that something has gone wrong. It might be—both hardware and software errors do happen—but they are much, much rarer than human errors. If our checking doesn't quickly reveal a small typographical error or the like, then we usually assume that the problem is with the computer or software. But we should consider one more possibility: It may be that we *think* we did everything right because we misunderstand the system and how it works, and so maybe we really *did* make a mistake. It's hard to admit, sometimes, that we've made a mistake, but at least the computer can't think less of us!

Using the Computer to Debug

Not only is the computer unable to debug itself, we can't debug it directly, either. That is, the error, even if it's our mistake, is internal to the computer, either in the stored data or the software logic. To get information about the error, we have to ask the computer

Computer Pioneer Grace Hopper. Rear Admiral Grace Murray Hopper, a computer pioneer, popularized the term *bug* for a glitch in a computer system while she was working on the Harvard Mark computers in the 1940s. When the Mark II computer had a moth jammed in one of its relays (electro-mechanical switches), bringing the machine down, technicians taped the insect into the machine's logbook (see Figure 6.1).

Hopper was one of the inventors of a kind of software known as a *compiler*, which translates a programming language into machine instructions (see Chapter 9), and she greatly influenced the development of the programming language Cobol. Conscious of the physical limitations on computing, Hopper used a length of copper wire

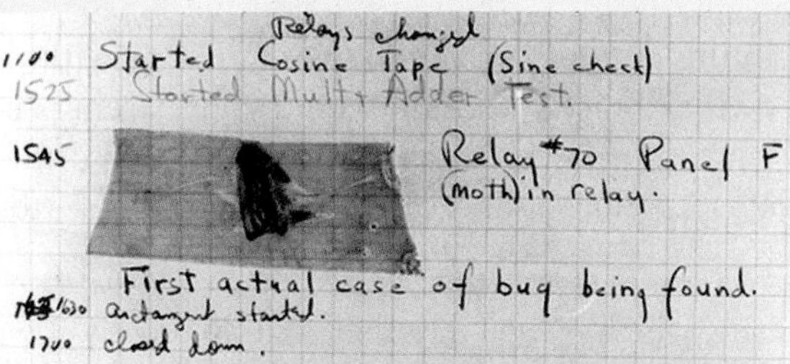

Figure 6.1 The Harvard Mark II logbook noting "First actual case of bug being found."

(approximately one foot long) to illustrate a "nanosecond" (1/1,000,000,000th of a second), because it is approximately the distance electricity can travel in that time.

A U.S. Navy ship was named in her honor.

to tell us what data it has stored, to run the faulty software, and so forth. We are *one step removed* from the failure and what's causing it, and we need the computer to help us find the problem.

Though there may be a bug in our software, most of the program works correctly. And, there are usually many ways to solve a problem. Accordingly, when trouble arises, we can often bypass the problem entirely. Bypassing an error with an alternative approach is called a **workaround**. Workarounds are essential when we use commercial software. Bugs in commercial systems are usually not fixed until an updated version is released, so we have to work around them until then.

A Dialog About Debugging

Imagine the following scenario. You are at the library quietly studying *Fluency*, when you notice you have a call from one of your parents. Stepping outside, you ask,

"What's up?"

"My computer is being attacked by hackers!"

"Really?"

"Yes! It's crawling with viruses and worms, STDs. Everything! What can I do?"

So, maybe your parent is being a little dramatic, but something is wrong, and you are being asked to help. This is a classic debugging situation that will let us discuss troubleshooting strategies in context.

What you know is that your parents have a high-speed connection, they use the Chrome browser, software like Flash is reasonably up-to-date because you upgraded them at the last break, and they are more proficient with computers than most of your friends' parents. That's all the information you have, and it's typical.

Debugging is solving a mystery. Just as we watch detectives solve mysteries in whodunits, we should watch ourselves debug. Why? Because this approach will probably reach a solution faster than if we aimlessly "try stuff." By purposely asking questions such as, "Do I need more clues (inputs)?"; "Are my clues reliable?"; and "What is a theory to explain the problem?" we focus better and will discover a solution faster.

In this example we cannot work directly with the problem. You're on campus, shivering by the library's front door, and your parent is back home. This is typical: Most debugging requires you to work indirectly. You cannot "see" the problem, and you must make queries—like asking your parent questions—to find out what's happening.

The first step in debugging is to check that the error is reproducible. Computers are deterministic, which means that they will do exactly the same thing every time if given the same input. But there is a tiny possibility that a one-time transient glitch caused the problem. If that happened, you're done because it won't repeat. So, start by trying to reproduce the problem. You ask your parent,

"What are you doing?"

"Well, I just paid the credit card bill, and then I tried to check the news at NPR."

"So you're on the Web?"

"Yes. The convenience of online banking! Don't you just love it?"

"Yeah, I'm sure I would if I only had some money. Okay, can you reload the page?"

"Did that. Same thing. I'm being attacked."

It's hard to believe that the National Public Radio Web site is attacking your home, but you at least know that whatever is happening is reproducible.

The next step is to be sure that you know exactly what the problem is. Mystery novels usually have a dead body, making the problem clear. The mystery is who murdered the person, not why the dead person failed to show up for work that day. But in computing, the computer may perform a sequence of operations *after* an error, and they must be eliminated first as the focal point of the debugging. For example, the reason there are no mailing labels printing from your printer may be due to a printer problem, but it could be due to a problem with the word processor or database that is sending the labels to the printer, or it could be that the file containing the addresses is empty; that is, there are no addresses to print. We don't want to debug the printer when the problem could be an empty file.

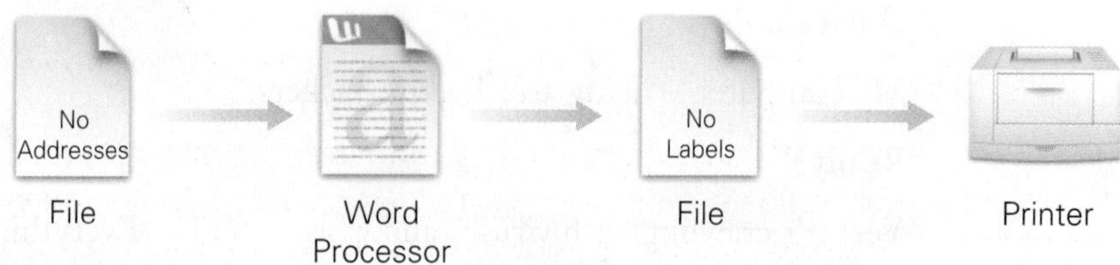

Determining exactly what's wrong is critical.

"How do you know you're being 'attacked'?"

"It says so, and I quote, 'An attacker on your network could be trying to get you to visit a fake (or potentially harmful) version of www.npr.org.' End quote. It doesn't get plainer than that!"

So the problem is that your parent received a warning of some unusual behavior, which sounds like a computer security issue of some sort. So, that's the problem.

A standard next step is to check all of the "obvious" error sources. Of course, if the error were all that obvious, you wouldn't be debugging—you'd have already fixed the problem. What kinds of errors are obvious depends on the problem, naturally, but checking inputs, connections, links, previous behavior, and so on are standard.

Ask your parent to check all of the obvious causes.

"Is the antivirus software still installed?"

"I guess. I didn't touch it."

"Let's assume it's okay. Do you think you've been tricked by a phishing scam?"

"I hate fishing!"

"No, 'phishing' with a p-h. Did you reply to any email that said your account will expire if you don't take immediate action?"

"No. Those things are always so lame. I just hit delete."

So, the antivirus software is working, and phishing isn't likely.

"Have you noticed any other strange behavior? Have there been any strange pop-ups or has your computer slowed down?"

"No. It's working fine. I just paid the credit card bill."

Nothing obvious is wrong.

It's now time to apply a basic strategy of debugging: Isolate the problem by dividing the operation into those parts that are working and those that are not. This means theorizing about where the problem is located and possibly gathering more information. At this point you should take nothing for granted. Limit the number of untested assumptions you make. The error could be anywhere. The goal is to eliminate as many possibilities as you can to focus on the failing part.

In your parent's case, something has caused this warning. Is it something on your parent's machine or from NPR? You ask,

"When did you last check NPR?"

"Oh, maybe an hour ago . . . okay . . . so, I'm a news junkie."

"It worked then? And there's been no other strange behavior?"

"None."

Everything seems to check out. This is a common situation when debugging. You analyze the problem, perhaps getting more data, and conclude that everything is okay. Except it's not. There's a bug somewhere. It's natural to become frustrated, but the best response is to review your analysis. You've made some assumptions, gathered data, performed some tests, interpreted the results, and made some deductions. Ask yourself:

"Is there a wrong assumption?" "Did I misunderstand the data?" "Did I make a wrong deduction?" It's important at this point to think objectively about the process. *A good approach is to step through the process from beginning to end, comparing what should be happening with what is happening.*

"Okay. So you paid the credit card. Was there *anything* strange about that?"

"No, unless you mean someone used the parents' credit card to buy new shoes."

"That's not strange at all. Wait till you see 'em! . . . Then what?"

"I tried to check NPR news."

"You clicked on the bookmark?"

"No, I just changed that URL line at the top to npr.org."

"And. . . ?"

"This notice flashed on the screen." [The parent, but not the student, sees Figure 6.2.]

"Saying. . . ?"

"'This is probably not the site you are looking for'—exclamation point!"

This is useful information, because if it's not the right site, then the message couldn't come from NPR. It must have come from Chrome. Why would Chrome intercept a request to NPR?

"Does it say what site you got?"

"Yes. It's weird. It's a248.e.akamai.net."

"But you typed www.npr.org, right? In the URL window?"

"Yes, I didn't even have to type the www part. It was already there . . . just the npr.org."

And now you've got it!

You know that when banking or paying credit cards bills, it is necessary to have a secure connection. Those use the https protocol, and that protocol is shown in the browser's location window as part of the URL. Your parent's change of

https://www.plastic-credit.com

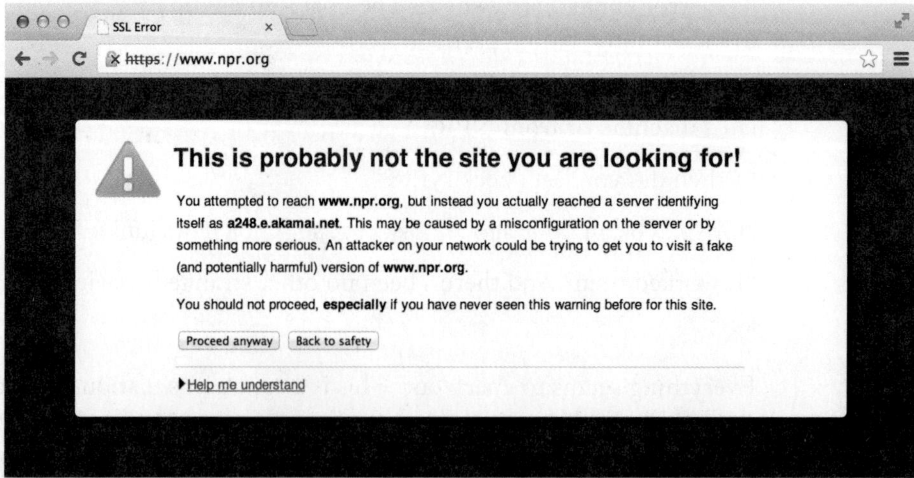

Figure 6.2 Diagnostic message from Chrome, seen by the parent in the story.

to

https://www.npr.com

resulted in a secure connection request to NPR. They don't support secure connections apparently.

"You left the 's' in there!"

"What?"

"Does the URL say h-t-t-p-*s*?"

"It does!"

"Thought so."

". . . and it's in red . . . I hadn't even noticed . . . and it has a little line through it. What's that all about?"

"When you were banking, you had a secure connection. When you typed in npr.org you left the https there. They don't do secure connections. And Chrome told you that you were doing something you didn't want to do."

"So I'm not being attacked?"

"No. You're fine. Keep using your bookmarks and tabs."

And you head back inside to finish reading Chapter 6 of *Fluency with Information Technology*.

Debugging Recap

The key point of the debugging illustration is that there is a semi-organized process to follow to find out what's wrong. The following are key points that can apply in other debugging situations:

- Make sure that you can reproduce the error.
- Determine the problem exactly.
- Eliminate the "obvious" causes.
- Divide the process, separating the parts that work from the part that doesn't.
- When you reach a dead end, reassess your information, asking where you may be making wrong assumptions or conclusions, then step through the process again.
- As you work through the process from start to finish, make predictions about what should happen and verify that your predictions are fulfilled.

This is not a guaranteed-to-work process, but it is a useful set of guidelines. Debugging requires tough, logical reasoning to figure out what's wrong. But, it's possible to do, and though it is not as entertaining as deducing whodunit from the clues in a mystery novel, there is a certain satisfaction to figuring out the answer.

Closer Examination. Watching yourself debug as if you were a mystery detective is important. It helps you be more objective—is the debugger (you) chasing the wrong lead?—and it helps you separate yourself from the process, reducing frustration. Thinking about what you are doing is a good idea generally, of course. After all, Socrates said, "The unexamined life is not worth living."

Fixing HTML Bugs: A Case Study

To illustrate the debugging principles in action, imagine that we've developed a simple page in HTML. Our goal page is shown in Figure 6.3, but the results we're getting are shown in Figures 6.4–6.7, depending on which browser we look at. Obviously, there is an error somewhere. The buggy HTML code we've written is shown in Figure 6.8.* We can study the HTML very, very closely and "brain out" where the error is, or we can use the debugging strategy just discussed. You can follow along online with our debugging process using the files from pearsonhighered.com/snyder. (Notice that software keeps changing, so the current browser versions may show different behavior.)

Jackie Joyner-Kersee -- All-Time Best Female Athlete

It sounds bold to claim that Jackie Joyner-Kersee is the absolute best female athlete, but consider this: She competed in the heptathlon, a track and field event that combines scores from seven different sports. She won two Olympic gold medals in heptathlon (and a silver), and still holds the world record for greatest number of points ever scored: 7,291.

How good was she? First, she competed in heptathlon, meaning she was Olympic caliber in 100m hurdles, 200m, 800m, high jump, long jump, javelin and shot put. Also, she won Olympic gold in long jump and two bronzes. Add to that two World Championship golds in heptathlon and two golds in long jump, and a long jump gold in the Pan American Games. She also played starting forward all four years of college at UCLA in basketball.

Jackie Joyner-Kersee Competing in High Jump

No One Better. But probably the most impressive fact about her abilities is that only two other women have ever been able to score more than 7000 points in heptathlon, Carolina Klüft (7032) of Sweden and Larisa Turchinskaya (7007) of the Soviet Union. For comparison, the table at right lists the seven sports of heptathlon, JJK's 7291-year (1988), her personal best, and the performance needed in each of the seven sports to earn 1000 points. (The scoring in heptathlon is bizarre.)

Event	JJK in 1988	Personal Best	1K Points
100 m hurdles (s)	*12.69*	12.61	13.85
high jump (m)	*1.86*	1.93	1.82
shot put (m)	15.80	16.00	17.07
200 m (s)	*22.56*	22.30	23.80
long jump (m)	*7.27*	7.49	6.48
javelin throw (m)	45.66	50.08	57.18
800 m (s)	128.51	128.51	127.83

JJK Stats -- Italic Shows Events Where JJK Beat 1K

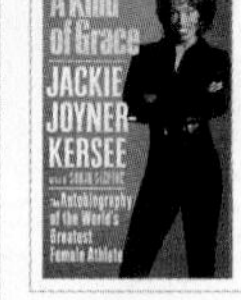

Inspiration Jackie Joyner-Kersee has said in her autobiography *A Kind of Grace* that as a young girl she was inspired to be a versatile athlete by a movie about Babe Didrikson Zaharias, who was a track star, basketball player and pro golfer, and ironically, considered the All-Time Best Female Athlete before JJK.

Figure 6.3 The target page displayed (correctly) with Firefox 25.0.

*The JJK page illustrates one tag we have not previously discussed, the <div> tag, which is used to set up coherent blocks or divisions on the page. It's a good one to learn, so check the references. Here it groups together the image, its caption, the table, and the book cover, and then they are "floated" as a unit to the right side of the page; it's very handy. Hint: There are no bugs connected with the <div> tag, so you can safely ignore it.

Jackie Joyner-Kersee -- All-Time Best Female Athlete

It sounds bold to claim that Jackie Joyner-Kersee is the absolute best female athlete, but consider this: She competed in the heptathlon, a track and field event that combines scores from seven different sports. She won two Olympic gold medals in heptathlon (and a silver), and still holds the world record for greatest number of points ever scored: 7,291.

Jackie Joyner-Kersee Competing in High Jump

How good was she? First, she competed in heptathlon, meaning she was Olympic caliber in 100m hurdles, 200m, 800m, high jump, long jump, javelin and shot put. Also, she won Olympic gold in long jump and two bronzes. Add to that two World Championship golds in heptathlon and two golds in long jump, and a long jump gold in the Pan American Games. She also played starting forward all four years of college at UCLA in basketball.

No One Better. But probably the most impressive fact about her abilities is that only two other women have ever been able to score more than 7000 points in heptathlon, Carolina Klüft (7032) of Sweden and Larisa Turchinskaya (7007) of the Soviet Union. For comparison, the table at right lists the seven sports of heptathlon, JJK's 7291-year (1988), her personal best, and the performance needed in each of the seven sports to earn 1000 points. (The scoring in heptathlon is bizarre.)

JJK Stats -- Italic Shows Events Where JJK Beat 1K

Event	JJK in 1988	Personal Best	1K Points
100 m hurdles (s)	*12.69*	12.61	13.85
high jump (m)	*1.86*	1.93	1.82
shot put (m)	15.80	16.00	17.07
200 m (s)	*22.56*	22.30	23.80
long jump (m)	*7.27*	7.49	6.48
javelin throw (m)	45.66	50.08	57.18
800 m (s)	128.51	128.51	127.83

JJK autobiography

Inspiration Jackie Joyner-Kersee has said in her autobiography *A Kind of Grace* that as a young girl she was inspired to be a versatile athlete by a movie about Babe Didrikson Zaharias, who was a track star, basketball player and pro golfer, and ironically, considered the All-Time Best Female Athlete before JJK.

Figure 6.4 The buggy page displayed with Firefox 25.0; notice the differences with Figure 6.3.

Jackie Joyner-Kersee -- All-Time Best Female Athlete

It sounds bold to claim that Jackie Joyner-Kersee is the absolute best female athlete, but consider this: She competed in the heptathlon, a track and field event that combines scores from seven different sports. She won two Olympic gold medals in heptathlon (and a silver), and still holds the world record for greatest number of points ever scored: 7,291.

Jackie Joyner-Kersee Competing in High Jump

How good was she? First, she competed in heptathlon, meaning she was Olympic caliber in 100m hurdles, 200m, 800m, high jump, long jump, javelin and shot put. Also, she won Olympic gold in long jump and two bronzes. Add to that two World Championship golds in heptathlon and two golds in long jump, and a long jump gold in the Pan American Games. She also played starting forward all four years of college at UCLA in basketball.

JJK Stats -- Italic Shows Events Where JJK Beat 1K

Event	JJK in 1988	Personal Best	1K Points
100 m hurdles (s)	*12.69*	12.61	13.85
high jump (m)	*1.86*	1.93	1.82
shot put (m)	15.80	16.00	17.07
200 m (s)	*22.56*	22.30	23.80
long jump (m)	*7.27*	7.49	6.48
javelin throw (m)	45.66	50.08	57.18
800 m (s)	128.51	128.51	127.83

No One Better. But probably the most impressive fact about her abilities is that only two other women have ever been able to score more than 7000 points in heptathlon, Carolina Klüft (7032) of Sweden and Larisa Turchinskaya (7007) of the Soviet Union. For comparison, the table at right lists the seven sports of heptathlon, JJK's 7291-year (1988), her personal best, and the performance needed in each of the seven sports to earn 1000 points. (The scoring in heptathlon is bizarre.)

Inspiration Jackie Joyner-Kersee has said in her autobiography *A Kind of Grace* that as a young girl she was inspired to be a versatile athlete by a movie about Babe Didrikson Zaharias, who was a track star, basketball player and pro golfer, and ironically, considered the All-Time Best Female Athlete before JJK.

Figure 6.5 The buggy page displayed with Safari 6.0.

Jackie Joyner-Kersee -- All-Time Best Female Athlete

It sounds bold to claim that Jackie Joyner-Kersee is the absolute best female athlete, but consider this: She competed in the heptathlon, a track and field event that combines scores from seven different sports. She won two Olympic gold medals in heptathlon (and a silver), and still holds the world record for greatest number of points ever scored: 7,291.

How good was she? First, she competed in heptathlon, meaning she was Olympic caliber in 100m hurdles, 200m, 800m, high jump, long jump, javelin and shot put. Also, she won Olympic gold in long jump and two bronzes. Add to that two World Championship golds in heptathlon and two golds in long jump, and a long jump gold in the Pan American Games. She also played starting forward all four years of college at UCLA in basketball.

Jackie Joyner-Kersee Competing in High Jump

JJK Stats -- Italic Shows Events Where JJK Beat 1K

Event	JJK in 1988	Personal Best	1K Points
100 m hurdles (s)	*12.69*	12.61	13.85
high jump (m)	*1.86*	1.93	1.82
shot put (m)	15.80	16.00	17.07
200 m (s)	*22.56*	22.30	23.80
long jump (m)	*7.27*	7.49	6.48
javelin throw (m)	45.66	50.08	57.18
800 m (s)	128.51	128.51	127.83

No One Better. But probably the most impressive fact about her abilities is that only two other women have ever been able to score more than 7000 points in heptathlon, Carolina Klüft (7032) of Sweden and Larisa Turchinskaya (7007) of the Soviet Union. For comparison, the table at right lists the seven sports of heptathlon, JJK's 7291-year (1988), her personal best, and the performance needed in each of the seven sports to earn 1000 points. (The scoring in heptathlon is bizarre.)

Inspiration Jackie Joyner-Kersee has said in her autobiography *A Kind of Grace* that as a young girl she was inspired to be a versatile athlete by a movie about Babe Didrikson Zaharias, who was a track star, basketball player and pro golfer, and ironically, considered the All-Time Best Female Athlete before JJK.

Figure 6.6 The buggy page displayed with Chrome 30.0.

Jackie Joyner-Kersee -- All-Time Best Female Athlete

It sounds bold to claim that Jackie Joyner-Kersee is the absolute best female athlete, but consider this: She competed in the heptathlon, a track and field event that combines scores from seven different sports. She won two Olympic gold medals in heptathlon (and a silver), and still holds the world record for greatest number of points ever scored: 7,291.

How good was she? First, she competed in heptathlon, meaning she was Olympic caliber in 100m hurdles, 200m, 800m, high jump, long jump, javelin and shot put. Also, she won Olympic gold in long jump and two bronzes. Add to that two World Championship golds in heptathlon and two golds in long jump, and a long jump gold in the Pan American Games. She also played starting forward all four years of college at UCLA in basketball.

Jackie Joyner-Kersee Competing in High Jump

JJK Stats -- Italic Shows Events Where JJK Beat 1K

Event	JJK in 1988	Personal Best	1K Points
100 m hurdles (s)	*12.69*	12.61	13.85
high jump (m)	*1.86*	1.93	1.82
shot put (m)	15.80	16.00	17.07
200 m (s)	*22.56*	22.30	23.80
long jump (m)	*7.27*	7.49	6.48
javelin throw (m)	45.66	50.08	57.18
800 m (s)	128.51	128.51	127.83

JJK

No One Better. But probably the most impressive fact about her abilities is that only two other women have ever been able to score more than 7000 points in heptathlon, Carolina Klüft (7032) of Sweden and Larisa Turchinskaya (7007) of the Soviet Union. For comparison, the table at right lists the seven sports of heptathlon, JJK's 7291-year (1988), her personal best, and the performance needed in each of the seven sports to earn 1000 points. (The scoring in heptathlon is bizarre.)

Inspiration Jackie Joyner-Kersee has said in her autobiography *A Kind of Grace* that as a young girl she was inspired to be a versatile athlete by a movie about Babe Didrikson Zaharias, who was a track star, basketball player and pro golfer, and ironically, considered the All-Time Best Female Athlete before JJK.

Figure 6.7 The buggy page displayed with Internet Explorer 10.0.

```
<!doctype html>
<html>
 <head> <title>Jackie Joyner-Kersee</title>
 <meta charset="UTF-8"/>
   <style>
    body     {background-color:ivory; font-family:helvetica;
              color:sienna; padding-left:80px;width:825px}
    h2       {text-align:center}
    img      {padding:6; border-width:1px; border-style:solid;
              border-color:burlywood}
    table    {outline:solid burlywood thin;font-size:14px }
    th       (text-align:center;border-width:1px; border-style:solid;
              border-color:burlywood;padding:3px}
    td       {text-align:right;background-color:white;
              border-width:1px; border-style:solid;
              border-color:burlywood;padding:2px}
    td.jjk   {background-color:tan; color:white;}
    caption  {caption-align:bottom;padding-top:4px}
    span.au  {color:gold}
    span.ag  {color:silver}
    span.bz  {color:orange}
   </style>
 </head>
 <body>
   <h2 style="color:darkred"> Jackie Joyner-Kersee -- All-Time Best Female Athlete</h2>
    <div style="float:right;padding-left:6px">
    <p style="text-align:center"><img src="pic/jjkHiJump.jpg" alt="JJK competes in high jump" width="500" /><br/>
       <span style="font-size;small"> Jackie Joyner-Kersee Competing in High Jump</span><br/></p>
    <img src="jjkKindGrace.jpg" alt="JJK autobiography" width="100" style="float:right;"/>
    <table>     <caption>JJK Stats -- Italic Shows Events Where JJK Beat 1K</caption>
     <tr><th>Event</th><th>JJK in 1988</th><th>Personal Best</th><th>1K Points</th></tr>
     <tr style="color:red"><td>100 m hurdles (s)</td><td><i>12.69</i></td><td>12.61 </td><td>13.85 </td></tr>
     <tr style="color:blueviolet"><td>high jump (m)</td><td><i>1.86</i></td><td>1.93 </td><td>1.82 </td></tr>
     <tr style="color:blueviolet"><td>shot put (m)</td><td>15.80  </td><td>16.00 </td><td>17.07 </td></tr>
     <tr style="color:red"><td>200 m (s)</td><td><i>22.56</i></td><td>22.30 </td><td>23.80 </td></tr>
     <tr style="color:blueviolet"><td>long jump (m)</td><td><i>7.27</i></td><td>7.49 </td><td>6.48 </td></tr>
     <tr style="color:blueviolet"><td>javelin throw (m)</td><td>45.66 </td><td>50.08 </td><td>57.18 </td></tr>
     <tr style="color:red"><td>800 m (s)</td><td>128.51 </td><td>128.51 </td><td>127.83</td></tr>
   </table>
   <p> <br/> It sounds bold to claim that Jackie Joyner-Kersee is the absolute best female athlete, but
       consider this: She competed in the heptathlon, a track and field event that combines scores from
       seven different sports. She won two Olympic <span class="au">gold</span> medals in heptathlon
       (and a <span class="ag">silver</span>), and still holds the world record for greatest number of
       points ever scored: 7,291.</p>
    <p><b style="color:darkred">How good was she?</b> First, she competed in heptathlon, meaning
        she was Olympic caliber in 100m hurdles, 200m, 800m, high jump, long jump, javelin and shot
        put. Also, she won Olympic <span class="au">gold</span> in long jump and two <span class="bz">bronzes.
        </span> Add to that two World Championship <span class="au"> golds</span> in heptathlon and two
        <span class="au">golds </span> in long jump, and a long jump <span class="au">gold </spam> in the
        Pan American Games. She also played starting forward all four years of college at UCLA in basketball. </p>
    <p><b style="color:darkred">No One Better. </b>
        But probably the most impressive fact about her abilities is that only two other women have ever
        been able to score more than 7000 points in heptathlon,  Carolina Klüft (7032) of Sweden and
        Larisa Turchinskaya (7007) of the Soviet Union. For comparison, the table at right lists the seven
        sports of heptathlon, JJK's 7291-year (1988), her personal best, and the performance needed in
        each of the seven sports to earn 1000 points. (The <a href="http://en.wikipedia.org/wiki/Heptathlon">
        scoring in heptathlon </a> is bizarre.)</p>
   <p><b style="color:darkred">Inspiration</b> Jackie Joyner-Kersee has said in her autobiography <i>A Kind
        of Grace</i> that as a young girl she was inspired to be a versatile athlete by a movie about Babe Didrikson
        Zaharias, who was a track star, basketball player and pro golfer, and ironically, considered the All-Time
        Best Female Athlete before JJK.</p>
 </body>
</html>
```

Figure 6.8 The buggy HTML code.

6.1 Some of These Things Are Kind of Different. Check the pages in Figures 6.3–6.7. Find something similar and something different between Figure 6.3 and the versions in Figures 6.4–6.7.

Look At the Page Closely

The best way to get started, especially when looking at a page that someone else has written, is to study the output closely to see where the errors are. The goal is to notice features that are right and features that are wrong. The first point is that the four browsers display the buggy page differently—none of them agree! All browsers should show a correct page exactly the same, but once the page is buggy, anything can happen. Firefox (Figure 6.4) doesn't display any formatting in the body text; Chrome (Figure 6.6) and Internet Explorer (Figure 6.7) don't either, though their spacing differs from Firefox. Safari (Figure 6.5) shows formatting, but it's very strange; it seems to change into yellow text late in the second paragraph. Sometimes it's possible to find a difficult bug by comparing how different browsers show it. In the present cases, however, that's not too useful. We will work with Firefox.

Notice that although the fancy formatting of the table isn't working, there are other things wrong, too. The browsers disagree about whether the caption should be inside of the table, or outside.

6.2 Not Perfect. The difference mentioned in the text between the correct (Figure 6.3) and the incorrect (Figure 6.4) page in Firefox is the coloring of the text. What are the other differences?

Error 1. As we begin watching ourselves debugging the HTML, we recall that the first step is to be sure we can reproduce the error. So, we close our browser and reopen the file. Unfortunately, the results are the same. There is definitely a problem with our HTML.

Determine the Exact Problem. The next step is to determine the problem exactly. In the case of debugging HTML, identifying the problem is simple: just look at the displayed page. Here, as is typical, there are multiple bugs, so we need to pick one to concentrate on. We choose *the missing book cover image*.

Eliminate the Obvious. Once we know what the problem is, we look for the "obvious" causes and eliminate them. What's the most obvious problem with a missing image? The file is not where it should be, so the browser can't find it. So, we check to see that the image is in the pic folder, which it is.

The next most obvious error is misspelling the file name. So, we check our HTML (Figure 6.8) to find

```
<img src="jjkKindGrace.jpg" alt="JJK autobiography" width="100" style="float:right;"/>
```

and immediately we see the problem: the path is messed up—it doesn't mention the pic folder.

6.3 Get on the Right Path. How should the image tag be corrected?

And after fixing the tag, the image is there. It was an obvious mistake, so checking the "obvious" problems is smart. One error down! It's satisfying to have already fixed one bug without too much effort!

Focusing the Search

We return to the "determine the problem step" and continue with the next bug.

Determine the Exact Problem. This time we choose the *no styling* problem. It's the main problem with the page, so it's smart to prioritize it. Also, it's important to solve because styling influences many features of the page—the other bugs we have noticed could be due to the bad styling, too.

Eliminate the Obvious. The most obvious HTML error is to forget an end tag; that is, to forget the matching "slash-tag." Because the styling isn't working we guess the </style> is missing or messed up, but checking the page, we see that it (and every other tag) is matched. So that simple tactic fails.

While we're looking at the styling tags, we notice that not all of the styling is wrong—the background color and text color are working; so are other features of the body and h1 elements. So, *some* styling is happening.

Our next idea is to ask the computer for help, so we go to the Web Console (*Tools* > *Web Developer* > *Web Console*). This is where Firefox lists the problems it finds while it renders the page, and says how it is handling them. (Mozilla gives a tutorial for this tool including a short video on its use: https://developer.mozilla.org/en-US/docs/Tools/Web_Console.) For the JJK page we get a list of four errors Firefox discovered, as illustrated in Figure 6.9.

Error 2. The first diagnostic says there is some sort of problem with the "padding" property in line 9:

```
img     {padding:6; border-width:1px; border-style:solid;
         border-color:burlywood}
```

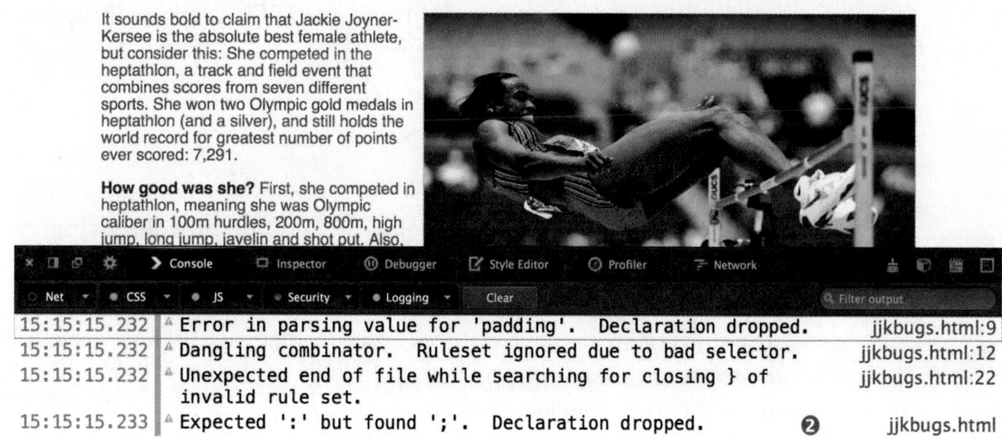

Figure 6.9 Web Console report for the buggy JJK page.

So, what is it? Just looking at the line, we notice that the padding specification doesn't say what unit the padding is measured in, though the border-width does. Checking the definition of the padding property (www.w3schools.com/css/css_padding.asp), we notice that the amount can be specified in several different units. So, obviously, we need to give which unit we use.

Correcting the units problem gives a nice border around the images. It also eliminates that diagnostic from the Web Console.

6.4 A Whole New Image. How should the image element be corrected?

Error 3. Pushing on, the next diagnostic says, "Dangling combinator. Ruleset ignored due to bad selector." This is a typical diagnostic—gibberish that means nothing to us. It does say, "ruleset ignored," confirming that Firefox isn't bothering with some of our style commands. If only we knew what a "bad selector" is. We could try doing a Web search to find out, but that is an if-all-else-fails idea. We'll push on to the next diagnostic.

The next diagnostic reads "Unexpected end of file while searching for closing } of invalid rule set." That seems to say that we have left out a closing brace, which probably *is* useful to know, and it's killing off the styling process. So, the obvious thing is to look for the forgotten brace. Unfortunately, all of the closing braces are there, so that doesn't solve the problem. But, the diagnostic gives one more bit of data: "jjkbugs.html 22", which points us to line 22 of our file. So we patiently count the lines (Figure 6.8, because lines start numbering at the top) and we find that line 22 is the closing </style> tag, which we've already checked. So, we push on.

Divide Up the Process. The next step is to separate those parts of the system that work from the part that does not. This is not always possible to do perfectly, but we should try. In the present case our focus is on the styling section. We are looking for a "dangling combinator"—whatever that is—that stops the styling. Here's what to do.

Process to Separate Working and Failing Style Elements. Step through the style section one element at a time. From your HTML editor (Notepad++ or TextWrangler), do the following for each element:

1. Delete the entire element
2. Save the file
3. Refresh the Firefox display
4. Check to see that the only thing different is the styling of the removed element
5. Undo the deletion to restore the file to its original form

If removing an element restores other formatting, then we have found the element that is stopping the styling, and we can fix it. That is, we will separate the part that is broken from the parts that are working.

As a result of performing this sweep, we find that the th element is the culprit, because once it is eliminated other styling features such as the table become visible, as we see in Figure 6.10. This is definitely progress!

Jackie Joyner-Kersee -- All-Time Best Female Athlete

It sounds bold to claim that Jackie Joyner-Kersee is the absolute best female athlete, but consider this: She competed in the heptathlon, a track and field event that combines scores from seven different sports. She won two Olympic gold medals in heptathlon (and a silver), and still holds the world record for greatest number of points ever scored: 7,291.

How good was she? First, she competed in heptathlon, meaning she was Olympic caliber in 100m hurdles, 200m, 800m, high jump, long jump, javelin and shot put. Also, she won Olympic gold in long jump and two bronzes. Add to that two World Championship golds in heptathlon and two golds in long jump, and a long jump gold in the Pan American Games. She also played starting forward all four years of college at UCLA in basketball.

Jackie Joyner-Kersee Competing in High Jump

No One Better. But probably the most impressive fact about her abilities is that only two other women have ever been able to score more than 7000 points in heptathlon, Carolina Klüft (7032) of Sweden and Larisa Turchinskaya (7007) of the Soviet Union. For comparison, the table at right lists the seven sports of heptathlon, JJK's 7291-year (1988), her personal best, and the performance needed in each of the seven sports to earn 1000 points. (The scoring in heptathlon is bizarre.)

JJK Stats -- Italic Shows Events Where JJK Beat 1K

Event	JJK in 1988	Personal Best	1K Points
100 m hurdles (s)	*12.69*	12.61	13.85
high jump (m)	*1.86*	1.93	1.82
shot put (m)	15.80	16.00	17.07
200 m (s)	*22.56*	22.30	23.80
long jump (m)	*7.27*	7.49	6.48
javelin throw (m)	45.66	50.08	57.18
800 m (s)	128.51	128.51	127.83

Inspiration Jackie Joyner-Kersee has said in her autobiography *A Kind of Grace* that as a young girl she was inspired to be a versatile athlete by a movie about Babe Didrikson Zaharias, who was a track star, basketball player and pro golfer, and ironically, considered the All-Time Best Female Athlete before JJK.

Figure 6.10 JJK page with the th element removed; most styling is now "working," though it is not yet all correct.

So, what's wrong with the th element? The Web Console report said that it didn't find a closing brace, but it has one.

```
th      (text-align:center;border-width:1px; border-style:solid;
         border-color:burlywood;padding:3px}
```

To figure out what is wrong with this line, we have several options. We can repeat the process we just went through, eliminating parts of this line to see which one is busted. Another approach might be to reenter the text, because occasionally files get odd, unprintable characters ("gremlins") that are hard to locate. Plus, retyping requires that we consider each part of the styling again, carefully. And in doing that we make a discovery!

It's hard to see, but, oddly, this element doesn't have an *opening* brace! It is actually a parenthesis, not a brace. We fix the opening brace and fix the problem! But why was the browser looking for a *closing brace* when the problem was a missing opening brace? It's a mystery and we may never find the answer. But, we did find the error using the separation process. It's a good tool to remember.

Notice that the th element is on line 12 of the HTML file, and the Web Console did tell us in the diagnostic to look on line 12. We didn't pay attention earlier, but we will going forward.

Nearly Perfect

VideoNote

The Case of the Missing Bracket

We have found a tough bug; it wasn't tough to fix, just tough to locate. There are several other problems with the page, however. We can simply find the HTML code for each broken feature and see if we can figure out what's wrong. It's a continuation of the pick-a-bug-and-eliminate-the-obvious process. But having been successful with the Web Console, we return to it with the third correction in place (see Figure 6.11).

Error 4. The next diagnostic says "Unknown property 'caption-align'" on line 18. The idea was to put the caption on the bottom, but apparently this is the wrong property. Again, checking the references (www.w3schools.com/cssref/pr_tab_caption-side.asp) we discover that the property we want is caption-side:bottom. And fixing it places the caption as intended. Notice that this diagnostic wasn't even listed in the original list, because it was hidden by the th error. It is common for one bug to hide another.

Interestingly, some text editors or Integrated Development Environments (IDEs), which are tools to help people write code, often help by the way they highlight the text. For example, while working, if you type

```
td       {text-align:right;background-color:white;
           border-width:1px; border-style:solid;
           border-color:burlywood;padding:2px}
td.jjk  {background-color:tan; color:white;}
caption  {caption-align:bottom;padding-top:4px}
span.au  {color:gold}
```

and notice that the caption-align text is not highlighted like the other properties, you might guess that you've made a mistake. Correcting it shows the right highlighting.

```
td       {text-align:right;background-color:white;
           border-width:1px; border-style:solid;
           border-color:burlywood;padding:2px}
td.jjk  {background-color:tan; color:white;}
caption  {caption-side:bottom;padding-top:4px}
span.au  {color:gold}
```

The system knows that you are writing HTML (by the file extension), and so can parse your text properly. When it finds properties, it looks them up in the official list. Finding them, it highlights them. Caption-align is not in the list.

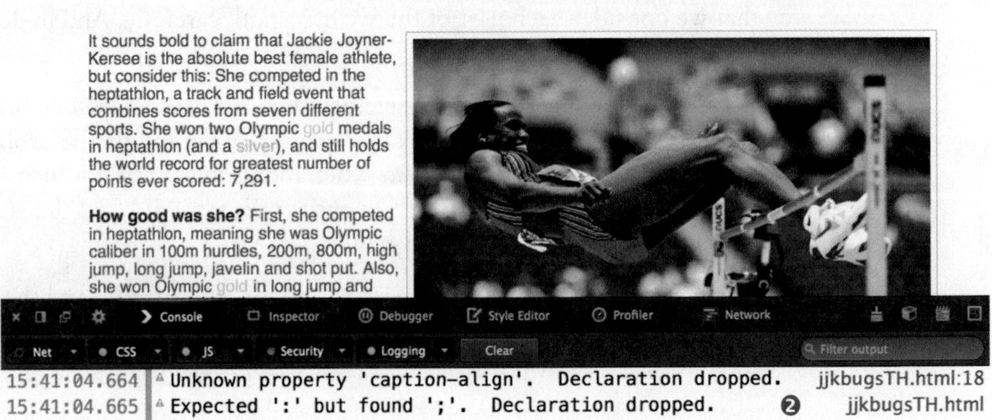

Figure 6.11 Web Console for the JJK page after the third correction.

The last two diagnostics of Figure 6.11 are not very useful because they don't say where the errors are.

Error 5. To find the next error, which is the wrong colored text in the second paragraph (Figure 6.10), we simply find that place in the code where the problem begins:

Wrong color begins here

```
</span> Add to that two World Championship <span class="au"> golds</span> in heptathlon and two
<span class="au">golds </span> in long jump, and a long jump <span class="au">gold </spam> in the
Pan American Games. She also played starting forward all four years of college at UCLA in basketball. </p>
```

It is immediately obvious what the mistake is! (It would be wonderful to stop spam so easily!) Fixing this typo removes the miscolored text.

6.5 A Better End Tag. How should the text be corrected?

Error 6. We almost have the exact page that was intended. The only remaining problem is the caption for the high jump image. This should be small; it is styled by

```
<span style="font-size;small"> Jackie Joyner-Kersee Competing in High Jump</span><br/></p>
```

And now, we recall the last two diagnostics in Figure 6.11. At the time they seemed strange, but obviously (now) they were trying to tell us that we have another typo, a semicolon instead of a colon between this property, font-size, and its value, small. Fixing that produces our target page.

Debugging the JJK Page: A Postmortem

We debugged the mistakes in the Jackie Joyner-Kersee page by applying our debugging guidelines. They were useful even though the bugs turned out not to be serious enough to require that we apply the full process. What did we do?

- Checked that the book cover file was in the pic folder—it was.
- Checked the spelling of the file, but found that the path left out the pic part. Fixed.
- Checked that the end (/) tags were all present—they were.
- Clicked the Web Console to get diagnostics.
- Checked padding, and noticed that the unit had not been set. Fixed.
- Returned to the Web Console to find two mysterious diagnostics.
- Checked that the closing braces were all present—they were.
- Separated working from failing code by a process of delete, check, undo—found th had stopped styling.
- Checked the th element, and eventually spotted the opening parenthesis. Fixed.
- Looked at the Web Console again to find new diagnostics.
- Looked up "caption-align" to find it should be "caption-side." Fixed.
- Checked the wrongly colored text, and spotted a typo in the end tag. Fixed.
- Checked the caption's small font specification, and spotted a colon typo. Fixed.

There were six errors on the page, but only one of which was truly serious and challenging to find.

There is a common debugging feature that we didn't encounter here: *"Correcting" text that isn't actually wrong because of having made a wrong conjecture as to what the error is.* When we're lucky, we end up changing the program text from correct to correct; when we're unlucky, we change it from correct to incorrect. In that case, we have to "back out" and restore the original. It's annoying, but it's the nature of debugging.

Hiding Other Errors. Notice that the errors we found were different from the errors we thought we had originally. We thought that the missing lines and the missing background colors in the table were separate errors, but they were both the result of the `th` error. The `th` error hid the `caption-align` error. Also, the main styling error hid the "spam" error, in Firefox and IE10 at least. This is very common in debugging. It's why programmers never say that they are "down to the very last bug" . . . that bug could be hiding one more.

Asking the System to Help. Notice that the most effective technique in our debugging exercise—after thinking logically—was to use the browser's Web Console feature. We used it effectively to hone in on three errors. We could have even used it more effectively if we had better understood what the gibberish was actually talking about, like not finding a closing brace! It's not a magic wand, but whatever it is trying to tell us does have some nugget of value.

We didn't try the Validator, but it wouldn't have been much help on this page. The only error it would find in the original code is the "spam" bug, which would help, but it was trivial to find without the Validator.

For certain kinds of errors the Page Source shows color- and font-coded HTML source that tells us how the browser interprets the page. It's also a good thing to check because it can reveal an error directly.

In general, one of the most powerful debugging techniques is to find ways for the computer to tell us the meaning of the information it stores or the effects of the commands it executes. Having the computer say how it's interpreting our instructions can separate the case in which we give the right command—but mess up expressing it—and giving the wrong command. This is an important difference for finding a bug.

Little Errors, Big Problems. Thirteen characters were changed: `pic/(px side n :`. The HTML file has 4701 characters, which means that the incorrect fraction of the program was 13/4701 = 0.0027, or less than 0.3 percent. With such a small amount of text making such a large difference in the program, we really must be precise.

In Which Case. Generally, file references for Windows and Mac are not case sensitive, but for UNIX systems they are. Because you do not know which operating system will host your Web page, it is essential to make the case of the file references match the names.

No Printer Output: A Classic Scenario

Debugging HTML is possible because we know and write HTML, but we don't create most computer systems, and they are extremely complex, way beyond our understanding. A smartphone or standard personal computer and its software are more complex than the space shuttle in several ways. As users, we have little idea how something so complex works; how is it possible to troubleshoot a system we don't understand?

Of course, we cannot debug software and information systems at the detailed level used by programmers and hardware engineers. If there is a basic, conceptual error in the system, we probably won't find it. But we don't have to. Before we come in contact with a system, it is tested extensively. This testing doesn't eliminate all errors, but it probably means that the "standard operations" used by "average" users are run through their paces many times. Systems should be bug-free, and we should be able to depend on the software.

Putting It to the Test. As noted in Chapter 2, "getting out and getting back in" often works when an application is not operating correctly. The reason this method works is related to how software is tested. Beginning with a fresh configuration, the testing proceeds "forward" into the application, with the common operations getting the most attention. So the most stable part of a system is the part that is reachable from an initial configuration—the part you first meet when you're "getting back in."

To illustrate debugging a system without understanding it, consider a classic debugging scenario: You try to print a document and nothing comes out of the printer. This is a common problem. What you know about the context of the problem is that a cable connects the computer/printer system, part of the system is mechanical, the flow of information is from one device to the other, and the system has worked in the past.

Applying the Debugging Strategy

The printing problem is solved just like the earlier problems were solved: *reproduce the error*, *understand the problem*, and *check the obvious causes*. These steps include checking the printer's control panel, the paper, the cartridges, the cable connections, the file to be printed, the installation of the printer driver (that the correct printer dialog box comes up when the *Print* command is issued), whether others can print if this is a shared printer, and whether you can print a different document. If these steps do not solve the problem, you may think it's time to ask for help. You've already gone further than most users, so it's not embarrassing, but you can do more.

Pressing On

Take the next step in the debugging strategy: *Try to isolate the problem*. This is daunting because you don't really understand how printing works. Not to worry. It's still possible to make progress.

Because you have printed before, you know your computer is configured correctly. You try to print a simple document like a text file, but it's the same story: The printer driver's dialog box comes up, asks how many copies you want, and so forth—you reply 1, click **Print**, and the machine appears to compute for a moment. But when you check the printer, nothing's there. What is happening to your output?

Thinking through what you imagine to be the process, you guess that when you click **Print**, the printer driver must convert the file into the form suitable for the printer. Because the computer runs briefly after you click **Print**, it's a safe bet that it's doing something like a conversion. Then your computer must send the converted file to the printer. Does it go? Surely, if the computer tried to send the file to the printer and the printer didn't acknowledge getting it, the computer would tell you to plug in the printer. Or would it? Suppose you unplugged the printer from the computer and tried again to print. You run this experiment and the same thing happens! The printer can't even receive the converted file, and there are no complaints. What's happening? Where is the file?

Perhaps the computer is saving the converted file. Why? Shouldn't it print if it's told to print? This is a little odd, because it's not asking you to plug in the printer. Could the other files you tried to print be waiting too, even though the printer was plugged in earlier? So, you start looking around for the stranded file(s). You locate the printer driver's printing monitor (*Start > Devices and Printers* on the PC; among the active programs on the Mac). When you open this monitor, you find a list of all the files you've tried to print recently. They're not printing—they're just listed.

The Print Queue

You have discovered the **print queue** for your machine, a place where printing tasks wait before being processed. You didn't even know that computers *have* print queues, but apparently they do. It's obvious that your file is stalled in the printing queue. While "clicking around," you explore the monitor application, discovering that the queue is "turned off" or possibly "wedged." (The actual description for "turned off" varies from system to system.) Though machines are different, the situation is the same: The computer's settings tell it to queue your converted files rather than print them immediately. How it got into this state you may never know. The best approach is to cancel or trash all of the jobs in the queue, because there are probably many duplicates, and restart the queue. That is, configure the printer so that it tries to print your files immediately rather than queuing them. Your printing problem may be solved! Or have you forgotten to reconnect the cable to your printer?

6.6 No Response. Another possibility when discovering the print queue with a long list of files is not that it has accidentally been turned off, but that the monitor reports the printer is not responding. What should you do then?

Calling Tech Support?

Summarizing the situation, you boldly tried debugging the printing operation in spite of the fact that it's complicated and you know almost nothing about how computers print. You correctly assumed that the software is okay. You discovered that computers use a print queue, though it's a mystery why. The queue can stop or stall, but by using the print monitor you can restart it. Locating the problem involved the standard debugging strategy applied with courage and common sense, and the results were successful. Obviously, there are many problems that are not solved using this approach—those that actually require some technical knowledge—but you should always assume that the standard debugging strategy will work. When you've applied it without complete success, is it time to call tech support.

Sleep on It. Professionals know that when they can't find a bug, it's time to take a break. Whether our minds continue to work on the problem subconsciously or that returning refreshed to the problem clears our thinking, briefly getting away from the problem helps.

Ensuring the Reliability of Software

Anyone who uses computers regularly knows that software contains bugs, and that even catastrophic errors—crashes—occur occasionally. Most of these errors are just an annoyance. But computers control life-support systems and other medical apparatus, airplanes, nuclear power plants, weapons systems, and so on. Errors in these systems are potentially much more serious—"crash" is not a metaphor. How do we know the software running safety-critical systems is perfect? We don't! It's a sobering thought.

Safety-Critical Applications

Any system, whether mechanical or electronic, that supports life or controls hazardous devices or materials should work flawlessly. Accepting anything less seems reckless. But it is easier to say that we want perfection than it is to achieve it.

Hardware Failures. To understand the issues, we need to distinguish first between hardware failures and software failures. In general, hardware failures can be resolved using techniques such as **redundancy**. For example, three computers can perform all the computations of a safety-critical system and make decisions based on majority vote. If a failure in one computer causes it to come up with a different answer, the other two overrule it. The chance that the identical error would happen in each computer simultaneously is infinitesimally small. Another technique, dubbed *burn in*, exploits the so-called "infant mortality" property of computer hardware failures caused by manufacturing problems: Most errors show up after only a few hours of operation. A computer that has a record of successful operation is likely to continue to operate successfully. Overall, such techniques give us reasonable confidence that the hardware will work properly.

Software Failures. Software is another matter. Compared with mechanical and electronic systems, software is amazingly complex. The number of possible configurations that a typical program can define grows exponentially and quickly becomes unimaginably large even for small programs. All states that the software can get into, known as **reachable configurations**, cannot be examined for their correctness. This reality poses a serious problem for programmers and software engineers: How can they be sure their programs work correctly?

Like all engineers, programmers begin with a **specification**—a precise description of the input, how the system should behave, what the output should be. The specification doesn't say how the behavior is to be achieved necessarily, just what it should be. Using various design methods, programmers produce the program. The program can be tested with sample inputs, and the outputs can be checked against the specification. If they do not match, there is a bug and the program must be fixed. *A program is said to be correct if its behavior exactly matches its specification.*

Though we have a tidy definition for correctness, there are two problems to achieving it, and both are showstoppers. First, it is not possible to know if the specification is perfect. Second, even if it were, it is not possible to establish correctness by testing. These two facts mean that we cannot *know* whether a program is correct, even if it is. Programmers and software engineers have developed many ingenious tools and technologies, including testing, to locate bugs and improve software. These can and do give us confidence that the program closely approximates its specification. But confidence, not certainty, is the best we can do.

Hard Fact of Software. Programming pioneer Edsger Dijkstra first stated this fundamental fact: Program testing reveals only the presence of bugs, never their absence.

The Challenge. What can we do about the fact that we can't prove that the software we use is correct? There are two aspects to consider.

- We must accept that software may contain bugs despite Herculean efforts of programmers and software engineers to get it right. So, we must monitor our software usage, be alert to unusual behavior that can indicate bugs, and be prepared to limit the harm that they can do.
- Because programmers and software engineers are aware of the challenge to produce correct software, poorly tested software is simply unprofessional; users should demand high-quality software, refuse buggy software, and be prepared to change to better software.

Thus, we must be cautious and informed users and take our business to those who produce the best product.

Fail-Soft and Fail-Safe Software

Returning to the problem of software that controls safety-critical systems, what should the standard of quality be? The software may be perfectly correct, but we can't be sure. We *can* limit the harm that may result from using imperfect software. If we know that software is safe—that the life-support system does not cause patients to die, and the nuclear power plant software will not cause a meltdown—then perhaps we are less concerned about bugs. The idea of **safe software** changes the focus from worry about program correctness to concern about the consequences of errors in the software.

Testing and other techniques can give us confidence that software works "under normal circumstances," so safety focuses on what happens in unusual circumstances. It is difficult to test software under unusual circumstances, as when an earthquake damages a nuclear power plant. So, there are two design strategies: fail-soft and fail-safe. **Fail-soft** means that the program continues to operate, providing a possibly degraded level of functionality. **Fail-safe** means that the system stops functioning to avoid causing harm. The basic strategy, therefore, is to continue to operate as long as productive service is safely provided, but when that isn't possible, to avoid negative outcomes by stopping entirely.

Perfectly safe software is just as impossible as correct software, since the only way for the software to avoid all harm is not to do anything at all—not even start the nuclear power plant. Using software to control potentially dangerous systems means taking a risk, just like crossing a bridge or riding an elevator.

Community Debugging

It may happen at some point that no matter how hard you have tried, you can't find the bug. You've followed the debugging guidelines thoroughly, you've "slept on it," and still the bug resists discovery. There is still one more possibility depending on what the problem is.

If the bug involves "publicly available software"—either a system or a characteristic of a generally available language—then someone else has probably found the problem before you. There are hundreds of chat sites where exasperated people post their problems, and other community-minded people offer help. If your problem has surfaced before, then a simple Web search should locate a place where the solution is discussed. Sometimes—as with the Web Console—these can get a little technical, but like the Web Console, it's not necessary to understand everything that's being said for it to be useful to you.

Unfortunately, none of the problems of this chapter, the https problem, the HTML of the JJK page, or the printer problem, qualifies as generally available software failing or an obscure language feature. For the JJK page, our problems were simple mistakes of our own sloppy typing. But, asking the community is a good tactic to keep in mind.

SUMMARY

This chapter began by emphasizing why being precise is important when using computers. The standard of precision is higher than in most other situations, so being careful and exact makes using computers easier. We learned the following:

- What debugging is and why we need to know how to do it.
- Basic debugging strategy, including the whys and hows of debugging.
- To debug a Web page, using the Error Console of the document that shows how the computer interprets the HTML.
- How to analyze our debugging performance, noting that debugging involves both correct and incorrect conjectures.
- That it's possible to debug a sophisticated system like a computer printer with little more than a vague idea of how it works, by using our standard debugging strategy applied with common sense and courage.
- That it is practically impossible to have bug-free software. This doesn't mean that we must quit using computers or accept bugs, but we must watch for unusual behavior that might indicate bugs and take precautions to limit the harm that they can cause.

TRY IT SOLUTIONS

6.1 These answers are illustrations; there are several similarities and differences between each pair of figures.

	Similar	**Different**
6.3–6.4	Both pages are indented from the left edge	Image caption in small font vs. caption in large font
6.4–6.5	Both pages use the same main figure	Text is all brown vs. text with yellow sentences
6.5–6.6	Both pages give the same text	The table has a border vs. no border
6.6–6.7	Both pages use the same colors for the different events	The pages have different spacing

6.2 In addition to (1) the text being colored wrong, (2) an image is missing, (3) there is no line around the main image, (4) the image caption is in a large font, (5) the table has no lines, (6) the table has no background color in the cells, and (7) the table caption should be at the bottom of the table.

6.3 `<img src="pic/jjkKindGrace.jpg"` . . . everything following is unchanged.

6.4 `img {padding:6px;` . . . everything following is unchanged.

6.5 Change the end tag from `</spam>` to `</span>`.

6.6 The printer's software seems to be "wedged," so cycling the power for the printer—turning it off for five seconds and then turning it back on—is the best response.

REVIEW QUESTIONS

Multiple Choice

1. The first step in the debugging process is to
   a. check for obvious errors
   b. reproduce the problem
   c. isolate the problem
   d. determine the exact problem
2. Computers do exactly the same thing every time when given the same input. What is this property called?
   a. fail-safe
   b. correct
   c. deterministic
   d. reproducible
3. Most software
   a. contains bugs
   b. is bug free
   c. contains no known bugs
   d. works exactly as it should all the time
4. When using computers, what is the most common source of problems?
   a. hardware failures
   b. human error
   c. Internet outages
   d. software failures
5. What does the "s" stand for in `https`?
   a. secure
   b. site
   c. safe
   d. standard
6. When testing, it is never possible to establish the ________ of a program.
   a. output
   b. run time
   c. correctness
   d. author

7. Not only is the computer unable to _______ itself, we can't _______ it directly, either.
    a. power
    b. create
    c. correct
    d. debug
8. What built-in tool in most browsers can help you debug a Web page?
    a. validator
    b. error console
    c. error tracker
    d. bookmark
9. How do we know the software running safety-critical systems is perfect?
    a. by using the debugging process
    b. by using a special kind of software to test it
    c. by letting users try the software before it is released
    d. we can't

Short Answer

1. You should expect _______ when interacting with software.
2. An alternative approach to get around a problem is called a(n) _______.
3. A(n) _______ program continues to operate when there is a problem, although its efficiency may be degraded.
4. A(n) _______ program shuts down to avoid causing problems.
5. Computers don't understand what we _______, only what we _______.
6. Bugs in commercial software are usually fixed _______.
7. Computers are _______, which means that they will do exactly the same thing every time if given the same input.
8. _______ is the most obvious HTML error.
9. Errors in HTML code are generally not tough to _______, just tough to _______.
10. Program testing reveals only the _______ of bugs, never their _______.

Exercises

1. Explain in detail why error messages produced by a computer do not usually explain exactly what the problem is.
2. Use debugging strategies that you have been using since grade school to check the math on this problem (* means multiplication)

    $N = -((12 + 6) - 7 * 4 + ((9 - 2) * 3)/7)$
    $N = 18 - 7 * 4 + 7 * 3/7$
    $N = 11 * 4 + 21/7$
    $N = 44 + 25/7$
    $N = 49/7$
    $N = 7$

3. Design several workarounds for the computer printing error. Pretend it's your term paper and it has to be printed. How would you get around the problem that the computer and the printer aren't printing?

4. Describe a time when you "debugged" something in your life (it doesn't need to relate to computers).
5. Suppose your friend's personal music player (such as an iPod) isn't playing any songs. Explain the process you would go through to debug the problem. List at least eight questions you would ask, and explain how each applies to the debugging guidelines.
6. Explain the differences between fail-soft and fail-safe.
7. Why is debugging a better approach than aimlessly "trying stuff"?
8. List five questions you should ask yourself while debugging.
9. Why do programmers never say they are "down to the very last bug"? Provide a concrete example that illustrates this using HTML (your example should be your own, and not come directly from this book).
10. Explain in detail three things you can try if you have followed the debugging process and are still unable to fix the problem.

INTERVIEW

with

Vinton G. Cerf

Vinton G. Cerf is vice president and chief Internet evangelist at Google. Widely known as one of the "Fathers of the Internet," Cerf is the co-designer of the TCP/IP protocols and the architecture of the Internet. With his colleague Robert Kahn, Cerf received the U.S. National Medal of Technology in 1997 for co-founding and developing the Internet. In 1994 and 1998 respectively, Kahn and Cerf were honored as Marconi Fellows. They received the ACM Alan M. Turing award in 2004 for their work on the Internet protocols. In November 2005 they received the Presidential Medal of Freedom. In 2008 they received the Japan Prize.

Vint Cerf served as chairman of the board of the Internet Corporation for Assigned Names and Numbers (ICANN) from 2000–2007 and is a Fellow of the IEEE, ACM (and its current president), American Association for the Advancement of Science, the American Academy of Arts and Sciences, the American Philosophical Society, the International Engineering Consortium, and the Computer History Museum. He is a member of the National Academy of Engineering.

Cerf holds a Bachelor of Science degree in Mathematics from Stanford University and Master of Science and Ph.D. degrees in Computer Science from UCLA. He also holds honorary Doctorate degrees from 18 universities.

How did you get started in all of this?

My interest in computing was piqued by a visit arranged by my father to System Development Corporation in 1958 where the Semi-Automated Ground Environment (SAGE) system was housed. This was a tube-based computing system developed by the RAND Corporation and spun out as System Development Corporation in 1957 to program and operate for the U.S. Air Force. I was fascinated by the idea that radar information from the Distant Early Warning system located in northern Canada could be transmitted electronically to the SAGE system and analyzed to detect Russian bombers coming over the North Pole. I was 15 at the time.

In 1968, the U.S. Defense Advanced Research Projects Agency (then called ARPA, now DARPA) released a Request for Quotation for an Interface Message Processor (IMP) with which to implement the ARPANET. Professor Leonard Kleinrock [at UCLA] concurrently proposed to create and operate a Network Measurement Center that would be used to compare measured performance of the ARPANET with the queuing theoretic models that Kleinrock and his students were developing. I became the principal programmer for that effort. In the meantime, Stephen Crocker became the head of the Network Working Group (NWG) that included graduate students from at least a dozen universities whose computer science departments were supported by ARPA. Crocker led the effort to create the protocols used to allow host computers on the ARPANET to communicate with one another, despite the wide variations in computer hardware and operating systems that existed at that time. I participated with others in this work.

During the time I worked on the Network Measurement Center, Robert Kahn, a senior member of the staff at Bolt, Beranek and Newman (BBN, the maker of the IMP) and one of his colleagues, David Walden, came to visit UCLA after the first IMPs were installed at UCLA, Stanford Research Institute (SRI), University of California at Santa Barbara, and University of Utah. This four-node network formed the nascent ARPANET.

By the fall of 1973, we had developed an architecture and protocol (Transmission Control Protocol or TCP) that would form the basis of the Internet design. The Institute of Electrical and Electronic Engineering (IEEE) published our paper in May 1974. By December of 1974, my students and I had fleshed out the details of the TCP design and we began experimental implementations in 1975, working with BBN and University College London. These implementations demonstrated various flaws and the protocol continued to evolve, finally being split into the basic Internet Protocol (IP) and a revised version of the TCP. The suite of protocols that grew up around these basic components became known as the TCP/IP protocol suite.

The actual roll out of the Internet occurred on January 1, 1983, when all the hosts on the ARPANET were converted to run only TCP/IP protocols.

Did you imagine that the Internet protocol would become as pervasive as it is today when you first designed the protocol?

At the time that Bob Kahn and I were working on open networking in 1973, our research community had had several years of experience with the ARPANET, its host-to-host protocol (NCP for Network Control Program), and several application protocols including file transfer protocol (FTP), telecommunications network protocol (TELNET), and electronic mail protocol (eventually the Simple Mail Transport Protocol or SMTP). TELNET was in use to allow remote access to any time-sharing system on the ARPANET. Files were exchanged using FTP, and networked email, which had been invented by Ray Tomlinson at BBN and elaborated upon by several of the NWG participants, was in use.

I don't think I fully appreciated what would happen when nearly 2 billion people got online and the World Wide Web (WWW) application became a dominant force. The latter was invented in 1989 by Tim Berners-Lee and Robert Cailliau at the European Particle Physics Laboratory CERN, and spread rapidly after the first commercial browser, Netscape Navigator, was developed by Marc Andreessen, who had worked with his colleague, Eric Bina, at the National Center for Supercomputer Applications (NCSA) on an earlier graphical WWW browser they called Mosaic. The availability of commercial Internet service did not emerge until 1989, and personal computers were around only since about 1984.

And what do you now envision for the future of the Internet?

It is clear that an increasing amount of access to the Internet will take place by way of mobile systems. Many sensor networks will be connected to the Net as will appliances around the house, the office, in the car, and things we carry with us. Higher speed access will enable increasing amounts of audio, video, and interactive applications, including a considerable amount of collaborative entertainment games as well as scientific and business collaboration with online instruments and shared documents (word processing, spreadsheets, presentations, etc.). More scientific instruments (telescopes, electron microscopes, spectrometers, particle accelerators, and so on) will be placed online, allowing for rapid access to scientific data. Increasing fractions of published material will be available and searchable online, and retrospective digitization will make much of the world's information discoverable in fractions of a second. Translation of written languages is improving, making ever-more information accessible. Spoken interactions with Internet applications are also improving with time. Perhaps some day we will be able to have conversations with Internet-based systems that will help us find what we need. One can readily anticipate that more transactions of all kinds will take place online. There is already strong evidence that social networking is creating new forms of personal interactions in the general population.

What challenges do you face?

At Google, the biggest challenges have to do with keeping up with the rapid influx of information in the World Wide Web, the increasing demand for streaming audio and video applications, the increasing use of collaborative interactions, and the need for language translation. Capturing all the world's written material and indexing it to make it discoverable is a daily challenge. The basic Internet design, now about 36 years old, needs further adaptation for meeting the demand for increased numbers of devices on the Net. A new version of the Internet Protocol, version 6 (IPv6), must be deployed before the present version (IPv4) runs out of unique address space. There are many vulnerabilities in the system (especially the hosts at the edges of the Internet) that must be remedied. Privacy is a major concern and new techniques are needed to insure it.

Do you have any advice for students studying IT?

Information technology continues to thrive as a field in which new ideas can still be transformative. Just a brief look at the last 15 years illustrates the point. During that time we have seen the rise of Yahoo!, Google, eBay, Amazon, Skype, YouTube, Facebook, MySpace, and a host of other new companies whose founders have taken ideas and turned them into reality through the magic of networked software. The network has no limits—it is an endless software frontier. If you can imagine it, you can program it and make it accessible on the network.

What do you think about an Interplanetary Internet?

In 1998, I met with a small group of engineers from the Jet Propulsion Laboratory hosted by the California Institute of Technology. We began to explore what might be needed in the way of networked communication resources if manned and robotic exploration of the solar system continued to accelerate. We asked ourselves what might the solar system be like in 100 years, by which time perhaps some forms of colonization or at least persistently manned laboratories might be found on the surface of planets or their moons, or in orbit around them. We concluded that it would be useful to design a set of protocols that could operate across the solar systems with the same degree of interoperability that the terrestrial Internet provides. We quickly discovered that the traditional TCP/IP protocol suite would not work well at interplanetary distances, and that disruption of communication caused by normal celestial motion or by solar storms or even local mobility (like the rovers on Mars) dictated a new design. We developed something we called the Bundle Protocol, which is the interplanetary equivalent of the Earth's Internet Protocol.

PART 2

Algorithms and Digitizing Information

CHAPTER

PART 2

INTRODUCTION

BEING SKILLED with information technology, you are prepared to learn a few of the underlying concepts that make computing possible. Like black holes in astronomy or natural selection in ecology, the underlying scientific phenomena are interesting. The difference is, computing concepts have direct applicability to your daily life.

In Part 2 you will learn how information is represented—from basic bits, through sound and video, to virtual reality. We explain what a transistor is, and how a few million of them can process information. And we introduce the fundamental idea of an algorithm, although you've already encountered several in Part 1. By the end of Part 2 you will have an intuitive understanding of what's happening inside a computer and how it stores information. If I've been successful, the mystery of computing—how a chunk of silicon can do all of the things we expect—should be gone.

CHAPTER 7

Representing Information Digitally

Bits and the "Why" of Bytes

learning objectives

- Explain the link between patterns, symbols, and information
- Determine possible PandA encodings using a physical phenomenon
- Encode and decode ASCII
- Represent numbers in binary form
- Compare different encoding methods
- Explain how structure tags (metadata) encode the *Oxford English Dictionary*

CHAPTER 7

Most of the fundamental ideas of science are essentially simple and may as a rule be expressed in a language comprehensible to everyone.

—ALBERT EINSTEIN

Omnibus ex nihilo ducendis sufficit unum. (*To create everything from nothing, one is sufficient.*)

— GOTTFRIED WILHELM VON LEIBNIZ

MOST PEOPLE know that computers and networks record and transmit information in *bits* and *bytes*. From basic English, you can guess that bits probably represent little pieces of information. But what are bytes? And why is "byte" spelled with a *y*? In this chapter we confirm that bits do represent little pieces of information, we define bytes, and, by the end, we explain the mysterious *y*. But the chapter is much more fundamental than these basic concepts. It describes how bits and bytes—the atoms and molecules of information—combine to form our virtual world of computation, information, and communication. (Multimedia is covered in Chapter 8.) We even explain how information exists when there is nothing, as when Sherlock Holmes solves the mystery using the information that "the dog didn't bark in the night."

The first goal of this chapter is to establish that digitizing doesn't require digits—any set of symbols will do. You will learn how pattern sequences can create symbols, and discover that symbols can represent information. The next goal is to learn the fundamental patterns on which all information technology is built: the presence and absence of a phenomenon. Called the PandA encoding here, this meeting of the physical and logical worlds forms the foundation of information technology. We then define bits, bytes, ASCII and binary numbers. Finally, we describe the digitization of the *Oxford English Dictionary* to show how metadata is added to content so computers can help us use it.

Digitizing Discrete Information

The dictionary definition of *digitize* is to represent information with digits. In normal conversation, *digit* means the ten Arabic numerals 0 through 9. Thus, digitizing uses whole numbers to stand for things. This familiar process represents Americans by Social Security numbers, telephone accounts by phone numbers, and books by ISBN numbers. Such digital representations have probably been used since numerals were invented. But this sense of *digitize* is much too narrow for the digital world of computing.

Digital Man. The first person to apply the term *digital* to computers was George Stibitz, a Bell Labs mathematician. While consulting for the U.S. military, he observed that "pulsed" computing devices would be better described as digital because they represent information in discrete (that is, separate) units.

Limitation of Digits

A limitation of the dictionary definition of *digitize* is that it calls for the use of the ten digits, which produces a whole number. But in most cases the property of being numeric is unimportant and of little use. Numbers quantify things and let us do arithmetic, but Social Security numbers, phone numbers, and ISBN numbers are not quantities. Having a larger telephone number does not make you a better person. So, when we don't need numbers, we don't need to use digits. But what else can we use to digitize?

Alternative Representations

Digitizing in computing can use almost any symbols. For example, the North American telephone number 888 555 1212 could be represented as *** %%% !@!@. This encoding, rather than using {1, 2, 3, 4, 5, 6, 7, 8, 9, 0}, uses the symbol set {!, @, #, $, %, ^, &, *, (,)}. These symbols are simply the uppercase digit characters on a U.S. QWERTY keyboard. If we use the symbol set { ▶, ▼, ◀, ⏩, ■, ⏪, ⏭, ▲, ⏮, ⏸ } the phone number is represented as: ▲ ▲ ▲ ■ ■ ■ ▶ ▼ ▶ ▼. This could be called *player encoding* because it uses the standard symbols from music players. These symbols work just as well as the digits as long as the telephone keypad is relabeled, as shown in Figure 7.1. The reason the encoding works is that a phone number's digits simply tell us which sequence of keys to press. Any ten distinct symbols will work as long as the keypad is labeled properly.

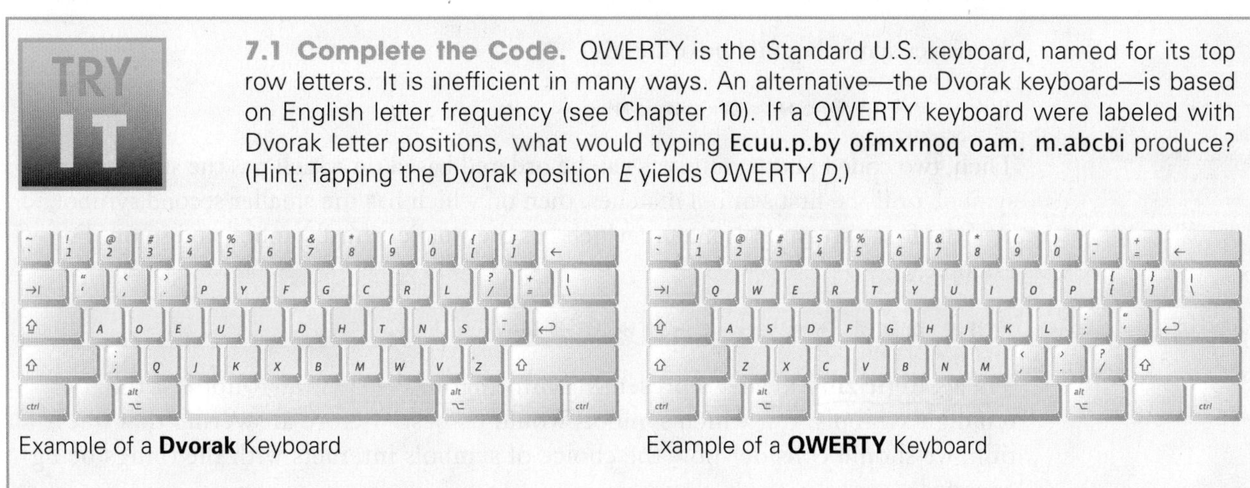

7.1 Complete the Code. QWERTY is the Standard U.S. keyboard, named for its top row letters. It is inefficient in many ways. An alternative—the Dvorak keyboard—is based on English letter frequency (see Chapter 10). If a QWERTY keyboard were labeled with Dvorak letter positions, what would typing **Ecuu.p.by ofmxrnoq oam. m.abcbi** produce? (Hint: Tapping the Dvorak position *E* yields QWERTY *D*.)

Example of a **Dvorak** Keyboard

Example of a **QWERTY** Keyboard

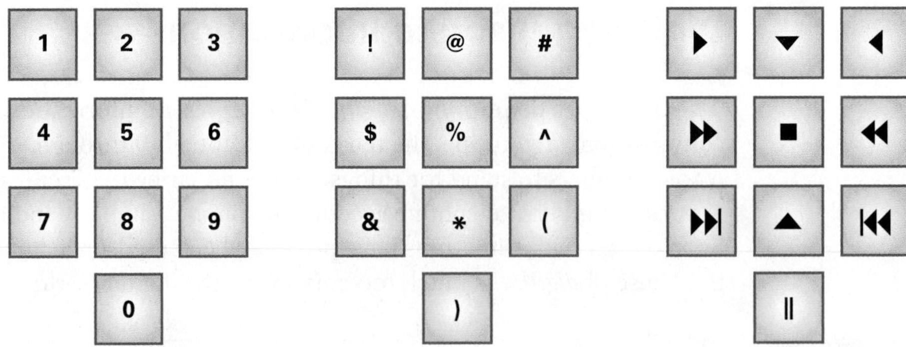

Figure 7.1 Three symbol assignments for a telephone keypad.

Symbols, Briefly

One practical advantage of digits over other less familiar symbols is that digits have short names. Imagine speaking your phone number as "asterisk, asterisk, exclamation point, closing parenthesis, exclamation point . . . " In fact, as IT has adopted these symbols, the names are getting shorter. For example, computer professionals often say exclamation point as *bang* and asterisk as *star*. Instead of saying "eight, eight, eight, five, five, five, one, two, one, two" we could say "star, star, star, per, per, per, bang, at, bang, at," which is just as brief. So, the advantage of brevity is not limited to digits.

Ordering Symbols

Another advantage of digits for encoding information like telephone numbers is that the items can be listed in numerical order. This feature is rarely used for the kinds of information discussed here; for example, telephone books are ordered by the name of the person rather than by the number. But sometimes ordering items is useful.

To place information in order by using symbols (other than digits), we need to agree on an ordering for the basic symbols. This is called a **collating sequence**. In the same way that the digits are ordered

0 < 1 < 2 < 3 < 4 < 5 < 6 < 7 < 8 < 9

the player symbols could be ordered

II < ▶ < ▼ < ◀ < ▶▶ < ■ < ◀◀ < ▶▶| < ▲ < |◀◀

Then, two coded phone numbers can be ordered based on which has the smaller first symbol, or if the first symbol matches, then on which has the smaller second symbol, or if the first two symbols match, which has the smaller third symbol, and so on. For example,

▲ II II ■ ■ ■ ▶ ▼ ▶ ▼ < ▲ ▶▶| ▶▶| ■ ■ ■ ▶ ▼ ▶ ▼

Today, **digitizing** means representing information by symbols—not just the ten digit symbols. But which symbols would be best? Before answering that question, we should consider how the choice of symbols interacts with the things being encoded.

Information Representation

Fundamentally, we acquire information when we observe the presence or absence of a phenomenon. The phenomenon can be anything—light, charge, magnetism, pressure, velocity, color, and on and on. Even steam and bubbles reveal information.

The presence of steam coming from coffee means it is very hot; the absence of steam coming from coffee means it's not very hot. The absence of bubbles in a cola drink means it is "flat" or stale; the presence of bubbles means it is "sparkling," recently opened. The solid form of water is cold; water that is not solid is not "freezing" cold.

We adopt the definition that **information** is *the presence or absence of a phenomenon at a specific place and time*. Often the "place and time" conditions are either understood or unimportant, and so are not always stated.

For example, in Chapter 1 (Figure 1.2) we described how a punch card reader detects the presence or absence of a hole punched in a paper card. It is reading information that was stored in the form of punched (present) or unpunched (absent) positions on the card.

The definition is specialized to *digital* information, because we separate our observations into just two cases: present or absent. So, steam conveys that the coffee is very hot (present) or not very hot (absent). If there is no steam the drink may have cooled only enough to be "drinkable," or it may have cooled to room temperature; the absence of steam will not tell us. The range of temperature possibilities that a drink might have illustrates **analog** information, which is covered in Chapter 8.

This **PandA** definition—mnemonic for presence and absence—describes information that is "black" or "white." The coffee is either steaming, meaning it is very hot, or it is not steaming, and is not very hot. There is no in-between "warm" option. This means that in the process of observing the phenomenon, we must definitely decide if it's present or absent. "Not steaming very much" is not a choice. It is, or it isn't.

No Barking. With digital information, presence and absence are equally important. Sherlock Holmes uses the absence of a phenomenon to solve the disappearance of a prize racehorse in the story "Silver Blaze." In the vicinity of the stable during the night (place and time), the phenomenon (barking watchdog) was not detected (absent), implying to Holmes the dog knew the thief, who had to be Simpson, the owner. Holmes reasons that barking "present" implies the thief is not known to the household; barking "absent" implies the opposite. There is information even though the phenomenon is absent.

The PandA Problem

Table 7.1 Possible interpretations of the two PandA alternatives

Present	Absent
True	False
1	0
On	Off
Yes	No
+	–
Black	White
For	Against
. . .	. . .

A **bit** is the information produced in one PandA observation. Noting whether steam is coming from a cup of coffee yields one bit, which will mean either "very hot" or "not very hot" in that case. The two possible alternatives make PandA observations a **binary** system.

7.2 Specific Information. North Atlantic lobsters have green-brown shells when alive. Specify the bit of information for "lobster cooked."

Though we often name bits by their direct meaning (see Table 7.1), we mostly find it too cumbersome to say "present" or "absent" or "very hot" or "not very hot." So, we name the two alternative outcomes "0" and "1". Which is which? It doesn't matter as long as we're consistent. They only name the two options. (It is common for 1 to be "present" and 0 to be "absent," but there is no law requiring it.)

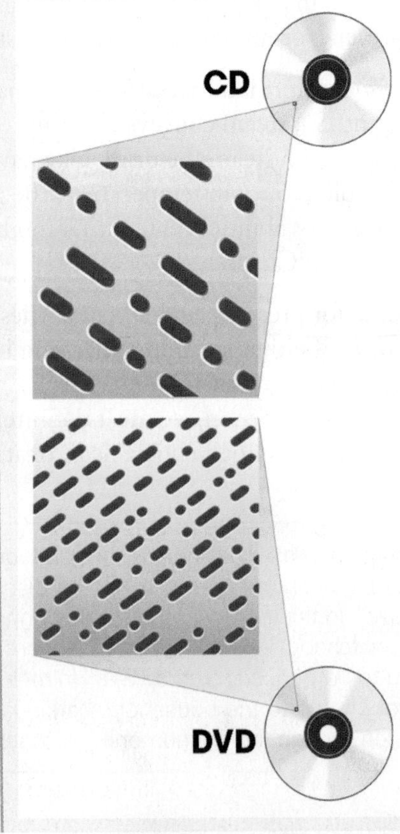

Encoding Bits on a DVD. The Digital Versatile Disc (DVD) is a familiar digital storage technology for music and video, and the successor to the compact disc (CD). Developed by Philips, Sony, Toshiba, and Panasonic in 1995, DVDs use the same concepts as CDs, but they pack the bits closer together. Here's how they work.

DVDs are made of clear plastic that is forced into a round mold, something like a round waffle maker, having a smooth bottom and a bumpy top. When the plastic hardens and is removed from the mold, the topside bumpy pattern is covered with aluminum to make it shiny. A protective layer is put over the aluminum and the "label" is printed on the top.

The bumps encode the information. Because they are read from the bottom of the DVD, the bumps are called *pits*. The regions between the pits are called *lands*. A laser beam is focused up through the plastic onto the land surface. The beam reflects off of the aluminum and back to a sensor that detects whether the beam is striking a land (clean signal comes back), or a pit (laser light is scattered), or is changing between them. The change signals a 1 bit.

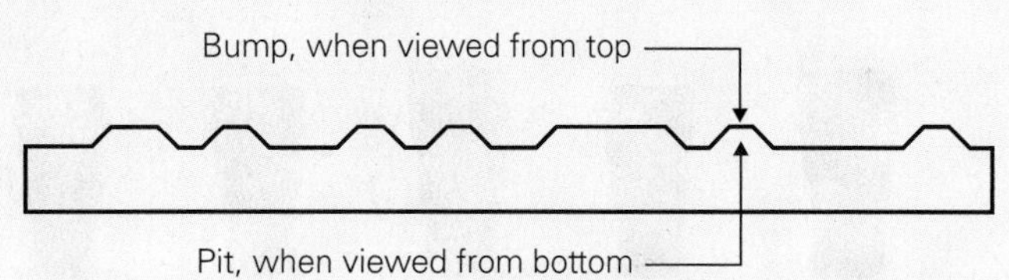

The pits are arranged in a line that begins at the *inner* edge of the DVD and spirals out to the *outer* edge. (Notice that this inside-out layout is the opposite of how vinyl records are arranged.)

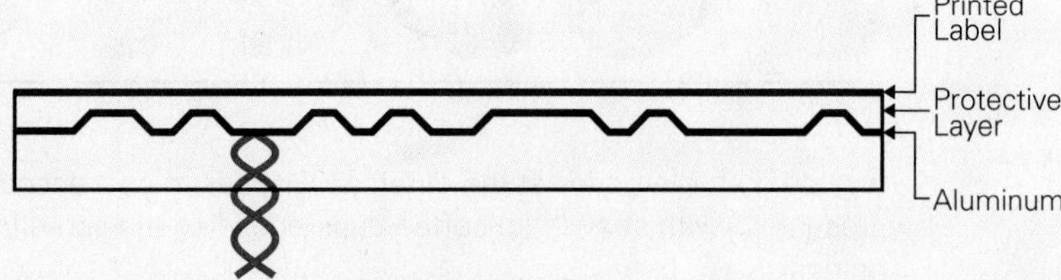

The DVD improves on the CD, and the numbers tell the whole story. Basically, the pits are smaller and the spacing between tracks is smaller. Other technical changes make DVDs more durable to scratches and fingerprints. And, of course, Blu-ray is the next step in applying this optical-reader technology.

Property	CD	DVD	Blu-ray
Smallest pit	0.83 μ	0.4 μ	0.32 μ
Track separation	1.6 μ	0.74 μ	0.32 μ
Capacity	0.65 GB	4.7 GB	25 GB
Data rate	1.2 Mb/s	10.8 Mb/s	36.5 Mb/s

Beyond the Physical World

In the logical world of thinking and reasoning, the concepts of true and false are important. Propositions such as "If the year is evenly divisible by 4, then it is a leap year" can be expressed and combined with other propositions such as "2016 is evenly divisible by 4" to draw conclusions such as "2016 is a leap year." Logic is the foundation of reasoning and thinking, and naturally, the foundation of computing.

The abstract concepts of "true" and "false" as used in logic can be associated with presence and absence of a phenomenon. This makes it possible to build computers based on digital information, and use the physical world to implement the logical world.

Memory

We all know memory is composed of bits, but what does that mean? Recalling that a bit embodies the information observed about a phenomenon (present or absent) at a specific place and time, we correctly assume memory is composed of some such observable phenomenon. In addition to the "bit" definition, memory requires the ability to *set* the phenomenon to be either *present* or *absent*.

For example, suppose we are at a diner watching people walk by outside. We can keep track of which direction they pass by placing straws in glasses. The phenomenon will be "glass with straw," and *present* will mean a pedestrian walking right. Because we can insert or remove a straw, we can set the phenomenon to remember whichever direction

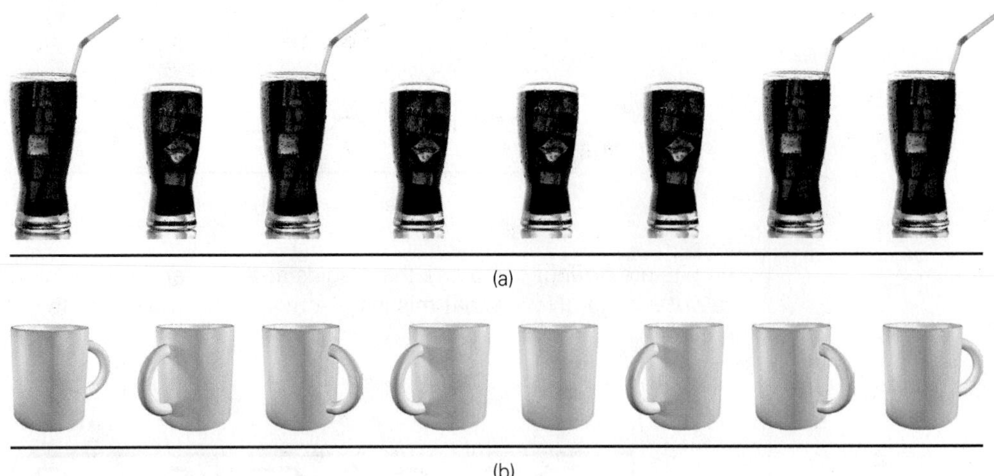

Figure 7.2 Memories at the diner. (a) Glasses of cola encoding the history of passersby: present = "with straw"; (b) coffee cups encoding the same information: present = "handle on right."

is needed, so this is a memory. Figure 7.2(a) records that the first, third, seventh, and eighth person to walk by were going right. The others were not going right. Notice that the "place" part of the definition matters in this case.

Figure 7.2(b) records the same information with coffee mugs. Present is "handle on right," which we associate with walking to the right. Notice that this is NOT the same as saying "the handle shows the direction of the passerby." This is because cup five doesn't have its handle visible. When the phenomenon is "handle on right" everything works out, because no visible handle just means absent. The person passing wasn't going right. The point: the cups are memory bits, which we interpret as recording the direction of passage. They don't *directly* record the direction.

Positive Presence. The use of physical phenomena to represent information sometimes poses problems because there might be more than two alternatives. For example, a magnetic material might not be magnetized at all, or it can have positive polarity or negative polarity; that is, there are three possibilities. In such situations, engineers adopt one state such as positive polarity to mean "present" and all other states to mean "absent."

7.3 Bits of Orange. The sequence of glasses below records information in several different ways. Assuming that present represents 1, identify what the phenomenon is to represent these binary sequences: (a) 101101011, (b) 000001011, and (c) 100110101.

Table 7.2 Number of symbols possible from *n* bits in sequence

n	2^n	Symbols
1	2^1	2
2	2^2	4
3	2^3	8
4	2^4	16
5	2^5	32
6	2^6	64
7	2^7	128
8	2^8	256
9	2^9	512
10	2^{10}	1,024

Bits in Computer Memory

Memory is arranged inside a computer as a very long sequence of bits. That is, places where the physical phenomenon encoding the information can be set and detected. For example, if the memory is implemented with a long sequence of transistors, which can be separately charged or discharged, then the phenomenon can be "transistor charged." Both states can be set, allowing any information to be encoded.

Combining Bit Patterns. Single bits are a limited resource for representing information. That is, we can represent things with only two values: votes (*aye*, *nay*), personality types (*A*, *B*), baseball games (*won*, *loss*). To encode the alphabet, for example, we need groups of bits to create enough symbols so that there is one for each letter. When bits are arranged into *n*-length sequences, we create 2^n symbols. Table 7.2 relates the length of the bit sequence to the number of possible symbols.

For example, to represent the four bases of DNA—adenine (A), guanine (G), cytosine (C), and thymine (T)—we need four symbols; $4 = 2^2$, so, two bits. The symbols are: 00, 01, 10, and 11. We can assign the symbols to the bases however we wish. But, if we assign them as A = 00, G = 01, C = 10, and T = 11, then each base pairs with its complement (00, 11 and 01,10); that is, it pairs with the base with its bits "flipped."

Binary and Hex

Because 0 and 1 are available, it makes better sense for computers to represent numbers in base 2, that is, the **binary number system**, than to use bits to represent decimal digits. Some early computers tried decimal, but it was slow and cumbersome.

Binary

So, computers count in binary, which means it must be pretty easy. As Table 7.3 shows, counting in binary is like counting in decimal, except limiting yourself to using just 0 and 1. Obviously, 0 in binary is 0 in decimal, and 1 in binary is 1 in decimal. So, counting in binary from 0 we have

0, 1, 10, 11, 100, 101, 110, 111, 1000 . . .

Table 7.3 Sixteen symbols of the 4-bit PandA representation.

Decimal	PandA	Binary	Hex
0		0000	0
1		0001	1
2		0010	2
3		0011	3
4		0100	4
5		0101	5
6		0110	6
7		0111	7
8		1000	8
9		1001	9
10		1010	A
11		1011	B
12		1100	C
13		1101	D
14		1110	E
15		1111	F

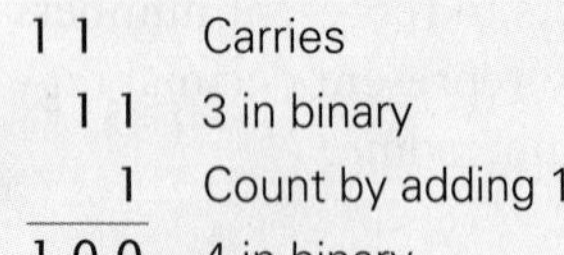

by simply adding 1 at the rightmost bit position. The rule is: Adding 1 to a 0-bit position makes it 1; adding 1 to a 1-bit position makes it 0, and carries 1 to the next higher (left) position, where the rule is applied again. This makes sense if we check the PandA column, where empty is 0 and filled is 1.

7.4 Count One More. If your new computer thinks it is 100111 days old, how old will it be tomorrow?

Hex

While we're learning to count in strange numbering systems, let's take a moment to learn base 16, or the **hexadecimal numbering system**. "Hex," as it's known, is important because of its close relationship to binary, which we explain below.

As a base 16 numbering system, hex has 16 numerals, which it gets by first sharing the decimal digits, and then using the first six Latin letters. So the digits—they should probably be called *hexits*—are:

0, 1, 2, 3, 4, 5, 6, 7, 8, 9, A, B, C, D, E, F

1 1	Carries
F F	255 in hex
1	Count by adding 1
1 0 0	256 in hex

The rule for counting in hex is basically the same as decimal and binary. The carry only applies for F: adding 1 to F gives a 0 in the hex position, and a carry of 1 to the next higher (left) hex position. As the illustration at left shows, hex is much more economical in terms of the number of digits needed for a given number than is binary.

Changing Hex Digits to Bits and Back Again

Although computers have no problem with binary, one problem humans have is that it is difficult to write down or remember long sequences of bits. For example, these 32 bits are a computer instruction

1000 1110 1101 1000 1010 0011 1010 0000

It's possible to write them down accurately, but doing so takes a lot of care and checking to be positively sure that they're right. (Remember, computers don't like mistakes!) It's hexadecimal that saves our sanity.

As you can see in Table 7.3, every four-bit binary sequence corresponds to some hexadecimal numeral. This perfect match allows us to translate back and forth between groups of four bits and hex digits. So, thinking of the binary sequences above as groups of four-bit sequences, we can convert each to hex, resulting in

8E D8 A3 A0

The hex digit 8, for example, corresponds to binary 1000, and E corresponds to binary 1110; the remaining bits are related in the same way.

7.5 Casting a Hex. Convert the hex F00D 4 A BEE to binary using substitutions from Table 7.3. Going the other way, decode this binary 0000 1111 1111 0010 1010 1101 1000 into hex.

Digitizing Numbers in Binary

The two earliest uses of the PandA representation—or binary representation—were to encode numbers and keyboard characters. These two applications are still extremely important, but now representations for sound, images, video, and other types of information are almost as important. In this section we talk about how numbers are encoded as binary; in the next section we introduce how text is represented. We'll discuss how the other forms of information are encoded in Chapter 8.

Binary Numbers Compared with Decimal Numbers

Binary numbers are different from decimal numbers by being limited to two digits rather than the customary ten digits. The number of digits—the **base** of the numbering system—is really the only difference. The other features distinguishing binary from decimal relate to that one difference.

The Beauty of Binary. Gottfried Wilhelm von Leibniz (1646–1716) was a famous German mathematician who, independent of Newton, invented calculus. In 1679 he wrote, *Despite its length, the binary system, in other words counting with 0 and 1, is scientifically the most fundamental system, and leads to new discoveries. When numbers are reduced to 0 and 1, a beautiful order prevails everywhere.*

For example, in decimal numbers, we use a **place value** representation, where each "place" represents the next higher power of 10, starting from the right. In binary, it's the same idea, but with higher powers of 2.

Place Value in a Decimal Number. Recall that to find the quantity expressed by a decimal number, the digit in a place is multiplied by the place value and the results are added. For example, in Table 7.4, the result is one thousand ten, found by adding from right to left: the digit in the 1's place (0) multiplied by its place value (1), plus the digit in the 10's place (1) multiplied by its place value (10), and so on: $0 \times 1 + 1 \times 10 + 0 \times 100 + 1 \times 1000$.

Place Value in a Binary Number. Binary works in exactly the same way except that the base of the power is not 10 but 2, because there are only two digits, not ten. Therefore, instead of the decimal place values, 1, 10, 100, 1000, . . . , resulting from the successive powers of 10, the binary place values are 1, 2, 4, 8, 16, . . . , resulting from the successive powers of 2.

Power	Decimal	Binary
0	$1 = 10^0$	$1 = 2^0$
1	$10 = 10^1$	$2 = 2^1$
2	$100 = 10^2$	$4 = 2^2$
3	$1000 = 10^3$	$8 = 2^3$
4	$10{,}000 = 10^4$	$16 = 2^4$
. . .	. . .	. . .

Table 7.4 The decimal number 1,010 representing one thousand ten =1,000 + 10

10^3	10^2	10^1	10^0	Decimal Place Values
1	0	1	0	Digits of Decimal Number
1×10^3	0×10^2	1×10^1	0×10^0	Multiply place digit by place value
1,000	0	10	0	and add to get a decimal 1,010

Table 7.5 The binary number 1010, representing the decimal number ten = 8 + 2

2^3	2^2	2^1	2^0	Binary Place Values
1	0	1	0	Bits of Binary Number
1×2^3	0×2^2	1×2^1	0×2^0	Multiply place bit by place value
8	0	2	0	and add to get a decimal 10

Thus, if we are given a binary representation, we can find the (decimal equivalent) value if we multiply the digit times the place value and add the results just like we do in decimal. See Table 7.5, which shows that 1010 in binary has the value ten in decimal: $1 \times 8 + 0 \times 4 + 1 \times 2 + 0 \times 1$.

7.6 Counting on Your Fists. According to the joke, humans count with their fingers, which is why we have decimal; computer people count with their fists, which is why we have binary. Assign 0 and 1 to the fists below to make binary six.

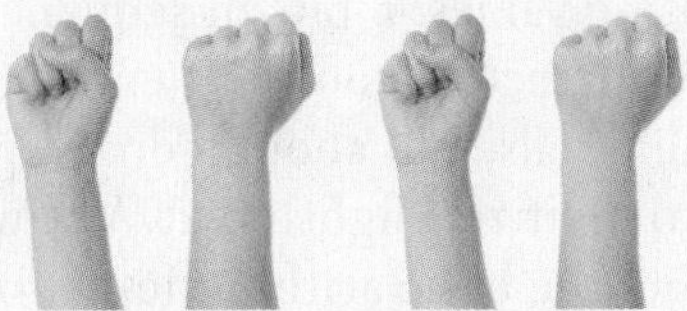

2nd Base. The "base" of a numbering system, 10 for decimal and 2 for binary, is also called its **radix**.

Because powers of 2 don't increase as fast as powers of 10, binary numbers need more places than decimal numbers to represent the same amount. So, for example, representing one thousand ten as a binary number requires ten bits, as shown in Table 7.6. Compare Table 7.6 with Table 7.4.

Converting a Binary Number to a Decimal Number. Because the bit is either a 0 or a 1, the "multiply the digit times the place value" rule is especially easy in binary—a 1 means include the place value and a 0 means "forget it." So, to convert a binary number to its decimal equivalent, just add the place values for the places with 1's. Thus, in Table 7.6, if we start with the highest place value, we have 512 + 256 + 128 + 64 + 32 + 16 + 2 is decimal 1010.

Table 7.6 Binary representation of the decimal number one thousand ten = 11 1111 0010

2^9	2^8	2^7	2^6	2^5	2^4	2^3	2^2	2^1	2^0	Binary Place Values
1	1	1	1	1	1	0	0	1	0	Bits of Binary Number
1×2^9	1×2^8	1×2^7	1×2^6	1×2^5	1×2^4	0×2^3	0×2^2	1×2^1	0×2^0	Multiply place bit by place value
512	256	128	64	32	16	0	0	2	0	and add to get decimal 1,010

Spacing Out. When writing long decimal numbers, North Americans usually separate groups of three digits with a comma for readability. Binary numbers, which are usually even longer, are grouped in four-digit units, separated by a space, as in, "The binary number 11 1111 0010 represents the decimal number 1010." Notice that grouping by fours makes converting to hex (3F2) especially easy.

7.7 Alternating. What decimal number is the binary number 1 0101 0101?

Digitizing Text

Remember that the number of bits determines the number of symbols available for representing values: n bits in sequence yield 2^n symbols. And, as you've learned, the more characters you want encoded, the more symbols you need. Roman letters, Arabic numerals, and about a dozen punctuation characters are about the minimum needed to digitize English text. We would also like to have uppercase and lowercase letters, and the basic arithmetic symbols like +, –, *, /, and = But, where should the line be drawn? Should characters not required for English but useful in other languages, like German (ö), French (é), Spanish (ñ), and Norwegian (ø), be included? What about Czech, Greek, Arabic, Thai, or Cantonese? Should other languages' punctuation be included, like French (« ») and Spanish (¿)? Should arithmetic symbols include degrees (°), pi (π), relational symbols (≤), equivalence (≡), and for all (∀)? What about business symbols: ¢, £, ¥, ©, and ®? What about unprintable characters like backspace and new line? Should there be a symbol for smiley faces (☺)? Some of these questions are easier to answer than others. We want to keep the list small so that we use fewer bits, but not being able to represent critical characters would be a mistake.

Assigning Symbols

The 26 uppercase and 26 lowercase Roman letters, the 10 Arabic numerals, a basic set of 20 punctuation characters (including blank), 10 useful arithmetic characters, and 3 nonprintable characters (new line, tab, and backspace) can be represented with 95 symbols. Such a set is enough for English and is accessible using the keys on a basic "Latin" keyboard. To represent 95 distinct symbols, we need 7 bits because 6 bits gives only $2^6 = 64$ symbols. Seven bits give $2^7 = 128$ symbols, which is more than we need for the 95 different characters. Some special control characters, used for data transmission and other engineering purposes, must also be represented. They are assigned to the remaining 33 of the 7-bit symbols.

An early and still widely used 7-bit code for the characters is **ASCII** (pronounced AS·key). ASCII stands for American Standard Code for Information Interchange. The advantages of a "standard" are many: computer parts built by different manufacturers can be connected, programs can create data and store it so that different programs can process it later, and so forth. In all cases, there must be an agreement as to which character is associated with which symbol (bit sequence).

Extended ASCII: An 8-Bit Code

As the name implies, ASCII was developed in the United States. By the mid-1960s, it became clear that 7-bit ASCII was not enough because it could not fully represent text from languages other than English. Therefore, IBM, the dominant computer manufacturer at the time, decided to use the next larger set of symbols, the 8-bit symbols, as the standard for character representation. Eight bits produce $2^8 = 256$ symbols, enough to encode English and the Western European languages, their punctuation characters, and a large set of other useful characters. The larger, improved encoding was originally called Extended ASCII, as shown in Figure 7.3; today it is known by the curious name of **ISO-8859-1**. The original ASCII is the "first half" of Extended ASCII; that is, 7-bit ASCII is the 8-bit ASCII representation with the leftmost bit set to 0. Though Extended ASCII does not handle all natural languages, it does handle many languages that derived from the Latin alphabet; the ASCII of Figure 7.3 is also known as *Latin-1*. Handling other languages is solved in two ways: recoding the second half of Extended ASCII for the language's other characters, and using the multibyte Unicode representation.

VideoNote
ASCII Hidden Messages

ASCII	0000	0001	0010	0011	0100	0101	0110	0111	1000	1001	1010	1011	1100	1101	1110	1111
0000	NU	SH	SX	EX	ET	EQ	AK	BL	BS	HT	LF	YT	FF	CR	SO	SI
0001	DL	D1	D2	D3	D4	NK	SY	EΣ	CN	EM	SB	EC	FS	GS	RS	US
0010		!	"	#	$	%	&	'	(	)	*	+	,	-	.	/
0011	0	1	2	3	4	5	6	7	8	9	:	;	<	=	>	?
0100	@	A	B	C	D	E	F	G	H	I	J	K	L	M	N	O
0101	P	Q	R	S	T	U	V	W	X	Y	Z	[	\	]	^	_
0110	`	a	b	c	d	e	f	g	h	i	j	k	l	m	n	o
0111	p	q	r	s	t	u	v	w	x	y	z	{	|	}	~	DT
1000	80	81	82	83	IN	NL	SS	ES	HS	HJ	YS	PD	PV	RI	S2	S3
1001	DC	P1	PZ	SE	CC	MM	SP	EP	Q8	QQ	QA	CS	ST	OS	PM	AP
1010	AO	¡	¢	£	¤	¥	¦	§	¨	©	ª	«	¬	-	®	¯
1011	°	±	^{2}	^{3}	´	µ	¶	·	¸	^{1}	º	»	¼	½	¾	¿
1100	À	Á	Â	Ã	Ä	Å	Æ	Ç	È	É	Ê	Ë	Ì	Í	Î	Ï
1101	Ð	Ñ	Ò	Ó	Ô	Õ	Ö	×	Ø	Ù	Ú	Û	Ü	Ý	Þ	β
1110	à	á	â	ã	ä	å	æ	ç	è	é	ê	ë	ì	í	î	ï
1111	ð	ñ	ò	ó	ô	õ	ö	÷	ø	ù	ú	û	ü	ý	þ	ÿ

Figure 7.3 ASCII, the American Standard Code for Information Interchange.

Note: The original 7-bit ASCII is the top half of the table; the whole table is known as Extended ASCII (ISO-8859-1). The 8-bit symbol for a letter is the four row bits followed by the four column bits (e.g., A = 0100 0001, while z = 0111 1010). Characters shown as two small letters are control symbols used to encode nonprintable information (e.g., BS = 0000 1000 is backspace). The bottom half of the table represents characters needed by Western European languages, such as Icelandic's eth (ð) and thorn (þ).

VideoNote
Binary to ASCII Decoding

IBM's move to 8 bits was bold because it added the extra bit at a time when computer memory and storage were extremely expensive. IBM gave 8-bit sequences a special name, **byte**, and adopted it as a standard unit for computer memory. (*Octet* is used as a synonym for byte.) Bytes are still the standard unit of memory, and their "8-ness" is noticeable in many places. For example, recent computers are "64-bit machines"—not 60-bit or 65-bit—so their data paths (the part that processes most instructions) can handle 8 bytes at a time.

The Ultimate. Although ASCII and its variations are widely used, the more complete solution is a representation, called *Unicode*. It uses more than one byte (up to four) to encode about 100,000 symbols, enough for *all* languages. The actual encoding into bytes is given by the Unicode Translation Format or UTF-8.

ASCII Coding of Phone Numbers

Let's return to the phone number 888 555 1212, whose representation concerned us at the start of the chapter. How would a computer represent this phone number in its memory? Remember, this is not really a number, but rather, it is a keying sequence for a telephone's keypad represented by numerals; it is not necessary, or even desirable, to represent the phone number as a numerical quantity. Because each of the numerals has a representation in ASCII, we can express the phone number by encoding each digit with a byte. The encoding is easy: Find each numeral in Figure 7.3 and write down the bit sequence from its row, followed by the bit sequence from its column. Therefore, the phone number 888 555 1212 in ASCII is

0011 1000 0011 1000 0011 1000
0011 0101 0011 0101 0011 0101
0011 0001 0011 0010 0011 0001 0011 0010

You can use Figure 7.3 to check this encoding. This is exactly how computers represent phone numbers. The encoding seems somewhat redundant because each byte has the same left half: 0011. The left halves are repeated because all of the numerals are located on the 0011 row of the ASCII table. If only phone numbers had to be represented, fewer bits could be used, of course. But there is little reason to be so economical, so we adopt the standard ASCII.

Notice that we have run all of the digits of the phone number together, even though when we write them for ourselves we usually put spaces between the area code and exchange code, and between the exchange code and the number. The computer doesn't care, but it might matter to users. It's easy to add these spaces and other punctuation.

7.8 Numbers as Letters. Encode the phone number (888) 555-1212 in ASCII, including the punctuation. (Notice that there is a space before the first 5.) To find the answer, locate each character in Figure 7.3 and write the four bits at the left of the row and the four bits at the top of the column. For example, the open parenthesis—(—is in the third row and corresponds to 0010 1000.

Two Bits, Four Bits. The term *byte* has motivated some people to call 4 bits—that is, half a byte—a *nibble*.

Table 7.7 NATO broadcast alphabet designed not to be minimal

A	Alpha	H	Hotel	O	Oscar	V	Victor
B	Bravo	I	India	P	Papa	W	Whiskey
C	Charlie	J	Juliet	Q	Quebec	X	X-ray
D	Delta	K	Kilo	R	Romeo	Y	Yankee
E	Echo	L	Lima	S	Sierra	Z	Zulu
F	Foxtrot	M	Mike	T	Tango		
G	Golf	N	November	U	Uniform		

Advantages of Long Encodings

Although we usually try to be efficient by using the shortest symbol sequences to minimize the amount of memory needed to store and transmit information, not all letter representations should be short. Consider two familiar examples.

NATO Broadcast Alphabet

The code for the letters used in radio communication is purposely inefficient, so that the letters are distinctive when spoken amid noise. The NATO broadcast alphabet, shown in Table 7.7 and used in air traffic communication, encodes letters as words; that is, the words are the symbols, replacing the standard spoken names for the letters.

For example, *Mike* and *November* replace "em" and "en," which can be hard to tell apart. This longer encoding improves the chance that letters will be recognized when spoken under less than ideal conditions. The digits keep their usual names, except nine, which is frequently replaced by *niner*.

It's Greek to Me. There are dozens of phonetic alphabets for English and many other languages. The NATO alphabet, used for air traffic control, begins with "alpha," raising the question, "What is the first letter of the Greek phonetic alphabet?" Alexandros.

Bar Codes

The familiar bars of the Universal Product Codes (UPC) illustrate another example of using more than the minimum number of bits to encode information. In the UPC-A encoding, seven bits are used to encode the digits 0–9, as shown at the left, though these digits could be represented with four. To understand how the coding works, know that UPC encodes the manufacturer (left side) and the product (right side). As shown in Table 7.8, different bit combinations are used for each side. Notice, however, that one side is the **complement** (switch 0's and 1's) of the other side. The bit patterns were chosen to appear as different as possible from each other.

The extra bits solve an important problem. Different encodings for each side make it possible to recognize whether the code is right side up or upside down. For example, if the scanner, reading left to right, reads 0001001, it knows it read the bars upside down.

Table 7.8 Bit encoding for bars for the UPC-A encoding; notice that the two sides are complements of each other, that is, the 0's and 1's are switched.

Digit	Left Side	Right Side
0	0001101	1110010
1	0011001	1100110
2	0010011	1101100
3	0111101	1000010
4	0100011	1011100
5	0110001	1001110
6	0101111	1010000
7	0111011	1000100
8	0110111	1001000
9	0001011	1110100

How?

The only way to interpret that sequence of bits as a legal encoding reading forwards or backwards in Table 7.8 is to notice that it is an 8 read right to left. So, the bars must have been upside down.

The First Product Ever Scanned. The first commercial transaction using the bars of the Universal Product Code (UPC) occurred at 8:01 AM on June 26, 1974, at Marsh's supermarket in Troy, Ohio. The product was a 10-pack of Wrigley's Juicy Fruit chewing gum.

UTF-8

As mentioned above, characters for non-Latin based languages use Unicode. The Unicode Transformation Format (UTF) is the way characters are represented for the Web and other applications requiring international information exchange. It is a variable-length coding of characters that allows all of the Unicode characters to be expressed. By *variable length* we mean that a different number of bytes is used depending on the character. Although it is pretty easy to understand, there is no reason to learn it completely. The main idea is that ASCII—that is, the "top half" of Figure 7.3—is expressed as one byte. All of those characters will have a first bit of 0. Any other characters will use 2, 3, or 4 bytes, and each of those bytes will all start with 1. That's all you need to know about how UTF-8 works.

Because UTF-8 can encode all characters, you can have any characters you want on your Web page, so every language can use it. Furthermore, languages such as Finnish that can use the main Latin alphabet benefit from having 8-bit characters, and only require extra bytes (usually just two) to encode the letters not in ASCII. It's not a win for everyone, however, because languages involving another full alphabet—for example, Cyrillic or Greek—need at least two bytes for most characters. There are ways of bypassing this doubling of the bit encoding, so other languages are not as inconvenienced. But everyone on the planet can read the UTF-8 version. See Figure 7.4 for a small illustration of a Web page that loads on your computer thanks to UTF-8.

لماذا لا يتكلمون اللّغة **العربية** فحسب؟
Защо те просто не могат да говорят **български**?
Per què no poden simplement parlar en **català**?
他們爲什麼不說中文（台灣）？
Proč prostě nemluví **česky**?
Hvorfor kan de ikke bare tale **dansk**?
Warum sprechen sie nicht einfach **Deutsch**?
Μα γιατί δεν μπορούν να μιλήσουν **Ελληνικά**;
Why can't they just speak **English**?
¿Por qué no pueden simplemente hablar en **castellano**?
Miksi he eivät yksinkertaisesti puhu **suomea**?
Pourquoi, tout simplement, ne parlent-ils pas **français** ?
למה הם פשוט לא מדברים **עברית**?
Miért nem beszélnek egyszerűen **magyarul**?
Af hverju geta þeir ekki bara talað **íslensku**?
Perché non possono semplicemente parlare **italiano**?
なぜ、みんな日本語を話してくれないのか？
세계의 모든 사람들이 한국어를 이해한다면 얼마나 좋을까?
Waarom spreken ze niet gewoon **Nederlands**?
Hvorfor kan de ikke bare snakke **norsk**?
Dlaczego oni po prostu nie mówią po **polsku**?
Porque é que eles não falam em **Português (do Brasil)**?
Oare ăştia de ce nu vorbesc **româneşte**?
Почему же они не говорят **по-русски**?
Zašto jednostavno ne govore **hrvatski**?
Pse nuk duan të flasin vetëm **shqip**?
Varför pratar dom inte bara **svenska**?
ทำไมเขาถึงไม่พูด**ภาษาไทย**
Neden **Türkçe** konuşamıyorlar?

Figure 7.4 "Why can't they just speak ______?" A portion of a Web page, www.trigeminal.com/samples/provincial.html, displaying that question expressed in more than 125 languages. Can you name all of them in this partial list?

Not only does Unicode solve displaying natural languages, it works for "odd ball" characters too. It allows us to display characters like ⋱ and ⋰ even though we may have no idea what their proper use is. They are in the list (U+22F0 and U+22F1, respectively) and so we can use them. This fact has led to some rather bizarre ideas, such as writing text upside down using the characters of the very strange International Phonetic Alphabet (IPA):

¿sıɥʇ pɐǝɹ noʎ uɐɔ

In the normal orientation, these are letters harvested mostly from the IPA, but they are readable upside down too!

The Metadata and the OED

So far, we have used bits to digitize numbers and letters. Together these forms of encoding handle much of the content that interests people; other types of content like images, sound, and video are covered in Chapter 8. However, the digitizing—converting the content into binary—is only half of the problem of representing information.

The other half of the problem is to describe the information's properties. Specifically, we must encode characteristics of the content, including the following:

How is the content structured?

What other content is it related to?

Where was it collected?
What units is it given in?
How should it be displayed?
When was it created or captured?

And the list goes on and on. Such information *describes* other information, and is just as important as the numbers and text that we've already encoded.

Information describing information is called **metadata**. Although metadata joins numbers and letters as the third basic form of data, it does not require its own binary encoding. Rather, other means based on letters and numbers are used to specify metadata; the most common way to give metadata is with **tags**. For example, in Chapter 4 when we wrote HTML, we were defining the metadata to describe how to display the content. The tag form will concern us for the rest of this chapter, but here we briefly think of metadata more abstractly.

Properties of Data

An important property of metadata is that it is *separate* from the information that it describes. For example, we have only discussed the ASCII representation of letters, and not how they are displayed, say, as Times New Roman font. *How they are displayed* is metadata. Rather than fill a file with Times New Roman, we fill the file with the letters and note with tags how it should be displayed. As you know, separating the content from the metadata does not "lock in" a specific form of display, making it easy to change the display by just changing the metadata.

The Price of Metadata. The price of a product is metadata. When a price tag is attached to a product it binds the object and its metadata. Attaching a price is appropriate for unique products such as art, but it's an uncommon practice for manufactured items. Merchants use the bar code, the Universal Product Code (UPC), on products, and they store the price in a database. That separates the product from the price metadata. When the product is scanned, a computer looks up the price. The separation enables stores to discount products without needing to remark the price on each one.

Using Tags for Metadata

The *Oxford English Dictionary* (*OED*) is the definitive reference for every English word's meaning, etymology, and usage. Because it is comprehensive, the *OED* is truly monumental. The printed version is 20 volumes, weighs 150 pounds, and fills 4 feet of shelf space. In 1857, the Philological Society of London established the goal of producing a complete list of all English words. They expected that the completed dictionary would comprise 6,400 pages in four volumes. By 1884, with the list completed only up to *ant*, it became clear to James Murray, the lexicographer in charge, that the effort was much more ambitious than they originally thought. The first edition, completed in 1928, long after Murray's death, filled 15,490 pages and contained 252,200 entries. In 1984, the conversion of the *OED* to digital form began.

7.9 How Much Is a Pound? The ASCII for the character "£," the symbol for the British pound, is A3 in hex and 1010 0011 in binary. What's the decimal value of the binary number 1010 0011; that is, how much is a £?

Now imagine that you have typed in the entire *OED* as a long sequence of ASCII characters from A through the end of the definition for *zyxt*, the last word in English. That task would take one person about 120 years. The result would be a digitized dictionary, but in the form of a very long sequence of ASCII characters. Would a computer be able to help us use it?

Suppose we want to find the definition for the verb *set*, which is notable for having the longest entry in the *OED*. The searching software (as described in Chapter 2) would look for *s-e-t* and find it thousands of times. This is because *set* is part of many words, like clo*set*, hor*set*ail, and *set*tle, and *set* is used in many definitions, for example, "*match-point* in tennis is the final score ending the present game, *set*, and match."

We can solve the first problem—avoiding *s-e-t* within words—by ignoring all occurrences that do not have a punctuation character or space before and after the *s-e-t*. The software can do that. But how does it find the definition for *set* among the thousands of true occurrences of the word *set* in other definitions? The software processing the text file, unable to understand the dictionary's contents, would have no clue which one it is.

People use a number of cues to find information in the dictionary, such as alphabetic order and the fact that a new definition begins on a new line, and the defined word is printed in bold. Though we could insert HTML-like tags for new lines or boldface type, a better solution is to use the tags to describe the *structure* of the dictionary's content. That is, incorporate metadata.

Structure Tags

A special set of tags was developed to specify the *OED*'s *structure*. For example, <hw> is the *OED*'s tag for a *headword*, the word being defined. As usual, because tags surround the text like parentheses, there is a closing *headword* tag, </hw>. Thus, the place in the *OED* where the verb *set* is defined appears in the tagged text file of the dictionary as

<hw>set</hw>

Other tags label the pronunciation <pr>, the phonetic notations <ph>, the parts of speech <ps>, the homonym number <hm> for headwords that sound the same, and so forth. There are also tags to group items, such as <e> to surround an entire entry and <hg> to surround a head group (that is, all of the information at the start of a definition). In the printed *OED*, the first entry for the verb *set* begins

set (sɛt) *v.*[1]

giving the word being defined, the pronunciation, the part of speech (verb), and the homonym number (1). We expect it must be tagged as

<e><hg><hw>set</hw> <pr><ph>s&epsilont</ph></pr>, <ps>v</ps>.<hm>1</hm></hg>

Notice the use of the escape code (&epsilon) for the epsilon character in the pronunciation, which is similar to the use of & for accented letters in HTML (Chapter 4). Also, the </e> is not shown because it must be at the very end of the entry.

With the structure tags in the dictionary, software can use a simple algorithm to find easily the definition of the verb *set:* Search for occurrences of <hw>set</hw>, which indicate a definition for set, check within its head group for <ps>v</ps>, which indicates that it is a verb form of set being defined, and then print (formatted) all of the text within the <e> and </e> tags.

Of course, the tags do not print. They are included only to specify the structure, so the computer knows what part of the dictionary it is looking at. But in fact, structure tags are very useful for formatting. For example, the boldface type used for headwords can be automatically applied when the dictionary is printed based on the <hw> tag. No <b> tag needed. In a similar way, the italics typeface can be applied in the part of speech. The parentheses surrounding the pronunciation and the superscript for the homonym number are also generated automatically. Thus, knowing the structure makes it possible to generate the formatting information.

The opposite is not true. That is, formatting tags do not usually tell us enough about a document to allow us to know its structure. In the *OED* example, though boldface is used for headwords, it is also used for other purposes, which means that just because a word is boldface does not mean it is a headword. In fact, because some formatting information, like <italic>, has both structural and nonstructural occurrences, the *OED* digitization includes some formatting information with the structural information. The structure is more important, but most complex documents use both types of tags.

Although it started long ago, the *Oxford English Dictionary* remains current. In 2011, OMG and LOL were added, making them officially part of the English language. Check their entries at www.oed.com/view/Entry/291168 and www.oed.com/view/Entry/293068.

OMG
LOL
OED

Sample OED Entry

Figure 7.5 shows the entry for *byte*, together with its representation, as it actually appears in the file of the online *OED*. At first, the form looks very cluttered, but if you compare it with the printed form, you can make sense of the tags. The tags specify the role of each word of the dictionary. So, for example, to find the first time the word *byte* was used in print, the software searches for <hw>byte</hw>, then looks for the quote date tags, <qd> and </qd>, to find that the first use of the word was in 1964. Structure tags help the software help the user.

Because the tag characters are included with the content characters, they increase the size of the file compared with plain text. The entry for *byte* is 841 characters, but the tagged code is 1,204 characters, almost a 50 percent increase.

byte (baIt). *Computers.* [Arbitrary, prob. influenced by bit sb.[4] and bite sb.] A group of eight consecutive bits operated on as a unit in a computer.

1964 ***Blaauw*** & ***Brooks*** in *IBM Systems Jrnl.* III. 122 An 8-bit unit of information is fundamental to most of the formats [of the System/360]. A consecutive group of *n* such units constitutes a field of length *n*. Fixed-length fields of length one, two, four, and eight are termed bytes, half-words, words, and double words respectively. **1964** *IBM Jrnl. Res. & Developm.* VIII. 97/1 When a byte of data appears from an I/O device, the CPU is seized, dumped, used and restored. **1967** ***P. A. Stark*** *Digital Computer Programming* xix. 351 The normal operations in fixed point are done on four bytes at a time. **1968** *Dataweek* 24 Jan. 1/1 Tape reading and writing is at from 34,160 to 192,000 bytes per second.

<e><hg><hw>byte</hw> <pr><ph>baIt</ph></pr></hg>. <la> Computers</la>. <etym> Arbitrary, prob. influenced by <xr><x>bit</x></xr> <ps>n.<hm>4</hm></ps>and <xr><x>bite</x> <ps>n.</ps></xr></etym> <s4>A group of eight consecutive bits operated on as a unit in a computer.</s4><qp><q><qd>1964</qd><a>Blaauw</a> & <a>Brooks</a><bib>in</bib> <w>IBM Systems Jrnl.</w> <lc>III.122</lc> <qt>An 8-bit unit of information is fundamental to most of the formats <ed>of the System/360</ed>.&es.A consecutive group of <i>n</i> such units constitutes a field of length <i>n</i>.&es.Fixed-length fields of length one, two, four, and eight are termed bytes, halfwords, words, and double words respectively. </qt></q><q><qd>1964</qd> <w>IBM Jrnl. Res. & Developm. </w> <lc>VIII. 97/1</lc> <qt>When a byte of data appears from an I/O device, the CPU is seized, dumped, used and restored.</qt></q><q><qd>1967</qd> <a>P. A. Stark</a> <w>Digital Computer Programming</w> <lc>xix. 351</lc> <qt>The normal operations in fixed point are done on four bytes at a time.</qt></q> <q><qd> 1968</qd> <w> Dataweek</w> <lc>24 Jan. 1/1</lc> <qt>Tape reading and writing is at from 34,160 to 192,000 bytes per second.</qt></q></qp></e>

Figure 7.5 The OED entry for the word *byte* (top panel), together with the representation of the entry in its digitized form with tags (bottom panel).

Why "Byte"?

As informative as the *OED* definition is, it doesn't answer that nagging question: Why is *byte* spelled with a *y*? To understand the charming nature of the answer, we need to know that computer memory is subject to errors (a zero changing to a one, or a one to a zero), caused by such things as cosmic rays. Really. It doesn't happen often, but often enough to worry computer engineers, who build special circuitry to detect and correct memory errors. They often add extra bits to the memory to help detect errors—for example, a ninth bit per byte can detect errors using parity.

Parity refers to whether a number is even or odd. To encode bytes using **even parity**, we use the normal byte encoding, for example, *1010 0010*, and then count the number of 1's in the byte. If there is an even number of 1's, we set the ninth bit to 0; if there is an odd number, we set the ninth bit to 1, for example, *1010 0010 1*. The result is that all 9-bit groups have even parity, either because they were even to begin with and the 0 didn't change that, or they were odd to begin with, but the 1 made them even. Any single bit error in a group causes its parity to become odd, allowing the hardware to detect that an error has occurred, although it can't detect which bit is wrong using this parity scheme.

So, why is *byte* spelled with a *y*? The answer comes from Werner Buchholz, the creator of the word and the concept. In the late 1950s, Buchholz was the project manager and architect for the IBM supercomputer, called Stretch. For that machine, he explained, "We needed a word for a quantity of memory between a bit and a word." (A "word" of computer memory is typically the amount required to represent computer instructions; on modern computers, a word is 32 bits.) Buchholz continued, "It seemed that after 'bit' comes 'bite.' But we changed the 'i' to a 'y' so that a typist couldn't accidentally change 'byte' to 'bit' by the single error of dropping the 'e'." No single letter change to *byte* can create *bit*, and vice versa. Buchholz and his engineers were so concerned with memory errors that he invented an *error-detecting name* for the memory unit!

SUMMARY

We began the chapter by learning that digitizing doesn't require digits—any symbols will do. We explored the following:

- PandA encoding, which is based on the presence and absence of a physical phenomenon. Their patterns are discrete; they form the basic unit of a bit. Their names (most often 1 and 0) can be any pair of opposite terms.
- A bit's 0 and 1 states naturally encourage the representation of numbers in base 2, that is, binary.
- 7-bit ASCII, an early assignment of bit sequences (symbols) to keyboard characters. Extended or 8-bit ASCII is the standard.
- The need to use more than the minimum number of bits to encode information.
- How documents like the *Oxford English Dictionary* are digitized. We learned that tags associate metadata with every part of the *OED*. Using that data, a computer can easily help us find words and other information.
- The mystery of the *y* in *byte*.

TRY IT SOLUTIONS

7.1 Different symbols, same meaning

7.2 The phenomenon is "lobster shell is bright red"; presence means cooked, absence means not cooked.

7.3 (a) contains juice, (b) has orange slice, and (c) short glass

7.4 101000 days

7.5 1111 0000 0000 1101 0100 1010 1011 1110 1110

0FF 2 A D8

7.6 Fingers visible is 1; fingers not visible is 0 to make 0110.

7.7 The binary number 1 0101 0101 is 256 + 64 + 16 + 4 + 1 = 341.

7.8 0010 1000 0011 1000 0011 1000 0011 1000 0010 1001

0010 0000 0011 0101 0011 0101 0011 0101 0010 1101

0011 0001 0011 0010 0011 0001 0011 0010

7.9 A £ is 128 + 32 + 2 + 1 = 163 as a binary number.

Multiple Choice

1. How many symbols can be represented by four bits?
   a. 12
   b. 16
   c. 36
   d. 256
2. PandA representation is what kind of system?
   a. decimal
   b. binary
   c. hexadecimal
   d. byte
3. What was used to help structure the digitized *Oxford English Dictionary*?
   a. bytes
   b. sets
   c. ASCII
   d. tags
4. This defines how characters relate to each other when they are compared.
   a. digitizing
   b. binary sequence
   c. collating sequence
   d. information representation
5. When using physical phenomena to encode information, name one potential solution if there are more than two alternatives.
   a. there is no solution
   b. adopt them all as present
   c. adopt one as present and all the other alternatives as absent
   d. adopt them all as absent
6. Information describing information is called
   a. special information
   b. metadata
   c. special-data
   d. formatting
7. K bits in a sequence yield how many symbols?
   a. K^2
   b. 2^K
   c. K
   d. 2

Short Answer

1. PandA is short for _______.
2. _______ encode information on DVDs and CDs.
3. Hexadecimal is base _______.
4. Grouping binary digits in groups of four makes converting to _______ easier.

5. _______ is the name we use for the two fundamental patterns of digital information based on the presence and absence of a phenomenon.
6. Information is said to be _______, or distinct; there is no gray.
7. The number of digits is the _______ or the _______ of the numbering system.
8. The more symbols you want, the more _______ you need.
9. _______ is representing information with symbols.

Exercises

1. Make a list of the numbers you use that are not treated as numbers (e.g., phone numbers).
2. Create a list of 10 different PandA encodings that are different from those presented in this chapter.
3. Encode (800) 555-0012 in ASCII, including punctuation.
4. This chapter mentions that it does not matter whether 0 represents present or absent. Explain in detail why this is the case.
5. Translate the following hexadecimal into binary and then into ASCII: 68 65 78 61 64 65 63 69 6D 61 6C
6. Encode the following ISBN number in ASCII: 978-3-16-148410-0
7. You have discovered the following string of binary ASCII code; figure out what they mean: 01010111 01100001 01111001 00100000 01110100 01101111 00100000 01100111 01101111 00100001
8. Explain the relationship between the number D and

9. Explain why radio broadcasters use longer encoding to transmit information.
10. Explain why the NATO broadcast alphabet represents digitization. Then explain why it was designed to be minimal.
11. Explain how Buchholz created an error-detecting name for the memory unit.
12. Without metadata, why would it be hard to search for “set” in a digitized dictionary?

CHAPTER 8

Representing Multimedia Digitally

Light, Sound, Magic

learning objectives

- Explain how RGB color is represented in bytes
- Understand the difference between "bits" and "binary numbers"
- Change an RGB color by binary addition
- Discuss concepts related to digitizing sound waves
- Explain data compression and its lossless and lossy variants
- Explain the meaning of the Bias-Free Universal Medium Principle

CHAPTER 8

Blue color is everlastingly appointed by the Deity to be a source of delight.

—JOHN RUSKIN, 1853

Science will never be able to reduce the value of a sunset to arithmetic.

—DR LOUIS ORR, 1960

DIGITIZING DATA HAS in our study so far been limited to letters, numbers, and metadata. As you well know, there's a lot more digital information available than those three. Photos, audio, and video come to mind immediately. However, these don't seem to work like letters, numbers, and metadata. When you Skype with friends, what are the bits doing? It doesn't seem to involve letters, numbers, or metadata. Does it even involve bits? In this chapter we round out the digitization discussion by covering these other forms of digitized information, collectively known as **multimedia**. We will find out that they still apply the same principles we've seen with letters and numbers to encode information into bits. All of the discussion will lead us to a profound conclusion: Bits are it!

We begin this chapter by looking at color. You will learn how a color is displayed and encoded in bits, and how software makes colors darker or lighter. This process—a basic part of digital photo editing software—is little more than doing arithmetic on binary numbers. Changing the color of an image and performing other modifications illustrates these concepts. Next, we discuss JPEG and MPEG and the need for compression techniques for images and video. We go on to discuss optical character recognition to emphasize the advantages of encoding information in digital form. And finally, the whole topic of digital representation is summarized in one fundamental principle.

Digitizing Color

In Chapter 7 we discussed the binary encoding of keyboard characters to create the ASCII representation, but we (and the creators) didn't pay much attention to which bit patterns are associated with which characters. It's true that in ASCII the numerals are encoded in numeric order, and the letter sets are roughly in alphabetical order, but the assignment is largely arbitrary. The specifics of the keyboard character encoding don't matter much (as long as everyone agrees on them) because the bytes are used as units. We rarely manipulate the individual bits that make up the pattern for the characters. For encoding other information, however, manipulating the individual bits is essential, and so the assignment cannot be arbitrary.

8.1 Not in This Case. About the only situation in which programmers manipulate the bits of letters is to change them into lowercase—it's done for matching and searching. Looking back at Figure 7.3, can you discover what change is needed to make the uppercase ASCII alphabet into the corresponding lowercase?

Color and the Mystery of Light

Pixels (from *picture elements*) are small points of colored light arranged in a grid to form a computer display. Each pixel is formed from three colored lights: red, green, and blue. They are referred to by their first letters, **RGB**, and always in that order.

By turning on one light at a time, we can display the three colors red, green, and blue. Turning off all of them makes black. All other colors are made by using different amounts, or **intensities**, of the three lights. Figure 8.1 illustrates the colors produced by full-intensity colored light.

For example, *white* results from turning on all three lights at high intensity. It may seem odd that combining red, green, and blue produces white, but it is similar to stage lighting, where colored lights combine to form a pure white light. The three colors do not have to be red, green, and blue, but they are standard.

8.2 Light Sabers. Suppose a red light saber crosses a blue light saber. What color are they at the place where they cross, from the audience's point of view?

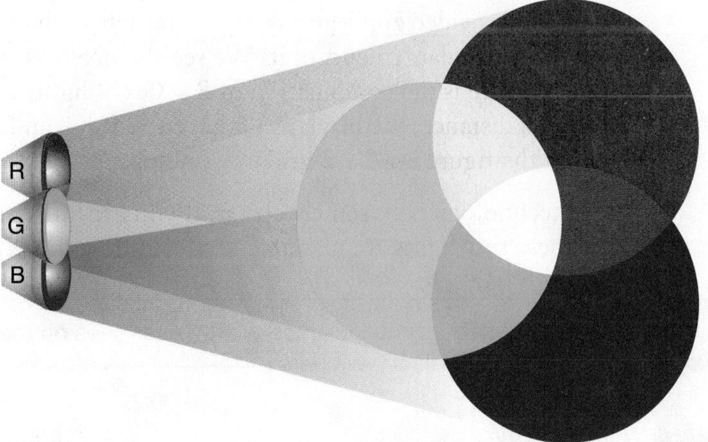

Figure 8.1 Combining full intensity RGB light to create different colors.

Yellow = R + G?

But, it is not only that R + G + B = white that is odd. Notice from Figure 8.1 that combining red and green makes yellow. This is very odd because we were taught in elementary school that red and yellow are primary colors—you don't make them out of anything. Also, in elementary school we learned how to make green paint from yellow paint and blue paint. (We called it blue, but it is really light blue, or *cyan*.) So, then why do R + G = yellow pixels?

The mystery is solved by understanding that there is a difference between colored light and colored paint. Paint, like any colored surface, reflects some colors and absorbs others. So, when white light (R + G + B) strikes paint, some light is absorbed—we can't see it—and some light is bounced back, that is, reflected. We see the reflected color.

In the case of a pixel, the light shines directly at our eyes. Nothing is absorbed. Nothing is reflected. We just see the pure colored light. The exact color is determined by the intensity of each color.

Green Paint = Blue + Yellow

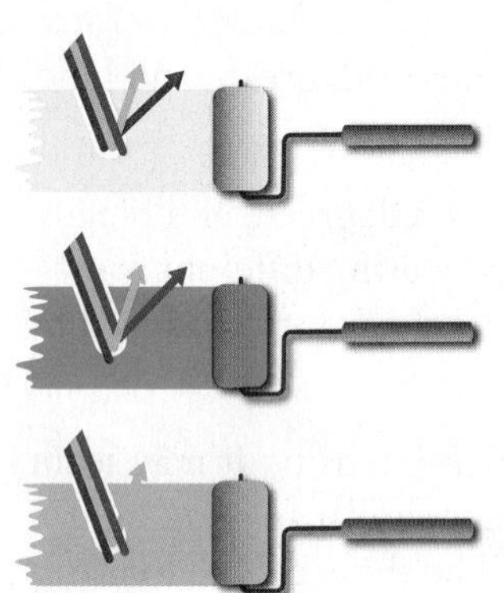

To see how combining light works with pigment, imagine white light striking yellow paint. Because it is yellow, the colors *reflected* back when white light (R + G + B) strikes it must be R and G. B must be absorbed.

When white light (R + G + B) shines on cyan paint, it reflects G and B light, as we can figure out from Figure 8.1, and it absorbs R.

When we mix yellow pigment and cyan pigment in art class, the white light (R + G + B) is handled as follows: The yellow absorbs B, none is reflected; the cyan absorbs R, none is reflected. The only thing left to reflect—which both yellow and cyan reflect—is G.

Voila! Yellow paint plus cyan paint produces green paint. Just as we learned in art class!

Making a Big Display

To finish our discussion of pixels and colored light, look at Figure 8.2 to see a thin film transistor (TFT) form of liquid crystal display (LCD), known as an *active matrix* display. These are the standard "flat" or "thin" displays used for laptops, phones, and most familiar video applications. At the far left in the figure is an arrow pointer; to its right are two enlargements of it. We see the pixels as red, green, and blue colored lights. Because white is the combination of R + G + B light, we see that the colored pixels are white at a distance; the black pixels have the R, G, and B subpixels turned off. At the far right in the figure is a 2 × 2 grid of white pixels.

LCD technology is extremely clever. If you are interested, read about it online to see how these tiny lights are manufactured and how they are controlled. It's amazing.

8.3 Colored Light. Describe what a user sees on the screen when viewing the pixels shown here.

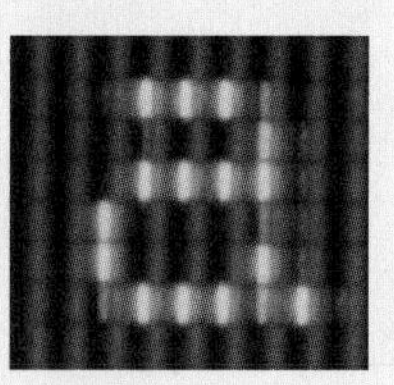

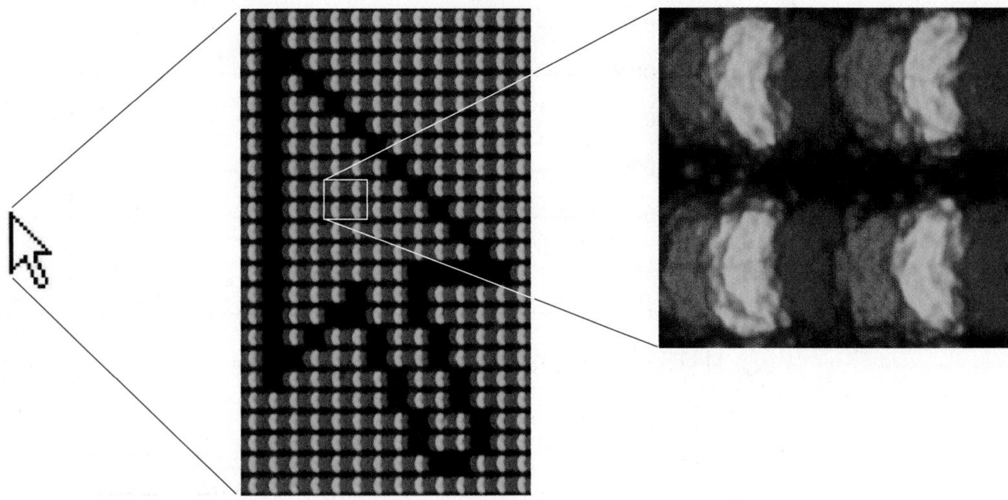

Figure 8.2 At the left is a standard arrow pointer; the other two images are close-ups of its LCD pixel grid. The enlargement in the middle shows the RGB-triple lights that make pixels. Most are at full intensity creating the white background, and some are turned off (zero intensity) to create the arrow outline. A 2 × 2 white pixel region is further enlarged at the right.

Thinking About Intensities

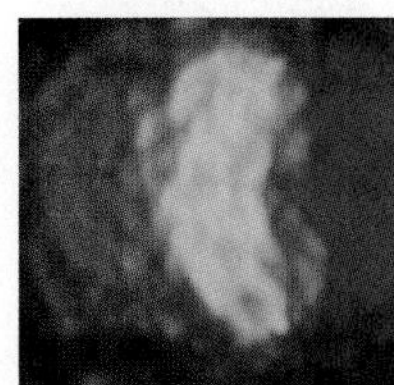

Some people—Leibniz was one—get pretty excited about binary, but for most of us, they're just bits. If we think of them as controlling the intensity of the light of a subpixel (a color), however, the idea has some interest. Consider a blue subpixel. The 8 bits specifying its intensity have position values:

```
128  64  32  16  8  4  2  1
```

These values specify how bright the blue should be. If we want the subpixel to be "half on," that is, "half intensity," we write

```
128  64  32  16  8  4  2  1
  1   0   0   0  0  0  0  0
```

to say we want 128 units of power. If we want the pixel "three quarters on," then we write

```
128  64  32  16  8  4  2  1
  1   1   0   0  0  0  0  0
```

because 3/4 of the 256 range of values is 192 = 128 + 64. We would get 7/8 of the intensity by setting the next bit, and so forth. Obviously, by adding only half as much power as the previous bit, the effect is less, but each position contributes, as shown in Figure 8.3.

8.4 Dim Bulb. What is the binary setting needed to show a red subpixel at 1/4 of its brightness, as shown here?

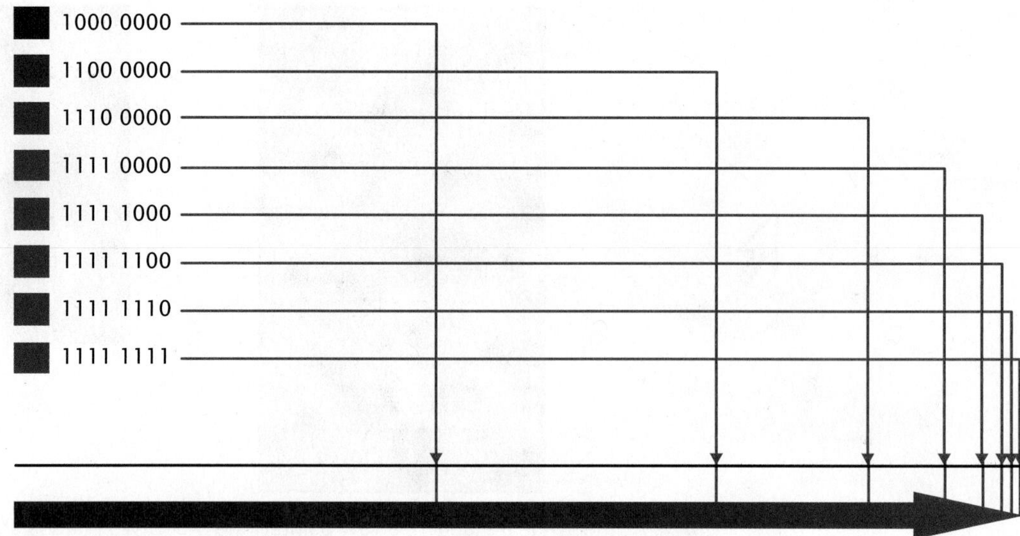

Figure 8.3 Progressively increasing the intensity for a blue subpixel; each bit contributes half as much power as the bit to its left.

Black and White Colors

The intensity of the R, G, and B lights just discussed are the binary numbers stored in a byte: 8 bits. So, representing the color of a single pixel requires 3 bytes. Using binary numbers means that the smallest intensity is 0000 0000, which is 0, of course, and the largest value is 1111 1111. To figure out what decimal number that is (and to refresh ourselves on binary numbers from Chapter 7), we add the place values for the 1's,

$$\begin{aligned} 1111\ 1111 &= 2^7 + 2^6 + 2^5 + 2^4 + 2^3 + 2^2 + 2^1 + 2^0 \\ &= 128 + 64 + 32 + 16 + 8 + 4 + 2 + 1 \\ &= 255 \end{aligned}$$

which tells us that the range of values is 0 through 255 for each color.

As stated above, black is the absence of light,

0000 0000 0000 0000 0000 0000 *RGB bit assignment for black*
red byte, green byte, blue byte

while white

1111 1111 1111 1111 1111 1111 *RGB bit assignment for white*
red byte, green byte, blue byte

has full intensity for each color. Between these extremes is a whole range of intensity.

Super Powers. Powers of two, $2^n = 2 \times 2 \times \ldots \times 2$, are common in computing because of binary. For that reason, computer people quickly learn their powers.

2^0	1	2^4	16	2^8	256	2^{12}	4,096	2^{16}	65,536	2^{20}	1,048,576
2^1	2	2^5	32	2^9	512	2^{13}	8,192	2^{17}	131,072	2^{21}	2,097,152
2^2	4	2^6	64	2^{10}	1,024	2^{14}	16,384	2^{18}	262,144	2^{22}	4,194,304
2^3	8	2^7	128	2^{11}	2,048	2^{15}	32,768	2^{19}	524,288	2^{23}	8,388,608

Decimal to Binary

So far, we have converted binary to decimal. The algorithm for converting decimal to binary is the opposite, of course. Basically, it "finds which powers of 2 combine to make the decimal number." The following table clarifies this:

Number being converted										
Place value	512	256	128	64	32	16	8	4	2	1
Subtract										
Binary Number										

We'll discuss the algorithm in a moment, but first, to build the table we fill the second row with powers of 2. But, how many powers of 2? *All of the powers of 2 less than the number we want to convert.* So, the table shown above works for any decimal number up to 1,023, because the next power of 2 is 1,024. You'll see why this is the rule as soon as we've done our first conversion.

8.5 Very Powerful. To convert decimal 206 to binary, which powers of 2 will be needed for the table?

The algorithm begins by placing the number to be converted—we'll illustrate with 365—into the top-left square, shown in green.

Number being converted	365								
Place value	256	128	64	32	16	8	4	2	1
Subtract									
Binary Number									

The algorithm has two cases based on a comparison of the number being converted and the place value.

1. **If the place value is smaller:** Subtract. Enter a 1 in the binary number row for that column (because that place contributes to the binary form of the number), and move the remainder (the result of the subtraction) to the top of the next column.
2. **If the place value is larger:** Don't subtract. Enter a 0 in the binary number row for that column and move the number to be converted right one square.

Continue with the columns in order until all of the binary digits have been created.

The first two steps of the conversion of 365 to binary illustrate the two cases of the algorithm.

Number being converted	365	109	109						
Place value	256	128	64	32	16	8	4	2	1
Subtract	109								
Binary Number	1	0							

Starting out, the place value (256) is less than 365, so the first case applies; we subtract and enter a 1 into the binary number row. The resulting 109 goes to the top of the next column. But now, the place value is larger than the number 109 to be converted (128 is larger than 109), so the second case applies. We enter a 0 in the developing binary number, and shift the 109 right one position. The full computation produces 1 0110 1101.

Number being converted	365	109	109	45	13	13	5	1	1
Place value	256	128	64	32	16	8	4	2	1
Subtract	109		45	13		5	1		0
Binary Number	1	0	1	1	0	1	1	0	1

So, why, when we set up the table, do we fill in all powers of 2 less than the number to be converted? Because the binary number will be a combination of the powers of 2 that add up to the decimal number—that's what it means to represent a number in binary—and so we must check them all to see if they contribute to the number.

8.6 Decimal Conversion. Convert the decimal number 206 to binary using the algorithm and its table.

Lighten Up: Changing Colors by Addition

Returning to our discussion of color representation, the extreme colors of black and white are easy, but what color does the following represent?

1100 1110 1100 1110 1100 1110

red byte	green byte	blue byte

First, notice that each byte contains the decimal value 206, which you recognize from the Try It 8.6 conversion. So, the mystery color is the color produced by the specification RGB (206,206,206). Like black and white, the mystery color has equal amounts of red, green, and blue, and it is closer to white than black. In fact, it is a light gray ■. All colors with equal intensities of the RGB subpixels are a shade of gray if they are not black or white. It's just a question of whether they're closer to black or white.

1100 1110	binary representing decimal number	206
+ 1 0000	binary representing decimal number	16
1101 1110	binary representing decimal number	222

Figure 8.4 Adding 16 to a binary value to lighten RGB intensities.

To Increase Intensity: Add in Binary

To make a *lighter* color of gray, obviously we change the common value to be closer to 255. Suppose we do this by increasing each of the RGB values by 16—that is, by adding 16 to each byte—as shown in Figure 8.4.

The result in Figure 8.4 is found by simply setting the 16's place value—that is, changing it from 0 to 1—because as a power of 2, it now contributes to the intensity. When the increase is applied to each color, the result is

1101 1110 1101 1110 1101 1110

red byte	green byte	blue byte

which is a lighter shade of gray. By the way, we can add or subtract any amount as long as the result is not less than 0 or greater than 255.

Lighter Still: Adding with Carry Digits

Imagine that we want the color lighter still by another 16 units of intensity for each RGB byte. Adding another 16 isn't quite as easy this time. The 16's position in the binary representation 1101 1110 of decimal 222 is already filled with a 1. So, we "carry" to the next higher place (see Figure 8.5).

The result gives color intensities of

1110 1110 1110 1110 1110 1110

red byte	green byte	blue byte

Notice that if we'd simply added 32 to 206 originally, we'd have ended up with the same result—the gray with each intensity set at 238.

We just illustrated the binary addition process. As with other aspects of binary, binary addition is actually the same as decimal addition, except with two digits only. We work from right to left, adding corresponding digits in each place position and writing the sum below. Like decimal addition, there are two cases. Sometimes, we can add the two numbers in a place and the result is expressed as a single digit. That was the case the first time we added 16 to the RGB byte: We added 1 + 0 in the 16's place and the result was 1.

1	carry digit	
1101 1110	binary representing decimal number	222
+ 1 0000	binary representing decimal number	16
1110 1110	binary representing decimal number	238

Figure 8.5 Adding 16 to the binary representation of the intensity 222, requiring a carry.

Table 8.1 Summary of the rules for binary addition. The carry-in is added to the two operands, A and B, to give the place digit and carry-out.

Carry-in	0	0	0	0	1	1	1	1
A	0	1	0	1	0	1	0	1
B	0	0	1	1	0	0	1	1
Place digit	0	1	1	0	1	0	0	1
Carry-out	0	0	0	1	0	1	1	1

Other times, when we add two digits in a place their sum is larger than can be expressed by a single digit, so we must carry to the next higher place. That was the case the second time we added 16 to the RGB byte: We added 1 + 1 in the 16's place, which is 10 in binary. We wrote a 0 in the place and carried the 1 to the next higher digit. Because there may be a carry involved, it is best to think of adding as involving three digits in each place: the two digits being added plus (possibly) a carry.

More Geek Humor. A widely repeated remark goes, "There are 10 kinds of people in the world . . . those who know binary and those who don't."

Adding a Summary. Binary addition held no surprises. It actually *was* like decimal addition limited to 0 and 1. Though we usually focus on adding two bits, it's best to think about adding three bits: two digit bits and a carry-in from the previous place. And, though we usually focus on producing one result bit, it's best to think of producing a result bit and a carry-out bit. Table 8.1 summarizes all of the cases.

8.7 Checking Binary. Compute this addition:

Binary addition is so easy even computers can do it!

```
  110 1001
+ 110 0011
```

Computing on Representations

Though we have focused on binary representation, conversions between decimal and binary, and binary addition, the previous sections have also introduced another fundamental concept of digital representation: the idea of *computing on representations*. When we made gray lighter, we showed how digital information—for example, the RGB settings of a pixel—can be changed through computation. For a better understanding of the idea, consider the more involved example that follows.

Old Photographs

Imagine that you scanned a photo of your great-great-grandmother (GGGM). What is the photo in terms of RGB pixels? It is a grid of pixels, let's say 600 × 800. Each pixel is 3 bytes, giving the color specification of that position, and the subpixels of a pixel have the same value because they are gray. It's a great picture, but it needs a little work!

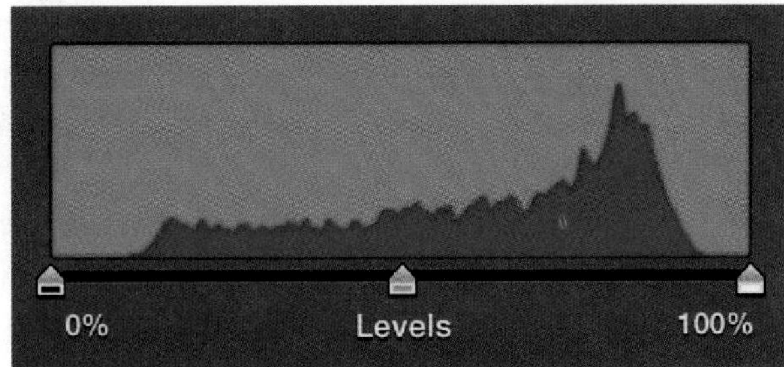

Figure 8.6 The Levels graph for the GGGM photo; the horizontal axis is the 256 pixel values, and the vertical axis is the number of pixels in the image with that value.

Increasing Brightness and Contrast

Photo manipulation software usually gives the ability to increase the brightness and contrast of photos, and this one looks like it could use those enhancements. *Brightness* refers to how close to white the pixels are; *contrast* is the size of the difference between the darkest and lightest portions of the image. What? Isn't black 0000 0000 0000 0000 0000 0000, the darkest, and white, 1111 1111 1111 1111 1111 1111, the lightest? It's true that they are the most extreme encodings, but an image may not have any true black or true white pixels in it. In fact, photo manipulation software often gives the values of the pixels in a clever Levels graph (see Figure 8.6).

In the pixel distribution of the GGGM photo, 0 percent is called the *black point*, or all zeroes in an unmanipulated picture, and 100 percent is the *white point*, or all ones. The midpoint is called the *gamma point*—let's not think about why—and it is the midpoint in the pixel range. From the graph we see that this photo's pixels are clumped in the middle gray range, with no extremes of white or black; it doesn't have much contrast and it's not very bright.

Let's consider brightening it first. What does that mean? We want all the pixels to be nearer intense white, but to keep their relative relationships. So, if we add, say 16, to each pixel, then a pixel in her cheek, which is 197, 197, 197 ■, would become 213, 213, 213 ■. It doesn't look like a huge change, but when applied everywhere, the image brightens noticeably.

Binary Addition

Okay, back to binary. We can apply (and review) the binary given in the last section. Let's implement the addition of 16 to 197. First of all, what is 197 in binary? Our table tells us

Number being converted		197	69	5	5	5	5	1	1
Place value		128	64	32	16	8	4	2	1
Subtract		69	5				1		0
Binary Number		1	1	0	0	0	1	0	1

that it is 1100 0101, ■; of course, 16 is a power of 2, so it is simply 1 0000. Writing the addition in the usual form

1100 0101	binary representing decimal number	197
+ 1 0000	binary representing decimal number	16
1101 0101	binary representing decimal number	213

the addition works as always. We can check the result using our binary to decimal algorithm to see that the result is 213. Changing all three bytes makes that pixel lighter, ■.

To increase brightness for the rest of the picture, we add 16 to all pixels. A pixel in her wrist has a gray value of 157 ■, which is 1001 1101 in binary. It presents a carry situation:

1	carry digit	
1001 1101	binary representing decimal number	157
+ 1 0000	binary representing decimal number	16
1010 1101	binary representing decimal number	173
↑		

The resulting gray value is 173, ■.

After adding 16 to all pixels, we have the brighter image shown in Figure 8.7(b). In terms of the Levels graph in Figure 8.6, we have shifted the entire graph 16 positions to the right, as shown in Figure 8.8(b).

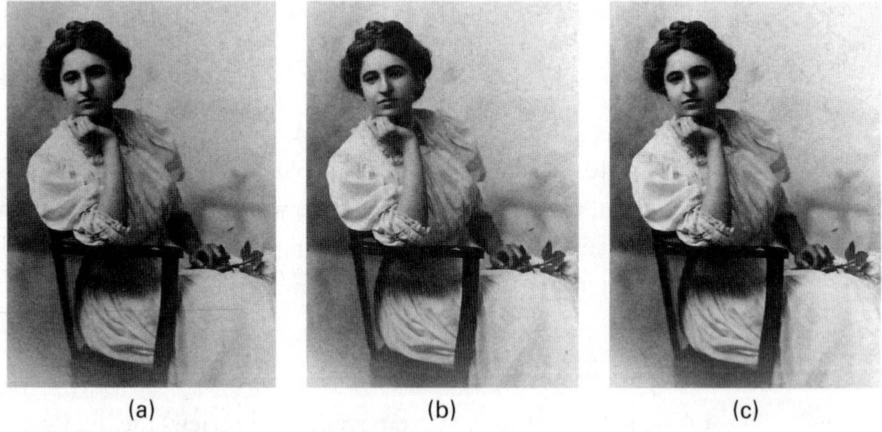

Figure 8.7 Three versions of the GGGM photo: (a) original, (b) brightened by "adding 16," and (c) contrast improved by increasing highlights more than shadows.

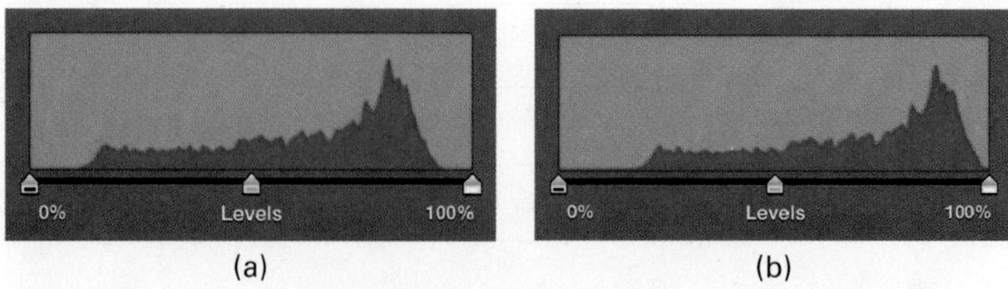

Figure 8.8 Levels graph for GGGM photo: (a) original and (b) after brightening by adding 16. Notice that the graph is simply shifted right by 16.

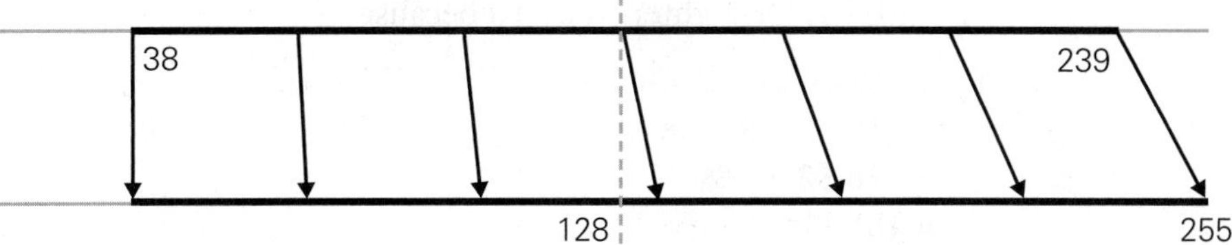

Figure 8.9 "Stretching" the pixel values right from the range 38–239 to 38–255.

Contrast

The photo got lighter when we added brightness, but it hasn't improved enough. We don't need the whole thing to be lighter as much as we need to increase the difference between the light parts and the dark parts, that is, increase the contrast. We can do that by using similar ideas.

Our goal is not to shift the Levels diagram right, but rather to "stretch it out" toward the right. That is, we want to add an amount to each pixel as we did before, but this time we need to add a smaller amount for dark pixels and a larger amount for light pixels. By leaving the dark pixels pretty much the same, and increasing the light pixels, we increase the contrast between the dark and light areas of the image (see Figure 8.7(c)).

To understand adding different amounts to each pixel, see the diagram in Figure 8.9. The (solid) upper line shows the pixel values as they are in the original Levels graph, as shown in Figure 8.6. The smallest pixel value is 38 and the largest is 239. The arrows show how we want to increase the amount we lighten each pixel gradually so that they span the range 38 to 255.

It's easiest to think about the operation as converting the original value to a new value, and to use Figure 8.9 as a guide. For every original pixel P_o, we subtract the amount of the lower end of the range; in our case that's 38,

$P_o - 38$

giving us its position along the dark part of the top line. That tells how much to increase each pixel position; smaller (darker) numbers get lightened less than larger (lighter) numbers. Then we multiply by the size of the new interval divided by the size of the old interval. This is how much to stretch the old range (38–239) so that it just matches the new range (38–255):

$$\frac{(255-38)}{(239-38)} = \frac{217}{210} - 1.08$$

Finally, we add the low end of the original range back in again, to return each pixel to its new position along the second line. This gives us the equation for the value in each pixel position of the new image:

$P_n = (P_o - 38)*1.08 + 38$

rounding to a whole number. Checking, we verify that pixel value 38 isn't changed at all, and pixel value 239 is changed to 255. Additionally, pixel 197 is lightened by 13 because

$$\begin{aligned} P_n &= (197 - 38) * 1.08 + 38 \\ &= 159 * 1.08 + 38 \\ &= 171.72 + 38 \\ &= 209.72 \\ &= 210 \end{aligned}$$

and pixel 157 is lightened by 10 because

$$P_n = (157 - 38) * 1.08 + 38$$
$$= 119 * 1.08 + 38$$
$$= 128.52 + 38$$
$$= 166.52$$
$$= 167$$

The result, shown in Figure 8.7(c), is quite nice. Your great-great-grandmother's hair is dark, and the detail in her sleeve is accentuated. It's possible to increase by more or less than 1.08, of course. (Image processing software usually gives us a slider.) Here, we chose 1.12 and made sure that any value that exceeded 255 was set to 255.

Of course, the computer is performing all of these multiplications in binary, which works like decimal multiplication, as you probably guessed. We will leave the details of binary multiplication to computer engineers.

Adding Color

So far, we have not used the RGB characteristics of our image encoding. But now we will add color by changing the subpixels by different amounts. Whenever the 3 bytes differ in value, we can perceive color. We will continue our idea of changing the pixels by different amounts on different parts of the photograph. As is standard in image manipulation, recognize three parts of the photograph:

Pixel Type	R Change	G Change	B Change
Highlights	+8	0	–4
Midrange	+9	+6	–4
Shadows	+15	0	–6

The amount shown is the amount by which I propose to change the subpixels. These settings produce an effect similar to "antique" in image processing software, a slightly pink-brown tint known as sepia.

But, how do we define the three different regions of the image? We can define "highlights" as the lightest 25 percent of the pixels and "shadows" as the darkest 25 percent of the pixels. We do this by counting the pixels.

A useful fact is that there are 600 × 800 = 480,000 pixels total in this photo. If we start at pixel value 38 and find the number of 38 pixels and add that number to the number of 39's and the number of 40's, . . . until we get a total of about 120,000, we know that that's the boundary between the shadows and the midrange portions of the image. In the GGGM photo, the largest shadow subpixel value is 134. Starting at the other end, at 255, and doing the opposite gets us the boundary between the highlights and the midrange. The largest midrange pixel is 233 (see Figure 8.10).

To summarize, the highlights, midrange, and shadows are defined as follows:

Highlights 25%	255–234	121,339
Midrange 50%	233–135	239,540
Shadows 25%	134–38	119,121

The approximate nature of these ranges will not affect the quality of the image.

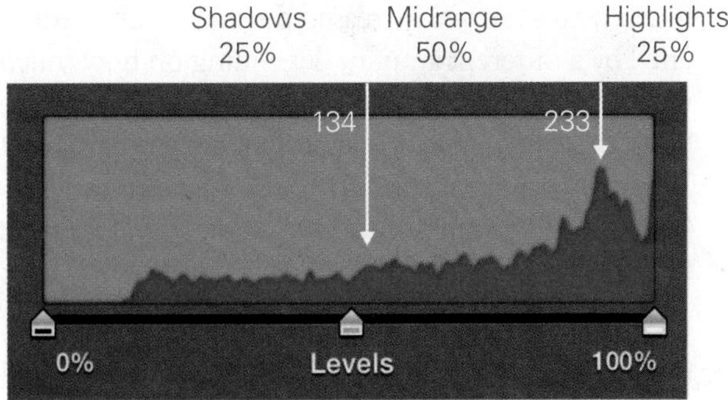

Figure 8.10 The Levels graph for the image in Figure 8.7(c), and boundaries between the highlights, midrange, and shadows.

The algorithm to colorize the image (see Figure 8.11) is simple. For each pixel, get the red subpixel (any one will work) and check its range. Then, using the color modifications given above for that portion of the image, adjust the color of each subpixel.

8.8 Getting the Gray Out. Using the coloring algorithm, give the new value for a pixel with a gray value of 1010 1100.

Summary of Digital Color

Color is represented by three quantities: red intensity, green intensity, and blue intensity, or RGB. Together, these three values form a pixel; the constituent parts are called subpixels. Standard computer equipment assigns 1 byte to each intensity, giving a range from 0 to 255. The intensities are given as binary numbers, which allows software to "compute on the image."

Using a scanned black-and-white photo, we manipulated it in several ways. We brightened it by adding 16 to each subpixel. This preserved the gray color—all three subpixels have the same value—and pushed each pixel closer to white. The picture was brighter, but not

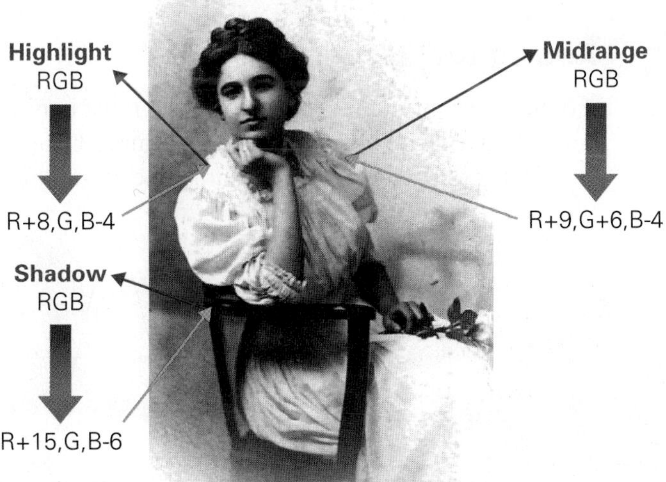

Figure 8.11 The gray is changed to sepia by checking each pixel, deciding if it's a highlight, midrange or shadow, and replacing the pixel with a corresponding revised RGB assignment.

much better. So, we increased the contrast by redefining each pixel so they would be brightened by a different amount depending on how much larger it was than the darkest subpixel value of 38. The darks changed little, but the highlights were lightened as before. Finally, we "split the RGB values" so that they were no longer the same, causing the image to be colored. We applied an algorithm to adjust the color differently over different parts of the image. Commercial image processing software is more sophisticated when it performs these transformations, generally to produce a more artistic effect, but the process is exactly the same.

And as we transformed the image, we learned the basics of binary arithmetic, which—it turned out—we already knew, because we know decimal arithmetic. It's the same, just limited to 0 and 1.

Digitizing Sound

In this section we discuss digitizing again, but this time we focus on digitizing sound rather than images because it is equally interesting and slightly easier. The principles are the same when digitizing any "continuous" information.

An object—think of a cymbal—creates sound by vibrating in a medium such as air. The vibrations push the air, causing pressure waves to emanate from the object, which in turn vibrate our eardrums. The vibrations are transmitted by three tiny bones to the fine hairs of our cochlea, stimulating nerves that allow us to sense the waves and "hear" them as sound. The force, or intensity of the push, determines the volume, and the **frequency** (the number of waves per second) of the pushes is the pitch. Figure 8.12 shows a graph of a pure tone sound wave. The horizontal axis shows time and the vertical axis shows the amount of positive or negative sound pressure.

From a digitization point of view, the key is that the object vibrates continuously, producing a continuously changing wave, which is called **analog** information. As the wave moves past, say, a microphone, the measured pressure changes smoothly. When this pressure variation is recorded directly, as it was originally by Thomas Edison with a scratch on a wax cylinder, and then later with vinyl records, we have a continuous (analog) representation of the wave. In principle, all of the continuous variation of the wave is recorded. Digital representations work differently.

Analog to Digital

To digitize continuous information, we must convert the data to bits. For a sound wave, we use a binary number to record the amount that the wave is above or below the 0 line at a given point on our graph; that is, the amount of positive or negative sound pressure.

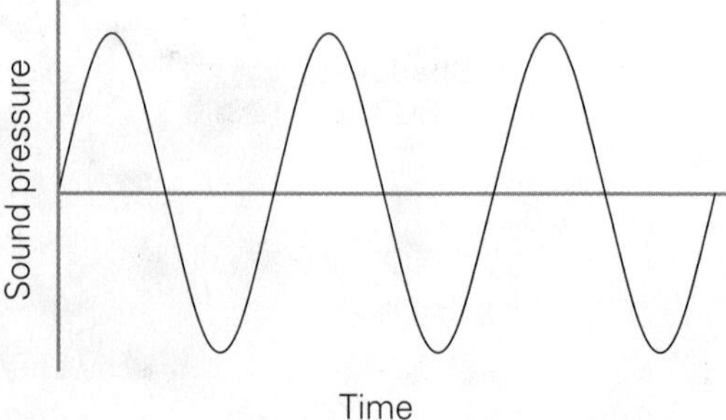

Figure 8.12 Sound wave. The horizontal axis is time; the vertical axis is sound pressure.

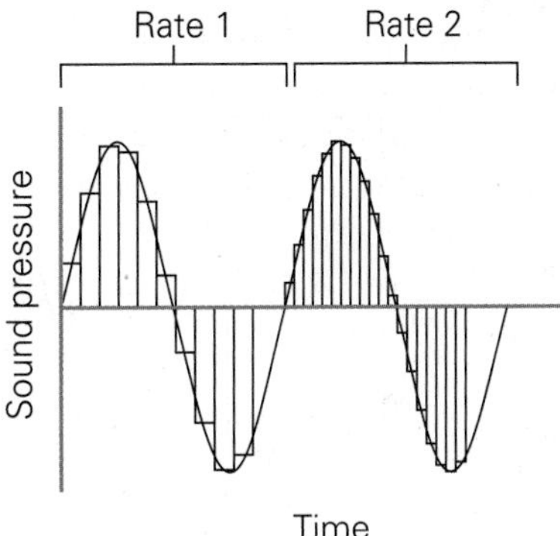

Figure 8.13 Two sampling rates; the rate on the right is twice as fast as that on the left.

But at what point do we measure? There are infinitely many points along the line, too many to record every position of the wave.

Sampling. So, we **sample**, which means we take measurements at regular intervals. The number of samples in a second is called the **sampling rate**, and the faster the rate, the more accurately the wave is recorded (see Figure 8.13).

How Fast a Sampling Rate? To get a good recording of the wave, we need a sampling rate that is related to the wave's frequency. For example, if the sampling were too slow, sound waves could "fit between" the samples and we would miss them entirely.

Fortunately, we have guidelines for the sampling rates. In electrical engineering, the **Nyquist rule** says that a sampling rate must be at least twice as fast as the fastest frequency. And what is the fastest frequency we can expect? Because humans can hear sound up to roughly 20,000 Hz, a 40,000 Hz sampling rate fulfills the Nyquist rule for digital audio recording. For technical reasons, however, a somewhat faster-than-two-times sampling rate was chosen for digital audio, 44,100 Hz.

ADC-CoDec-DAC. The digitizing process works as follows: Sound is picked up by a microphone (called a *transducer* because it converts the sound wave into an electrical wave). This electrical signal is fed into an **analog-to-digital converter (ADC)**, which takes the continuous wave and samples it at regular intervals, outputting for each sample binary numbers. These numbers are compressed (see Figure 8.14) and stored in memory.

The process is reversed to play the sound: The numbers are read from memory into the decompressor, which produces binary numbers suitable for playing. These are input to a **digital-to-analog converter (DAC)**, which creates an electrical wave by interpolation between the digital values—that is, filling in or smoothly moving from one value to another. The electrical signal is then input to a speaker, which converts the electrical wave into a sound wave, as shown in Figure 8.14.

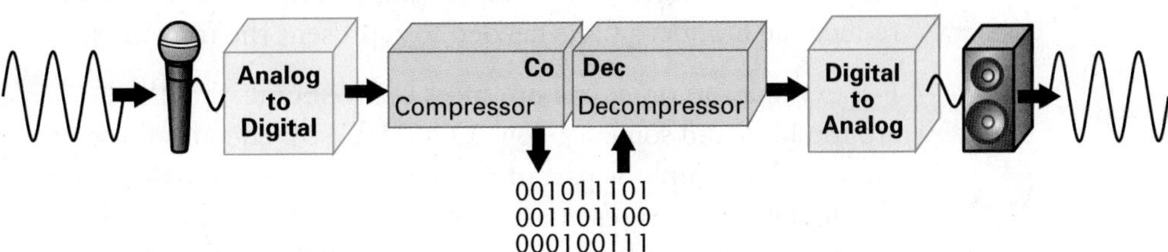

Figure 8.14 Schematic for analog-to-digital and digital-to-analog conversion.

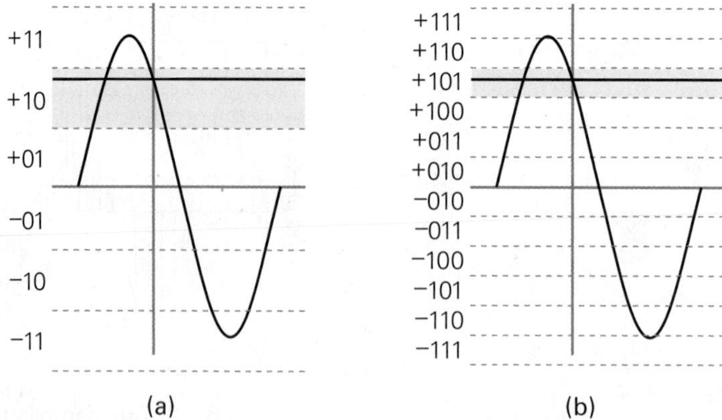

Figure 8.15 (a) Three-bit precision for samples requires that the indicated reading at the (blue) sample point is approximated as +10. (b) Adding another bit makes the sample twice as accurate.

How Many Bits per Sample? The problem of digitizing is solved except for describing how accurate the samples must be. To make the samples perfectly accurate, we would need an unlimited number of bits for each sample, which is impossible. But to start, we know that the bits must represent both positive and negative values, because the wave has both positive and negative sound pressure. Second, the more bits there are, the more accurate the measurement is. For example, with only 3 bits, one of which is used to indicate whether the sign is + or –, we can encode one of four positions in either direction (they align at 0). With so few bits, we can only get an approximate measurement, as shown in Figure 8.15(a). If we used another bit, the sample would be twice as accurate. (In Figure 8.15(b), each interval is half as wide, making the illustrated crossing in the "upper" half of the interval.)

Using more bits yields a more accurate digitization. The digital representation of audio typically uses 16 bits, meaning that 2^{16} = 65,536 levels are recorded, 2^{15} =32,768 for positive values and 32,768 for negative values.

Unforgiving Minute. How many bits does it take to record a minute of digital audio? There are 60 seconds of 44,100 samples of 16 bits each, times two for stereo. That's 84,672,000 bits, or 10,584,000 bytes, more than 10.5 megabytes. An hour is 635 MB! That number, 635 MB for an hour of audio, determined the size of the original compact disc design.

Advantages of Digital Sound

A key advantage of digital information (as demonstrated earlier in the chapter) is that we can compute on the representation.

MP3 Compression. One computation of value is to *compress* the digital audio; that is, reduce the number of bits needed to represent the information.

For example, an orchestra produces many sounds that the human ear can't hear—some are too high and some too low. Our ADC still encodes these frequencies—not to annoy our dog, but simply as part of the encoding process. By computing special functions on the digital audio representation, it's possible to remove these waves without harming the way the audio sounds to us. This is the sort of compression used for MP3. In MP3 we typically get a **compression ratio** of more than 10:1, which means that the number of bits is reduced to about one-tenth of what it was. So, a minute of MP3 music typically takes less than a megabyte to represent. This makes MP3 popular for Internet transmission, because it has lower bandwidth requirements. We discuss bandwidth—the rate at which bits are transmitted—shortly.

Another computation is to "fix" a recording in the same way we "fixed" our GGGM picture. If someone coughs during a quiet moment of Verdi's *Requiem*, we can remove the offending noise from the recording. Performances can be sped up or slowed down without affecting pitch, volume, and so on.

MP3. The "sound track" of a digital video in the MPEG representation is known as MPEG level 3, or MP3.

Reproducing the Sound Recording. Another key advantage of digital representations over analog is that they can be reproduced exactly. As discussed in Chapter 2, we can copy the file of bits that make up an audio performance without losing a single bit of information. When the original and the copy are played by the same system, they sound exactly the same. With analog representation, the copy is never as exact as the original, and because of wear, a second (or third or one-hundredth) playing of the same version is never as good as the first. Digital recordings never have these problems as long as the bits remain stable.

Digital Images and Video

A digital image is a long sequence of RGB pixels. Of course, the picture is two dimensional, but we think of the pixels stretched out one row after another in memory, which is one dimensional. How many pixels are there? For an 8 × 10 image scanned at 300 pixels per inch, there are 80 square inches, each requiring 300 × 300 = 90,000 pixels for a grand total of 7.2 megapixels. At 3 bytes per pixel, it takes 21.6 MB of memory to store one 8 × 10 color image. That's more memory than personal computers came with in the 1990s.

Receiving this photo over a baseline cable modem (typically 1.5Mbs) takes 115.2 seconds, or almost two minutes; a wireless phone (LTE) connection (averaging 3–6Mbs) can cut that to a little less than a minute; and a dialup connection—don't even ask!—takes more than 51 minutes (longer than the average college class). So, how do people without fast connections see screen-size pictures in seconds when surfing the Web?

Image Compression

Compression means to change the representation in order to use fewer bits to store or transmit information. For example, faxes are usually long sequences of 0's and 1's that encode where the page is white (0) or black (1). Rather than sending all the 0's and 1's, we can use run-length encoding to take advantage of the fact that the sequences of 0's and 1's tend to be long. **Run-length encoding** uses binary numbers to specify how long the first sequence (run) of 0's is, then how long the following sequence of 1's is, then how long the following sequence of 0's is, and so on. This works best for long sequences of 0's and 1's, and most of the time run-length compression is a big win.

Run-length encoding is a **lossless compression** scheme, meaning that the original representation of 0's and 1's can be perfectly reconstructed from the compressed version. The first number says how many 0's to write down, the second number says how many 1's to write down next, the third number says how many 0's to write down next, and so forth. The opposite of lossless compression is **lossy compression**, meaning that the original representation cannot be exactly reconstructed from the compressed form. MP3 is lossy because the high notes cannot be recovered—but it doesn't matter since we can't hear them anyway.

Tom's Diner. The MP3 lossy compression technique works because people cannot perceive any difference between the original and the compressed versions. In trying to evaluate their lossy techniques, the engineers who developed MP3 compression ran listener studies using the song *Tom's Diner* by American songwriter Suzanne Vega. The song refers to her experiences in a New York City diner. She sings the song a cappella, making it easy to detect problems with the encoding. You can listen to it as an MP3 at **www.youtube.com/watch?v=nLedFWpF9EA**.

Suzanne Vega

Color Table		
1	FF 00 00	
2	FF FF FF	
3	00 FF 00	
	. . .	

Hungary

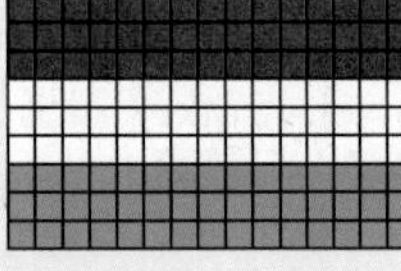

Italy

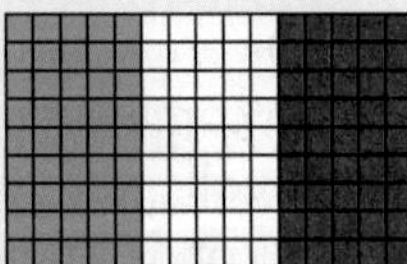

GIF Encoding. The Graphics Interchange Format (GIF) is a standard encoding for icons, cartoons, and simple art. GIF is a lossless encoding scheme that pushes the idea of run-length encoding beyond the runs-of-0's and runs-of-1's. There are three ideas that make GIF encodings work. First, the number of colors is limited to 256, which is plenty for simple art. (Transparent is also allowed so the background can show through.) The use of 256 allows for the second idea: Do not represent colors as 3-byte RGB triples, but make a table of colors, put the RGB into the table, and refer to the colors by their 1-byte index—their number in the table (see the table at the left). These two ideas give a simple encoding, which records runs of colors.

For example, the file `huFlag`, which gives the size of the image in pixels followed by the list of runs expressed as *length:color* pairs (lc-pairs), where *color* is an index into the table

huFlag: [15 × 9] 45:1, 45:2, 45:3

can be decoded into a 15 × 9 pixel Hungarian flag. The flag's first three rows are each 15 consecutive red pixels, making a run—when we stretch out the pixels into a sequence—of 45; the white and green bands are similar. Italy's flag, however, is not encoded as succinctly.

itFlag: [15 x 9] 5:3,5:2,5:1,5:3,5:2,5:1,5:3,5:2,5:1,
5:3,5:2,5:1,5:3,5:2,5:1,5:3,5:2,5:1,
5:3,5:2,5:1,5:3,5:2,5:1,5:3,5:2,5:1

and requires groups of three of the *length:color* pairs to encode a row in the flag, implying that it needs nine groups of three. This illustrates GIF's preference for horizontal bands of color rather than vertical bands. Computing the costs we have

Direct pixel encoding	9 × 15 pixels × 3 RGB bytes	=	405 bytes
Hungarian Flag	3 lc-pairs × 2 bytes + 12 bytes (table)	=	18 bytes
Italian Flag	9 × 3 lc-pairs × 2 bytes + 12 bytes (table)	=	66 bytes

showing the advantage of even this simple scheme. (A table entry is 4 bytes.)

The third idea is to add Lempel-Ziv-Welch (LZW) compression, which looks for pixel patterns like 5 green, followed by 5 white, followed by 5 red, and encodes them into the table so the pattern can be indexed, just like the colors. This idea gets the Italian flag to an encoding approximating that of the Hungarian flag, but it is rather involved. However, the idea will obviously help, especially with vertical bands like the Italian flag.

PBS Digital Studios Animated GIFs: Birth of a Medium

Regarding the pronunciation of "GIF," the inventor, Steve Wilhite said, "The *Oxford English Dictionary* accepts both pronunciations. They are wrong. It is a soft 'G,' pronounced 'jif.' End of story."

JPEG

MP3 is probably the most famous compression scheme, running a close second is the familiar JPG. JPEG—we often leave out the e, especially for file extensions, but it's officially there—was invented by the Joint Photographic Experts Group of the ISO. JPEG (pronounced JAY·peg) is a lossy compression technique that exploits the same kinds of "human perception" characteristics that MP3 does, only for light and color.

Specifically, humans are quite sensitive to small changes in brightness, technically known as **luminance**. So, when compressing images, the brightness features of a photo must be preserved or we will notice a difference between the uncompressed and compressed versions. However, people are not sensitive to small differences in color, technically referred to as **chrominance**. So, if the sky or other large region of color is made up of pixels that are the same except for the "small (least significant) bits" to the right, then one representative color can be chosen for the whole region, allowing one pixel to "stand in" for many.

The technique works until the region becomes so large that the difference becomes perceptible where one region meets the next region. For example, the upper square becomes darker gradually from top to bottom, but most of us see it as "all blue." However, when all pixels in the top half are changed to match the top row, as shown in the lower square, we see a noticeable line across the middle; pixels on each side differ enough to be noticeable.

JPEG is capable of a 10:1 compression without detectable loss of clarity simply by keeping the regions small (see Figure 8.16). But, often greater compression is possible. As you know, in consumer software, JPEG comes with a slider control for selecting the amount of compression, so it is possible to experiment with levels greater than 10:1. The benefit is smaller files, but eventually the picture begins to "pixelate," or as the slang goes, it gets "jaggies." The original image in Figure 8.16 (a) required 202 KB at full resolution delivered from the camera. A 10:1 compression—the 20 KB file in Figure 8.16 (b)—preserves all features of the photo at this size. At 20:1, the 10 KB file image in Figure 8.16 (c) could be acceptable for some purposes, though now pixelation is evident—for example, the sand looks like blobs and as the orange sculpture becomes shaded, and we see the smooth change break into solid blocks. Eventually, the 25:1 compression (8 KB) in Figure 8.16 (d) completely pixelates, producing art in another form. Notice the effect on memory: Saving 180 KB with the 10:1 compression caused no apparent harm; saving the next 10 KB made a detectable difference, and saving the last 2 KB completely changed the image. We can fool our perception, but to a limited degree.

(a) (b) (c) (d)

Figure 8.16 Life Saver sculpture at the beach (400 × 300 pixels): (a) original 202 KB, (b) 10:1 compression (20 KB), (c) 20:1 compression (10 KB), (d) 25:1 ratio (8 KB).

MPEG Compression Scheme

MPEG, the compression scheme of the Motion Picture Experts Group of the ISO, is the same idea as JPEG applied to motion pictures. On the one hand, it seems like an easier task because each image—each frame—is not seen for very long, so we should be able to get away with even greater levels of single-image compression. On the other hand, the problem seems more difficult because it takes many stills to make a movie. In MPEG compression, JPEG-type compression is applied to each frame, but then "interframe coherency" is used. Because two consecutive video images are usually very similar, MPEG compression only has to record and transmit the "differences" between frames. This results in huge amounts of compression. So, MPEG and other compression schemes only need moderate amounts of bandwidth, allowing us to watch videos on YouTube and Vimeo.

The familiar QR Code is a two-dimensional, optically readable encoding that is more versatile than bar codes. Developed in 1994 by Denso Wave, a subsidiary of Toyota, to track parts in factories, the QR Code was ingeniously designed to be read quickly and in different orientations. QR Codes can handle Japanese Kanji characters, and they allow four different levels of error correction; greater correction requires more bits. The most aggressive error correction can recover the content when as much as 30 percent of the code is damaged or lost. For example, lay a pencil across this QR code, covering up some of the bits; your scanner should still be able to read it.

Capacity

Data Type	*Max Content**
Numeric only	7,089 characters
Alphanumeric	4,296 characters
Binary (8-bit)	2,953 bytes
Kanji/Kana	1,817 characters

*Largest size, smallest error correction

Error Correction Options

EC Level	*% Restored**
L	7%
M	15%
Q	25%
H	30%

*Amount of loss that can be recovered

QR Codes have a very involved structure that only a computer can love. Notice first that the code shown above has a (required) 4-unit "quiet space" around it where nothing can be printed. Figure 8.17 shows the standard layout of the components (a); these include three position symbols (b) with their own "quiet spaces" in the three specific corners; the format information (c), given twice; the "dotted lines" (d) are timing patterns; and the area shown in gray (e) encodes the content and error correction. The bits are assigned starting in the lower right corner, and are laid out two bits at a time in a pattern (f) that continues (moving left) except where the other components are in the way. The actual bit assignments are determined by the kind of information encoded and the level of error correction.

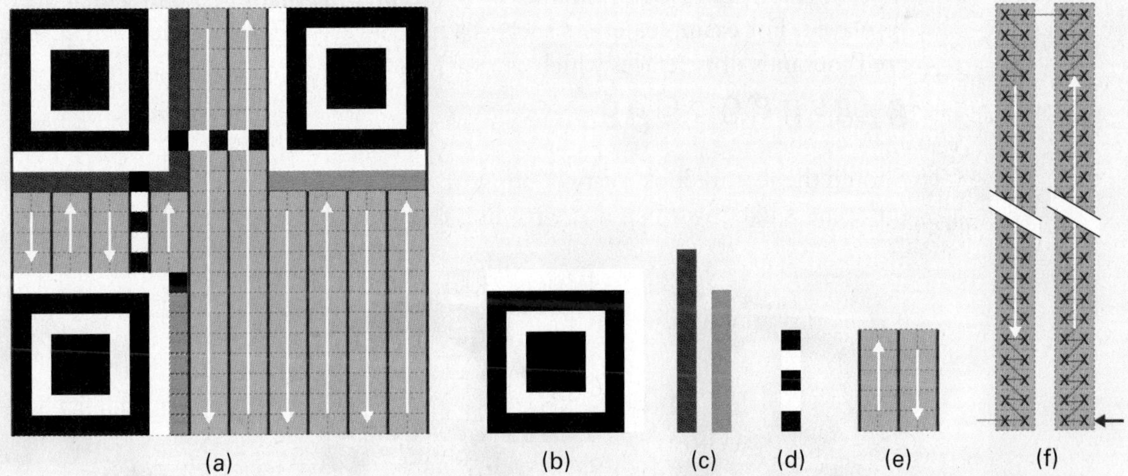

Figure 8.17 Structure of a QR Code: (a) the overall layout, (b) a position symbol with its 1-unit "quiet" region, (c) the two separate copies of format information, (d) timing symbols, (e) data area, and (f) double-bit assignment pattern, which begins in the lower right corner of the layout shown in (a) and continues.

So, what does the QR Code above say? As you can verify with your phone or other mobile device, it says, "The 'qr' probably stands for 'quite remarkable.'" Make your own QR Codes at www.qrstuff.com/.

8.9 Perfect Timing. The QR Code shown at right, is the Japanese text 連邦政府軍のご協力により、君達の基地は、全てCATSがいただいた。, which is from the video game *Zero Wing*, and was famously and incorrectly translated into English as "All your base are belong to us." How many black squares are there in the timing row (or column) of this code?

Optical Character Recognition

Different forms of digital information have different advantages. For example, a JPG image of a page of text only describes how to color the screen's pixels to display the page; it won't, for example, let you search for a word in the picture. To do that, the pixels must be converted to text, a process known as **optical character recognition (OCR)** (see Figure 8.18).

The computer scans groups of pixels looking for edges where the color changes. It forms these into distinct **features**—parts of a character to be recognized. For example, a "hole," a "vertical stroke," and a "horizontal stroke" might be identified as features for this a. Lines and holes are patterns that can be recognized by noting how edges form connections. Given the features, a **classifier** matches them to the alphabet to determine which are close, perhaps finding a strong correlation with a, a weaker one with d, perhaps, and an even weaker one with 6. Finally, after picking the most likely characters, some optical character recognizers check the context, trying to decide if the combination makes sense.

Optical character recognition must work despite the many styles in which printed text is displayed. For example, letters such as a have a very different italic form, *a*. Also, there are thousands of typefaces which can vary widely as in

gggggggggg

Should the feature look for two loops, or one loop with a tail? We hardly notice differences like this when we're reading text, but OCR software must.

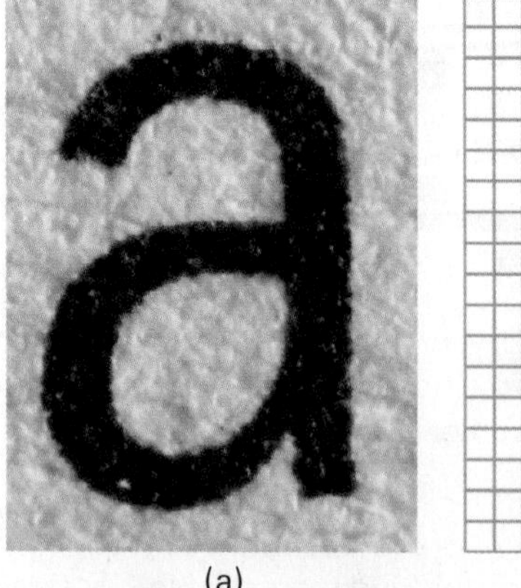

(a)

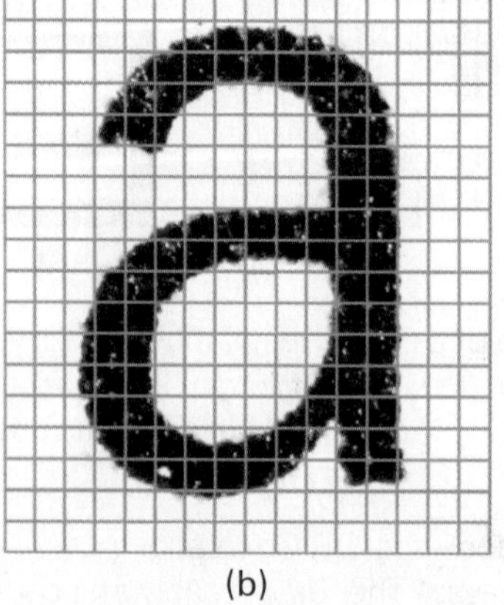

(b)

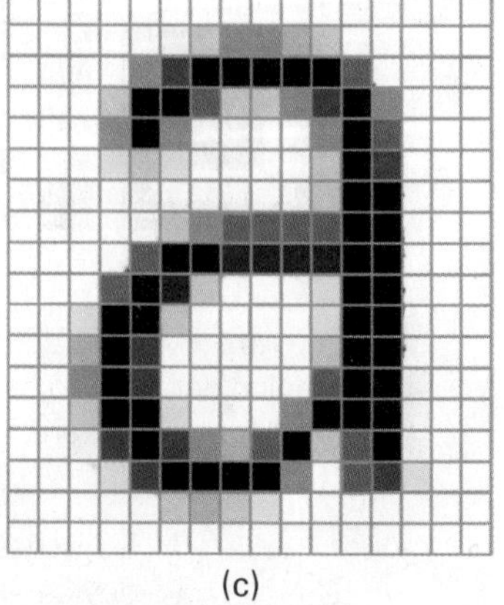

(c)

Figure 8.18 Lowercase, sanserif a: (a) shows the analog letter as it appears on the printed page; (b) the letter overlaid by a grid showing where the image will be sampled; and (c) shows the letter in its digital form as it might appear after being captured by a scanner or camera. Each pixel is an estimate of how dark the corresponding area is.

Text-to-Speech Technology. Perhaps the most significant application of optical character recognition is Raymond Kurzweil's text-to-speech reading machines developed for the blind and partially sighted. First produced in 1976, the reading machine uses a flatbed scanner—a technology originally developed by Kurzweil—to scan reading material, recognize it as text, and then speak it using a voice synthesizer. Scanning, font-independent optical character recognition, large-vocabulary dictionaries, and speech synthesis, all of which Kurzweil had to create for his devices, are now standard technologies. For the disabled, the reader and its inverse, the speech-to-text machine, have dramatically improved personal lives and career opportunities. Says the blind musician Stevie Wonder, who credits the reader with changing his life, "It gave blind people the one life goal that everyone treasures, and that is independence."

Ray Kurzweil with the Kurzweil Personal Reader, a 1988 version of his invention.

Raymond Kurzweil received the National Medal of Technology and the Lemelson-MIT Award for Innovation, which is similar to a Nobel Prize for inventors. (See the interview following Chapter 10 for observations by Ray Kurzweil.)

Today Kurzweil's technology is packaged as a smartphone; photograph the text with the camera, then listen to it as it's read to you.

Beginning Reader. In 1954, J. Rainbow demonstrated an optical character reader that could recognize uppercase typewritten characters at the rate of one letter per minute.

OCR Technology

Though optical character recognition is a very sophisticated technology, it has become mainstream. You may already have an OCR app, but if not they are easy to find with a Web search.

Commercial OCR business applications include sorting mail and banking. The U.S. Postal Service uses a system that locates the address block on an envelope or card, reads it in any of 400 fonts, identifies its ZIP code, generates a nine-digit bar code, sprays the bars on the envelope, sorts it, and, with only a 2 percent error rate, processes up to 45,000 pieces of mail per hour. In banking, the magnetic numbers at the bottom of the check have been read by computers since the 1950s; now OCR is used to read the *handwritten* digits of the numeric check amount to verify that a data entry person has interpreted the amount correctly. That is, the computer checks the person.

Human Character Recognition. As you probably know, those "fuzzy, wiggly" text-deciphering problems we must solve to access Web sites are called **captchas**. They are there to keep out "spambots," the programs that post ads, bait visitors to malware sites, and deliver other undesirable junk. As annoying as captchas are, they successfully protect sites most of the time.

CAPtCha
[captcha]

But it is a battle of wits. While some programmers work hard to make captchas easy for humans to recognize but difficult for computers, the hackers who write spambot programs are working hard to recognize them. It's a war in which the advantage shifts back and forth. In Autumn 2013 a startup called Vicarious claimed to be able to solve Captchas with 90% accuracy using artificial intelligence techiques. Captchas have gotten "fuzzier" to keep the spambots at bay, but before they get so fuzzy even people can't read them, sites are implementing a "next generation" system called **reCaptcha**.

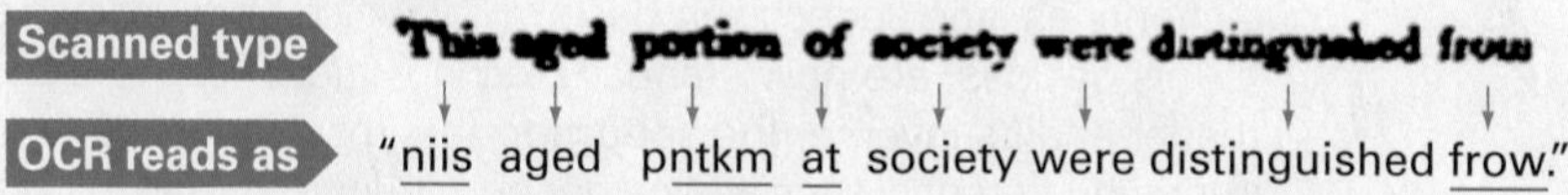

This idea works as follows: Instead of purposely creating fuzzed-up words, reCaptcha uses words from real books with poor printing that OCR systems can't figure out and have problems interpreting. The reCaptcha system asks a group of people two words—one known and one unknown. If those who got the known word right generally agree on the unknown word (a few errors are okay), they are allowed to enter the site, and the reCaptcha can add that word to its "known" word list. This process then helps the digitized book to be corrected.

Multimedia Challenges

Despite the ingenuity of audio and video compression, online video chat software still occasionally loses frames, pixelates images, and garbles words. This is not a surprise. Compression technologies are battling on our behalf to give a smooth, uninterrupted conversation against the forces of latency and bandwidth.They are formidable foes.

The Challenge of Latency

Latency—the time it takes for information to be created or delivered—greatly influences our experience with technology. When Web pages do not load instantly, we get frustrated as we sit, watching the spinner. But waiting is usually the extent of our inconvenience. In video and voice communication, long latencies ruin the experience. No one will chat when the words are lost, or it takes seconds (rather than milliseconds) to redraw the speaker's image.

For Internet-related latencies, the causes typically are either a slow server or network congestion. Compression doesn't help either one get the first packet to your computer. For loading Web pages, however, it does help complete the task quicker. Reducing latency is a common engineering goal, but there is an *absolute limit* to how fast information can be transmitted: the speed of light. Eventually, the virtual world is constrained by the physical world.

The Challenge of Bandwidth

Closely related to latency is **bandwidth**—a measure of how much information is transmitted per unit of time. Bandwidth is related to latency in that a given amount of information (for example, 10 MB) transmitted with a given bandwidth (for example, 5 MB/s) determines the (best) latency by dividing the amount by the bandwidth; in this case, 10/5 = 2, or 2 seconds of latency. Other delays can extend the latency beyond this theoretical best. Higher bandwidth usually means lower latency. (The rule eventually fails for speed-of-light and switching-delay reasons.)

Bits Are It

Looking back over this and previous chapters, we have seen that 4 bytes can represent many kinds of information, from four ASCII keyboard characters to numbers between zero and about 4 billion. This is not an accident, but rather a fundamental property of information, which we summarize in this principle:

Bias-Free Universal Medium Principle: *Bits can represent all discrete information; bits have no inherent meaning.*

Bits: The Universal Medium

The first half of the principle—all discrete information can be represented by bits—is the universality aspect. Discrete things—things that can be separated from each other—can be represented by bits. At the very least, we can assign numbers to each one and represent those numbers in binary. But, as we saw with color, it's possible to be much smarter. We assigned the RGB colors so the intensity could be increased or decreased using binary arithmetic. This representation of color is much more organized than simply saying, "Black will be 0, purple will be 1, yellow will be 2," and so on. As a result of organizing the representation in a sensible way, we can *easily* compute on it, making changes like brightening the image. Of course, if the information is continuous—that is, if it is analog information like sound—it must first be made discrete by an analog-to-digital conversion. But once digitized, this information, too, can be represented by bits.

Bits: Bias-Free

The second half of the principle—bits have no inherent meaning—is the bias-free aspect. Given a bit sequence

0000 0000 1111 0001 0000 1000 0010 0000

there is no way to know what information it represents. The meaning of the bits comes entirely from the **interpretation** placed on them by us or by the computer through our programs. For example, the 4 bytes could be a zero byte followed by the RGB intensities (241, 8, 32) ■. Or, the 4 bytes could be an instruction to add two binary numbers. As a binary number, the bits work out to 15,796,256.

So, bits are bits. What they mean depends on how the software interprets them, which means they work for any kind of information. Storage media need to store one pair of patterns only: 0 and 1. The principle explains why, for example, a single transmission medium—the TCP/IP packet—is all that's needed to deliver any kind of digital information across the Internet to your computer: text, photos, or MP3 tunes. It delivers bits and that's enough.

Bits Are Not Necessarily Binary Numbers

Since the public first became aware of computers, it has been "common knowledge" that computers represent information as binary *numbers*. Experts reinforce this view, but it's not quite right. Computers represent information as bits. Bits can be *interpreted* as binary numbers, as you've seen, which is why the experts are not wrong. But the bits do not always represent binary numbers. They can be interpreted as ASCII characters, RGB colors, or an unlimited list of other things (see Figure 8.19).

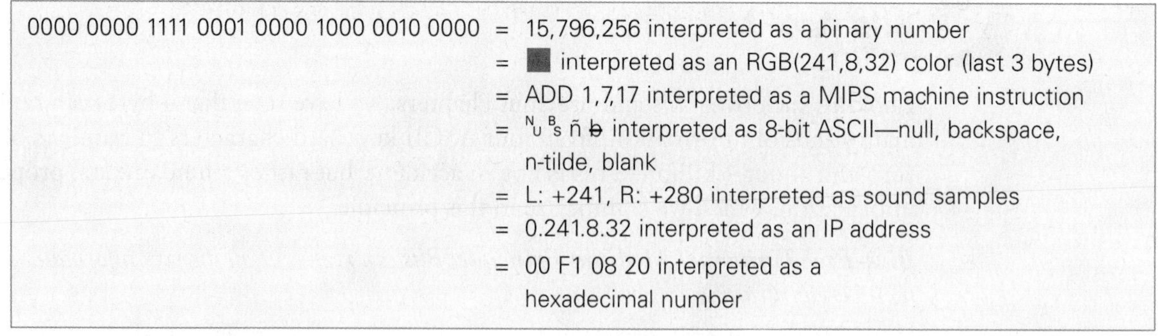

0000 0000 1111 0001 0000 1000 0010 0000 = 15,796,256 interpreted as a binary number
= ■ interpreted as an RGB(241,8,32) color (last 3 bytes)
= ADD 1,7,17 interpreted as a MIPS machine instruction
= ␀ ␈ ñ ␢ interpreted as 8-bit ASCII—null, backspace, n-tilde, blank
= L: +241, R: +280 interpreted as sound samples
= 0.241.8.32 interpreted as an IP address
= 00 F1 08 20 interpreted as a hexadecimal number

Figure 8.19 Illustration of the principle that "bits are bits." The same 4 bytes shown can be interpreted differently.

Programs often perform arithmetic on the bits, as you saw when we modified the GGGM image; but often they do not, because it doesn't make sense with the intended interpretation of the information. Computers represent information with bits. They are an amazing medium.

SUMMARY

In this chapter we considered how different forms of information are represented in the computer. You learned the following:

- With RGB color, each intensity is a 1-byte numeric quantity represented as a binary number.
- Binary representation and binary arithmetic are the same as they are for decimal numbers, but they are limited to two digits.
- The decimal equivalent of binary numbers is determined by adding their powers of 2 corresponding to 1's.
- We can use arithmetic on the intensities to "compute on the representation," for example, making gray lighter and colorizing a black-and-white picture from the nineteenth century.
- When digitizing sound, sampling rate and measurement precision determine how accurate the digital form is; uncompressed audio requires more than 80 million bits per minute.
- Compression makes large files manageable: MP3 for audio, JPEG for still pictures, and MPEG for video. These compact representations work because they remove unnecessary information.
- Optical character recognition technology improves our world.
- The Bias-Free Universal Medium Principle embodies the magic of computers through universal bit representations and unbiased encoding.

TRY IT SOLUTIONS

8.1 For the alphabet, changing the third bit from the left to a 1 makes a letter lowercase.

8.2 The light sabers make magenta (or pink).

8.3 The user sees a white lowercase "a" on a blue background.

8.4 0100 0000 0000 0000 0000 0000

8.5 2^7 down to 2^0; that is, 128, 64, 32, 16, 8, 4, 2, 1

8.6 110 1110 = 128 + 64 + 8 + 4 + 2

8.7

```
  110 1001
+ 110 0011
 1100 1100
```

8.8 This RGB is midrange, so 1010 1100 + 1001, 1010 1100 + 110, 1010 1100 – 100, which equals 1011 0101 1011 0010 1010 1000

8.9 Eleven squares. According to Wikipedia, a more accurate translation is, "With the help of Federation Forces, all of your bases have been taken over by CATS."

REVIEW QUESTIONS

Multiple Choice

1. Put the following binary values representing the intensity of green in order from least intense to most intense: 1111 1100, 1111 1111, 1100 0000, 1111 0000
   a. 1111 1100, 1111 1111, 1100 0000, 1111 0000
   b. 1111 1111, 1100 0000, 1111 0000, 1111 1100
   c. 1111 1111, 1111 1100, 1111 0000, 1100 0000
   d. 1100 0000, 1111 0000, 1111 1100, 1111 1111
2. The RGB setting for blue is (0 is off, 1 is on)
   a. 0000 0000 0000 0000 0000 0000
   b. 1111 1111 0000 0000 0000 0000
   c. 0000 0000 1111 1111 0000 0000
   d. 0000 0000 0000 0000 1111 1111
3. People tend to be sensitive to small changes in _______, but not to small changes in _______.
   a. brightness, color
   b. color, brightness
   c. brightness, contrast
   d. color, contrast
4. Analog information is
   a. discrete
   b. continuous
   c. random
   d. digital
5. According to the Nyquist rule, the sampling rate for sound should be roughly
   a. half of what humans can hear
   b. the same as what humans can hear
   c. twice what humans can hear
   d. three times what humans can hear

6. The accuracy of a digitized sound is determined by
   a. the sampling rate
   b. the precision of the sample
   c. the size of the digitized file
   d. all of the above
7. A digital-to-analog converter
   a. changes digital information to analog waves
   b. converts continuous sound to digital sound
   c. converts sound to an electrical signal
   d. sets approximated values
8. Do GIF files display vertical or horizontal bands better?
   a. vertical
   b. horizontal
   c. neither
   d. both
9. Jessica Simpson's "A Little Bit" is 3 minutes 47 seconds long. How many bits is this?
   a. 1,411,200
   b. 40,042,800
   c. 84,672,000
   d. 320,342,400
10. Raymond Kurzweil is known as the inventor of
    a. computer science
    b. text-to-speech generation
    c. image compression
    d. virtual reality

Short Answer

1. RGB values are usually stored as three _______.
2. _______ is the limit that defines the maximum rate that information can be transmitted.
3. All colors with equal intensities of RGB subpixels are either _______, _______, or shades of gray.
4. _______ is the term used when digital values are converted to create an analog sound.
5. _______ sound removes the highest and lowest samplings as part of its compression algorithm.
6. Pixel color is determined solely by the _______ of the color.
7. In OCR, each pixel is an estimate of how _______ the corresponding area is.
8. On the computer, _______ means to store or transmit information with fewer bits.
9. A process that allows the computer to "read" printed characters is called _______.
10. To increase the _______ of a photo, you should increase the difference between the light and dark parts.
11. When converting analog sound to digital sound, using _______ bits yields a more accurate digitization.
12. JPEG is to still images what _______ is to motion pictures.

13. The ______ states that bits can represent all discrete information even though the bits have no meaning of their own.
14. GIF images are limited to ______ colors.

Exercises

1. Explain the phrases "bits are it" and "bits have no inherent meaning."
2. In the decimal to binary algorithm presented in this chapter, how do you determine what power of two to start the "place values" row of the table?
3. Convert 1492 and 1776 to binary and then compute their addition, displaying the answer in binary. Show your work.
4. In binary, add 1011, 1001, 110, and 1100.
5. Convert 168 and 123 to binary and then compute their addition. How many bytes does it take to represent each number? How many bytes are needed for the answer?
6. What process could you use to remove "red eye" from a photo? Explain your algorithm in great detail.
7. Explain how a picture with 300 pixels per inch could be converted to a picture with 100 pixels per inch.
8. Give three applications of OCR systems.
9. For music sold on CD, explain how a singer's voice in the recording studio reaches the earphones on your computer.
10. Why are JPEG, MPEG, and MP3 considered algorithms?
11. What will the best latency be for 225 KB to be transmitted with a bandwidth of 25 KB per second? Explain your answer.
12. State five kinds of information that can be represented with four bytes of information. Be creative, recall information discussed in previous chapters, and explain each kind in detail.
13. Explain how colored light and colored paint differ. Provide concrete examples in your explanation.
14. Provide three advantages of using digital sound over analog sound. Are there any disadvantages? Explain your answer in detail.
15. Assuming you had a small file of 0's and 1's as follows, use run-length encoding to compress this file.

```
0000 0000 1100 0000
1111 1111 0011 1111
0011 1111 0000 0000
1100 0000 0000 0000
```

16. MP3 is a lossy compression that loses some pieces of information. Why is it okay to lose this information?
17. Devise an algorithm that allows you to remove certain letters from the following sentence and yet retain its clarity, making it understandable by most humans: "Ultimately, new technical advances transform every facet of human life and society."

CHAPTER 9

Principles of Computer Operations

Following Instructions

learning objectives

- Explain what a software stack represents and how it is used
- Describe how the Fetch/Execute Cycle works, listing the five steps
- Understand the function of the memory, control unit, arithmetic/logic unit (ALU), input unit and output unit, and program counter
- Discuss the purpose of an operating system
- Explain the purpose of a compiler
- Describe how large tasks are performed with simple instructions
- Explain why integration and photolithography are important in integrated circuits

CHAPTER 9

Don't worry about people stealing an idea. If it's original, you will have to ram it down their throats.

—HOWARD AIKEN

In their capacity as a tool, computers will be but a ripple on the surface of our culture. In their capacity as intellectual challenge, they are without precedent in the cultural history of mankind.

—EDSGER DIJKSTRA

THIS CHAPTER INTRODUCES two key inventions in information technology that rank among the top technological achievements of all time: computers and integrated circuits (ICs). Both are complex and sophisticated topics, but both are based on easily understood ideas. Pushing those ideas to their limits makes the technology complex and sophisticated, and that is definitely beyond our needs. But we should learn the main ideas, because there is no magic. True, it is amazing that a small square of silicon with no moving parts can follow instructions and do all the wonderful things it does for us, but there is no magic. By learning those principles, we can explain our familiar Web search "all the way down to the electrons."

We begin with a quick look at contemporary software development, since we're most familiar with apps *running* on computers. The glimpse gives a clearer picture of how to instruct a computer. Then, we discuss the Fetch/Execute Cycle. Next, we describe the parts of a computer, how they're connected, and, briefly, what each does. We outline how these parts execute instructions, and give a detailed example that shows that computers operate straightforwardly. Next, we discuss software translation and operating systems to explain how a computer's primitive abilities can achieve impressive results. Finally, we explain the "big ideas" behind integrated circuits and how semiconductor technology works.

There's an App for That

Most of us use computers during every waking minute of the day. Our phones contain several computers, and by serving so many of our personal needs—talking to others, finding our way to an unfamiliar destination, entertainment, monitoring our bodies, photography, and so on—we are continually using computation. It seems almost like magic that computers can be so versatile. Of course, it isn't magic. Our phones are a beautifully engineered application of a few basic principles. And so are our laptops, cameras, tablets, iPods, desktops, GPS navigators, TVs, and all the other electronic devices we use. Although making the "magic" happen requires amazing engineering, the principles themselves are easy enough for all to understand. Let's leave the engineering to someone else, and take a look at the principles of computation.

The Usual Suspects

At the end of this chapter I describe what your computer is doing in the first few nanoseconds at the start of an app. It gives insight into how the "magic" actually works. You're already familiar with many of the "characters" of this story. Here's the whole list in preparation for filling in more details.

The Processor. Because of the computer's popular success, the term "computer" has many different informal meanings. So, we refer to the device that does the actual computing by its technical name, **processor**; equivalent terms in common use are **computer**, **microprocessor**, **central processor**, **CPU** (**central processing unit**), and **core**. The processor does the work; that is, it follows the program's instructions.

The Operating System. A raw processor is capable of doing almost nothing interesting. It adds, subtracts, moves data from here to there, etc. It's simple and fast. The **operating system (OS)** is the software that makes the computer into a useful device. It performs operations common to all apps, like loading programs, sharing memory with multiple apps, locating files, and many other tasks.

The Software. The "magic" of computing is revealed in **apps**—programs—for our phones, laptops, tablets, and other devices. The hardware simply follows the program's instructions, so someone—programmers, of course—must write the instructions. Whatever these software developers say, the computer will do. So, programmers get much of the credit for the "magic."

Instructions. What are computer instructions like? Probably not "Do Today's Homework." They are ridiculously simple. So simple that it seems like nothing useful could be done with such tiny operations. But, run billions of them every second, and Presto!, the app is useful. Obviously, that's why we want fast computers.

The Fetch/Execute Cycle. This odd-sounding term refers to the process of executing an instruction; that is, doing what the instruction specifies. Instruction **execution** is the proper term for what processors do. The term comes from viewing the program as commanding the computer; in fact, instructions were called "orders" in early computers. Another common term for performing computer instructions is instruction "interpretation."

Memory. As we learned in Chapters 7 and 8, bits are a universal medium for information, and they are commonly referred to as 0 and 1. Of course, it's the memory that stores the billions of 0s and 1s. Both programs and data are encoded as bits. As it is computing, the Fetch/Execute Cycle gets program and data bits from the memory, and puts data bits back into the memory.

Component Hardware. We've already seen how the RGB display converts bits into images on the screen (Chapter 8). A few other hardware parts are interesting, too. The most fundamental are the transistors and the silicon chips that implement them. Their operation is also based on familiar ideas; they are simply amazing.

Software Isn't So Hard

We know that apps are software, but what does that mean? When you get a new app, you get an extremely long sequence of bits. Often millions and millions of them. Although a team of programmers created the bits, they didn't type each one; we'll explain how they are produced below. At the moment, though, we are interested in what those programmers do to create the software.

Figure 9.1 shows an example of application code that displays a splash screen. A *splash screen* is an image that displays before an application starts running, and this one fades in, fades out, and then goes on to the actual application. This is code provided by Microsoft, written in the programming language C# (pronounced C-sharp, rather than C-hash), and it is typical of app programming.

Notice a few characteristics of the software.

- The code is very sparse—each line has only a few symbols on it. It doesn't take a lot of typing to create software.
- Most of the blue-colored words are normal English words, such as `using`, `if`, `this`, `true`, and `false`. They name facilities available to programmers in C#. Other languages use a similar set of words for their similar facilities.
- Many of the words in the program are normal English words run together, like `SetAndStartTimer()`. These are programmer-chosen names referring either to operations, as in this case, or to data values, like `fadeOut`.

Although it doesn't take much to type these "few" symbols, they are very, very specific. Make one typo, and your program has a bug.

Deciding On What to Do

At this point the code in Figure 9.1 probably looks like total gibberish, but even though you may not be a programmer, it's possible to guess what it's doing. For example, in several places the programmer—let's call him or her Taylor because it's shorter than "programmer"—makes a test. Testing and acting on the outcomes is very common in algorithms, so all languages have an instruction called `if`. It asks a true/false question, and if the computer finds the answer is true, it does one thing, and if the computer finds the answer is false, it does something else.

Halfway through the code, where Taylor is making the image fade in, there is the test:

```
if (this.Opacity < 1.0)                          if-statement and its test
{
   this.Opacity += 0.02;                         Instruction if the test outcome is true
}
// After fadeIn complete, begin fadeOut
else                                             else-statement–what to do otherwise
{
   fadeIn = false;                               Instructions (2) if the test outcome is false
   fadeOut = true;
}
```

```
SplashScreen1.cs 2.79KB
/****************** Module Header *********************\
* Module Name: SplashScreen1.cs
* Project:     CSWinFormSplashScreen
* Copyright (c) Microsoft Corporation.
\*******************************************************/

#region Using directives
using System;
using System.Drawing;
using System.Windows.Forms;
#endregion

namespace CSWinFormSplashScreen
{
  public partial class SplashScreen1 : Form
  {
    System.Windows.Forms.Timer t = new System.Windows.Forms.Timer();
    bool fadeIn = true;
    bool fadeOut = false;

    public SplashScreen1()
    {
      InitializeComponent();
      ExtraFormSettings();
      // If we use solution2 we need to comment the following line.
      SetAndStartTimer();
    }

    private void SetAndStartTimer()
    {
      t.Interval = 100;
      t.Tick += new EventHandler(t_Tick);
      t.Start();
    }

    private void ExtraFormSettings()
    {
      this.FormBorderStyle = FormBorderStyle.None;
      this.Opacity = 0.5;
      this.BackgroundImage = CSWinFormSplashScreen.Properties.Resources.SplashImage;
    }

    void t_Tick(object sender, EventArgs e)
    {
      // Fade in by increasing the opacity of the splash to 1.0
      if (fadeIn)
      {
        if (this.Opacity < 1.0)
        {
          this.Opacity += 0.02;
        }
        // After fadeIn complete, begin fadeOut
        else
        {
          fadeIn = false;
          fadeOut = true;
        }
      }
      else if (fadeOut) // Fade out by increasing the opacity of the splash to 1.0
      {
        if (this.Opacity > 0)
        {
          this.Opacity -= 0.02;
        }
        else
        {
          fadeOut = false;
        }
      }
        // After fadeIn and fadeOut complete, stop the timer and close this splash.
      if (!(fadeIn || fadeOut))
      {
        t.Stop();
        this.Close();
      }
    }
  }
}
```

Figure 9.1 Program in C# to display a splash page that fades in, then fades out.

The actual "test question" is in the parentheses following the word if; the rest of this code says what to do based on the outcome. Taylor is checking the *opacity* of this screen's image, that is, how transparent it is. If Opacity is **1.0** or greater, it's not transparent at all; otherwise it's somewhat transparent. The test is

```
this.Opacity < 1.0
```

Either it is or isn't less, so there are two outcomes.

If Opacity is less than **1.0**, the image must still be partially transparent and is still fading in. That's the true outcome, so the computer is told to increase the opacity in the next instruction, this.Opacity += **0.02**. That makes it less faded by a little bit. If the outcome of the test is false—the Opacity is **1.0** or more, meaning the image is completely faded in—Taylor says what to do in that case using an else instruction. It's the "otherwise" case. Taylor says to switch activities and begin fading out, using the instructions fadeIn = false and fadeOut = true. These instructions will be reused every few milliseconds, so the image fades in, becomes completely opaque, and then fades out.

This is how programmers make computers test data, and based on the outcome, follow one of two alternate sets of instructions.

Software Layers

In addition to the code we just looked at, millions and millions of *other* instructions will execute to make the app's image fade in and out, and it's likely Taylor didn't write any of them. For example, the image fades in 50 increments controlled by a timer. This timer is software available in the operating system's *software stack* that Taylor can use without having to write the code for it; it has already been developed and is available for immediate use. To see what's happening, recall the idea of a software stack discussed in Chapter 1 and look at the Microsoft software stack in Figure 9.2.

In the figure, the apps (not shown) are above the programming languages like C#. The actual hardware is not shown, but it is below the OS. In between are layers of common software that apps use. The "layers" are only a conceptual grouping of software that performs similar activities. Because a given layer is built with code from the levels below, they are organized from more primitive (lower levels) to more general and sophisticated (upper levels).

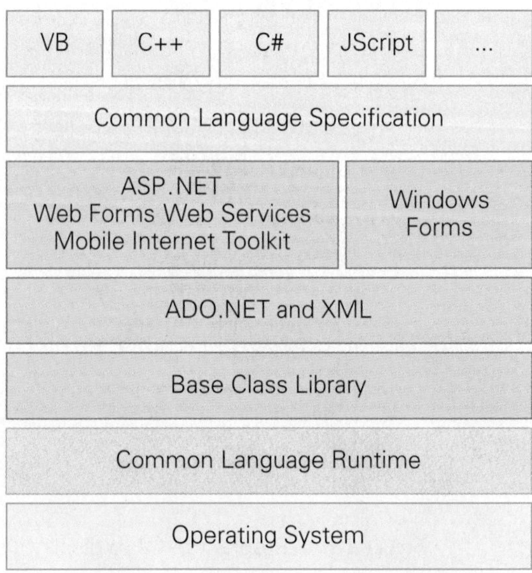

Figure 9.2 Software stack for Windows.NET.

We see that in the code of Figure 9.1, Taylor lists three lines starting with the word using.

```
#region Using directives
using System;
using System.Drawing;
using System.Windows.Forms;
#endregion
```

Such lists help the system find items or whole layers from the software stack that Taylor uses in the code. For example, the System.Windows.Forms layer (mentioned third) is where the timer code and the code setting the opacity level of a screen image are found. Someone previously wrote programs to set the timer, start it, awaken the app when it "goes off," and so on. These programs are available for Taylor and everyone else to use.

The splash screen illustrates two powerful ideas (referenced in Chapter 1) that explain why software keeps getting better and better.

Shared Effort. By sharing libraries of programs that implement commonly needed operations, programmers can dramatically reduce their effort and leverage other programmers' knowledge. These existing programs allow programmers to focus on their new and interesting apps rather than repeatedly writing the same code someone else has already written when they need to do the same operation. Not surprisingly, then, thousands of programmers have contributed to each of your favorite apps.

Wide Use and Consistency. Software available in the stack can have wide dissemination. For example, when spellchecking code developed for word processors was added to the software stack, it became available to use in any application in which users type words. Furthermore, users see it working the same way in each app because it's the same code. And if there is a bug in the code, or an improvement to be made, updating that single instance allows all apps to benefit at once.

Programming Pioneers. The first American programmers, those who wrote and ran the programs on the ENIAC, were women: Kathleen McNulty Mauchly Antonelli, Jean Jennings Bartik, Frances Snyder Holberton, Marlyn Wescoff Meltzer, Frances Bilas Spence, and Ruth Lichterman Teitelbaum. They were recruited from the ranks of "computers," humans who used mechanical calculators to solve complex mathematical problems before the invention of electronic computers.

Clockwise above from top: Kathleen McNulty Mauchly Antonelli, Jean Jennings Bartik, Frances Snyder Holberton, and Marlyn Wescoff Meltzer

At right from top: Frances Bilas Spence (also pictured on right in photo of ENIAC), Ruth Lichterman Teitelbaum

Instruction Execution Engine

There is more to say about converting programs into a form a computer can actually execute, but we can't do that until we understand what form that ought to be. So, we next look at the processor as an instruction execution engine, which brings us to the Fetch/Execute Cycle.

The Fetch/Execute Cycle

Calling a computer an "instruction execution engine" suggests the idea of a machine cycling through a series of operations, performing an instruction on each round. And that's pretty much the idea. The "engine" is the **Fetch/Execute Cycle**, which is implemented in hardware. The Fetch/Execute Cycle (or F/E Cycle for short) consists of getting the next instruction, figuring out what to do, gathering the data needed to do it, doing it, saving the result, and then repeating the cycle again and again. Overall it's a simple process, but repeating it billions of times a second accomplishes a lot.

The five steps of the Fetch/Execute Cycle have standard names, and because these operations are repeated in a never-ending sequence, they are often written with an arrow from the last step to the first showing the cycle (see Figure 9.3). The step names suggest the operations described in the previous paragraph. But the F/E Cycle is a little more complicated than that. What is an instruction like? How is the next instruction located? When instructions and data are fetched, where are they fetched from, and where do they go?

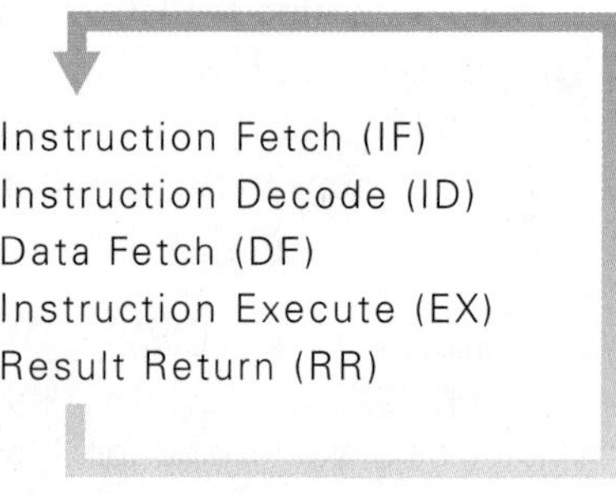

Instruction Fetch (IF)
Instruction Decode (ID)
Data Fetch (DF)
Instruction Execute (EX)
Result Return (RR)

Figure 9.3 The Fetch/Execute Cycle.

Anatomy of a Computer

To understand how the Fetch/Execute Cycle works, it helps to look at how a computer's parts are arranged. All computers, regardless of their implementing technology, have five basic parts or subsystems: the memory, control unit, arithmetic/logic unit (ALU), input unit, and output unit. These are arranged as shown in Figure 9.4. *Note:* It is just a coincidence that there are five steps to the F/E Cycle and five subsystems to a computer—they're related, of course, but not one-to-one.

Let's check the characteristics of these five subsystems.

Memory. Memory stores both the program while it is running and the data on which the program operates. Memory has the following properties:

- **Discrete locations**—Memory is organized as a sequence of discrete locations, like apartment building mailboxes. In modern memory, each location is composed of 1 byte (that is, a sequence of 8 bits).

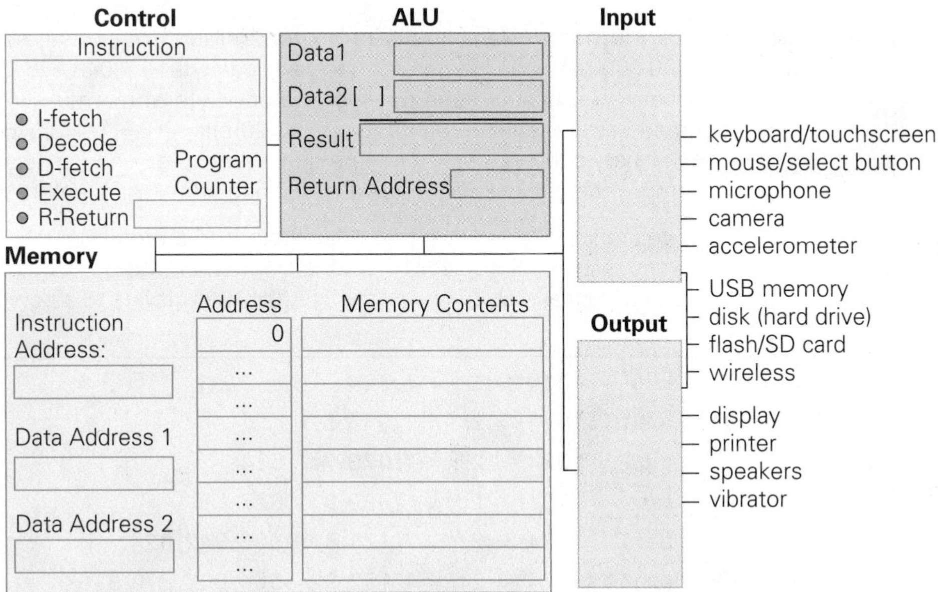

Figure 9.4 The five principal subsystems of a computer—the control unit, memory, ALU, input unit, and output unit—with typical input and output devices shown.

- **Addresses**—Every memory location has an address, like a mailbox, although computer memory addresses are whole numbers starting at 0.
- **Values**—Memory locations record or store values, like a mailbox holds a letter.
- **Finite capacity**—Memory locations have a finite capacity (limited size), so programmers must keep in mind that the data may not "fit" in the memory location.

Byte-Size Memory Location. These properties are displayed in Figure 9.5, which shows a common visualization of computer memory. The discrete locations are represented as boxes. The address of each location is displayed above the box, and the value or contents of the memory locations are shown in the boxes.

The 1-byte size of a memory location is enough to store one ASCII character (letter, numeral, or punctuation symbol), or a whole number less than 256. Therefore, a single computer memory location has very limited capacity. To overcome this limitation, programmers simply use a sequence of memory locations, and ignore the fact that they all have separate addresses; that is, programmers treat the address of the first location as if it were the address of the whole block of memory. For example, blocks of 4 bytes are used as a unit so frequently that they have a name, memory **words**.

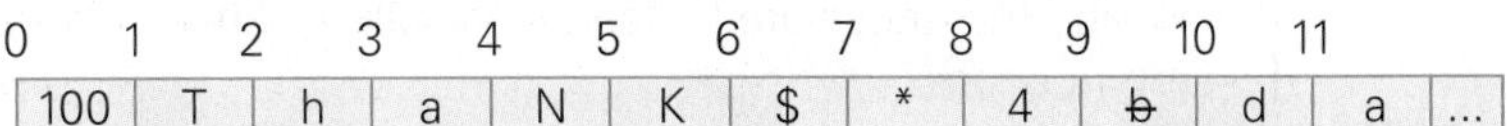

Figure 9.5 Diagram of computer memory illustrating its key properties: Discrete locations of byte-size memory, each with an address and each *containing* a value.

Free Memory. *Mega-* is the prefix for "million," of course, so a megabyte should be 1,000,000 bytes of memory. In fact, a megabyte is 1,048,576 bytes. Why such a weird number? Computers need to associate one byte of memory with every address. A million addresses require 20 bits. But with 20 bits, 2^{20} = 1,048,576 addresses are possible with binary counting. So, to ensure that every 20-bit address is associated with a byte of memory, the extra 48,576 bytes are included "free." All memory includes such a "bonus."

For reference, the number that is equivalent to a prefix is given in Figure 9.6. Generally, a prefix refers to a power of 1,000, except when the quantity (for example, memory) is counted in binary; for binary quantities, the prefix refers to a power of 1,024, which is 2^{10}.

1000^1	kilo-	$1024^1 = 2^{10}$ = 1,024	milli-	1000^{-1}
1000^2	mega-	$1024^2 = 2^{20}$ = 1,048,576	micro-	1000^{-2}
1000^3	giga-	$1024^3 = 2^{30}$ = 1,073,741,824	nano-	1000^{-3}
1000^4	tera-	$1024^4 = 2^{40}$ = 1,099,511,627,776	pico-	1000^{-4}
1000^5	peta-	$1024^5 = 2^{50}$ = 1,125,899,906,842,624	femto-	1000^{-5}
1000^6	exa-	$1024^6 = 2^{60}$ = 1,152,921,504,606,876,976	atto-	1000^{-6}
1000^7	zetta-	$1024^7 = 2^{70}$ = 1,180,591,620,717,411,303,424	zepto-	1000^{-7}
1000^8	yotta-	$1024^8 = 2^{80}$ = 1,208,925,819,614,629,174,706,176	yocto-	1000^{-8}

Figure 9.6 Standard prefixes from the Système International (SI) convention on scientific measurements.

Random Access Memory. Computer memory is called random access memory (RAM). The modifier "random access" simply means that the computer can refer to the memory locations in any order. RAM is measured in megabytes (MB) or gigabytes (GB). A large memory is preferable to a small memory because there is more space for programs and data.

Beauty of Prefixes. Prefixes "change the units" so that very large or small quantities can be expressed with numbers of a reasonable size. A well-known humorous example concerns Helen of Troy from Greek mythology "whose face launched 1,000 ships." The beauty needed to launch one ship is one-thousandth of Helen's, that is, 0.001 Helen, or 1 milliHelen.

In summary, memory is like a sequence of labeled containers known as locations: The address is the location's number in the sequence; the value or the information stored at the location is the container's contents; and only so much can fit in each container.

9.1 Finding the Right Address. If the address of the first byte in the following sequence is 1020, what is the address of the last byte?

42 72 65 61 6B 27 73 20 6F 76 65 72 2E

Knowing that these are hexadecimal values, check Figure 7.3 to see what this memory is remembering.

Control Unit. The control unit of a computer is the hardware implementation of the Fetch/Execute Cycle. Its circuitry fetches an instruction from memory and performs the other operations of the cycle on it.

Figure 9.4 shows that the control unit has two registers, that is, places to store a word or two of memory. The first register is the *instruction register*, which is where the control unit keeps the instruction that it's working on. The other register, the *program counter (PC)*, gives the memory location of the next instruction that the control unit will work on.

The control unit begins a Fetch/Execute Cycle by fetching the instruction at the memory location specified by the PC. The next step is to decode the instruction, that is, figure out what operation it is requesting. In addition, the control unit figures out where in the memory the data for the instruction is located, and where the result should go (once it's computed). Next, in the third (Data Fetch) step, the control unit asks the memory to send those data values to the ALU (explained next). The ALU then "does the math" in the fourth (Instruction Execute) step, producing the result. Finally, the control unit tells the ALU to send the result back to the memory to the address that it figured out in the decode step. That completes a cycle, so it starts another.

Arithmetic/Logic Unit (ALU). As its name suggests, the arithmetic/logic unit (ALU) does the "math." The ALU is the part of the computer that generally does the actual computation during the Instruction Execute step of the F/E Cycle. So, if the instruction is ADD, the ALU is given the two numbers to add, and does so. A circuit in the ALU can add two numbers—an amazing capability when you think about it. The circuit uses logic gates—simpler circuits that implement operations like AND and OR—to perform binary addition operations (see Table 8.1). There are also circuits for multiplying two numbers, circuits for comparing two numbers, and so on. You can think of an ALU as carrying out each machine instruction with a separate circuit.

Most computer instructions perform some kind of math, that is, most instructions transform data. But information processing can also include simply moving data—some instructions transfer data without changing it—though instructions for data transfer don't usually use the ALU. Computers have instructions for both transforming and transferring information.

For instructions that use the ALU, it is clear what the Data Fetch and Result Return steps of the Fetch/Execute Cycle must do. Data Fetch gets the values from memory for the ALU so it can perform operations like ADD and MULTIPLY. These values are called **operands**. The instruction provides the addresses where the data is to be found. When the ALU completes the operation, producing a sum or product or other value, the Result Return step moves that answer from the ALU to the memory at the address specified in the instruction.

Input Unit and Output Unit

These two components, which are inverses of each other, and therefore easily discussed together, are the wires and circuits through which information moves into and out of a processor. A computer without input or output—that is, the memory, control, and ALU sealed in a box—is useless. Indeed, from a philosophical perspective, we might question whether we can say it "computes."

The Peripherals. As shown in Figure 9.4, many kinds of devices—called **peripherals**—connect to the processor's input/output (I/O) ports, providing it with input or receiving its output. These peripheral devices are not considered part of the processor; they are specialized gadgets that encode or decode information between the processor and the physical world. The keyboard encodes our keystrokes into binary form. The display decodes information from the computer's memory using RGB representation, as described in Chapter 8. In general, the peripherals handle the physical part of the operation, sending or receiving the binary information the computer uses.

Wires or a cable from the peripheral to the processor connects to the input unit or the output unit. These units handle the communication protocol with the peripherals. As a general rule, think of the input unit as moving information from the peripheral into the memory, and the output unit as moving information from the memory and delivering it to the device.

Portable Memory, Hard Drives, Networking. Some peripherals are difficult to classify as an input device or output device. For example, memory units, like USB flash drives, can both receive information from the processor and send information to it. So, they connect to the input and output subsystems. Wireless and other networking technologies are similar in that they send and receive information. The value of these devices—both memories and networking—is that they greatly extend the power of the processor. They can have much greater capacity (disks, SDcards, etc.) than the processor's primary memory, allowing them to store more apps and photos. And they give much greater range (via networking), allowing processors to get input and send output across the world.

9.2 Another Device. Figure 9.4 shows several devices attached to the I/O subsystems that are typical of a phone or laptop. If a CD/DVD drive were shown, how would it attach to the I/O units?

A Device Driver for Every Peripheral. Most peripheral devices are "dumb" because they provide only basic physical translation to or from binary signals. They rely on the computer for further processing, which is almost always required to make the peripheral operate in an "intelligent way." So, as I type the letters of this sentence, signals are sent from the keyboard of my laptop indicating which keys my fingers press. When the computer receives information that I've pressed the *w* and the Shift key simultaneously, the computer—not the keyboard—converts the *w* keystroke to an uppercase *W*. Similarly, keys like Ctrl and Backspace are just keys to the keyboard. Added processing by a piece of software called a **device driver** gives the keyboard its standard meaning and behavior. Find them referenced on the next-to-bottom layer in Figure 1.8.

Machine Instructions

Computer instructions are much more primitive than the commands Taylor gives the computer when he or she programs. A typical machine instruction has the form

```
ADD 4000, 2000, 2080
```

which appears to command that three numbers, 4,000, 2,000, and 2,080, be added together, *but it does not*. Instead, the instruction asks that the two numbers stored in the memory locations 2000 and 2080 be added together, and that the result be stored back into memory location 4000. So the Data Fetch step of the Fetch/Execute Cycle must get the two values at memory locations 2000 and 2080, and after they are added together by the ALU, the Result Return step stores the answer in memory location 4000.

No one person invented the computer, though several researchers were working on "calculation research" in the late 1930s and early 1940s. In Berlin, Germany, Konrad Zuse built several increasingly sophisticated computer designs, culminating in the Z4. In Bletchley Park, England, Alan Turing developed the Enigma code-breaking machine (the Bombe), and Tommy Flowers built the Colossus Mark 2, also for code breaking. In the United States, John V. Atanasoff of Iowa State College built the Atanasoff-Berry Computer (ABC), with graduate student Clifford E. Berry. Their ideas were used by J. Presper Eckert and John Mauchly of the University of Pennsylvania to build ENIAC, the Electronic Numerical Integrator And Calculator. All of these machines contain ideas that contributed to the von Neumann Architecture, the usual name given to the basic computer design. The name makes it sound like John von Neumann invented it, but he did not; his role was explaining it in clear but abstract terms.

Clockwise from top left: J. Presper Eckert and John Mauchly, John V. Atanasoff, Clifford E. Berry, Alan M. Turing, Tommy Flowers, and Konrad Zuse.

Large Numbers. Fitting these three operand addresses—4000, 2000, and 2080—into one 32-bit instruction word is not literally possible because they require at least 36 bits to represent them. I have simplified this example. Computers actually use separate load and store instructions, which solve the "problem." We will always assume they fit.

This fundamental property of computer instructions bears repeating: The instruction

```
ADD 4000, 2000, 2080
```

does *not* command the computer to add the numbers following ADD. Rather, the instruction commands the computer to add the numbers stored in memory locations 2000 and 2080, whatever those numbers are. Because different values could be in those memory locations each time the computer executes the instruction, a different result could be computed each time.

The concept is that computer instructions encode the memory addresses of the numbers to be added (or subtracted or whatever), not the numbers themselves, and so they refer

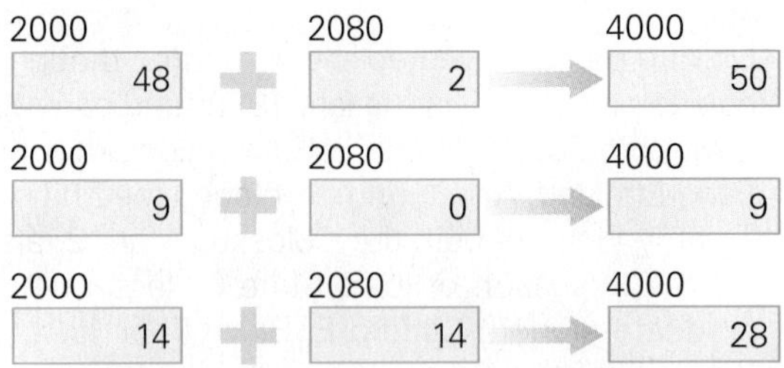

Figure 9.7 Illustration of a single **ADD** instruction producing different results depending on the contents of the memory locations referenced in the instruction.

to the values *indirectly*. The indirection means that a single instruction can combine any two numbers simply by placing them in the referenced memory locations (see Figure 9.7). **Indirect reference**—referring to a value by referring to the address in memory where it is stored—is fundamental to a computer's versatility.

9.3 Same Data, Different Operations. Using the data from Figure 9.7, execute the multiply instruction `MUL 4000, 2000, 2080` and (read this carefully) the subtract instruction `SUB 4000, 2080, 2000`.

The Program Counter: The PC's PC

One aspect of the Fetch/Execute Cycle not yet explained is how a computer determines which instruction to execute next.

Address of the Next Instruction

Recall that when the Fetch/Execute Cycle executes a program, the instructions are stored in the memory. That means every instruction has an address, which is the address of the memory location of the first byte of the instruction. (Instructions of current computers use 4 bytes, or one word.) Computers keep track of which instruction to execute next by its address. This address, stored in the control part of the computer, should probably be called the *next instruction address*, but for historic reasons it is actually known by the curious term **program counter**, abbreviated PC. (Computer engineers build personal computers (PC) with printed circuit (PC) boards that have processors with program counters (PC), so they use the PC abbreviation a lot. In the rest of this chapter, PC means program counter.)

The Instruction Fetch step of the F/E Cycle transfers the instruction from memory at the address specified by the program counter to the decoder part of the control unit. Once the instruction is fetched, and while it is being processed by the remaining steps of the cycle, the computer prepares to process the next instruction. It assumes that the next instruction is the next one in sequence. Because instructions use 4 bytes of memory, the next instruction must be at the memory address PC + 4, that is, 4 bytes further along in sequence. Therefore, the computer adds 4 to the PC, so that when the F/E Cycle gets around to the Instruction Fetch step again, the PC is "pointing at" the new instruction.

Branch and Jump Instructions

This scheme of executing instructions in sequence seems flawed: Won't the Fetch/Execute Cycle blaze through the memory executing all the instructions, get to the last instruction in memory, and "fall off the end," having used up all of the instructions? This won't happen unless the program has a bug, because computers come with instructions called *branch* and *jump* that change the PC. After the control unit prepares for the next instruction in sequence by adding 4 to the PC, the Instruction Execute step of the current (branch or jump) instruction resets the PC to a new value. This overrides the selection of the next instruction in sequence and makes the PC address some other instruction in memory. The next instruction is fetched from that memory location on the next round of the F/E Cycle, allowing the processor to go back and repeat instructions it has executed before.

Instruction Execution

To illustrate the process of executing instructions, let's follow the execution of a typical ADD instruction.

Stepping Through ADD

Breaking IT Down

Figure 9.8 shows the situation before the Fetch/Execute Cycle starts the next instruction. Specifically, the program counter (PC) is set to the address, 800, of the instruction we will be executing.

According to the cycle given in Figure 9.3, the process of instruction execution begins with Instruction Fetch (IF), which moves the instruction at the address given by the PC from the memory unit to the control unit. (See Figure 9.9, where the instruction address is 800 and the sample instruction is ADD 4000, 2000, 2080.) The bits of the instruction are placed into the decoder circuit of the control unit. Once the instruction is fetched, the PC can be readied for fetching the next instruction. For today's computers whose

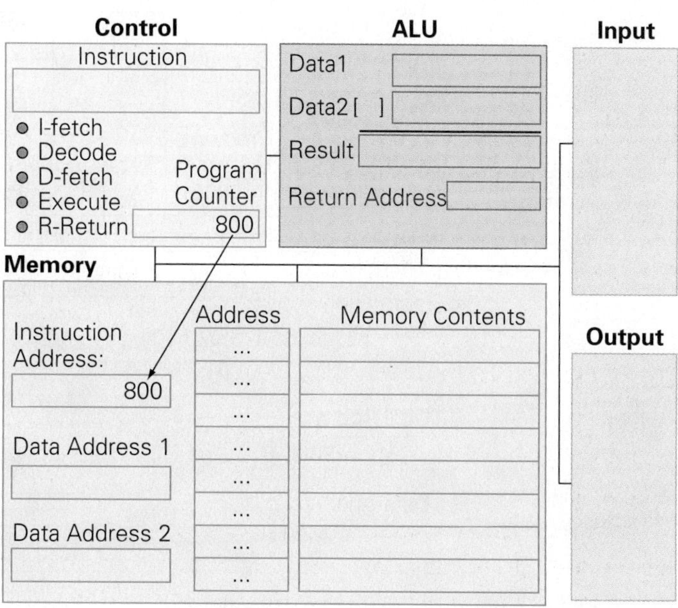

Figure 9.8 The processor before executing the instruction in memory location 800.

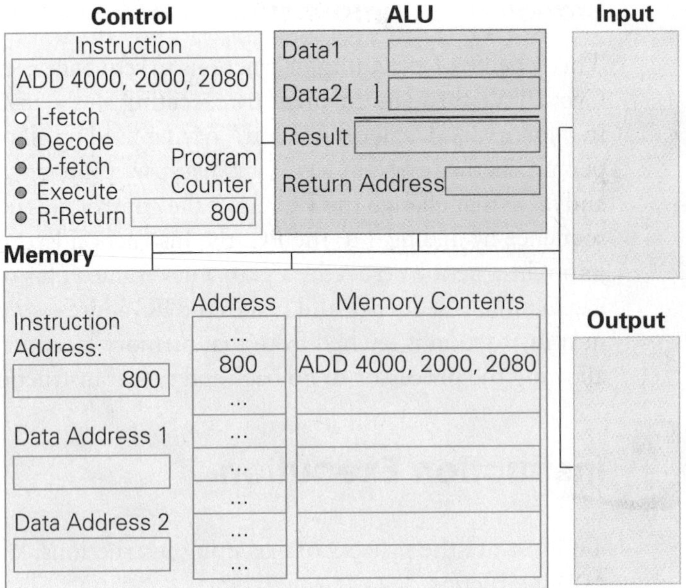

Figure 9.9 Instruction Fetch: The instruction addressed by the PC is moved from memory to the control unit.

instructions are 4 bytes long, 4 is added to the PC. (The updated PC value is visible in the Data Fetch configuration, as shown in Figure 9.11 and those that follow.)

Figure 9.10 shows the Instruction Decode (ID) step, in which the processor is set up for later steps in the cycle. Analyzing the bits of the instruction, the decoder finds the memory addresses of the instruction's data, the source operands. Like ADD, most instructions operate on two data values stored in memory, so most instructions have addresses for two source operands. These two addresses (2000, 2080) are passed to the circuit that will fetch the operand values from memory during the next (Data Fetch) step. Simultaneously, the decoder finds the destination address, the place in memory where the answer will be sent

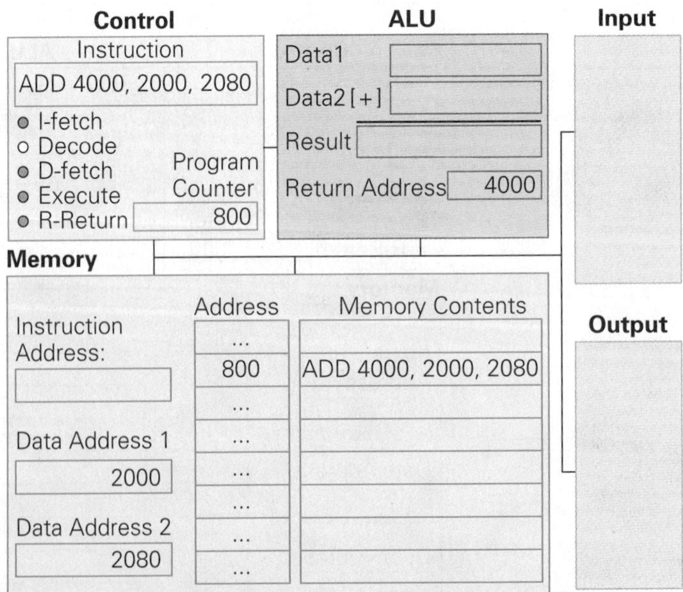

Figure 9.10 Decode: The instruction is analyzed and the processor is configured for later steps: the data addresses are sent to the Memory, the operation (+) is set in the ALU, and the result return address is set.

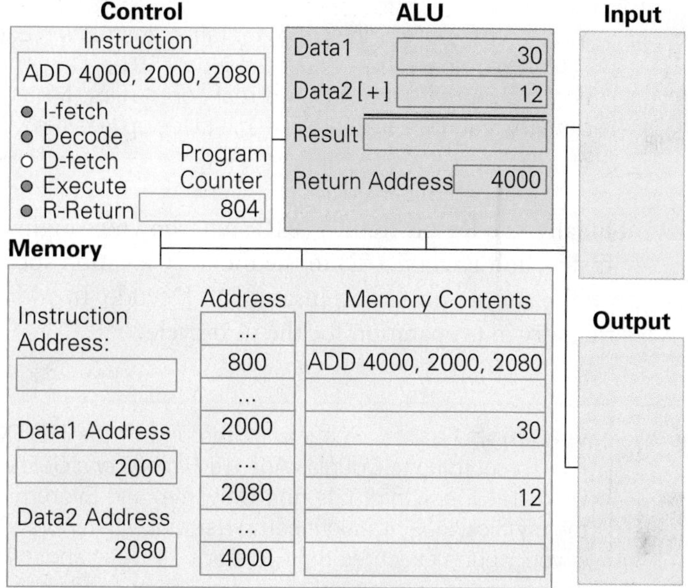

Figure 9.11 Data Fetch: The values for the two operands are fetched from memory and stored in the ALU.

during the Result Return step. That address (4000) is placed in the result return register. Finally, the decoder figures out what operation the ALU should perform on the data values (addition) and sets up the ALU appropriately for that operation.

Figure 9.11 shows the Data Fetch (DF) step. The data values for the two source operands are moved from the memory into the ALU. These values (30 and 12) are the data that the instruction will work on in the next (Instruction Execute) step.

The Instruction Execute (EX) step is illustrated in Figure 9.12. The operation—set up during the Instruction Decode step—performs the computation. In the present case, the addition circuit adds the two source operand values to produce the answer, 42. This is the actual computation.

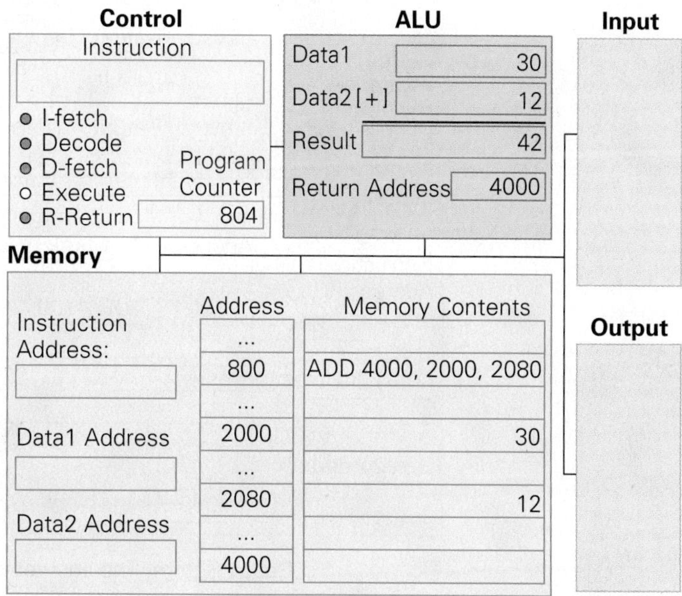

Figure 9.12 Instruction Execute: The addition operation is performed.

Micro Computer. In our presentation, Instruction Execution—the "compute" part of the Fetch/Execute Cycle—accounts for only 20 percent of the time spent executing an instruction; it averages even less on real computers. Measured by silicon area, the ALU—the circuitry that does the computing—takes up less than 5 percent of a typical processor chip.

Finally, the Result Return (RR) step, shown in Figure 9.13, returns the result of Instruction Execute (42) to the memory location specified by the destination address (4000) and set up during Instruction Decode. In addition, the PC address is sent to the memory in preparation for the next cycle.

9.4 Much Faster. In our walk through of the F/E Cycle the answer computed was 42, which according to Douglas Adam's *Hitchhiker's Guide to the Galaxy* is "The Answer to the Ultimate Question of Life, the Universe, and Everything." Adams reveals in the book that the mythical Deep Thought computer took 7.5 million years to get the answer; the computer in your phone executes the five steps above in about 7.5 nanoseconds. If there are a billion nanoseconds in a second and 31 million seconds in a year, how many times faster is your phone at computing 42 than Deep Thought?

The Clock's Ticking

What makes the Fetch/Execute cycle "go"? Nearly all processors use an electronic clock, and the step advances with each "tick." In principle, then, it takes five clock ticks to execute each instruction. In practice, processors typically run much faster than that.

The faster the clock, the faster the processor, which is why computer vendors always mention their processor's speed. Today, clock speeds are measured in gigahertz units; that is, in billions of cycles per second. A typical laptop's clock runs at a rate in the 1–3 gigahertz range; phones are generally less than one gigahertz.

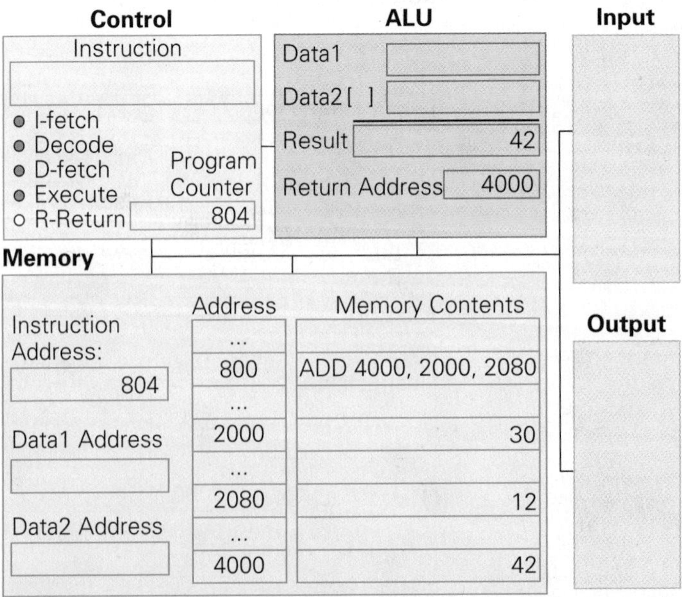

Figure 9.13 Result Return: The answer is returned to the memory, and the program counter's updated value is sent to the memory in preparation for the next fetch.

The reason processors run faster than the five ticks per cycle is computer engineers **pipeline** the Fetch/Execute cycle. In the same way that a car assembly line doesn't make one car at a time, start to finish, the steps of the F/E cycle are not run start to finish before the next cycle starts. In fact, on most computers a new F/E cycle begins on *each* tick. So, immediately after each instruction fetch (IF)—and before the remaining four steps are completed—the next instruction is fetched. This greatly speeds up the processor.

The idea of pipelining, though it seems intuitive, is more complicated than car assembly, because instructions are dependent on each other. Computing a*b+c requires a MULT instruction followed by an ADD instruction. The result of the a*b multiplication is needed to add to c. When the F/E cycle executes completely before the next one starts, there's no problem. But in pipelining, the tick after the MULT starts, the ADD starts. The result of a*b will not be available yet when the Data Fetch for the ADD happens. So if the ADD has to wait on the multiplication, what was the advantage to starting the ADD right away? Computer engineers have solved this and other much greater complications. (The ADD doesn't actually wait!) As a result, the design of a pipelined processor should be counted as one of the great Wonders of the World.

Many, Many Simple Operations

The ADD instruction has been reduced to five very primitive steps that can be accomplished by electronic circuitry. As a result of that decomposition, we can have computers work for us. But executing an addition is a very small accomplishment. What else can computers do?

Computers "know" very few instructions. That is, the decoder hardware in the controller recognizes, and the ALU performs, only about 100 or so different instructions. And there is a lot of duplication. For example, different instructions are used for different kinds of data: one instruction adds bytes, a different instruction adds whole words (4 bytes), a third adds "decimal" numbers, and so on. Altogether, there are only about 20 *different* kinds of operations. Everything that computers do must be reduced to some combination of these primitive, hardwired instructions. They can't do anything else.

The ADD instruction has average complexity, and MULT (multiply) and DIV (divide) instructions are at the screaming limit of complexity. Typical instructions are:

- Shift the bits of a word (4 bytes) to the left or right, fill the emptied places with zeros, and "throw away" the bits that "fall off the end."
- Compute the logical AND, which tests if pairs of bits are both true (1), and the logical OR, which tests if at least one of two bits is true.
- Test if a bit is zero (or nonzero), and jump to a new set of instructions based on the outcome.
- Move information around in memory.
- Sense the signals from input/output devices.

They are all very primitive.

Because there are no instructions like

```
Check_spelling_of_the_document_beginning_at_memory_location 884
```

processors achieve success with speed. Typical laptops run 1–2 billion instructions in a second; the typical phone may get a half billion done in that time. Thus, rather than powerful instructions that knock off homework assignments in five ticks, processors succeed by executing huge numbers of very, very simple instructions each second.

That just leaves the problem of converting the code of Figure 9.1 into zillions of primitive operations, which brings us back to software.

Stop! If the Fetch/Execute Cycle is an infinite loop, how does a computer stop? Early computers actually had Start and Stop buttons, but modern computers simply execute an "idle loop" when there's nothing to do. The instructions keep checking to see if there's anything to do, like process a mouse click or keystroke. And, they're capable of "going to sleep," that is, powering down (almost) to "off."

Translation

We introduced the F/E cycle to understand what a processor's instructions are like. Now we know that, like ADD 4000, 2000, 2080, they include a very simple operation, two addresses saying where operands (data) are, and another address saying where the result is to go. These will obviously be expressed in binary, and for modern computers they must fit inside, as mentioned earlier, a 4-byte word, that is, in 32-bits. We gave just such an instruction in Chapter 8:

```
0000 0000 1111 0001 0000 1000 0010 0000
```

Without going into the rather complicated details of the encoding, this sequence specifies an add operation with two data operand addresses and a destination address. So, in some computer the imagined instruction of memory word 800 discussed above is this bit sequence.

We now have a conversion to perform. Our favorite programmer, Taylor, wrote the code

```
this.Opacity += 0.02
```

in order to make the image on the screen more opaque. As we'll see, this is an addition very similar to the one analyzed above. But to perform the addition, the processor needs this code

```
0000 0010 1001 1000 1010 0000 0010 0000
```

not Taylor's. Therefore, we need to translate the former into the later. It is a huge translation, because Taylor's code apparently has so little in common with the binary code. How can the translation be done?

Assembly Language

Happily—because it helps us explain the translation—there is an intermediate form between Taylor's code, which is known as **source code**, and the bits that processors need, which is known as **object code**, also known as **binary code** or, often, just **the binary**. The intermediate form is called **assembly code**, and it is written in an **assembly language**. We will see where it gets its name in a moment.

Assembly language is an extremely primitive programming language for writing the binary code of a computer in *symbolic* form, that is, with *words* rather than 0s and1s. So, rather than writing

```
0000 0010 1001 1000 1010 0000 0010 0000
```

a programmer could write the equivalent

```
ADD Opacity, TwoCths, Opacity //Increasing opacity by 0.02
```

It has an operation (ADD), two data value names (TwoCths and Opacity), and it has a result name, Opacity again. This looks very similar to the machine instruction we followed, except that it uses words rather than numbers for the addresses, and one operand and the destination are the same, which is okay. The computer will need numerical addresses for names like Opacity, so in assembly language it is possible to write address definitions,

```
Opacity   float4 0.0    //Opacity is the address of a decimal number 0.0
TwoCths   float4 0.02   //TwoCths is the address of the decimal constant 0.02
```

The lines say that these two names should be the addresses of word-long memory locations, one with the starting value of 0.0 and the other with the value 0.02. It's easier to write Opacity for the address rather than a number like 2080 in binary, that is, 1000 0010 0000. So, assembly language is easier to use than the machine language that it is equivalent to.

In summary, "halfway" between the source code Taylor wrote and the binary code the computer needs are a few lines of assembly code, one of which is very similar to both, but not quite.

Compiling

The process of converting Taylor's C# code into the assembly code is called **compiling**. There is a C# compiler, and one for every other production programming language. Compilers are a very sophisticated technology—beyond our interest—but we can get the idea using our simple example.

Source-to-Source Translation. When Taylor wrote the code

```
this.Opacity += 0.02;
```

to increase the Opacity, he or she used a programming shortcut for the text

```
this.Opacity = this.Opacity + 0.02;
```

That is, both lines mean the same thing: increase Opacity by 0.02. It doesn't seem like much of a simplification, but this is an extremely common command for programmers to write. So, any shortcut is good.

Source-to-source translation means to compile legal program text into equivalent—but simpler for the compiler—legal program text. Although the compiler still has to compile the simpler code, the technique allows programmers to make shortcuts to speed up their task. And a compiler is just another program, so let it do work.

"Lowering" to Assembly Language. When the compiler considers the statement

```
this.Opacity = this.Opacity + 0.02;
```

it recognizes this as *three-address code*: an operator (+) with two data operands (Opacity, 0.02) and a result destination (Opacity). That seems a lot like the assembly form of the instructions the processor needs. So, the compiler

1. Notes the operation (+),
2. Finds the addresses of the data operands (Opacity), or if the address is being used for the first time, defines it, as shown in the last section; and finally,
3. Builds a line of assembly language code, producing

   ```
   ADD Opacity, TwoCths, Opacity
   ```

The assembly code is saved for the final assembling step. Incidentally, the "this" that we've seen so often just helps the compiler locate the correct address for Opacity.

The addition was easy because computers have an addition instruction. Many computers do not have a comparison instruction, so how does the compiler handle the if-test

```
this.Opacity < 1.0;
```

Cleverly, the compiler converts it into the three-address code for a subtraction. How does this work? If we compute Opacity–1.0 and get a negative number as a result, Opacity is smaller than 1; if the result is 0 or positive, then it is 1 or more. That is, a negative number means true; a nonnegative number is false. So, the compiler generates a subtract assembly instruction

```
SUB TestTemp, Opacity, DecOne
```

which subtracts 1.0 from Opacity and saves the answer in TestTemp, which is a memory location for such simplifications. TestTemp will be used to pick between the if-statements (true) and the else statements (false).

In summary, a compiler uses several techniques to produce assembly language code.

Assembling. Assembly code is just a symbolic form of binary code. That is, we get the convenience of writing words rather than long sequences of binary bits. Addition is ADD rather than 0000 0000. Similarly, we can use names like Opacity for addresses, not the binary form of 2080.

An **assembler** is a program that creates binary memory words by replacing our symbolic letters, like ADD, with their binary equivalent 0000 0000. It matches the words of the program and substitutes the binary for them. When it has *assembled* all of the bits for the instruction, the assembler saves the bits in the binary object file and goes on to the next line. Naturally, the process is called *assembling*, and was invented with the very earliest computers, because everyone quickly gets tired of writing long bit sequences. Assembly language saves us from bits.

Originally, all programs were written in assembly language. Today, only those computer scientists who build compilers read and write assembly language, but only to make their compilers work. It's better than reading and writing binary, but it's very primitive.

Principles of Operation, the Summary. When this discussion started, we said that your snazzy new app, which you just downloaded, arrived as an extremely long sequence of bits, millions and millions usually. Obviously, those bits are the translation as just described of the programmer's code. That means that if your app has a splash page that fades in and then fades out, it will contain a bit sequence similar to

```
... 1000 1111 1001 0100 0000 0011 0111 0100
    1000 1111 1001 1000 0000 0001 1010 1100
    0000 0010 1001 1000 1010 0000 0010 0000
    1010 1111 1001 0100 0000 0001 1001 0000 ...
```

which includes a sequence of 32 (by now very familiar) bits. We know where they came from, and how the compiler and assembler created this specific sequence from the code Taylor wrote. Further, we know what the computer will do with them. It'll take one "revolution" of the Fetch/Execute Cycle to interpret this instruction. Although there is a lot to the entire process, each part is straightforward.

Integrated Circuits

So far in this chapter we have revealed some rather astonishing facts: It is possible to create very complex applications (reasonably easily) using the software stack and a modern programming language; it is possible to translate the code into bits so a five-step process can execute it; and that five-step process can be pipelined. But, I've saved the best two facts—how integrated circuits and semiconductors work—for last. We'll look at integrated circuits first.

Integrated circuits (ICs) are important because the technology allows extremely complex devices to be made cheaply and reliably. Two characteristics of ICs make this possible: integration and photolithography. Oh, yes. There is one other (much less significant) property: Integrated circuits are also very small.

Miniaturization

Modern computer clocks can run at GHz rates because their processor chips are so tiny. That means that each step of the Fetch/Execute Cycle must finish in less than a nanosecond. The farthest electrical signals can travel in a nanosecond is about one foot (30 cm), and in a computer much more has to happen to the signals than simple transmission. Early computers, which filled whole rooms, could never have run as fast as modern computers because their components were farther apart than one foot. Making everything smaller has made computers faster by allowing for faster clock rates.

Integration

But the real achievement of microchip technology is not miniaturization, but **integration**. It is impossible to overstate its significance. T. R. Reid, in his book *The Chip*, called the invention "a seminal event of postwar science: one of those rare demonstrations that changes everything."

To appreciate how profound the invention of integrated circuitry is, understand that before integration, computers were made from separate parts (discrete components) wired together by hand. The three wires coming out of each transistor, the two wires from each resistor, the two wires from each capacitor, and so on, had to be connected to the wires of some other transistor, resistor, or capacitor. It was very tedious work. Even for printed circuit boards in which the "wiring" is printed metallic strips, a person or machine had to "populate" the board with the discrete components one at a time. A serious computer system would have hundreds of thousands or millions of these parts and at least twice as many connections, which were expensive and time consuming to produce, error prone, and unreliable. If computers were still built this way today, they would be rare.

The "big idea" behind integrated circuits is really two ideas working together. The first idea is that the active components—transistors, capacitors, and so forth—and the wires that connect them, are manufactured from similar materials by a single (multistep) process. So, rather than making two transistors and later connecting them by soldering a pair of their wires together, IC technology places them side by side in the silicon, and at some stage in the fabrication process—perhaps while some of the transistor's internal parts are still being built—a wire connecting the two is placed in position. The crux of integration is that the active and connective parts of a circuit are built together. Integration saves space (promoting speed), but its greatest advantage is that it produces a single monolithic part for the whole system all at once without hand wiring. The resulting "block" of electronics is extremely reliable.

Photolithography

The second idea behind integrated circuits is that they are made by **photolithography**, a printing process. Here's how it works. Making a chip is like making a sandwich: Start with a layer of silicon and add layers of materials to build up the transistors, capacitors, wires, and other features of a chip. For example, wires might be made of a layer of aluminum. But the aluminum cannot be smeared over the chip like mayonnaise covers a sandwich; the wires must be electrically separated from each other and connect to specific places. This is where photolithography comes in.

Transistors and other features of a chip are created in a series of steps that begin by depositing a layer of material, say aluminum, on the silicon (see Figure 9.14). That layer is covered by a light-sensitive material called **photoresist**, and a mask is placed over it. The mask (like a photographic negative that works like a sun print) has a pattern corresponding to the features being constructed. Exposure to (ultraviolet) light causes open areas to harden; unexposed areas do not and can be washed away leaving the pattern. Hot gases etch the original layer, and when the remaining photoresist is removed, the pattern from the mask—and the new features—remain.

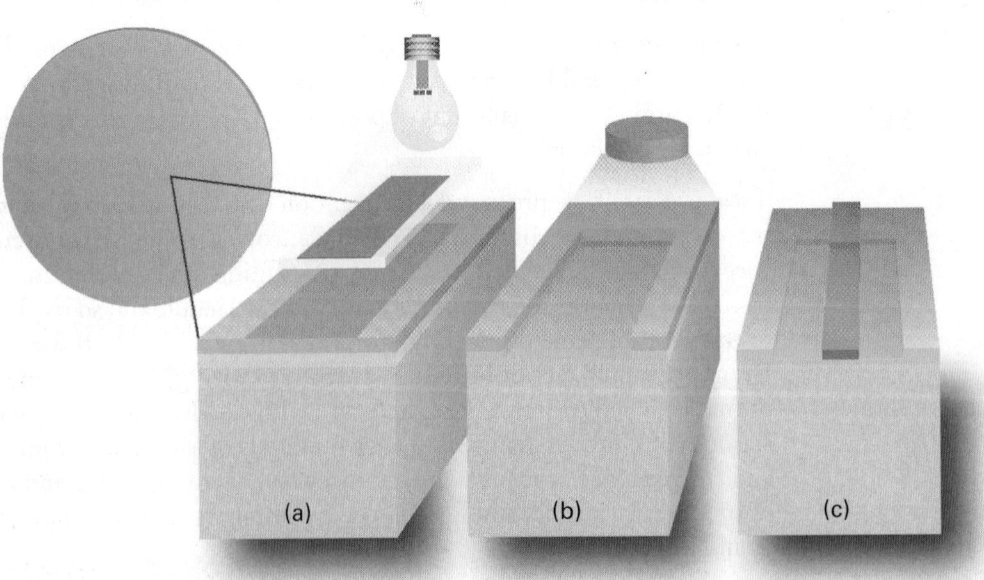

Figure 9.14 Early steps in the fabrication process. (a) A layer of photoresist (blue) is exposed to UV light through a pattern mask (light blue), hardening the exposed areas; (b) after washing away the unexposed photoresist, hot gases etch away (nearly all of) the exposed layer; and (c) the remaining resist is washed away and other layers are created by repeating the patterning and etching processes. In later stages of the fabrication process, (d) "impurities" (green) such

IC Man. Jack Kilby shared the 2000 Nobel Prize in Physics for inventing the integrated circuit. Kilby worked for the electronics firm Texas Instruments. New to the staff, Kilby hadn't accrued summer vacation time, so while the other employees were away on their holidays, he invented integrated circuits.

Using borrowed and improvised equipment, he conceived of and built the first electronic circuit in which all of the components, both active and connective, were fabricated in a single piece of semiconductor material. On September 12, 1958, he successfully demonstrated the first simple microchip (shown below), which was about half the size of a paper clip. Kilby went on to pioneer applications of microchip technology, co-inventing both the hand-held calculator and a portable thermal printer.

Jack Kilby with his lab journal

First integrated circuit

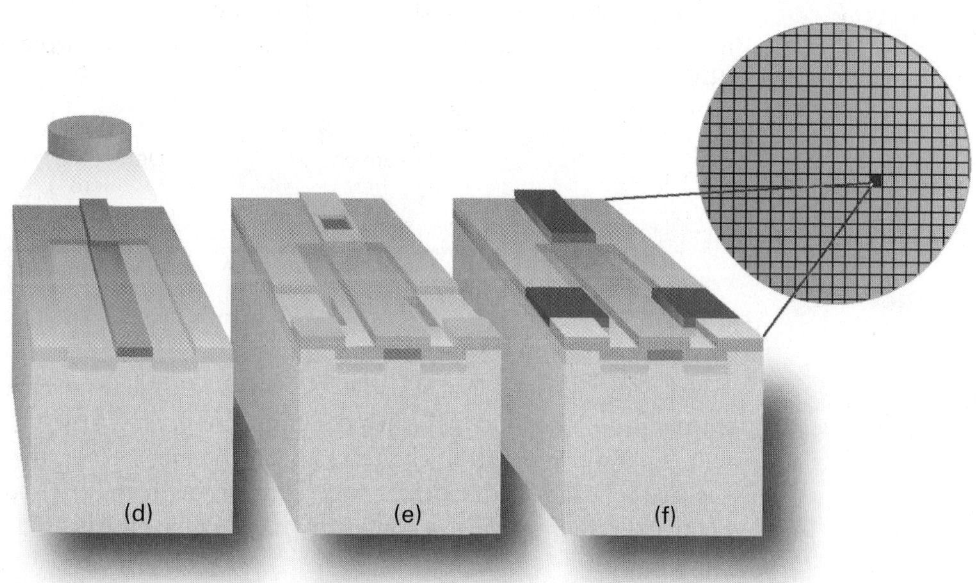

as boron are diffused into the silicon surface in a process called doping, which improves the availability of electrons in this region of the silicon. (e) After additional layering, etching exposes contact points for metal wires, and (f) a metal (dark blue) such as aluminum is deposited, creating "wires" to connect to other transistors. Millions of such transistors form a processor chip occupying a small square on the final fabricated wafer.

The key aspect of photolithography is that regardless of how simple or complicated the wiring is, the cost and amount of work required to produce a chip are the same. Like a page of a newspaper, which costs the same to print whether it has 5 or 5,000 words, the cost of making integrated circuits is not related to how complicated they are. Thanks to the photolithographic process, computers and other electronics can be as complicated as necessary.

How Semiconductor Technology Works

Semiconductor technology works because of two cool properties of physical materials: the field effect and silicon's semiconducting property.

Field Effect

As we all know from combing our hair with a nylon comb on a dry day, objects can be charged positively or negatively. The comb strips off electrons from our hair, leaving the comb with too many electrons and our hair with too few. Because like-charges repel, our hair "stands on end" as each hair pushes away from its neighbors; however, opposites attract, so the comb pulls the hair toward it. This effect that charged objects have on each other without actually touching is called the **field effect**. The field effect is handy for controlling a semiconductor.

Semiconducting Elements

Silicon is a **semiconductor**, meaning just what its name implies—it sometimes conducts electricity and sometimes does not. The ability to control when semiconductors do and don't conduct electricity is the main process used in computer construction. How could you use silicon this way?

Imagine a wire, a regular aluminum wire that conducts electricity nicely. If we present a charge at the left end of the wire, it is conducted to the right end, as expected. Now make a break in the wire, and at the break, connect the two ends to a piece of silicon (Si).

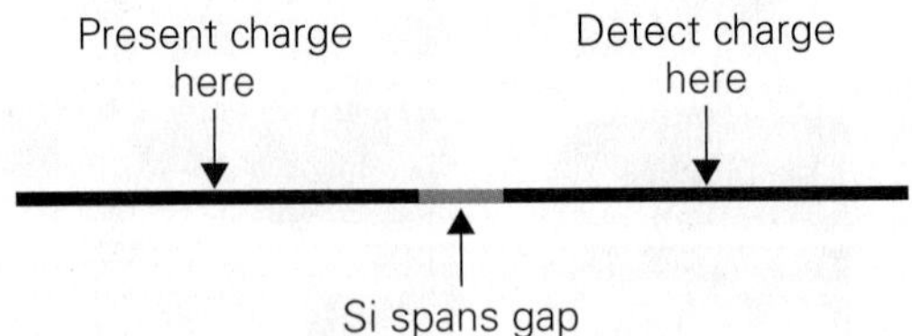

Now, if we present a charge at the left end, we will detect a charge at the right end only if the silicon is conducting. If it's not conducting, no charge will be detected at the right end. So, if we can control when the silicon conducts or not, then we can control whether the charge makes it to the right end. That's enough of a trick to build a computer. We control whether the silicon conducts with the field effect.

Field Effect Transistors

The idea of silicon spanning the gap between two ends of a wire is exactly what's happening inside a **field effect transistor**. Figure 9.15 shows the inside of a metal oxide semiconductor (MOS) transistor. This is the part we made when discussing the silicon fabrication process above. Here's what we're looking at.

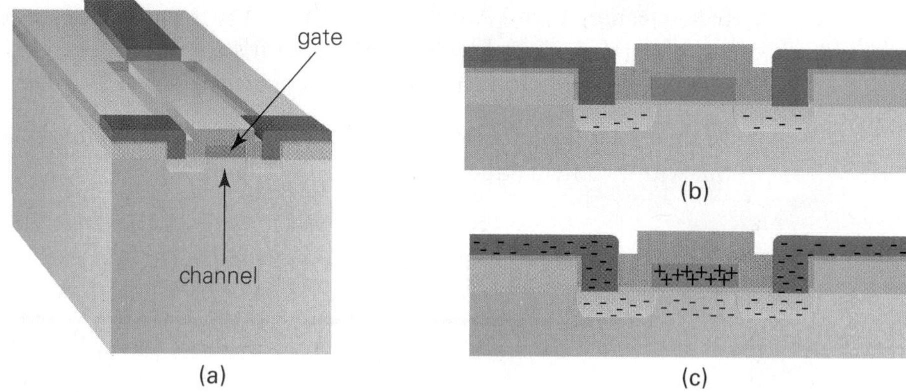

Figure 9.15 Operation of a field effect transistor. (a) Cross-section of the transistor of Figure 9.14(f). (b) The gate (red) is neutral and the channel, the region in the silicon below the gate, does not conduct, isolating the wires (blue); (c) positively charging the gate attracts electrons into the channel by the field effect, causing the channel to conduct and connecting the wires.

The wires (blue) on the left and right have been separated, and connected to the silicon by small tubs (light green) of especially conductive (doped) silicon. The tubs conduct charge nicely, but they are not connected and the wire ends are separated, so they cannot conduct left to right. We will focus on the region in the silicon between the two tubs, which is called the **channel**.

Above the channel is a red **gate**, which is actually just another metal wire. It is separated from the silicon by a thin layer of glass (an insulator), so the gate isn't going to help the two ends of the wire connect, either. As long as the gate remains neutral (9.15(b)), the wire ends are separated. But, when the gate is positively charged (9.15(c)), the field effect attracts electrons from the silicon block below, because they are attracted by the opposite charge on the gate. Immediately, there are enough electrons in the channel to make a connection between the tubs. And presto! Charge flows from the wire at left, through the tub, across the channel, into the next tub and onto the wire on the right. Connection! If we remove the positive charge from the gate, making it neutral again, the electrons disperse, and the wire ends become disconnected.

Notice that there are no moving parts. Also, the blue wire, controlled by the gate, can be the gate of another transistor further down the line. This is possible because in addition to the transistors just described—they are *n*-channel MOS transistors—there are also *p*-channel MOS transistors that are identical, except the signs are all flipped. (The *n* is for negative; *p* is for positive.) So, the negative wire can be the gate of a *p*-channel device; they work the same, but with opposite charges. Incidentally, **metal oxide semiconductors (MOS)** transistors get their name from the arrangement of their parts, seen vertically: the gate is **metal**, the glass insulator is silicon di**oxide**, and the silicon is the **semiconductor**.

Implementing ALU Operations

Now that we know how transistors work, we can see them "do the math" in the arithmetic/logic unit. Consider the AND instruction; we saw the AND operation in Chapter 5. The instruction has a form similar to an ADD instruction: AND ANS, A, B. When both A and B are true, the ANS should be true; otherwise it should be false because one or the other (or both) of A, B are false. Usually in computers, 0 represents false and 1 represents true, meaning that if A and B are both 1, then the answer is 1; otherwise it is 0. It might seem that there is little call for AND, but it's commonly used by compilers; it is likely to be the next operation after the subtraction instruction SUB discussed earlier.

In the ALU, the circuitry to execute the AND operation might use a wire like we've seen, but with two field effect transistors.

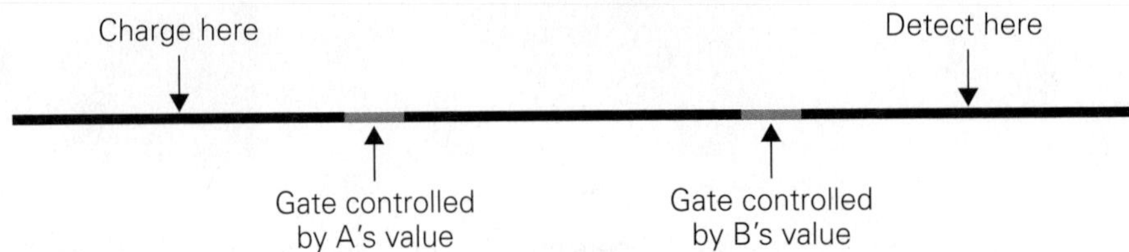

The first will be controlled by the value of A, and the other controlled by B's value. The circuit will have the property that when either value is 1, the gate of its transistor will be charged and it will conduct; for 0 values it will not conduct. The computation is now really easy.

For AND instructions, the ALU sets the charge on the first transistor according to the data fetched for A (1 means conduct, 0 means passive), and the second transistor is set in the same way based on the data fetched for B. Then a charge is presented at the left end. If the charge is detected at the right end, then the answer is true—the result register is set to 1—because both transistors must have been conducting, meaning the two values must be 1. If no charge is detected, the answer is false—the result register is set to 0—because one or both of the gates must be passive, the transistors are not conducting, and so one or both of A, B must be false.

Using only two transistors, we are able to perform one of the instructions found on all processors. Clearly, other instructions are much more complex and require many more transistors. Simple or complex, processors "do the math" with electronics.

9.5 OR Circuitry. Processors also have an instruction OR ANS, A, B, which is true if either of A or B is true (or both); it's false only if both are false. Using a split wire, show where MOS transistors should be positioned to compute this instruction, assuming the gate conducts when the operand value is 1.

Combining the Ideas

You have just clicked on that new app. The operating system for your computer retrieves the long sequence of bits from the flash memory or hard drive, and places them in the processor's memory. These bits are the compiled form of a program, written in C#, Java, C++, JavaScript, or another modern programming language. The OS runs the app, which begins by displaying a splash screen. The splash image fades in, and then fades out. The fading in is achieved by increasing the opacity of the image in small degrees.

The code to do that contains an if statement that tests to see if the opacity still needs to be increased. It asks if (this.Opacity < 1.0). A compiler converted this comparison into an assembly instruction of the form

```
SUB TestTemp, Opacity, DecOne
```

An assembler mapped the parts of this instruction into bits, assembled them into an instruction word, and added it to the binary object file, which you are now running. When the program counter gets to this instruction, the processor will execute it in five steps:

1. **IF** Fetch the instruction stored at the memory location specified by the program counter and place it in the control part of the computer.
2. **ID** Decode the instruction, setting the operation in the ALU, identifying the operand data addresses and sending them to the Memory, and saving the result return address. The PC is also advanced to reference the next instruction.
3. **DF** The operand data values are fetched from memory.
4. **EX** The subtraction operation is performed on the data values.
5. **RR** The result is returned to memory.

Assuming the instruction following the subtract must determine whether the outcome was negative or non-negative, the ALU will have to compute an AND.

In the ALU circuitry for the AND two transistors break a wire: one controlled by the sign bit of the TestTemp memory location, and the other one controlled by the constant 1. When a charge is presented at one end of the wire, being detected at the other end determines whether the outcome is true or false. If the charge is detected, the result is true and the address of the instruction following the if-test, now in the PC, is run; if it is not detected, the result is false, and the address of the instructions for the else statement replaces the PC value, and they are run next.

That's it, from applications to electrons. It is a sequence of interesting and straightforward ideas working together to create computation. No single idea is *the* key idea. They all contribute. *The power comes from applying the ideas in quantity*: Application programs and operating systems are composed of millions of machine instructions, the control unit executes billions of cycles per second, memories contain billions of bits, processors have hundreds of millions of MOS transistors, and so on.

Ours has been a simple but accurate description of a computer. To achieve their impressive speeds, today's computers are dramatically more complex than explained here. But the abstraction—the logical idea of how a computer is organized and operates—is as presented.

A Good Idea. Is the Fetch/Execute cycle the only way to compute? No. Your brain "computes" and it's unlikely that it uses an F/E cycle. But it is a fundamental way of computing, and is used in many situations besides processor chips. For example, the Android software stack (see Figure 1.7) has a program called the Dalvik virtual machine. This is a program that in software implements an F/E cycle for Java "byte code"—primitive software instructions that are higher level than hardware instructions. So, the hardware F/E cycle interprets the simple instructions of the Dalvik virtual machine interpreting more complicated instructions of a Java program, which may also use these same ideas for even more complicated "instructions."

SUMMARY

This chapter began by describing Taylor's code for an app's splash page. You learned the following:

- Modern software is written in a language using familiar terms and operations, though they are expressed very briefly; the code relies heavily on the software stack.
- The repeating process of the Fetch/Execute Cycle fetches each instruction (indicated by the PC), decodes the operation, retrieves the data, performs the operation, and stores the result back into the memory.
- This process is hardwired into the control subsystem, one of the five components of a processor.
- The memory, a very long sequence of bytes, each with an address, stores the program and data while the program is running.
- The ALU does the actual computing.
- The input and output units are the interfaces for the peripheral devices connected to the computer.
- Machine instructions do not refer to the data (operands) directly, but rather indirectly. Thus, different computations can be done with an instruction, just by changing the data in the referenced memory locations each time the instruction is executed.
- Programmers use sophisticated programming languages to create complex applications software as well as operating systems.
- The basic ideas of integrated circuits are integrating active and connective components, fabrication by photolithography, and controlling conductivity through the field effect.

TRY IT SOLUTIONS

9.1 The address of 2E is 1032, or if you interpreted 1020 as a hexadecimal number, 102C. The bytes spell out "Break's over."

9.2 The CD/DVD drive attaches to both the input and output units because it can both read and write.

9.3 Only the contents of location 4000 change; for multiply, 96, 0, 196; for subtract, –46, –9, 0.

9.4 The equation is 7.5×10^6 years / 7.5 nanoseconds. Because the "7.5" is the same in both numbers, the answer reduces to figuring how many nanoseconds there are in a million years: 10^6 years $\times$ (3.1×10^7)sec/year $\times$ $10^9 = 3.1 \times 10^{22}$ times faster. . . it's a pretty speedy phone.

9.5

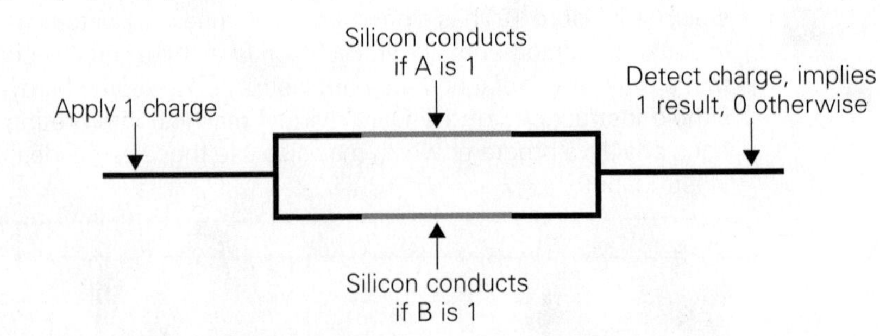

REVIEW QUESTIONS

Multiple Choice

1. A machine instruction uses how many bytes of memory?
   a. 1
   b. 2
   c. 4
   d. 128
2. Converting code that a programmer writes into assembly code is called
   a. compiling
   b. assembling
   c. F/E cycle
   d. integrating
3. What has made computers faster?
   a. making everything out of silicon
   b. making everything smaller
   c. making everything farther apart
   d. making the F/E cycle more complicated
4. Which of the following is used for input and output?
   a. keyboard
   b. hard disk
   c. mouse
   d. printer
5. The processor has how many moving parts?
   a. too many to count
   b. 8
   c. 2
   d. 0
6. From smallest to largest, the correct order of prefixes is
   a. giga, kilo, mega, tera
   b. kilo, mega, giga, tera
   c. tera, kilo, mega, giga
   d. kilo, mega, tera, giga
7. Modern computers know
   a. only a few instructions
   b. a couple dozen instructions
   c. about a hundred instructions
   d. thousands of instructions
8. Rerunning a program with the same data produces
   a. different results depending on the time of day
   b. exactly the same result every time
   c. different results depending on which computer it is run on
   d. the same results most of the time but sometimes it is different

9. If `this.Opacity += 1.0;` increases the opacity, what line of code would decrease the opacity?
   a. `this.Opacity = 1.0;`
   b. `this.Opacity -= 1.0;`
   c. `this.Opacity ++ 1.0;`
   d. `this.Opacity -- 1.0;`
10. Which of the following characteristics of a computer depends on the number of Fetch/Execute Cycles it performs per second?
    a. memory size
    b. price
    c. speed
    d. ALU

Short Answer

1. _______ deterministically execute instructions to process information.
2. Without the _______, the processor is not capable of doing anything interesting.
3. _______ is an acronym for the name of the location where computer programs run and data is stored.
4. The _______ part of the computer is the hardware part of the Fetch/Execute Cycle.
5. In addition to fetching instructions, the F/E cycle also fetches _______.
6. The math in the computer is done by the _______.
7. The _______ encodes keystrokes into binary form for the computer.
8. The computer's clock speed is measured in _______.
9. Every memory location has a(n) _______.
10. The _______ keeps track of the next instruction to execute.
11. A(n) _______ sometimes conducts electricity and sometimes does not.
12. The flow of electricity in a channel in a semiconductor is controlled by a(n) _______.
13. _______ is a long list of words, more accurately, a long series of 0's and 1's that make up a computer program.
14. A_______ is required for every peripheral connected to your computer.
15. _______ is a program that extends the operations a computer can perform beyond the hardwired machine instructions.
16. The active and connective parts of a circuit are built _______.

Exercises

1. What is the speed of the processor on your personal computer? Explain where you found this information.
2. How many bits in a kilobyte? Megabyte? Terabyte? (Express as numbers and as powers of 2.)
3. Explain what an "idle loop" is in your own words. When does a computer start this kind of loop?

4. Where does the Fetch part of the cycle get its instructions from? How does it know exactly where to go? Explain your answer in detail.
5. Explain the process of photolithography and why it changed computers so drastically.
6. Computers cannot read high-level programming languages. Explain how a programmer can be understood by a computer.
7. Explain the following instruction: `ADD 3000, 1050, 1900`.
8. List the five steps in the Fetch/Execute cycle, and describe each. Explain how these steps correspond to eating at a restaurant.
9. A megabyte is 1,048,576 bytes. Explain why it is not 1,000,000.
10. List 10 devices that can be connected to a computer, and classify each as “input”, “output”, or “I/O”.

CHAPTER 10

Algorithmic Thinking

What's the Plan?

learning objectives

- Explain similarities and differences among algorithms, programs, and heuristic solutions
- List the five essential properties of an algorithm
- Use the *Intersecting Alphabetized List* algorithm to:
  - Follow the flow of the instruction execution
  - Follow an analysis explaining why an algorithm works
- Demonstrate algorithmic thinking by being able to:
  - Explain the importance of alphabetical ordering for solutions
  - Explain the importance of the barrier abstraction for correctness

CHAPTER 10

The most beautiful thing we can experience is the mysterious. It is the source of all true art and science.

—ALBERT EINSTEIN, 1930

We are faced with insurmountable opportunity.

—WALT KELLY (POGO), 1970

AN *ALGORITHM* is a precise, systematic method for producing a specified result. As we've learned, computers must be given instructions for everything they do, so all they do is run algorithms. We normally call them *programs*, which are algorithms customized to do a specific task. Naturally, programmers and software developers care a lot about algorithms. But, they matter to the rest of us, too. Many of the problems we must solve personally are solved by algorithms, from describing how to achieve a clever effect in video editing to correcting mistakes in a term paper. Algorithms are solutions. And the best part is that by writing out the method carefully, some other agent—another person or a computer—can do the work. Which is, of course, the reason computers are such powerful and useful tools.

In this chapter, we familiarize ourselves with algorithms and become more adept at reading them, writing them, and evaluating them. We start by learning about Jean-Dominique Bauby, a man whose hospital care required the need of algorithms. Next we review algorithms we already know—how we learn them and how we use them. After that, we consider some defining characteristics of algorithms. Then, we study an algorithm we use every day; because it is an "industrial-strength" algorithm, it illustrates how an algorithm can exist in different forms, and why we prefer some algorithms over others. Finally, we consider how we know an algorithm does what it claims. Again, a simple illustration makes the point.

Algorithms

In this section, we begin with simple, intuitive examples to continue our earlier discussion of algorithms. You already know that algorithms are important in our study. Now you'll find out they're even more familiar than you might have realized.

Writing One Letter at a Time

The book (and movie) *The Diving Bell and the Butterfly* tells the true story of a French man who became paralyzed from his chin down. He couldn't write. He couldn't talk. He couldn't even swallow. All he could do was turn his head a few degrees and blink his left eyelid. But he could think. And amazingly, *he* wrote the book about himself just by blinking his left eyelid!

The man, Jean-Dominique Bauby (we will refer to him as J-DB; see Figure 10.1), wrote in *The Diving Bell and the Butterfly* that to be so paralyzed was like wearing the heavy suit and metal helmet deep sea divers wore in the days before SCUBA gear. He suffered from a condition called Locked-In Syndrome: his body was useless but his mind was active. He compared his thoughts to a butterfly, flitting quickly from one topic to the next. The idea became the title of his book.

Before he was paralyzed, J-DB was editor-in-chief at the fashion magazine *Elle* and an accomplished writer. So, it is not surprising that he wrote a book. What is surprising is that simply by blinking his left eye, he was able to communicate well enough to write at all. His problem—writing by blinking—will give us a situation to study algorithms.

Homemade Algorithms

Whenever J-DB wanted to say something, he had to spell it out letter by letter. To assist him, his nurses and visitors would say the alphabet, or point to the letters of the alphabet on a card, and when they got to the right letter, he blinked. Then, they would go on to

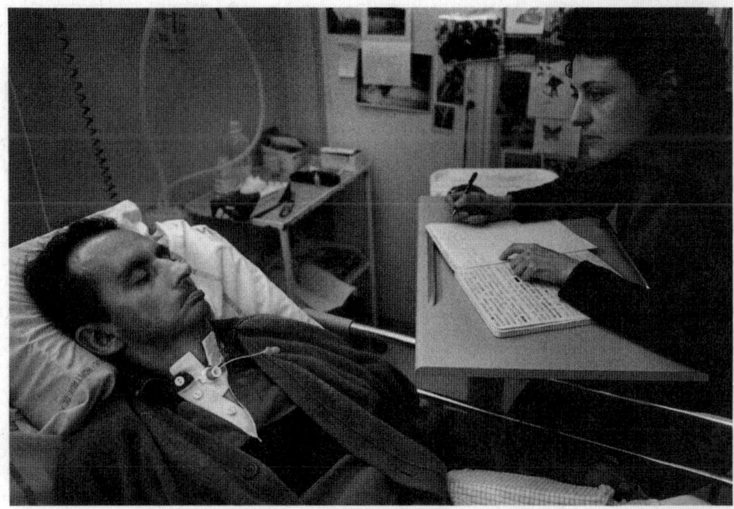

Figure 10.1 Jean-Dominique Bauby "dictates" to his assistant Claude Mendibil.

Figure 10.2 Anne Consigny as Claude Mendibil, J-DB's assistant, in the movie *The Diving Bell and the Butterfly*. She shows J-DB the alphabet; when she points to the right letter, he blinks his left eyelid.

the next letter, starting over with the alphabet (see Figure 10.2). It is a slow process. Try it!

This process is an algorithm invented by his nurses. It illustrates important points about algorithms:

- We use and invent algorithms all the time to solve our problems; it doesn't take a degree in computer science to create algorithms.
- Although the algorithm doesn't seem to compute in the popular imagination of computing—where are the numbers, the mathematical formulas?—it does; it creates the content for a document, namely J-DB's book.
- The agent running the algorithm is not a computer. It's a nurse, and J-DB is the user. Often the agent that "runs" the algorithm is a person rather than a computer.
- And as we are about to see, there are better and worse variations of this algorithm.

These observations emphasize the point that an algorithm is not an exotic creation requiring years of study and deep scientific knowledge, but rather a familiar concept that we use all the time without realizing it or thinking about it.

10.1 Yes or No? For yes/no questions, J-DB and the nurses used the rule one blink for "no" and two blinks for "yes." In Chapter 7 you learned that the presence/absence of a blink is enough to indicate one bit of information, so his 1-blink/2-blink protocol for yes/no seems wasteful—it could have been no-blink/1-blink. Can you figure out the practical reason why this wouldn't work for encoding his answer?

Many Questions; Fewer Questions

One way that the process was sped up was "word completion," in which the attendant said the word she guessed J-DB was trying to spell. This familiar autocomplete technique—for example, URL completion on the Web and word completion when texting—can save a lot of effort if you're blinking letters. However, there is an additional way to speed up blink-communication.

Frequency Order. Notice that in the photograph of Figure 10.2 the letters are not listed in alphabetical order. You might guess that because J-DB is French, the order **e s a r i n t u l o m d p c f b v h g j q z y x k w** is how the French say the alphabet, but it's not. Like all people who use the Latin alphabet, the French use the standard **a b c** . . . sequence, too. The letters in the photograph are given in **frequency order** for French. That is, the letters are listed by how often they are used in written French—most to least. So, **e** is the most frequently used letter in French, **s** is next most frequent, then **a**, **r**, **i**, and so forth.

Ordering English. The alphabet's frequency ordering for English differs from French, of course. The following is the generally accepted order: **e t a o i n s h r d l u c m f w y p v b g k q j x z**. It differs slightly by writer and topic; Dickens's *A Tale of Two Cities* has the following letter order: **e t a o n i h s r d l u m w c f g y p b v k q x j z**, that is, **n** and **i** exchange, as do **s** and **h**.

Asking—or pointing to—the letters in frequency order is smart, because it means that J-DB's assistant usually tried fewer letters. There is no guarantee, of course. The frequency ordering is an average, found by counting the number of times each letter occurs on thousands and thousands of pages of French text. Not every collection of French words has the same frequency, but it works pretty well. Let's give an example.

How Good Is Frequency Order? The famous French saying, "the more things change, the more they stay the same,"

Plus ça change, plus c'est la même chose,

can be communicated by the algorithm just described. We illustrate how well the frequency ordering works by counting how many letters a person must ask to communicate the saying compared to communicating it using the normal alphabetical ordering. How do they compare?

Similar Frequencies. Of the first 12 most frequent letters, 11 are the same in English and French, though in different order, of course. In fact, there is considerable similarity among European languages.

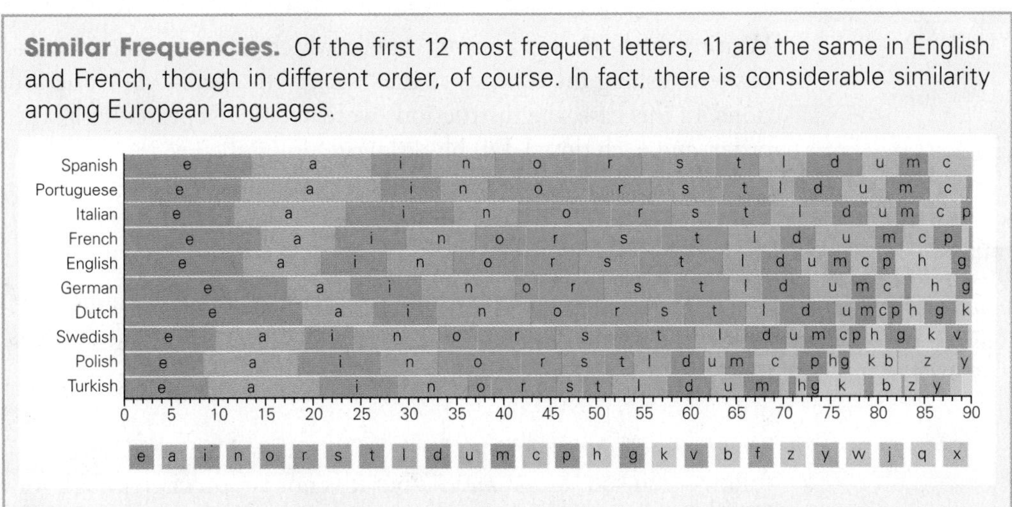

To begin, we start with the first word, *plus*. To find **p**, we ask **e s a r i n t u l o m d p**, and determine that **p** is located after pointing to 13 letters. Next, we look for **l**, asking **e s a r i n t u l**, so **l** takes 9 letters. We find that **u** takes 8, and **s** is the second letter.

So, to communicate the first word, *plus*, requires us to ask 13 + 9 + 8 + 2 = 32 letters. A computer program can finish the process for us, and finds that the total for the whole sentence is 247.

10.2 Say "Thank You". How many letters must you speak to communicate *merci* using the French frequency ordering: **e s a r i n t u l o m d p c f b v h g j q z y x k w**?

Now, we run the same experiment using the normal alphabetical order **a b c** . . . . Repeating the process from before, we ask **a b c d e f g h i j k l m n o p** to find that in this order **p** is letter 16, **l** is 12, **u** is 21, and **s** is 19. So, communicating *plus* using the normal alphabetical ordering takes 16 + 12 + 21 + 19 = 68, which is more than twice the 32 letters needed than when using the French frequency ordering. The computer program finds that for the whole sentence the normal alphabetical order requires 324 tries.

10.3 Say "Thank You" Again. How many letters must you speak to communicate *merci* using the normal alphabetical ordering: **a b c d e f g h i j k l m n o p q r s t u v w x y z**?

So, asking in frequency order required 247 letters compared to 324 for alphabetical order. Claude Mendibil and the other people assisting J-DB were very smart to use the frequency ordering. It saved him many, many blinks, which shortened the time it took to write *The Diving Bell and the Butterfly*. Such ideas are used in text compression.

10.4 Working an Abacus. Show that frequency order is not always faster by computing how many letters are needed to spell *abacus* using the English frequency ordering: **e t a o i n s h r d l u c m f w y p v b g k q j x z** and the normal alphabetical ordering.

Writing the book was a *computation* in which J-DB was the user and the assistant pointing to or asking the letters was the "agent," the person or thing following the instructions. In this case, the instructions were simple: Repeatedly ask the alphabet in frequency order, and each time J-DB blinks, write down the letter.

Writing Algorithms

Creative Communication

We have just seen an **algorithm**—a precise, systematic method for producing a specified result—in action. The process of constructing words and sentences by asking the letters one at a time is an algorithm.

The *Letter Search* algorithm for J-DB presented here is clear enough for people to follow—you spelled out *merci*—but it is not yet precise enough for a computer. As you know, computers are clueless. For a method to be precise enough for a computer to follow, *everything* needs to be spelled out. Programmers make algorithms perfectly precise for computers by writing them in a programming language. That's how the count for the whole quote was determined. People *do* have a clue, so many things can be left out of the explanation; for example, after finding a letter, a computer has to be told to go back to the beginning of the letter sequence to start looking for the next letter. People figure that out by themselves.

Helping the Clueless. What does it take to explain the *Letter Search* algorithm well enough that a computer can follow it? Express it in a programming language. Figure 10.3 shows a program written in the programming language Python to count the number of guesses using the French frequency ordering. Explaining it in Python takes 21 lines.

```
inny = open('textFR.txt','r')
content = inny.readline()
seq = "esarintulomdpcfbvhgjqzyxkw"
n = len(content)
count=0
tot = 0
while content != '':
    i =0
    while i<n:
        j=0
        while j<26:
            if content[i] == seq[j]:
                tot=tot+j+1
            j=j+1
        i=i+1
    count+=i
    content = inny.readline()
    n=len(content)
print tot
print count
print "done"
```

Figure 10.3 Python program to compute the number of questions needed to reveal the content of textFR.txt using the French frequency ordering.

Algorithms Versus Programs

The variations on the *Letter Search* algorithm illustrate an important point. Both letter search using frequency order (LSFREQ) and letter search using alphabetical order (LSALPHA) are examples of programs. **Programs** are algorithms that have been specialized to a specific set of conditions and assumptions, and are (usually) written in a specific programming language. The original explanation of an assistant asking the letters and J-DB blinking at the right moment was a *Letter Search* algorithm. LSFREQ and LSALPHA both use the *Letter Search* algorithm, but each has been specialized to a different sequence. This doesn't seem like a big difference, and it's not. We could write a letter search program that inputs the letter sequence to follow before it starts. It would be a different program from LSFREQ or LSALPHA, but it would still use the *Letter Search* algorithm.

So, programs are algorithms, and now you know the small difference between the two. In most cases, however, we do not need to make the distinction and can use the terms interchangeably.

In our discussion of the *Letter Search* algorithm, we focused on the two different orders of asking letters—frequency and alphabetic. This is typical. Every computational task has many ways of being solved. Computer professionals spend much of their time figuring out how well a solution works, or how to improve it. And it's important that they find a fast solution: When you're waiting for a computer to finish its task, you don't want to wait longer than necessary.

Experience with Algorithms

Because programs are algorithms and all of the applications you use daily are programs, you obviously *use* algorithms all the time. But, you regularly learn algorithms, too.

Weird Word. *Algorithm* is a strange word. (It's an anagram of logarithm!) It comes from the name of a famous Arabic textbook author, Abu Ja'far Mohammed ibn Mûsâ al-Khowârizmî (780–840 AD). He was a Persian scientist, mathematician, and astronomer, but he didn't invent the word "algorithm." The end of his name, al-Khowârizmî, means native of Khowârism (today it is Khiva, Uzbekistan). Over the centuries, references to his famous book corrupted the end of his name into *algorithm*. (At right, a 1983 Russian postage stamp marked the 1,200th anniversary of his birth.)

Textbook Examples of Algorithms

So far, we have studied several algorithms in this book.

Placeholder Technique. In Chapter 2 we described a three-step process that allows us to edit "colliding letter sequences"; for example, we corrected the use of *etc*. The input is a text file in need of editing. Use Find and Replace to:

1. Protect "good" letter sequences by replacing them with a placeholder symbol like #.
2. Edit the "bad" letter sequences as needed.
3. Restore the "good" letter sequences wherever there is a placeholder symbol.

The result is a revised text.

Binary to Decimal Conversion. In Chapter 7 we explained how to convert a number represented in binary into its decimal value. The input is a binary number; the process is as follows: For all of the digits in the binary number:

1. Whenever there is a 1, write down the place value for its position in decimal.
2. Add up those place values.

The result is the decimal value of the number represented in binary.

Binary Addition. Chapter 8 included several algorithms, one of which was binary addition. The input is two binary numbers with their right ends aligned. For each digit position, starting at the right,

- add as for decimal numbers, but limit resulting digit positions to less than two.

The result is the sum of the two numbers.

For the binary operations, you were the agent—the person or thing that followed the instructions; for the placeholder (and also the colorizing of Chapter 8), you and the computer worked together. You gave the instructions, and the computer did the work.

Algorithms Versus Heuristic Processes

There are processes given in this book that are not algorithms. The Web Searching section of Chapter 5 describes a process for finding information on the WWW using a search engine. That process, which had many "do this, then do that" type steps, was *not* an algorithm. Why? An algorithm is a "systematic method for producing a specified result." The searching process of Chapter 5 is not systematic. It is purposeful, and directed toward finding information, but it is not *guaranteed* to find it. That is, the process could fail; the information could be there, but following the steps might not find it. Algorithms always work, and they work by being systematic. They either get the specified answer or they report back that no such answer exists, and they are correct in what they answer.

So, if the Web search process of Chapter 5 isn't an algorithm, what is it? Web searching is a heuristic process. **Heuristic** is another weird word, this one meaning a helpful procedure for finding a result. The steps are guidelines, called **heuristics** that contribute to finding a solution. They are not guaranteed to work 100 percent of the time. A heuristic process is often the best we can do in cases where there is no known algorithm.

Inventing Algorithms

Most of the algorithms you know you developed yourself, simply by thinking through what is required to achieve your goal. For example, think of all of the things you know how to do with your phone, or with complex applications like video editing software. When someone asks your help with a "How do I . . . " question, you will likely answer with an algorithm. For your answer to be successful, it is important that your algorithm have a few basic properties.

Algorithms—A Basic Concept

We want our algorithms to be successful. Because they are written for some*one* or some*thing* else to follow, it is important that they are precise.

A Definition

As discussed in Chapter 1, an algorithm must have five properties:

- Input specified
- Output specified
- Definiteness
- Effectiveness
- Finiteness

Input Specified. The **input** is the data to be transformed during the computation to produce the output. We specify the type of data, the amount of data, and the form of the data that the algorithm expects.

Output Specified. The **output** is the data resulting from the computation, the intended result. Often the output description is given in the name of the algorithm, as in "Algorithm to compute a batting average." As with input, we must specify the type, amount, and the form the output will have. A possible output for some computations is a statement that there is no output—that is, there is no possible solution.

Definiteness. Algorithms must specify every step and the order to perform them. **Definiteness** means specifying the sequence of operations for transforming the input into the output. Details of each step must be spelled out, including how to handle errors. Definiteness ensures that if the algorithm is performed at different times or by different agents (people or computers) using the same data, the output is the same.

Effectiveness. It must be possible for the agent to execute the algorithm mechanically without any further input, special talent, clairvoyance, creativity, help from Superman, and so on. Whereas definiteness specifies which operations to do, in what order, and when, **effectiveness** means that they are doable.

Finiteness. An algorithm must have **finiteness**; it must eventually stop, either with the right output or with a statement that no solution is possible. If no answer comes back, we can't tell whether the agent is still working on an answer or is just plain "stuck." Finiteness is not usually an issue for noncomputer algorithms because they typically don't repeat instructions. But, as you will see, computer algorithms often repeat instructions with different data.

Work Without End. "Long" division is an algorithm in which finiteness is important. For example, divide 3 into 10. As we add each new digit (3) to the quotient, the computation returns to the same situation. When should the algorithm stop?

```
   3.33
3)10.00
  9
  1 0
    9
   10
   ...
```

10.5 Faulty Directions. The shampooing instructions "lather, rinse, repeat" can't be an algorithm because of an obvious flaw. What is it?

A Closer Look

To discuss key ideas about algorithms, let's begin with an algorithm you probably use everyday: the Google query evaluation algorithm. Really? You are probably thinking that it's *waaay* too complicated to understand, but stay with me.

Query Evaluation

Recall from Chapter 5 that the *query processor* makes an ordered list of the pages that hit on the keywords of your search query. *Query evaluation* makes that list; ordering that list so it is most convenient for you is a separate task and not considered here. Figure 10.4

1. Parse the query.
2. Convert words into wordIDs.
3. Seek to the start of the doclist in the short barrel for every word.
4. Scan through the doclists until there is a document that matches all the search terms.
5. Compute the rank of that document for the query.
6. If we are in the short barrels and at the end of any doclist, seek to the start of the doclist in the full barrel for every word and go to step 4.
7. If we are not at the end of any doclist go to step 4.

Sort the documents that have matched by rank and return the top k.

Figure 4. Google Query Evaluation

Figure 10.4 Original query evaluation algorithm developed by Brin and Page to find the hits for a Google search; from their original paper, The Anatomy of a Large-Scale Hypertextual Web Search Engine (infolab.stanford.edu/~backrub/google.html).

shows the query evaluation algorithm invented by Sergey Brin and Larry Page, and presented in their original paper, *The Anatomy of a Large-Scale Hypertextual Web Search Engine*.

The first thing we notice about this algorithm is that it is not written in a programming language. It uses "normal" English—specifically, "tech speak" English. So, for example, the term "doclist" is the list of URLs associated with each keyword; we showed a simplified picture of doclists in Try It 5.1. The term "rank" means "page rank" (also discussed in Chapter 5); "seek" means to go to a position in a list (stored as a file on a disk). If we read the whole paper, we would know what "short barrels" and "full barrels" are, but even without those definitions, tech speak is easier to understand than, say, ancient Greek.

Long Form. When the Brin/Page algorithm was finally written in a programming language, it doubtless took tens of thousands of lines of code, explaining why humans prefer this seven-step description.

The paper presents its algorithm in tech speak first because only computers prefer to read code, and secondly, because the actual program would be too detailed for their purpose of explaining to people how query evaluation is supposed to go; they left out *a lot* of details that a computer would need to be told.

Here is the first fact about algorithms that is illustrated by query evaluation:

> **Algorithmic Fact 1.** Algorithms can be specified at different levels of detail. It is only necessary that the agent know the terms and operations used in the specification, and that they be within the agent's capability to perform (that is, effective).

The Brin/Page algorithm is written for technically trained people who have read the paper up to "Figure 4," so it meets the criterion. When you explain video editing or other complicated operations to your friends, you use terms you know they know and operations you know they can perform.

A fact that we recall from Chapter 9 is that programs are usually written in a programming language (PL), which is compiled into assembly language (AL), which is assembled into binary form. All three—PL, AL, and binary—are different forms of the same thing. Each one is more detailed than its predecessor, and is understandable to anyone or anything fluent in that language.

Use Your Vocabulary. English or any natural language is a very imprecise way to give an algorithm. Among its sources of imprecision are pronouns—he, she, they, them, and so on—and among them "it" is the worst, because we can't always be sure what it refers to. (The only pronoun Brin and Page used in their algorithm is the "royal *we*.") Using nouns instead of pronouns won't win any writing awards, but your algorithm will be more understandable.

Intersecting Lists

Algorithms always use *functions*—operations that the agent already knows how to perform—to simplify the algorithmic description. For example, Step 4 of the Brin/Page algorithm states, "Scan through the doclists until there is a document that matches all the search terms." They don't give instructions for performing a "scan through," but it's an operation that is critical to their solution; they assumed the agent's capability includes knowing how to do this right. Notice that this is not a case of an undefined word. "Scan" has its obvious meaning, but when it is necessary to match items on each list, the exact operation of the scan matters a lot.

A Familiar Solution

In fact, the Brin/Page algorithm is (essentially) the "intersect an alphabetized list (IAL)" algorithm given in Chapter 5, illustrated in Figure 5.2, and practiced in Try It 5.1 to build a hit list. So, you already know it!

Repeating the algorithm and figure from Chapter 5, and connecting it with the Brin/Page version shown in Figure 10.4, we have:

1. Put a marker such as an arrow at the start of each token's index list.	*This is B/P Step 3.*
2. If all markers point to the same URL, include it in the hit list, because all tokens are associated with the page.	*This is B/P Step 4; they then compute page rank (Step 5) for a hit and, when necessary, switch to full lists (Step 6).*
3. Move the marker(s) to the next position for whichever URL is earliest in the alphabet.	*B/P don't have this step; it is the "scan" that makes the algorithm advance through the lists efficiently.*
4. Repeat Steps 2–3 until some marker reaches the end of the list, then quit.	*This is B/P Step 7.*

The two solutions overlap a lot even though the IAL simply builds the hit list. The Brin/Page solution does the same thing, but it also computes the page rank along the way (Step 5), which we didn't worry about, and it needs a command (Step 6) to switch to the "full barrels" when a short one runs out. Otherwise, they use the same logic.

The functionality Brin/Page *assumed* in their algorithm was Step 3, moving through the lists in a particular way.

> **Algorithmic Fact 2.** Algorithms always build on functionality previously defined and known to the agent.

In our case, readers of the Brin/Page paper would know that the most efficient way to "scan through" looking for matches is to alphabetize the lists and proceed as specified in the *Intersecting Alphabetized Lists* algorithm.

Let's be clear about what their readers knew by giving an example of an algorithm that should *not* be used.

10.6 Helping Out. In the "textbook examples" shown earlier. The *Binary Addition* algorithm referred to previously defined functionality known to the agent. What is it?

How Not to Match

Another way to implement "scan" to find the needed matches—we call it No Alphabetized Lists (NAL)—starts with any lists and works like an odometer. (The lists can be alphabetized or not; the algorithm will ignore the ordering.) It places the arrow pointers at the start of each list, and then advances the pointer of one of the lists all the way to the end looking for a match at each step; it then advances the next list one position, and repeats what it has done up to this point. (Think of the odometer as starting at 00000 and finding the 10 hits, 00000, 11111, . . . , 99999.) This is an algorithm. It checks every combination of URLs, and so it finds the identical information that the IAL does. But it's MUCH slower.

How much slower? An example will convince you that it's a lot slower. Consider five 10-item lists. The IAL moves the pointer past each item of each list *once*, giving a worst-case number of steps as

IAL: 10 + 10 + 10 + 10 + 10 = 50

(We don't know what order the pointers will be advanced in, but it doesn't matter when we're only counting up how many advancements there are: At most ten for each list.)

But the non-alphabetized lists solution repeatedly visits the same items. Because it works like an odometer, our sample lists will require as many steps as sweeping through a five-digit odometer:

NAL: 10 × 10 × 10 × 10 × 10 = 100,000

Both solutions work. One solution is very efficient compared to the other.

10.7 Speed Limit. In the Try It 5.1 exercise there are three "doclists," each five URLs in length. How many steps do the IAL and NAL algorithms take to find matches for this size input?

So, when Brin and Page said "scan through the doclists," they knew that readers would use the IAL approach to find each match.

Summarizing the comparison between IAL and NAL, we have:

VideoNote

One Problem, Many Algorithms

> **Algorithmic Fact 3.** Different algorithms can solve the same problem differently, and the different solutions can take different amounts of time.

The feature that makes IAL better than NAL is obviously the alphabetical order. It allows us to skip many, many checks for matching that would fail.

Different Solutions

An important point to emphasize is that the IAL and NAL algorithms are *not* different versions of the same solution. They are *different solutions* that solve one problem differently. This is clear because they each require a different form of the input and rely on that input's characteristics. For the IAL, the doclists must be alphabetized. The NAL doesn't care if the doclists are alphabetized or not because it ignores the order when it runs. Using the added information allows the IAL to bypass unproductive tests.

The difference in running times for the IAL and NAL algorithms also points to the fact that they are different solutions: Different forms of the same algorithm will have the same running time.

Doing the Right Thing

We (and computer scientists generally) believe that the IAL solution is good in the sense of being clear and simple, and we've just argued that it is efficient. There is one main remaining question: How do we know that the algorithm works? That is, how do we know if it finds all of the hits?

Sometimes when we develop an algorithm to solve a problem, the solution doesn't have any loops in it. This makes it particularly easy to test—run it and see if the result is right. Done. But, most algorithms have loops and so they need a little bit of analysis to be sure they are right. Specifically, it is not enough to run it on an input; trying the program might reveal an error, but it might not. If the error involves a larger problem—and therefore, more looping—the small problem may work fine. Programs containing loops cannot be verified exhaustively, that is, by trying all cases, because there are infinitely many. We must be smarter.

A Strategy

The way to know that an algorithm works is to know why it works. That is, we know what property or properties the computation has that cause it to produce the right result every time, and we can explain how they do so. Discovering why an algorithm works might seem difficult, but usually it is not. As its creator, we will know why because we gave the algorithm the "correct" properties when we developed it.

So, our strategy for "knowing why it works" is as follows:

- Find one or more properties that ensure the algorithm works.
- Explain, using the program, why they make it work.

In the case of the Intersecting Alphabetized Lists problem, we need to be sure that if there are hits to be found, the algorithm will find them. (If there are no hits, then Step 2 will always fail, meaning the algorithm "works" in that case.) So, we assume that one or more hits are among the URLs in the lists we are given. That means that the same URL is in all of the lists.

Explaining Why IAL Works

The small example in Figure 10.5 of the IAL at work shows algorithm applied to six lists in columns A through F. Notice how Step 3, advance-the-arrow-of-the-earliest-URL in any list causes the arrows to move down the list until they all reach the same URL, Hit.com.

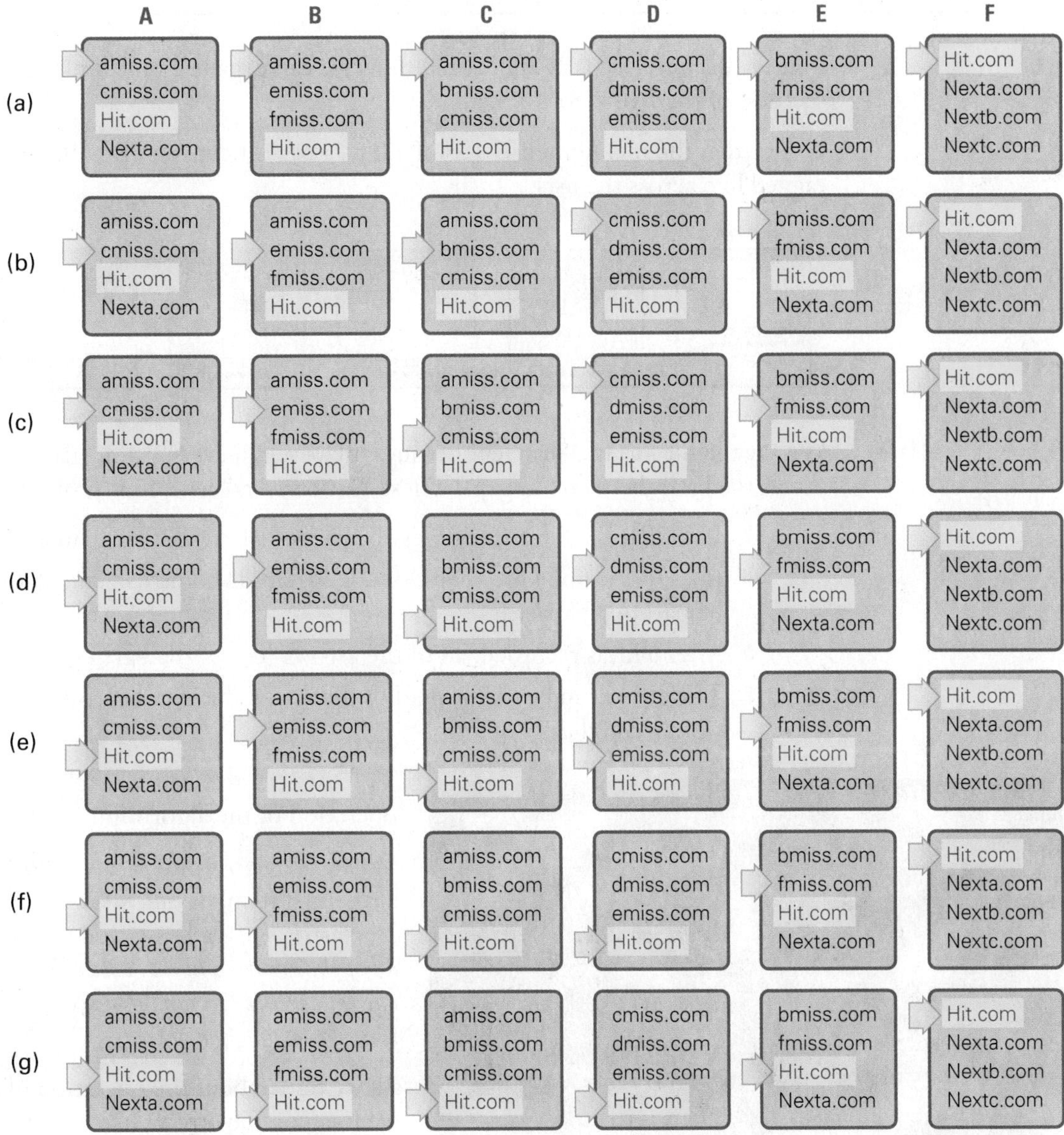

Figure 10.5 Progress of the Intersecting Alphabetized List computation for six keywords. For columns A through F, the activity described by each row is: (a) initial configuration, (b) pass amiss.com, (c) pass bmiss.com, (d) pass cmiss.com, (e) pass dmiss.com, (f) pass emiss.com, (g) pass fmiss.com.

By definition, that is a *hit*. If this example were longer, then the next step would show all of the pointers advancing together to the next item after Hit.com in their lists.

TRY IT

10.8 Taking More Hits. Suppose the example in Figure 10.5 were larger. Work out the next four steps assuming that the Hit.com hit has just been recorded.

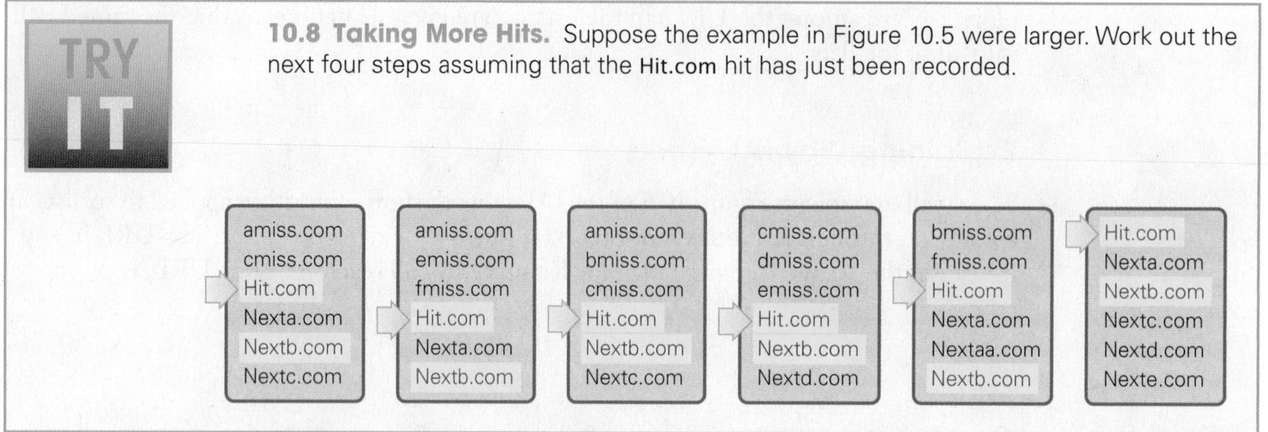

Figure 10.5 and Try It 10.8 illustrate how we can organize our thinking about the correctness of the IAL algorithm.

Notice that the highlighted URLs of a hit—both Hit.com and Nextb.com—each make a ragged line across the lists.

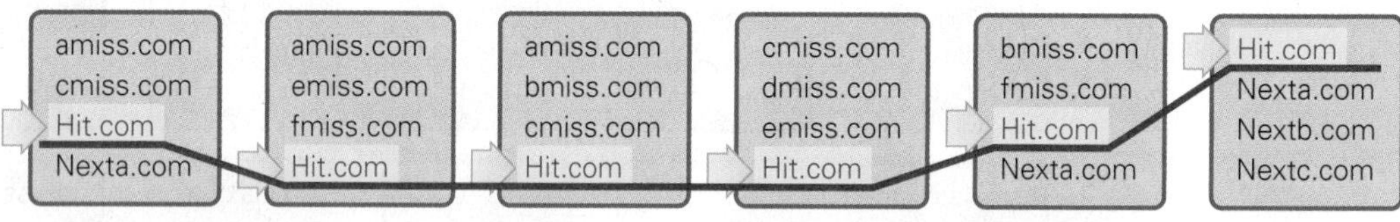

We say the hit forms a "barrier" because, by being in every list, it stretches all the way across the lists; there are no gaps. These "hit barriers" have four properties:

- If a URL is a hit, then it must be part of a barrier, that is, in each list.
- If a URL is not a hit, then the URL is not in some list, and so the URL can't be part of a barrier.
- After a hit is recorded, all of the arrows "cross" the barrier on the next step.
- The algorithm begins as if all of the arrows have just "crossed" a barrier, which we can call the *0th barrier*.

The barriers give us a way to think about the operation of the algorithm.

When the algorithm begins, all of the arrows are at the first item, having just crossed the 0th barrier. The arrows will advance, one URL at a time, and *all of the arrows will stay between two barriers: the one they just crossed and the next one, which is the hit they are looking for next.*

As we think about the operation of the algorithm, we imagine the arrows like members of a very strange marching band, each stepping forward when it's their turn, stopping when they reach the barrier, marching in place waiting for the others, and when they are all at the barrier, they all step across at once. They repeat the same behavior inside the barrier they just crossed and the next one. And so forth.

So, that's it. The arrows move forward between a pair of barriers. If there are no hits, the "barriers" are simply the start and the end. When they all get to a barrier, the hit is recorded and they all cross together, repeating the same protocol with the next pair of barriers.

Computer scientists often develop elaborate explanations for why their algorithms work, but, we've seen that it's not too hard to know why an algorithm works just by informal discussion. That's good enough for us.

Summary on Correctness

Anyone who creates an algorithm needs to know why it works. This involves finding the algorithm's correctness-preserving properties and explaining why they do the job. The explanation is always customized to the algorithm. Most of the time, we only need to explain this to ourselves, but we must always be able to do it if someone like a user asks, "Why does it work?"

SUMMARY

In this chapter we introduced algorithms, one of the most fundamental forms of thinking. You now understand the following:

- We use algorithms daily, and we continually create them as we instruct other people in how to do a task.
- Everyday algorithms can sometimes be unclear because natural language is imprecise.
- Algorithms have five fundamental properties.
- Algorithms can be given at different levels of detail depending on the abilities of the agent.
- Problems can be solved by different algorithms in different ways.
- Algorithms always work—either they give the answer or say no answer is possible—and they are evaluated on their use of resources such as space and time.
- The *Intersecting Alphabetized Lists* (IAL) algorithm is used in Web searching and is preferred over other solutions.
- Properties of the *Intersecting Alphabetized Lists* algorithm are used to explain why it works.

TRY IT SOLUTIONS

10.1 Because the nurses couldn't be sure that J-DB was listening or understood the question, they first needed to know if he was answering the question, and then they needed to know the answer. So, two bits were needed, and they are encoded well: no blink = "not answering" and blink = "answering." When he's answering, then no blink = "no" and blink = "yes." So, one blink works out to "I'm answering and the answer is no."

10.2 *Merci* requires asking 35 letters when using the French frequency ordering.

10.3 *Merci* requires asking 48 letters when using the normal alphabetical ordering.

10.4 *Abacus* requires asking 58 letters when using the English frequency ordering, and only 47 using the normal alphabetical ordering.

10.5 The operation is infinite because there is no indication when to stop.

10.6 The functionality is decimal addition.

10.7 The IAL takes 5 + 5 + 5 = 15 steps; the NAL takes 5 × 5 × 5 = 125 steps.

10.8 Step 1, all arrows move to the next item; Step 2, A, B, E, and F advance; Step 3, E advances; and Step 4, a hit is recorded, and all move to the next item.

Multiple Choice

1. An algorithm is a(n)
   a. list of general nonspecific steps to produce an output
   b. logarithm
   c. systematic method for producing a specified result
   d. math problem
2. Algorithms are used by
   a. only computers
   b. only humans
   c. various agents
   d. no one, they are not real
3. Algorithms must always
   a. produce output
   b. produce output or state that there is no solution
   c. produce input or state that there is no solution
   d. state that there is no solution
4. Algorithms are guaranteed to work
   a. 99.9 percent of the time
   b. 100 percent of the time
   c. depends on the computers they are running on
   d. 50 percent of the time
5. When writing an algorithm in a natural language it is helpful to use ________ instead of ________.
   a. programming language, natural language
   b. nouns, pronouns
   c. abbreviations, actual words
   d. nouns, adjectives
6. If an algorithm is performed with the same data, at different times with different agents the output will be
   a. the same
   b. different
   c. sometimes different and sometimes the same
   d. impossible to tell

7. How many algorithms can solve one specific problem?
   a. only one
   b. many
   c. it depends on the type of algorithm

Short Answer

1. Programs containing _______ cannot be verified exhaustively.
2. A program is an algorithm that has been _______.
3. Algorithms must be _______; they eventually stop with the right output or a statement that no solution is possible.
4. Algorithms must be definite. They must specify ordered steps, including details on how to _______.
5. The steps in algorithms must be _______ so that the agent is able to do it.

Exercises

1. This chapter describes how Jean-Dominique Bauby wrote a book by winking. Explain what he was doing in terms of PandA concepts as he is being presented the alphabet.
2. Explain why the Web searching process in Chapter 5 isn't an algorithm. What is the Web searching process called if not an algorithm?
3. State whether the following properties hold for the placeholder technique. Be sure to include details to support your answer.
   a. input
   b. output
   c. definiteness
   d. effectiveness
4. Explain how detailed an algorithm needs to be.
5. The IAL requires the agent to advance the arrow for the alphabetically earliest URL. Show that the IAL is effective by explaining how an agent would know which list has the "alphabetically earliest" URL, and so must have its arrow advanced.
6. What makes IAL (intersect an alphabetized list) faster than NAL (no alphabetized lists)?
7. Give the steps for checking your email inbox.
8. Explain the five proprieties of your algorithm for Exercise 7 (input specified, output specified, definiteness, effectiveness, and finiteness).
9. Develop an algorithm for brushing your teeth. Then explain the correctness of your algorithm, detailing why it works.
10. Why is it not enough to make sure an algorithm works by running it on a few inputs? How can you ensure that an algorithm will always produce the correct output or state that there is no solution for the given input?

INTERVIEW

with

Ray Kurzweil

Inventor, author, and futurist Ray Kurzweil is a modern-day Thomas Edison. He was the principal developer of many break-through innovations: the first omni-font optical character recognizer, the first print-to-speech reading machine for the blind, the first flat-bed scanner, the first text-to-speech synthesizer, the first music synthesizer capable of recreating the grand piano and other orchestral instruments, and the first commercially marketed large-vocabulary speech recognition system. Ray has successfully founded and developed businesses in optical character recognition, music synthesis, speech recognition, reading technology, virtual reality, financial investment, medical simulation, and cybernetic art. His Singularity prediction about rapid technological change is the subject of both his book and movie entitled *The Singularity Is Near*. In addition to scores of other national and international awards, Ray received the 1999 U.S. National Medal of Technology, the nation's highest honor in technology; was inducted into the National Inventors Hall of Fame in 2002; and received the Arthur C. Clarke Lifetime Achievement Award in 2009. Ray's Web site, KurzweilAI.net, is a leading resource on artificial intelligence.

Do you have a "favorite story" to tell about one of your inventions?

We announced the Kurzweil Reading Machine, which was the first print-to-speech reading machine for the blind, on January 13, 1976. I remember this date because Walter Cronkite, the famous news anchor for CBS News, used it to read his signature sign-off that evening "And that's the way it was, January 13, 1976." It was the first time that he did not read this famous phrase himself.

I was subsequently invited to demonstrate this new reading machine on the *Today Show*. We only had one working model and we were nervous about demonstrating it on live television since there was always the possibility of technical glitches. They responded that it was live or nothing.

We arrived at the *Today Show* studio very early in the morning and set up the reading machine. Sure enough, it stopped working a couple of hours before show time. We tried various easy fixes that failed to rectify the problem. So our chief engineer frantically took the machine apart. With electrical pieces scattered across the studio floor, Frank Field, who was to interview me, walked by and asked if there was a problem. We said that we were just making a few last minute adjustments.

Our chief engineer put the machine back together, and it still was not working. Then, in a time-honored tradition of repairing delicate technical equipment, he picked up the machine and slammed it into the table. It worked perfectly from that moment on, and the live demonstration and interview went without a hitch.

Stevie Wonder happened to catch me on the broadcast, and called our office wanting to stop by and pick up his own reading machine. Our receptionist did not believe it was really the legendary musical artist, but she put him through anyway. We were just finishing up our first production unit, so we rushed that to completion. Stevie stopped by, stayed several hours to learn how to use it, and went off with his new Kurzweil Reading Machine in a taxi. That was the beginning of a [more than] 30-year friendship that continues to this day. A few years later, Stevie was instrumental in my launching Kurzweil Music Systems, Inc.

Your inventions range from the Kurzweil 250 to a nutritional program that cured you of type 2 diabetes. Is there a tie that binds your many inventions?

My original, and still primary, area of technology interest and expertise is a field called "pattern recognition," which is the science and art of teaching computers to recognize patterns. It turns out that the bulk of human intelligence is based on our remarkable ability to recognize patterns such as faces, visual objects, speech, and music. Most of my technology projects are related to recognizing patterns, for example, character recognition and speech recognition. Even my work in music synthesis was influenced by pattern recognition. We had to answer the question as to what patterns cause humans to recognize sounds as coming from a particular type of instrument, such as a grand piano.

I quickly realized that timing was important for my inventions, and began to develop mathematical models of how technology develops over time. This endeavor took on a life of its own. By using these models, I was able to make predictions about technologies 10 to 30 years into the future, and beyond. From these efforts, I realized that the twenty-first century was going to be an extraordinary time in advancing human civilization. This insight has been a major motivation for me to find the means to live long enough, and in good health, to experience this remarkable century.

I also realized that one of the areas of technology that is accelerating is health and medical technology. Therefore the tools we will have to keep ourselves healthy will grow in power and sophistication in the years ahead. It is important, therefore, to keep ourselves healthy using today's knowledge so that we are in good shape to take advantage of the full flowering of the biotechnology revolution, which is now in its early stages.

Many of your past predictions about the future of technology have "come true." How is it that you are able to make such specific and accurate predictions?

Most futurists simply make predictions without a well-thought-out framework or methodology. I have been studying technology trends for more than a quarter century, and have been developing detailed mathematical models of how technology in different fields evolves. I have a team of people gathering data to measure the key features and capabilities of technologies in a wide array of fields, including computation, communications, biological technologies, and brain reverse engineering. From this work, it has become clear that technologies, particularly those that deal with information, are growing at a double exponential rate (that is, the rate of exponential growth is itself growing exponentially). Typically, an information-based technology at least doubles its capability for the same unit cost every year.

The other important issue is that very few people realize that the pace of technical change, what I call the paradigm shift rate, is itself accelerating. We are doubling the pace of technical change every decade. I once spoke at a conference celebrating the 50th anniversary of the discovery of the structure of DNA. We were all asked what changes we foresaw for the next 50 years. With very few exceptions, the other speakers used the amount of change in the last 50 years as a guide to the amount of change we will see in the next 50 years. But this is a faulty assumption. Because the rate of change is accelerating, we will see about 30 times as much change in the next 50 years as we saw in the last half century.

In your book *The Age of Spiritual Machines,* you foresee a future where computers have exceeded human intelligence. How and when do you expect this to come about?

We can separate this question into two questions: When will computers have the computational capacity (the "hardware" capability) of the human brain? Secondly, when will we have the content and methods (the "software") of human intelligence?

In my book *The Age of Spiritual Machines*, which came out in 1999, I said we would achieve the computational capacity of the human brain for about $1,000 by 2019. I estimate this capacity to be about 100 billion neurons, times about 1,000 interneuronal connections per neuron, times 200 calculations per second per connection, or about 20 million billion calculations per second. This was considered a controversial projection in 1999, but there has been a sea change in perspective on this issue since that time. Today, it is a relatively mainstream expectation that we will have sufficient computational resources by 2019. Computers are at least doubling their speed and memory capacity every year, and even that rate is accelerating.

The more challenging issue is the software of intelligence. A primary source of what I call the "templates" of human intelligence is the human brain itself. We are already well along the path of reverse engineering the brain to understand its principles of operation. Here also we see exponential advance. Brain scanning technologies are doubling their resolution, bandwidth, and price-performance every year.

Knowledge about the human brain, including models of neurons and neural clusters, is doubling every year. We already have detailed mathematical models of several dozen of the several hundred regions that comprise the human brain. I believe it is a conservative projection to say that we will have detailed models of all the regions of the brain by the mid-2020s.

By 2029, we will be able to combine the subtle powers of pattern recognition that the human brain excels in, with several attributes in which machine intelligence already exceeds human capabilities. These include speed, memory capacity, and the ability to instantly share knowledge. Computers circa 2029, possessing human levels of language understanding, will be able to go out on the Web and read and absorb all of the available literature and knowledge.

Will these computers of the future have human emotions?

Indeed, they will. Emotional intelligence is not a side issue to human intelligence. It is actually the most complex and subtle thing we do. It is the cutting edge of human intelligence. If a human had no understanding of human emotions, we would not consider that person to be operating at a normal human level. The same will be true for machines. Already, there is significant interest in teaching computers about human emotions: how to detect them in humans and how to respond to them appropriately. This is important for the next generation of human-machine interfaces. As we reverse engineer the human brain, and understand how the different regions process information, we will gain an understanding of what our emotions mean. A very important benefit of this endeavor will be greater insight into ourselves.

What drawbacks do you foresee for the future you envision?

Technology is inherently a double-edged sword. All of the destruction of the twentieth century (for example, two world wars) was amplified by technology. At the same time, we are immeasurably better off as a result of technology. Human life expectancy was 37 years in 1800 and 50 years in 1900. Human life was filled with poverty, hard labor, and disease up until fairly recently.

We are now in the early stages of the biotechnology revolution. We are learning the information processes underlying life and disease, and are close to developing new treatments that will overcome age-old diseases, such as cancer, heart disease, and diabetes. This same knowledge, however, can also empower a terrorist to create a bioengineered pathogen. There is no easy way to separate the promise from the peril, as both stem from the same technology. We will see similar dilemmas with nanotechnology (technology in which the key features are less than 100 nanometers) and with artificial intelligence.

The answer, I believe, is to substantially increase our investment in developing specific defensive technologies to protect society from these downsides. We can see a similar battle between promise and peril in the area of software viruses. Although we continue to be concerned about software viruses, the defensive technologies have been largely successful. Hopefully we will be able to do as well with biotechnology and other future technologies.

Could you offer some advice to students with regard to keeping pace with information technology and perhaps with regard to inventing it?

This is a very exciting time to be embarking on a career in science and technology. The pace of change and the expansion of new knowledge is greater than at any time in history, and will continue to accelerate. The impact of science and technology goes substantially beyond these subjects themselves. Ultimately, new technological advances will transform every facet of human life and society.

I would advise students to

1. Obtain a strong background in math, as this is the language of science and technology. Math also represents a way of thinking that leads to discovery and understanding.
2. Become an ardent student of technology and technology trends. Build your inventions for the world of the future, not the world you see in front of you today.
3. Focus on a particular area of science or technology that particularly fascinates you. The days when one person could master all of science and technology are long gone. However, as you focus, don't put on the blinders to what is going on in fields around you.
4. Follow your passion.

PART 3

Data and Information

CHAPTER

PART 3

INTRODUCTION

OUR UNDERSTANDING of computing deepens as we become more versatile users. With greater knowledge and wider experience, it's wise to consider the bigger picture, noticing how computing can be used and abused. In Part 3 we discuss topics such as privacy, viruses, and passwords.

Although we cover important topics like spreadsheets and databases—how they store, structure, and deliver information that interests us—we also talk about the social implications of computation. Social networks, crowdsourcing, and other new uses of technology provide a context to discuss how computers have improved our lives.

Two important topics covered in Part 3 are especially active in the "public debate" about computing: privacy and security. We present the technical description of each topic, as well as both sides of the debate. Every computer user is personally interested in privacy and security. It is important to be informed.

CHAPTER 11

Social Implications of IT

Computers in Polite Society

learning objectives

- Give examples of how social networking technology can improve society
- Describe several tips associated with netiquette and explain the benefits of following them
- Discuss the requirements of a good password and how to achieve them
- Name three permitted/not permitted uses of licensed software
- Explain what rights are granted to material that is copyrighted

CHAPTER 11

I hear that a new order of Knighthood is on the tapis—O.M.G. (Oh! My God!)—Shower it on the Admiralty!

—ADMIRAL JOHN FISHER TO WINSTON CHURCHILL, 1917, THE EARLIEST USE OF OMG

No matter how well you know the rules of netiquette, you will eventually offend someone who doesn't.

—DON RITTNER

THIS CHAPTER is about the use of computers in social settings, but it doesn't discuss the basics of cell phones, text messaging, email, video chat, blogs, YouTube, Reddit, Facebook, Twitter, rating sites (Digg), multiperson games, or other popular technologies. You are using them already; no explanation is necessary. We *will* discuss the benefits and risks of the social use of computers. We mention how to be good online citizens through habits known as *netiquette*. And we discuss how to protect your online privacy. As you enjoy the social benefits of the Internet, however, others in the online society do not share your interest in friendship and fun. They have goals like burying you in spam, bullying you, spying on your personal information, taking over your computer, defrauding you, and other decidedly anti-social behavior. This chapter and Chapter 12 explain such hazards and offer ways to protect yourself. By being forewarned, social computing can continue to be very enjoyable.

The original developers of the Internet envisioned it as an important tool for commerce, government, education, the military, and public service. (Recall that the first top-level domain names were .com, .gov, .edu, .mil, .int, .org, and .net.) The developers formed a tightly knit community of a few hundred people in which the members were respectful, trustworthy, and interdependent; there was little abuse or bad behavior. Of course, they used the Internet for social purposes, and they played games online. Nevertheless, they were probably shocked to see the explosion of social applications that evolved when the user community expanded from hundreds online to hundreds of millions online. With the expansion, things had to change.

The Power of the Crowd

Let's begin by stating a fact: The Internet has brought substantial and positive changes to society. Social interactions have been extended well beyond the experiences that our parents and grandparents could enjoy. Though it would be interesting to consider these social transformations deeply, we will limit our discussion to a few representative examples of "positive change" brought by the World Wide Web.

Crowdsourcing

Crowdsourcing refers to solving a problem or achieving a goal by combining the contributions of a large, unconstrained volunteer population. Wikipedia is perhaps the most famous of the crowdsourcing enterprises. The goal, of course, is to build a database of all knowledge. It's a gigantic global effort. And, in most ways the crowd-produced Web site is superior to traditional encyclopedias such as the *Encyclopedia Britannica*.

Be a Martian

Another example of crowdsourcing is the Be a Martian Project, where volunteers help NASA by tagging images from the Mars rovers (see Figure 11.1). It's fun, and helpful, and with a little practice, it's possible to get pretty good at it. Crowdsourcing is a new phenomenon made possible by the free and easy communication enabled by the Internet. The crowd is obviously important because it increases the number of people

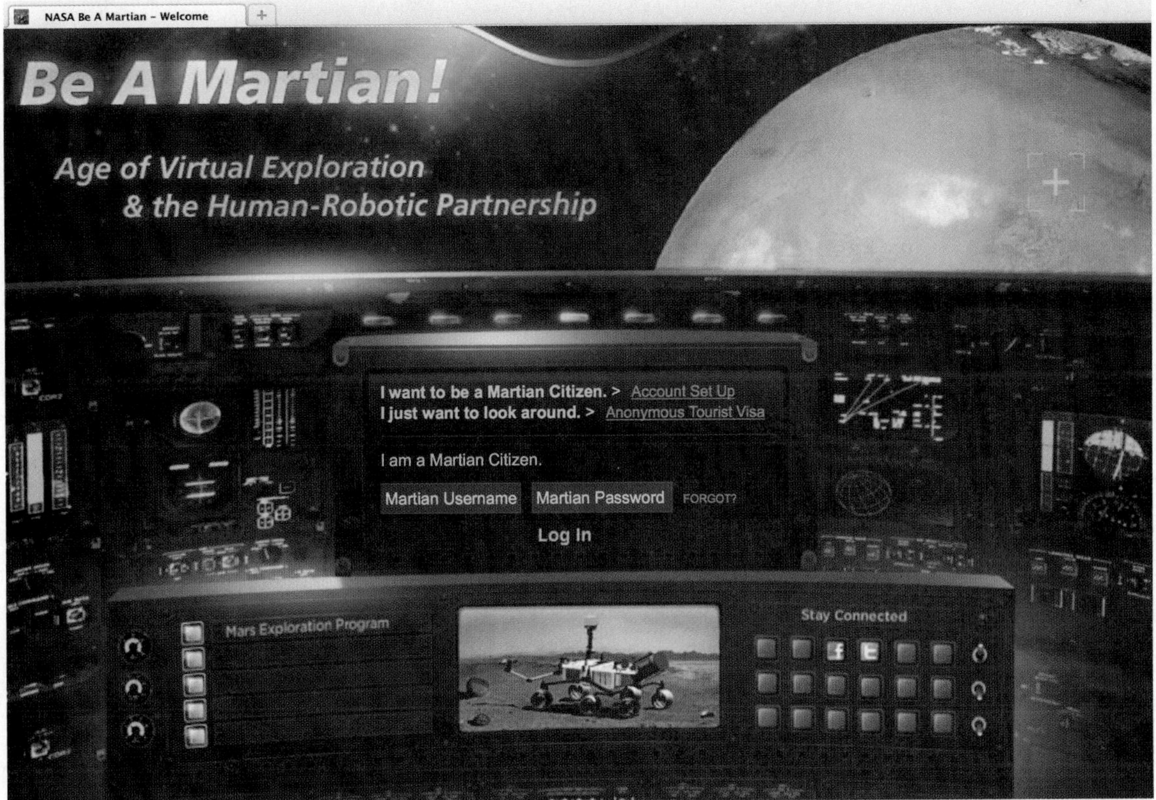

Figure 11.1 Cockpit image from NASA's Be a Martian welcome page, beamartian.jpl.nasa.gov/welcome.

working on a project, a benefit for the people with the problem (for example, NASA). It has been said that by opening up the project to a wide variety of people, participants will have a wide variety of skill sets. This means that volunteers might actually be faster and more efficient at the task than the people originally working on it. More importantly, their skills and knowledge might lead to a better solution, as Wikipedia proves in most cases. What's in it for the participants? Everyone has his own motives, of course. Obviously, it's fun. There are points to earn and prizes to win. More fundamentally, participants receive a sense of satisfaction that they are contributing to the project. And, many of the projects require skills that are more challenging than other leisure activities like watching TV. Even gaming can contribute to making the world a better place.

Foldit

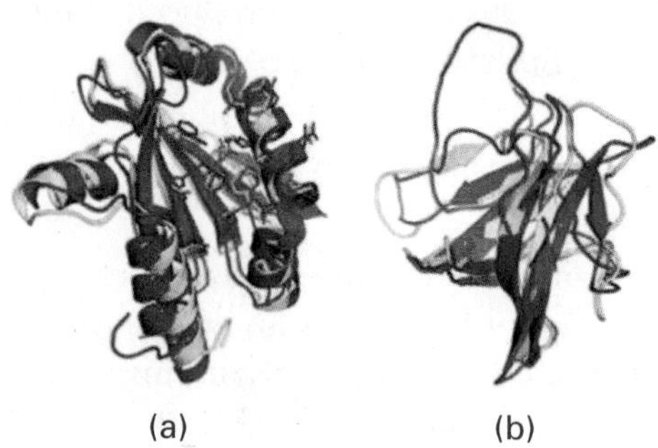

Figure 11.2 The protein monomeric retroviral protease, one subject of the Foldit video game.

Foldit is a game program in which teams compete to fold a protein. Proteins are complex molecules that manage most activities of life. Made of amino acids, proteins get all twisted as they float around in cells (see Figure 11.2). How they fold largely determines how they work. Medicine doesn't "know a protein" until it knows how it folds. The Foldit program works on proteins that are important to AIDS, cancer, and Alzheimer's research.

And Foldit's success is amazing. As reported in an article in which scientists and gamers were co-authors (*Nature Structural & Molecular Biology*, September 18, 2011),

> *Following the failure of a wide range of attempts to solve the crystal structure of M-PMV retroviral protease by molecular replacement, we challenged players of the protein folding game Foldit to produce accurate models of the protein. Remarkably, Foldit players were able to generate models of sufficient quality for successful molecular replacement and subsequent structure determination. The refined structure provides new insights for the design of antiretroviral drugs.*

The protein, monomeric retroviral protease, is "critical for reproduction of the AIDS virus" according to *Scientific American*. Amazingly, scientists had been trying to figure out how this protein folds for a *decade*. Using the crowdsourced strategies from the game, the structure was solved in *three weeks!*

You have now donated 60 grains of rice.

Civic Participation—Freerice

Foldit is not the only way to "do good" and compete. Other games such as Freerice.com have a double purpose: learning and donating. For example, in its vocabulary game, the player is given an English word and four possible definitions; picking the right answer donates 10 grains of rice. That doesn't seem like much, but answering is fun and addictive, and millions of people play. Other variations cover a wide range of subjects including the humanities, sciences, and other languages besides English The U.N. World

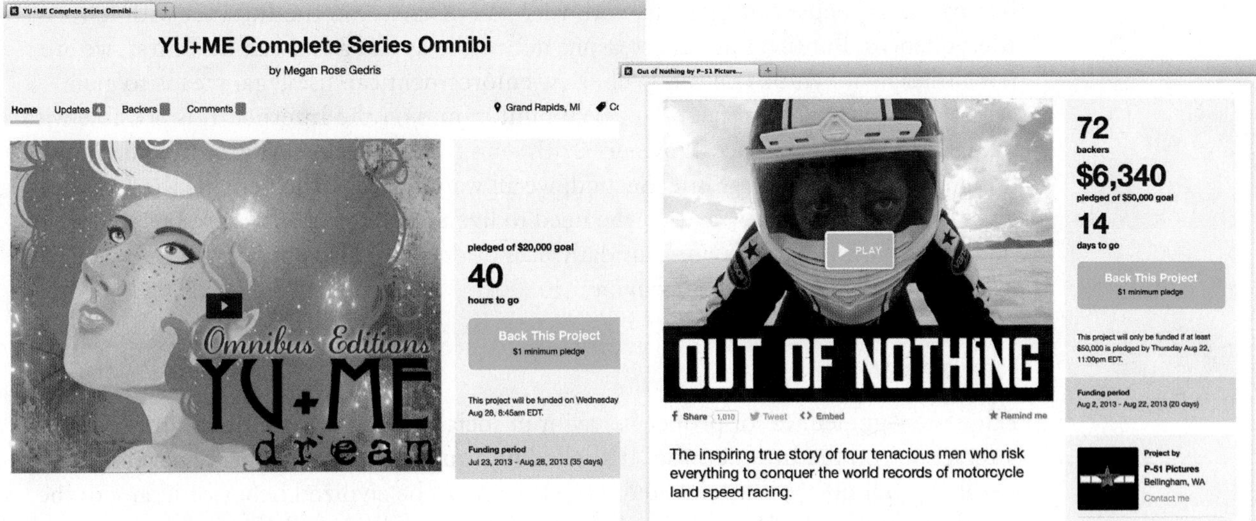

Figure 11.3 Kickstarter pitches to publish a Web comic on paper in two volumes, and to make a video about four guys pushing the limits in motorcycle racing.

Food Program is the beneficiary of all of the rice, and many people eager to improve their vocabularies and test and expand their knowledge about other topics have been provided a constructive way to learn.

Kickstarter

Kickstarter.com is another Web site in which the society can contribute to helping others (see Figure 11.3). At Kickstarter people with creative projects pitch their ideas: They say what they'll do, how much money they need to do it, why it's important, and so on. Donors can contribute a small or large amount toward the goal. If the goal is achieved the project is funded; otherwise, the donors get their money back. Basically, if the project doesn't attract enough support, it's abandoned; if it does, there is quick funding.

All of these sites harness the interest, help, and generosity of the community to further important societal goals. Crowdsourcing is one way in which the Web has improved the world. Thanks to crowdsourced music videos, it's also a lot of fun, too.

Out on Good Behavior

In normal society, people learn proper behavior from their families, relatives, religion, and community. Acting badly offends others and makes them mad. They remember the bad behavior, and punish the offenders in large and small ways. "Acceptable behavior" evolves to smooth social interactions. It's easier to live with people who recognize a basic level of courtesy and respect. It's social pressure, and it works.

The online world we live in today is different in many ways. First, our range of interactions is much broader than it was when we lived in villages; we may never meet face-to-face with the people we interact with online. Second, our families and relatives influence our online behavior very little, and many of our families are not well equipped to teach good online behaviors. Third, we can be anonymous on the Internet. If no one knows who we are, we can behave as badly as we want. Right?

It is true that people can get away with very bad behavior on the Internet with few consequences. But there are two reasons not to "be as bad as we can be." First, we are not entirely anonymous on the Web. Law enforcement can use legal means to gain access to the identities of people who commit crimes on the Internet. It is possible with the help of Internet service providers (ISPs) and companies like Microsoft and Google to figure out who's who online. Second, we all want to enjoy the benefits the Internet gives us. So, in the same way that the need to live together socially caused us to develop standards of civilized behavior, our daily uses of the Web also encourage us to behave within bounds of reasonable behavior.

Netiquette

Etiquette—guidelines for proper behavior in social situations—applies to our social interactions on the Internet, too. It's called **netiquette**. It was originally developed for email use, but now it is interpreted more broadly to be civilized behavior in any of the social settings on the Web. Table 11.1 gives some standard guidelines.

Netiquette matters because the people we interact with online are mostly our friends, family, and coworkers. These are the people we normally treat well in nonelectronic situations, so it is wise to be aware of how our digital interactions might be misinterpreted or have an adverse impact.

Specific Guidelines for Email

Our personal use of electronic communication (SMS, Twitter, Facebook) can be guided by the persona we wish to project to our contacts. But at work, we should follow rules of

Table 11.1 Netiquette guidelines for responsible behavior

Guidelines	Responsible Behaviors
Act as if you are there in person	Display your best side: In online interactions don't say or do things that you wouldn't say or do to the person face-to-face.
Remember that you aren't there in person	In face-to-face conversation, facial expressions, pauses, volume, emphasis, body language, and so on convey meaning that is not available in email, messaging, or other online situations. Explain yourself more completely. Avoid writing that can be misunderstood—"I can't praise her cooking enough"—and use notations like smilies—**emoticons**—to flag humor. Before sending or posting very emotional content, sleep on it.
One-on-one talks	Never forward email or other private communication without the sender's permission.
Delete doesn't remove content	Because copies are kept (to recover from crashes), most Web content is still accessible after it has been deleted. Watch what you post—your boss or your future boss may see it. Think carefully about Facebook and Twitter posts.
Don't waste your friend's resources	Sending long rambling "musings" or huge image files wastes your friend's time and slows network connections or possibly server space. Be thoughtful. Don't send, or at least warn about the file size ahead of time.
Avoid flame wars	**Flame wars** are nasty online exchanges in which a few people fight, but others see cc's or the post. Don't continue a flame war; contact a flamer separately.
Confirm addressees	Before clicking **Send** when emailing, check that the "To" list is correct. If you accidentally send a personal reply to a group—by clicking **Reply All** when you meant to click **Reply**—follow up immediately with an apology.

respect and good behavior so as to meet general business practice. Here are some additional habits to adopt.

Ask About One Topic at a Time. An email message requiring a response from the receiver should treat only one topic. For example, don't ask your boss when your raise begins in the same email that you ask if you left your brown sweater in her office. Because most of us handle one matter at a time, the reader of a one-topic message can respond to the matter and then delete or archive the mail. With multiple topics, it is likely that one or more will be dropped or ignored. For example, you'll find out you did forget the sweater, but your request for a start date of your raise might be ignored. The subject line of the email can describe that one topic. Email is cheap; it costs no more to send two messages than one. But managing one-topic messages is much easier for everyone.

Include Context. An all too common email reply, unfortunately, is "Yes." We all like to get positive email, of course, but the unfortunate part is we've forgotten the question. The subject line is no help; it reads, *Re: Question.*

Any email-reading software worth two bits gives you a way to include the original message in a reply. Including the question with the reply is a courtesy. It provides the context for your answer, so you can give a short reply without leaving the receiver clueless. And, when you're answering, it is sensible to put your reply *before* the included context, so the receiver doesn't have to look for it.

Use an Automated Reply. When you are unable to answer your email for a few days, it is polite to set up an **automated reply** saying you are away, and perhaps indicating when you expect to read your email again. The automated reply, called a **vacation message** in the earliest mailers, is generally available from your mail server. The benefit of using the vacation message is that readers know why you're not responding. Otherwise, they may think you are lazy or that they are being ignored or snubbed.

Answer a Backlog of Emails in Reverse Order. When we keep up with reading our email, we usually answer messages in the order they're received. But if we haven't answered our email for a while and our inbox is brimming, it's best to answer email in *reverse* order of its arrival. Many of the oldest messages will have "timed-out." That is, we may not have to answer a message because a more recent follow-up message supersedes it. Or we may receive a "forget it" message sent by someone who received our vacation message and realized they couldn't wait for a reply. Not answering such email saves time and saves our correspondent aggravation. For example, when your boss sends a message asking for everyone's availability for a future meeting, it is unnecessary and somewhat embarrassing to reply when a later message sets the time for the meeting. Answering email in reverse time-order allows us to read these resolution messages before we read the original. There's only one caution: Avoid the temptation to quit and never finish reading the backlog.

Clarifying Ownership of Email. As a general rule, most people assume that when they send email, it is private. It is impolite and inconsiderate to forward email without getting the sender's permission. Asking permission to forward email gives the sender a chance to review the message to decide if there is something in it that should not be passed along. The sender's opinion is important because although the mail may look innocent to you, other readers may react differently and the sender may know that. Remember that most email in the United States is *not* a private conversation. Companies, colleges, and other organizations can (under most circumstances) review emails sent or *received* by the members of their organization; that is, *your* personal email account might be private, but your readers' may not be (see Chapter 12).

Use Emoticons. Finally, the point of email is to communicate clearly. Because email (and texts) are casual writing, we often don't choose the right word (*le mot juste*!), causing others to misunderstand us. Emoticons (smilies) can help by being a small indicator of your intent. It may be that some people overuse them, especially emoji, but usually, they help. It's better to use more rather than fewer.

Origin and Development of the Smiley. The earliest known use of typographical rendering of emotion is from the British humor magazine *Puck* from 1881. Typesetters were the only people who could use smilies then, and mostly they didn't.

TYPOGRAPHICAL ART.

We wish it to be distinctly understood that the letter-press department of this paper is not going to be trampled on by any tyranical crowd of artists in existence. We mean to let the public see that we can lay out, in our own typographical line, all the cartoonists that ever walked. For fear of startling the public we will give only a small specimen of the artistic achievements within our grasp, by way of a first instalment. The following are from Studies in Passions and Emotions. No copyright.

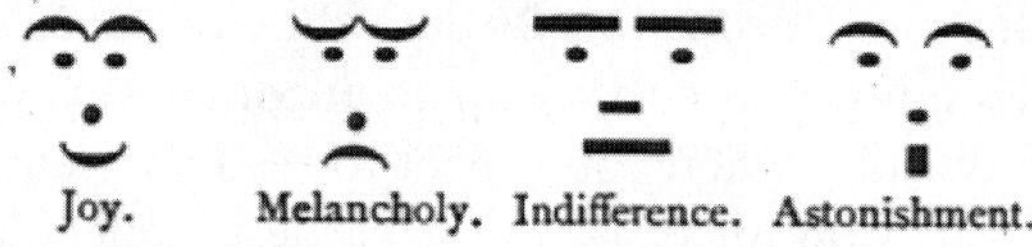

The use of smilies in electronic communication was proposed by Scott Fahlman in a 1982 email. Once defined, the idea took off.

```
19-Sep-82 11:44    Scott E  Fahlman             :-)
From: Scott E Fahlman <Fahlman at Cmu-20c>

I propose that the following character sequence for joke markers:

:-)

Read it sideways.  Actually, it is probably more economical to mark
things that are NOT jokes, given current trends.  For this, use

:-(
```

Please, Don't Be Offended

The guidelines just described help you avoid making social mistakes, because there is no value in offending people. But, "offense" involves two people. So, avoid *being offended*, too, through tolerance, patience, and respect for differences. Perhaps the best description of this perspective comes from the policies page of a CSS discussion Web site, and is reprinted in Figure 11.4.

The "Offensensitivity" perspective can be summarized as follows:

- Your post will be seen by people all over the world, and you will see posts from people all over the world.

Offensensitivity

(The word "offensensitivity" was, so far as I'm aware, first used by Berke Breathed in *Bloom County*.)

When posting to `css-discuss`, **remember that your message will be sent to (literally) thousands of people all over the world**. They all have likes and dislikes as individual as your own. They will also be offended by certain things which you may not find remarkable. While you can't foresee every potential area of conflict, there are certain guidelines that are fairly obvious: avoid swearing, cultural insults, blasphemy, proselytizing, and things of that nature. If you wouldn't say it out loud in front of your grandmother while in a place of worship, then you probably shouldn't say it on the list either.

At the same time, recognize that you are receiving messages from (literally) thousands of people all over the world. They all have likes and dislikes as individual as your own. They will also not find remarkable certain things by which you may be offended. Odds are that they probably didn't set out to offend you on purpose, so try taking a deep breath and counting to a nice high number if you feel a rising sense of offense. If, after this calming break, you still feel you must say something, **e-mail the poster directly** (and not on the list) to explain your feelings calmly, reasonably, and above all clearly without attacking them. They may be unaware of the effect of their words, so this is your chance to educate them. If you just slag them for being "insensitive," you may get flamed in return and create a resolve to keep offending you just for being so uptight and irrational (from their point of view).

Above all, remember that other people are about as likely to change their basic natures and habits as you are to change yours. You may at some point have to make a choice between tolerating other people's views and participating in the list. Please make this choice privately, and follow through quietly. Thank you.

Figure 11.4 A portion of the policies page at www.css-discuss.org/policies.html.

- You can easily and unintentionally offend them; they can easily and unintentionally offend you.
- The "problem" is our different cultures, social norms, backgrounds, religions, assumptions, and so forth. You're not wrong; they're not wrong. And they are no more likely to change their thinking than you are. Be tolerant. Be respectful.

Using the Web with an open mind and maturity can avoid considerable nastiness.

Expect the Unexpected

Expecting the unexpected is a valuable survival skill in life and in computing. When something unexpected happens, we should not only notice it, but we should also ask ourselves "Why did that happen?" or "What's going on?" By being alert, by wondering about the unexpected event, and by analyzing what might have caused it, we may discover an advantage, avoid harm, learn something new, or, perhaps most important, save ourselves from looking like total dummies! So, an essential skill in the social world of computing is to *expect the unexpected*.

The Onion

As discussed in Chapter 5, we need to be skeptical when using the World Wide Web, and "expecting the unexpected" helps. A good illustration comes from *The Onion* (www.theonion.com). As a humor magazine specializing in news satire, *The Onion* produces outrageous "news" stories that seem *almost* believable. Until you think about it. Is it possible that Neil Armstrong, the man who has been celebrated since 1969 as the first man to walk on the moon, would have said 40 years later that it was all a fake? No. It would really be unexpected if it were true. But rather than asking if it makes sense—and when not sure, checking for confirmation—many people simply believe it and repeat it.

Among those who have been taken in by *The Onion* are the *New York Times* (and many other newspapers around the world), former senator John Kerry and other politicians, FOX Nation, MoveOn.org and other advocacy organizations, and innumerable people posting to their Facebook accounts. It's harmless, but it is embarrassing to be fooled; we would all rather be "in the know."

Suspicious Activity

Being alert to unexpected information like an *Onion* article may save embarrassment, but other kinds of online activity are of greater concern. Is your software "acting" strange? Is your computer "behaving" unusually? These could be indicators of a software problem such as disk fragmentation or, more ominously, a computer virus infection. If the behavior continues after a reboot, you may need some help.

Other cases of unexpected behavior concern your interactions on the Web. "Stuff happens" online, and as you learned in Chapter 3, the Internet is designed to recover. So, you can expect that occasionally a site will be down or mail will go undelivered. Such problems are rare, however, and usually quickly resolved. But, suppose you got this message from your email provider:

Your message was not sent

Suspicious activity has been detected on your account. To protect your account and our users, your message has not been sent.

If this error continues, please contact your eMail Customer Care for further help.

We apologize for the inconvenience.

It is unexpected. Your previous email was sent with no problem. It *is* possible that there could be some type of cyber intrusion into your account (see Chapter 12), and your email provider is blocking your mail while it works on resolving it. But, like all unexpected behavior, you should think about it and do a little checking. What should you do?

Perhaps the first check you need to run is to test whether any *other* mail can be sent. So, try sending a "Hello" message to a friend or yourself. If it is *not sent*, then there is a problem with the general mailer operation, and you will have to wait for it to be resolved. If your "Hello" mail *is sent*, then either there was a transient error (an unrepeatable "out of the blue" event), or something else has prompted this message. Perhaps the best next move is to visit your email provider's site and their tech blog to check what they say there.

Unexpectedly Flaky. Occasionally a familiar application will do something strange, such as slowing down, "forgetting" changes, misaligning the cursor, or failing in other ways. Such behaviors are unexpected and often immediately precede a crash. When you notice your software "acting strange," act immediately: Save *to a new file name*, exit, and restart. The problem is usually just with the software, but it could be with the instance; a new file name avoids overwriting your previously saved version.

Creating Good Passwords

One day electronic hardware may reliably detect who we are when we come in contact with a computer, and there will be no need for **passwords**. Meanwhile, passwords are a key part of our daily interaction with computers. This section considers selecting, changing, and managing passwords as well as password principles that can make your daily computer usage easier. Chapter 12 deals with the related topic of computer security.

The Role of Passwords

The point of a password, of course, is to limit computer or software system access to only those who know a not-likely-to-be-guessed sequence of keyboard characters. So, obviously, it is necessary to select such a sequence. We'll discuss how to choose an effective password momentarily, but first let's discuss how they work.

How Passwords Work

You might think the computer system stores the password you choose, and then each time you log into your account, it compares what you entered with what it has stored. That's almost right, but not quite. There is a serious flaw with that scenario. If the account numbers and passwords were stored together inside the computer as **cleartext**—that is, the way you typed them and readable to you—a snoop could find them and use them to access your account.

Instead, your password should be stored encrypted—although not every company does so. **Encrypted** information has been recoded to hide its meaning. Your password is transformed into a **ciphertext** that cannot be easily read. For example, if the password is drowsSap, it might be encrypted by changing each letter to be the next letter in the alphabet. That is,

drowsSap $\xrightarrow[\text{change\_each\_letter\_to\_next}]{}$ espxtTbq

The ciphertext is saved. Normally, the encryption technique used is called a **1-way cipher**, meaning that it is not easy (or possible) to decrypt. This cipher (to be discussed further in Chapter 12) is not one way, and it's not strong either—that is, it's not secure.

Notice that in a 1-way cipher, no one knows your password except you. The computer doesn't know it—it only knows the encrypted version. It verifies that you know it by encrypting what you type in, and comparing that to the encrypted version it keeps with your account. If you forget the password, it's lost for good!

11.1 One Way Only. One-way ciphers are not reversible; they cannot be decoded. Our drowsSap example doesn't have that property, as you can easily show by figuring out what vsdpssfdu is, if it was encrypted by the same technique.

So, how can your password be "recovered" when you lose it? For systems using a 1-way cipher, it cannot be. The system administrator—often called the **superuser**—sets a new, known password. If you say you've forgotten your password, he or she tells you a new one and asks you to change it. Once changed, you are again the only person who knows it.

What stops someone from asking to have any account's password changed? "Security questions." At school or at work the system administrator may know you personally, and when you ask to have your password changed, he or she simply does it. The superuser knows the account belongs to you. But online, where there are millions of users, what proof does anyone have that you are the owner of the account? Security questions—"What is your favorite pet's name?"—can provide some evidence. By answering one or more security questions correctly, you give the system a basis for thinking the account is yours.

A Thoughtful Question. If the security question is "What's your favorite pet's name?" and you have plastered your pet's name all over your social media account, it wouldn't be that difficult for someone to claim to be you, say they forgot their password, be challenged by the security question, and guess the answer. Then they have access to your account. To be secure, pick a question whose answer you have not publically disclosed.

Poor Passwords

A good password is one that no one is likely to guess, but which you can easily remember. Many of us focus on the "easy to remember" part, and choose a nickname, our house number, or our boy or girl friend's name. These may be easy to remember, but someone familiar with us (or our profile) could easily guess them. Other weak passwords include short passwords (`x`), obvious number or letter sequences (`123`), and standard single dictionary words (`password`).

It may seem hopeless to think of a password that cannot be easily guessed. After all, aren't computers extremely fast? Why couldn't someone program a computer to try all possible combinations of keyboard characters? Of course, computers are extremely fast and generating all possible combinations is possible, at least until the password gets long. But, the software system that asks for passwords will not allow zillions of attempted logins. If the correct password isn't presented after several attempts, the system assumes it's not a real user, but rather an attempt to bypass the password process. It then notifies the superuser or takes some other preventative action.

Therefore, the main concern is to avoid a password that someone familiar with you or your profile could guess after a few attempts. Strong passwords are easy to create, as we now explain.

Creating Quality Passwords

There are two goals when creating a password: It must be easy to remember and hard to guess. We solve these problems as follows:

VideoNote
How Many Passwords?

- Easy to remember—pick a topic from which all of your passwords are chosen
- Hard to guess—compress, scramble, and recode a password phrase to be unintelligible

These two requirements are easy to work through.

Easy to Remember

To avoid forgetting a password—or more typically, forgetting where you wrote down your password so you wouldn't forget it—pick a topic that you will *always* use to pick passwords. Sample topics might be

movies
favorite sport
favorite hobby
foreign country
famous author
. . .

Using one topic helps you remember passwords because they will be associated in your mind. So, imagine that you pick movies as your topic. Then you can build a password based on

May The Force Be With You

The Matrix Trilogy

Hollywood

. . .

Then, when you try to remember your password, you will know where to start thinking.

The topic should be broad like "movies" so that there are many possible words and phrases to use. Most importantly, pick a topic and stick with it. It's a brain aid for you. Even if some of your passwords cannot be used because others know them, there will still be many more related terms to choose from.

Hard to Guess

Long passwords are harder to guess than short ones, so our rules begin with a length requirement:

Rule 1: Choose a password that is eight characters or more.
Rule 2: Include numbers and letters (and if allowed, symbols like % and *).
Rule 3: Mix upper- and lowercase letters.
Rule 4: Avoid "dictionary words."

It's worth thinking about your password rather than picking one impulsively.

Our heuristic for generating a good password can be illustrated in three examples. The basic strategy will be to pick a *phrase*, not just a word, and then modify it in a directed way so that to someone else it is a meaningless sequence of symbols. This lowers the chance that someone can guess it.

EXAMPLE 1

Begin with the quote "May the force be with you"	
Drop the "the", it's boring:	Mayforcebewithyou
Change May, the fifth month, to 5:	5forcebewithyou
Change "for" to 4:	54cebewithyou
Change "you" to u:	54cebewithu
Change "cebe" to CB:	54CBwithu

EXAMPLE 2

Begin with the title "The Matrix Trilogy"	
Drop the "The", it's boring:	MatrixTrilogy
Change the "tri" letters to 3:	Ma3x3logy
Change 3 x 3 to 9:	Ma9logy
Change which letters are capitalized:	ma9Logy
Change "y" to "EE":	ma9LogEE

EXAMPLE 3

Begin with the name "Hollywood"	
Change "oo" to 2o:	Hollyw2od
Change "ll" to 2l:	Ho2lw2od
Change "w" to 2u:	Ho2l2u2od
Change "o" to zero:	H02l2u2od
Change capitalization:	h02l2u2oD

These examples illustrate the kinds of changes that a phrase, quote, or title can go through to become a password. The transformations can also use foreign languages (2 ⇔ dos), Roman numerals (V ⇔ 5), chemistry (fe ⇔ iron), and so on. Anything you know about. Perhaps the most ingenious idea is to have an obvious transformation (Ratatouille → Ratatoui2le) but not to make it. Instead, go for another change (Ratatouille → Ratatwoe) that spans a larger set of letters.

It's Okay to Be Elite. You may be familiar with the form of writing called Leet or Eleet or Leet Speak. In Leet, normal keyboard characters are replaced with different characters that kind of look similar. For example, use 6 instead of G. Leet is written *1337* in Leet. Check Wikipedia for a dictionary of Leet spelling. Changing *some* characters to Leet is a very handy transformation.

Would anyone guess 54CBwithu, ma9LogEE, or h02l2u2oD? Probably not. Would you remember them? They may not be easy to remember when someone else creates them by this process, but when *you* create them yourself, they are surprisingly easy to remember.

11.2 Create a Password. Using transformations like those in the examples, change the word password into a better password. Limit yourself to three transformations.

One final comment: It is possible to be too clever. So clever, in fact, that you can't remember the password you developed. Some imaginative people can keep transforming a letter string for a very long time. This is unnecessary for the purposes of a password, though it may be fun as a game! Our examples used four to five transformations, which should be plenty. After all, your adversary won't know the original phrase or the topic, probably.

Managing Passwords

People with high-security jobs must follow the password policies of their employers. For the rest of us, we don't need especially strong passwords, but we will have to use them frequently. How can we keep them all straight?

Perfect Recall. Should you keep a copy of your password written down somewhere? Some people must and others don't bother. You should decide if you're confident in your ability to remember—or rederive—your password, and decide accordingly.

One strategy is to have three passwords to use in a variety of circumstances, and always use one of them. Classify them as follows:

1. Four-digit numerical password—for PINs and *not* "obvious"
2. Six-letter/digit password—when little risk if compromised, such as Yahoo! mail account
3. Eight+ symbol password—for cases where serious risk exists, such as online banking

The password construction heuristic described earlier is appropriate for the third case.

These three types should handle normal situations you encounter. By using the passwords repeatedly, you will have no problem remembering them. If you forget which one you used, there will be only two other possibilities to try.

These passwords can be used for years, even though security experts tell us to change them periodically. Occasionally, you may be asked to change a password—especially if the system has been compromised. The password you must change is one of the three above. To avoid having to remember another password, begin using the new password. This requires you to change it wherever you have used the old password in the past. Chances are that you won't remember all these places, so change it at the sites you do remember, and the others when you revisit them. Eventually, the password will be changed everywhere and you can forget the old one.

Spam

Unsolicited commercial email, popularly known as **spam**, is a serious annoyance for regular computer users. Without doing anything to provoke it, a person can be sent more than 100 spam messages a day. There are laws against spam in many places, and spammers are prosecuted, but it still persists.

Unwanted Input. The term *spam* is widely believed to derive from a *Monty Python* skit in which the word "spam" was chanted by Vikings to drown out restaurant conversation, humorously showing that unwanted input impedes legitimate communication.

A **spam filter**, software that separates legitimate mail from spam, provides excellent protection against the problem. Examples include SpamAssassin and PureMessage. In most cases, the service that provides your email account—your school or company, for example—has a spam filter installed; it may be working without your knowledge.

The spam filter software processes email messages as they arrive, separating the spam from the legitimate mail, which it places in your inbox. Because a program cannot possibly understand the content of the email (see our discussion of the Turing test in Chapter 22), determining if email is spam is really just a program's best guess. The program scans the email and assigns a score that measures how many properties typical of spam are also properties of the email. If the score is above the user threshold, the email is considered spam and moved to a separate folder, called the *spam quarantine*. Users can check the quarantine to be sure no legitimate mail is being stopped.

Table 11.2 How spam thresholds affect email delivery

Change Threshold	Effect on Legitimate Messages	Effect on Spam
Higher	Fewer legitimate messages quarantined	More spam gets through to inbox
Lower	More legitimate messages quarantined	Less spam gets through to inbox

Controlling Spam

After a spam filter scores the email, it is delivered to your inbox if the score is below your spam threshold. Because determining whether email is spam or not is only a guess, some mistakes are inevitable. Setting the threshold lets you control how to handle the "close calls." Because messages are assigned more points when they have more properties typical of spam, a lower threshold amounts to saying, "I will call a message spam based on fewer properties." Raising the threshold amounts to saying, "I want more evidence that a message is spam before it's quarantined." Table 11.2 summarizes the effects of these choices.

As a general rule, once you have found the threshold you're comfortable with, you will rarely have to adjust it again.

Comfort Range. When using a new spam filter, check the quarantine faithfully for legitimate messages for the first few weeks. The best case is no good messages in the quarantine and little spam getting through to the inbox; the threshold is set just right. Otherwise, adjust the threshold up or down and continue to check the quarantine until satisfied.

Scams

Many things people want to do are easy to do with computers: finding information (Google), keeping up with friends (Twitter), buying merchandise (Amazon), and so forth. Other things people want to do, including cheating others, are also easy with computers. Scams are common in our online life, so we must be aware of them.

Nigerian Widow Scam

The Nigerian Widow scam is so common that it has become a widely understood reference in popular culture (see Figure 11.5). The scam is technically known as

SUBJECT: URGENT RESPONSE

DEAR SIR

IT IS WITH HEART FULL OF HOPE THAT I WRITE TO SEEK YOUR HELP IN THE CONTEXT BELOW. I AM MRS. MUNIRAT ABACHA THE SECOND WIFE OF THE FORMER NIGERIA HEAD OF STATE, LATE GENERAL SANI ABACHA, WHOSE SUDDEN DEATH OCCURRED ON 8TH OF JUNE 1998.

HAVING GOTTEN YOUR PARTICULARS FROM THE FAMILY LIBRARY , I HAVE NO DOUBT ABOUT YOUR CAPACITY AND GOOD WILL TO ASSIST US IN RECEIVING INTO YOUR CUSTODY (FOR SAFETY) THE SUM OF US$20MILLION WILLED AND DEPOSITED IN MY FAVOR BY MY LATE HUSBAND, PLUS 24 CARAT GOLD DUST WORTH USD$5M.

...

Figure 11.5 Beginning of a typical "Nigerian Widow" scam email.

an **advance-fee fraud**, but most international law enforcement officials refer to it as the **419 fraud** after its section number in Nigerian Criminal Code.

The 419 scam works like this:

- Someone you never heard of claims to have great wealth that they cannot access ($25,000,000).
- They ask your help in transferring the money, usually out of their country.
- For your help, they intend to give you a large share (20 percent) of the money.
- They emphasize that the operation is confidential—tell no one.
- After you agree to help, things go wrong with the transfer.
- They need some money to bribe officials or pay various fees before they can get the money out.
- You give them the money thinking you will get much more in the future. This is the "advance fee" part.
- The scammers need more and more money as time passes.
- Eventually you threaten them, and they disappear.

The scam has many, many variations—search the Web for the latest variations—but they all require urgency, secrecy, and your money.

Just the Facts, Lady. Reading the 419 scam in Figure 11.5, one might wonder if there really was a Sani Abacha from Nigeria or a Munirat Abacha. In fact, Sani Abacha was a Nigerian dictator who died in 1998, apparently of a heart attack. His wife was Mariam Jidah; there is no evidence he had a second wife. Munirat Abacha seems to be a name made up for these scam letters.

Unfortunately, the 419 scam has been extremely successful for the scammers. The U.S. Secret Service claims Americans lose tens of millions of dollars every year to this scam. There are whole Web sites dedicated to combating the Nigerian Widow scam (www.419scam.org), but it continues to thrive. In a recent variation, the email says that you have won a lottery in another country (see Figure 11.6). This should sound very suspicious: How many foreign lotteries do you usually enter? How often do people hit lottery jackpots? Yet another variation simply announces that for your shipment to be sent, they need personal identification for customs purposes (see Figure 11.7). Were you expecting a shipment from Ghana? But, people continue to take the bait.

Obviously, any email that appears to give you something for nothing can safely be deleted. The world just doesn't work that way.

Different Story, Same Fraud. The Nigerian Widow scam is not new. The same fraud, known as the Spanish Prisoner scam, was used extensively in the 1920s. The story was that an extremely wealthy man was locked in a Spanish jail, and his family promised riches in gratitude to anyone who helped him escape. Of course, the helper would pay for one failed attempt after another.

We are pleased to inform you of the release of the SPANISH SWEEPSTAKE LOTTERY/INTERNATIONAL PROMOTION PROGRAM for the Year 2012. Your email address drew the lucky numbers 01-04-12-21-25-32 that consequently won the lottery in the 3rd category. You have therefore been approved for a lump Sum Pay of £5.500, 000.00 Five Million Five Hundred Thousand Great British Pounds Only) in cash Credited to File Ref number EUR-891/7700p. This is from A Total Cash Prize of £100,000.000.00 (One Hundred Million Great British Pounds only) Shared among International winners in this category.

Your fund is now deposited with a financial institution (Royal Bank Of Canada London United Kingdom insured in your name. Please note that your claim and batch number are the key to your funds, your are to keep this confidential until your claim has been processed and your money remitted to your account as this is part of our protocol to avoid double claiming or unwarranted taking an advantage of this program by participants. All participants were selected through a computer ballot system drawn from 25,000 names from Africa, Asia, Europe and America as part of our international promotion program that we conduct once in a month. We hope with a part of your prize, you will take part in assisting the less privileged in the society.

PAYMENT OF PRIZE AND CLAIM

Remember all prize money must be claimed within Six (6) Month of this notice. Six 6) Month, all funds will be returned to the Ministerio De Economia Y Hacienda as unclaimed.

Stated below is your identification numbers:

Batch Number: EUR-401/709p
Pin Number: EUR -23 811

These numbers fall within the England Location file. Urgently email your full name and mobile Number/Pin/Batch number to our fiduciary agent in London via his contact details below to claim your prize.

Overseas Claims/Exchange Online Payment Unit
Contact Dr. C Gibson
Mobile: + 44 7700089 Telephone +447024033 Office Fax: +447024063
Office Address: 300 Oxford Street London W1A1EX United Kingdom
Email: 18@hotmail.com
Email: 18@hotmail.com

Congratulation again from all members of our staff and thank you for being part of our promotion program

Yours faithfully,
Mrs. Janet Hessian, Network Online Coordinator.

WARNING!!!!!

Do not tell people about your Prize Award until your money is successful handed over to you to avoid disqualification that may arise from double claim. You may also receive similar e-mails from people portraying to be other Organizations or Network Inc. This is solely to collect your personal information from you and lay claim over your winning.

Figure 11.6 A recent variation of the advance-fee fraud claiming the recipient is a lottery winner.

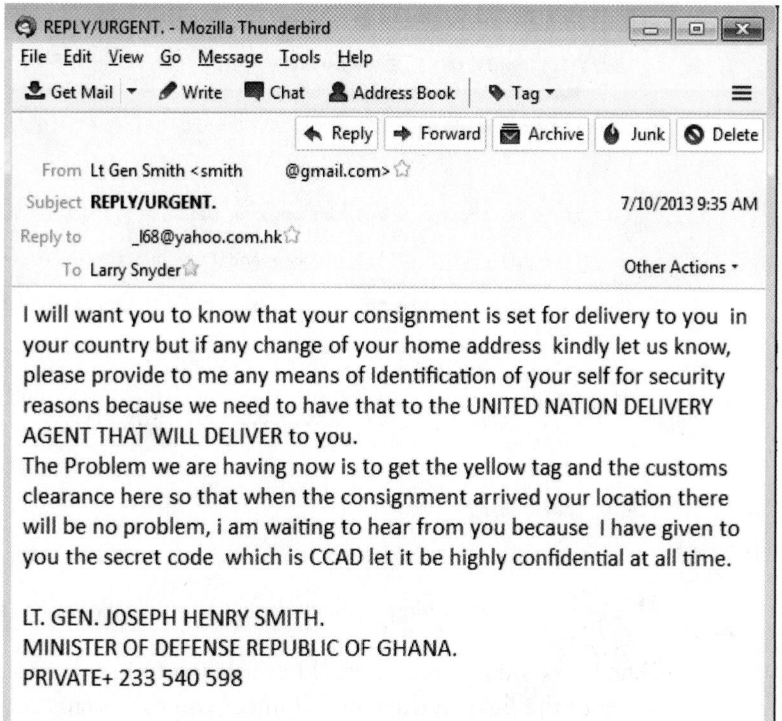

Figure 11.7 A request for personal identification to complete a shipment from Ghana.

Phishing

If someone walked up to you and said, "Give me your Social Security number, your driver's license number, the passwords to all of your computer accounts, credit card numbers, . . . ," you would laugh. You would not consider giving such sensitive information to any random person. If the person is wearing a nice blue suit and has a badge in his or her pocket indicating an agent from the FBI, you still wouldn't give that data, at least not until you verified that they really were from the FBI, and on what legal authority they are asking for this information.

But every day, people voluntarily give up such personal information. It is a mystery why they would be so skeptical in person, but so trusting online.

The term for the social engineering process of convincing trusting people to give up personal data voluntarily is called **phishing**, short for *password harvesting fishing*. The scam works as follows.

Spam email is sent out designed to look like it comes from a reputable organization, such as a bank, PayPal, or eBay. The mail uses actual content from the reputable organization's site, such as logos, images, and fonts. Some go to such extremes as to use the actual Help Line 1-800 phone number. It's easy to be taken in.

The text of the message makes one of several claims on behalf of the reputable organization:

- Your account has been accessed by unauthorized people.
- You are owed money.
- There has been a security breach, which they are trying to fix.
- They are performing an audit and find possible problems with your account.
- A phishing scam has been detected and they're trying to fix it (see Figure 11.8).

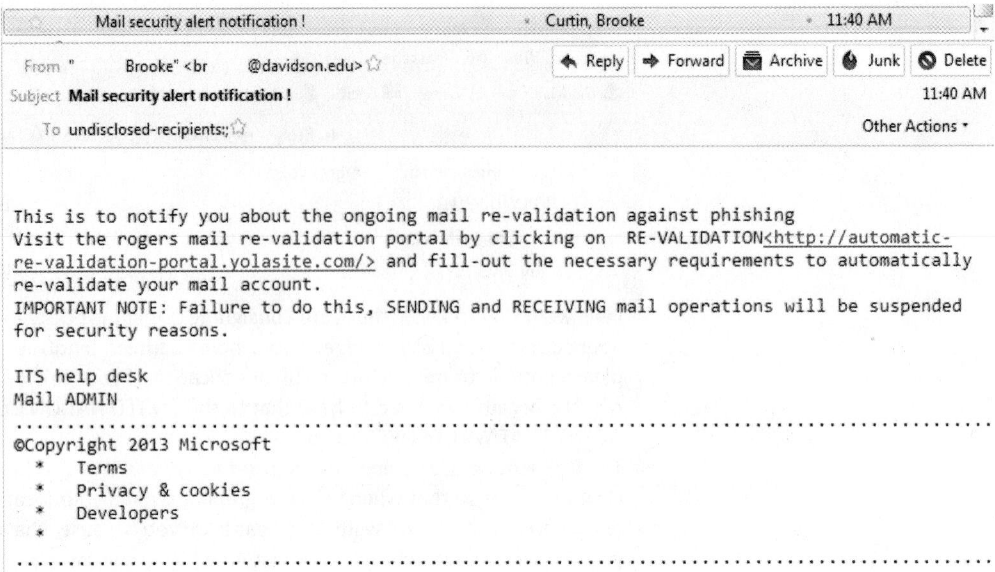

Figure 11.8 A phishing scam claiming to be validating email accounts against a phishing scam.

The list could go on and on. They ask you to log on to a Web site to resolve the issue. Most of the links in the email connect you to a bogus site that looks like it might be from the reputable organization, but in fact it's a phishing site. See how realistic Figure 11.9 appears. It asks you to give your account numbers, password, and other private information. The scammers simply collect the data you enter.

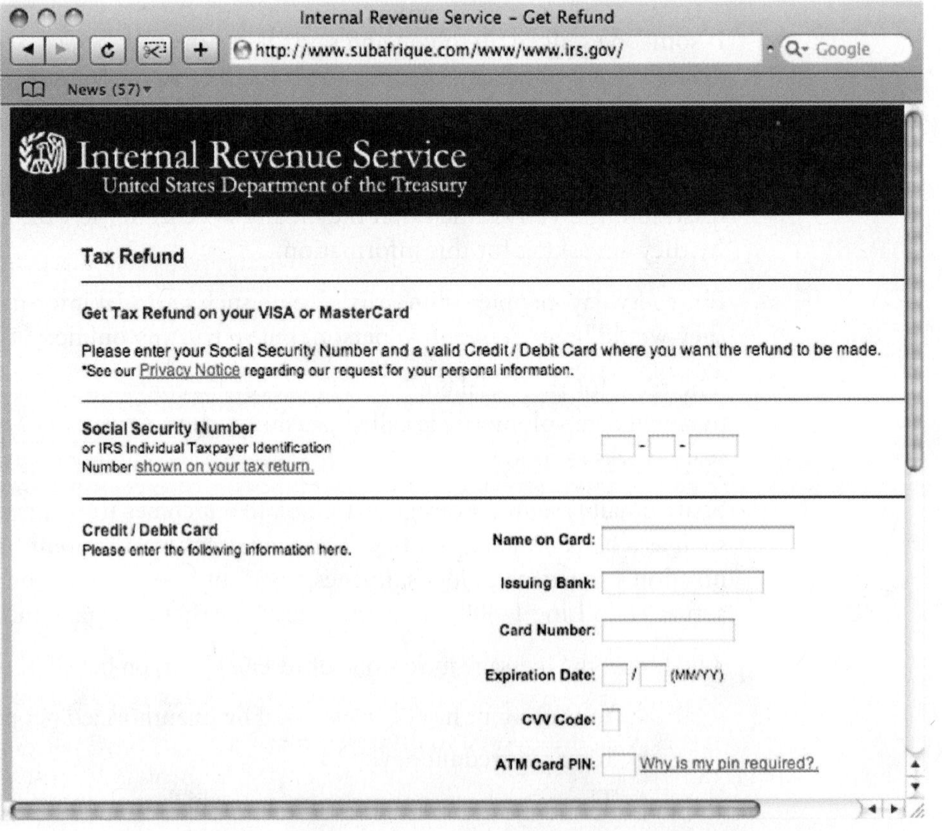

Figure 11.9 An example of a fraudulent email phishing attempt claiming to be from the tax people at the U.S. Internal Revenue Service; notice that the domain is not the IRS, but www.subafrique.com.

11.3 UPS and Downs of Phishing. Take the SonicWALL Phishing Quiz, and explain why the UPS email is legitimate: **www.sonicwall.com/phishing/**.

The End of the Phishing Story

Phishing was first described in 1987, when the Internet was in use but before the World Wide Web was invented. It's a good assumption that it is not going away.

Your best defense is your own skepticism. How likely is it that you are owed money you don't know about, or that a company bothers its customers to do an audit? You can protect yourself from phishing by doing the following:

- Open attachments only when you know who sent them and why.
- Only give information online when you have initiated the transaction yourself by going to the company.
- Before entering information, think: "How did I get to this company?" Typing their URL or Web search are okay; clicking a link in an email or a social network site is not.
- Pay attention to the domain name of the company—in the IRS example, it is subafrique.com and www.irs.gov is a folder name.

Many people never lose information in phishing trips; you can avoid it, too.

The risk in phishing scams is identity theft, which is discussed in Chapter 12.

Protecting Intellectual Property

Like land or Rover or a Land Rover, information is something that can be owned. Information, including photographs, music, textbooks, and cartoons, is the result of the creative process. The act of creation gives the creator ownership of the result in the United States and most of the world. Sometimes there are multiple forms of ownership. If on her tour Adele sings a song written by Paul Simon, he owns the words and music, and she owns the performance. If a person creates something while working for a company, the company generally owns the information. All such human creations are called **intellectual property** to distinguish them from real estate, pets, cars, and other stuff that can be owned.

The two aspects of intellectual property that we are interested in here are software licensing and copyrighted material on the Web. Each affects how you can use information technology.

Licensing of Software

When you buy software, you load it onto your machine without giving much attention to the legal mumbo jumbo that you agree to by opening the package or downloading the file. (Sure, lawyers probably read the fine print, but the rest of us don't.) If you were to read it, you'd discover a remarkable fact: You didn't buy the software—you actually leased it. That is, **software licenses** tend to give you the use of the software, but the ownership remains with the company that is marketing it. (Of course, every license is different, forcing us to discuss the topic generally. To be sure about your particular agreement, check your software license.) We are not interested in why this is the case; rather, we want to know how such agreements constrain our behavior.

Use of the Software. If the agreement allows us to use the software, we can use it on at least one computer, and we may be permitted to use it on all of the computers we own. The fact that we use it personally generally means that we use one instance at a time. Installing several instances for convenience may be okay. But, if the number of computers it can be installed on is restricted, then we should explore purchasing an alternative license—the family plan, for example—to cover other computers.

Don't Sell It or Give It Away. Because you don't *own* commercial software, you cannot give it to your friend. If you do, you would violate the terms of the contract that you agreed to when you opened the software package or downloaded it. But even if you simply bought software from a friendly programmer you met in the computer lab, you probably still can't give it away. The programmer created the software—it's his or her intellectual property—and the programmer has full copyright protection. Like a photographer who creates a stunning picture, the programmer's ownership of the software allows copies to be made and sold to people like you. You buy a photograph to frame and enjoy; you buy software to run and enjoy. Unless the programmer gives you the *explicit* right to copy and distribute the software, you cannot sell it or even give it away.

Try Before You Buy. Finally, there is **shareware**, which is software that is usually distributed over the Internet. You can download a free copy, and you can copy it and give it to your friends. The idea of shareware is that you can try out the software, and if you like it and use it, you pay the person who created it. (The price is listed.) It's a great system because it gives individual programmers a chance to distribute their often well-built and effective software, and because you can try it before you purchase it. But it is an honor system. If you use the software, you should pay for it. It is unethical to download software on the implied promise of paying for it if you use it, and then to use it without paying. Prices are generally very modest, and the software is often exceptionally good.

Open Source Software

Software from vendors like Microsoft and Adobe is *proprietary*, meaning the vendors keep the source code (program) private; when you get a copy to install, you receive only the binary code for your computer model and operating system (see Chapters 9 and 22). The other kind of software—software for which the program is publicly available—is known as **open source** software. For example, the Mozilla browser software is open source. Firefox, SeaMonkey, Web, MozBraille (Web page rendering for the visually impaired), and other browsers are built on top of it. As a result, personal copies of Firefox, for example, are free. Many, many useful programs are open source.

Open source seems not to make sense: Who pays for the technology and how can a company make money if the product is publicly available? Companies developing technology often make their products open source to promote wide distribution; they make their money selling specialized versions to corporate clients, providing customer support, and selling other software that interfaces to it. Advocates of open source point out that if the software is publicly available, other people work on it and improve it, a point that is repeatedly borne out. After all, who would have the resources to build a Braille browser from scratch? When looking for new software, find out what open source software is available for your problem.

Copyright on the Web

When a person writes a term paper, builds a Web page, or creates a sculpture, he or she automatically owns the **copyright** on that "work" in the United States and most nations of the world. It's the creator's copyright, unless the creation is "work for hire," in which case the owner is the person who paid the creator, usually a company. For example, if you create a personal Web page, you own the copyright, but if you build a Web page as part of your job, your employer owns it. Posting information on the Web is a form of publishing, and though Internet copyright and other law is not fully developed yet, it is a good assumption that information on the Web is owned by someone.

No © 'em. At one time, to claim copyright, you had to include the phrase "© Copyright *dates* by *author/owner*. All Rights Reserved." That's no longer necessary for works produced after March 1, 1989. However, the copyright notice is still used as a reminder and reference.

What rights are included in a copyright? Obviously the right to copy it, but surprisingly, there are others. Copyright protects the owner's right to do the following:

- Make a copy of the work
- Use a work as the basis for a new work, called *creating a derivative work*
- Distribute or publish the work, including electronically
- Publicly perform the work, as in music, poetry, drama, or video or audio recording
- Publicly display the work, as in displaying an image on a computer screen

It is the very act of creating the intellectual property that creates these rights. No application or approval is required. The work doesn't require the © symbol. It's copyrighted the moment it's finished.

Notice the second item in the list: using the work to create a derivative work. This is an important aspect of copyright because it prevents someone from, for example, changing each of the *Simpsons* characters in some small way—aging them, perhaps—and then claiming to have created a new dysfunctional cartoon family. Only their creator, Matt Groening, has the right to change the characters. You might be tempted to bypass copyright law by restating a work in your own words, but if your creation is too much like the original, you've produced a derivative work rather than new intellectual property.

Free Personal Use. Of course, just because someone else owns a work doesn't mean that you can't use and enjoy it. Obviously, the fact that they've published it on the Web means that you are free to read, view, or listen to it. Printing it so that you can read it on the bus is okay, as is filing a copy on your computer for future *personal* enjoyment. You can mail the URL to your friends—the URL, not the content—notifying them of the information. Such applications are why the information was published on the Web in the first place.

When Is Permission Needed? Many sites have a written copyright policy. Sometimes the information is placed in the **public domain**, meaning that it is free for anyone to use, in any form. This is convenient because it means that you can treat the information as your own. You can even sell it if you have a buyer. Sometimes owners state that the information can be republished or used in other forms, as long as you cite the source. They retain ownership, but you get to use it. All you have to do is follow their guidelines. And, of course, some sites—those that don't state otherwise—retain all rights to the Web-published information under the applicable copyright laws.

Generally, if you want to use works in one of the five ways listed above from a site that reserves its rights, you must get permission from the owners of the information. Using such copyrighted property without permission is illegal, of course. But the fact that a site retains the rights to its information should not keep you from asking for permission. Many sites routinely give permission; their purpose in requiring you to ask for it is to control the distribution of their works. It takes only a little effort to ask.

The Concept of Fair Use. Between the free personal use and the need to get permission is a gray area in which limited use of copyrighted materials is allowed without getting permission. This is known as the concept of "fair use." **Fair use** is recognized in copyright law to allow the use of copyrighted material for educational or scholarly purposes, to allow limited quotation of copyrighted works for review or criticism, to permit parody, and a few other uses. For example, I can quote one of the most widely known computer instructions, David Bowman's command in Stanley Kubrick's *2001: A Space Odyssey*,

"Open the pod bay doors, HAL."

without getting the permission of the present owner (Warner Brothers), because I am using the quotation for the educational purpose of instructing you about fair use. This is true even though this book is a commercial application of the quoted material. And you would be allowed to use similar brief quotations in class assignments, for example. Indeed, fair use provides many opportunities for using copyrighted material for socially beneficial purposes. The problem is that it can be very unclear just when fair use applies.

When Is It Fair Use? The following questions are applied to determine whether a given use of copyrighted information constitutes fair use.

1. What is the planned use?
2. What is the nature of the work in which the material is to be used?
3. How much of the work will be used?
4. What effect would this use have on the market for the work if the use were widespread?

What constitutes fair use is complex and subject to disagreements by fair-minded Web users, lawyers, and even judges. Indeed, in 1997 a two-year Conference on Fair Use (CONFU) struggled mightily with the interpretations and failed to clarify the matter fully. It is beyond the scope of this book to delve into the nuances of deciding fair use. But the University of Maryland publishes a very useful guideline; when in doubt, check it out: www.umuc.edu/library/libhow/copyright.cfm.

Violating the Copyright Law

Many people say that it is all right to use copyrighted material for noncommercial purposes, but that's false. You break the law whether you sell the material or not, though commercial use usually results in larger fines or damages when you're sued. Because the penalties for copyright infringement are substantial—up to $150,000 per act—it pays to be careful. By far the best approach is to think up your own material—that is, create intellectual property with your own intellect. You're not required to ask for anyone else's permission, and you enjoy copyright protection too!

Uncopyrightable Fact. Facts cannot be copyrighted. For example, "*Uncopyrightable* is the longest English word without repeated letters" is a fact, and so is uncopyrightable.

No Harm in Asking. When asking for copyright permission, state what works you are interested in, such as "the photograph on your page . . . /greatpix/elvis/"; how you would like to use the works, such as "put copies on my personal Web page at . . . "; and any other relevant information, such as "I want to colorize his suede shoes so they are actually blue." You can use the template in Figure 11.10 for the letter—just revise the red text.

To: Date:

I am writing to you to request permission to use the material described below. This material will be posted on a Web site that receives approximately 30 hits per month. The URL is

www.bloghoster.com/mySuperPage.html.

The material will be posted on July 1st and will remain on the Web site for an indefinite period. I am asking permission for the nonexclusive, worldwide right to publish this material.

Description: Include title, author and source of the work (if from a book, give the ISBN; if from a Web site give the complete URL), and a copy of the work if possible (the text or art you want to use).

Full credit will be given to the source. A release form appears below along with space for indicating your desired credit line.

If you do not control these rights in their entirety, please let me know to whom else I should write. Thank you.

Sincerely,

Your Name

Your Contact Information

I warrant that I have the right to grant the permission to republish the material specified above.

Permission is granted by: ____________________

Title: ____________________

Address: ____________________

Date: ____________________

Preferred Acknowledgment: ____________________

Figure 11.10 Sample request for copyright permission; revise the red text. Find the file at pearsonhighered.com/snyder.

Creative Commons

We began this chapter by discussing some amazing social advances resulting from the World Wide Web. Since then, we've been covering difficulties when using it socially, including spam and phishing. Now we are back to another improvement: the Creative Commons.

Most countries have copyright laws with the default, "All rights reserved" to the author. Although copyright law changes from time to time, it seems to be getting more restrictive, at least in the United States. And, we must live with it. That generally means, based on what we've just discussed, that to use someone's Web-published work, we must contact them for permission or other details of how they intend to exercise their intellectual property rights. It is a drag. And it limits sharing. And to the extent that other people's creations inspire creativity in us, it limits that, too. Enter the Creative Commons.

Allow Copying and Distribution

The Creative Commons (CC) has as its goals both to increase the sharing of intellectual property and to inspire greater creativity. To do this, they have developed licenses that allow works to be shared easily: When a creator posts his or her work on the Web with a CC license, people are allowed to copy and distribute it. Everyone knows immediately what the rules are for using it. This saves the burden of contacting the creator, and because the licenses emphasize making the work widely available, most work is available with few limitations.

The Creative Commons (creativecommons.org) licenses are not the same as putting work into the public domain. Placing a work in the public domain gives up all rights, which is the "No rights reserved" case. The CC licenses are middle ground: the author keeps "some rights reserved" but others are given away.

What to Keep, What to Give

A copyright owner—that could be you!—can choose among several options for a Creative Commons license:

ATTRIBUTION: Others are allowed to copy, distribute, perform, remix, or otherwise modify the work, as well as create other work based on it, as long as you get credit for it.

NONCOMMERCIAL: Others are allowed to copy, distribute, perform, remix, or otherwise modify the work, as well as create other work based on it, as long as the result is not for sale.

NO DERIVATIVE WORK: Others are allowed to copy, distribute, perform, or use the work in another way, as long as those are verbatim; no derivative works can be created from it.

SHARE ALIKE: Others are allowed to distribute derivative works only under a license identical to the one governing your work.

A standard CC license has been shortened to **CC BY-NC-SA** as text, or iconographically,

making it extremely easy to understand what your rights are regarding reuse.

11.4 Ask Permission? Could I mash up an image covered by the CC BY-NC-SA license, that is, create a derivative work, and use it in this book if I attributed the original image to its creator?

The Creative Commons licenses are a great idea and they are having a tremendous impact on making the information on the Web more universal.

Creative Commons Summary

Here is a summary checklist of the CC concepts and implications:

- Creators keep the copyright to their work.
- CC developed licenses for the general "good"; they get no extra rights beyond other users.
- CC provides tools for tagging your work with the license link.
- CC licenses allow copying, distributing, and performing.
- Attribution, which most CC licenses have, gives credit to the creator.
- Creators can waive any of the rights they keep for themselves.

The Creative Commons is communal.

SUMMARY

The chapter began with a discussion of crowdsourcing and other benefits of the Internet. It moved on to some of the hazards. You learned that thoughtful email users limit messages requiring an answer to one topic, include context, and do not forward private messages or broadcast email indiscriminately. We continued our discussion about the following:

- "Expecting the unexpected" as a useful survival skill. The challenge is to think about the unexpected event and correctly determine whether and how to respond.
- Spam, scams, and phishing. They are everyday occurrences, but skepticism is a handy tool to avoid trouble.
- Creating an easy-to-remember password. The approach emphasized selecting passwords that are connected to a common topic. It is smart to choose simple passwords when little security is needed and to choose more obscure passwords when there is greater risk.

- Characteristics of copyright. When we create intellectual property, we immediately have copyright protection of it. When others hold the copyright, we may be restricted on how we can use it. Asking permission is always the safest thing to do.
- And we learned about the Creative Commons licenses. It provides a simple way to create and share intellectual property within the existing laws. It promotes a creative and communal environment on the Web.

TRY IT SOLUTIONS

11.1 urcorrect

11.2 There is no single answer. Possible answers include:

password → pa2sword → pa2s2uord → pa2s2uORD

password → tossword → 2ssword → 2sSabres

password → noFword → properword → 4perWord

password → pass2uord → pass2uOhare → ATCOhare

11.3 What was your score? Did you check the items you missed?

11.4 No. I could create a derivative work—that's allowed—but it would have to carry the same license, which prevents the use of the derived work to be used commercially. Authors can waive their rights, so I might get permission to use my mashed-up image from the owner.

REVIEW QUESTIONS

Multiple Choice

1. When you forget your password
   a. the system administrator gives you a one-time password to use and then prompts you to create a new password
   b. the system administrator looks up your password
   c. the system administrator unscrambles your password and gives it to you
   d. the system administrator assigns a new password for you to use
2. Copyrighted material may be used
   a. only in nonprofit instances
   b. only when written permission is granted
   c. if proper credit is given to the owner
   d. without permission in limited circumstances
3. If you commit a crime on the Internet, who can determine your real identity?
   a. your parents
   b. your school officials
   c. no one, you are anonymous
   d. the law
4. When emailing, how many topics should you limit each individual email to?
   a. no more than three
   b. one
   c. any number is fine as long as you explain each one in detail
   d. it depends on the recipient

5. When using a 1-way cipher, who knows your password?
   a. only you
   b. you and your administrator
   c. you, your parents, and your administrator
   d. you, your administrator, and the government
6. Under most circumstances, what prevents a stranger from resetting your user password?
   a. the site administrator
   b. the government
   c. security questions
   d. nothing
7. Most people assume that when you send email it is
   a. semi-private
   b. private
   c. public
8. In what order should you answer a backlog of emails?
   a. normal order
   b. reverse order
   c. it does not matter
9. Can passwords stored in systems using 1-way cipher be recovered?
   a. yes, sometimes
   b. yes, always
   c. no
   d. it depends on whose password it is
10. What cannot be copyrighted?
   a. facts
   b. opinions
   c. new ideas
   d. old ideas

Short Answer

1. _______ is etiquette for the Internet.
2. A(n) _______ is a programmed response to your email that's sent when you are away.
3. The individual who controls access to a computer system, including logins and passwords, is called a(n) _______.
4. _______ are nonmaterial, human creations that people can claim ownership to.
5. New work created from existing work is called a(n) _______.
6. Information in the _______ is free for anyone to use.
7. _______ is the illegal use of email to scam users into surrendering their personal information—usually items like Social Security numbers, bank account numbers, and credit card numbers.
8. You don't buy software, you _______ it.
9. Before posting very emotional content you should _______.
10. Computers store passwords, but they are _______ for security.

Exercises

1. Explain crowdsourcing. Give at least three examples of crowdsourcing projects. Describe at least three benefits of crowdsourcing.
2. What is lacking in email communication as compared to face-to-face communication? Explain your answer in detail.
3. Explain what the following quote means in detail: "Avoid being offended."
4. What is this password: BH9oH2won0? (*Hint*: It was a popular 1990s TV show.)
5. Devise a year's worth of passwords based on a common theme.
6. Some Web sites won't allow you to reuse an old password when changing your current one. If the administrator does not store your past passwords, how does it know if one of your new passwords matches an old password? Explain your answer in detail.
7. Explain the following phrase in detail: "It is a mystery why they would be so skeptical in person, but so trusting online."
8. For each of the following, determine whether the practice is legal, illegal, or iffy. Also state whether it follows netiquette rules. Defend your answers.
   a. You sell a copy of a computer game to a friend.
   b. You forward an email from your boss to a coworker without permission
   c. You sell your old PC with the software still on it, but you keep the original copies of the software.
   d. You download a piece of shareware but don't pay for it.
   e. You frequently use a piece of shareware but don't pay for it.
   f. You install your company's software on your home computer.
   g. You frequently play a freeware game.
   h. You install software on your computer and the laptop of your college-bound sibling using the same disk.
   i. You copy a picture posted on Tumblr and add it to your personal Web page.
   j. You buy one license and install it on computers throughout a lab.
9. For each of the following, determine whether the practice is legal or illegal.
   a. You create a comical, big-eared cartoon rodent.
   b. You publish a Web page without including a copyright notice.
   c. You write a sequel to *Titanic*.
   d. You include a link to a Web page in your term paper.
   e. You include a paragraph from the *Fluency* text in your term paper.
   f. You accept money for a derivative you made of a piece of artwork with a noncommercial Creative Commons license
   g. You scan the autographed picture of your favorite band and put it on your Web site.
   h. You put a sound bite from a movie on your phone's ring tone.
   i. You put a sound bite from a movie into your class presentation.
   j. You use parts of your friend's term paper from last semester in your term paper.
10. How many possible eight-character passwords can be created using only uppercase letters and numbers?

11. Change the quote "How am I not myself?" to a strong password. Explain your process in detail.
12. Explain in detail everything you should check before sending an email. Make sure to explain the importance of checking each item.
13. Explain how vendors make a profit from open source software.

CHAPTER 12

Privacy and Digital Security

Shhh, It's a Secret

learning objectives

- Explain the meaning of privacy; discuss the issues surrounding privacy of information
- List and explain the meaning of the OECD Fair Information Practices
- Discuss the issues concerning U.S. privacy: opt-in/opt-out options and data security
- List the ways a computer can be compromised
- Explain the security methods used in public key cryptosystems (PKCs)
- Perform simple encryption from cleartext to ciphertext and perform the reverse decryption

CHAPTER 12

I've never looked through a keyhole without finding someone was looking back.

—JUDY GARLAND, COMMENTING ON HER LACK OF PRIVACY, 1967

They who can give up essential liberty to obtain a little temporary safety deserve neither liberty nor safety.

—BENJAMIN FRANKLIN, 1755

I think computer viruses should count as life. I think it says something about human nature that the only form of life we have created so far is purely destructive. We've created life in our own image.

—STEPHEN HAWKING, 1994

PRIVACY is a fundamental human right. The United Nations Universal Declaration of Human Rights recognizes privacy in Article 12. The constitutions of Australia, Hungary, and South Africa, among others, state a right to privacy. Though privacy is not explicitly mentioned in the U.S. Constitution, the U.S. Supreme Court has accepted privacy as a right implied by other constitutional guarantees. And privacy is a right that matters to all of us. No matter how exemplary our lives may be, there are aspects of it we would prefer to keep secret. And they are no one else's business. When those aspects interact with information technology, the issues of electronic privacy and security become important. There is much more than our passwords that we want to keep to ourselves.

In this chapter we discuss privacy and security. To begin, we consider a business transaction as a basis for understanding the topic of privacy and for considering who has an interest in collecting our private information. We look at how private information can be kept private, and we list the principles of privacy, including the principles from the Organization for Economic Cooperation and Development (OECD). Then, we explore the differences between how the principles are followed in the United States and in other countries. Next, we consider cookies and tracking as two ways privacy is threatened, and we discuss the problem of identity theft.

The next topic is malware, followed by a discussion of the security risks to network-connected computers and phones. After we have learned what they are, what they can do, and how we "catch" them, we give guidelines on how to protect yourself.

Encryption is the next topic. After learning encryption vocabulary, we study simple encryption examples. Public key cryptosystems (PKCs) are studied as a means of achieving more convenient security for Internet-related situations. PKC systems seem at first to offer almost no protection, and then they seem to offer so much protection that it's impossible to decrypt what was encrypted. We resolve the dilemma and explain why these protocols are truly secure.

Finally, we consider how to keep your information secure from computer disasters.

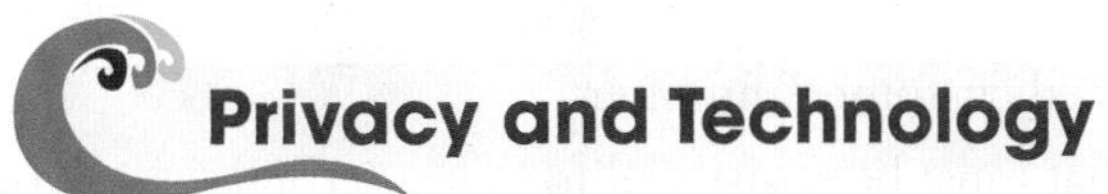

Privacy and Technology

In a primitive society *with no technology*, privacy is easy to understand and to achieve: Do something that is unobserved by others, and it's private; otherwise it's public. Technology—as always, neither good nor bad—helps both to gather information on others and to protect our privacy. It may not be good or bad, but it definitely complicates matters.

Modern Devices and Privacy

Supreme Court Justice Louis D. Brandeis was one of the first people to worry about how technology affects privacy. He described privacy as the individual's "right to be left alone." He also wrote (with Samuel D. Warren) in the *Harvard Law Review*:

> *The [original] narrower doctrine may have satisfied the demands of society at a time when the abuse to be guarded against could rarely have arisen without violating a contract or a special confidence; but now that* ***modern devices*** *afford abundant opportunities for the perpetration of such wrongs without any participation of the injured party, the protection granted by the law must be placed upon a broader foundation. [Emphasis added]*

He is saying that in the past it was hard for people's privacy to be violated without their knowledge, but using *modern devices*, people's privacy can be violated without their knowing it. The amazing thing about Warren and Brandeis's comments is that they were written in 1890. The modern devices they referred to were the first portable cameras and the faster film permitting short-exposure photographs. They continued,

> *While, for instance, the state of the photographic art was such that one's picture could seldom be taken without his consciously "sitting" for the purpose, the law of contract or of trust might afford the prudent man sufficient safeguards against the improper circulation of his portrait; but since the latest advances in photographic art have rendered it possible to take pictures surreptitiously, the doctrines of contract and of trust are inadequate to support the required protection.*

What would Warren and Brandeis have thought about phone cameras, the ever-present surveillance camera, Tumblr, YouTube, and full-body scanners? Their important point is that your image—and more generally, information about you—deserves "sufficient safeguards against improper circulation." It's a nineteenth-century formulation of a twenty-first-century concern.

Information Sources and Uses

Buying a product at a store generates a transaction, which produces information. The merchant can gather the date and time of the purchase, the product, the cost, and possibly information about other products in the same "market basket." Is this information connected to a specific customer? Paying with cash generally ensures anonymity; that is, the buyer is not connected with the purchase, though cash payments in small towns or even in neighborhood stores where "everyone knows everyone" probably aren't anonymous. However, in other transactions purchases definitely can be (and are) linked to the customer:

- Paying by check, credit card, or debit card
- Purchasing through mail order or on the Internet

- Providing a "preferred customer" number
- Buying a product that must be registered for a service agreement or warranty

If you're buying socks, you probably don't care if this information is recorded. If you're buying *Dating for Total Dummies*, you probably do. You want your book purchase to be private.

But what is private? It's not easy to define; we'll give a formal definition later. For now, we'll examine the *Dating for Total Dummies* transaction.

Controlling the Use of Information

The *Dating for Total Dummies* problem comes down to, "Who controls the use, if any, of the transaction information?" There is a spectrum spanning four main possibilities.

1. **No Uses.** The information ought to be deleted when the store is finished with it (for example, when the payment has cleared), because there is no further need for it.
2. **Approval or Opt-In.** The store can use it for other purposes, but only if you approve the use.
3. **Objection or Opt-Out.** The store can use it for other purposes, but not if you object to a use.
4. **No Limits.** The information can be used any way the store chooses.

This spectrum, which ranges from No Uses to No Limits, includes other intermediate points, too.

There is also a fifth possibility, call it *Internal Use*, where the store can use the information to conduct business with you, but for no other use. "Conducting business with you" might mean keeping your address on file so that they can send you announcements about book readings. It would not include giving or selling your information to another person or business, but it may not require your approval either.

If the transaction took place in Australia, Canada, Europe, Hong Kong, New Zealand, or several other countries, the law and standards would place it between (1) and (2) on the spectrum, but very close to (1). If the transaction occurred in the United States, the law and standards would place it between (3) and (4) on the spectrum, but very close to (4). Perhaps of greater concern, many Americans apparently *assume* that there is a privacy law that is close to the fifth case, internal use. We will return to these different standards in a later section, but first we must understand the concept of privacy.

A Privacy Definition

As important as it is, privacy is difficult to define. It is more than Brandeis's right "to be left alone." Generally, privacy concerns four aspects of our lives: our bodies, territory, personal information, and communication. Of these, only the last two concern us here. We adopt this definition:

Privacy: *The right of people to choose freely under what circumstances and to what extent they will reveal themselves, their attitude, and their behavior to others.*

This definition emphasizes first that it is the person who decides the "circumstances" and the "extent" to which information is revealed, not anyone else. The person has the control. Second, it emphasizes that the range of features over which the person controls the information embodies every aspect of the person—themselves, their attitudes, and their behaviors. Adopting such an inclusive definition is essential for covering situations of importance.

Returning to our earlier example, buying *Dating for Total Dummies* was an act, covered by behavior, included in our privacy definition. Notice that it doesn't automatically imply the No Uses classification. We may decide that the fact that the book was paid for with a credit card rather than cash—that is, with an identifying form of payment as opposed to an anonymous one—was evidence of a willingness by the buyer to reveal the fact of the purchase. Or we could decide that the form of payment has no bearing on whether the information should be revealed; permission to reveal it must be explicitly given.

Enjoying the Benefits of Privacy

Now that we have the definition, what are the threats to privacy? There are only two basic threats: government and business. A third threat, snooping or gossiping private parties, will be handled by security and encryption, that is, by keeping the information secret. Historically, the governmental threat—a regime spying on its citizens—worries people the most, probably because when it happens the consequences are very serious. The business threat is a more recent worry, and its IT aspects even newer still. There are two types of business threats: surveillance of employees and the use of business-related information, including transaction information, for other purposes.

Voluntary Disclosure

In principle, a person can enjoy perfect privacy by simply deciding not to reveal anything to anyone; that is, to be a hermit, though that probably would mean living alone on a remote island, surviving on coconuts and clams. But most of us interact with many people and organizations—businesses, employers, and governments—to whom it is in our interest to reveal private information. That is, we freely choose to reveal information in exchange for real benefits.

- We tell our doctors many personal facts about ourselves so they can help us stay healthy.
- We allow credit card companies to check our credit record in exchange for the convenience of paying with a card.
- We permit our employer to read email we send at work, understanding that we are using the employer's computer, Internet connection, and time; that the email system is there for us to use on the job; and that we have no need or intent to send personal email.
- We reveal to the government our religion—though not in the United States—our parents' names and birthplaces, our race and ethnicity, and so on for the purposes of enjoying the rights of citizenship.

How private can we be when we reveal so much about ourselves, our attitudes, and our behavior?

Social Networking. Today, the most common way to share personal information is on social networking sites. We voluntarily reveal ourselves to be a friend, to make friends, to share with our friends. Of course, it's publicly available for everyone to see—friends, relatives, employers, and government investigators to name a few. As we will learn at the end of the chapter, the information may survive forever despite our best efforts to delete or remove it. So, it is wise to consider what to post on a social networking site. As they say, "If you wouldn't present it on TV, don't publish it on the Web."

Fair Information Practices

It is possible to reveal information about ourselves to other people and organizations and still enjoy considerable privacy, but it depends on what happens to the information after we've revealed it. If they keep the information confidential, use it only for the purposes for which they gathered it, and protect it from all threats, our privacy is not seriously compromised. We receive the benefits and preserve our privacy. It's a good deal.

But if those people or organizations are free to give or sell the information to anyone else, they are also revealing information about us. Our privacy is compromised. It's not enough to trust the people we give the information to. There must be clear guidelines adopted for handling private information, so that we have standards by which to judge whether the trust is warranted. For that, we have the Fair Information Practices principles.

OECD Fair Information Practices

In 1980 the Organization for Economic Cooperation and Development (OECD)—an organization of (currently) 34 countries concerned with international trade—developed an eight-point list of privacy principles that became known as the Fair Information Practices. They have become a widely accepted standard, forming a reasonably complete solution to the problem of keeping information private while at the same time revealing appropriate information to businesses and governments. We all have an interest in these principles becoming law. The principles also give a standard that businesses and governments can meet as a "due diligence test" for protecting citizens' rights of privacy, thereby protecting themselves from criticism or legal action. The OECD principles, listed in Table 12.1, are a practical implementation of privacy protection in the presence of computer technology.

Table 12.1 A brief explanation of the OECD's Fair Information Practices guidelines.

Limited Collection	There should be limits to the personal data collected; data should be collected by fair and lawful means, and with the knowledge and consent of the person whenever possible.
Purpose	The purposes for collecting personal data should be stated when it is collected; the uses should be limited to those purposes.
Quality	The data should be relevant to the purpose of collection; it should be accurate, complete, and up-to-date.
Use Limitation	Personal data should not be disclosed or used for purposes other than stated in the Purpose Principle, except with the consent of the individual or by the authority of law.
Security	Personal data should be protected by reasonable security measures against risks of disclosure, unauthorized access, misuse, modification, destruction, or loss.

Openness	There should be general openness of policies and practices about personal data collection, making it possible to know of its existence, kind, and purpose of use, as well as the contact information for the data controller.
Participation	An individual should be able to (a) determine if the data controller has information about him or her, and (b) discover what it is. If the request is denied, the individual should be allowed to challenge the denial.
Accountability	The data controller should be accountable for complying with these principles.

An important aspect of the OECD principles is the concept that the **data controller**—the person or office setting the policies—must interact with individuals about their information, if any, and must be accountable for those policies and actions.

12.1 Mistakes Were Made. Each year Americans are allowed a free credit check to learn their "credit score" and check for errors. Which Fair Information Practice(s), if they applied in the United States, would require this?

Is There No Privacy?

Despite being a fundamental human right, privacy is not enjoyed in much of the world at the OECD standard for both government- and business-held information (see Figure 12.1). This is somewhat surprising because privacy is well understood, its IT implications are clear, OECD standards have been implemented and work well, and so all that's left to do is to enact laws and enforce them in those places not now enjoying privacy. What's the problem?

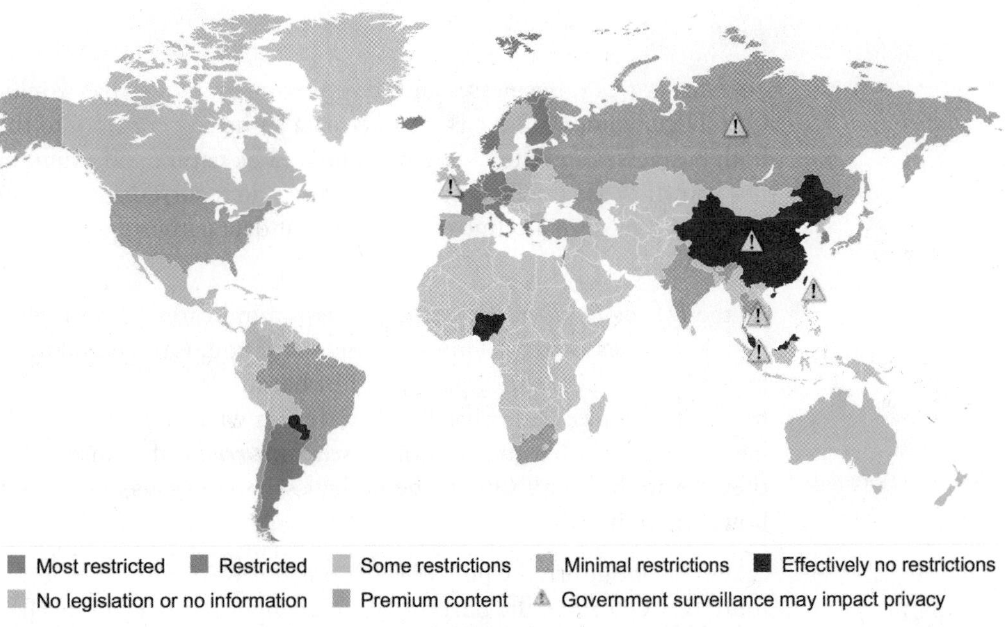

Figure 12.1 Comparison of privacy and data protections by country.

The privacy standards of the Fair Information Practices conflict with the information gathering goals of businesses and governments. That fact provides a powerful constituency to line up against countries adopting OECD privacy standards, and can be assumed to explain why the standards are not more widespread.

Who *Is* Protected?

In 1995, in a landmark advancement for privacy, the European Union (EU) issued the European Data Protection Directive, a benchmark law incorporating the OECD principles. In the next few years, the member countries adopted it. Many non-EU countries, such as Australia, Canada, Hong Kong, and New Zealand, have also adopted laws based on OECD principles.

Europe's adoption of these standards is important because one provision in the EU directive requires that data about EU citizens be protected by the standards of the law even when it leaves their country. Non-EU countries that want information on EU citizens must show that they have privacy laws consistent with the OECD principles. Switzerland, a non-EU country, applied and was approved. The United States applied and was not. What sorts of laws protect U.S. privacy?

The United States has no OECD-like law. Its few privacy laws speak to specific situations. This is a hit-or-miss approach that is known as *sectoral*, meaning that it applies to different sectors of society. For example, the Health Insurance Portability and Accountability Act (HIPAA) protects an American's personally identifiable health information. Automobile registration information is also private by a specific law, as is the privacy of video rental titles by another specific law.

Most sectors—social media, to pick one—are not covered by privacy laws, and without broad OECD-like coverage, the EU isn't likely to approve the United States. This is a huge headache for multinational companies doing business with OECD countries. In order to accommodate the laws of other countries, they must establish a **safe harbor**, meaning that the company complies with OECD standards for citizens of EU countries.

Business as Usual

So, what are U.S. businesses and the government doing that wouldn't be consistent with OECD guidelines? There is *extensive* data gathering contrary to the OECD rules by both businesses and the U.S. government. The nature and extent of the abuse is usually not known to the public because companies do it surreptitiously, and U.S. government's *Patriot Act* makes it a crime even to say that data gathering is taking place. But, examples are available.

As the *Dating for Total Dummies* discussion indicates, almost every store and company you do business with has information about you. Clearly, many do nothing with it beyond making sure they get paid. But because of their "Web presence," many businesses have a link to a privacy policy. It says what they do with the information they have. To know what they're doing, *you must read it*, because there is no standard and they are all different. Often, the policy essentially says, "We use the information however we like."

A key test about privacy polices is the opt-in/opt-out test. Because of the Use Test (the fourth OECD rule), the purpose of gathering the data can't be changed without your permission. That is, you need to say it's okay, and the technical description of that—to

opt-in to the change—allows the purpose to be changed. (The original purpose was presumably to implement a transaction like a purchase, which is different than, say, selling it to another business.) **Opt-out** is the opposite: the purpose can be changed unless you disapprove of the new use.

As the standards require, companies serious about privacy assume *by default* the opt-in standard: you want them to limit the information's use. A-Check America is an example; their privacy statement (www.acheckamerica.com/about-us/privacy.aspx) covers all of the items on the OECD list above. Other companies assume it's okay to change the use, and give you the option to opt out on their privacy page; that is, they assume you don't care about your privacy. The grocery store conglomerate Kroger has—in many ways—a respectable privacy policy (www.kroger.com/company_information/Pages/privacy_policy.aspx); they even support a safe harbor for EU transactions, although they are very specific that their high level of privacy applies *only* to the EU customers; they require U.S. citizens to write—as in a letter—to opt out. Most other sites simply say, "By using our site you agree to our privacy policy." That is, you accept what we do, or leave. Apparently, Americans are not concerned about how information is used. Perhaps they should be.

An Ocean of Differences. The privacy laws in the United States are so far from meeting the EU's privacy directive that the Federal Trade Commission (FTC) has spent years negotiating with the EU to help multinationals with moving information across the Atlantic. There are three main sticking points. The *opt-in/opt-out* choice creates a problem, because no one but the individual should decide it's okay to change the purpose; that is, the default should be "no other use," but in most situations in the United States, the default is effectively "no limits."

Compliance and enforcement is a problem because the EU's directive requires that compliance be monitored and enforced. The FTC and better business groups want "self-regulation," despite the fact it obviously isn't working, and violating privacy rights in the United States carries almost no penalties. Finally, *coverage* is an issue, because the OECD rules in the EU apply to virtually all stored and transmitted information with only rare exceptions; the sectoral approach of the United States leaves most information unprotected. So, the present solution is that multinational companies that need to deal with EU data must adhere to a set of negotiated polices on data protection: a safe harbor. If they do, the EU accepts that its citizens' privacy is being respected.

Targeted by Target

Data mining—known informally as "Big Data"—is the statistical analysis of huge information archives. It is a powerful tool to extract a business advantage from customer data. It is so effective that retailer Target can figure out if a woman is pregnant from her buying habits, *even if she didn't buy a pregnancy-test kit or tell anyone about it.*

Target—like most companies with a loyalty card—assigns each shopper a unique code used to track everything they buy. According to a February 2012 *New York Times* article, whenever a shopper uses a credit card or a coupon, fills out a survey, mails in a refund, calls the customer help line, opens an email Target sent, or visits its Web site, Target will record it and link it to their unique guest ID.

By analyzing customers' accumulated buying habits, Target developed a list of "about 25 products that, when analyzed together, allow them to assign each shopper a 'pregnancy prediction' score." Examples include purchasing more unscented lotion than in the past, or buying lots of supplements like calcium, magnesium, and zinc, or getting a purse large enough to double as a diaper bag. Notice that buying lotion or supplements is not enough; the purchases must represent a change in behavior compared to the past history. It takes a lot of data and analysis, but the score is remarkably accurate.

In one case a father in Minnesota complained to Target that his daughter had received an advertising flyer for maternity clothing and other expectant-mother products, and claimed the store was trying to promote teen pregnancy. As it turned out, his teenage daughter was already pregnant, a fact the score had predicted, but he had not yet been told.

This story makes clear how effective data mining can be when there is a complete enough shopping history. Notice that although Target can (and possibly does) buy much more extensive data about the background of its customers—ethnicity, size of family, jobs, and so on—the data used in the "pregnancy prediction" score is apparently just the data gathered as part of conducting business with customers, as in the *Dating for Total Dummies* example. (It must be emphasized that, although the ads may have caused a humiliating invasion of privacy, Target seems to be operating within the applicable U.S. privacy laws.)

Government, as Usual

In June 2013 Edward Snowden—an analyst for the U.S. National Security Agency (NSA)—revealed that the U.S. government was collecting complete metadata records from telephone carriers. (Recall from Chapter 7 that metadata is data about data, such as when a call was made, the number it was to, and so on; it doesn't include the content.) Further, using a surveillance program called PRISM, Snowden said the NSA was gathering data of Americans' online activity from Facebook, Microsoft, Google, and other large tech companies. This development took Americans by surprise, but it was also a shock overseas, because the records included calls and data from countries with OECD privacy laws, such as Germany.

According to the NSA, the justification for the collection is the U.S. Patriot Act of 2001. Before the passage of the Patriot Act, Americans enjoyed reasonable protection from government snooping by the standards of the OECD. The Patriot Act ended that.

This is a developing situation: It is so far unknown whether the allegations are true, what use if any is being made of the information, what the repercussions are within and outside of the United States, and a myriad of other unanswered questions. As the situation unfolds, find reliable up-to-date information at the Electronic Privacy Information Center (www.epic.org/privacy/) and the Electronic Freedom Foundation (www.eff.org).

Tracking

In electronic privacy, **tracking** is used in two different ways and is supported by two different technologies.

Online tracking is the practice of a Web site automatically sending details about your visit—what products or other items you clicked on, for example—to other content providers so that they can target ads or show you products (that appear from your clicks to be) in line with what you are looking for.

Cell phone tracking refers to the positioning information available from mobile devices used to map your physical location and movements.

Online Tracking

The consequences of being tracked online are not yet fully understood. The practice is clearly gathering much more complete information about your Web surfing habits than has ever been recorded before. We can assume these recipients include advertisers and marketing organizations trying to understand consumer behavior, but without any limitations on tracking, anyone could arrange to follow your "click stream."

It may be that you have nothing to hide, and you are happy to see ads and be offered products that you're interested in. On the other hand, where you go online and what you do at a site is no one's business but yours.

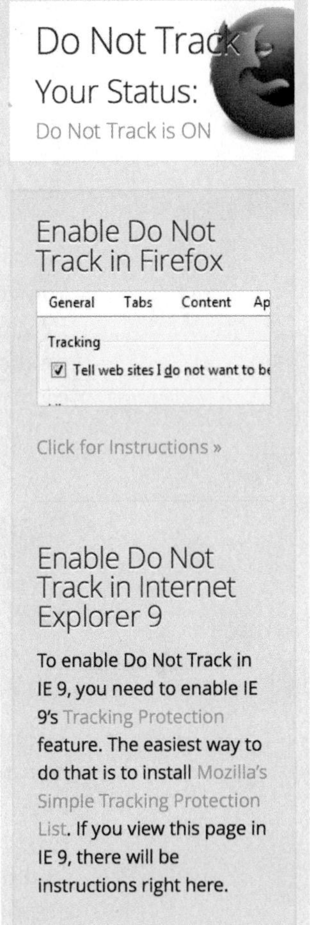
Do Not Track
Your Status:
Do Not Track is ON
Enable Do Not Track in Firefox
General Tabs Content
Tracking
Tell web sites I do not want to be
Click for Instructions »
Enable Do Not Track in Internet Explorer 9
To enable Do Not Track in IE 9, you need to enable IE 9's Tracking Protection feature. The easiest way to do that is to install Mozilla's Simple Tracking Protection List. If you view this page in IE 9, there will be instructions right here.

"Do Not Track." HTTP has a "Do Not Track" flag telling Web servers your tracking preferences. If the flag is set, your browser will tell the Web server, and it is up to the server to honor your request. We assume they do. Firefox makes it easy to set, and strongly encourages you to do so, even for other browsers. Recent versions of Internet Explorer come with the flag already set to "Do Not Track." Chrome lets you set it in a multistep process, although the accompanying information says Google continues to ignore it. If you would prefer not to be tracked, set the flag in each browser you use—it's easy, as the Fluency TIP explains.

FLUENCY
TIP

Set "Do Not Track." In Firefox—our browser of choice—navigate from Tools > Options > Privacy, and click the first item under Tracking. Click **OK** and you're done. Setting the flag on all browsers is easy, and the steps are illustrated at the Electronic Freedom Foundation's site: www.eff.org/deeplinks/2012/06/how-turn-do-not-track-your-browser.

Even More Private. The "Do Not Track" concept has been controversial because on the one hand understanding consumer behavior is commercially very valuable, but on the other hand, people don't want anyone following them around, not even electronically. Furthermore, we don't know if users' wishes are being respected. Google and other advertising companies flatly say they will ignore it.

Motivated by giving more certain protection to users, two other safeguards have been developed:

- **Industry initiatives.** The National Advertising Initiative (NAI) opt-out program is an industry-supported method allowing users to tell their member companies that they do not want to be tracked. To participate, check their opt-out page: www.networkadvertising.org/choices/. The Digital Advertising Alliance has a similar program (see www.aboutads.info/choices/).

- **Privacy initiatives.** A privacy company called Abine.com claims 600 companies are tracking consumers, and they offer a blocker called DoNotTrackMe, available for free (and easy) download at their site, www.abine.com/dntdetail.php. Interestingly, because they limit tracking traffic, they claim Web pages will also load faster.

The issues surrounding privacy and understanding consumer behavior are continuing to develop.

Private Browsing. Notice that tracking is a separate matter from "private browsing," known as InPrivate (IE), Private Browsing (Firefox and Safari), and Incognito (Chrome). Private browsing is a "client side" facility, meaning it only concerns the information stored on the computer you are using, not what the servers do. In private mode, all cookies and cached files retrieved during a session, as well as the history of the session itself, are deleted at the end, which makes it useful when you're using a public computer at, say, a library.

Cell Phones

It's possible to determine where a cell phone is (roughly)—even if "location services" (GPS) is turned off—based on its proximity to cell phone towers. What happens to the location data, which could allow a person's movements to be tracked and archived? Privacy groups wanted to know.

In order to determine what carriers know, how long they keep the information, and how frequently they are asked to turn it over to the police and the government, a huge Freedom of Information Act (FOIA) request was launched in 2010. Eventually, the results were provided (see Figure 12.2). Carriers need to save all of the information in the figure for some period of time simply to conduct their businesses in a responsible way, and to respond to legally authorized inquires. Is that the limit of how the information is used?

Ahead of the Curve. The privacy FOIA request predated Snowden's claim that the phone companies are handing over their metadata directly to the NSA. So, why the big worry? The companies keep it for quite a while—that's known—and the NSA is keeping it permanently. So? The purpose changed from conducting business—the reason it was gathered—to some other purpose not involved with conducting business. That fact makes it a privacy issue.

There is a huge difference between the phone carriers keeping their own records for purposes of conducting business, and an organization getting all of the records and integrating them. The "prudent man"—in Brandeis's quaint terminology—can change to a carrier whose retention policies he prefers. When all phone records are archived by one agency, there is no choice; everyone has been involuntarily opted in to one or more new uses. What are they?

And, once the records are integrated, the database becomes a tempting resource to apply to all sorts of new purposes, which most people would find unacceptable. For example, *The Wall Street Journal* reported that some NSA employees have checked on the calls their "love-interests" make.

At the moment, the extent of the privacy impact of phone tracking remains undetermined.

	Verizon	T-Mobile	AT&T/Cingular	Sprint	Nextel	Virgin Mobile
Subscriber Information	Post-paid: 3–5 years	5 years	Depends on length of service	Unlimited	Unlimited	Unlimited
Call detail records	1 rolling year	Pre-paid: 2 years Post-paid: 5 years	Pre-paid: varies Post-paid: 5–7 years	18–24 months	18–24 months	2 years
Cell towers used by phone	1 rolling year	Officially 4–6 months, really a year or more.	From July 2008	18–24 months	18–24 months	Not retained—obtain through Sprint
Text message detail	1 rolling year	Pre-paid: 2 years Post-paid: 5 years	Post paid: 5–7 years	18 months (depends on device)	18 months (depends on device)	60–90 days
Text message content	3–5 days	Not retained	Not retained	Not retained	Not retained	90 days (search warrant required with "text of text" request)
Pictures	Only if uploaded to Web site (customer can add or delete pictures any time)	Can be stored online and are retained until deleted or service is canceled	Not retained	Contact provider	Contact provider	Not retained
IP session information	1 rolling year	Not retained	Only retained on non-public IPs for 72 hours. If public IP, not retained.	60 days	60 days	Not retained
IP destination information	90 days	Not retained	Only retained on non-public IPs for 72 hours. If public IP, not retained.	60 days	60 days	Not retained
Bill copies (post-paid only)	3–5 years, but only last 12 months readily available	Not retained	5–7 years	7 years	7 years	n/a
Payment history (post-paid only)	3–5 years, check copies for 6 months	5 years	Depends on length of service	Unlimited	Unlimited	n/a
Store Surveillance Videos	Typically 30 days	2 weeks	Depends. Most stores carry for 1–2 months	Depends	Depends	n/a
Service Applications	Post-paid: 3–5 years	Not retained	Not retained	Depends	Depends	Not retained

Figure 12.2 Retention periods for information held by cellular phone providers.

Cookies

Cookies are a standard computer science concept originally used by Netscape engineers to connect the identity of a client across a series of independent client/server events. Here's the problem cookies solve.

VideoNote

The Cookies That Knew Too Much

Appearing To Stay Connected

Figure 12.3 illustrates the Web server's view of the client/server relationship (discussed in Chapter 3). Imagine this is your bank's server and that you are paying bills online, which makes you a client. The server is helping many clients at once, and to know who's who, the server stores a **cookie**—a record containing seven fields of information that uniquely identify a customer's session—on your computer. Cookies are exchanged between the client and the server on each transmission of information, allowing the server to know which of the many client computers is sending information.

Many sites use cookies, even when the interaction is not intended to be as secure as a bank transaction. For example, the National Air and Space Museum sent me this cookie

```
www.nasm.si.edu FALSE / FALSE 2052246450 CFTOKEN 89367880
```

while I was writing this book. The meaning of the fields is unimportant, except to note that the first is the server and the last is the unique information identifying my session. Cookies are an elegant way for servers to give clients the illusion they are the only one being served.

Though cookies serve a useful purpose—and most of us want to enable cookies so we can bank online—**third-party cookies** are a key way Web surfing behavior is tracked. The first two parties are you and the Web site you're visiting; the third party is a company—often an ad agency hired by the server company to place ads—that records where you've visited, based on the history you left as recorded in their database built with third-party cookies.

Generally, accepting cookies makes for more effective use of the Web, but it is wise to block third-party cookies (in your browser's privacy settings) if you haven't set the Do Not Track flag.

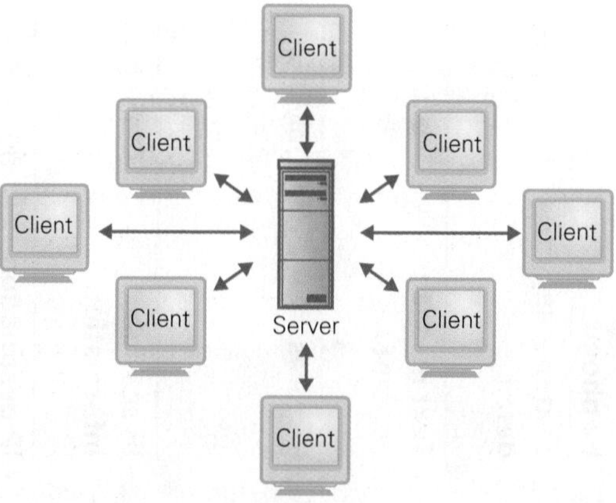

Figure 12.3 Server's view of the client/server relationship.

The Right to Be Forgotten

As we note at the end of this chapter, once information is online it is probably there forever, even if you try to delete it. And there are times when, perhaps, it should be deleted.

Imagine a Connecticut nurse with a clean police record, who gets busted with her two grown sons with a small amount of marijuana, scales, and plastic bags. It's her first offense, and her case is dismissed when she agrees to go to drug counseling. From the legal point of view, it's as if the arrest never happened according to the law. She applies for a job, her potential employer finds the newspaper headline, "Nurse and Sons Arrested," and she's not hired. That's a problem for the real person of this story: the law sees it as never having happened, but she's being punished anyway.

The question is, how should the historic fact of her arrest be handled so as not to jeopardize her future? It was true when the newspaper printed it; they made no mistake. The fact that the court dismissed her case didn't change that. But, the court's action removed her arrest in the eyes of the law. Shouldn't it be removed from the public record, that is, the newspaper, as well? After all, she has not been convicted of anything; her police record is still clean. Doesn't the nurse have a right to have the whole situation forgotten?

Like several other topics in this chapter, the matter has not been fully worked out. One possibility is that the newspaper could add an update to the online version, since that is the version search engines will find; it's analogous to online news that is updated after its original post. Another possibility is for the article to have a flag that search engines see, which would bury the article deeper in the hit list. The historic record hasn't changed, but it is harder to find it in a casual search. Certainly any solution that stops her from paying the penalty for a crime she hasn't been convicted of would be welcome.

Identity Theft

We have focused most on the Use Limitation principle of the Fair Information Practices, which focuses on changing the use of information, but the Security principle has become at least as important. The Security principle states that those who hold private information are obligated to maintain its privacy against unauthorized access and other hazards. Americans do not enjoy protection from this principle either.

There is a steady stream of news items about companies allowing secure data—passwords, Social Security numbers, credit card numbers, and other sensitive information—to be stolen. An illustrative example, because it's old enough that we know how it turned out, is the information broker ChoicePoint. In February 2005 the company announced that personal data it holds on 145,000 Americans had been, in the company's words, "viewed by unauthorized parties." ChoicePoint keeps data on people's credit rating, and initially they only admitted that information on 32,000 people had been "viewed." This smaller number apparently referred only to the Californians on the list, because California has a law requiring notification of security violations. Public pressure forced ChoicePoint to admit to and notify the larger population.

The Electronic Privacy Information Center (EPIC), a privacy watchdog, stated the situation more plainly: "ChoicePoint, which recently admitted it sold personal information on 145,000 Americans to identity thieves, also sold such information on at least 7,000 people to identity thieves in 2002."

How can this private information be used? One possibility is **identity theft**—the crime of posing as someone else for fraudulent purposes. Because information from a company like ChoicePoint includes credit card numbers, Social Security numbers, bank account numbers, and employers, a thief has no more difficulty applying for a credit card or a loan than does the person whose information it actually is. It's the victim, however, who ends up with a ruined credit rating and large debts.

If you believe someone has taken sensitive identifying information of yours, check the Federal Trade Commission's Web site for easy to understand guidance on what to do: www.consumer.ftc.gov/features/feature-0014-identity-theft.

Over 800 identity thefts were attributed to the ChoicePoint event; presumably the number would have been much larger had the victims not been notified so they could take preventative actions. Though the Federal Trade Commission resolved the matter with ChoicePoint by negotiating $10 million in civil fines and $5 million in consumer redress, it is likely that identity theft will remain a serious issue.

The Snowden revelations have shaken the IT community, and many companies and groups are taking action on behalf of user privacy. As we go to press, several Web companies, e.g., Twitter, have recently upgraded to encrypted communication (see below). Adopt such upgrades immediately.

Digital Security

Computer security is a topic that is in the news almost daily: Some organization's Web site has just been hacked, or some new trick dupes social media users into giving away their personal information. With such a relentless discussion of security, it's easy to become bored and ignore it completely. But, somewhere between "security 24-7" and "forget it," there is a level of attention that is just right. You should be informed of the risks and take the precautions. Once you've protected yourself, it's back to watching viral puppy videos. This section discusses the risks and precautions.

Macintosh Is Safe. Not. It is widely assumed that security failures only happen to Windows machines, but that's false. Macs do a better job of security—that's true—but they are attacked, too. Macs also need virus protection, and Mac users need to follow all of the precautions discussed here.

Understanding the Problem

A standalone (unconnected) computer in a secure location for which honest and trusted programmers wrote all of the software has few security issues; the computer is a reliable and trustworthy helper. It's a situation, however, that's extremely rare. For the rest of us, our computers are connected to the Internet all the time, they are not physically secured, and we probably don't know a single person who wrote the software we use continually. We have a problem. The goal of computer security is to keep our computing experiences as close to the first case as possible without changing (much) how we use computers daily.

Installing Software. Installing software is the greatest risk you can expose your computer to. Only install software from the vendor company's site or an official App Store, and *only* if you're sure you are at their site (because you Googled it, or Binged it, or Yahooed it, or typed in the URL yourself—what's difficult about typing f-l-a-s-h-.-c-o-m?).

The Risks What can happen? Most computer security risks can be classified into four groups.

- *Mischief* includes everything from simply infecting a computer and moving on, to causing a nuisance, erasing files, trashing software, and so on. Generally, the benefit to the "perp" is unclear.
- *Information theft* includes stealing personal information such as addresses, account numbers, passwords, documents, email, and other records. The benefit to the "perp" is access to the accounts, or selling the documents to others.
- *Spying* includes everything from surreptitiously recording videos of the user to logging keystrokes to find passwords, compromising secure online activities like banking, and other invasive activities. The "perp's" main benefit is actively capturing information, which is often easier than locating it statically on the machine; a credit card security code is an example.
- *Resource theft* includes taking over the computer (making it a "zombie") so it can participate in a "botnet" generating spam, denial of service attacks, and other unsavory activities. The "perp" can sell the service to spammers, intercept legitimate ads and replace them with their own, turn the botnet into an income-producing activity, and other such malicious behavior.

If any of these happens to your computer, it will be the start of a very bad day. Notice that all of these risks are virtual—they do not require physical access to the machine.

Evolution of Viruses and Worms. Since the 1950s, computer scientists have known how to write programs that make exact copies of themselves; it's not that hard or interesting. On November 2, 1988, it got interesting. Robert Tappan Morris, Jr., a graduate student in computer science at Cornell University, lost control of a self-reproducing program, and the general public learned for the first time that programs can make their own copies. Morris's program was supposed to replicate once on each computer and send itself along to others—making it a worm. But, due to an unfortunate bug, it kept reproducing, filling up the computer's memory and hard disk. It infected 6,000 computers—10 percent of the Internet at the time—before it was stopped. The damage had to be cleaned up manually and cost millions of dollars. Morris was convicted and got three years of probation, 400 hours of community service, and a $10,000 fine.

Viruses and worms have been big news since. In 1999 the Melissa virus spread by an infected MS Word .doc file; it caused $80 million damage and got the author, David L. Smith, 20 months in prison. At the time, everyone was warned, *Don't open* .doc *attachments if you don't know who they're from.* Almost exactly a year after Melissa, the I Love You virus used the same trick—and it was even worse!

Terms and Jargon

Reading about security compromises is often difficult because of all of the jargon and odd terminology. The following list will help you understand the most commonly used terms and jargon.

- **Malware** is the general term for software that harms computers in the risks listed above; everything we discuss here concerns malware.
- A **virus** is a program such as a screen saver or game that might be shared but which contains code to reproduce itself when the program runs; viruses "ride along" in other software.
- A **worm** is a program that is often embedded in an email attachment. It reproduces itself and sends a copy to everyone on your contact list, thereby propagating and moving on its own.
- **Exploit** is the verb used to describe when software takes advantage of bugs in standard commercial software to install itself and perform its unsavory activities. There is a long list of such bugs, but a famous one is "buffer overflow," in which more data is trying to be stored than the space allotted for it can hold. This bug can create an entry point for malicious software.

- A **Trojan** is an unasked-for "gift"—like the horse of ancient Greece—that is a malicious program performing unauthorized activities. Trojans arrive with downloads of seemingly benign software, like "sharing" software from sites with "free stuff" such as music or wallpaper.

These are the principle ways malware gets into your computer.

What Does Malware Do?

The computer security community focuses on the three worst activities from malware, which are used to implement the Spying and Resource Theft risks listed above:

- **Backdoors** are software that "pokes a hole" in the computer, creating an access path allowing the attackers who produced the malware to run any program they want on your computer without being stopped by your computer's defenses. Such computers are usually set up to participate in a botnet.
- **Trojans** are software capable of so many unauthorized activities they're classified by type. Trojan keyloggers record every key you type, looking for passwords and other private information; Trojan FakeAVs pretend to be antivirus software, but they extort money from users to "fix" the problem it creates; and Trojan bankers watch for banking and credit card activity to capture account numbers and passwords. These are just a few of the types of Trojans; there are about two dozen others.
- **Rootkits** are software that infects your computer and then fights back against its security systems! If you manage to stop the infection, a rootkit can restart itself, copy itself, or even move itself. Rootkits purposely conceal themselves, which often makes removal nearly impossible.

The first thing that these malicious systems do is to lower the security defenses of the computer so they don't get detected or caught.

These three forms of "bad behavior" can be combined. For example, a backdoor can download a Trojan banker to your machine; it sits quietly gathering your accounts and passwords, and when asked by the "mothership," it sends the data in.

Allô, C'est Foncy. Mobile devices are subject to all of the security issues described here. An early mobile botnet known as Foncy was implemented in France in 2012. It used a backdoor, a Trojan, and a rootkit. Once set up, it sent texts to "premium" phone numbers (like 900 numbers in North America), causing the owner of the phone to be charged the premium, which was remitted to the "bad guys." The alleged perpetrators were quickly arrested by French police, although Foncy had reportedly already infected 2,000 phones and earned €100,000.

Prevention

Attacks by people with malicious intent can happen to us if we are not cautious. What can we do to prevent these? This section gives practical, usable advice to protecting yourself.

Play It Safe

The biggest problem—in fact, almost the only problem—in computer security is us. People who practice safe computing rarely have a problem; those who don't repeatedly have to pay someone to *sanitize* their computer. Sometimes we behave impulsively—maybe hoping to get something for free—and end up infecting the computer.

What's a person to do?

No Free Lunch. In June 2013, Coner Myhrvold described his fascinating experiment revealing the extent to which grabbing "free stuff" off the Web trashes your computer (see arstechnica.com/information-technology/2013/06/download-me-saying-yes-to-the-webs-most-dangerous-search-terms/). His results are a "cautionary tale."

His experiment: Using ten extremely popular search terms, he Googled each. Then he clicked on the first ten search hits with Firefox running on a freshly installed version of Windows 7 for each, and when he got to the site (landing page), he installed whatever "free stuff" it offered. He then analyzed what was sent and installed on his computer. See his results in Table 12.2.

The first column shows the search terms—definitely popular. Next is the number of links leading to downloads, out of the total landing pages with links. Third is the count of *infected* files received, and the final column tells what they were infected with. Notice he got 835 infected files from 5 free music sites! Also, two malware files were installed: a backdoor (Hijacker) and a Trojan. But Myrhvold summarized the real problem:

"Adware such as iLivid wreaked havoc on my PC speed and performance despite the fact that I installed several free programs [. . .] that promised the exact opposite. *Post install, my computer was effectively unusable.* Just opening the Web browser took *several minutes* because of the slate of adware running startup and background processes" (emphasis added).

(Continued)

Table 12.2 Results for search terms from Myhrvold's "Free Stuff" experiment.

Keywords	Results	Infected Files	Threats Detected by Lavasoft Ad-Aware
"free wallpaper"	2/6	11	Adware, Adware Installer, unwanted programs, miscellaneous
"free screensaver"	8/10	191	Hijacker, Adware, Adware Installer, unwanted programs, cookies, miscellaneous
"free games"	2/10	45	Adware, Adware Installer, cookies
"free game cheats"	0/1	0	N/A
"free word unscrambler"	0/10	0	N/A
"free e-cards"	0/10	0	N/A
"free lyrics"	5/10	608	Adware, Adware Installer, toolbar, cookies
"free music downloads"	5/10	835	Trojan, Adware, Adware Installer, toolbar, browser, plug-in, miscellaneous

Safe Computing Checklist

Among the points security specialists continually make is that we will be safe if we just pay attention to what we're doing and understand the risks that go with it. Here are their most important bits of advice.

- **Turn off Bluetooth when not in use.** Bluetooth wireless is subject to many vulnerabilities, including nearby parties listening to calls and placing calls through your device. If you must use it, turn it *completely* off—not just "invisible" mode—when you're not in a conversation.
- **Keep your phone and other computers locked.** It may seem like you are always holding your phone, but you do put it down occasionally, making it possible for someone else to pick it up. Keeping it locked is a tiny hassle considering the personal data you have stored on it. . . or, considering the chance of loss or theft, do you want your sensitive information stored there in the first place?
- **Do not automatically click on email attachments.** Email attachments such as .jpg files are basically data and are generally safe, but many other files also contain program code. "Bad guys" embed malware in the file's program code. When you open such files, the code runs and a worm or virus can be released. Table 12.3 is a list of dangerous file types that should never be opened (as attachments) until you're sure they're safe.
- **Never enter sensitive information in a pop-up.** Pop-ups are the main way malware gathers information; sites legitimately gathering sensitive information, say, for credit card purchases, use forms discussed in (Chapter 18). Most pop-ups are a nuisance, so turning them off entirely isn't a bad idea; in Firefox, go to *Tools* > *Options* > *Content* > *Block pop-up windows*.
- **Thinking of getting something for nothing? Think again. . . .** As the accompanying Back Story about Coner Myhrvold's experiment indicates, downloading free stuff can be extremely risky. But, we all like freebees. The security advice: Don't download until you've done your homework and have convinced yourself you're getting something of value from a legitimate site.

Table 12.3 File extensions that can carry malware, primarily for Windows OS. (Recall that the file extension is the letter sequence following the last dot in the file name.)

Extension	Description
.386	Virtual Device Driver (Windows 386 enhanced mode)
.3gr	VGA Graphics Driver/configuration files
.add	Adapter Driver file
.ade	Microsoft Access project extension
.asp	Active Server Page
.bas	Microsoft Visual Basic class module
.bat	Batch file
.chm	Compiled HTML Help file
.cmd	Microsoft Windows NT command script
.com	Microsoft MS-DOS program
.cpl	Control Panel extension
.crt	Security certificate
.dbx	Database Index
.dll	Dynamic Link Library
.exe	Program file
.fon	Font file
.hlp	Help file
.hta	HTML program
.inf	Setup information
.ins	Internet Naming Service
.isp	Internet communication settings
.js	JavaScript file
.jse	JavaScript encoded-script file
.lnk	Shortcut
.mdb	Microsoft Access program
.mde	Microsoft Access MDE database
.msc	Microsoft Common Console document
.msi	Microsoft Windows Installer package
.msp	Microsoft Windows Installer patch
.mst	Microsoft Windows Installer Transform file
.ocx	Microsoft Object Linking
.pcd	Corel Adaptec CD Creator image file
.pif	Shortcut to MS-DOS program
.reg	Registration entries
.scr	Screen saver
.sct	Windows Script Component
.shb	Shell Scrap object
.shs	Shell Scrap object
.url	Internet shortcut
.vb	Visual Basic Script file
.vbe	Visual Basic Script-encoded file
.vbs	Visual Basic Script file
.vxd	Microsoft Windows Virtual Device Driver
.wsc	Windows Script Component
.wsf	Windows Script File
.wsh	Windows Script Host Settings file

- **Know where you're going.** When you're surfing, it's always possible for Web links to appear to be connecting you to one place, when they're actually sending you somewhere else. Recall from Chapter 4 that anchor tags have the form:

  <a href="http://bad.site.com/reallybad"> http://neat.siteOn.net/cool.html </a>

  and on the screen you will see http://neat.siteOn.net/cool.html. But when you click the link, the computer takes you to http://bad.site.com/reallybad, as instructed. It's a pretty simple trick. If you Copy/Paste the anchor text (blue), you go to the link you want and aren't surreptitiously redirected to the bad link. By that means, you can avoid being tricked. Or, use Firefox and hover over the link to see the URL displayed at the bottom of the window; that's where you're going if you click.
- **Be somewhat skeptical.** Social engineering (phishing) takes many forms, but there is just one goal: to get you to voluntarily give up your private information so they can grab your money. In Chapter 11 we studied email gimmicks and scams; Myrhvold's experiment illustrates being duped by the allure of free stuff. With a little bit of skepticism—is this deal really what it seems to be?—it's possible to avoid getting hooked.
- **Use extreme care when visiting notorious sites.** Music sharing, sports gambling, and pornography sites are notorious as sources of "electronic infection." Minimizing visits minimizes risk.

Following the experts' advice shouldn't be particularly difficult.

Oops, Now I've Done It!

Following the above precautions should be sufficient to keep the "bad guys" from your computer(s), but just in case something *really bad* does happen, security experts are clear:

- **Turn off** your computer *immediately*; malware cannot run on a computer that isn't running. For phones, that means *completely* off, not just "standby."
- **Using some other computer**, do a Web search to find out what to do under the circumstances. Use search terms such as the *kind* of site you visited (its name may be too specific), as in "music sharing," and the symptoms you encountered.
- **Use an external source for the OS to reboot.** Cleaning up the mess will require restarting the computer, but do that from an external source such as a CD or USB memory; for example, Kaspersky has a free rescue disk (see support.kaspersky.com/4162).

If it's too difficult to clean up the mess, the computer may need to be wiped, so you'll be glad you have a backup (see below).

Free? Really? Although we've advised against expecting to get anything for free, there are many safe and legitimate freebees on the Web. There is an abundance of free software, textbooks, games, and so forth online, but to avoid malware sites and to be sure you've found legitimate items, you need to do a little research. Examples:

- **Free software.** Great software is available for free because it is *open source*, for example, Firefox. Generally, the programs are created in the spirit of openness and sharing traditional in computing. (Research: www.gnu.org/philosophy/free-sw.html). Find a good list at www.en.wikipedia.org/wiki/Free_Software_Directory.)
- **Free textbooks.** Hundreds of quality textbooks are available online (unfortunately not this one) thanks to California State University's affordable learning initiative. (Research: als.csuprojects.org/home. Find a list of topics and titles at als.csuprojects.org/free-etextbooks.)
- **Free games.** The famed game company EA (Electronic Arts) seems to be offering free games based on Adobe Flash (www.ea.com/uk/1/play-free-games). Is this the real site or is it fake? (Research: Recall from Chapter 5 that www.internic.net/whois.html gives the owner of a Web site. We check and find: Registrant: Electronic Arts Inc., 209 Redwood Shores Parkway, Redwood City, CA 94065, which according to Wikipedia is their address.)
- **Free lunch.** There's no such thing.

Inform Yourself. You may be surprised at the number of file extensions in Table 12.2. If so, then it may be that you have "file extensions" hidden. Operating systems give us the ability to show or hide file extensions, and you *must* show them to avoid being tricked. Here's why. A file attachment with the apparently harmless name myNewCar.jpg could really be named myNewCar.jpg.exe, and the OS is hiding the (real) extension because you have that property set. Click on the file, and your computer is at risk. On Windows 7: *Control Panel > Folder Options > View > Hide extensions . . . .* For Mac OSX: *Finder Preferences > Advanced > Show All File . . . .*

Plan of Action

In the previous sections we have explained what can go wrong. The only remaining matter is what can be done about it. Here is a checklist of actions sensible users can take.

- Run "modern" software, because it is more security sensitive. This is especially true of operating systems; if you're still using Windows XT, it's time to move on.
- When updates are available for your software, install them; besides fixing bugs, they usually have security fixes.
- Install anti-virus software; it's not expensive and definitely worth the price.
- Set your Wi-Fi router to security level of at least WPA2 (see below).
- Password-protect your phones and computers with appropriate passwords as explained in Chapter 11.
- Use your knowledge of computer security risks as you surf, and be wise.

Safe computing is pretty easy.

Encryption

In your daily computing, say when you're at a coffee shop surfing the Web, you would prefer that your activities be private, or shared only with the person sitting next to you. But, your wireless is using a radio to send your keystrokes and mouse clicks to the shop's hotspot. Every computer in the room receives those signals, and if the communication wasn't encrypted—that is, recoded to hide its true meaning—everyone could follow your whole session. So, it's obvious you need encryption. But, how does it work?

12.2 Caesar Cipher. The idea of encrypting a message by shifting its letters a fixed amount in the alphabet (our example in Chapter 11 shifted by one) is called a *Caesar Cipher*, because Julius Caesar used it, according to the historian Suetonius, who claimed Caesar shifted by three letters:

A B C D E F G H I J K L M N O P Q R S T U V W X Y Z
D E F G H I J K L M N O P Q R S T U V W X Y Z A B C

Suetonius gave away Caesar's secret, but Caesar was probably smarter than that—did he encrypt his message and then to keep Suetonius clueless, encrypt it again? USM OZ CUXQY!

The Key to Encryption

The Caesar Cipher was perfect for emperors of antiquity, but with the availability of computers, it's better to use more modern techniques. A key component of encryption is the *key*. And it comes in two forms: private and public.

Quite Insecure. A Caesar Cipher that *shifts by* 13 positions forward is known as ROT13( ), and is used on Internet sites to encrypt text such as answers to contests. Notice that ClearText(x) = ROT13(ROT13(x)) in our 26-letter alphabet.

Keys

In encryption, a **key** is a "magic number" used to transform text, called **cleartext**, into gibberish, called a **ciphertext**. Both the sender and receiver—the two ends of the communication—must agree on the key, because it will be used to encode the cleartext, and decode the ciphertext back to cleartext.

Supposing the two communicators have agreed on a key, then the basic process is a five-step algorithm:

1. The sender breaks the message into groups of letters.
2. "Multiply" each group of letters (the bits are just treated as a number) times the key.
3. Send the "products"—the results from the "multiplications"—to the receiver.
4. The receiver "divides" the "products" by the key to recreate the groups.
5. Assemble the groups into the message.

This works because of a fact you know: Multiplying any number by another number, and then dividing the result by the same number gives the original number back. Right?

6 x 4 = 24

24 / 4 = 6

Such facts provide the "reversibility" of encryption that makes them 2-way ciphers. Because only the sender and receiver know the key (in this case, 4), the products are just useless numbers to anyone snooping the transmission.

What's happening in the five-step algorithm is a **secure communication** (see Figure 12.4 for a schematic of the idea). The sender takes the cleartext and encrypts it using the key, making it into gibberish or ciphertext (Steps 1 and 2). The ciphertext is transmitted (Step 3). The receiver gets the gibberish, and reverses the transformation, that is, decrypts it, to recreate cleartext (Steps 4 and 5).

Encrypting Example

To see the encryption/decryption algorithm in action, let's work a small example. Suppose the message we want to send is MEET @ 9 and the key is 13.

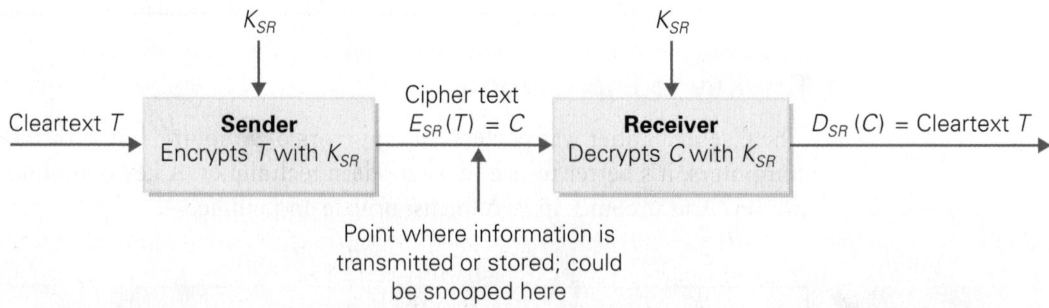

Figure 12.4 Schematic diagram of a cryptosystem. Using a key K_{SR} known only to them, the sender encrypts the cleartext information to produce a ciphertext, and the receiver decrypts the ciphertext to recover the cleartext. In the middle, where the content is exposed and can be snooped, it is unintelligible.

Here's how it works:

ASCII convert

1. Visiting www.branah.com/ascii-converter and typing in MEET @ 9, we learn that these eight letters (blanks are letters, too!) in ASCII have the decimal values: 77 69 69 84 32 64 32 57
2. Grouping the decimal values into *pairs*, we "multiply" each pair by the key, 13:
   7769 × 13 = 100997
   6984 × 13 = 090792
   3264 × 13 = 042432
   3257 × 13 = 042341
   (The "leading zeros" make all numbers six digits.)
3. Send the "products"—100997 090792 042432 042341—to the receiver.
4. The receiver "divides" by the key, 13:
   100997/13 = 7769
   090792/13 = 6984
   042432/13 = 3264
   042341/13 = 3257
   and types in the digits 77 69 69 84 32 64 32 57 to the www.branah.com/ascii-converter program to get the ASCII: M E E T @ 9.
5. Reassembling the message, MEET @ 9.

So, in the privacy of her own computer, the sender converted her message MEET @ 9 to 100997 090792 042432 042341. The public could see those numbers when she sent them, but they looked like gibberish. Then, in the privacy of his own computer, the receiver converted them to the message, MEET @ 9. The message was in cleartext only when it was private.

12.3 Another Message. Suppose you sent the message just encrypted/decrypted to someone, and received back: 101257 042640 099645 087997. What is the message you received?

Private Key Encryption

The technique just explained is called **private key encryption**, or **symmetric key cryptography**. The example, to be simple enough for us to study, is very, very, very small. Real encryption systems use much longer blocks (hundreds of letters), and much larger keys. Also, they use other transformational techniques besides multiplication and division. But the ideas are exactly the same, and so it is safe to think of encryption as working by the algorithm just discussed.

In the algorithm above, I put quotations around "multiply," "products," and "divides," because they are not the only operations that can be used for encryption. All that is needed is for an operation to have an inverse: divide is the *inverse* of multiply. So, there are many encryption algorithms.

Private key encryption works very well, and it is used a lot. But, there is one small problem: The sender and receiver have to agree on the key, which means they need to communicate somehow. Normally, they can just meet face-to-face ahead of time, and agree.

But, for online communication agreeing on a key could be a showstopper, because the sender and receiver don't usually meet face-to-face. They can't exchange an encrypted communication using a private key, because they haven't chosen one yet. That's why they're trying to communicate. Whoops!

But, thanks to a great mathematician and several enterprising computer scientists, the problem has been solved!

Public Key Encryption

The solution: Publish the key. Really! See Figure 12.5 for a schematic diagram. If the receiver publishes the key on his Web site, the sender can grab it, and encrypt the message. Then she sends the encrypted message to the receiver. He uses his key to decrypt it, and read her message. Slick, right?

Well . . . couldn't the "bad guys" go to the Web site, too, get the key, grab the transmission, and decrypt it? They have the same access to the key that the sender and receiver do. True . . . but it's not just any key.

It's a public key, and it has some very astonishing properties. The public key is two special prime numbers multiplied together. (If you've forgotten, a prime number is *evenly* divisible only by itself and 1. Like 13.)

In a **public key cryptosystem** (PKC), the receiver publishes the special key, *K*. Then, the following occurs:

1. The sender breaks up the message into blocks as before.
2. The sender cubes each block—yup, raises it to the third power—and divides by *K*, the special public key, keeping only the remainders—the stuff that's left after division.
3. The remainders are transmitted.
4. The receiver raises each remainder to a high power determined by the prime numbers and known only to him.
5. The receiver divides each by *K*, too, and saves only the remainders, which are—surprisingly—the original blocks!
6. The receiver assembles the message.

It's a little more complicated than our multiplication encryption algorithm above, and it's a tough process to do with a calculator. But computers are pretty good with the math!

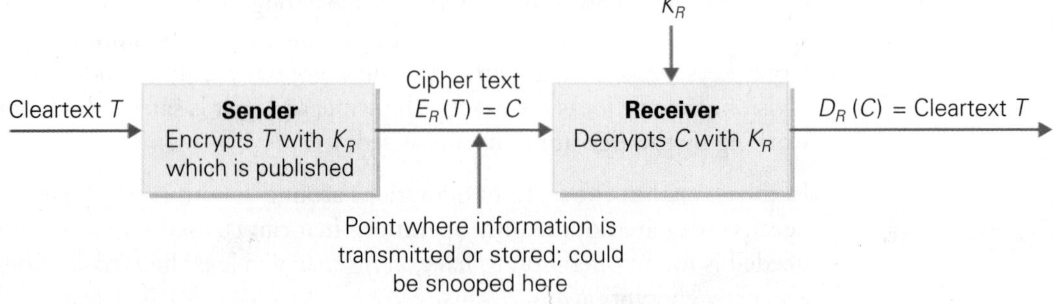

Figure 12.5 Public key cryptosystem. The sender uses the receiver's public key K_R to encrypt the cleartext, and only the receiver is able to decrypt it to recover the cleartext.

Even so, it doesn't seem like this would work, because in Steps 2 and 5, after dividing by the magic key *K*, the main part of the number is tossed, and only the remainder is kept. It's kind of like baking bread, slicing it up, tossing the slices, and keeping the crumbs. How could this possibly work?

The Genius of PKC

Thanks to Leonard Euler (OY·ler), we know that the prime numbers and the cubing in Step 2 have wonderful properties that make the six-step public key cryptosystem work. We won't go into the math, but two computer scientists—Whitfield Diffie and Martin Hellman—recognized that these properties would make a public key encryption technology work. Then, three more computer scientists—Ron Rivest, Adi Shamir, and Len Adleman—developed one of the popular PKC algorithms, **RSA**, which is outlined above.

The Take-Home Message

Public key cryptosystems are very smart, and if you are good at math and interested, check Appendix B, where the technique is explained more completely. It's mind-boggling! For the rest of us, this is what we need to know:

Public key cryptosystems let people exchange a key over an unprotected channel, and that key can be the private key that is used in the simpler private key protocols.

That is, PKC solves the key exchange problem—getting the private key to the other person—and once that's done, the simpler private key algorithm works fine.

Leonard Euler. An eighteenth-century mathematician, Euler is so awesome that his face has appeared on Swiss money and several stamps. For the record (it's not on the test), here is Euler's theorem that makes our public key example work:

Theorem: Let p and q be distinct primes, $K = pq$, $0 < T < K$, and $r > 0$.

If $T^{r(p-1)(q-1)+1}$ is divided by K, the remainder is T.

T is the block of cleartext, K is the public key, and $r = 2$ in our example; the encrypted message sent over the "snoopable" channel is the remainders of T^3/K.

Factoring Is Hard

How do we know that PKC systems work? Looking at Euler's formula—but you don't have to—mathematicians will tell you that K, the magic public key, is just two prime numbers, p and q, multiplied together. They'll say, correctly, that it is possible to figure out those two numbers—a process called *factoring*—from the published key. Maybe in theory, but in practice, probably not.

Although computer scientists are not certain, most believe that factoring is a very tough computation; that is, if the numbers p and q are large—maybe 60 digits apiece—it is impractical to factor them no matter how big and bad your computer is. So, the PKCs just use big prime numbers, and no one has figured out how to factor them fast. That fact is what keeps the PKC process safe.

Crack the Code and Win! In 1977, shortly after inventing their scheme, Rivest, Shamir, and Adleman issued a challenge to the world: break the small ciphertext they encrypted with their public key RSA129—the 129 refers to the number of digits of their key—and win $100. This was a bold challenge because, although there was no known way to factor a 129-digit key quickly, maybe someone could invent a better factoring algorithm. The best-known method at the time wasn't much better than the grammar school technique of dividing consecutive prime numbers into the number, looking for one that divides evenly. If computer scientists were clever enough to come up with public key encryption in the first place, they could probably come up with better ways to factor. In fact, in 1981 Carl Pomerance did invent a new factoring method that gave some hope, though all the while other computer scientists were trying to prove that the factoring process could never be improved much. Pomerance's algorithm was better, but it didn't crack the code. Eventually, Arjen Lenstra and Mark Manasse organized an effort, which in 1994, using better algorithms, the Internet, and the improved speed of computers, cracked the RSA129 cipher. Their strategy took eight months and used nearly one thousand computers from around the world. But this wasn't the end of public key cryptosystems—it only revealed the factors of a single public key. Most of us don't have one thousand computers or eight months to spend trying to snoop a single credit card transaction. Even if the secret is extremely important—a missile code, for example, or the outcome of the final episode of some TV drama—and the code cracker has the resources of the U.S. government, the RSA scheme is still secure because all it takes to make things harder for code crackers is to increase the size of the key.

The difficulty of factoring increases dramatically as the key length grows. It has been estimated that increasing the key to 250 digits—that is, doubling its length—would increase the cracking time 100,000,000 times. Keys can be increased to 300 or 400 digits or more if one hundred million times harder is not enough. Larger keys do not seriously complicate the problem for the encryption and decryption processes compared to their impact on increasing the factoring time. When RSA129 was cracked—an effort dubbed the largest computation of all time—everyone was waiting breathlessly to know what the secret message was. It turned out to be THE MAGIC WORDS ARE SQUEAMISH OSSIFRAGE.

Back to the Coffee Shop

Our discussion started with you in a coffee shop planning to use the wireless connection. We said that wireless uses radio signals, so every computer in the coffee shop can listen to the signals. So, the first question:

Q1: Does the coffee shop wireless use encryption?

Many "free Wi-Fi" hot spots do not. You can tell when your modem tells you that a wireless connection is available, it will name the wireless security protocol. If it doesn't say anything—if it doesn't ask for a password when you first use it—then there isn't any, and all of your signals are going to everyone as cleartext. If you're reading the news with your browser *and there are no other apps running on your machine*, who cares? If you're planning on using any other application, it may be a problem. This brings us to the second question:

Q2: When do I need to encrypt my wireless signals?

Most experts will tell you, "Always!", and it *is* good advice, but the coffee shop may not be using encryption, and you *do* want to read your email, which you must log into with your password. Will someone snoop that? Luckily, even if your wireless connection isn't encrypted, your application may be. On the Web, for example, when the URL begins with https, the "s" means secure (recall the scenario in Chapter 6). This technology is the **secure socket layer (SSL)**, which is often indicated by a lock icon somewhere in the browser window. So, for example, your free email account is likely to use this kind of secure communication. This is probably good enough to read email at the coffee shop even without any better encryption. And finally, our third question:

Q3: If the coffee shop doesn't need secure wireless, do I need it for my wireless router?

Absolutely! First, you will use your own system for more secure transactions like banking. Second, many of us live near others who could piggyback onto your unsecured system. They are happy for you to pay their Internet video streaming charges. Third, even if your neighbors are not going to use your Internet, they can install software that allows them to watch everything you do, like typing passwords. (Remember, many applications do not use SSL when asking for your password.) So, absolutely, you need to install a security barrier with your router.

Secure wireless technology has been under attack in recent years, with many systems—WEP and WEP2—being completely compromised. Today, WPA2—Wi-Fi Protected Access 2—is solid and recommended. When installing your router, setting a WPA2 password is probably enough to give your system adequate protection.

Recent versions of Firefox come with **HTTPS Everywhere** installed, and set to on; check the navigation bar. (It's also available for Chrome.) This is a good feature because it automatically sets up a secure connection whenever possible and even if you forget to request it. See https://www.eff.org/https-everywhere.

Redundancy Is Very, Very, Very Good

As the saying goes, "Life is uncertain; eat dessert first." Uncertainty poses physical security challenges for networking and computer use generally.

Uncertainty results from lightning strikes that cut power, earthquakes and other natural disasters, terrorist attacks, accidents, and simple entropy—the tendency of things to "run down." To the list of physical risks, add the potential logical problems of program bugs, operator errors—*How could I have done that?!*—computer viruses, worms, backdoor assaults, and many more. Each of us would like to avoid such disasters. Life is uncertain, so it makes sense to take precautions.

Alternate Superstition. People can be superstitious, believing, for example, that thinking about a disaster can make it happen. Naturally, repressing such thoughts is sensible. But believing a different superstition—that taking precautions against disasters, like saving often, prevents them—may make more sense in computing. They're both superstitions, of course, but the second one reduces the harm when it turns out to be wrong, which it will.

Protecting Your Data

The situation in personal computing has become much better in recent years thanks to two developments: the cloud, and large external disk drives.

The Cloud. A massive online data storage site is referred to as a **cloud**. Large companies, such as Amazon, Google, and Microsoft, that have big data centers (see Figure 5.3) provide a reliable data storage service. This is what people mean when speaking of storing their information "in the cloud." And it is a good backup choice for your smartphones and computers, because they are already Internet connected. Many phones and computers come with the ability to back up to a cloud, usually the vendor's cloud. Doing so effectively solves the data reliability problem.

The "cloud" solution works like free email accounts such as Yahoo! and Gmail: The companies' computers store the information for you and they take responsibility for keeping it available to you, though the service may not be free.

Clouds use very clever redundant encodings of data and are set up to handle the continual failure of processors and disks. See Figure 5.3. The data centers are staffed with teams of technicians who pretty much guarantee that what you store will be there the next time you want it. Data centers are often located in remote sites where physical harm is less likely, and they are very secure. They are about as reliable as anything gets.

Privacy advocates have raised questions about the cloud, because some cloud services companies also happen to be famous data miners. However, the cloud services companies have given their assurances. If you are concerned, encrypt your sensitive data before storing it.

Terabyte Disks. The cost of digital storage has plummeted so far in recent years that it is possible for people to own several trillion bytes of storage. Even better, these can have a Wi-Fi connection to a network, so you don't even have to plug in anything to do a backup once they're connected to the router. It's like a private cloud, but—unfortunately—without the tech support!

If you regularly use your phones and computers in one location—home or work—then they can be set up to back up to a wireless external hard drive located there. It's just as convenient as the commercial cloud.

The other value of terabyte disks for people with zillions of photos or lots of movies is that the disks provide a handy place to keep all those files. And, thanks to wireless, they're easy to retrieve.

Backups and Recovery

It seems like making a backup should take a long time, considering the gigabytes of travel photos and the number of honors thesis drafts stored on your computer. The reason backing up is usually fast is that only the files and folders that changed since the last backup need to be backed up. The unchanged files are still there from before.

A Two-Step Recovery Program. The process is this: The first time, a **full backup** copy of everything must be saved. After that a **partial backup** of the changed files and folders is enough.

Later, if a rootkit forces your computer to be wiped clean, the backup can restore your disk to the point of the most recent backup. Beginning at the root of the directory (folder) hierarchy (see Chapter 3), the files are copied, and each one is verified to be the most recent. That protocol, when it's complete, will reproduce the external memory state to the point of the last backup.

12.4 Backup Plan. Imagine that a computer with the following file structure is backed up for the first time:

FOLDER: Desktop

newCarPhoto.jpg

FOLDER: Stuff

oldCarPhoto.jpg

ChrisLetter.doc

Then, the ChrisLetter document is edited, the oldCarPhoto image is deleted, and a new file, insurance.pdf, is added in that folder. Say what information the archiving software would copy in a partial backup.

On the Road. Of course, in exceptional cases—when you are traveling, perhaps—you can back up manually by simply copying your folders and files to flash (USB) memory or a DVD. Remember, you don't have to back up:

- Information that can be recreated from some permanent source, such as software
- Information that was saved but that has not changed—last year's email archive, for example
- Information that you don't care about, such as your Web cache or old versions of term papers

Of course, if you upload your digital photos from your camera to your computer—they're easier to view—and also leave them in the camera's memory, too, you already have a backup copy of those.

Recovering Deleted Information. An important aspect of maintaining consistent backups is that "delete doesn't actually delete very much." Here is why. Backups are usually kept a very long time, often outliving the life of the computer that created the information in the first place. This is handy. If you accidentally delete important files, file restoration is a very desirable and helpful service. So, deleting a file that is in the archive means that it is not truly gone. For example, in Try It 12.4, notice that oldCarPhoto.jpg is still in the full backup, and so could be recovered even though it was deleted.

Of course, backups can save evidence of crimes or other inappropriate behavior, too. Computer users have hastily tried to delete incriminating files in hopes of covering up undesirable activity only to learn later that the files like oldCarPhoto.jpg can be recovered from the backups. Unlike paper files, digital copies of files are easy to create and cheap to store, so it can be difficult to eradicate all copies of digital information.

Email is especially dangerous if you're trying to hide inappropriate behavior, but it's especially helpful if you're trying to discover it: Two copies of email are produced immediately when the **Send** button is clicked—one in the sender's sent mail folder, and one somewhere else, which is probably impossible for the sender to delete.

Furthermore, if that email is around for more than a few hours, it will probably be backed up. Of course, your own backups have this same permanence property. Perhaps the Information Age will promote good behavior.

Gone, but Not Forgotten. Emptying trash on a personal computer is another example when delete does not truly delete. Computers keep a *free list* of available disk storage blocks, and they take blocks from it whenever they write data. Emptying trash usually adds the trashed files' blocks to the free list, allowing them to be reused but without changing their contents. Until the blocks are overwritten, experts can recover the information. To completely remove files, choose "Secure" *Empty Trash* on Macintosh, or grab a "secure delete" application such as Eraser for the PC.

After discussing a privacy scenario, we defined privacy as the right of individuals to choose freely under what circumstances and to what extent they will reveal themselves, their attitudes, and their behaviors. We learned the following:

- Revealing personal information can be beneficial, so the people and organizations that receive the information must keep it private. The guidelines for keeping data private have been created by several organizations, including the Organization for Economic Cooperation and Development (OECD).
- Guidelines often conflict with the interests of business and government, so some countries like the United States have not adopted them. Because the United States takes a sectoral approach to privacy, adopting laws only for specific business sectors or practices, much of the information collected on its citizens is not protected by OECD standards.
- The Do Not Track flag should be set, and DoNotTrackMe should be installed to avoid third parties building a profile of your Web surfing behavior.
- The best way to manage privacy in the Information Age is to have OECD-grade privacy laws.
- There are two key features of encryption: private key and public key techniques.
- Public key cryptography (PKC) is an amazing idea built on familiar concepts.
- Computer scientists have not yet proved the invincibility of the RSA scheme, but it can be "made more secure" simply by increasing the size of the key. This has little effect on the encryption and decryption processes, but it greatly increases the problem of finding the prime factors that make up the key.
- Viruses and worms cause damage. We can reduce the chance of infection by installing and running anti-virus software. We must be aware of hoaxes and phishing scams.
- We can implement a plan of action to ensure that our personal computers remain private and secure.
- Backing up computer files is an essential safeguard. It ensures that your files will survive for a long time, even if you don't want them to.

Privacy and security topics have not been fully resolved in the public forum, and both pose daunting challenges. Laws and policies are still under construction. Privacy seems to be waiting for the broad adoption of the OECD safeguards for both business and government information gathering. Security seems to be waiting for a way for parties to communicate securely by mechanisms fully within their control, yet that can be compromised in extraordinary circumstances of public importance.

TRY IT SOLUTIONS

12.1 Quality and Participation.

12.2 The message USM OZ CUXQY! decrypted once is RPJ LW ZRUNV! Decrypting that yields: OMG IT WORKS!

12.3 101257 / 13 = 77 89

042640 / 13 = 32 80

099645 / 13 = 76 65

087997 / 13 = 67 69

and typing that in to www.branah.com/ascii-converter gives MEET @ 9.

12.4 ChrisLetter.doc, insurance.pdf, Stuff_file_list, and Desktop_file_list would be backed up; the latter two directory lists would be backed up because items they contain are backed up.

REVIEW QUESTIONS

Multiple Choice

1. Private browsing does not store data on
   a. the computer itself
   b. the server
   c. both the computer itself and the server
   d. neither the computer itself and the server
2. True or false: Macs do not need virus protection software because it is built into the OS.
   a. true
   b. false
   c. depends on the type of Mac
   d. no computers need virus protection software
3. Which of the following is an example of identity theft?
   a. taking a test for someone else
   b. using your older sibling's ID
   c. posing as someone you're not to vote
   d. all of the above
4. What is the greatest risk you can expose your computer to?
   a. connecting to the Internet
   b. installing software
   c. not locking your phone when it is not in use
   d. using online banking

5. You discover that credit information about you is inaccurate. Which principle does this violate?
   a. Limited Collection
   b. Quality
   c. Security
   d. Openness
6. Which Fair Information Practice provides for ways to correct your faculty credit record?
   a. Quality
   b. Purpose
   c. Participation
   d. Accountability
7. Data on EU citizens is
   a. not as secure as data on U.S. citizens
   b. protected even outside of the EU
   c. not protected by OECD principles
   d. protected in Europe but not outside of it
8. What is the biggest problem in computer security?
   a. ourselves
   b. the government
   c. businesses
   d. our friends
9. Information from people in EU countries can be shared outside of the EU, providing the business or government follows the principles of
   a. Don't ask, don't tell
   b. Safe Harbor
   c. Fair Information Practices
   d. Opt-in/opt-out
10. When should you enter sensitive information in a pop-up?
    a. when it is a site you use regularly
    b. when using an online banking site
    c. only when it is absolutely necessary
    d. never
11. Digital encryption is
    a. only used for passwords
    b. easily broken by computer experts
    c. the use of math to make communication unreadable to snoops
    d. all of the above
12. Social networking
    a. is not private
    b. can be viewed by potential employers
    c. allows members to present themselves to others and to interact with them
    d. all of the above

Short Answer

1. Privacy is the right of people to choose freely under what circumstances and to what extent they will reveal themselves, their attitude, and their behavior to others.
2. In regard to information technology, privacy is primarily concerned with _______ and _______.

3. _______ is an anonymous form of payment.
4. The _______ serve as a guideline for protecting personal privacy in regard to international trade.
5. The _______ provides a benchmark by which businesses can measure how well they are protecting the privacy of individuals.
6. A(n) _______ is responsible for maintaining personal information and is held accountable for it.
7. The Fair Information Practices standards conflict with the information gathering goals of _______ and _______.
8. The _______ act ended Americans reasonable protection from government snooping.
9. A(n) _______ is a combination of encryption and decryption.
10. _______ is information before it is encrypted.
11. The _______ cryptosystem is the best-known public key cryptosystem.
12. Setting _______ in your browser may stop certain Web sites from tracking you.
13. _______ is software that monitors and records details of computer usage.
14. _______ contain code that reproduces itself when the program runs.
15. The difficulty of factoring _______ as the key grows in size.

Exercises

1. Explain in detail the following statement from the chapter: "the EU directive requires that data about EU citizens be protected by the standards of the law even when it leaves their country." Also, list the top few countries with the most privacy laws.
2. There are several national "sweepstakes" that deliver big prizes to winners. To be a part of these contests, you must register and provide your address (so they can deliver your check on national TV!). What potential privacy concerns are involved with such contests?
3. Credit card companies track your transactions. How can they abuse this?
4. What flaws exist in a sectoral approach to privacy?
5. Based on existing legislation, who appears to have more influence: businesses or individuals?
6. Explain how a simple serial number stored in a cookie can be used to store personal information.
7. Is compliance without enforcement effective?
8. Discuss the different approaches to privacy taken by the European Union and the United States.

CHAPTER 13

The Basics of Spreadsheets

Fill-in-the-Blank Computing

learning objectives

- Explain how data is organized in spreadsheets
- Describe how to refer to spreadsheet rows, columns, and cell ranges
- Explain relative and absolute references
- Apply concepts of relative and absolute references when filling a formula
- Explain the concept of tab-delimited input and output

CHAPTER 13

The purpose of computing is insight, not numbers. (1961)
The purpose of computing numbers is not yet in sight. (1997)

—RW HAMMING (1915–1997)

THIS CHAPTER introduces spreadsheets. There is a simple reason why we care about spreadsheets: They are the "app" we use when no one else cares about a computation except us. That is, personally interesting computations are most easily implemented using spreadsheets. If other people cared about the computations, too, someone would write an application. But, for our one-of-a-kind computations, we need to figure it out for ourselves. Spreadsheets are our tool.

This chapter introduces the basic ideas of spreadsheets. Because they make computer users so effective, especially in business, spreadsheets have become very sophisticated. This chapter introduces you to the basic ideas, making them personally useful. If you need more power, you'll have a great foundation for learning more, such as the advanced spreadsheet techniques introduced in Chapter 14; if not, you'll be acquainted with a very versatile tool.

We begin by introducing the basics of using spreadsheets, including constructing lists, sorting them, naming cells, and controlling the format of the entries. Next, we add numeric information to our spreadsheet and learn how to manipulate it, which teaches you about formulas, relative and absolute references, and functions. Computing new numbers from numbers already in the table is what spreadsheets do best and, luckily, it is an extremely easy facility to learn and use. After learning these basic concepts, we practice them on "everyday" problems; that is, tasks of personal interest: We build a time zone "cheat sheet" to avoid calling our friends in the middle of the night; we build a table to get the best deal when we buy pizza; and we develop data for helping to decide how much money to borrow for a "big ticket" purchase like a car or sound system. None of these tasks is so difficult as to require a computer, but since we're using a computer anyway, we can solve them quickly to our personal satisfaction. Finally, we use the Best Picture Oscar winners list to practice manipulating data in a spreadsheet.

Arranging Information

Commonly, textual information is organized into lists, as we know from making shopping lists, invitation lists, "to do" lists, class lists, and so on. As a running example, we'll use a list of migratory birds:

Short-tailed shearwater
Swainson's hawk
Wheatear
Arctic tern
Willow warbler
Long-tailed skua

Looking at the list, you see that it contains six bird names. Although you may not be too familiar with birds, you probably figured out the category because you know that hawks and warblers are birds and the items appear on separate lines. The names themselves are quite diverse as text: a single word name, double word names, hyphenated names, and even a possessive. Because the computer doesn't have your knowledge, it needs to be told the extent of each entry; that is, how much text there is in each entry. The separate line cue helps, but if the entries were lengthy, they would spill to another line and then that cue wouldn't work.

Kinda the Same. Spreadsheet software is available from many sources. The content of this chapter applies generally to Microsoft Excel, OpenOffice, and Google Docs. Every system is different in how it presents the operations to users—menus, ribbons, icons, and so forth—and all with different defaults. To reach the greatest number of students, this chapter's content is presented in "Excel Classic form," which uses menus and is compatible with a variety of installed systems. Users of Excel 2010/2013 can quickly and easily find the equivalent operations under the obvious ribbons—basics under *Home*, formulas under *Formulas*, and so forth; when operations are in less obvious places, the ribbon is given in brackets [*View*] in green.

An Array of Cells

To help us create a list, spreadsheets give us an array of **cells** that we fill in to set up our list.

	A	B	C	D
1				
2		Short-tailed shearwater		
3		Swainson's hawk		
4		Wheatear		
5		Arctic tern		
6		Willow warbler		
7		Long-tailed skua		
8				

The lines are part of the UI; they help us and the computer agree on what an item is and how the positions of items are related to each other.

Notice that four of the six items in the list do not fit within the lines provided. Even though it takes more space to display the entry than the computer provides, entries *do not* straddle cells. Each occupies only the cell into which it is typed, as is shown when we enter test data in the cells to their right.

	A	B	C	D
1				
2		Short-tailed she	Test data	
3		Swainson's haw	to see what	
4		Wheatear	happens	
5		Arctic tern	when long	
6		Willow warbler	entries can't	
7		Long-tailed sku	spill	
8				

The test data, which blocks the long entries from spilling to the empty cells on the right, indicates that entries that are too long are clipped. (Items only spill when the cells to their right are unused.) We can either let the entries be clipped, or make the cells wider, as explained later in Table 13.1. We choose the latter.

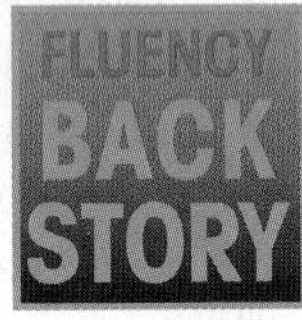

Automatic Accounting. Spreadsheets were invented by Dan Bricklin and Bob Frankston in 1978. Their system was called VisiCalc and it ran on the Apple II. The screenshot at the right is the VisiCalc display at its launch in 1979.

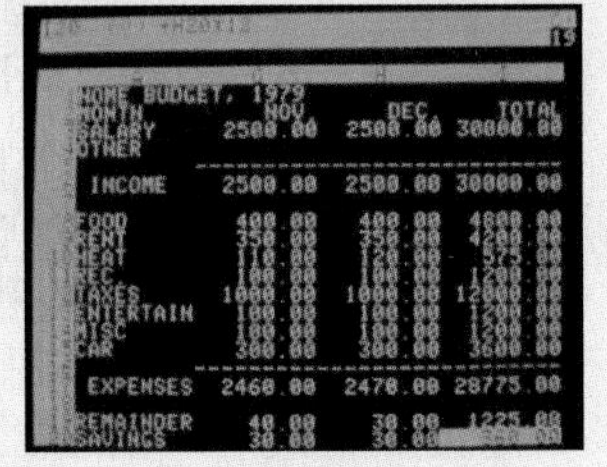

Sorting the Data

A common operation on any list, especially when it gets long, is to alphabetize or sort it. Spreadsheet software makes sorting easy. We must specify which items to sort, so naturally, we must select the list. We select the list by dragging the cursor across the cells; the resulting selection is indicated with highlighting.

	A	B	C	D
1				
2		Short-tailed shearwater		
3		Swainson's hawk		
4		Wheatear		
5		Arctic tern		
6		Willow warbler		
7		Long-tailed skua		
8				

Table 13.1 Common spreadsheet operations in recent versions of spreadsheet software; for Excel 2010 and 2013 check the tab shown in brackets.

Operation	Using Excel. . .	Using OpenOffice. . .
Change column width manually	Place cursor at right side of column name, then drag	Place cursor at right side of column name, then drag
Change column width automatically	*Format > Column > Autofit Selection* [*Home*]	*Format > Column > Optimal Width . . .*
Cut, copy, paste contents	Standard: ^X, ^C, ^V	Standard: ^X, ^C, ^V
Fancy formatting	*Format > Cells . . .* [*Home*]	Format > Cells . . .
Clear cells	*Edit > Clear > All* [*Home*]	*Edit > Delete Contents . . .*
Delete columns, rows	*Edit > Delete . . .* [*Home*]	*Edit > Delete Cells . . .*
Hide a column	*Format > Column > Hide* [*View*]	*Format > Column > Hide*

Note: All spreadsheet applications provide these common operations; explore your system.

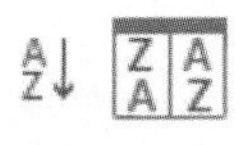

All of the items inside the blue box are selected, including the white item, which is a different color only because it was the first cell selected, that is, it's the place where the dragging began. The *Sort . . .* operation is found among the menu items, and is often shown as an icon somewhere in the UI. It allows us to choose ascending or descending order. Sorting our list of birds in ascending order produces the following result.

	A	B	C	D
1				
2		Arctic tern		
3		Long-tailed skua		
4		Short-tailed shearwater		
5		Swainson's hawk		
6		Wheatear		
7		Willow warbler		
8				

Notice that the sorting software orders the list alphabetically on the first letter of the entry, not on the type of bird, for example, "hawk." This is consistent with the spreadsheet view that the cell entries are "atomic" or "monolithic" from the computer's point of view, meaning that the computer does not consider any of their constituent parts. If the list contained both Swainson's hawk and Swainson's warbler, they would appear together in sorted order. But if we wanted those birds to be grouped with the hawks and the warblers respectively, then it would be necessary to sort on the second part of the name. That would require the type of the bird (e.g., "hawk" or "warbler") to be in a separate cell—in its own column.

Adding More Data to the List

Our list is not so complete. We will leave the common names in a single column, but we'll add the scientific names using two columns, one for genus and one for species.

	A	B	C	D	E
1					
2		Arctic tern	Sterna	paradiasaea	
3		Long-tailed skua	Stercorarius	longicaudus	
4		Short-tailed shearwater	Puffinus	tenuirostris	
5		Swainson's hawk	Buteo	swainsoni	
6		Wheatear	Oenanthe	oenanthe	
7		Willow warbler	Phylioscopus	trochilus	
8					

As you know, scientific names are usually written in italics. Spreadsheets give us the ability to format cell entries with the kinds of formatting facilities found in word processors, such as italics, bold, font styles, font sizes, justification, colored text and backgrounds, and so on. Naturally, the formatting facilities are found under the *Format* menu [*Home*]. We italicize the scientific names and right justify the genus name so it looks like it is paired with the species name.

Naming Rows and Columns. Now suppose we want to alphabetize on the second column, the genus. We begin by selecting the whole list because that is the information we want to reorder. With three columns selected, how do we specify that the second column is the one to sort on rather than the first column?

	A	B	C	D	E
1					
2		Arctic tern	*Sterna*	*paradiasaea*	
3		Long-tailed skua	*Stercorarius*	*longicaudus*	
4		Short-tailed shearwater	*Puffinus*	*tenuirostris*	
5		Swainson's hawk	*Buteo*	*swainsoni*	
6		Wheatear	*Oenanthe*	*oenanthe*	
7		Willow warbler	*Phylioscopus*	*trochilus*	
8					

Spreadsheet programs automatically provide a naming scheme for referring to specific cells. The columns are labeled with letters and the rows are labeled with numbers. This allows us to refer to a whole column, as in column C, or to a whole row, as in row 4, or to a single cell by specifying both the column letter and the row number, as in cell B2. Thus, when we request to sort the entries, the sorting software displays a *Sort* UI.

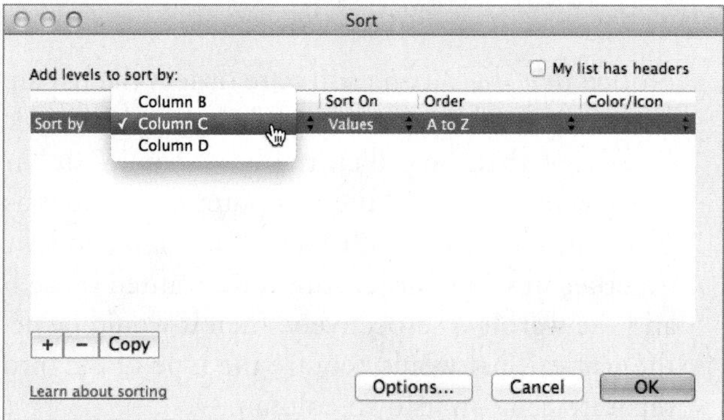

We choose to sort the selected rows based on entries in column C (which contains our *genus* entries) by clicking the directional arrows. This produces the following result:

	A	B	C	D	E
1					
2		Swainson's hawk	*Buteo*	*swainsoni*	
3		Wheatear	*Oenanthe*	*oenanthe*	
4		Willow warbler	*Phylioscopus*	*trochilus*	
5		Short-tailed shearwater	*Puffinus*	*tenuirostris*	
6		Long-tailed skua	*Stercorarius*	*longicaudus*	
7		Arctic tern	*Sterna*	*paradiasaea*	
8					

Note that the naming scheme allows us to refer to a group of cells by naming the first cell and the last cell and placing a colon (:) in between, as in "the cells B2:D7 are highlighted in the figure." This kind of reference is called a **cell range**.

13.1 New Range. What is the cell range for the scientific names of the birds whose common name includes "-tailed"?

Headings. Though the software provides names for referring to cells, it is convenient for us to name the rows and columns with more meaningful names. For example, we can label the columns with the type of information entered.

	A	B	C	D	E
1		**Common Name**	**Genus**	**Species**	
2		Swainson's hawk	*Buteo*	*swainsoni*	
3		Wheatear	*Oenanthe*	*oenanthe*	
4		Willow warbler	*Phylioscopus*	*trochilus*	
5		Short-tailed shearwater	*Puffinus*	*tenuirostris*	
6		Long-tailed skua	*Stercorarius*	*longicaudus*	
7		Arctic tern	*Sterna*	*paradiasaea*	
8					

Summarizing, spreadsheets are formed from cells that are displayed to the user as rectangles in a grid. Information is entered in a cell and treated as an elemental piece of data no matter how long it is or if it contains spaces or other punctuation symbols. Generally, we build a list of items that can be sorted simply by selecting them and requesting the sorting operation. If multiple columns must be sorted, we select all of the information to be reordered, request *Sort*, and specify the column to sort on when the UI asks for it. Spreadsheets automatically provide a labeling for specifying the column/row position of any element in the grid, but it is also convenient to add our own, more meaningful names. Table 13.1 gives other common operations useful for lists.

Computing with Spreadsheets

Though spreadsheets don't have to contain a single number to be useful, their most common application is to process numerical data. Numerical data is usually associated with textual information, too, so most spreadsheets have both. For example, suppose our bird migration spreadsheet has been further filled out, as shown in Figure 13.1.

The `Migration` column gives the end points of the bird's semiannual migration route, the `Distance` column gives the approximate length of that flight in kilometers, and `Length` gives the size of the bird (length) in meters. In the following discussion, the `Genus`, `Species`, and `Migration` columns will be hidden: *Format* > *Column* > *Hide* [*View*].

Writing a Formula

Suppose we want to find out how far the Swainson's hawk flies in miles rather than kilometers. Because one kilometer is 0.621 miles, we must multiply the value in cell `F2` by 0.621 to find out. We can perform this specific computation with a calculator, but we will probably want to know the distances in miles for all of the migration flights. So, we

	B	C	D	E	F	G
1	**Common Name**	**Genus**	**Species**	**Migration**	**Distance(Km)**	**Body Length(m)**
2	Swainson's hawk	*Buteo*	*swainsoni*	USA-Argentina	13500	0.52
3	Wheatear	*Oenanthe*	*oenanthe*	Alaska-E. Africa	13500	0.16
4	Willow warbler	*Phylioscopus*	*trochilus*	Chukotka-S. Africa	15500	0.11
5	Short-tailed shearwater	*Puffinus*	*tenuirostris*	Tasmania-Bering Strait	12500	0.43
6	Long-tailed skua	*Stercorarius*	*longicaudus*	N. Greenland-Southern Ocean	16000	0.51
7	Arctic tern	*Sterna*	*paradiasaea*	Greenland-Antarctic	19000	0.35
8						

Figure 13.1 Bird migration spreadsheet.

decide to create a new column for the distance in miles and instruct the spreadsheet how to compute it.

	A	B	F	G	H	I
1		Common Name	Distance(Km)	Length(m)	Distance(Mi)	
2		Swainson's hawk	13500	0.52		
3		Wheatear	13500	0.16		
4		Willow warbler	15500	0.11		
5		Short-tailed shearwater	12500	0.43		
6		Long-tailed skua	16000	0.51		
7		Arctic tern	19000	0.35		
8						

What entry do we want in position H2? We'd like it to be equal to F2 × 0.621, so we type

=F2*0.621

which appears in the H2 window and the *Edit Formula* window on the edit bar above.

SUM fx =F2*0.621

	B	F	G	H	I
1	Common Name	Distance(Km)	Length(m)	Distance(Mi)	
2	Swainson's hawk	13500	0.52	=F2*0.621	
3	Wheatear	13500	0.16		
4	Willow warbler	15500	0.11		
5	Short-tailed shearwater	12500	0.43		
6	Long-tailed skua	16000	0.51		
7	Arctic tern	19000	0.35		
8					

Notice that we use an asterisk (*) for the multiplication symbol rather than a times sign or dot. When we press Enter or Return, the value in H2 is the result of the computation, that is, 8,383.5 miles.

	B	F	G	H	I
1	Common Name	Distance(Km)	Length(m)	Distance(Mi)	
2	Swainson's hawk	13500	0.52	8383.5	
3	Wheatear	13500	0.16		
4	Willow warbler	15500	0.11		
5	Short-tailed shearwater	12500	0.43		
6	Long-tailed skua	16000	0.51		
7	Arctic tern	19000	0.35		
8					

We have just instructed the spreadsheet software to compute the value in cell H2 by telling it what the cell should equal. We did this by typing a formula into the cell. Formulas, which begin with an equal sign (=), define the value for the entry based on the values of other entries. We used numbers (0.621), cell references (F2), and standard arithmetic operations (*) as found on a calculator. If we ever change our estimate of the distance Swainson's hawks migrate, that is, change the value in F2, then the spreadsheet software will *automatically change* the value in H2 to reflect the revision.

Equal Opportunity. When we type characters into a cell, the spreadsheet software needs to know if we are entering data that should be stored, or if we are giving it a formula saying how to compute information for that cell. The equal (=) is the indicator: It's a formula if it starts with =; otherwise it's data.

Consider the formula a bit more. We entered the formula = F2*0.621 into cell H2. The cell contains this formula, not 8383.5. We can prove this by clicking H2 and checking the *Edit Formula* window.

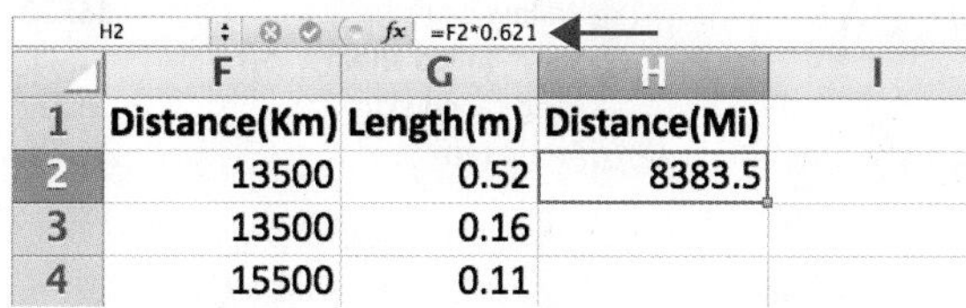

H2 | =F2*0.621

	F	G	H	I
1	Distance(Km)	Length(m)	Distance(Mi)	
2	13500	0.52	8383.5	
3	13500	0.16		
4	15500	0.11		

Then, by temporarily changing the value in F2 from 13,500 to, say, 14,000, we notice that H2 automatically increases to 8694.

By specifying this formula, we have defined an equation

H2 = F2 × 0.621

just as we would in algebra. Recall that such an equation means that both sides of the equal sign refer to the same value. So, entering the formula into H2 means that we want the cell to have the value of F2 * 0.621 now and forever. Because F2 presently contains the data 13,500, cell H2 displays as 8383.5. When we change the value of F2, the value of H2 must change, because the equality must be preserved. Thus, when we put a formula into a cell (the right side of the equation), the computer does the math and displays its value (the left side of the equation).

13.2 One Size. A meter is equal to 100 centimeters. Write the formula for converting the body length of Swainson's hawk to centimeters.

Repeating a Formula

We can specify a similar computation for cell H3 and the other cells in that column by entering them in the same way.

Copy/Paste. Thinking about it, however, we might guess that *Copy/Paste* will work to replicate the equation to other cells. So, we select cell H2, which, in Excel, is indicated by dashes around the box. Other spreadsheet software simply shows a solid box around the item.

	F	G	H	I
1	Distance(Km)	Length(m)	Distance(Mi)	
2	13500	0.52	8383.5	
3	13500	0.16		
4	15500	0.11		

The cell's contents are shown in the *Edit Formula* window. We *Copy* this cell (^C), select the remaining cells in the column by dragging the mouse across them, and *Paste* (^V). The result shows all of the distance values computed. This is quite a bit of computation for very little effort on our part.

Notice that in the *Edit Formula* window the equation shows as F3*0.621. This corresponds to the computation for the cell H3, the first of the highlighted cells (white) into which we pasted the formula. And we notice a curious thing: Whereas the formula we pasted was F2*0.621, the formula was transformed into F3*0.621 when it was pasted

H3 f_x =F3*0.621

	B	F	G	H	I
1	Common Name	Distance(Km)	Length(m)	Distance(Mi)	
2	Swainson's hawk	13500	0.52	8383.5	
3	Wheatear	13500	0.16	8383.5	
4	Willow warbler	15500	0.11	9625.5	
5	Short-tailed shearwater	12500	0.43	7762.5	
6	Long-tailed skua	16000	0.51	9936	
7	Arctic tern	19000	0.35	11799	
8					
9					

into H3; it was transformed into F4*0.621 for H4, and so on. This is exactly what we want for this column, namely that the value in column H is based on the corresponding values in column F. The software makes this transformation for us automatically. (This is explained later in the Transforming Formulas section.)

Filling. It's possible for these computations to be performed even more easily! Let's go back and redo them from the point where we had just entered the formula for the Swainson's hawk.

	F	G	H	I
1	Distance(Km)	Length(m)	Distance(Mi)	
2	13500	0.52	8383.5	
3	13500	0.16		
4	15500	0.11		

Notice in the image that the highlighted cell H2 is outlined in color, but there is also a small box or tab beyond the cell's lower-right corner (near the cursor). This is called its **fill handle**. We can grab this handle with the cursor and "pull" it down the column, applying the operation we just performed on H2 to those cells.

	B	F	G	H	I
1	Common Name	Distance(Km)	Length(m)	Distance(Mi)	
2	Swainson's hawk	13500	0.52	8383.5	
3	Wheatear	13500	0.16	8383.5	
4	Willow warbler	15500	0.11	9625.5	
5	Short-tailed shearwater	12500	0.43	7762.5	
6	Long-tailed skua	16000	0.51	9936	
7	Arctic tern	19000	0.35	11799	
8					
9					

This process is known as **filling**. It's automated copying and pasting! Filling is a shortcut that allows us to replicate, that is, *Copy/Paste*, the contents of the cell with the fill handle, saving us from explicitly setting each cell in the column or manually using the *Copy/Paste* operations. Whenever the fill handle is visible on a highlighted cell, the contents can be replicated by filling.

13.3 Give an Inch. Suppose we would also like to see the birds' body lengths measured in inches. Knowing that a meter is 39.37 inches, what steps do we perform to add this information in column I of the spreadsheet?

Transforming Formulas: Relative Versus Absolute

The software automatically transforms the formulas as it pastes them or fills them into a cell because we used a **relative cell reference** when we wrote F2. Spreadsheets allow two kinds of cell references—relative and absolute—and we must be careful which we use. The **absolute cell reference** to this cell is `$F$2`; it tells the software never to change the reference when filling or pasting. Here's what's happening.

Relative means "relative position from a cell." When we pasted the formula `= F2*0.621` into `H2`, the software noticed that cell `F2` is two cells to the left of `H2`. That is, the formula refers to a cell in the same row, but two cells to the left. Because this is a relative reference, the software preserves the relationship of "two cells to the left in the same row" between the position of the referenced cell and the cell where the formula is pasted. So, when we *Paste* or fill this same formula into `H3`, the software transforms the formula so it still refers to the cell two cells to the left in the same row; that is, the formula is changed to `= F3*0.621`. Similarly, this occurs whenever a relative formula is pasted or filled.

	B	F	G	H	I
1	Common Name	Distance(Km)	Length(m)	Distance(Mi)	
2	Swainson's hawk	13500	0.52	=F2*0.621	
3	Wheatear	13500	0.16		
4	Willow warbler	15500	0.11		
5	Short-tailed shearwater	12500	0.43		
6	Long-tailed skua	16000	0.51		
7	Arctic tern	19000	0.35		
8					

	B	F	G	H	I
1	Common Name	Distance(Km)	Length(m)	Distance(Mi)	
2	Swainson's hawk	13500	0.52	=F2*0.621	
3	Wheatear	13500	0.16	=F3*0.621	
4	Willow warbler	15500	0.11	=F4*0.621	
5	Short-tailed shearwater	12500	0.43	=F5*0.621	
6	Long-tailed skua	16000	0.51	=F6*0.621	
7	Arctic tern	19000	0.35	=F7*0.621	
8					

An absolute reference always refers to the fixed position—the software never adjusts it.

Because there are two dimensions—columns and rows—there are actually two ways a formula can be relative. This makes four cases:

`F2`—column and row are both relative

`$F2`—absolute column, but relative row

`F$2`—relative column, but absolute row

`$F$2`—column and row are both absolute

For example, assume cell `A1` contains 1. When the formula `= A$1 + 1` is filled from `A2` down column `A` into new rows, the formula is untransformed and 2's are computed, because the cell's row reference (`$1`) is absolute and the column reference, though relative, didn't change as we filled down the column into new rows. All cells refer to the same cell, `A1`. But when that formula is filled from `B1` across row 1 into new columns, the relative column reference (`A`) is transformed, `= B$1 + 1`, `= C$1 + 1`, `= D$1 + 1`, and so on, and the numbers 2, 3, 4, . . . are computed.

	A	B	C	D	E	F	G
1	1	2	3	4	5	6	
2	2						
3	2						
4	2						
5	2						
6	2						
7	2						
8							

The spreadsheet software preserves the relative position in whichever dimension(s) you specify, and leaves absolute references unchanged.

Use Squiggle. In Microsoft Excel, a handy way to prove that cells actually contain formulas—and not the result of computing the formula—is to type Ctrl-~. This displays all of the contents of the spreadsheet's cells, including the formulas.

Cell Formats

Although it is amazing that the migratory birds fly so far twice a year, it is perhaps even more impressive that the smaller birds do it. One analysis that a biologist might make to take both distance and size into consideration is to divide the bird's size into the distance flown. This *flying score* measures each bird in a way that allows a more equal comparison.

We will use the distance in kilometers (column F) and length in meters (column G) so that the "meters" cancel out giving a "unitless" score. As before, we define a new column and enter the equation into the first cell. After finding the hawk's score, we fill the column with the formula, computing the results.

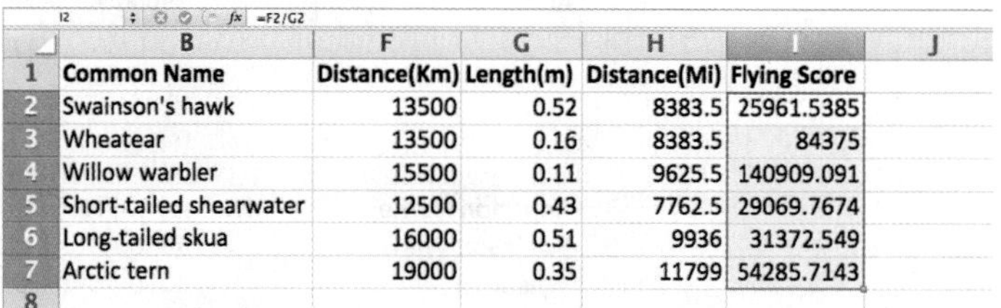

	B	F	G	H	I	J
1	Common Name	Distance(Km)	Length(m)	Distance(Mi)	Flying Score	
2	Swainson's hawk	13500	0.52	8383.5	25961.5385	
3	Wheatear	13500	0.16	8383.5	84375	
4	Willow warbler	15500	0.11	9625.5	140909.091	
5	Short-tailed shearwater	12500	0.43	7762.5	29069.7674	
6	Long-tailed skua	16000	0.51	9936	31372.549	
7	Arctic tern	19000	0.35	11799	54285.7143	
8						

The scores are somewhat difficult to read because they have too many digits, or as a mathematician might say, more digits than are significant. For the numbers to be useful, we need to format them, say, by making them whole numbers.

All spreadsheet software provides control over the format of the information displayed. For example, Excel displays this UI for formatting cells.

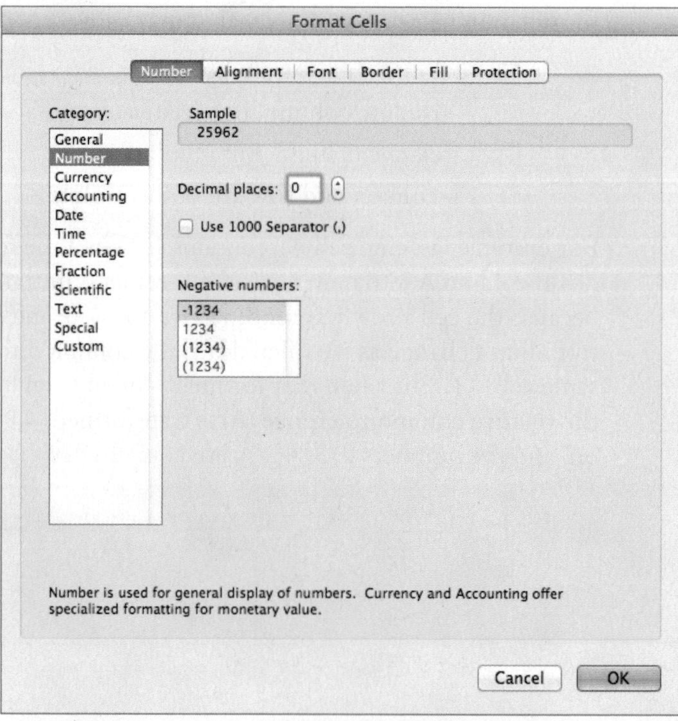

This UI gives us control over the types of information in the fields (*Category*); control over the number of decimal digits for the *Number* category chosen; control over setting the "1000s" separators (commas for North America); and control over the display of negative numbers.

When we reduce the number of decimal digits to 0, that is, specify whole numbers only, we get this result.

I2 fx =F2/G2

	B	F	G	H	I	J
1	Common Name	Distance(Km)	Length(m)	Distance(Mi)	Flying Score	
2	Swainson's hawk	13500	0.52	8383.5	25962	
3	Wheatear	13500	0.16	8383.5	84375	
4	Willow warbler	15500	0.11	9625.5	140909	
5	Short-tailed shearwater	12500	0.43	7762.5	29070	
6	Long-tailed skua	16000	0.51	9936	31373	
7	Arctic tern	19000	0.35	11799	54286	
8						

This confirms our intuition that smaller birds score higher even if they don't fly the longest distances.

Functions

Picking the Willow warbler as the most amazing flier is based on its being the maximum value in the Flying Score column. Visually finding the maximum for this column is easy to do, but it's more difficult to do for the other columns because the entries have the same number of digits; also, the list could be much longer. So we set up the spreadsheet to compute the maximum.

Finding the Maximum

Spreadsheet software provides **functions** for computing common summary operations such as totals (sum), averages, maximums (max), and many others. To use these functions, we give the function name and specify the cell range to be summarized in parentheses after it. For example, we write

```
=max(I2:I7)
```

in a cell at the bottom of column I, and label that row with the "Maximum" caption.

SUM fx =max(i2:i7)

	A	B	F	G	H	I	J
1		Common Name	Distance(Km)	Length(m)	Distance(Mi)	Flying Score	
2		Swainson's hawk	13500	0.52	8383.5	25962	
3		Wheatear	13500	0.16	8383.5	84375	
4		Willow warbler	15500	0.11	9625.5	140909	
5		Short-tailed shearwater	12500	0.43	7762.5	29070	
6		Long-tailed skua	16000	0.51	9936	31373	
7		Arctic tern	19000	0.35	11799	54286	
8							
9	Maximum:					=max(i2:i7)	
10							

The formula directs the software to find the largest value in the cell range I2:I7, that is, the Flying Score column. There is a full list of function names under *Insert* > *Insert Function. . . .* [*Formulas*].

The Easy Case. Functions and column letters are not case sensitive in spreadsheets, so we can type them however we wish. The software stores the result as uppercase, which is how it's displayed after its initial entry.

Having computed the maximum for Flying Score, we can figure the maximum of the other columns as before, by filling. That is, we grab the I9 cell by its fill handle and pull it left to column F. The result is curious.

I9 fx =MAX(I2:I7)

	A	B	F	G	H	I	J
1		Common Name	Distance(Km)	Length(m)	Distance(Mi)	Flying Score	
2		Swainson's hawk	13500	0.52	8383.5	25962	
3		Wheatear	13500	0.16	8383.5	84375	
4		Willow warbler	15500	0.11	9625.5	140909	
5		Short-tailed shearwater	12500	0.43	7762.5	29070	
6		Long-tailed skua	16000	0.51	9936	31373	
7		Arctic tern	19000	0.35	11799	54286	
8							
9	Maximum:		19000	1	11799	140909	
10							
11							

The "1" in the Length column is a whole number rather than 0.52, the largest of the two-decimal-digit fractions in column G. Why? Because the maximum value computation in the Flying Score column inherits the whole number setting from before. When we drag it across to the other columns, it brings its formatting with it. So, the software looks for the largest value in Length, finds that it is 0.52, and then rounds it to a whole number, that is, 1. Formatting this cell so that it displays numbers with two decimal digits fixes the problem.

For completeness, let's also compute the average for each column using the average function. The result requires some additional formatting in the last two columns.

	A	B	F	G	H	I	J
1		Common Name	Distance(Km)	Length(m)	Distance(Mi)	Flying Score	
2		Swainson's hawk	13500	0.52	8383.5	25962	
3		Wheatear	13500	0.16	8383.5	84375	
4		Willow warbler	15500	0.11	9625.5	140909	
5		Short-tailed shearwater	12500	0.43	7762.5	29070	
6		Long-tailed skua	16000	0.51	9936	31373	
7		Arctic tern	19000	0.35	11799	54286	
8							
9	Maximum:		19000	0.52	11799	140909	
10	Average:		15000	0.35	9315	60995.61	
11							

Displaying Hidden Columns

Notice that we have three hidden columns between B and F: the columns with the genus, species, and migration data. When we "unhide" these columns, ... The final spreadsheet, slightly adjusted in formatting, is shown in Figure 13.2.

	B	C	D	E	F	G	H	I
1	Common Name	Genus	Species	Migration	Distance(Km)	Length(m)	Distance(Mi)	Flying Score
2	Swainson's hawk	*Buteo*	*swainsoni*	USA-Argentina	13500	0.52	8383.5	25962
3	Wheatear	*Oenanthe*	*oenanthe*	Alaska-E Africa	13500	0.16	8383.5	84375
4	Willow warbler	*Phylloscopus*	*trochilus*	Chukotka-S Africa	15500	0.11	9625.5	140909
5	Short-tailed shearwater	*Puffinus*	*tenuirostris*	Tasmania-Bering Strait	12500	0.43	7762.5	29070
6	Long-tailed skua	*Stercorarius*	*longicaudus*	N Greenland-Southern Ocean	16000	0.51	9936	31373
7	Arctic tern	*Sterna*	*paradiasaea*	Greenland-Antarctic	19000	0.35	11799	54286
8								
9	Maximum				19000	0.52	11799	140909
10	Average				15000	0.35	9315	60995.61
11								

Figure 13.2 Final spreadsheet for the migratory birds.

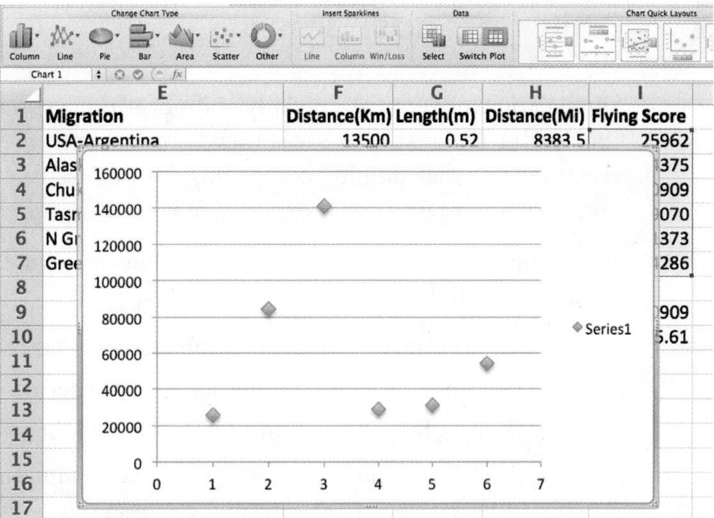

Figure 13.3 The Flying Score graph after selecting an XY-Scatter Plot chart with "points."

Charts

Spreadsheets organize our data and compute new values, but often it is helpful to see the results graphically when comparing values. Spreadsheet software makes creating charts remarkably easy.

The process is to select the values to be plotted and then select the type of chart under the *Insert* menu/ribbon. To see how it works, let's select the items in the Flying Score column. When we click the *Chart* choice of *Insert*, the software gives us a choice of graph styles, as shown across the top of the UI in Figure 13.3. To get an idea of what the graph will look like with our data, we select the "points" form and get the completed chart. Notice that the program, detecting that the column has a heading (how does it know?), uses the heading to label the point as a key to the right.

Clicking on any part of the graph displays a pop-up window that offers editing options; choosing a background fill and changing the font results in the chart shown in Figure 13.4.

Figure 13.4 The final formatted chart displaying the Flying Score.

Daily Spreadsheets

Some people use computers daily and never use a spreadsheet; others use spreadsheets constantly. The rest of us are somewhere in between: Spreadsheets are convenient and versatile tools that simplify computing. In this section we look at a few personal applications as a way to gain more experience with using spreadsheets.

Many opportunities exist to use spreadsheets to organize our personal information, including the following:

- Track our performance in our personal exercise program—distances, time, reps
- Set up an expense budget for the next term
- Keep a list of books and DVDs we've lent to others
- Follow our favorite team's successes by importing the season schedule and annotating it with wins and losses and our own comments about the games
- Record flight hours or dives after each flying or scuba lesson
- Document expenses such as travel, or income such as tips, for income tax purposes
- Save records generated while online banking

Spreadsheets can even serve as an address book or recipe file.

Here are more ways to apply spreadsheets in personally relevant ways.

Time Zone Cheat Sheet

As mentioned at the beginning of the chapter, one reason to be interested in spreadsheets is that they help us compute things that no one but us cares about—they help with personal computations. (They're pretty handy for lots of other tasks, too.) Let's demonstrate this point and practice series fill to solve a "personal computation."

Solving a Problem of Personal Interest

Video chatting—Skype or gChat—is a popular way for people to stay in touch. It's interactive, making it better than email or texting, and it's better to see and hear your buddies than to hear them only. The problem is that some people you want to chat with live in different time zones, which means that it's not always convenient for them to chat when you want to, because they may be sleeping, working, or studying. To help to plan your chat sessions, it's handy to have a "cheat sheet" that provides the local time of where the people you're likely to chat with live. (A "cheat sheet" is a reminder of information you need to know, but don't want to figure out each time you need it.)

The key to creating this spreadsheet is **series fill**. Often, when we use spreadsheets, we use certain data that are "special," such as days, dates, and time. When the software fills these values, it *automatically increments* them, that is, it automatically adds 1 as it fills each cell. The spreadsheet knows that Monday follows Sunday, that February 1 follows January 31, and that 12:00 PM follows 11:00 AM. Some systems assume, when they see values like "Sunday," that it's not just text data, but rather it's one of these special data types, and they use series fill automatically. Series fill is always available: In systems with menus, *Edit* > *Fill* > *Series. . .*, or click [↓] under the *Home* ribbon. If you type `Sunday`

	A	B	C	D	E	F
1	Will	** ME **	Gram & Pops	Chris	Uncle Dave	Kiyomi
2	10:00 PM	12:00 AM	2:00 AM	3:00 AM	11:00 AM	5:00 PM
3	11:00 PM	1:00 AM	3:00 AM	4:00 AM	12:00 PM	6:00 PM
4	12:00 AM	2:00 AM	4:00 AM	5:00 AM	1:00 PM	7:00 PM
5	1:00 AM	3:00 AM	5:00 AM	6:00 AM	2:00 PM	8:00 PM
6	2:00 AM	4:00 AM	6:00 AM	7:00 AM	3:00 PM	9:00 PM
7	3:00 AM	5:00 AM	7:00 AM	8:00 AM	4:00 PM	10:00 PM
8	4:00 AM	6:00 AM	8:00 AM	9:00 AM	5:00 PM	11:00 PM
9	5:00 AM	7:00 AM	9:00 AM	10:00 AM	6:00 PM	12:00 AM
10	6:00 AM	8:00 AM	10:00 AM	11:00 AM	7:00 PM	1:00 AM
11	7:00 AM	9:00 AM	11:00 AM	12:00 PM	8:00 PM	2:00 AM
12	8:00 AM	10:00 AM	12:00 PM	1:00 PM	9:00 PM	3:00 AM
13	9:00 AM	11:00 AM	1:00 PM	2:00 PM	10:00 PM	4:00 AM
14	10:00 AM	12:00 PM	2:00 PM	3:00 PM	11:00 PM	5:00 AM
15	11:00 AM	1:00 PM	3:00 PM	4:00 PM	12:00 AM	6:00 AM
16	12:00 PM	2:00 PM	4:00 PM	5:00 PM	1:00 AM	7:00 AM
17	1:00 PM	3:00 PM	5:00 PM	6:00 PM	2:00 AM	8:00 AM
18	2:00 PM	4:00 PM	6:00 PM	7:00 PM	3:00 AM	9:00 AM
19	3:00 PM	5:00 PM	7:00 PM	8:00 PM	4:00 AM	10:00 AM
20	4:00 PM	6:00 PM	8:00 PM	9:00 PM	5:00 AM	11:00 AM
21	5:00 PM	7:00 PM	9:00 PM	10:00 PM	6:00 AM	12:00 PM
22	6:00 PM	8:00 PM	10:00 PM	11:00 PM	7:00 AM	1:00 PM
23	7:00 PM	9:00 PM	11:00 PM	12:00 AM	8:00 AM	2:00 PM
24	8:00 PM	10:00 PM	12:00 AM	1:00 AM	9:00 AM	3:00 PM
25	9:00 PM	11:00 PM	1:00 AM	2:00 AM	10:00 AM	4:00 PM

Figure 13.5 The time zone cheat sheet (assuming "me" lives in LA) for five buddies; "sunset gold" indicates yesterday, "sunrise magenta" indicates tomorrow.

and you want to copy the word *Sunday*, that is, you don't want to treat it as a special type of data, then don't use series fill. Simply *Copy/Paste*.

A convenient way to use series fill is to enter the first two items of the series into adjacent cells, select the two cells, and then pull on the handle to fill either the row or column. This double-cell fill indicates a series, where the amount of increment between successive items is not necessarily +1, but the difference between the pair.

Series fill makes creating this cheat sheet a simple task. Figure 13.5 shows the spreadsheet we will be creating. Imagine that you live in Los Angeles, your grandparents live in Chicago, your best friend Chris goes to school in Boston, Uncle Dave is in the military in Europe, your foreign exchange friend Kiyomi lives in Tokyo, and your brother Will lives in Hawaii, though no one is quite sure what he's doing there besides surfing.

The cheat sheet has a column for each buddy, and it is set up so that each row gives the same time in each time zone. To use it, find your time in the yellow column and then read off your buddies' times in the row. For example, when it is 1:00 PM for you, it is 11:00 AM for Will, and it is 6:00 AM tomorrow for Kiyomi.

Getting Started, Then Filling In

To create the cheat sheet, begin by placing the headings at the top; you get the clearest table if the people are listed in order, either East to West or West to East (as shown here). Under *your name* enter midnight, using the time format you prefer; if you like AM/PM time, type 12:00 AM (the space is important), but if you prefer international time (a\k\a military time), type 12:00. Fill down the column to the end of the day.

Next, to fill in the time zones for your buddies, use the "Set date and time" feature of your computer. Suppose that it is 3:15 PM where you live, and you change the time zone of your computer to another location where one of your buddies lives, say Chicago where your grandparents live. The current time in Chicago shows 5:15 PM. So, in the column for your grandparents, in the position opposite your 3:00 PM, place 5:00 PM, because that is the time there when it's 3:00 PM where you are (see part a of Figure 13.6). Next, grab the fill handle and fill the column up and down. The spreadsheet software assumes that rows above are earlier and rows below are later, which is exactly what you want.

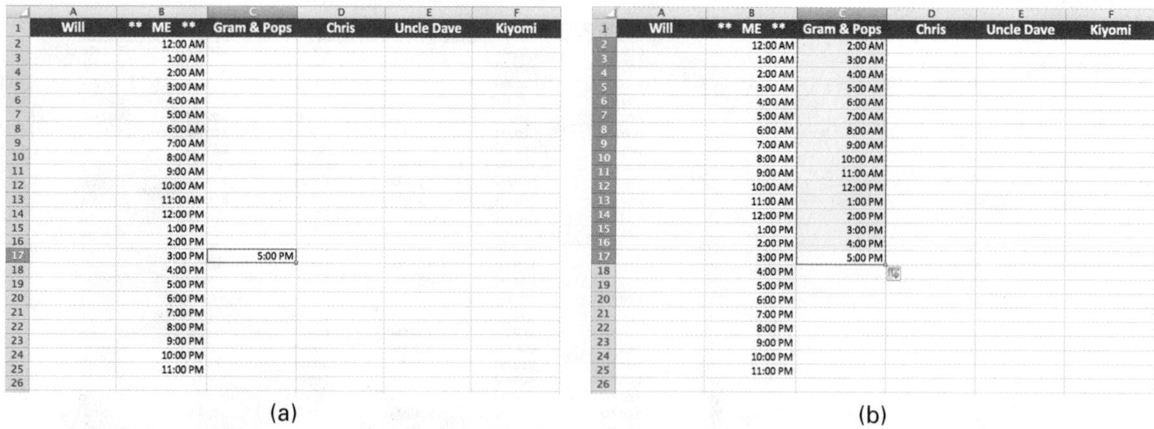

Figure 13.6 Adding the time zone for a buddy (a) prior to filling, and (b) after filling "up."

Repeat the same process for the other buddies on your list. If it's now 3:16 PM where you live, and you change to Boston time, where Chris lives, and get 6:16 PM, you know that in Chris's column, opposite your 3:00 PM cell should be 6:00 PM. Enter that into the cell, fill up and fill down. Chris is done. Very quickly you can set everyone's time zone.

13.4 The Time of Your Life. Suppose that rather than making this spreadsheet at 3:15 PM, you are working on it at 9:45 AM. When you look up the time in Chicago, it shows 11:45 AM. Explain how to construct the grandparents's column (a) at 9:45 AM. (b) Suppose you're working on the spreadsheet at 10:45 AM and the time in Chicago is now 12:45 PM; give the process.

Finish Up

Finally, add colors to the cells that refer to "yesterday" and "tomorrow" to remind you of day changes. Any cells that *start* a column and contain "PM" times refer to yesterday—a color suggestive to you of sunset would be good. Any cells that end a column and contain "AM" times refer to tomorrow—a color that reminds you of dawn is a good choice. Adding a horizontal line between morning and afternoon may also be helpful.

That's it! It takes just a few minutes, it's good spreadsheet practice, and it can be kept handy on your desktop. It can also be printed, and posted near your computer or kept in your wallet or purse. (It saves the embarrassment of counting on your fingers!) No one else wants this information except you, and you produced it very quickly.

Pizza Discount Table

Imagine that your local pizza shop tries to encourage more business by giving a "frequent pizza buyers" discount. You and your friends definitely qualify!

The shop's discount is based on how many pizzas a customer purchased the previous month: no discount for none or one, 5 percent for two or three, 10 percent for four or five, 15 percent for six or seven, and 20 percent for eight or more. The store sells pizza in three sizes: 10", 12", and 14", and charges according to their area: $7.85, $11.30, and $15.39.

A Plan

You and your friends decide to pool your purchases for the month, designating one person as the pizza buyer. That makes everyone's purchases count toward the discount.

Frequent Pizza Buyer Promotion				
Last Mo.	Discount		Size	Price
0–1	None		10"	$7.85
2–3	5%		12"	$11.30
4–5	10%		14"	$15.39
6–7	15%			
8 or more	20%			

Now, you decide to strategize on how best to buy pizza. To figure out a good plan, you need the spreadsheet shown in Figure 13.7. So, let's see how to build it using relative and absolute references.

The Requirements

The spreadsheet shown in Figure 13.7 tells what the store will charge for each size pizza based on the "frequent pizza buyer" category. The table has headings across the top of the columns for the category, and headings down the side of the rows for size. Below the column headings in the blue cells is the amount of the discount, and to the right of the row headings in the magenta cells is the undiscounted price for each size. An entry in the table is found by multiplying the blue amount in that column by the magenta amount in that row. So, what we want in the first cell of the spreadsheet is

D4 = D3 × C4

but the obvious command, =D3*D4, is not a good choice for the formula to compute it because it uses relative references only. It does work for this *one* cell, but we want it to work for the whole table. If we move the formula to other positions with *Copy/Paste* or filling, as we did before, all of the references—the D, the C, the 3, and the 4—will change. But to compute the correct value in each cell, we must always refer to the blue row and the magenta column. They can't change. Let's analyze how we can do that.

Absolute References

To analyze what's happening, consider how we compute E6. Following the blue-row-times-magenta-column rule, we want the value to be

E6 = E3 × C6

Comparing what we want in D4 and E6

D4 = D3 × C4
E6 = E3 × C6

	B	C	D	E	F	G	H
1							
2	PIZZA	Last Month	0 or 1	2 or 3	4 or 5	6 or 7	8 or more
3	Size		1	0.95	0.9	0.85	0.8
4	10 Inch	$7.85	$7.85	$7.46	$7.07	$6.67	$6.28
5	12 Inch	$11.30	$11.30	$10.74	$10.17	$9.61	$9.04
6	14 Inch	$15.39	$15.39	$14.62	$13.85	$13.08	$12.31
7							

Figure 13.7 Table showing the price per pizza for three different sizes based on the number purchased during the previous month.

we see the tinted terms are the same for both cells, allowing them to refer to the blue row and the magenta column. In our commands to the computer, these tinted terms must always be the same for all cells in our table. That means we need absolute references for them, and so we will give the colored characters a $ when we command the computer.

Relative References

The other thing we notice from the two equations

D4 = D3 × C4
E6 = E3 × C6

is that the position, which is given on the left, is also used on the right side in the places that were not previously tinted. That is, these refer to the current position. So, they must use relative addressing, because we want them to change as we fill them into other cells. We will *not* attach a dollar sign to them.

Combining both pieces of information, we conclude that if we want

D4 = D3 × C4

we need a formula that mixes both absolute and relative addressing. That is, we want to type into cell D4 the formula =D$3*$C4, which allows the first term, D$3, always to refer to the third (blue) row, and allows the second term, $C4, always to refer to the C (magenta) column. Because of the orange and purple relative references, the references will always be to the row and column of the cell getting the formula. Filling as before will create the table.

Notice that with such a discount scheme, a group of friends who normally buy 14" pizzas each month, might be smart to buy two 10" pizzas instead of one 14" pizza. (It's more pizza.) Buying four large pizzas in a month allows them to buy next month's 14" pizzas at $13.85 each. By buying eight 10" pizzas, they will be able to buy next month's 10" pizzas at $6.28 each, or $12.56 for two.

13.5 Too Much Crust? Someone complains that the plan to buy two small pizzas instead of one large pizza results in too much crust and not enough cheese. We can estimate the amount of crust by computing the perimeter (edge) of the pizza, which we know from math class is πd, where d is the diameter or size of the pizza (pie). To fill in the table below with the amount of crust (3.14 × size) times the number of pizzas, first give what we want in cell B2, and then what to type into cell B2 that can be filled to the other cells to complete the table. You will mix absolute and relative references.

	A	B	C	D	E
1	Pizza	1	2	3	4
2	8				
3	10				
4	14				

Paying Off a Loan

Suppose you are considering a large purchase, which may or may not have woofers. Your uncle has agreed to lend you the money, but ever the businessman, he's charging you 5 percent interest; it's better than the credit card! To decide how much to borrow, you want to create a spreadsheet of the monthly payments required for different amounts borrowed for different time periods. The spreadsheet setup follows the strategy of the last section: Fill a row across the top with different numbers of payments, and fill a column with different amounts.

	A	B	C	D	E	F	G
1							
2		Payments	6	12	18	24	
3		$1,000					
4		$1,500					
5		$2,000					
6		$2,500					
7		$3,000					
8		$3,500					
9		$4,000					
10		$4,500					
11		$5,000					
12							

Among the functions available with spreadsheets is the "payment" computation, PMT. Navigate *Insert* > *Function. . .* , locate the *Financial* category, and then scroll down to click on PMT [*Formulas* > *Financial*].

We are offered a dialog box, though the exact form varies significantly from system to system.

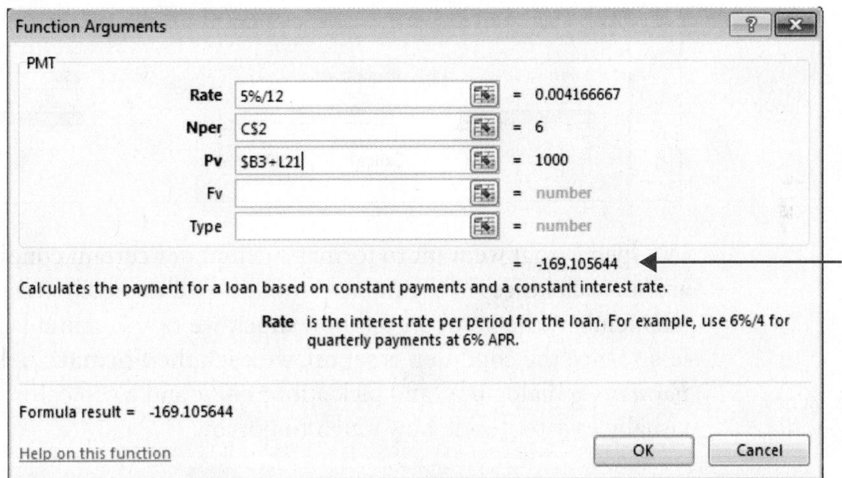

The inputs to the function are the monthly interest Rate, which is 1/12th of the annual rate your uncle is charging, so the proper entry is 0.05/12 or 5%/12. The number of payments (Nper) is the amount in row 2 for this column, and the present value, or the amount of the loan (Pv), is the amount in column B for this row. We enter the numbers. As in the previous section, the inputs mix absolute and relative references to refer to the row and column entries. So, Nper is C$2 because we always want to reference row 2, and Pv is $B3 because we always want to reference column B. The formula result, shown at the bottom of the UI, is the amount required to repay $1,000 in six payments (see arrow). Notice that the result is negative, because the payment is a cost to you.

Filling the formula down the column and across the rows results in a table with red, parenthesized values, which is the default display form for negative numbers.

	A	B	C	D	E	F	G	H
1								
2		Payments	6	12	18	24		
3		$1,000	($169.11)	($85.61)	($57.78)	($43.87)		
4		$1,500	($253.66)	($128.41)	($86.67)	($65.81)		
5		$2,000	($338.21)	($171.21)	($115.56)	($87.74)		
6		$2,500	($422.76)	($214.02)	($144.45)	($109.68)		
7		$3,000	($507.32)	($256.82)	($173.34)	($131.61)		
8		$3,500	($591.87)	($299.63)	($202.23)	($153.55)		
9		$4,000	($676.42)	($342.43)	($231.12)	($175.49)		
10		$4,500	($760.98)	($385.23)	($260.01)	($197.42)		
11		$5,000	($845.53)	($428.04)	($288.90)	($219.36)		
12								

If we don't like the parentheses, we can reformat the entries as follows.

Repaying a Loan

Perhaps, because the table is intended to help us decide how much to borrow, the best way to display the entries is to display them in two colors: Green for those within our budget and red for those over our budget. Deciding that a payment of $250 per month is a comfortable limit, we click *Format > Conditional Formatting. . .* [*Home*]. and get a UI requesting this information. Again, its form varies from system to system.

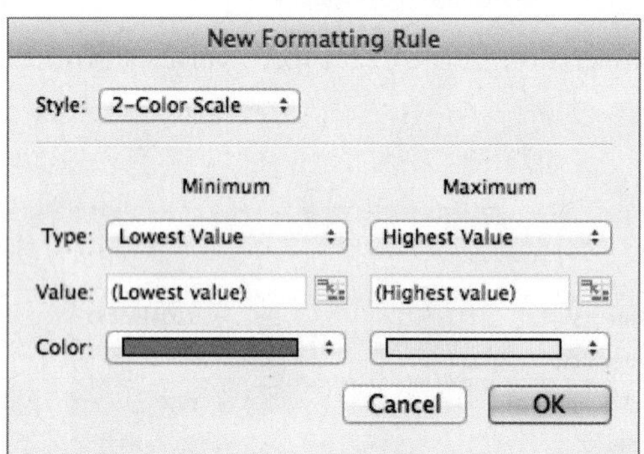

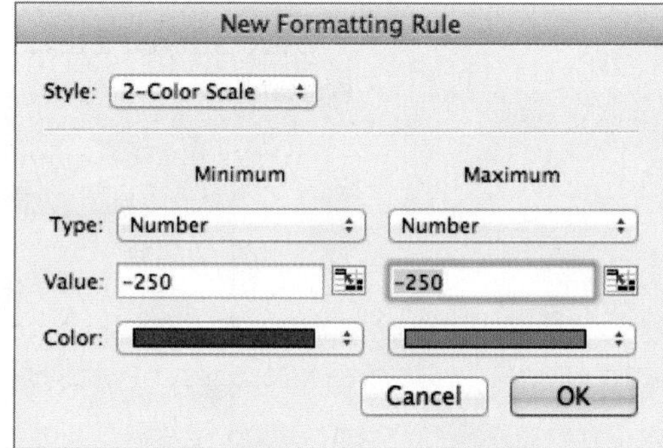

How Your Money *Could* Grow

We specify that we want to format a cell under certain conditions. The condition—there are several choices in the menu—should "fire" for cells greater than or equal to –250. (Remember, the numbers tell how much we *pay*, so a number closer to 0 means paying less.) Once the condition is set up, we click the **Format. . .** button in the *Conditional Formatting* dialog box, and pick a font color and a cell color. The final result makes it visually easy to decide how much to borrow.

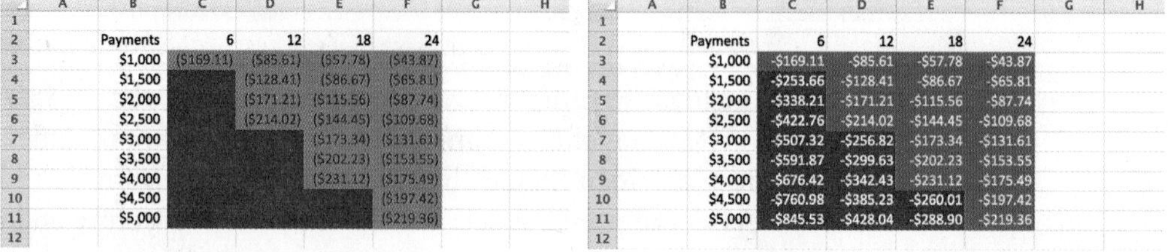

	A	B	C	D	E	F	G	H
1								
2		Payments	6	12	18	24		
3		$1,000	($169.11)	($85.61)	($57.78)	($43.87)		
4		$1,500		($128.41)	($86.67)	($65.81)		
5		$2,000		($171.21)	($115.56)	($87.74)		
6		$2,500		($214.02)	($144.45)	($109.68)		
7		$3,000			($173.34)	($131.61)		
8		$3,500			($202.23)	($153.55)		
9		$4,000			($231.12)	($175.49)		
10		$4,500				($197.42)		
11		$5,000				($219.36)		
12								

	A	B	C	D	E	F	G	H
1								
2		Payments	6	12	18	24		
3		$1,000	-$169.11	-$85.61	-$57.78	-$43.87		
4		$1,500	-$253.66	-$128.41	-$86.67	-$65.81		
5		$2,000	-$338.21	-$171.21	-$115.56	-$87.74		
6		$2,500	-$422.76	-$214.02	-$144.45	-$109.68		
7		$3,000	-$507.32	-$256.82	-$173.34	-$131.61		
8		$3,500	-$591.87	-$299.63	-$202.23	-$153.55		
9		$4,000	-$676.42	-$342.43	-$231.12	-$175.49		
10		$4,500	-$760.98	-$385.23	-$260.01	-$197.42		
11		$5,000	-$845.53	-$428.04	-$288.90	-$219.36		
12								

Importing Data

Much of the data we are interested in comes from some other source, that is, we didn't produce it. This probably means it has already been organized, and so may already exist in a spreadsheet or in a table in another application. Call this **foreign data**—data from another application that we want to import into a spreadsheet. Though importing previously formatted data into a spreadsheet can be tricky, there are guidelines to make it easier.

Tab-Delimited Data

As a rule, spreadsheets prefer to import foreign data as **tab-delimited text**. "Text" means ASCII text, that is, files with .txt extensions. Because they are text files, numbers like *100* are represented as three numeral characters rather than as a single binary number. This allows the spreadsheet software to convert the ASCII form into whatever internal number representation it prefers. "Tab-delimited" means that each cell's entry is **delimited** (ends with) a tab in the file, and each row is delimited with a return (the symbol that results from pressing Return or Enter on the keyboard). Other delimiters are recognized, too, such as spaces and commas. Spreadsheets can output their lists as tab-delimited text. Copying and pasting tab-delimited text is a simple way to import foreign data.

Lists with some other form can often be converted into the preferred tab-delimited form by copying the foreign data into a text editor or word processor and editing it using *Search/Replace*, possibly using the placeholder technique introduced in Chapter 2. The goal is to substitute a tab or other preferred delimiter for a delimiter in the file that the spreadsheet software doesn't understand. Writing the result to a text file eliminates any formatting characters from the word processor.

Another important source of data is the World Wide Web. The information is already in text form—so that condition is fulfilled—and often it is formatted with HTML table tags, as described in Chapter 4. It seems it should be possible to *Copy* a table from HTML and *Paste* it into a spreadsheet. For some browser-spreadsheet combinations it works, but for others it doesn't. It all depends on how the browser delimits "copies" taken from the source. If you try to *Copy/Paste* table data from the Web and it doesn't work, try another browser before beginning the tedious task of reformatting the foreign data by other means. You'll probably get lucky.

Guidelines for importing foreign data:

- *When possible, save foreign data as tab-delimited ASCII text in a file with a* .txt *extension.*
- *When foreign data comes from the Web, select a browser that supports* Copy/Paste *of tagged tables.*
- *When the foreign data format is messed up, use a text editor with* Search/Replace, *apply the placeholder technique, and copy the revised data into a file with a* .txt *extension. Import the resulting file.*

For example, suppose you want a custom bus schedule. Transportation schedules often include more data than we need, so if we grab a copy of the whole schedule from the Web, we can trim and edit it to match our needs in a spreadsheet. Visiting the city's Web page, we locate the bus schedule and *Copy* it, as shown in Figure 13.8, and then *Paste* it into the spreadsheet.

We only want the departure time from our stop and the arrival time at campus. By deleting columns we can create a simple two-column schedule. Adding the two columns for the return trip produces a custom schedule, as shown in Figure 13.9.

Arranging Columns

Spreadsheets are designed to manipulate rows and columns of information easily. Most other applications are good with rows, but not columns. For example, it is common in

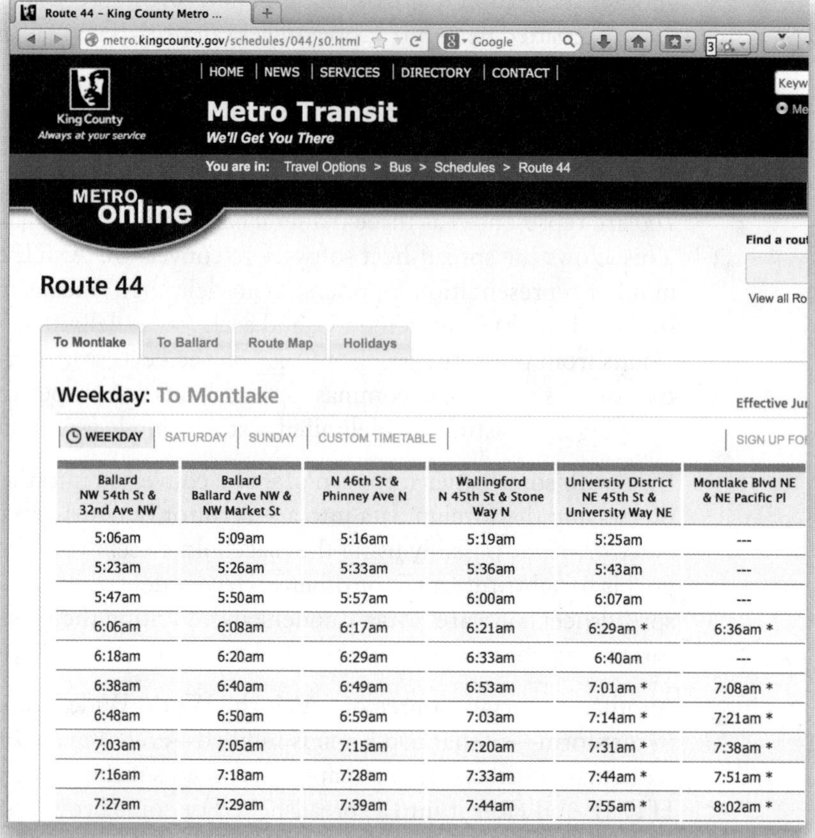

Ballard NW 54th St & 32nd Ave NW	Ballard Ballard Ave NW & NW Market St	N 46th St & Phinney Ave N	Wallingford N 45th St & Stone Way N	University District NE 45th St & University Way NE	Montlake Blvd NE & NE Pacific Pl
5:06am	5:09am	5:16am	5:19am	5:25am	---
5:23am	5:26am	5:33am	5:36am	5:43am	---
5:47am	5:50am	5:57am	6:00am	6:07am	---
6:06am	6:08am	6:17am	6:21am	6:29am *	6:36am *
6:18am	6:20am	6:29am	6:33am	6:40am	---
6:38am	6:40am	6:49am	6:53am	7:01am *	7:08am *
6:48am	6:50am	6:59am	7:03am	7:14am *	7:21am *
7:03am	7:05am	7:15am	7:20am	7:31am *	7:38am *
7:16am	7:18am	7:28am	7:33am	7:44am *	7:51am *
7:27am	7:29am	7:39am	7:44am	7:55am *	8:02am *

Figure 13.8 Bus schedule from the Web selected for copying.

	A	B	C	D
2				
3	Home	School	School	Home
4	5:23 AM	5:43 AM	5:46 AM	6:04 am *
5	5:47 AM	6:07 AM	6:01 AM	6:20 am *
6	6:06 AM	6:29 am *	6:16 AM	6:35 am *
7	6:18 AM	6:40 AM	6:27 AM	6:46 am *
8	6:38 AM	7:01 am *	6:39 AM	6:58 am *
9	6:48 AM	7:14 am *	6:46 AM	7:05 am *

Figure 13.9 Customized schedule with "to campus" in white, "from campus" in green.

word processing to present a list of information, one item per line, as in this list of Best Picture winners (starting with the first award in 1929), which includes Oscar awards / nominations, director, and year.

> *Argo*, 3 / 7, Ben Affleck, 2012
> *The Artist*, 5 / 10, Michel Hazanavicius, 2011
> *The King's Speech*, 4 / 12, Tom Hooper, 2010
> *The Hurt Locker*, 6 / 9, Kathryn Bigelow, 2009
> *Slumdog Millionaire*, 8 / 10, Danny Boyle, 2008
> *No Country for Old Men*, 4 / 8, Joel & Ethan Coen, 2007
> . . .

Though the lines may not be intended as a table, when each one contains the same information in the same order, we naturally align it into a table in our minds. Adding new rows is easy. Inserting or rearranging the columns is a headache. Spreadsheets can help.

To manipulate columns in an application not well suited to the task, we must create a consistently delimited text file of the data, and import it into a spreadsheet, as described earlier. (Most entries are delimited with commas, so only the slash (/) presents a problem.) We then manipulate the list and write out the file as text. After being revised in the spreadsheet, the file can be returned to the application. We will illustrate this idea by rearranging the columns of the movie list.

For example, suppose we want to reorder the columns so the year follows the movie, and change the *awards / nominations* data so it reads, for *Argo*, "3 of 7 Oscars."

To begin:

- Make a file containing only the list.
- Use *Search/Replace* to replace every space-slash-space (" / ") with a comma (","), so that the numbers will get separate columns.
- Import the file into the spreadsheet.

The result is shown in Figure 13.10.

Using *Cut* and *Paste* we move the last column to become the second column.

	A	B	C	D	E	F
1						
2		Argo	2012	Ben Affleck	3	7
3		The Artist	2011	Michel Hazanavicius	5	10
4		The King's Speech	2010	Tom Hooper	4	12
5		The Hurt Locker	2009	Kathryn Bigelow	6	9
6		Slumdog Millionaire	2008	Danny Boyle	8	10
7		No Country for Old Men	2007	Joel & Ethan Coen	4	8
8						

We also use a new column to combine the awards and nominations into one phrase. The formula uses an operation called **concatenate**, which means to join pieces of text together, one after the other. We will join four pieces of text together (ƀ is our symbol for a space): the number of awards, the text " of " (ƀofƀ), the number of nominations, and the text " Oscars" (ƀOscars),

awards " of " *nominations* " Oscars"

	A	B	C	D	E	F	G
1							
2		Argo	Ben Affleck	3	7	2012	
3		The Artist	Michel Hazanavicius	5	10	2011	
4		The King's Speech	Tom Hooper	4	12	2010	
5		The Hurt Locker	Kathryn Bigelow	6	9	2009	
6		Slumdog Millionaire	Danny Boyle	8	10	2008	
7		No Country for Old Men	Joel & Ethan Coen	4	8	2007	
8							

Figure 13.10 The movie list imported into a spreadsheet.

This is expressed by the formula

= concatenate(e2," of ",f2," Oscars")

For the movie *Argo*, the formula produces

	A	B	C	D	E	F	G	H
1								
2		Argo	2012	Ben Affleck	3	7	3 of 7 Oscars	
3		The Artist	2011	Michel Hazanavicius	5	10		
4		The King's Speech	2010	Tom Hooper	4	12		
5		The Hurt Locker	2009	Kathryn Bigelow	6	9		
6		Slumdog Millionaire	2008	Danny Boyle	8	10		
7		No Country for Old Men	2007	Joel & Ethan Coen	4	8		
8								

The function concatenate can join any number of text pieces, and is a handy tool for combining words and numbers.

13.6 Director's Cut. Write the spreadsheet formula to be placed in H2 that would produce the contents "Ben Affleck, director" and that could be filled down column H to apply to all directors. (Ignore the plural for the Coen brothers.)

The result, after filling into column G, is shown in Figure 13.11(a). This revised column converts two columns of data to a phrase that can replace them. We move the two numerical columns to the end of the table (we need to keep them or the concatenate formula won't work) and reorder the columns as we intend, as shown in Figure 13.11(b).

To complete the table, we want to *Cut* and *Paste* the Oscars column into column E and throw away the last two data columns. But if we do that, the data that the Oscars column depends on will be gone. What we must do is *Paste* the Oscars as *values*, that is, as text, into column E. So, we use *Edit > Paste Special. . .* [*Home > Paste*] and select *Values*. This converts the Oscars column from formulas to text (see Figure 13.11(c)) so that the spreadsheet no longer depends on the data columns. Now, the "working columns" can be removed, producing the final result (see 13.11(d)).

This completes our revisions, and we can copy the final results from our spreadsheet to our document.

Argo, 2012, Ben Affleck, 3 of 7 Oscars
The Artist, 2011, Michel Hazanavicius, 5 of 10 Oscars
The King's Speech, 2010, Tom Hooper, 4 of 12 Oscars
The Hurt Locker, 2009, Kathryn Bigelow, 6 of 9 Oscars
Slumdog Millionaire, 2008, Danny Boyle, 8 of 10 Oscars
No Country for Old Men, 2007, Joel & Ethan Coen, 4 of 8 Oscars
. . .

The result achieves our intended columnar modifications. When we explain the process in complete detail it seems complicated, but it takes only a few minutes to put it into a spreadsheet, fix it, and copy the reformatted text into the document.

	A	B	C	D	E	F	G
1							
2		Argo	2012	Ben Affleck	3	7	3 of 7 Oscars
3		The Artist	2011	Michel Hazanavicius	5	10	5 of 10 Oscars
4		The King's Speech	2010	Tom Hooper	4	12	4 of 12 Oscars
5		The Hurt Locker	2009	Kathryn Bigelow	6	9	6 of 9 Oscars
6		Slumdog Millionaire	2008	Danny Boyle	8	10	8 of 10 Oscars
7		No Country for Old Men	2007	Joel & Ethan Coen	4	8	4 of 8 Oscars

(a)

	A	B	C	D	E	F	G	H
1								
2		Argo	2012	Ben Affleck		3	7	3 of 7 Oscars
3		The Artist	2011	Michel Hazanavicius		5	10	5 of 10 Oscars
4		The King's Speech	2010	Tom Hooper		4	12	4 of 12 Oscars

(b)

	A	B	C	D	E	F	G	H	I
1									
2		Argo	2012	Ben Affleck		3	7	3 of 7 Oscars	
3		The Artist	2011	Miche		5	10	5 of 10 Oscars	
4		The King's Speech	2010	Tom H		4	12	4 of 12 Oscars	
5		The Hurt Locker	2009	Kathry		6	9	6 of 9 Oscars	
6		Slumdog Millionaire	2008	Danny		8	10	8 of 10 Oscars	
7		No Country for Old Men	2007	Joel &		4	8	4 of 8 Oscars	

Paste Special

Paste

All	All using Source theme
Formulas	All except borders
Values	Column widths
Formats	Formulas and number formats
Comments	Values and number formats
Validation	Merge conditional formatting

(c)

	A	B	C	D	E
1					
2		Argo	2012	Ben Affleck	3 of 7 Oscars
3		The Artist	2011	Michel Hazanavicius	5 of 10 Oscars
4		The King's Speech	2010	Tom Hooper	4 of 12 Oscars
5		The Hurt Locker	2009	Kathryn Bigelow	6 of 9 Oscars
6		Slumdog Millionaire	2008	Danny Boyle	8 of 10 Oscars
7		No Country for Old Men	2007	Joel & Ethan Coen	4 of 8 Oscars
8					

(d)

Figure 13.11 Revising the movie list. (a) Constructing the phrase; (b) reordering the main columns; (c) creating the text form of the phrase with *Paste Special. . .* ; and (d) the completed table.

SUMMARY

In this chapter we explored the basic ideas of spreadsheets. We learned the following:

- Spreadsheets present an array of cells, each of which is capable of storing one data item: a number, a letter sequence, or a formula.
- Numbers and text can be formatted so that they display as we prefer—proper font, correct number of digits, and so on.
- The power of spreadsheets comes from entering formulas that calculate new values based on the values in other cells.

- The formula is one side of an equation, which the computer solves for us, preserving the equality whenever the numbers that the formula depends on are changed and displaying the new value in the cell.
- In addition to performing arithmetic on the cells, we can apply functions to individual items or to whole cell ranges.
- Both relative and absolute references to cells are needed depending on the circumstances.
- In addition to sorting, there are functions for finding totals, averages, the maximum or minimum, and others.
- Spreadsheets are a practical tool for routine computing.
- It's easy to teach ourselves more about spreadsheets simply by trying them with courage.
- Spreadsheets may be the most useful software for personal computing.

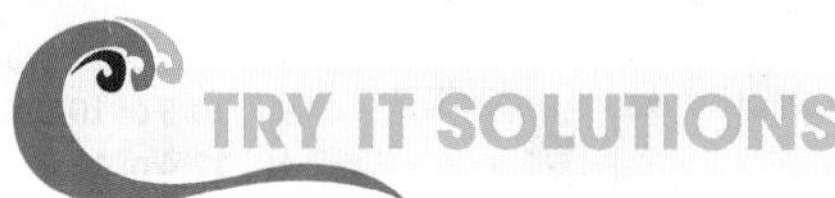

TRY IT SOLUTIONS

13.1 The cell range is C5:D6, because the two birds with "-tailed" in their names are in rows 5 and 6, and the scientific names span columns C and D.

13.2 The formula is = G2*100.

13.3 *Step 1.* It's recommended to label the next column, I, with an appropriate heading, though it is not actually required.

Step 2. Enter the formula = G2*39.37 in cell I2, which computes the length of Swainson's hawk in inches; it's 20.28 inches.

Step 3. Click once on cell I2 to select it, and drag the fill handle down the column to fill in the lengths of the other birds.

13.4 (a) Place 11:00 in the grandparents's column in the cell opposite the 9:00 AM cell in your column; fill up, fill down. (b) Place 12:00 PM in the grandparents' column in the cell opposite the 10:00 AM cell in your column, fill up, fill down.

13.5 $B2 = 3.14 \times A2 \times B1$ and the command is = 3.14*$A2*B$1.

13.6 The formula is =concatenate(D2, ", director").

Did you remember the space after the comma?

REVIEW QUESTIONS

True/False

1. Text too wide to fit into a cell is truncated.
   a. true
   b. false
   c. not enough information
2. Cells in a spreadsheet are 10 characters wide.
   a. true
   b. false
   c. not enough information

3. Relative cell references change as associated values change.
   a. true
   b. false
   c. not enough information
4. *Copy/Paste* will duplicate a formula, but it won't utilize relative and absolute cell references.
   a. true
   b. false
   c. not enough information
5. The small box or handle in a selected cell's lower-right corner is used to move the contents of a cell.
   a. true
   b. false
   c. not enough information
6. A cell reference cannot contain a relative and an absolute reference at the same time.
   a. true
   b. false
   c. not enough information
7. Column references in cell ranges must be typed using uppercase.
   a. true
   b. false
   c. not enough information
8. To change a relative cell reference to an absolute reference, you should use the ampersand (&).
   a. true
   b. false
   c. not enough information
9. Spreadsheet columns can be hidden but rows cannot.
   a. true
   b. false
   c. not enough information
10. A spreadsheet can import any kind of data.
    a. true
    b. false
    c. not enough information

Multiple Choice

1. Functions and column letters are ________ in formulas.
   a. case sensitive
   b. not case sensitive
   c. case sensitive if you put a $ in the formula
   d. not case sensitive if you put a $ in the formula
2. How many different ways are there to combine absolute and relative references to a single cell?
   a. 4
   b. 1
   c. 6
   d. 2

3. Respectively, rows and columns are designated with
   a. numbers, letters
   b. letters, numbers
   c. numbers, numbers
   d. names, numbers

4. Which of the following is a valid range of cells?
   a. D1:D4
   b. C3:D5
   c. A1:E1
   d. all of the above

5. Which of the following is not a valid range of cells?
   a. A1>A5
   b. C3–C8
   c. 3B:6B
   d. all of the above

6. How many cells are in the range B2:D7?
   a. 6
   b. 12
   c. 18
   d. unknown

7. Spreadsheet formulas start with
   a. +

   b. =
   c. @
   d. !

8. Delimited cell entries mean
   a. cell entries that begin with a certain character
   b. cell entries that contain a certain character
   c. cell entries that do not contain a certain character
   d. cell entries that end with a certain character

9. What function would you use to change the color of certain cells based on the value stored inside of them?
   a. sort
   b. text formatting
   c. cell formatting
   d. conditional formatting

10. Which of the following is a completely relative cell reference?
    a. J4
    b. $J4
    c. J$4
    d. $J$4

11. If the formula =$B$3 * .062 is copied from cell B4 to B5, the result will be
    a. =$B$4 * .062
    b. =$B$3 * .062
    c. =B5 * .062
    d. an error

12. If $G5 appeared in a formula, you'd know
    a. the G is absolute and the 5 is relative
    b. the G is relative and the 5 is absolute
    c. both are relative
    d. both are absolute

Short Answer

1. If a cell does not start with an equal sign then the cell contains ______.
2. Cell entries are ______; that is, the computer will not consider any of their constituent parts.
3. The ______ statement finds the maximum value in column J for rows 3–7 (assume the cells are filled with numerical values).
4. The ______ statement finds the minimum value in row 8 for columns A–E (assume the cells are filled with numerical values).
5. A rectangular group of one or more cells is called a(n) ______.
6. The small box in the lower-right corner of a selected cell (or range of cells) is called the ______
7. A(n) ______ cell reference automatically transforms a formula when it is pasted or filled.
8. A(n) ______ cell reference retains a reference to a fixed position when it is pasted or filled.
9. Data imported into a spreadsheet should generally be ______.
10. Using ______ automatically fills and increments values.
11. ______ are formulas built into a spreadsheet to make it easier to create calculations.
12. Use the ______ function to find the average of a range of cells.
13. Use the ______ function to find the largest of the numbers in a range of cells.
14. A ______ is a range of cells filled with increments of a certain type of data.
15. The PMT( ) function returns a(an) ______ because it's money you owe.
16. To change the formatting on a chart you should ______ on that item to access the appropriate menus.
17. ______ means "join letter sequences together."

Exercises

1. What two types of information do cells in a spreadsheet contain? Explain how the spreadsheet knows the type of the information.
2. Look through the list of functions for a spreadsheet. Make a list of 10 functions and how you could use them.
3. List five ways in which you could use a spreadsheet to organize your personal life. Be specific to your life and do not use any of the examples discussed in this chapter.
4. Use a spreadsheet to create a checkerboard. Resize the rows and columns of a spreadsheet to make eight rows and eight columns of equal size. Color alternate squares red and black. Print it in color.

5. Count the number of each color in a bag of M & M's. Create a spreadsheet from this. Write down each color and put the number of M & M's of that color in the cell next to it. Change the color of the cells to match the color of the M & M's. Write a formula to find the total. If you want, create a pie chart. Select the colors and the numbers.
6. Create a spreadsheet to display the classes in your plan of study. Use a column for each semester and enter the classes below it.
7. Modify the spreadsheet for Paying Off a Loan. Change it so you can enter the interest in a cell and have the cell in your formula. Test it to see how changes in the interest rate affect your ability to repay the loan.
8. Go to www.tides.info/. Select a location and get the tide charts for the current month. Copy the data and paste it into a spreadsheet. Change the formatting to suit your tastes.
9. Create a personal budget. Put income in its own column. Total it. Put expenses in another column. Total it. The more accurate you are, the closer your budget will be. There should be at least a little money left over at the end of the month just in case!
10. Create a GPA calculator. Enter your classes in one column. Next to it enter the number of credits. Next to that enter the grade points earned for that class. (Usually it's one point per credit for a D, two per credit for a C, three per credit for a B, and four per credit for an A.) Total the credits and the grade points. The GPA is grade points divided by credits.
11. Explain in detail why the author chose to create a spreadsheet of different time zones of his friends when instead he could have just looked up their time zone information each time on an appropriate Web site.
12. Navigate to www.imdb.com/chart/top in your favorite browser. Determine how to move the data shown into a spreadsheet. Sort all the movie titles alphabetically, then turn the background of every cell red that corresponds to a movie that was rated below 8.0.

CHAPTER 14

Advanced Spreadsheets for Planning

"What If" Thinking Helps

learning objectives

- State the two basic design criteria for creating effective spreadsheets
- Explain how conditional formatting of spreadsheet entries applies an interpretation to spreadsheet information
- Explain conditional formulas, and their components and behavior
- Perform "what if" analysis with a spreadsheet
- Use AutoFiltering and advanced filtering to customize spreadsheet lists
- Explain the importance of symbolic naming of spreadsheet cells

CHAPTER 14

Informed decision-making comes from a long tradition of guessing and then blaming others for inadequate results.

—SCOTT ADAMS

Part of the inhumanity of the computer is that, once it is competently programmed and working smoothly, it is completely honest.

—ISAAC ASIMOV

THE INTRODUCTION to spreadsheets in Chapter 13 taught only the most basic operations. Based on that explanation, you could be excused for wondering how it is that spreadsheets are the "most useful general-purpose computer application." They seem so limited. But you'll soon see that's not the case; in this chapter we introduce advanced spreadsheet techniques. This chapter's study shows that spreadsheets not only help us organize and analyze our data, but they also allow us to explore possibilities that might arise and to work out strategies for reacting to those changes. These advanced spreadsheet concepts are just as easy to learn as the basic topics of Chapter 13 were, and they allow us to look into the future.

Spreadsheets are often taught using business applications, but we use a "running example" with more personal interest: a spreadsheet to plan a road trip. Perhaps you are the sort of person who likes spontaneous travel and thinks a detailed plan spoils the fun. Or maybe you like to have a carefully plotted itinerary. Either way, the plan helps us to understand important constraints on our travel, such as time and money. Once we know those limits, the trip can be either spontaneous or scheduled.

So far, the spreadsheets we have created have been used only once, rather than being saved and used again and again. When a spreadsheet becomes a basic tool of our everyday work or recreation, it must be useful and convenient. That means it needs good design, and we will present a couple of important design guidelines in this chapter.

The advanced features we discuss concern using spreadsheets *conditionally*. These include adjusting the formats or values of cells based on various circumstances; for example, we may wish to flag values that are "out of bounds." We will also *filter* our spreadsheets, including or excluding data as our analysis requires. Another analytical tool supports "what if" experimentation; that is, the spreadsheet helps us examine alternatives and see the consequences of various decisions.

Common Tools. Spreadsheet software is available from many sources, each system with a different set of facilities. The presentation in this chapter is designed to maximize its applicability to different systems. To reach the greatest number of students, this chapter's content is presented in "Excel Classic form," which uses menus and is compatible with a variety of installed systems. Users of Excel 2010/2013 can quickly and easily find the equivalent operations under the obvious ribbons—basics under *Home*, formulas under *Formulas*, and so forth; when operations are in less obvious places, the ribbon is given in brackets [*View*] in green.

Designing a Spreadsheet

When we make a spreadsheet to find an answer and then delete it, it hardly matters what form it has as long as the computation is right. When a spreadsheet is used repeatedly, it doesn't just give answers; it becomes a tool of planning, analysis, and decision-making. To be effective, the spreadsheet must be well designed, being as informative and flexible as possible. We give design guidelines that further these goals after we describe the data we will use in our sample spreadsheet.

The Trip

The data we use in our example is about two friends, Pat and Alex, who know that it's not possible to drive to the North Pole, but wonder if it's possible to drive to the Arctic Circle. Turning to the Web, they find the following:

- There is an Arctic Circle Street in Rockford, Illinois (a false start).
- A highway crosses the Arctic Circle in the Yukon Territory of Canada, between Dawson and the Northwest Territories town of Fort McPherson.
- The trip to Fort McPherson is 3,512 miles from their home in Chicago, and takes 67 hours of driving time (see Figure 14.1).
- The highway is unpaved over several hundred miles of the distance.

Obviously, the given driving time is continuous, which they do not plan to do. So they decide to make a spreadsheet to figure out how long it will take and how much it will cost. We use their spreadsheet as our example in this chapter.

Traveling Companion. Read the following sections at a computer and build the spreadsheets along with the text; it is an extremely effective way to learn these concepts. Moreover, when finished, you will have a spreadsheet to use to plan your travels. Find all the necessary files at pearsonhighered.com/snyder.

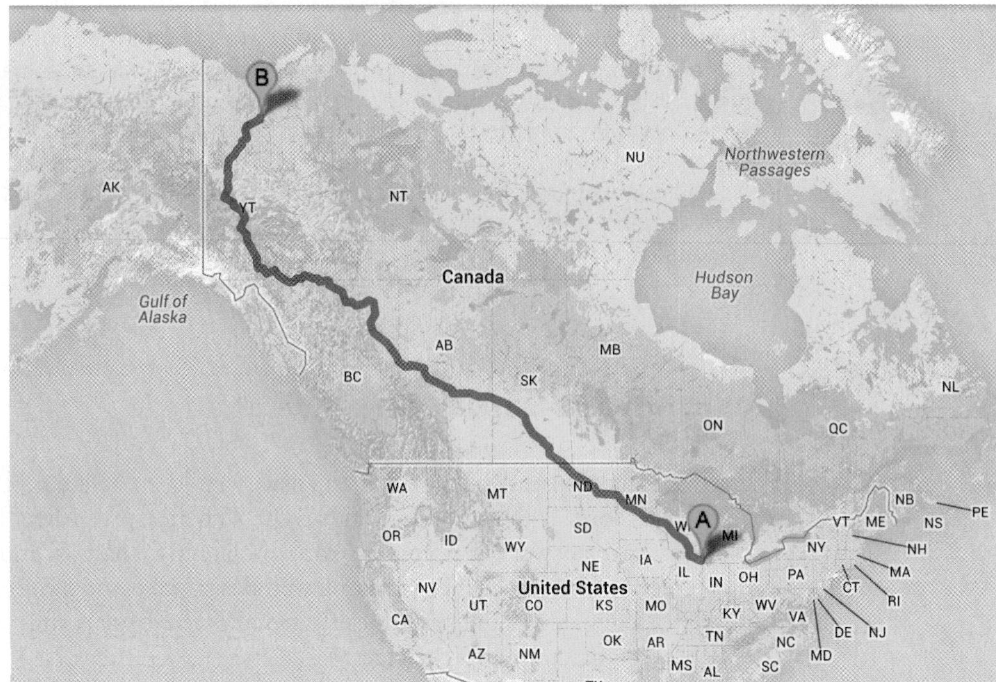

Figure 14.1 Google map directions for a trip from Chicago, Illinois (pin A), to Fort McPherson, Northwest Territories (pin B).

Design Guidelines

We adopt two basic principles for setting up effective spreadsheets:

Focus on Form: *Make the form logical, the layout clean, and the entries clear and easy to use.*

Because a spreadsheet is for people to use in solving problems and not for a computer, it must be easy to understand and easy to work with. This makes the form of the presentation of data key. Arrange the data logically, which for English speakers generally means the following:

- Descriptive information should be on the top and left sides
- Summary information should be on the bottom and right sides

Fonts should be clear, possibly different for headings and data. Colors—for both font and fill—should be used in moderation, so that they attract attention to the important aspects of the sheet but aren't a distraction. Use a separate sheet for each table—multiple sheets don't cost more and individual sheets make working with multiple tables more manageable. Hiding information that isn't needed in the current context is also a good way to make a spreadsheet clear and easy to use.

Explain Everything: *It should be possible to know immediately what every cell means.*

Initially, the rule implies that we say where the data comes from, and include meaningful column headings and identifying information about the rows. Cells and ranges are assigned symbolic names (explained later) so the content can be referenced directly without also specifying its position. For summary information cells, choose modifiers like *total* and *largest*. For computations, include comments with the cells explaining the assumptions made when creating the formulas.

Not only are these useful principles for spreadsheets, but also they apply generally to Web page design and many other IT applications. Throughout this chapter, there will be many opportunities to apply these rules.

At the Top of Its Game. Spreadsheets are extremely powerful. Theoretically, they are as powerful as any programming language, but they are much more intuitive to use. As proof that spreadsheets are up to any task, a Canadian accountant named Cary Walkin wrote a video game using a spreadsheet! See it at http://carywalkin.ca/2013/03/17/arena-xlsm-released/.

Initial Spreadsheet: Applying the Rules

Pat and Alex are trying to figure out how much time and money the trip will cost, so it seems as though they could pull together a spreadsheet to compute the answer and then throw it away. But because it turns out that the trip is too expensive for just the two of them, they will need to find others to join them. Thus, they will keep revising the spreadsheet and showing it to others as part of an effort to encourage participation. Accordingly, they should concentrate on applying the design rules to make the spreadsheet flexible, credible, and self-explanatory.

Applying the rules is straightforward. The data they have is for a five-day trek from Chicago to Dawson, Yukon Territory. From there, they will drive to the Arctic Circle and back to Dawson that night, where they expect to celebrate in the town's renovated 1890's Gold Rush saloons. Using online mapping software, they formulate the following segments:

Chicago to Carrington, ND:	778 miles	12 hours, 2 minutes
Carrington to Battleford, SK:	620 miles	11 hours, 6 minutes
Battleford to Fort St. John, BC:	648 miles	11 hours, 26 minutes
Fort St. John to Watson Lake, YK:	555 miles	11 hours, 17 minutes
Watson Lake to Dawson, YK:	601 miles	11 hours, 55 minutes
Round-trip Dawson to Arctic Circle:	484 miles	14 hours

The friends are interested in how much the trip will cost, so they add a column for fuel costs, which they find on the Web (www.gasbuddy.com). Part of the trip is through the United States, of course, where gas is priced by the gallon in U.S. dollars, and part of the trip is through Canada, where petrol (gas) is priced by the liter in Canadian dollars, so the spreadsheet lists where the price estimate comes from, as shown in Figure 14.2.

The principle of "focus on form" is evident in a variety of places. The spreadsheet in Figure 14.2 has a title listing the authors and stating the completion date. Columns are

Trip to the Arctic Circle
by Pat and Alex (Completed 23.June) "Let's Go!!"

Segment	Time Est.	Miles	Fuel Price Report	Fuel Price
Chicago to Carrington ND	12:02	778	US Chicago	$4.15
Carrington to Battleford SK	11:06	620	US Carrington ND	$3.65
Battleford to Fort St. John BC	11:26	648	CA Battleford SK	$1.27
Fort St. John to Watson Lake YT	11:17	555	CA Medicine Hat AB	$1.16
Watson Lake to Dawson YT	11:55	601	CA Fort Nelson BC	$1.57
Dawson to Dawson via AC	14:00	484	CA Yellowknife NT	$1.39

Figure 14.2 Initial spreadsheet for the Arctic Circle road trip.

assigned clear headings. The heading row is filled with a soft color that separates it from the content, which is preferable to intense colors that can distract. A clean, sans serif font presents the data justified in the cells, so the columns align and give a clean, neat appearance.

The principle of "explain everything" is illustrated by four comments, which explain the data sources. Comments are like sticky notes that can be added to cells. Their presence is denoted by the red triangle in the cell's upper right corner (see the headings in Figure 14.2). Hovering the cursor over the cell displays the comment.

Time Est.	M	Fuel Price
12:02		$4.15
11:06	620 US Carrington ND	$3.65

Alex & Pat: US prices in gallons CA prices in liters; each in local currency.

To insert a comment in Excel, select the cell and then navigate *Insert* > *New Comment* [*Review*]. The author's name is automatically placed at the beginning of the comment. To edit it, select the cell and navigate *Insert* > *Edit Comment*. To remove a comment, find it as an option for *Clear*, that is, navigate *Edit* > *Clear* > *Comments* [*Review* > *Delete*].

These two design principles will be exhibited throughout the remainder of the spreadsheet development.

14.1 Getting Gas. In the United States gas is priced in gallons and in Canada it is priced in liters. Referring to Figure 14.2, is the fuel in Medicine Hat, Alberta, cheaper or more expensive than gas in Chicago, Illinois, if the currencies are at par? (Hint: There are 3.78 liters in a gallon.)

Conditional Formatting

Another technique to make a spreadsheet more effective is to conditionally format the cells. In Chapter 13 you saw conditional formatting for calculating loan payments, where monthly payments within the budget were displayed in green and payments exceeding the budget were displayed in red. **Conditional formatting** allows us to *apply an interpretation to the data*—payments are within budget, payments are over budget—and express that interpretation in an easily perceived manner.

Cell Value Is Specifications

The Arctic Circle road trip spreadsheet has a variety of opportunities to use conditional formatting to help the friends understand the data. One observation about the trip is that there is considerable variance in how long they must travel on each segment; some days are much longer than others. To emphasize the long days, Pat and Alex decide to apply conditional formatting to the Time Estimate column: Any segment where the number of hours of driving is above average is interpreted as "long" and will be displayed in bold. They select the Time Estimate entries, and choose *Format* > *Conditional*

Formatting. . . [*Home*] to arrive at a dialog box (possibly of a different form) where they specify the following information.

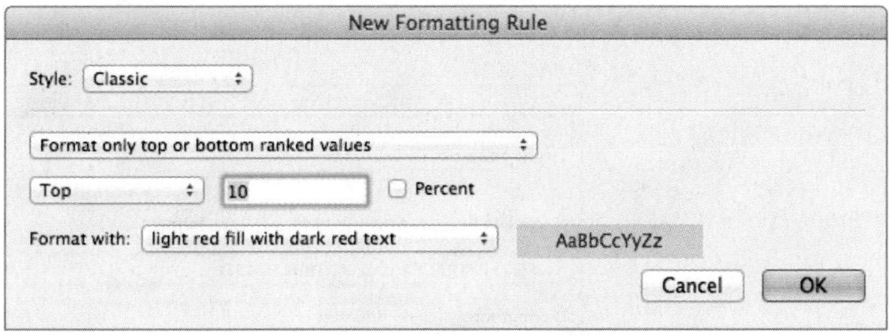

New Formatting Rule

Style: Classic

Format only top or bottom ranked values

Top 10 Percent

Format with: light red fill with dark red text AaBbCcYyZz

Cancel OK

This window lets users specify one or more conditions. If the program finds that these conditions apply to the cell, it formats the entry in the manner specified under *Format*. Users specify the condition by picking one of a set of relationships and filling in the limits. The default options for the Classic style are shown. The travelers edit the form to achieve the "make long days bold" formatting

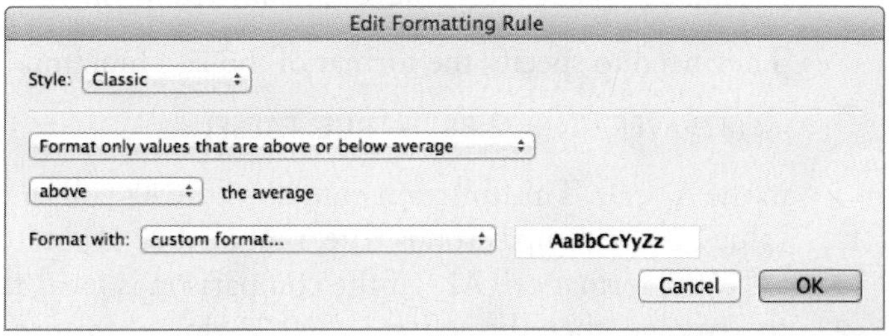

Edit Formatting Rule

Style: Classic

Format only values that are above or below average

above the average

Format with: custom format... **AaBbCcYyZz**

Cancel OK

and click **OK**, creating the result shown in Figure 14.3.

Formula Is Specifications

Although the large drive time *defines* a long segment, it is the travel—the segment—that is causing the long day. The friends want to highlight the information in the first column (A), Segment. It's possible to format those items based on the AVERAGE(B$2,B$7), which computes the average of the Time Estimate column, but there is a problem: The

Trip to the Arctic Circle

by Pat and Alex (Completed 23.June) "Let's Go!!"

Segment	Time Est.	Miles	Fuel Price Report	Fuel Price
Chicago to Carrington ND	**12:02**	778	US Chicago	$4.15
Carrington to Battleford SK	11:06	620	US Carrington ND	$3.65
Battleford to Fort St. John BC	11:26	648	CA Battleford SK	$1.27
Fort St. John to Watson Lake YT	11:17	555	CA Medicine Hat AB	$1.16
Watson Lake to Dawson YT	11:55	601	CA Fort Nelson BC	$1.57
Dawson to Dawson via AC	**14:00**	484	CA Yellowknife NT	$1.39

Figure 14.3 Arctic Circle road trip spreadsheet with conditional formatting for "long days."

value that must be compared to the average is B2, not A2. That is, in the Conditional Formatting window [*Home > Conditional Formatting > Highlight > More Rules . . .*], the friends must choose *Use a formula to determine which cells to format*.

Edit Formatting Rule

Style: Classic

Use a formula to determine which cells to format

=IF(B2>AVERAGE(B$2:B$7), TRUE, FALSE)

Format with: custom format... AaBbCcYyZz

Cancel OK

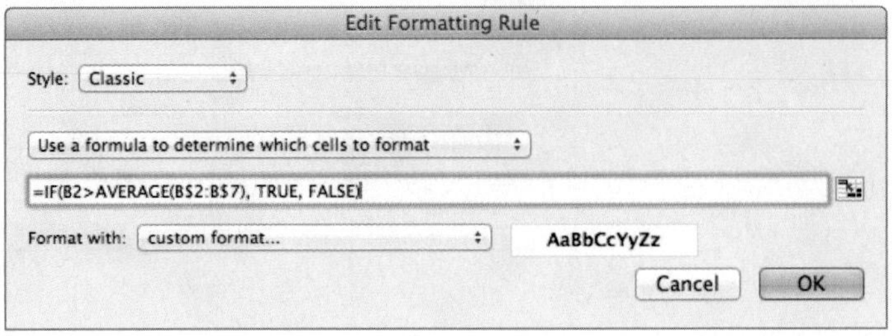

The friends need a formula that is true when the entry is to be formatted and false otherwise. The function they use to decide this condition is the IF( ) function, which has this general specification:

```
IF(condition, action_on_true_outcome, action_on_false_outcome)
```

They need to specify the format of the IF( ) function for the A2 cell, so they place

```
=IF(B2>AVERAGE(B$2:B$7), TRUE, FALSE)
```

in the A2 cell. This function compares the B2 cell to the average of the Time Estimate values; if the comparison is true, that is, if B2 is greater than the average, then the action is "TRUE, format cell A2"; if the comparison is false, that is, if B2 is less than or equal to the average, then the action is "FALSE, do not format cell A2."

To implement highlighting the Segment, the friends clear the conditional formatting of the Time Estimate column, select the Segment entries of column A, and enter the formula. The result is shown in Figure 14.4.

Distinguish Between the United States and Canada

Figure 14.5 illustrates one more instance of conditional formatting: The prices in the Fuel Price column given in Canadian dollars are italicized. Like the Segment formatting just considered, the Fuel Price formatting requires an IF( ) function in a formula. The complication, however, is determining when a price is in Canadian dollars, because it's not possible to determine that from the amount in the cell. However, the Fuel Price

Trip to the Arctic Circle

by Pat and Alex (Completed 23.June) "Let's Go!!"

Segment	Time Est.	Miles	Fuel Price Report	Fuel Price
Chicago to Carrington ND	12:02	778	US Chicago	$4.15
Carrington to Battleford SK	11:06	620	US Carrington ND	$3.65
Battleford to Fort St. John BC	11:26	648	CA Battleford SK	$1.27
Fort St. John to Watson Lake YT	11:17	555	CA Medicine Hat AB	$1.16
Watson Lake to Dawson YT	11:55	601	CA Fort Nelson BC	$1.57
Dawson to Dawson via AC	14:00	484	CA Yellowknife NT	$1.39

Figure 14.4 Conditional formatting to highlight trip Segments, whose Time Estimate is greater than average.

Report column has the property that it lists the source of the price quote in the first two letters of the cell, so whenever the country is CA, the price should be italicized.

To access letters of a cell value for such comparisons, the LEFT( ) function is provided, which has the specification

LEFT(text_value, num_chars)

This function "removes" from the left end of the letter sequence (text_value) the number of characters (num_chars) specified; of course, there is also a similar RIGHT( ) function. For the text_value the friends use D2, the Fuel Price Report; for the second parameter, they use 2. So, to do the match requires the formula

LEFT(D2, 2)="CA"

as the condition for the IF( ) function. Note that quotes are required around CA because it must be treated as a letter string. In words, the expression says, "Take the first two characters from the left end of the text in cell D2 and compare them to the letters "CA"." Placing the expression in an IF( ) function as the condition

=IF(LEFT(D2, 2)="CA", TRUE, FALSE)

produces the formatting decision: If the text and the string are equal, then format the cell—because the fuel price estimate is in Canadian dollars; if they are not equal (false), do not format the cell. So, to italicize the entries, the friends select the Fuel Price entries, click on *Conditional Formatting...*,

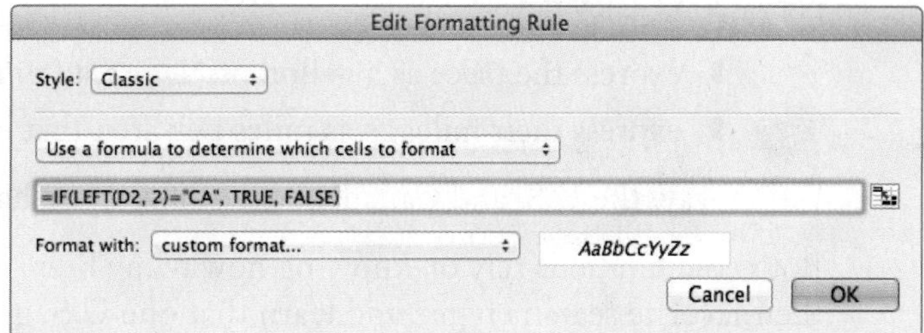

enter the IF( ) function into the formula window, and click **OK**, which yields the result shown in Figure 14.5. Notice that there was no change in formatting of the first two entries of Fuel Price because the first two letters in column D were not "CA" and so their formatting wasn't changed.

Finally, they add a comment to Segment explaining that highlighting means the estimated driving time is above average, and a comment to Fuel Price explaining that italic means the price is given in Canadian dollars for a liter of petrol.

Conditional Formulas

In the same way that the friends used an IF( ) function to change the formatting in response to certain conditions, they can make the entire computation of a cell contingent on the outcome of a condition using **conditional formulas**. This is essential for Pat and Alex, because they are using fuel measured in gallons and liters, and money measured in U.S. dollars and Canadian dollars. Figuring how much a tank of fuel costs requires precision. In this section, we explain how spreadsheets can compute conditional formulas and show how to use this capability to figure out the cost of each segment of the trip. The new column will be called Amount Paid. Before considering how to compute it, let's figure out exactly what the friends need to do.

Figuring the Amount Paid

First, we need to know how far the car typically travels on a unit of fuel, that is, its average mileage. Most drivers have some idea of the mileage they get, and Alex's old Subaru averages 22 miles per gallon (mpg). So, they figure the cost of the fuel as

*cost = price * distance/mpg*

and add a comment to the Amount Paid column stating that the assumed mpg is 22.

The distances listed in the spreadsheet are in miles because they were reported that way by the mapping software (used from the United States). If some distances were in miles and others in kilometers, the friends would have to convert one format to the other. Happily, that's not necessary.

Conversion to Miles per Liter. The friends do have to convert between liters and gallons. To compute the fuel cost, they will divide the distance by the mileage the Subaru gets, which gives the amount of fuel they need for each segment. Then they will multiply that number by the fuel price in that area. Because the mileage is known in "miles per gallon," they have a choice:

- express the price as a gallon price instead of a liter price, or
- express their mileage as miles per liter, that is, mpl.

Either way, the U.S. and Canadian cases have to be handled slightly differently.

Both computations rely on knowing how many liters are in a gallon, so the friends check their favorite search engine and learn that one U.S. gallon equals 3.788 liters. Choosing the second option, they compute

mpl = mpg/3.788

which for the Subaru's *mpg* = 22, makes *mpl* = 5.8.

Applying Two Cases, Conditionally. So, for cases where the two travelers know the price in gallons, they multiply it times distance/mpg; when they know the price in liters, they multiply it times distance/mpl. Obviously, this is a job for the IF( ) function. Like the previous conditional formatting example, the friends will test on the first two letters of the Fuel Price Report field. If the data is from the United States, they use the first computation, otherwise they use the second. The appropriate equation is

```
=IF(LEFT(D2,2)="US", E2*C2/22, E2*C2/5.8)
```

Notice that unlike before, this formula compares to "US". The result is an estimate of the total of the amounts paid for the fuel purchased for each segment, assuming the price of fuel is the average price of the location listed and the vehicle's mileage is 22 mpg. These assumptions are recorded in a comment. The entry is U.S. dollars in the United States and Canadian dollars in Canada, so the friends format Amount Paid with italics, as before. These results are shown in Figure 14.5.

Trip to the Arctic Circle
by Pat and Alex (Completed 23.June) "Let's Go!!"

Segment	Miles	Fuel Price Report	Fuel Price	Amount Paid
Chicago to Carrington ND	778	US Chicago	$4.15	$146.76
Carrington to Battleford SK	620	US Carrington ND	$3.65	$102.86
Battleford to Fort St. John BC	648	CA Battleford SK	*$1.27*	*$141.89*
Fort St. John to Watson Lake YT	555	CA Medicine Hat AB	*$1.16*	*$111.00*
Watson Lake to Dawson YT	601	CA Fort Nelson BC	*$1.57*	*$162.68*
Dawson to Dawson via AC	484	CA Yellowknife NT	*$1.39*	*$115.99*

Figure 14.5 Arctic Circle road trip spreadsheet with the Amount Paid column added. Notice that the Time Estimate column has been hidden, and that a comment noting the assumption of 22 mpg has been added to the Amount Paid heading.

Cost in One Currency

We give one more illustration of conditional formulas. For the friends to know the total cost estimate for their trip, it is essential to know the expenditures in one currency. Being Americans, they choose U.S. dollars. Therefore, they add a column, Cost. It will contain a copy of the Amount Paid cell when it's reported in U.S. dollars, and it will contain the U.S. dollar equivalent when the Amount Paid is reported in Canadian dollars. The computation uses the same ideas described earlier and will again use the IF( ) function.

Checking on the Web, Pat finds the exchange rate for Canadian currency to U.S.; it states that a Canadian dollar is worth $0.948 in U.S. dollars. Therefore, for each spreadsheet price given in Canadian dollars, they simply multiply the price times $0.948 to get the price in U.S. dollars.

Developing the IF( ) function needed for the Cost column (column G), they test column D as usual to determine if the price is in U.S. or Canadian dollars. The test for G2 is LEFT(D2,2)="CA". If it is Canadian, then they want F2*0.948, and if it is not, then they simply want F2, because it is already in U.S. dollars. The whole expression,

```
=IF(LEFT(D2,2)="CA", F2*0.948, F2)
```

results in an amount expressed in U.S. dollars. They fill the computation down the column and inspect to see that italicized amounts become slightly smaller in the Cost column.

14.2 Currency Exchange. Suppose the formula that corrects for currency differences were written =IF(LEFT(D2,2)="US", x, y). What must be entered for x and y to compute the same thing?

Finally, the friends enter the data for the return trip by the same route—not their first choice, but maybe the quickest and cheapest way home. After doing so, they add a SUM( ) function to compute the total cost of the trip. The result is shown in Figure 14.6.

Trip to the Arctic Circle
by Pat and Alex (Completed 23.June) "Let's Go!!"

Segment	Miles	Fuel Price Report	Fuel Price	Amount Paid	Cost
Chicago to Carrington ND	778	US Chicago	$4.15	$146.76	$146.76
Carrington to Battleford SK	620	US Carrington ND	$3.65	$102.86	$102.86
Battleford to Fort St. John BC	648	CA Battleford SK	*$1.27*	*$141.89*	$134.51
Fort St. John to Watson Lake YT	555	CA Medicine Hat AB	*$1.16*	*$111.00*	$105.23
Watson Lake to Dawson YT	601	CA Fort Nelson BC	*$1.57*	*$162.68*	$154.22
Dawson to Dawson via AC	484	CA Yellowknife NT	*$1.39*	*$115.99*	$109.96
Dawson to Watson Lake YT	601	CA Fort Nelson BC	*$1.57*	*$162.68*	$154.22
Watson Lake to Fort St. John BC	555	CA Medicine Hat AB	*$1.16*	*$111.00*	$105.23
Fort St. John to Battleford SK	648	CA Battleford SK	*$1.27*	*$141.89*	$134.51
Battleford to Carrington ND	620	US Carrington ND	$3.65	$102.86	$102.86
Carrington to Chicago IL	778	US Chicago	$4.15	$146.76	$146.76
				Total	$1,397.14

Figure 14.6 Arctic Circle road trip spreadsheet completed to the point of producing an estimate for fuel costs.

The friends are surprised that it's so expensive—and they have only accounted for the fuel cost. They still need to eat, they need to sleep somewhere besides in the Subaru, and they need to buy treats and souvenirs. They need a couple of friends to help share the costs!

14.3 Gas Tax. Suppose a gas tax has been levied in Alberta, Canada, that is, the places whose right-most letters are "AB." Define a formula for a `Fuel Surcharge` column in which 10 percent is added to any fuel quotations from Alberta, and all other quotations remain unchanged.

Naming: Symbolic Reference

In their development of conditional formatting and conditional formulas, the friends have referred, as usual, to B2, D2, E2, and so on. But this could lead to problems later on. Suppose they insert a column in the spreadsheet. Will the references adjust? Certainly, the earlier *comment* referring to column D will not adjust, thwarting their effort to make the spreadsheet clear. Additionally, they have embedded some assumptions—gas mileage, currency exchange rate—into the formulas. These quantities can change: Exchange rates change by the minute, and they might find another car with better gas mileage to drive. The spreadsheet has become too dependent on the specific positions and data used at the moment. If the goal is to use the spreadsheet repeatedly, it must be more insulated from such changes.

Defining Names

A helpful design methodology is to give names to the components of our spreadsheets. Computer scientists say it is better to refer to cells *symbolically*—that is, by name—than to refer to them *literally*—that is, by their explicit column/row position reference. A *name* is a word or phrase assigned to a cell or range of cells. Once the name has been

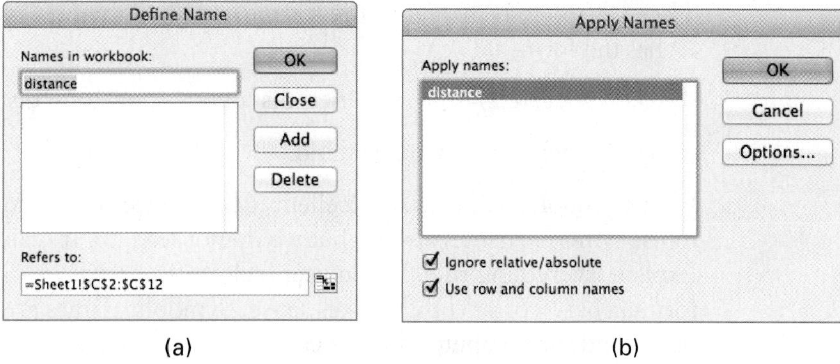

Figure 14.7 Name windows: (a) the Define Name window and (b) the Apply Names window.

assigned, it can be used wherever cell references would normally be used, such as in formulas. Using names reduces the chance of messing up range specifications, and minimizes the likelihood that errors will creep in when columns and rows are added later.

We illustrate this idea by revising the friends' spreadsheet to use names. After choosing *Insert > Name > Define . . .* , [*Formulas > Define Name*] we are presented with the Define Name window, shown in Figure 14.7(a). The range is automatically filled in for us based on our selection prior to choosing the command. Enter a name—it generally cannot contain spaces—and the software assigns the name to that range of cells. But this action has only *defined* a name; it is so far unused. Now, choosing *Insert > Name > Apply* [*Formulas > Define Name > Apply Names*] allows us to use the name, as shown in Figure 14.7(b). Clicking **OK** tells the software to look through the formulas, and wherever it finds a reference for the cells bound to a selected name—that is, in the range C2:C12 in this example—the symbolic name replaces the literal position in the formula.

Notice that we have chosen to name the column headed Miles with the range name of distance, because that is a somewhat better description. The point is that names are separate from the labels that we assign, though often we use the same word.

Applying Names

After clicking **OK** in the Apply Names dialog, the name distance is applied to the spreadsheet formulas. We can look at cells, for example F2, in which we have used the distance value, C2. We see the entry

```
=IF(LEFT(D2,2)="US", E2*distance/22,E2*distance/5.8)
```

in the formula bar, indicating that the name has been applied to this formula. In addition to being safer, it is easier to read and understand the formula when symbolic names are used.

To see how we could apply this idea to other parts of the spreadsheet, let's define some more symbolic names. We choose

```
priceSrc    D2:D12
fuelPrice   E2:E12
amtPaid     F2:F12
cost        G2:G12
```

Then we apply the names to the formulas. When the process is complete, the formula in F2 has the form

```
=IF(LEFT(priceSrc,2)="US", fuelPrice*distance/22,fuelPrice*distance/5.8)
```

which is much easier to understand.

Using symbolic names is an excellent idea, and we could adopt a design rule that says to use symbolic names always, but we do not have to. It is already implied by the earlier Explain Everything rule. When users select cell F2, for example, they should see in the formula bar a formula that makes sense. Symbolic names are easier for people to understand (and the computer doesn't care).

Make Assumptions Explicit

We haven't *completely* applied the idea of naming all of the quantities in the spreadsheet. The 22 (mpg) and 5.8 (mpl) are not constants of the universe like π; they are instance-specific quantities that our computation depends upon. We should make them symbolic, too.

The difference between the ranges we have named so far and these parameters to the formulas is that the latter do not correspond to cells. But, by assigning their values to cells and giving them names, they can be used to explore travel alternatives, as you will see in the next section.

Pat and Alex have established an area below the Segments entries where they listed their assumptions. They identified the three parameters used so far: mileage in gallons, mileage in liters, and exchange rate. An additional assumption, the number of travelers, doesn't show up in any formula, but they are pretty sure that the number of travelers will change, so they decide to add a cell for that number, too. Their assumptions area has the form

Assumptions	
Miles per gallon	22
Miles per liter	5.81
US-Canadian Exch Rate	0.948
Travelers	2

The friends assign names to the values to make it easier to replace in the formulas. The names are mpg, mpl, xchRate, and buddies. The mpl value is computed using the formula

```
=mpg/3.788
```

implying that it is dependent on mpg. (Because 5.81 is greater than 5.80 used previously, there will be a tiny difference in their fuel bill.)

14.4 Better Mileage. At 22 mpg, a liter of fuel carries the car 5.81 miles. At 25 mpg, how far can it go on a liter?

Finally, the constants used in the Amount Paid formula must be changed manually. We cannot use the *Insert > Name > Apply...* command, because the reference in the formula is to 22, not to a cell containing 22. So, we manually replace 22 by mpg in the formula bar, and fill the new formula into the other cells of the column. Of course, mpl and xchRate must also be changed manually as well. The modifications are visible in F2, which completes the naming.

```
=IF(LEFT(priceSrc,2)="US", fuelPrice*distance/mpg,fuelPrice*distance/mpl)
```

Once we name the bottom line fuelCost, we have revised the spreadsheet to name the relevant cells and ranges, an improvement that has taken a few minutes. If the names had been introduced as the entries were being developed, which is the way they should be used, the cost of using them would have been unnoticed.

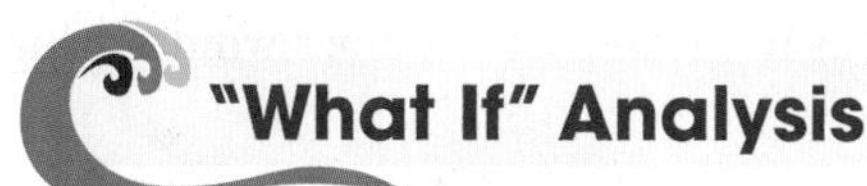

"What If" Analysis

Pat and Alex are a little surprised that driving to the Arctic Circle and back is going to cost them roughly $1,400 for fuel alone. They will need to find some travel companions to share the cost, but before doing that they need a better idea of what the whole trip will cost, and whether there are ways to control costs. Because spreadsheets recalculate everything whenever a number is changed, they are ideal for speculating on the consequences of change. Make a change, and notice what happens to the "bottom line."

Direct Experimentation

With their present spreadsheet, Pat and Alex can do some of this speculative analysis directly. It involves changing cells, looking to see what happens, and then undoing the change. It's cumbersome, but it's quick. (It's also smart to save the file before speculating.) They wonder about the following:

- The Subaru could be tuned up to get 25 mpg. How would that affect fuel costs?
- With more people and therefore more weight in the vehicle, maybe 22 mpg is too high. What is the effect of 20 mpg?
- A friend with a 30 mpg vehicle offered to drive; how would that change fuel costs?

By changing mpg, the friends discover that these assumptions change fuel costs to be $1,228, $1,536, and $1,024, respectively. Obviously, the cost of the trip is very sensitive to the efficiency of the vehicle. Using the same technique, they also discover that the trip is not very sensitive to the currency exchange rate, at least not within the range in which it is likely to fluctuate. So, waiting for the U.S. dollar to strengthen against the Canadian dollar won't help much.

The problem with experimenting directly with the spreadsheet is that it risks making permanent changes to the data and formulas that have been so carefully entered. Fortunately, there is a better way to experiment with a spreadsheet.

Scenarios

The speculative or **"what if" analysis** that the friends just performed is nicely supported in spreadsheet software by a tool called Scenarios. A **scenario** is a named alternative to a spreadsheet based on different inputs. A scenario is an aid to understanding changes in plans, like changes in gas mileage. And, it's safer than just changing entries. Let's see how the friends can use a scenario.

Tune-Up Scenario. Selecting the mpg cell, because we are exploring alternatives to the current mileage of 22, we navigate *Tools* > *Scenarios. . .* [*Data* > *What-If Analysis*] and arrive at the Scenario Manager window, as shown in Figure 14.8(a). This window is the principal interface to the Scenario facility: It is where we define new scenarios, edit them, and request summaries. Initially, there are no scenarios defined, of course, so we click **Add. . .** .

The Add Scenario window (Figure 14.8(b)) is the place to name a scenario. In addition, the software fills in the cell(s) that will change, and a comment as to who created it and when the scenario was defined. Clicking **OK** takes us to the Scenario Values window (Figure 14.8(c)),

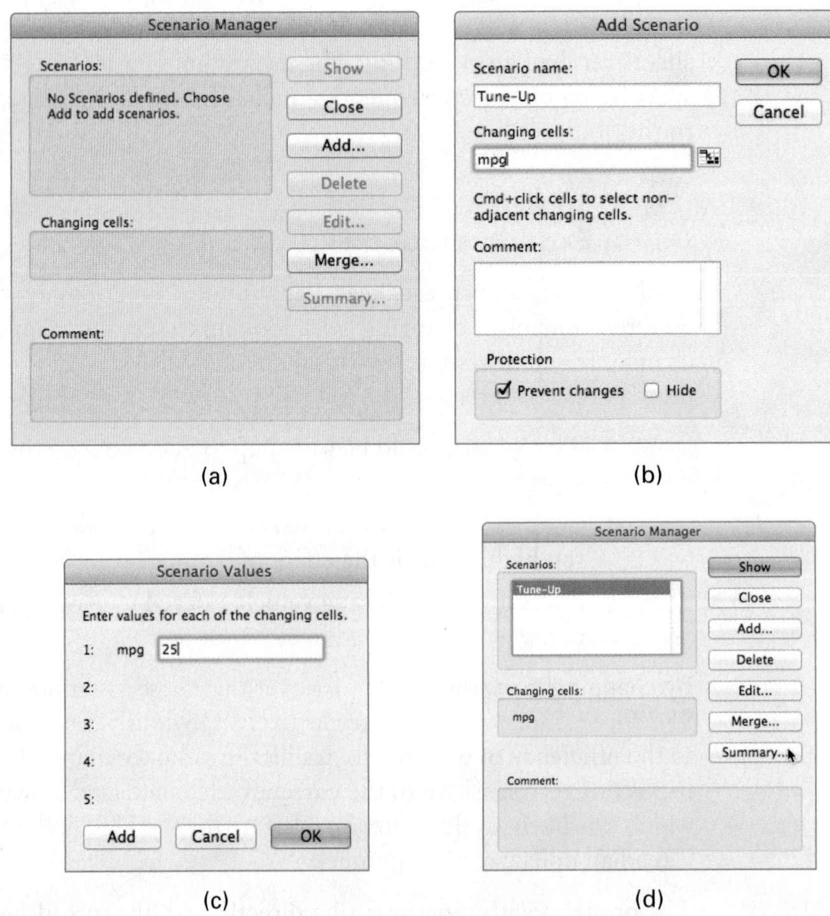

Figure 14.8 Dialog box sequence for adding a scenario to the Arctic Circle road trip spreadsheet: (a) Scenario Manager window, (b) an added scenario for a tune-up, (c) setting a "What if" value, and (d) requesting a summary report.

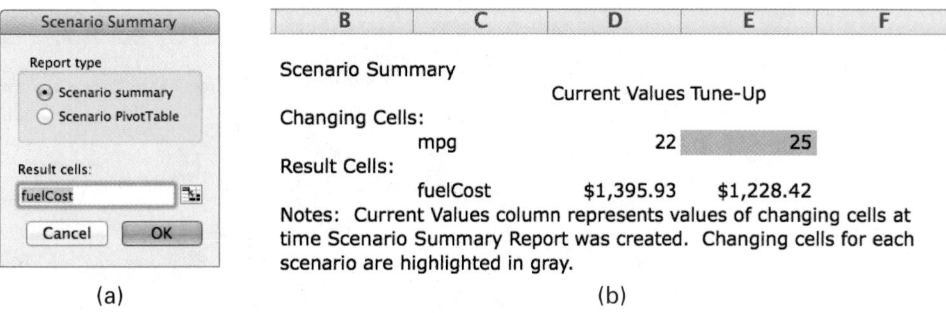

Figure 14.9 The Scenario Summary sheet showing the result of the Tune-Up scenario.

where we enter the alternative value for mpg. Notice that the symbolic name is used for the field, now that we have named the cells. Clicking **OK** takes us back to the Scenario Manager window (Figure 14.8(d)), where the newly added scenario can be seen in the list. We have created a scenario and archived it.

Having taken some effort to define the scenario, we can run it. Notice at the bottom of the Scenario Manager window (Figure 14.8(d)), there is a **Summary…** button. When we click it, a dialog box appears asking what cell we consider the "bottom line" of the computation. That is, supposing the scenario came to pass, what value are we most interested in? The software predicted that G14, which is our fuelCost, is the summary information we want to know about. We click **OK**, and are presented with the Scenario Summary sheet shown in Figure 14.9. The sheet nicely summarizes the base case (Current Values column) and the "bottom line" of our Tune-Up scenario. (The analysis implies that a tune-up would be beneficial if it were cheap enough, though it's probably a good idea to tune up a car before any long trip!)

The time required for the Tune-Up scenario setup may not seem like it is worthwhile, compared to simply changing the mpg cell and looking to see what happens. But, the benefits are coming.

14.5 Worth the Money? Although a tune-up might be smart, it could cost more than it was worth in fuel savings. Where is the breakeven point?

Traveling Companions Scenario. Because Pat and Alex want to consider the advantages of taking along one or more friends, they add, below their fuelCost cell, another cell with the cost per person, as in

Total	$1,395.93
Cost Each	$697.96

which is implemented by the formula =fuelCost/buddies. They name the per person fuel cost cell fuelPP. Then, they construct another pair of scenarios.

The xtraPassenger scenario follows the same protocol used for the Tune-Up scenario. Figure 14.10 shows the key steps. Notice first that in the Add Scenario window, Figure 14.10(a), two fields are specified as varying: mpg and buddies. Having two fields changing

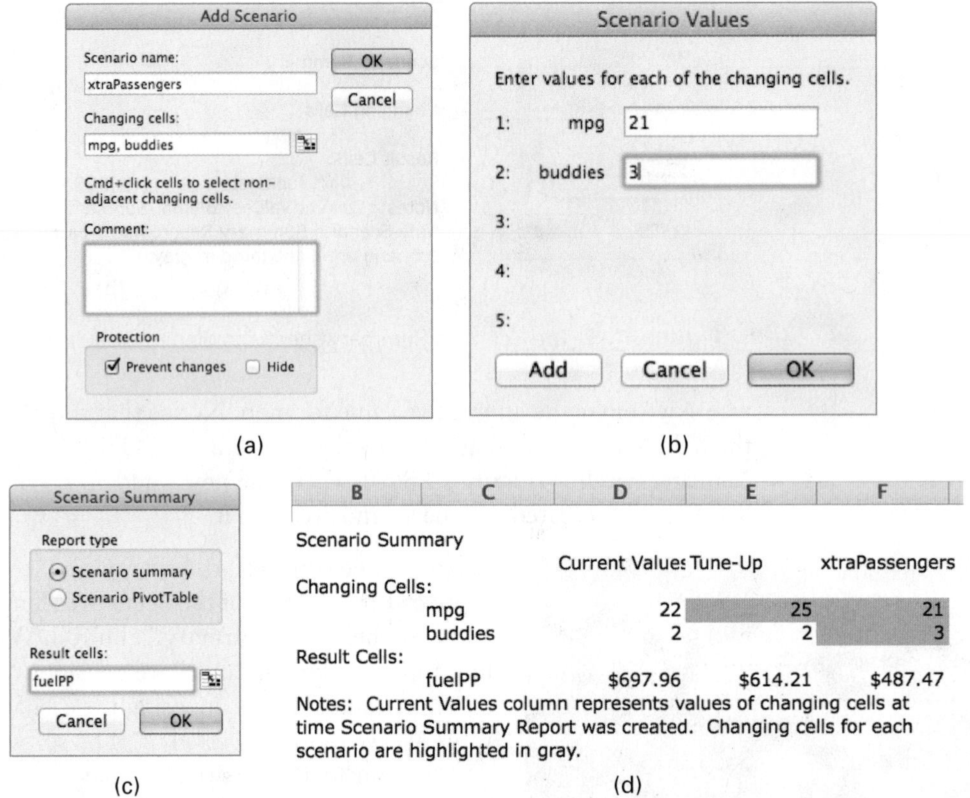

Figure 14.10 The xtraPassengers scenario and the effect on FuelPP.

means that in the Scenario Values window (Figure 14.10(b)), both values are listed with value fields. They set buddies to 3 and drop mpg to 21 because of the extra weight. Then, in the Scenario Summary window, Figure 14.10(c), they specify the fuelPP cell as the one they are most interested in. Finally, in the Scenario Summary sheet, Figure 14.10(d), the new scenario is presented with the earlier scenario and the base case. As expected, having another person along helps with costs, even if it harms the mileage a bit.

Obviously, a High Mileage scenario would be developed in the same way.

14.6 Heavy. The friends assumed that with an extra person in the car the mileage would drop a little, from 22 to 21, but there would be an extra person paying for fuel. How much did the extra person increase the fuel cost?

Analyzing a Model

The travelers have a good estimate of the fuel costs for their trip and the cost benefits of taking others along. But how much will the trip actually cost? To answer the question, they build a model that accounts for all of the foreseeable costs of the trip, and how these combine with fuel costs to produce the bottom line expense for going to the Arctic Circle. Here's what they do.

Trip to the Arctic Circle
by Pat and Alex (Completed 23.June) "Let's Go!!"

Lodging	Occp	Price	Lodging Expense
Campground	2	$28.00	$28.00
Provincial Park	2	$25.00	$25.00
Provincial Park	2	$25.00	$25.00
Wilderness	2	$0.00	$0.00
Hostel @ 22	2	$22.00	$44.00
Hostel @ 22	2	$22.00	$44.00
Wilderness	2	$0.00	$0.00
Provincial Park	2	$25.00	$25.00
Provincial Park	2	$25.00	$25.00
Campground	2	$28.00	$28.00
Total			$244.00
Total PP			$122.00

Trip to the Arctic Circle
by Pat and Alex (Completed 23.June) "Let's Go!!"

Extras	Cost
Contingency	$100.00
Tires	$180.00
Total	$280.00
Total PP	$140.00

Figure 14.11 The lodging and contingency data for the Arctic Circle road trip spreadsheet.

Formulating a Model. To start, they think a little more about the costs. To save lodging expenses, they decide to camp, which makes sense because they are headed into the wilderness and they own camping equipment. A few moments on the Web reveals that they can camp at public campgrounds, provincial parks, and, once they are in the wilderness, the wilderness itself. On the next page of their spreadsheet, they click together another table, shown in Figure 14.11.

In the Lodging table, there is an entry for each night the travelers spend on the road, saying where they are staying and how many people are covered by the `Price`. They will stay in a hostel in Dawson on the night they arrive and the next night, and because the price is given "per bed," the occupancy is listed as 1. In the other cases, it is listed as `buddies`. The lodging expense entries are computed as

```
=price*buddies/occupancy
```

which yields the total lodging expense, `lodgingPP`, when summed at the end of the column. Each person's share is found by dividing by `buddies`.

Regarding contingencies, `continPP`, there are tolls and probably an oil change at some point, but they decide that although "stuff happens," it will only total about $100. There is concern about the tread on the rear tires of the Subaru, and they decide to budget some new tires if needed. They compute the total of the entries and divide by `buddies`.

The Model. Finally, with more complete data available, the friends make one more table.

Trip to the Arctic Circle
by Pat and Alex (Completed 23.June) "Let's Go!!"

Expenses	Amt PP
Fuel	$697.96
Lodging	$122.00
Contingencies	$140.00
Total Est Cost	$959.96

This table summarizes the per person expenses of the spreadsheet. This is their model: It shows fuelPP, lodgingPP, and continPP subcomputations, and computes the grand total, called estTotal. It doesn't contain a food charge, because the friends decide that they would eat even if they stayed at home, so food isn't a direct cost of the trip.

Reusing Scenarios. Having set up the scenarios earlier, it's possible to rerun them to see how the total cost changes as the number of travelers increases. They navigate to the Scenario Manager and click **Summary. . .** again. When the Scenario Summary window appears, they change the "bottom line" to the estTotal cell, which is the one that matters now.

After clicking **OK**, they get the following report summarizing the model.

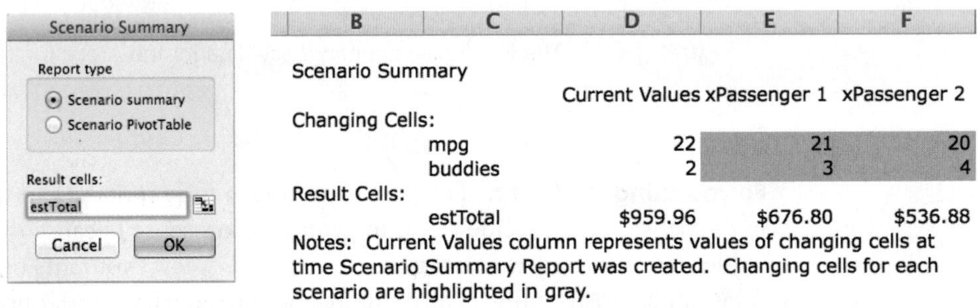

The model predicts the expenses to the extent that the estimates are correct. It is very convenient.

A Change in Plans. Pat and Alex quickly find the first friend interested in the Arctic Circle trip, provided they buy new tires before they leave. The next person they speak to is concerned about camping in places populated by bears, and prefers to stay at hostels. It's silly to stop at a hostel each night, drop off the friend, and then continue on to the campground. So they decide to run another scenario to see how staying in hostels would change the cost of the trip.

The Hostel Upgrade scenario requires a new field, camping.

Assumptions	
Miles per gallon	22
Miles per liter	5.81
US-Canadian Exch Rate	0.948
Travelers	2
Camping	Yes

This Yes/No field controls the occupancy of the Lodging table. That is, the occupancy data, which was previously defined to be the number of people who would stay in the campsite (buddies), becomes

=IF(camping="Yes", buddies, 1)

This formula specifies that everyone either stays in the campsite (Yes) or has a bed at the hostel (No). They add a comment describing the field's meaning.

Pat and Alex click to the Scenario Manager and request **Add. . .** to define a new scenario. This time the scenario must consider the effect of changing a whole range of values, the Price values; when the travelers are camping (Yes), the original data is correct,

B	C	D	E	F	G
Scenario Summary					
		Current Values	xPassenger 1	xPassenger 2	Hostel Upgrade
Changing Cells:					
	mpg	22	21	20	20
	buddies	2	3	4	4
	$J$2	$28.00	$28.00	$28.00	$22.00
	$J$3	$25.00	$25.00	$25.00	$22.00
	$J$4	$25.00	$25.00	$25.00	$22.00
	$J$5	$0.00	$0.00	$0.00	$22.00
	$J$6	$22.00	$22.00	$22.00	$22.00
	$J$7	$22.00	$22.00	$22.00	$22.00
	$J$8	$0.00	$0.00	$0.00	$22.00
	$J$9	$25.00	$25.00	$25.00	$22.00
	$J$10	$25.00	$25.00	$25.00	$22.00
	$J$11	$28.00	$28.00	$28.00	$22.00
	camping	Yes	Yes	Yes	No
Result Cells:					
	estTotal	$959.96	$676.80	$536.88	$673.88

Notes: Current Values column represents values of changing cells at time Scenario Summary Report was created. Changing cells for each scenario are highlighted in gray.

Figure 14.12 Hostel Upgrade Scenario Summary table for the Arctic Circle road trip spreadsheet.

but when they are not camping (No), the entries must show what a bed at the hostel costs.

When the Add Scenario window appears, they enter a name, Hostel Upgrade, and specify the changing cells' names.

The cells include the mpg and buddies as usual, the Price field of the Lodging table (J2:J11), and camping. Next, the Scenario Values window appears, and they enter their estimate of $22 per night for the hostels—they didn't take the time to find out the exact cost—and the other values, the last of which is No to camping. Clicking **Summary** results in the Scenario Summary table shown in Figure 14.12.

Notice the form of Figure 14.12. The changing values are shown with gray fill, and are presented for each of the scenarios without regard to whether they are part of the scenario. That is, even though the lodging prices didn't change in the extra travelers scenarios, they are displayed, because they changed in some scenario (Hostel Upgrade).

This model could be used to explore alternative scenarios.

Analyzing Data Using Filtering

Pat and Alex, joined by friends Chi and Ali, leave on their epic road trip to the Arctic Circle. With long hours to pass while driving across the Great Plains of central North America, Pat extends the spreadsheet to a new sheet to record entries for their travels (see Figure 14.13). They name the page the Travel Log.

The Travel Log is an example of a long list of entries that are interesting as a group—that's why they are in the list—and also as subgroups. The Filtering tool gives access to subsets of this information. For example, from time to time the friends are interested in seeing only certain entries of their Travel Log record, such as when they have purchased gas.

Road To Arctic Circle and Back: Stops
Pat, Alex, Chi, Ali

When	Seg No	Where	Reason	Buy	$	Amt	Mi	Remark
8/4/14 5:45	1	Ali"s house IL	Last pick-up					We're Off!
8/4/14 6:40	1	Toll Booth IL	Alex Fumbles	All tolls	X	$2.85		
8/4/14 8:05	1	DriveThru Joe IL	Espresso					Only driver
8/4/14 9:00	1	Beloit WI	Gas & Go	Gas	A	$34.50	241	
8/4/14 9:55	1	Madison WI	Snacks					
8/4/14 12:05	1	St. Paul MN	Gas & Go, Eat	Gas	P	$28.95	191	Subway
8/4/14 14:45	1	St. Cloud MN	Stretch/Photo					Pretty Here
8/4/14 15:30	1	Sauk Center MN	Snacks					
8/4/14 16:55	1	Fergus Falls MN	Gas & Go	Gas	P	$29.22	205	
8/4/14 19:45	1	Fargo ND	Photo in ND					Pat's First
8/4/14 20:25	1	Valley City ND	Supper					Junk Food
8/4/14 22:00	1	Carrington ND	Stay Night	Camp	C	$21.45		Great Start
8/5/14 7:25	2	Carrington ND	Gas	Gas	A	$37.42	252	
8/5/14 7:55	2	Sykeston ND	Photo					It's flat
8/5/14 10:05	2	Minot ND	Gas & Go, Snx	Gas	X	$19.64	135	Ice Cream
8/5/14 11:50	2	Portal ND	Photo in CA					Ali, Pat, 1st
8/5/14 12:25	2	Estevan SK	Lunch					
8/5/14 13:55	2	Weyburn SK	Gas & Go, Eat	Gas	A	*$33.82*	151	
8/5/14 15:45	2	Moose Jaw SK	Snacks					I Scream!

Figure 14.13 Start of the Travel Log of the Arctic Circle road trip. Seg No corresponds to a segment of the original plan (Sheet 1), $ refers to who paid a shared expense, and Mi is distance traveled since last fuel.

Auto Filtering Technique

Filtering, as its name implies, selects only certain rows from a list. It applies only to spreadsheet tables that have column headings, as the Travel Log does. Filtering lets users create a customized version of a spreadsheet list that is limited to the rows meeting some criterion. For example, to find out how many times they've stopped for gas, the travelers could look through the record in Figure 14.13 to find all the times and places where they filled up. Or they could filter the list, which is much easier.

The easiest form of filtering, called *AutoFilter*, is trivial to apply. Select any cell in the list, then choose *Data* > *Filter*. The result will be a redrawn spreadsheet list with triangle menu buttons by each column heading.

Road To Arctic Circle and Back: Stops
Pat, Alex, Chi, Ali

When	Seg No	Where	Reason	Buy	$	Amt	Mi	Remark
8/4/14 5:45	1	Ali"s house IL	Last pick-up					We're Off!
8/4/14 6:40	1	Toll Booth IL	Alex Fumbles	All tolls	X	$2.85		
8/4/14 8:05	1	DriveThru Joe IL	Espresso					Only driver

The triangle buttons give you options for filtering the list based on data in that column. Clicking a button opens the menu and presents the options, which include sorting columns, displaying rows containing a limited number of values, or displaying only those rows matching a specific value in the column. For example, clicking the **Buy** button presents the travelers with these options:

To find out when they've purchased gas, the friends select "gas" in the column, and the filter pulls out only those rows. It's quick and efficient.

So, to this point in the trip, the friends have purchased fuel six times. These rows can be filtered further. For example, by clicking the `$` menu selector and selecting `X`, a personalized version of the Travel Log `Gas` purchases is shown for Alex.

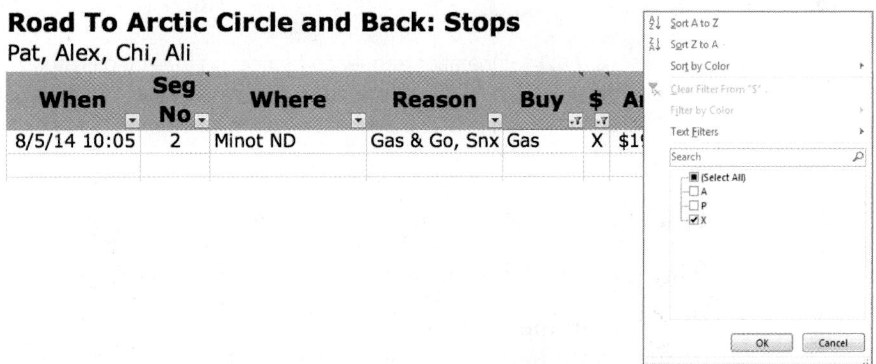

Notice that in Figure 14.13 Alex also paid tolls, but that is not reflected in this version of the table, because the first filter was `Buy` column matches `Gas`, and the second was `$` column matches `X`. Of course, the same result would have been found by executing the two filters in the opposite order.

These changes to the list are only logical, that is, the actual list has not been modified. We turn off the AutoFilter simply by selecting filtering again, that is, toggle it, and the original list will be redrawn.

Advanced Filtering Technique

AutoFiltering is easy because the software gives us access to a variety of standard filtering criteria. But most lists contain data that requires more refined analysis. We use the same interface, but we simply make the queries more complex.

Advanced Filtering Setup. For example, the travelers decide to analyze their gas purchases. To filter out the smaller gas purchases, they set the criterion in the mileage column to be greater than or equal to `175`. They start by choosing a criterion, namely Greater Than, and specify 175, leaving only longer distances, with the result shown in Figure 14.14.

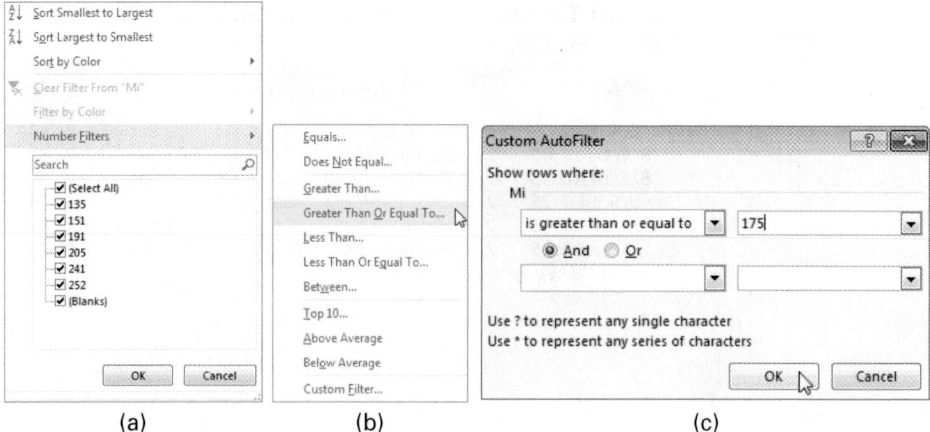

Road To Arctic Circle and Back: Stops
Pat, Alex, Chi, Ali

When	Seg No	Where	Reason	Buy	$	Amt	Mi	Remark
8/4/14 12:05	1	St. Paul MN	Gas & Go, Eat	Gas	P	$28.95	191	Subway
8/4/14 16:55	1	Fergus Falls MN	Gas & Go	Gas	P	$29.22	205	

(d)

Figure 14.14 Operation sequence for filtering to keep gas stops for distances over 175 miles: Clicking on MI's auto-filter followed by (a) hovering over "Numerical Filters", (b) hovering over "Greater than…", and (c) filling out the dialog box for the cut-off; (d) the result.

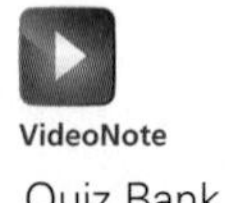

VideoNote
Quiz Bank

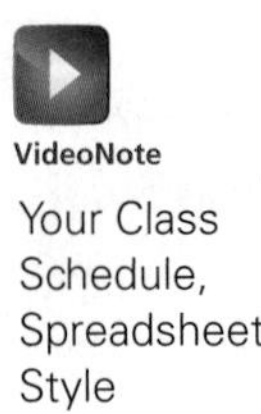

VideoNote
Your Class Schedule, Spreadsheet Style

Filtering on Multiple Criteria

The Advanced Filtering feature allows multiple criteria. It's quite intuitive.

To filter out the larger gas purchases, say those over 225 miles, simply requires adding another condition to the criteria for the Mi column, as shown in Figure 14.15.

Notice that in the figure the cursor is on the *And* choice for the connective between the two tests. This ensures that both conditions must be met for a row to be displayed, as we see in the result.

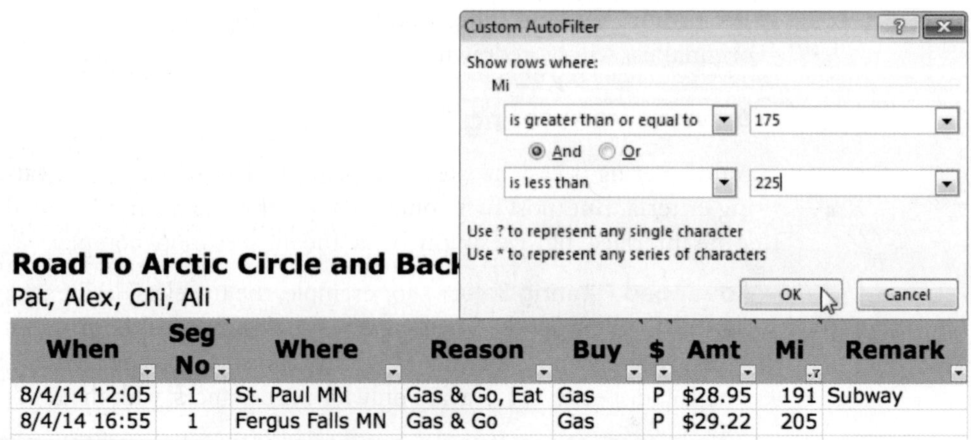

Road To Arctic Circle and Back
Pat, Alex, Chi, Ali

When	Seg No	Where	Reason	Buy	$	Amt	Mi	Remark
8/4/14 12:05	1	St. Paul MN	Gas & Go, Eat	Gas	P	$28.95	191	Subway
8/4/14 16:55	1	Fergus Falls MN	Gas & Go	Gas	P	$29.22	205	

Figure 14.15 Filtering a range of mileages between 175 and 225.

Figure 14.16 **Postcard**. Having fun, wish you were here! We made it to the Arctic Circle, saw bears on the Dempster "Highway" (ha!), and partied two nights in Dawson City, where we watched the sunrise over the Yukon River.

Filtering is extremely useful. For example, when the trip is over and the friends are settling their accounts, a list of each traveler's payments can be created, processed, and analyzed. In fact, when the trip is over, Pat and Alex can determine the accuracy of their original predictions about the trip's cost.

SUMMARY

This chapter has discussed several advanced spreadsheet techniques. You learned the following:

- Two basic principles underline the design of effective spreadsheets: (1) focus on form and (2) explain everything.
- Conditional formatting can apply an interpretation to the data in a spreadsheet so that it is easy to perceive.
- Conditional formulas using the IF( ) function allow complex, case-specific data definition and analysis.
- Naming the cells and regions of a spreadsheet allows the parts of a spreadsheet to be referenced in a convenient and less error-prone way.
- "What if" analysis is a particularly powerful application of spreadsheets in which the consequences of alternative information can be assessed.
- Filtering effectively customizes spreadsheet data to particular cases.

There are other handy spreadsheet operations that are not covered here, and for each of the techniques we *have* discussed, there are other applications. When you start using spreadsheets as a daily computing tool, you will undoubtedly migrate toward these more powerful features.

TRY IT SOLUTIONS

14.1 More expensive, because 3.788*1.16 = 4.39 > 4.15.

14.2 x = F2 and y = F2*0.948.

14.3 The formula is =IF(RIGHT(D2,2)="AB", E2 + 0.1*E2,E2).

14.4 6.60 mpl.

14.5 167.51 = 1395.93 – 1228.42.

14.6 $66.48 = 3*487.47 – 1395.93.

REVIEW QUESTIONS

Multiple Choice

1. In spreadsheets, names
   a. are used for cells
   b. are used for cell ranges
   c. can contain an underscore
   d. all of the above
2. All of the following are basic spreadsheet principles except
   a. logical form
   b. clean layout
   c. no text
   d. clear and easy to use entries
3. "Explain everything" in a spreadsheet means
   a. you should easily be able to tell what every cell means
   b. each cell and cell range should be labeled
   c. each formula should be explained with a label
   d. all of the above
4. Conditional formatting
   a. allows you to display information in more than one way
   b. allows you to write more than one formula for a cell
   c. automatically finds and flags errors in formulas and formatting
   d. all of the above
5. To get the first characters in a cell you should use the
   a. BEGIN( ) function
   b. START( ) function
   c. LEFT( ) function
   d. GET( ) function
6. Conditional formatting can change the
   a. text color
   b. text format
   c. cell color
   d. more than one of the above

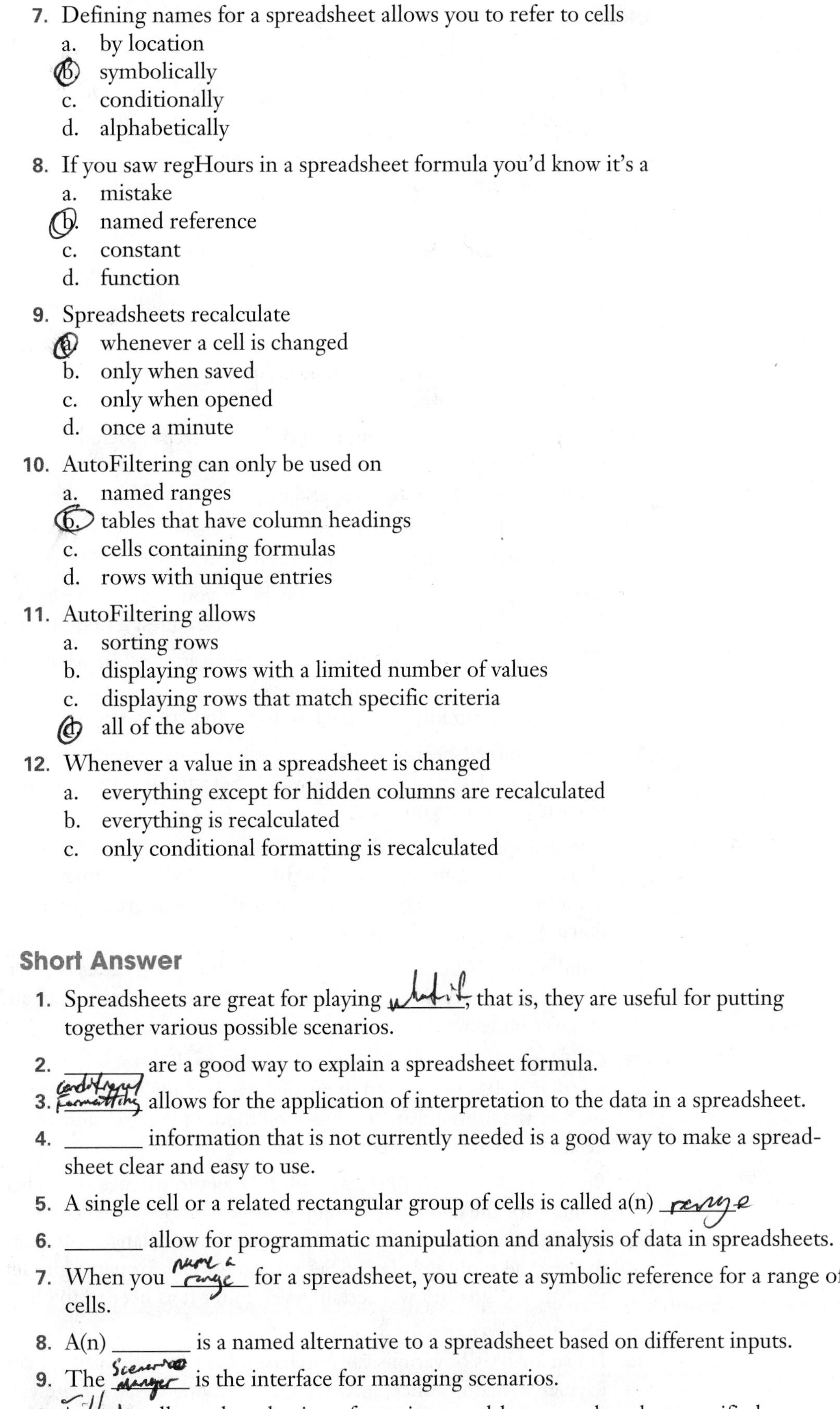

7. Defining names for a spreadsheet allows you to refer to cells
   a. by location
   b. symbolically
   c. conditionally
   d. alphabetically
8. If you saw regHours in a spreadsheet formula you'd know it's a
   a. mistake
   b. named reference
   c. constant
   d. function
9. Spreadsheets recalculate
   a. whenever a cell is changed
   b. only when saved
   c. only when opened
   d. once a minute
10. AutoFiltering can only be used on
    a. named ranges
    b. tables that have column headings
    c. cells containing formulas
    d. rows with unique entries
11. AutoFiltering allows
    a. sorting rows
    b. displaying rows with a limited number of values
    c. displaying rows that match specific criteria
    d. all of the above
12. Whenever a value in a spreadsheet is changed
    a. everything except for hidden columns are recalculated
    b. everything is recalculated
    c. only conditional formatting is recalculated

Short Answer

1. Spreadsheets are great for playing _______, that is, they are useful for putting together various possible scenarios.
2. _______ are a good way to explain a spreadsheet formula.
3. _______ allows for the application of interpretation to the data in a spreadsheet.
4. _______ information that is not currently needed is a good way to make a spreadsheet clear and easy to use.
5. A single cell or a related rectangular group of cells is called a(n) _______
6. _______ allow for programmatic manipulation and analysis of data in spreadsheets.
7. When you _______ for a spreadsheet, you create a symbolic reference for a range of cells.
8. A(n) _______ is a named alternative to a spreadsheet based on different inputs.
9. The _______ is the interface for managing scenarios.
10. _______ allows the selection of certain spreadsheet rows based on specified criteria.

Exercises

1. Create a spreadsheet to plan a trip.
2. Plan a trip using airlines, car rentals, and hotel stays. Don't forget to budget for sightseeing. Play "what if" with various scenarios.
3. Create a table to calculate free-throw percentages. Use IF( ) functions to prevent an error when no free throws are shot. Format the results using bold for percentages greater than or equal to 75 percent.
4. Create a spreadsheet for apartment costs based on the number of bedrooms, the number of roommates, and standard living expenses. Plot various scenarios depending on the price, number of roommates, and monthly expenses.
5. Create a spreadsheet to track your monthly expenses. Create categories for the expenses and filter them. Include columns for the day and date and track expenses by the day of the week.
6. Using the spreadsheet from the previous exercise, include data about your current bank balance. Write an IF( ) function that displays "GOOD" when the value is greater than or equal to zero, and displays "BAD" when the value is less than zero.
7. Organize your CD or DVD collection. Create categories as needed and filter by genre, year, ratings, producers, directors, and so on.
8. Create a spreadsheet to track the stats for your favorite basketball team. Create formulas as needed to calculate shooting percentages. Total the columns as needed.
9. Create a spreadsheet of multiple-choice questions. Use a column for the question, a column for each possible answer, a column for the correct answer, and a column for the topic. Set up filtering based on topic and correct answer.
10. Create a spreadsheet to track your eating habits. Use columns for food types, calories, time of day, and nutritional value. Set up filtering to see how much junk food you eat and when you eat it.
11. Create a spreadsheet to do a stock analysis. Track a stock's open, close, high, low, change, and volume. Track it for 30 days and see how many days are up and how many are down. Use conditional formatting with green for up days and red for down days.
12. Building on Exercise 5, create a monthly budget. Track your actual expenses to see how close you are. Use green for items that are under budget and red for those that are over budget.
13. Create a spreadsheet for your college classes. List each in its own row. Track whether a class is required or an elective. Include the semester it was (will be) taken. Include the prerequisites, delivery method, instructor, and grade. Filter them as needed to analyze your curriculum.
14. Building on Exercise 6, create a spreadsheet to balance your checkbook. Set up a column for the date, check number, payee, amount, and comment. Create one column to track deposits and another to track the balance. Write formulas as needed to keep the running balance. Set up conditional formatting to let you know when the balance falls below a certain level. Filter it as needed to see your spending habits.
15. Do an analysis of various car purchases. Compare the price, loan amount, payments, maintenance, insurance, and driving costs. Create various scenarios to determine which is the best buy.

CHAPTER 15

Introduction to Database Concepts

A Table with a View

learning objectives

- Explain the differences between everyday tables and database tables
- Use XML to describe the metadata for a table of information, and classify the uses of the tags as identification, affinity, or collection
- Understand how the concepts of entities and attributes are used to design a database table
- Use the six database operations: **Select**, **Project**, **Union**, **Difference**, **Product**, and **Join**
- Express a query using Query By Example
- Describe the differences between physical and logical databases

CHAPTER 15

Computers are useless. They only give answers.

—PABLO PICASSO

Now that we have all this useful information, it would be nice to do something with it. (Actually, it can be emotionally fulfilling just to get the information. This is usually only true, however, if you have the social life of a kumquat.)

—UNIX PROGRAMMER'S MANUAL

WE HAVE seen the benefits of using spreadsheets to organize lists of information. By arranging similar information into columns and using a separate row for each new list item, we can easily sort data, use formulas to summarize and compute values, get help from the computer to set up series, and so forth. Spreadsheets are very powerful, but with databases it's possible to apply even greater degrees of organization and receive even more help from the computer.

The key idea is to supply metadata describing the properties of the collected information. Recall that metadata is simply information describing (the properties of) other information. We have seen the idea of specifying metadata in Chapter 7, when we saw tags—the metadata—describe the content of the *Oxford English Dictionary*, enabling the computer to help us search for words and definitions. Some databases use tags for metadata, others use different kinds of metadata, but the same principles apply: Knowing the structure and properties of the data, the computer can help us retrieve, organize, and manage it.

In this chapter we distinguish between the everyday concept of a table and a relational database table. We will make the metadata tangible by using a notation called XML. Next, we explain how to set up the metadata for collections of information to create a database. The principles are straightforward and intuitive. After introducing basic table concepts, we present the five fundamental operations on tables and the Join operation. The convenience of Query By Example is illustrated using simple examples. Finally, the concepts of physical databases and logical databases are connected by the concept of queries, and we illustrate how to build a user's logical view from physical tables.

Differences Between Tables and Databases

When we think of databases, we often think of tables of information. For example, your iTunes or similar application records the title, artist, running time, and so on in addition to the actual MP3 data (the music). Your favorite song is a row in that table. Another example is your state's database of automobile registrations, which records the owner's name and address, the vehicle identification number (VIN), the license plate number, and such. The information about your car is stored as a row in the registration database table. And as a last example, the U.S. Central Intelligence Agency (CIA) keeps an interesting database called the World Factbook (see https://www.cia.gov/library/publications/the-world-factbook/index.html). They have a demographic table that records the country name, population, life expectancy, and so on. Information about the United States is kept as a row in the demography table.

Comparing Tables

To see the difference between these database tables and other forms of tables, such as spreadsheets and HTML tables, consider the row for Canada in the CIA's demographic database. This row is displayed as

Canada	34568211	1.61	5	80.1

in a table with column headings such as Country, Population, and Birthrate. In the file it is represented as

```
<demogData>
   <country>     Canada     </country>
   <population>34568211  </population>
   <fertility>   1.61       </fertility>
   <infant>      5          </infant>
   <lifeExpct>   80.1       </lifeExpct>
</demogData>
```

where the tags identify the country, population, fertility or birthrate, infant mortality rate (per 1,000 live births), and life expectancy. That is, we are shown a row of data as it appears in any other table, but inside the computer it has a tag identifying each of the data fields.

How does this data appear in other table forms? In a spreadsheet, the following is the row for Canada.

36	Cameroon	16900132	4.47	65	50.09
37	Canada	32805041	1.61	5	80.1
38	Cape Verde	410224	3.49	40	70.45

The entries for Canada are the same, but the software knows the values only by position, not by their meaning. So, if a cell is inserted at the beginning of the row, the data can shift right one position,

36	Cameroon	16900132	4.47	65	50.09	
37		Canada	32805041	1.61	5	80.1
38	Cape Verde	410224	3.49	40	70.45	

and the identity of the information is lost. Spreadsheets rely on position to keep the integrity of their data; the information is not known by its <country> tag, but rather as its A37 reference.

HTML tables are possibly even worse. The usual Web page presentation of the data for a table in which Canada is represented is

```
<tr>
   <td>Canada</td>
   <td>32805041</td>
   <td>1.61</td>
   <td>5</td>
   <td>80.1</td>
</tr>
```

where we recall that <tr> is a table row tag and <td> is a table data tag. These tags simply identify Canada's data as table entries with no other identity; that is, the same kind of <td> tags surround all of the different forms of data. HTML is concerned only with how to display the data, not with its meaning.

The Database's Advantage

The metadata is the key advantage of databases over other approaches to recording data as tables, because it enables content search. Suppose we want to know the life expectancy of Canadians. Database software can search for the <country> tag surrounding Canada. When it's found, the <country> tag will be one of several tags surrounded by <demogData> tags. These constitute the entry for Canada in the database. The software can then look for the <lifeExpct> tag among those tags and report the data that they surround as the data for Canada. The computer knew which data to return based on the availability of the metadata.

The tags for the CIA database just discussed fulfill two of the most important roles in defining metadata.

- **Identify the type of data:** Each different type of value is given a unique tag.
- **Define the affinity of the data:** Tags enclose all data that is logically related.

The <country>, <population>, and similar tags have the role of identification because they label the content. The <demogData> tag has the role of implementing affinity because it keeps an entry's data together—Canada's in this case. There are other properties of data that metadata must record, as you will see throughout this chapter, but these are perhaps the most fundamental.

XML: A Language for Metadata Tags

To emphasize the importance of metadata and to prepare for our own applications of database technology, let's take a moment to discuss the basics of **XML**. XML stands for the **Extensible Markup Language**, and like the Hypertext Markup Language (HTML) that you already know, it is basically a tagging scheme, making it rather intuitive. The tagging scheme used for the *Oxford English Dictionary* (*OED*) in Chapter 7 was a precursor to XML, and the demographic data of the last section was written in XML.

What makes XML easy and intuitive is that there are no standard tags to learn. *We think up the tags we need!* Computer scientists call this a *self-describing language*, because whatever we create becomes the language (tags) to structure the data. There are a few rules—for example, always match tags—but basically anything goes. Perhaps XML is the world's easiest-to-learn "foreign" language.

The same people who coordinate the Web—the **World Wide Web Consortium (W3C)**—developed XML. As a result, it works very well with browsers and other Web-based applications. So, it comes as no surprise that just as HTML must be written with a text editor rather than a word processor to avoid unintentionally including the word processor's tags, we must also write XML in a simple text editor for the same reason. Use the same editor that you used in Chapter 4 to practice writing Web pages: Notepad++ for Windows users and TextWrangler for Mac users.

Use a Text Editor for XML. Like HTML, XML should be written using a text editor like Notepad++ or TextWrangler rather than a word processor like Word or Word Perfect. Text editors use only the text you see, but word processors include other information to be avoided. Be sure the character encoding is set to "UTF-8."

An Example from Tahiti

After admiring the beauty of Tahiti—it's in the distance, beyond Moorea's Temae Beach—let's use XML to define tags to specify the metadata for a small data collection. Given the following size data (area in km^2) for Tahiti and its neighboring islands in the Windward Islands archipelago of the South Pacific,

Tahiti	1048
Moorea	130
Maiao	9.5
Mehetia	2.3
Tetiaroa	12.8

we want to record the metadata—that is, identify which data is an island name and which is the area. As usual, the tag and its companion closing tag surround the data. We choose <iName> and <area> as the tags and write:

```
<iName>Tahiti</iName>   <area>1048</area>
<iName>Moorea</iName> <area>130</area>
<iName>Maiao</iName>    <area>9.5</area>
<iName>Mehetia</iName> <area>2.3</area>
<iName>Tetiaroa</iName> <area>12.8</area>
```

These tags are used in the identification role. Notice that we chose <iName> rather than, say, <island name>. This is because XML tag names cannot contain spaces. But because both uppercase and lowercase are allowed—XML is case sensitive—we capitalize the "N" to make the tag more readable. All XML rules are shown in Table 15.1.

Though we have labeled each item with a tag describing what it is, we're not done describing the data. We need tags describing what sort of thing the name specifies and the area measures. That's an island, of course. So we enclose each entry with an <island> tag, as in

```
<island><iName>Tahiti</iName>     <area>1048</area> </island>
<island><iName>Moorea</iName>     <area>130</area>  </island>
<island><iName>Maiao</iName>      <area>9.5</area>  </island>
<island><iName>Mehetia</iName>    <area>2.3</area>  </island>
<island><iName>Tetiaroa</iName>   <area>12.8</area> </island>
```

The <island> tag serves in the affinity role to keep the two facts together; that is, Tahiti is grouped with its area and it is separated from Moorea and its area.

We're nearly done. The islands are not just randomly dispersed around the ocean. They are part of an archipelago, the proper name for a group of islands. So, we naturally invent one more tag, <archipelago>, and surround all of the islands with it. The result is shown in Figure 15.1.

Table 15.1 Rules for writing XML

Required first line	<?xml version="1.0" encoding="UTF-8"?> must appear as the first line of the file, starting in the first position.
First tag	The first tag encountered is the *root* element, and it must enclose all of the file's content; it appears on the second or possibly third line.
Closing tags	All tags must be closed.
Element naming	Observe these rules: • Names can contain letters, numbers, and underscore characters. • Names must not start with a number or punctuation character. • Names must not start with the letters xml (or XML, or Xml, etc.). • Names cannot contain spaces.
Case sensitivity	Tags and attributes are case sensitive.
Proper nesting	All tags must be well nested.
Attribute quoting	All attribute values must be quoted; paired single quotes (apostrophes) or paired double quotes are okay; use one type inside the other if needed; no "curly" quotes of any type.
White space	White space is preserved and converted to a single space.
Comments	XML comments have the form <!-- This is a comment. -->.

```
<?xml version = "1.0" encoding="UTF-8" ?>
<archipelago>
  <island><iName>Tahiti</iName>        <area>1048</area></island>
  <island><iName>Moorea</iName>        <area>130</area></island>
  <island><iName>Maiao</iName>         <area>9.5</area></island>
  <island><iName>Mehetia</iName>       <area>2.3</area></island>
  <island><iName>Tetiaroa</iName>      <area>12.8</area></island>
</archipelago>
```

Figure 15.1 XML file encoding data for the Windward Islands database. The first line states that the file contains XML tags.

Notice the first line of the file in Figure 15.1. This line, which uses the unusual form of associating question marks (?) within the brackets, identifies the file as containing XML data text. (It also states that the file's characters use the standard UTF-8 encoding; see Chapter 7.) This first line is required and must be the first line of any XML file. By identifying the file as XML, hundreds of software applications can understand what it contains. In this way, the effort to tag all of the information can be repaid by using the data with those applications.

Start Off Right with XML. XML files must be identified as such, and so they are required to begin with the text

```
<?xml version = "1.0" encoding="UTF-8" ?>
```

(or other encoding) as their first line and without leading spaces. The file extension should be .xml.

15.1 More Islands. Write an XML metadata coding for the following collection of data from the Galápagos archipelago.

For the items of the same type as the data from the Windward archipelago, use the same tags; for the elevation, the highest point on the island, create a new tag.

Island	Area	Elevation
Isabela	4588	1707
Fernandina	642	1494
Tower	14	76
Santa Cruz	986	846

Expanding the Use of XML

Given the XML encoding of two archipelagos—the Windward Islands and the Galápagos Islands—it seems reasonable to combine them.

To create a database of the two archipelagos, we place their data in the same file, one after the other (in the order we want them to appear). This might seem odd because the Windward Islands have only two data values—name and area—while the Galápagos Islands have three—name, area, and elevation. But this is okay. Both archipelago encodings use the same tags for the common information, which is the key issue to consider when combining them. Extra data is allowed and, in fact, we might want to gather the elevation data for the Windward Islands.

Browse It. The rules listed in Table 15.1 must be respected. Luckily, it is possible to ask Firefox to scan your file, and if there are problems, you will usually get an error message. Make sure the file extension is .xml, it has the mandatory first line, and then open it with Firefox. Having removed the </area> tag from Figure 15.1, Firefox flagged my error with this message:

```
XML Parsing Error: mismatched tag. Expected: </area>.
Location: file:///Users/lawrencesnyder/Desktop/tahiti.xml
Line Number 4, Column 44:

  <island><iName>Moorea</iName> <area>130</island>
-------------------------------------------^
```

With the two archipelagos combined into one database, we want to include the name of each archipelago to tell them apart easily. Of course, this means adding another tag for the name. We could use <name>, which is different from the <iName> tag used before. But in the same way that we added "i" to remind ourselves that it is an island name, it is probably wise to use the same idea to create a more specific tag name. Let's adopt the tag <a_name>. Notice the use of the underscore, which is an allowed punctuation symbol for XML. We will place the name inside the <archipelago> tag, since it is data about the archipelago.

Finally, we have two archipelagos and we need to group them together by surrounding them with tags; these tags will serve as the root element of our XML database. A **root element** is the tag that encloses all of the content of the XML file. In Figure 15.1 the <archipelago> tag was the root element, but now with two archipelagos in the file, we need a new tag to enclose them. They are both geographic features of our planet, so we will use <geo_feature> as the tag that surrounds both archipelagos. The final result of our revisions is shown in Figure 15.2.

Incidentally, XML doesn't care about white space—spaces, tabs, and new lines—when they are between tags. This allows us to format XML files to simplify working with them, but the indenting is only for our use.

```
<?xml version = "1.0" encoding="UTF-8" ?>
<geo_feature>

 <archipelago>
  <a_name>Windward Islands</a_name>
  <island><iName>Tahiti</iName>        <area>1048</area></island>
  <island><iName>Moorea</iName>        <area>130</area>  </island>
  <island><iName>Maiao</iName>         <area>9.5</area>  </island>
  <island><iName>Mehetia</iName>       <area>2.3</area>  </island>
  <island><iName>Tetiaroa</iName>      <area>12.8</area> </island>
 </archipelago>

 <archipelago>
  <a_name>Galapagos</a_name>
  <island><iName>Isabela</iName>      <area>4588</area> <elev>1707</elev></island>
  <island><iName>Fernandina</iName>   <area>642</area>  <elev>1494</elev></island>
  <island><iName>Tower</iName>        <area>14</area>   <elev>76</elev>  </island>
  <island><iName>Santa Cruz</iName>   <area>986</area>  <elev>846</elev> </island>
 </archipelago>

</geo_feature>
```

Figure 15.2 XML file for the Geographic Features database.

Attributes in XML

Recall that HTML tags can have *attributes* to give additional information, such as src and alt in <img /> tags. Our invented tags of XML can also have attributes. They have a similar form, and their values must always be set inside quotation marks. These examples show we can use either paired double quotes

```
<entry location="Hawai'i">Luau Restaurant</entry>
```

or paired single quotes

```
<entry location='"SoHo"'>Barney's NYC Bistro</entry>
```

depending on the content.

The best advice about attributes is to use them for additional metadata, not for actual content. So, we might write an attribute in the <area> tag for the units of measurement

```
<area unit="km2">
```

because it is a property of the data and isn't normally displayed.

Effective Design with XML Tags

XML is a very flexible way to encode metadata. As we have described the archipelagos, we have used a few basic guidelines to decide how to use the tags. To emphasize these rules, let's review what we said, encapsulating it into three encoding rules.

Identification Rule: Label Data with Tags Consistently. *You can choose whatever tag names you wish to name data, but once you've decided on a tag for a particular kind of data, you must always surround that kind of data with that tag.*

Notice that one of the advantages of enclosing data with tags is that it keeps the data together. For example, the island of Santa Cruz in the Galápagos is a two-word name, but we don't have to treat it any differently than the one-word island names because the tags keep the two words together.

Affinity Rule: Group Data Referencing an Entity. *Enclose in a pair of tags all tagged data referring to the same thing. Grouping it keeps it all together, but the idea is much more fundamental: Grouping makes an association of the tagged data items as being related to each other as features of the same thing.*

We applied this rule when we grouped the island name and area data inside <island> tags. We did this because both items referred to the same thing, the island. This is an important association, because the area data is not just area data about some random place on the earth; it is the area data for a specific place that is named Tahiti. This is an extremely important result from the simple act of enclosing data in tags.

When we added elevation data as an additional feature of islands, we included it inside the <island> tags for the same reason. As the elevation data shows, it is not necessary for every instance of an object to have data for the same set of characteristics.

Collection Rule: Group Instances. *When you have several instances of the same kind of data, enclose them in tags; again, it keeps them together and implies that they are instances of the same type.*

When we had two archipelagos, we grouped them inside a <geo_feature> tag, a collection tag.

Notice that the Collection Rule and the Affinity Rule are different. The Affinity Rule groups the data for a single thing—an island, for example. The Collection Rule groups the data of different instances of the same type—two archipelagos, for example. The difference is clear with the <archipelago> tag: The islands together identified a new thing or *entity*—the archipelago—and so it is an affinity tag keeping the information about the archipelago together; adding an identifying name with <a_name> justifies this view. The two instances of archipelagos don't make a new entity; they're simply collected together.

The XML Tree

Your Class Schedule, XML Style

The rules for producing XML encodings of information produce hierarchical descriptions that can be thought of as trees. (We interpreted hierarchies as trees in Chapter 3.) Figure 15.3 illustrates the tree structure of the encoding in Figure 15.2. The hierarchy is a consequence of how the tags enclose one another and the data.

Tables and Entities

You have seen how you can record metadata about a collection of data values using XML tags. For the moment, let's set aside the topics of tagging and XML, and focus directly on database table systems generally. I want you to understand the concepts of database organization and the value of metadata, not simply the way to encode that structure with tags. We'll return to tagging in Chapter 16, but for now, think of tables pure and simple.

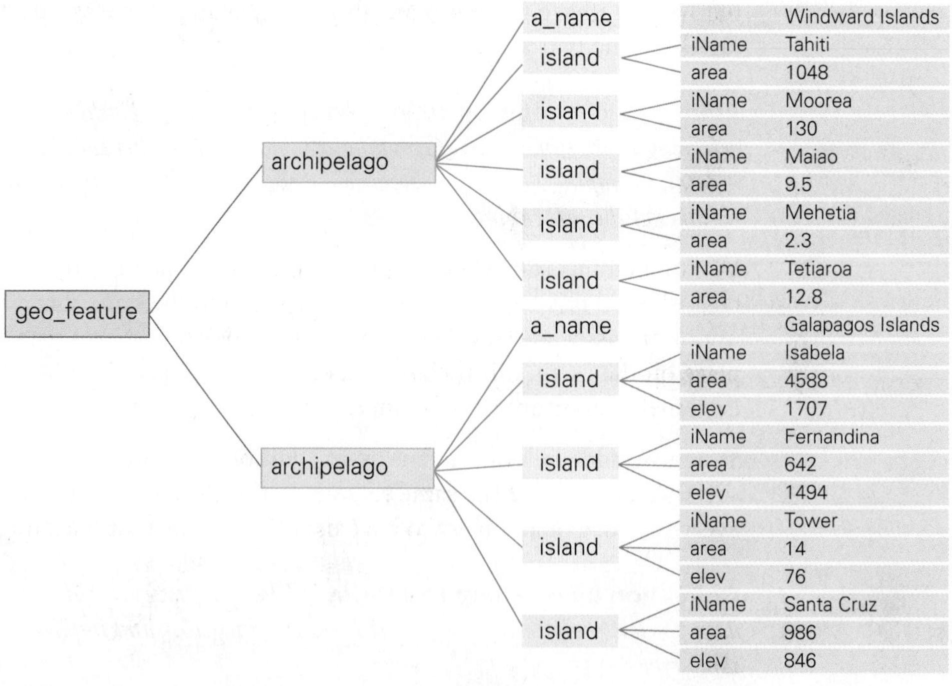

Figure 15.3 The XML displayed as a tree. The encoding from Figure 15.2 is shown with the root element (geo_feature) to the left and the leaves (content) shown to the right.

Entities

Database tables store information about entities. "Entity" is about as vague a word as "thing" and "stuff," but the inventors of databases didn't want to limit the kinds of information that can be stored.

Common Characteristics. To relate entities and attributes to the metadata discussion above, look at Figure 15.4, which shows the same information as the XML tagging in Figure 15.2, but in database table form.

Entities and *attributes* are unfamiliar terms for familiar ideas, so let's start out informally: Any group of things with common characteristics *that specifically identify each one* can be formed into a *database table*. For example, in a table of information about students, there will be a column for each of the characteristics: name, student ID, email address, and so on. Each column has a name or heading, like Name, ID, and email. Each student will be listed as a row with his or her value for each characteristic listed in the proper column, such as

Grant Pell, 20140001, grape@ude.edu

In database terminology, we call the characteristics in columns *attributes*, the rows *entities*, and the entries the *attribute values of the entity*.

Attributes Gone Wild. Unfortunately, *attribute* is an overused word in computing. In relational databases—the case we're interested in now and which are described later in this chapter—an attribute is a "column of a table," the "attribute name" is the column heading, and the "attribute values" are the entries. We use the term *tag attributes* when we mean the attributes of XML or HTML.

Now, a little more precisely. A **database table** contains a set of things with common **attributes** that uniquely identify each one. The rows of the database table are **entities**. The table has a column for each attribute. The column heading is the **attribute name**. A row lists the values for each attribute for an entity. So, Name and ID are attributes of any student generally, but "Grant Pell" and "20140001" define a specific student, called an **entity instance**. The whole table with its specific rows is said to be a **table instance**. We usually drop the "instance" when the distinction between abstract idea—entity—and a specific row of data—entity instance—is unimportant.

PacificIslands

ID	IslandName	Area	Elev	Archipelago
1	Tahiti	1048		Windward Islands
2	Moorea	130		Windward Islands
3	Maiao	10		Windward Islands
4	Mehetia	2		Windward Islands
5	Tetiaroa	13		Windward Islands
6	Isabela	4588	1707	Galapagos Islands
7	Fernandina	642	1494	Galapagos Islands
8	Tower	14	76	Galapagos Islands
9	Santa Cruz	985	846	Galapagos Islands

Figure 15.4 A database table instance (from Microsoft Access) representing the same information as shown in Figure 15.2.

What to Notice. The island example illustrates several features of entities that might not be obvious at first:

- The rows of a database table are all different, because the attributes uniquely identify each one.
- Even when we don't know the data for an attribute value—like the elevation for Tahiti—it is still a characteristic of an island.
- The conditions saying how to make a table of entities allows for any order of the rows.
- The conditions saying how to make a table of entities allows for any order of columns.
- The conditions allow for columns (as a whole) to be interchanged, and rows (as a whole) to be interchanged; the rearranged table is the same table instance as the original.
- A given table instance—a table containing a specific set of values—becomes a *different instance* if we add or remove rows, or change any value.
- Two rows can have the same value for some attributes, but not all attributes.

Also, for any given entity (row), the column headings are handy names for its values.

15.2 A Question of Elevation. If the database table in Figure 15.4 is updated to fill in the missing elevation entries, will it still be the same table instance as the original?

Properties of Entities

Defining tables as rows of "things you can tell apart by a fixed set of values (attributes)" seems so simple, yet it implies many properties. It even makes sense if there are no rows at all.

When Nothing Is Something. A curious property of database tables is that they can be empty. That is, the table has no rows. (Visualize the idea by deleting the last nine rows of the table in Figure 15.4.) It seems odd, but it makes sense. Once we agree that an entity is anything defined by a specific set of attributes, then in principle a table exists with a name and column headings, but no data. When we specify entity instances, we'll have rows. So, among the instances of any table is the "empty instance."

Also, notice that the table of Figure 15.4 handles hierarchical information differently than the XML of Figure 15.2: In Figure 15.4 we need another attribute to say which archipelago an island is in, but in Figure 15.2 that information was represented by another layer of enclosing tags. Computer scientists say that database tables *flatten* hierarchical information. This is one of the key differences between database tables and XML databases.

One of Several Types. In addition to having a name, attributes also have a **data type**, such as number, text, image, and so on. The data type defines the form of the

PacificIslands

	Field Name	Data Type
🔑	ID	AutoNumber
	IslandName	Short Text
	Area	Number
	Elev	Number
	Archipelago	Short Text

information that can be stored as an attribute value. By specifying the data type, database software can prevent us from accidentally storing the wrong type of information as a table entry. To connect the data type to the tagging discussed earlier, think of the type as a tag attribute, as in <iName type="text"> or <area type="number">. This data type metadata for a table is stored by database software as a companion table and is manipulated in the UI, as shown at left.

For the Record. Because databases are so important and long-studied, the concepts are known by several terms. The technical term for a row is a **tuple** (short *u*) from words like quintuple, sextuple, and septuple. Rows are often called **records**, a holdover from computing's punch-card days. Attributes are also known as **fields** and **columns**, and we use both of these terms here. An attribute's data type is sometimes referred to as its *format*. Tables are technically known as **relations**.

Every One Is Different

There are few limits on what an entity can be, but some things are not. Amoebas are not entities, because they have no characteristics that allow us to tell them apart. (Perhaps amoebas can tell each other apart, and if we could figure out how, then the characteristics on which they differ could be their attributes, allowing them to become entities.) Of course, one-celled animals *are* entities.

In cases where it is difficult to process the information specifically identifying an entity, we might select an alternate encoding. For example, killer whales can be distinguished by the arrangement of their black-and-white markings. Even though images can be stored in a database, it is difficult to compare two images to determine if they show the same whale. So, we assign names to the killer whales, which are easy for computers to manipulate, letting a human do the recognition and assign the name.

Thus, to summarize this section, entities are the data of databases.

The Science of Tables

Can there be a *science* of tables? Absolutely! And we briefly check it out to explain how some computational "magic" that you use daily works. Our goal is to understand its main ideas, not to become data scientists.

Relational Database Tables

By the "science of tables" I refer to the study of **relational databases**. The previous section introduced entities and database tables with some care, because they are what relational databases are built from. Although tables are technically called *relations*, but we'll continue to call them *database tables*.

Always Different. All of the properties that we've discussed—rows all different, columns interchangeable as a whole, and so on—apply. About the only thing we haven't mentioned about these tables is this:

The rows must always be different, even after adding rows. Always.

It's not enough that the rows be different for a given table instance. They must be different for every (meaningful) instance.

This *rows-always-different* requirement is reasonable. Here's why. The rows of a database table are supposed to be entities. Because we can always tell entities apart by some fixed number of properties (attributes), then no matter what things are in the table, each row should be different and any row that's added will be different from them, too. So, the rows-always-different requirement basically says, "Be sure the table has all of the attributes (columns) needed to tell the entities apart."

To see that some tables don't have enough attributes to fulfill the *rows-always-different* requirement, consider a table that doesn't work: A two-column table giving hair color and eye color for students at a school. We see in Figure 15.5(a) that when we try to add a second student with blond hair and blue eyes, we have a problem—there is already one in the table. As you well know, these two properties are not enough to tell all students in a school apart. We can fix the problem, of course, by adding more information, such as student name.

The requirement is very important, and to make sure it's always true, there is a "standard fix": A sequence number can be added to each row of any table, as shown in Figure 15.5(b). This sequence number guarantees that every row is different because it has a different number. We interpret this as saying student No. 1 has blond hair and blue eyes, as does student No. 5. Using names and other information produce more useful entities, of course, but database software will include a sequence number field for tables automatically. You may not always need it, but it's there.

Keys. Notice that both columns in Figure 15.5(a) contain repeated entries. By itself, repeated data in a column is not a problem. What went wrong is that the data in both positions of a row matched a row already in the table. Adding the sequence number (Figure 15.5(b)) fixed that problem because its entries in that column will always be different.

We are interested in columns in which all of the entries are always different, because they can be used to look up data. Such a column is called a **candidate key**. Referring to Figure 15.4, the Islands table, the sequence number (ID) is a candidate key, of course. The Archipelago column cannot be a candidate key because of the repeats. Although

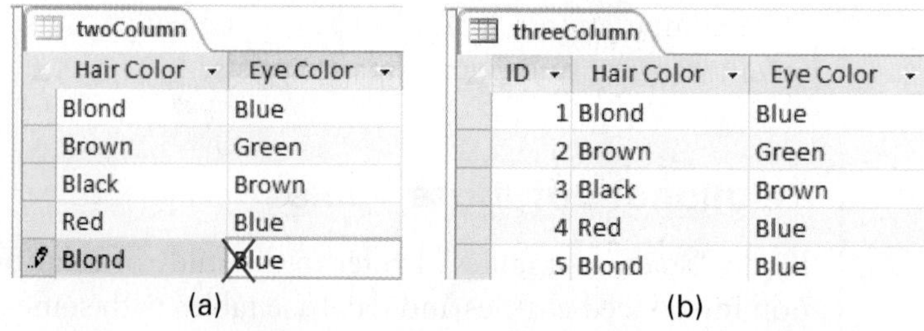

twoColumn

Hair Color	Eye Color
Blond	Blue
Brown	Green
Black	Brown
Red	Blue
Blond	Blue

(a)

threeColumn

ID	Hair Color	Eye Color
1	Blond	Blue
2	Brown	Green
3	Black	Brown
4	Red	Blue
5	Blond	Blue

(b)

Figure 15.5 Two database tables: (a) An attempt to add a row that violates the *rows-always-different* rule; and (b) a table with a sequence number (ID), ensuring that the rule will be fulfilled for every row.

the Area and Elev values are all different in the table shown, there may be islands in the Pacific of equal area or equal elevation, so they probably aren't candidate keys either. Is IslandName a candidate key? We might guess that it is, but Santa Cruz is also an island name in the San Bernardo archipelago. So, IslandName doesn't work either. Only the ID column is a candidate key.

However, a candidate key doesn't have to be just one column. It can be multiple columns taken together. So, IslandName and Archipelago *together* are a candidate key. That is, the pairs (Santa Cruz, Galápagos) and (Santa Cruz, San Bernardo) are different, and we expect that always to be true. So, the pair of columns is a candidate key.

Database software needs to know the **primary key**, which is the candidate key that the computer and user agree will be used to locate entities during database operations. The user specifies the primary key in the metadata UI. In Figure 15.6(a), the Code attribute has been designated as the primary key (notice the key symbol).

A Database Table's Metadata. Because database tables have attribute names—column headings—and data types for each attribute, it is possible to succinctly describe a database table with a **database scheme** or **database schema**, as shown in Figure 15.6. (Recall that historically, *attributes* were known as *fields* so, as here, we occasionally still see the term.)

In a database scheme the attributes are listed, one per row. For each attribute, the user specifies its data type and whether or not it is the primary key. It is also customary to include a brief description, as shown in Figure 15.6(a). Database systems consider the description optional, but database designers don't.

worldDatabase11

Field Name	Data Type	
CountryName	Short Text	Common English Name
🔑 Code	Short Text	Short Abbreviation
Capital	Short Text	Government
Longitude	Number	Capital Longitude: W < 0 < E
Latitude	Number	Capital Latitude: S < 0 < N
Population	Number	Recent Population Est
Area	Number	Area in square kilometers

(a)

wDB1

CountryNan	Code	Capital	Longit	Latitu	Population	Area
Austria	A	Vienna	16.37	48.20	8023244	83850
Afghanistan	AFG	Kabul	69.20	34.58	22664136	647500
Antigua and B	AG	Saint Johns	-61.50	17.30	65647	442
Albania	AL	Tirane	19.80	41.30	3249136	28750
Andorra	AND	Andorra la \	1.30	42.30	72766	450
Armenia	ARM	Yerevan	44.40	40.10	3463574	29800
Australia	AUS	Canberra	149.08	-35.10	18260863	7686850

(b)

Figure 15.6 The worldDatabase1 (wDB1) table: (a) the table's metadata, known as the database scheme, and (b) sample entries, ordered by Code. Notice in figure (a) that the primary key is Code.

The *database scheme is the database table's metadata*. Because all items in a column refer to the same attribute and have the same data type, this metadata is much more succinct than with tagging. But, be aware, this is not *all* of the metadata.

Electronic World. The data in Figure 15.6 comes from an open source database archive of world data that is available in many formats, probably including one for the database you're using. See www.dbis.informatik.uni-goettingen.de/Mondial/.

15.3 The Key Idea. Using your knowledge of geography, which of the attributes are candidate keys in this North American Political Units table?

NorthAmericaPoliticalUnits

Ctry	State/Prov	Capital	Largest City
US	Alabama	Montgomery	Birmingham
US	Alaska	Juneau	Anchorage
CA	Alberta	Edmonton	Calgary
	...	...	...
MX	Yucatán	Mérida	Mérida
CA	Yukon	Whitehorse	Whitehorse
MX	Zacatecas	Zacatecas	Zacatecas

Computing with Tables

To get information from database tables, we write a query describing what we want. A **query** is a command that tells the database system how to manipulate its tables to compute the answer, which will be a database table, of course. What else?

The database system "manipulates" its tables using simple operations. There are only six operations that we need to know. All database systems use these operations, but there are many small differences in the languages they use to express them. So, we outline the concepts first and then give an example of the actual commands later.

These operations, briefly defined in Table 15.2, take one or two database tables as input, D1 and D2, and produce a new table, DR, with a copy of the data. For example, to combine the rows in two tables, we write D1 + D2.

Table 15.2 Six operations on tables fundamental to database systems. D1 and D2 are database tables, and DR is the resulting database table.

Operation	Symbolic Form	DR Composed of
Project	D1 *c1,c2,. . . ,cn* → DR	Entire columns chosen from D1
Select	D1 *formula* → DR	All rows of D1 making *formula* true
Cross- Product	D1 × D2 → DR	All rows made by appending to all rows of D1, all rows of D2
Union	D1 + D2 → DR	All rows from D1 and D2; fields must be compatible
Difference	D1 – D2 → DR	All rows of D1 not also in D2
Join	D1 **Join** D2 **On** *D1.fieldi=D2.fieldj* → DR	When **fieldi** of a D1 row matches **fieldj** of a D2 row, the D2 row is appended to the D1 row and included in DR

$wDB1_{CountryName,\ Capital,\ Latitude}$ →

projectQuery

CountryNan	Capital	Latitu
Austria	Vienna	48.20
Afghanistan	Kabul	34.58
Antigua and B	Saint Johns	17.30
Albania	Tirane	41.30
...	...	0.00

Figure 15.7 Using the **Project** operation to form a table with three columns—**CountryName**, **Capital**, and **Latitude**—from wDB1.

In the following sections we elaborate on the definitions in Table 15.2 and give examples from the world database (wDB1) in Figure 15.6.

Project. The Project (pronounced *pro·JECT*) operation simply picks out and arranges columns from one database table to create a new, possibly "narrower," table. Figure 15.7 shows a three-column table created from wDB1 using the Project operation.

Select. The Select operation picks out rows according to specified criterion. Figure 15.8 shows the result of Select applied to rows from wDB1 where the formula is *Latitude > 60.*

Cross-Product. To illustrate Cross-Product, we define two small tables. Suppose we apply the Project and Select operations just illustrated together, except we revise the formula to *Latitude > 60 OR Latitude < –40*, which gives capitals in both Northern and Southern Hemispheres. The order in which the two operations are applied doesn't matter. The result is the three-row, three-column table in Figure 15.9(a), which we call extremes. Figure 15.9(b) shows another small table, called HemiNS, with only one column; it was typed in.

Cross-Product combines two tables in a process like multiplication, which is why we show it with a cross (×): For each row in the first table (extremes in this example), we make a new row by appending a row from the second table (HemiNS); all combinations are in the result, as shown in Figure 15.9(c). Because we pair all rows, a table with *m* rows crossed with a table with *n* rows will produce a table with *mn* rows, adding to the analogy with multiplication. (Now it's clear why we illustrate it with small tables.)

Although Project and Select seem like useful operations for picking out data from a table, Cross-Product seems odd and useless, because it combines data mechanically with no regard for whether the new rows make sense. That may seem true, but using Cross-Product with other table operators *is* powerful. For example, to label the hemispheres correctly, we can apply a Select operation to the Figure 15.9(c) database table using the formula

(*Latitude > 0 AND NS = 'North'*) OR (*Latitude < 0 AND NS = 'South'*)

$wDB1_{Latitude > 60}$ →

selectQuery

Countryl	Code	Capital	Longi	Latit	Populat	Area
Iceland	IS	Reykjavik	-21.93	64.13	270292	103000
Finland	SF	Helsinki	24.95	60.17	5105230	337030

Figure 15.8 Selecting the rows from **wDB1** that satisfy the formula *Latitude > 60.*

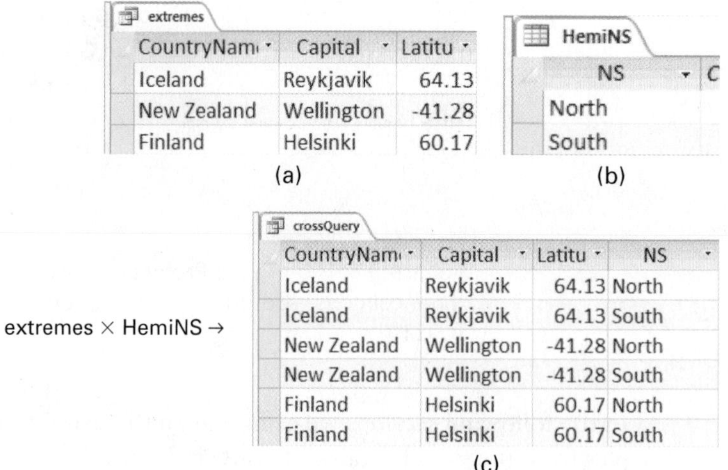

extremes

CountryNam	Capital	Latitu
Iceland	Reykjavik	64.13
New Zealand	Wellington	-41.28
Finland	Helsinki	60.17

(a)

HemiNS

NS	C
North	
South	

(b)

extremes × HemiNS →

crossQuery

CountryNam	Capital	Latitu	NS
Iceland	Reykjavik	64.13	North
Iceland	Reykjavik	64.13	South
New Zealand	Wellington	-41.28	North
New Zealand	Wellington	-41.28	South
Finland	Helsinki	60.17	North
Finland	Helsinki	60.17	South

(c)

Figure 15.9 The Cross-Product operation: (a) the extremes database table, (b) the HemiNS database table, and (c) the Cross-Product result of the two tables, called crossQuery.

This formula says that latitudes given by positive numbers should be labeled "North" and latitudes with negative numbers should be labeled "South" (see Figure 15.10). So, Select picks only those rows, and the result of these two operations together *does* make sense.

Summarizing these three commands, we took our original database table (extremes) and added new data to it from another database table (HemiNS). We did that by first constructing all possible pairings of rows with Cross-Product (×) and then selecting out those rows that made sense using Select. This idea—combine two tables to create an "all possibilities" database table, and then select only the meaningful results—is a powerful and frequently used database technique. We will see it again in a moment. But first, in keeping with the idea of multiplying, we check out add and subtract.

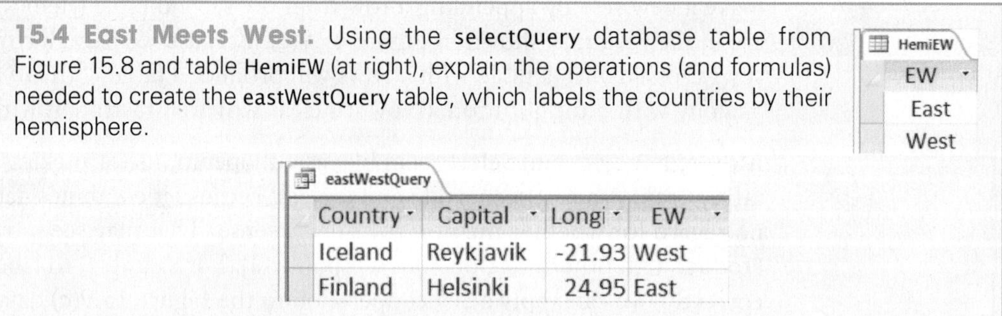

15.4 East Meets West. Using the selectQuery database table from Figure 15.8 and table HemiEW (at right), explain the operations (and formulas) needed to create the eastWestQuery table, which labels the countries by their hemisphere.

HemiEW

EW
East
West

eastWestQuery

Country	Capital	Longi	EW
Iceland	Reykjavik	-21.93	West
Finland	Helsinki	24.95	East

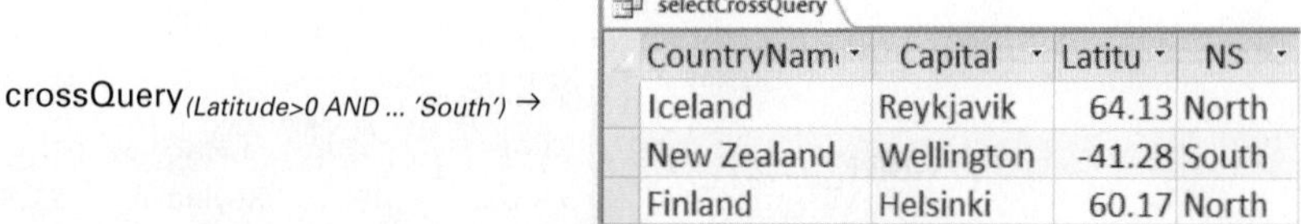

$\text{crossQuery}_{(Latitude>0\ AND\ \ldots\ 'South')}$ →

selectCrossQuery

CountryNam	Capital	Latitu	NS
Iceland	Reykjavik	64.13	North
New Zealand	Wellington	-41.28	South
Finland	Helsinki	60.17	North

Figure 15.10 Trimming the crossQuery table: a Select operation is applied to crossQuery with the formula (*Latitude* > *0 AND NS* = *'North'*) OR (*Latitude* < *0 AND NS* = *'South'*).

extremes

CountryName	Capital	Latitu
Iceland	Reykjavik	64.13
New Zealand	Wellington	-41.28
Finland	Helsinki	60.17

(a)

equatorial

CountryNan	Capital	Latitu
Kenya	Nairobi	-1.27
Ecuador	Quito	-0.22
Kiribati	Tarawa	1.40
Singapore	Singapore	1.30

(b)

extremes + equatorial→

exeq

CountryNan	Capital	Latitu
Kenya	Nairobi	-1.27
Ecuador	Quito	-0.22
Iceland	Reykjavik	64.13
Kiribati	Tarawa	1.40
New Zealand	Wellington	-41.28
Finland	Helsinki	60.17
Singapore	Singapore	1.30

(c)

Figure 15.11 The **Union** operation: (a) the **extremes** database table, (b) the **equatorial** database table—countries whose capital is within 1.5 degrees of the equator, and (c) the **Union** of the two, the **exeq** database table.

Union. The Union operation combines two tables with compatible attributes—that is, columns. The result has rows from both tables, and for any rows that are in both tables, only one copy is included in the result (see Figure 15.11).

Difference. The Difference operation is just the opposite of the Union. That is, the result of D1 – D2 contains the rows of the D1 table that are not also in the D2 table. Thus, the rows are unique to the D1 table. So, referring to the database tables of Figure 15.11, the equation

exeq – equitorial = extremes (*)

is true, as is

exeq – extremes = equitorial

(The first equation is starred, because it is referred to later.) Notice that for D1 – D2 the rows of D2 don't have to exist in D1. So, using exeq to remove rows from either extremes or equatorial

extremes – exeq = *<empty>*

results in an empty three-column table.

15.5 A World of Data. Recalling the database table projectQuery from Figure 15.7, describe the results of these two operations:

(a) projectQuery + exeq →

(b) extremes – equitorial →

Join. Finally, meet the Join operation. Join is really a combination of a Cross-Product operation followed by a Select operation. We saw this combination at work in Figures 15.9 and 15.10, although that example was a bit more complex than the basic Join operation.

Join takes two database tables, D1 and D2, and an attribute from each one, D1.a1 and D2.a2, specified by giving the table, followed by a dot, followed by the attribute name. Join crosses the two tables (that is, applies the Cross-Product operation), and then uses Select to find those rows of the cross in which the two attributes match. Thus, the formula is D1.a1 = D2.a2. The benefit of Join is that it puts tables together while matching up related data.

For example, suppose we have a table of cities with only four fields—ID, CityName, Country, and Population—where the Country attribute is given by the country code that we've seen above.

To add country names, capitals, and other data is easy by joining City with wDB1 and matching on the country code. The operation is

City **Join** wDB1 **On** City.Country = wDB1.Code

which produces the result shown in Figure 15.12.

Notice that in Figure 15.12 a second country code—SF—matches for the rows shown. Of course, every item in the City database table will be paired with some item in wDB1.

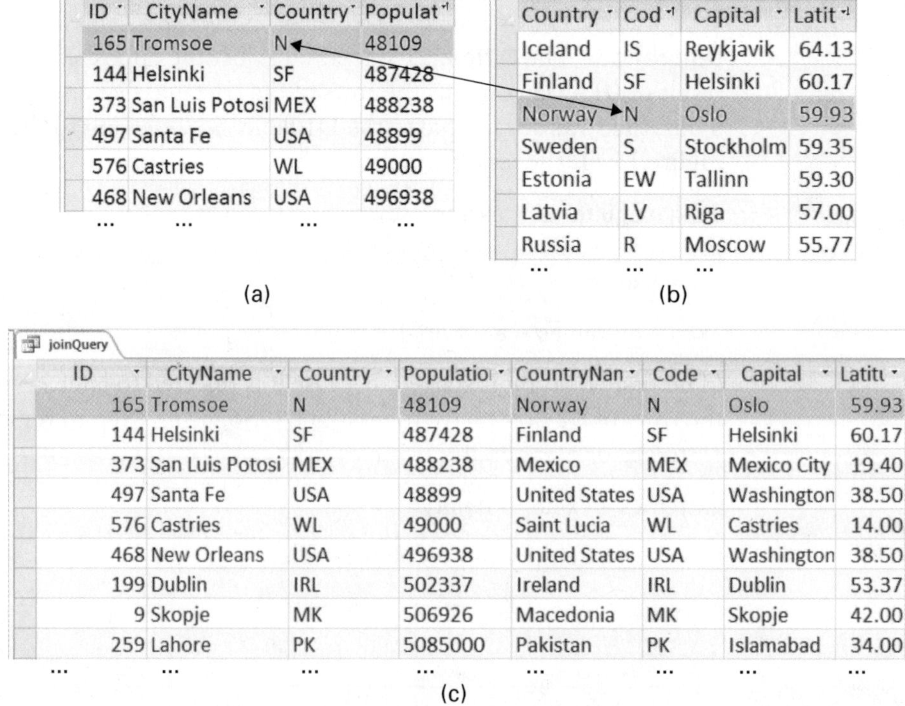

City

ID	CityName	Country	Populat
165	Tromsoe	N	48109
144	Helsinki	SF	487428
373	San Luis Potosi	MEX	488238
497	Santa Fe	USA	48899
576	Castries	WL	49000
468	New Orleans	USA	496938
...	...	...	...

(a)

wDB1

Country	Cod	Capital	Latit
Iceland	IS	Reykjavik	64.13
Finland	SF	Helsinki	60.17
Norway	N	Oslo	59.93
Sweden	S	Stockholm	59.35
Estonia	EW	Tallinn	59.30
Latvia	LV	Riga	57.00
Russia	R	Moscow	55.77
...	...	...	

(b)

joinQuery

ID	CityName	Country	Populatio	CountryNan	Code	Capital	Latitu
165	Tromsoe	N	48109	Norway	N	Oslo	59.93
144	Helsinki	SF	487428	Finland	SF	Helsinki	60.17
373	San Luis Potosi	MEX	488238	Mexico	MEX	Mexico City	19.40
497	Santa Fe	USA	48899	United States	USA	Washington	38.50
576	Castries	WL	49000	Saint Lucia	WL	Castries	14.00
468	New Orleans	USA	496938	United States	USA	Washington	38.50
199	Dublin	IRL	502337	Ireland	IRL	Dublin	53.37
9	Skopje	MK	506926	Macedonia	MK	Skopje	42.00
259	Lahore	PK	5085000	Pakistan	PK	Islamabad	34.00
...	...	...	...	...	...	...	...

(c)

Figure 15.12 A Join operation of City and wDB1: (a) the City database table in which the Country column uses Codes, (b) the wDB1 database table containing one row per country, and (c) the joinQuery database table created by the Join operation of City and wDB1, matching on City.Country = wDB1.Code. All rows of City will appear in joinQuery.

Ask Any Question

To illustrate the science we just introduced, let's apply it to a question typical of the sorts of things people wonder about. For example, you may wonder, "How many men from Africa have won an Olympic gold medal in the marathon?"

All of the records of all medalists of all the Olympics since they restarted in 1896 are kept in Lausanne, Switzerland, at the International Olympic Committee's headquarters. We could go there and check the records for the male marathon winner's country for each Olympics. It would be tedious, but doable. If the records are online, we could do the same thing online. Still tedious, still doable. But, we're people, so we're smart at figuring how to answer such questions.

A computer could answer this question for us, too. All we need to do is say what question we want answered. If we say it using the concepts just introduced, we get the answer back immediately. Let's see how.

Imagine that the database contains (at least) the two tables shown in Figure 15.13. The first table is a list of all men who have won Olympic medals over the years. All events are listed, and all medals are listed. The second is a list of African countries together with their country codes.

How could we use the operations discussed earlier to answer how many men from African countries have won gold medals in the marathon? Here is one solution:

1. Select only those rows from OlympicMen referring to the marathon:

   Select OlympicMen$_{Event\ =\ "Marathon"}$ → OMMarathon

   The result is the portion of OlympicMen in the box in Figure 15.13. Call the result OMMarathon.

2. Select only those rows from OMMarathon referring to gold medalists:

   Select OMMarathon$_{Medal\ =\ "Gold"}$ → OMMGold

   The result is a table with all marathon runners who were gold medal winners. Call the result OMMGold.

Games	Event	Athlete	Coun	Medal
1896	100 Meters	Thomas Burke	USA	Gold
1896	100 Meters	Fritz Hofmann	GER	Silver
...	...	...	...	...
1896	Marathon	Louis Spiridon	GRE	Gold
1896	Marathon	Vasilakos Kharilaos	GRE	Silver
...	...	...	...	...
2012	Marathon	Stephen Kiprotich	UGA	Gold
2012	Marathon	Abel Kirul	KEN	Silver
2012	Marathon	Wilson Kipsang	KEN	Bronze
...	...	...	...	...

(a)

Country	Code
South Africa	RSA
Kenya	KEN
Morocco	MOR
Uganda	UGA
...	...

(b)

Figure 15.13 Olympic database tables: (a) OlympicMen, lists all medalists in all events, and (b) AfricanCountries, contains countries and their three-letter codes (all data from Wikipedia).

3. Next, we need to figure out which marathon gold medalists come from African countries. We do that by crossing OMMGold with the AfricanCountries table, and keeping only the matches, which means we need a Join:

   OMMGold **Join** AfricanNations **On** OMMGold.Country=AfricanCountries.Code

   The result is a table of marathon gold medalists from Africa. Call the result Olympians.
4. As the last step, use the command Project $\text{Olympians}_{\text{Games, Athlete, Country}}$ → Ans to get the final result.

Notice that the first two operations could be combined if the formula was written as Event = "Marathon" **AND** Medal = "Gold"

The Answer Is. . . The Ans version of the Olympians database table is shown in Figure 15.14. Notice that the information about the event is gone, because it is the same (marathon) for each row—why display it? The same is true for medal (Gold). Also, the athletes are shown with their country's proper name, not its code. This information is available during the Join operation's matching, and makes the result a more understandable table.

Although these steps may seem complicated when first encountered, people who use databases every day can perform them quickly.

Wrap Up. Ta da! We've done it. We've shown how saying what question we want database software to answer is the solution to answering it. It's extremely clever. And easy. So easy, in fact, that most of the time the request comes not from a user, but from another computer. For example, when you are looking for airline tickets online, you give your departure and destination cities plus travel dates, and the software packages that into a database request. The database returns the answer, and the UI presents it to you as a long list of possible flights.

So, it may look like "magic," but it's only software built on the science of tables.

Olympians

ID	Games	Athlete	Country
1	1912	Ken McArthur	South Africa
2	1960	Abebe Bikila	Ethiopia
3	1964	Abebe Bikila	Ethiopia
4	1968	Mamo Wolde	Ethiopia
5	1996	Josia Thugwane	South Africa
6	2000	Gezahegne Abera	Ethiopia
7	2008	Samuel Wanjiru	Kenya
8	2012	Stephen Kiprotich	Uganda

Figure 15.14 The Ans version of the Olympians database table created from the tables in Figure 15.13.

15.6 Precious Metal. Using a database table named OlympicWomen containing all of the female medalists in all of the Olympic Games (structured like Figure 15.13(a)), write the query or queries needed to produce a table of African women who have won Olympic medals in the marathon since the event's inception in 1984.

AfriMaraWomen

ID	Games	Athlete	Country	Medal
1	1996	Fatuma Roba	Ethiopia	Gold
2	2000	Joyce Chepchumba	Kenya	Bronze
3	2004	Catherine Ndereba	Kenya	Silver
4	2008	Catherine Ndereba	Kenya	Silver
5	2012	Tiki Gelena	Ethiopia	Gold
6	2012	Priscah Jeptoo	Kenya	Silver

Summarizing the Science

The ideas we've introduced so far—the basics of tables, primitive operations on tables, and ways of combining operations to answer questions—show that "table science" is powerful. In this section we describe some of what the science tells us.

Joining Is Optional. Interestingly, although Join is both powerful and heavily used in practice, it is not really necessary. It is always possible to express what Join does using only Cross-Product and Select. For example, if we need

D1 **Join** D2 **On** D1.fieldi = D2.fieldj

we can replace it with

Select (D1 × D2)$_{D1.fieldi\ =\ D2.fieldj}$ →

Although they are equivalent, it is more convenient to use the Join operator.

Five Operations Do the Work. The five other table operations discussed above can be thought of as the operations that make relational databases work. That's the conclusion based on the following paraphrase of a fundamental property of relational databases:

Given a set of database tables for entities, the operations of Project, Select, Cross-Product, Union, and Difference are sufficient to create any database table derivable from them.

This means that, in practice, any question that can be answered by a table from a collection of database tables can be expressed as a query using those five operations.

The Relationship Metadata. Notice that as we used operations in queries—finding marathon winners, adding country names and capitals to world cities, and even making hemispheres explicit—we have exploited the fact that data in one table was related to data in another table. For example, in Figure 15.12, the Country data in City had the same meaning as the Code data in wDB1, allowing us to match on those two fields. We know this connection because we understand the content of the tables. To maximize the help the database system gives us, we need to tell the software about these relationships.

Informally, a **relationship** is a property of two attributes saying that there is a connection between their data values. For example, in Figure 15.13 the property between

OlympicMen.Country and AfricanNations.Code is that when they match, they refer to the same country. Thus, the letters UGA in OlympicMen.Country has the same meaning as the letters UGA in AfricanNations.Code, and it's a property of all of the content in those two columns.

We say explicitly that such relationships exist, because it isn't automatically true that matching letter sequences have the same meaning. For example, KEN means Kenya when it's in the AfricanNations.Code column, but it's a man's first name when it shows up in the OlympicMen.Athlete column (Ken McArthur). The database UI allows users to specify the relationships between attributes.

Relationships are metadata, and they are extremely valuable metadata. Relationships are responsible for many of the amazing things relational database can do. Scientists have studied the topic deeply and have classified many types of relationships. They are a fascinating topic, but except for one practical example below, we will leave the topic at that.

SQL: The Language of Databases

Many of your online activities—finding airline flights, for example—use the database concepts we've explained so far. A whole technology supports Web applications referencing databases. We place these ideas in a practical context by describing the main database language, SQL.

The most widely used database language is **SQL (Structured Query Language)**. As an illustration, Table 15.3 shows the basic operations of Table 15.2 as they are expressed in SQL. Notice that in SQL, the operations we called Project and Select are combined into one command called Select that uses WHERE to specify the formula. Also, SQL uses INNER JOIN rather than just Join because it has several different variations for joining data.

As an additional example, the Olympians table (Figure 15.14) is computed by the SQL query:

```
SELECT OlympicMen.Games, OlympicMen.Athlete, AfricanCountries.Country
FROM AfricanCountries INNER JOIN OlympicMen
   ON AfricanCountries.Code = OlympicMen.Country
WHERE (((OlympicMen.Event)="Marathon") AND ((OlympicMen.Medal)="Gold"));
```

which makes sense: The last line picks out the marathon gold medalists using our earlier "combined" formula, the FROM and ON statement is a join, and the SELECT statement chooses the needed fields we want to display.

Although there are tiny differences among database systems concerning the syntax and operation of SQL, the previous SQL commands one common way to create the tables used in this chapter.

Query By Example. Perhaps the easiest way to develop a query is with the Query By Example (QBE) facility available in Microsoft Access (see Figure 15.15(a)). The Access UI presents users with the opportunity to select the tables to be input to the query, such as OlympicMen and AfricanCountries.

Table 15.3 SQL queries implementing basic operations

Operation	SQL	Example
Project	**SELECT** wDB1.CountryName, wDB1.Capital, wDB1.Latitude **FROM** wDB1;	Figure 15.7
Select	**SELECT** wDB1.CountryName, wDB1.Code, wDB1.Capital, wDB1.Longitude, wDB1.Latitude, wDB1.Population, wDB1.Area **FROM** wDB1 **WHERE** (((wDB1.Latitude)>60));	Figure 15.8
Cross-Product	**SELECT** * **FROM** extremes, HemiNS;	Figure 15.9(c)
Union	**SELECT** * **FROM** extremes **UNION** **SELECT** * **FROM** equatorial;	Figure 15.11(c)
Difference	**SELECT** * **FROM** exeq **WHERE** Country **NOT IN** (**SELECT** Country **FROM** equatorial);	Equation (*) on page 24
Join	**SELECT** City.CityName, City.Country, City.Population, wDB1.ID. wDB1.CityName wDB1.Code, wDB1.Captial. wDB1.Latitude, wDB1.Logitude, wDB1.Population, wDB1.Area **FROM** City **INNER JOIN** wDB1 **ON** City.Country = wDB1.Code;	Figure 15.12(c)

Next, the attributes in the final result are listed from a drop-down menu in each column (see Figure 15.12(c)). Once these attributes have been selected, constraint formulas can be entered into the criteria row. Using this method, we specify the formulas for selecting rows of interest, such as Event = "Marathon" and Medal = "Gold".

Choosing the fields to be in the answer is about the easiest way to create a database table. There is only one more thing left to do. We must tell the database system that the attributes OlympicMen.Country and AfricanNation.Code refer to the same information. That says that a relationship exists between the two fields. All database systems provide mechanisms to define relationships. In the Query By Example UI that we are using in Access, we drag the field of one table (OlympicMen.Country, which becomes highlighted, see Figure 15.16(a)) to the field of the other table that it has a relationship with (AfricanCountries.Code, see Figure 15.16(b)).

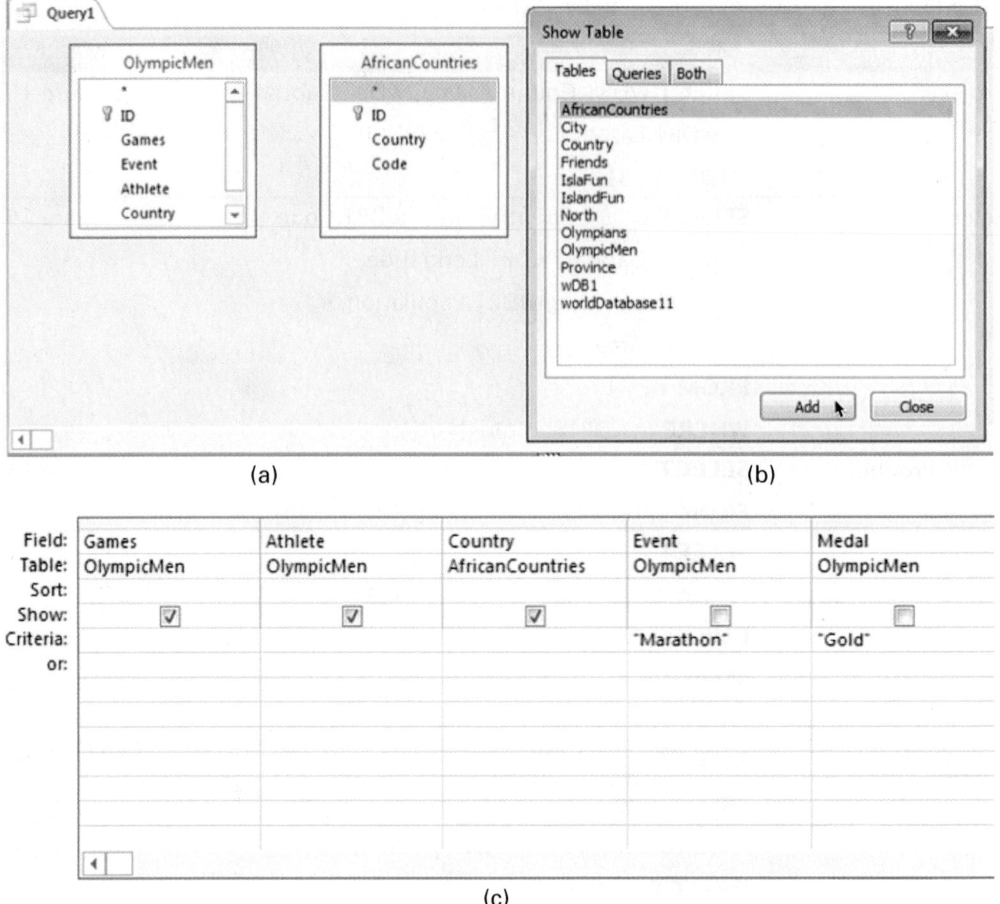

Figure 15.15 Programming **Olympians** in Query By Example in Microsoft Access: (a) choosing the tables that are input to the query from among, (b) the defined tables and queries of the database, and (c) specifying the fields, and limiting criteria.

On releasing the mouse, a line is drawn indicating the relationship. And with that, we are ready to run the query and build the table (Figure 15.14).

Stacks of Databases. The database concepts of this chapter are widely used by other apps. How widespread? Check Figure 1.7, the software stack of the Android phone, and find SQLite—a "phone-size" database system. Then check Figure 9.2, Microsoft's Windows. NET software stack, and find XML prominently situated in the middle layer.

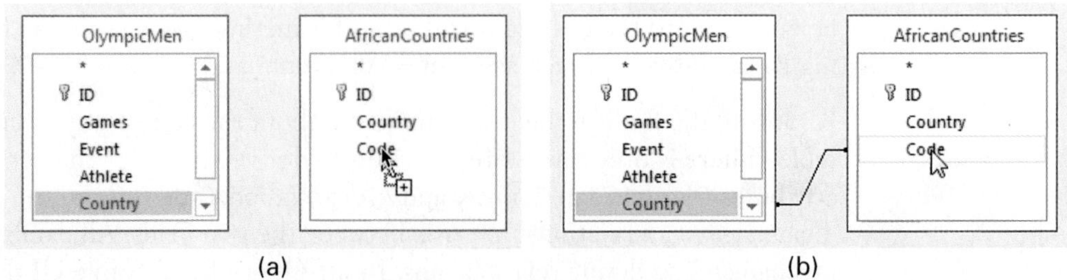

Figure 15.16 Speciying A Relationship in Query By Example: (a) select the **Country** field of **OlympicMen** and (b) after dragging it to the **Code** field of **AfricanCountries**, we see the line denoting the relationship.

Structure of a Database

You have learned that by using the five primitive operations and Join we can create tables from tables to answer questions about data in a database. But usually these operations are used in a slightly different way. We don't usually ask a single question and quit. Rather, we want to arrange the information of a database in a way that users see a relevant-to-their-needs view of the data that they will use continually. Figure 15.17 shows a schematic of this idea.

In the figure there are two forms of tables. The **physical database**, stored on the disk drives of the computer system, is the permanent repository of the database. The **logical database**, also known as the *view of the database*, is created for users on-the-fly and is customized for their needs. Why do we use this two-level solution? The answer requires that we look a little closer at the two groups of tables.

Physical and Logical Databases

The point of the two-level system is to separate the management of the data, which is typically done at the physical database level, from the presentation of the data, which typically involves many different versions for many different users.

Physical Database. The physical database is designed by database administrators in a way that makes the data fast to access. More importantly, the physical database is set up to avoid redundancy, that is, duplicating information. It seems obvious that data should not be stored repeatedly because it will waste space, but disk space is *extremely* cheap, implying that that isn't the reason to avoid redundancy. Rather, if data is stored in multiple places in the physical database, there is a chance—possibly, a good chance—that when it's changed in one place, it will not be changed in every other place where it is stored. This causes the data to become *inconsistent*.

For example, if your school stores your home address, and your major department also stores a separate copy of your address, then when you notify the school of your new residence, both addresses should be changed. But, with multiple copies, that might not occur. If the database contains two different addresses for you, then the school has no idea which address is correct; perfectly good information gets turned into garbage

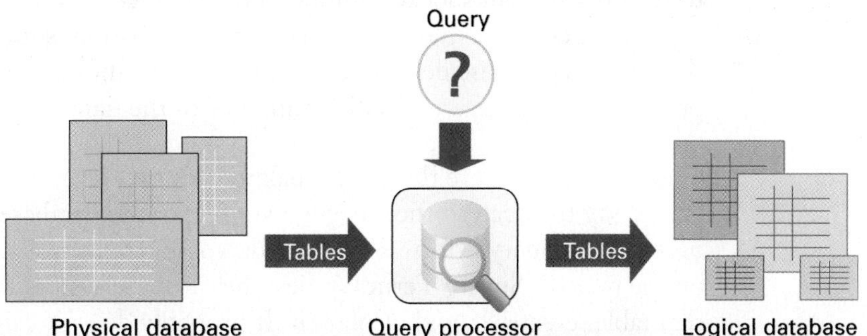

Figure 15.17 Structure of a database system. The physical database is the permanent repository of the data; the logical database, or view of the database, is the form of the database the users see. The transformation is implemented by the query processor, and is based on queries that define the logical database tables from the physical database tables.

because it is inconsistent. For this reason, database administrators make sure that there is only one copy of each piece of data. That is, data is not stored redundantly.

It might seem risky to keep only one copy of the data: What happens if it accidentally gets deleted or the disk crashes? Database administrators worry about this problem all the time, too, and have a process of making backup copies of the database, which they store in a safe place, *never to be used*. That is, until the data is accidentally deleted or the disk crashes—in other words—when the other copy is gone. They can retrieve lost data from the backup, but there is still only one copy.

Avoiding redundancy is obviously good, but keeping one copy seems to ignore the fact that multiple users need the information. The administration needs to send tuition bills, the dean needs to send notification that you "made the list," and the Sports Center needs to send you the picture of your photo finish; they all need your address. Where do they get their copy? That's where the logical database comes in.

Just One Copy. Notice that because your tunes or photos are stored in databases, when you create a playlist or slideshow that seems to have copies of the content, you are only collecting *references* to the single copy.

Logical Database. The logical database shows users the view of the information that they need and want. It doesn't exist permanently, but is created for them fresh every time they look at it. This solves the problem of getting everyone a copy of the address. It's retrieved from the one copy stored in the physical database, and provided to the users as needed, fresh every time. When you report your change of address, that one copy is changed, and everyone referencing it later gets the newest version.

Creating a new copy each time is essential, because if it were to be created once and then stored on the user's computer, then there would be two copies of the information again—the copy in the physical database and the one in the logical database—making the data redundantly stored. So, it never stays on the user's computer; it's always recreated. As a result, when you notify the administration that you moved in the morning, the dean can send you a congratulatory letter in the afternoon and have your correct address.

The other advantage of creating specialized versions of the database for each user is that different users want to see different information. For example, the Sports Center needs to record a student's locker number, but no other unit on campus cares about that. Similarly, the fact that a student is on academic probation is information that most users of the school's database don't need to know, and it should not be included in their view. In principle, each user wants a different view of the database.

Queries. Queries are the key to making this two-level organization work. Each user group, say the dean's office, needs a version of the database created for them. For each user table, a query is formulated in a database language, say SQL. When the dean clicks on the table of Spring Term Grades, the database system runs the query that defines that table, creates it, and displays it. It probably doesn't exist in that form in the physical database, but database operations can define how to create it from the data that is physically stored using the operations described above. On the next day, when the dean opens the table of Spring Term Grades again, a new copy will be created, which means, for example, that a grade change made the previous afternoon by some physics professor (and stored in the physical database) will be visible to the dean.

SUMMARY

In this chapter we followed a path from XML tagging through to the construction of logical views using QBE. You learned a lot, including the following:

- XML tags are an effective way to record metadata in a file.
- Metadata is used to identify values; it can capture the affinity among values of the same entity, and can collect a group of entity instances.
- Database tables have names and fields that describe the attributes of the entities contained in the table.
- The data that quantitatively records each property has a specific data type.
- The five primitive operations on tables—Select, Project, Union, Difference, and Product—are fundamental. These operations are sufficient to create any new tables from other database tables.
- Join is an especially useful operation that associates information from separate tables in new ways, based on matching fields.
- Relationships are the key to associating fields of the physical database.
- The physical database resides on the disk drive; it avoids storing data redundantly and is optimized for speed.
- There is a direct connection between the theoretical ideas of database tables and the software of database systems.

TRY IT SOLUTIONS

15.1 Using a tag name different from <elev> for the elevation is possible, but otherwise this is the one solution apart from spacing.

```
<?xml version = "1.0" encoding="UTF-8" ?>
<archipelago>
 <island><iName>Isabela</iName>      <area>4588</area> <elev>1707</elev></island>
 <island><iName>Fernandina</iName> <area>642</area>   <elev>1494</elev></island>
 <island><iName>Tower</iName>        <area>14</area>    <elev>76</elev></island>
 <island><iName>Santa Cruz</iName> <area>986</area>   <elev>846</elev></island>
</archipelago>
```

15.2 No, it will be a different instance. If any value is changed—say from nothing to something—it's a new instance.

15.3 For North America, any of Name, Capital, or Largest City could be the key, since they are all unique; that is, the column entries are unique. Name and Capital are better because they are not likely to change; conceivably, Largest City could change, say, one day being Kansas City for both Missouri and Kansas.

15.4 Using the database table selectQuery, use the Project operation on CountryName, Capital, and Longitude to form table1. Next, using the operation table1 x HemiEW, create a table of all row pairs, and call it table2. Finally, use the Select operation on table2 with the formula:

```
(Longitude > 0 AND EW='East') OR (Longitude < 0 AND EW='West')
```

15.5 (a) projectQuery + exeq = projectQuery because projectQuery contains the three columns for all rows in wDB1.

(b) extremes − equatorial = extremes because they share no rows, and so no rows are removed.

15.6 Begin with the Select OlympicWomen$_{Event="Marathon"}$ → OWMarathon. Next, use the Join operation as follows: OWMarathon **Join** AfricanCountries **On** OWMarathon.Country=AfricanCountries.Code. Then use the Project operation Olympians$_{Games,\ Athlete,\ Country,\ Medal}$ → to get the final result.

REVIEW QUESTIONS

Multiple Choice

1. Spreadsheets rely on this to keep the integrity of their data:
   a. metadata
   b. position
   c. the data itself
   d. column names
2. Which of the following is an invalid XML tag?
   a. <address>
   b. <stud ID>
   c. <cellPhone>
   d. <SSN>
3. Which of the following is a valid XML tag?
   a. <active?>
   b. <grad-date>
   c. <zip code>
   d. <DOB>
4. In database terminology, a set of entities refers to a
   a. field
   b. column
   c. table
   d. information
5. XML tags cannot contain
   a. spaces
   b. numbers
   c. underscores
   d. both spaces and numbers
6. True or false: Two rows in a table are allowed to have the same data for some attributes.
   a. true
   b. false
   c. it depends on the data itself
   d. it depends on who will be using the data

7. XML tags are
   a. case insensitive
   b. case sensitive
   c. it depends on the tag being used
8. True or false: Physical databases can have redundant data.
   a. true
   b. false
   c. it depends on the data
   d. it depends who will be using the data
9. Which tag encloses all of the content of an XML file?
   a. the root element
   b. <XML>
   c. <html>
   d. <content>
10. When is indenting required in XML files?
    a. always
    b. never
    c. only when sharing the XML file with others
    d. only when the XML files has 200 or more lines of tags
11. A database row is a
    a. value
    b. field
    c. query
    d. tuple or record

Short Answer

1. _______ is information describing other information.
2. A(n) _______ database uses tables to organize information.
3. XML tags cannot start with _______ or _______.
4. All XML tags must be _______.
5. Tag attributes should be used for _______, not _______.
6. Tag attributes have a name and a _______.
7. A column that will always have different values is a _______.
8. A join can be created using the operations _______ and _______.
9. A(n) _______ is a collection of table definitions that give the name of the table, a list of the attributes, and their data types, and identifies the primary key.
10. _______ is the most widely used database language.
11. Unlike databases, _______ rely on position to keep the integrity of their data.
12. XML is called a self-_______ language.
13. Every _______ can be described by XML.
14. Rows and columns in a database table can be _______ and it will still be the same table.
15. _______ tags group all data that is logically related.

Exercises

1. Using XML, tag your contact information and that of two friends. State the rule used for each tag.
2. Explain why you would want to use a database instead of a spreadsheet.
3. Use XML to define your class schedule.
4. When filling out Web forms, explain why they usually ask for your street address, city, and state in separate boxes.
5. Create a list of IDs you have that could be considered primary keys in a database.
6. Explain in your own words the difference between the Collection Rule and the Affinity Rule.
7. Use the data from your class schedule to define a database table.
8. Define the attribute names, data types, and optional comments needed to create a table that could be used as a datebook.
9. For the database in Exercise 8, give two examples of a column that will guarantee the uniqueness of each row (e.g., ID, name).
10. Write a database scheme for the contact information stored on your phone.
11. Create a table to store the information from your driver's license.
12. Using a text editor, create your own XML file containing CD or DVD information. Open the file in a browser.

CHAPTER 16

A Case Study in Database Organization

The iDiary Database

learning objectives

- Describe how to express metadata using XML
- Explain the relationship between XML and XSL
- Demonstrate the incremental creation of a database
- Explain the relationship between tags and templates
- Show how to use tag attributes to display images
- State how information is hidden in XML databases

CHAPTER 16

For a list of all the ways technology has failed to improve the quality of life, please press three.

—ALICE KAHN

MANY PEOPLE keep a diary, and in the Information Age it's natural to keep it in digital form. It's not a blog—that's for information to be shared with others. A diary is for one's own personal use, not for public entertainment. Traditionally, diaries have been text only, handwritten, and organized linearly. But in the world of online information, a digital diary can contain a wide variety of electronic information, including links to Web sites, photos, animations, as well as the daily record of one's private thoughts. In this new form, a diary is not a linear chain of text, but rather a personal database. And that fact makes it an ideal topic for a case study in creating databases, and an opportunity to learn database principles in a personally useful way.

In this chapter we build a diary database by applying the XML approach (see Chapter 15) to structure our data. That's our physical database. To display the iDiary, we let Firefox convert the XML to HTML so it can be viewed in the browser. The conversion uses a language based on XML, called the Extensible Stylesheet Language, or XSL. Because the idea is that each of us will personalize a diary to our own needs, the database of this chapter only illustrates the *principles*. It obviously can't be very "personal." So, we create a fictional diary built around someone's record of the most interesting thing learned each day. It's useful; all you need to supply are day-to-day experiences.

After illustrating an example of the database we will be building, we review XML by constructing a small database recording the foreign countries we have visited. We then introduce XSL to display the Travels database. Prepared with this knowledge, we incrementally build the iDiary database with its companion display information. We include text, titles, images, videos, and poetry to illustrate how irregular data can be organized in a coherent, rational way. Finally, we consider how our database facilities will be used each day.

Thinking About a Personal Database

To start, we analyze the problem of making a personal database that can store any (digital) information that catches our interest. Although we will be thinking about how to solve the technical problems of database design, the discussion will guide us in the organization of the chapter as well.

Regular Versus Irregular Data

Relational databases, as discussed in Chapter 15, can be expressed in neat tables with regular rows, attributes, keys, relationships, and so on. This regularity and the science of databases enable us to create queries in which computers do all of the difficult work of organizing and displaying the information we want to see. The key is the regularity of the data and the rigid structure imposed on it. Relational databases may be powerful, but very often the information we want to record isn't so regular. Our day-to-day lives aren't that regular. We need a more flexible approach. The iDiary database is an example of an irregular data collection.

All the Right Attributes. Despite being a chapter about databases, the heavy use of XML and HTML implies that the word "attribute" will generally mean *tag* attribute in this context.

We record things in the iDiary that we find interesting in our daily lives, which can be almost anything: text, photos, URLs of interesting sites, animations, poems, videos, and so forth. Because we don't want to limit the kinds of information we can store, we will use XML to specify the metadata, implying the database will be an XML tree. In tagging the items stored in the database (see Table 15.1), we will use the Identity, Affinity, and Collection rules described in Chapter 15. In this way, the computer can know what kinds of data it is storing for us.

Collecting information into a heap, however, is not enough organization. We need to impose some structure on the data. Organizing it helps us keep track of what we have, and it also helps the computer display it. Since it is natural to think of the iDiary being added to each day, we will organize the database in time sequence, that is, by date. That's not much structure compared to a relational database, but it will be enough to make our irregular data orderly enough to manage and be useful.

Physical Versus Logical

The XML tree will be our physical database. It's the structure into which we store the data. Because our database is mostly an archive rather than a "working database," we do not expect continuous revisions and updates, but only additions. That means we do not worry about the sorts of things that concern database administrators, like redundancy and access speed. All we want is convenience, which will still take a little preparation.

The logical database is, of course, our view of the iDiary. If it were a relational database, we could specify queries to show the information of interest to us, merging tables to have just the information of importance. But the XML tree is not a relational database. Although querying software is available for XML—called, unsurprisingly,

XQuery—we create instead a short description using the tagging language **XSL (Extensible Stylesheet Language)**, which picks out of the XML tree the data we want and says how to display it. XSL is an integral part of the XML effort to standardize Web databases. The XSL description converts the data into HTML so that it can be displayed on the screen using a browser.

As with all database views, the XSL approach gives us flexibility. We can decide to display everything in the XML tree, or we can choose instead only to display part of it—for example, the movie reviews—and leave everything else hidden. Therefore, the XSL description will be like our queries, plucking data from the physical database and showing us exactly what we want to see.

XHTML. The version of HTML for use with XML is called XHTML, but you don't need to learn a new version of HTML; the form we learned in Chapter 4 works for XHTML.

The iDiary

Our strategy will be to build the iDiary database and its stylesheet display together and incrementally. By beginning small and adding as we go, we will not be intimidated by any daunting task. Also, if our small database is working and we then add some new feature to it, causing it not to work, we know that the error is in the part that was just added. This is a reliable way to limit the problems of debugging a complicated system. Finally, the step-by-step approach mirrors the way in which databases and other systems are enhanced over time. The plan will ensure success and be a good example for independent database projects.

Use Firefox. This chapter uses browser features that are not available on some browsers (Chrome), or render with tiny, annoying errors. Use Firefox and it'll work great.

Figure 16.1a shows a sample from the database we are creating. To familiarize yourself with it, notice that the database is a long list of daily entries. The entries are quite diverse—science news, poetry, book reviews, and other topics. Not only are these few entries interesting, but we expect that over time this will be a rich archive of factoids that we want to remember.

Although we take much of the chapter to set up the iDiary, once built it is convenient to use and requires no further coding.

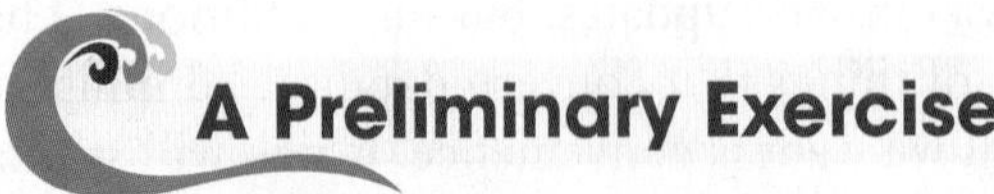

A Preliminary Exercise

We build the iDiary after the next section. First, we need to explore the ideas with a practice database, so we take a moment to construct a small application, which is a database of countries visited. This database will have a similar organization to the iDiary, but is much simpler, allowing us to focus on how it's done.

iDiary

iDiary: Journal of Interesting Stuff

This is a record of the most interesting thing I find out each day that's worth remembering. There's personal stuff in this database, too, but it's not gonna be displayed!

The Digital Diary

This will be fun! I start my digital journal today. So, to launch it with the right sentiment, I looked up what Henry David Thoreau wrote on the first day of his famous *Journal.* He wrote,

"'What are you doing now?' he asked. 'Do you keep a journal?' So I make my first entry today."

Which, I guess, is pretty much what I just said. Great minds ... !

11 August 2013

Human-powered Helicopter

It's so totally awesome! It's been a month since a Toronto team won the Sikorsky Prize, but OMG, I can't stop thinking about it! So, I start this journal with Di Vinci's dream-come-true!

Sikorsy requires: Be aloft 60 seconds; rise to 3 m; stay inside a 10m x 10m square. In the **winning flight** [at 3:30], 50 seconds are spent descending to avoid the perils of the downdraft!

12 August 2013

I ran across this today, and am saving it here so I don't lose track of it. It needs more reading.

Vesperting Cognitio

Natasha Trethewey

Overhead, pelicans glide in threes—
their shadows across the sand
dark thoughts crossing the mind.

Beyond the fringe of coast, shrimpers
hoist their nets, weighing the harvest
against the day's losses. Light waning,

concentration is a lone gull
circling what's thrown back. Debris
weights the trawl like stones.

All day, this dredging—beneath the tug
of waves—rhythm of what goes out,
comes back, comes back, comes back.

Figure 16.1a Part 1: An example of the planned iDiary.

13 August 2013

Potentially Hazardous Astroids

Wow! I read so much poetry, I missed yesterday's APOD! NASA has plotted the orbits of the inner planets, and potentially hazardous astroids. Hmm ... don't a lot of 'em cross Earth's orbit?

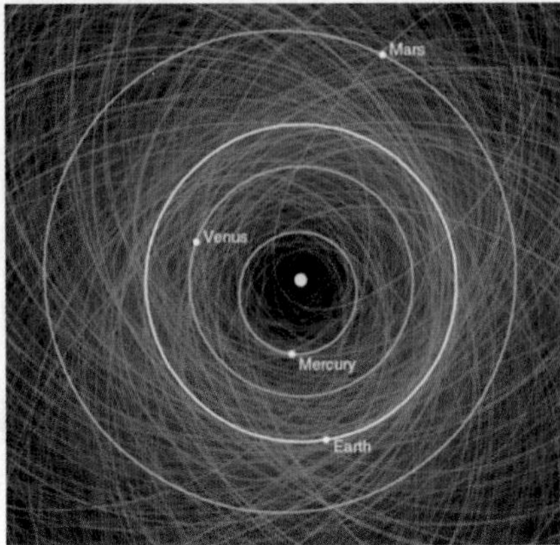

Here's the high resolution image. The Astronomy PIcture of The Day has to be about the BEST science site on the Internet. Thanks APOD! (*Sun not shown actual size.*)

14 August 2013

Science Finally Asks Permission

Last year I read *The Immortal Life of Henrietta Lacks* by Rebecca Skloot. Lacks was a poor African American tobacco farmer and mother of five, who died of cervical cancer in 1951 at age 31. Doctors at Johns Hopkins took cancer cells from her without permission. Because her cells continue to grow in the lab, they're key to medical research. Skloot profiles her and her family, stressing their confusion and hurt because her cells cured diseases; scientists got fame, she got nothing. HeLa cells, cited in 70,000 scientific papers, are *still* growing 60 years later. **Immortal!**

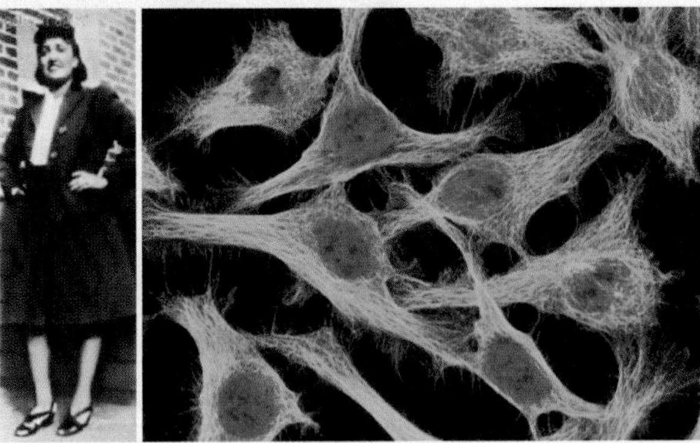

Her genome has now been sequenced. Today the National Institutes of Health set up a board to approve research with her genome; 2 family members sit on the board. Finally! **Hear NPR Here**

Figure 16.1b An example of the planned iDiary.

Use a Text Editor. Like HTML, XML and XSL files should be written using a text editor like Notepad++ or TextWrangler rather than a word processor like Word or Pages. As mentioned in earlier chapters, text editors give you only the text you see, while word processors include invisible tags.

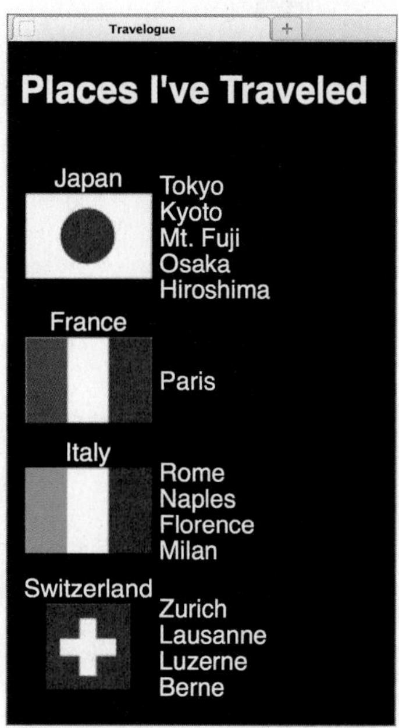

Figure 16.2 The display of the travels.xml file using the travelSS.xsl style information.

Travels Database

Imagine that in our international travels we have visited Italy, Switzerland, France, and Japan. Our database will list the countries, and for each country list a few places—usually cities—that we visited. We will use nontextual data by displaying the country's flag. The goal is shown in Figure 16.2.

The XML Definition. Our entries in the database will be a list of countries, and each will have a name and a tour that contains a list of sights. The name of the file containing the country's flag will be given as a tag attribute for the <name> tag. Therefore, the database will be a sequence of country instances with the following structure:

```
<country>
   <name flag="file.gif"> Country name </name>
   <tour>
      <sight> Sight name </sight>
      . . .
      <sight> Sight name </sight>
   </tour>
</country>
```

We use a standard text editor to enter the data into a file, tagging as we go. Recall that to identify the file as XML, we must give it the .xml file extension and include as the first line of the file this exact text:

```
<?xml version="1.0" encoding="UTF-8"?>
```

Recalling too that the root element is the Collective tag and encloses all items in an XML file, we make <travels> the root element of our tree, and within that we list countries using the structure just shown. Finally, we save the file as travels.xml.

Direct Check of XML. We can have Firefox display our XML as written by just opening the file, as shown in Figure 16.3. The browser looks for stylesheet

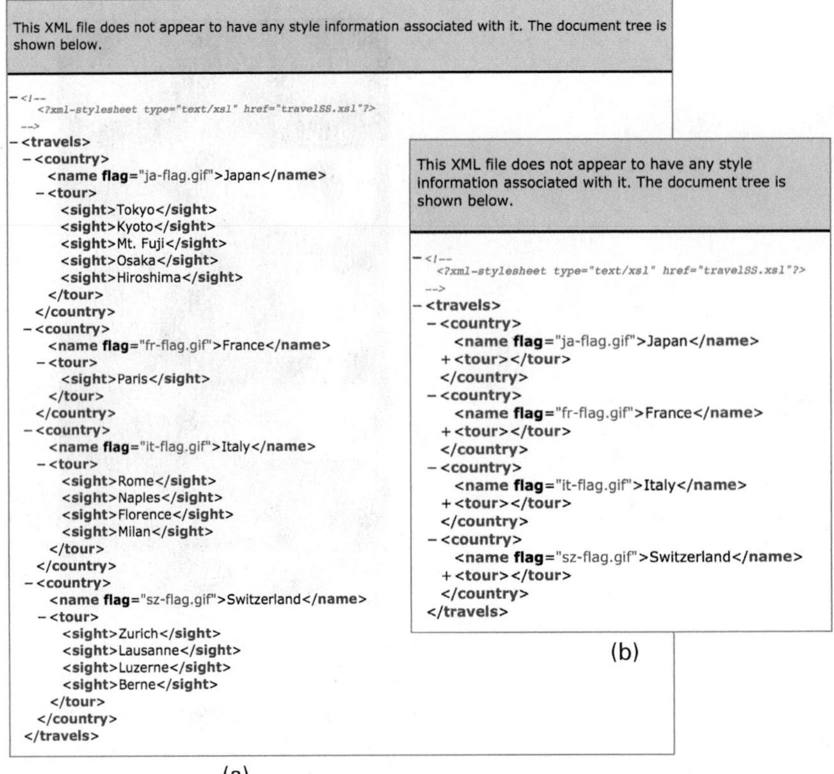

Figure 16.3 The display of the travels.xml file without a styling (XSL) file specified: (a) the initial display of the full file, and (b) using the active controls (– and +) to hide the tour information.

information—we explain that momentarily—and finding none, because we have commented out the second line, the browser shows the XML tree. The color coding helps us check that we have the structure right, and we verify that our intended organization is what the file contains. Notice that the display is *active* in that we can close and open tags used in the Affinity or Collection manner. For example, the inset in Figure 16.3 shows the result of closing the <tour> tags by clicking the minus (–) signs. Closing parts of the database allows us to see the <country> tags without the clutter of the <tour> tags.

Error Console. Recall that Firefox tells you what it doesn't like about your Web pages on the Web Console (*Tools > Web Developer > Web Console*). Consult it when, for example, it displays your XML completely unformatted.

Displaying the Travels with XSL

The message from the browser for the file in Figure 16.3 (at the top of the page) said that no style information was found. Style information tells the browser how to display a markup language like XML, just as it does in HTML. Using the style information, the tags are eliminated by the browser, and the information is displayed according to the style description. For example, the travels.xml file can be displayed as shown in Figure 16.2 using XSL, which is the language of style information. In this section we discuss how to do this.

Connecting XML with Style. Recall from Chapter 4 that Cascading Style Sheets allow an HTML page to have its style information included in an external file with a .css extension; the browser merges the .html and the .css files. XML uses the same idea, with the style information in an external file with an .xsl extension. So, we will put our style information in a file named travelSS.xsl. These two files get associated because we put in the XML file, as the second line, the text

```
<?xml-stylesheet type="text/xsl" href="travelSS.xsl"?>
```

which tells the browser, when it starts to process the XML file, where to find the style information. This is the line the browser didn't find in Figure 16.3. The line must be exactly as shown, except, of course, for the file name.

The Idea of XSL. Here's how XSL formats XML. The .xsl style file contains a series of rules on how to format the information in the .xml content tags. Expect one rule per tag. The rules are called **templates** in XSL, because they describe how the information is to look without actually having the information. (The information, of course, is in the XML content file.) How does the template describe how the information is to be displayed? It uses HTML. And this is what makes XSL so easy to learn: It is basically describing a page with the familiar HTML that we learned in Chapter 4.

Figure 16.4 shows this approach schematically. When the database (XML file) is opened in a browser, the database (DB) and stylesheet (SS) are input to a *transformer*—a part of the browser software. The transformer "walks" the XML tree, converting all of the tags to HTML according to the style template's specification. When an XML tag is found, the transformer looks up the template for that tag in the XSL stylesheet file, and does what the template says, producing more HTML. The HTML is accumulated to be displayed at the end. Usually, each template gives a bit of HTML and the transformer "stuffs in" the data from the XML file in the right places. Finally, when the "walk" of the XML tree is over, the HTML page is displayed.

XSL Templates. It's time to look at some XSL templates. Figure 16.5 shows the XSL file used to display the image in Figure 16.2. Notice that there are tags everywhere. This is because XSL is really just XML!

GAAAK! "XML! XSL! HTML! XSL is really XML! Is tagging computing's only idea? Help!" If you're confused and frustrated, know that others are sympathetic; they've felt just as overwhelmed as you may. Stay with it. It will become clear, and it *will* make sense. Thanks for your patience.

Notice in Figure 16.5 that the first line is the required first line of any XML file. The second line, also required, is a <xsl:stylesheet . . . > tag with tag attributes specifying the details of the stylesheet; these make it an XSL file. After that come the templates, one for each tag. Notice that because the <xsl:stylesheet . . . > tag is the root element of this XML file, it must be closed with </xsl:stylesheet> at the end of the file.

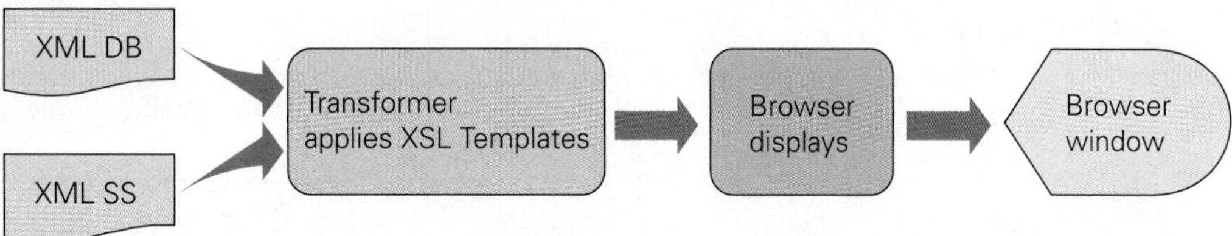

Figure 16.4 Schematic diagram showing how the XML database tree and the XSL style information are merged to produce HTML; the final HTML result is displayed by the browser.

Required Tags. As explained above, every XML file must start with the tag

<?xml version = "1.0" encoding="UTF-8"?>

and have **.xml** as a file extension. If the file is also an XSL file, the next tag must be

<xsl:stylesheet version="1.0" xmlns:xsl="http://www.w3.org/1999/XSL/Transform">

on the second line, and the extension should be **.xsl**. Be exact: spaces, case, and all!

```
<?xml version="1.0" encoding="utf-8" ?>
<xsl:stylesheet version="1.0"
  xmlns:xsl="http://www.w3.org/1999/XSL/Transform">

<xsl:template match="travels">
  <html >
    <head><title>Travelogue</title>
        <meta http-equiv="Content-Type"
               content="text/html; charset=utf-8"/>
      <style type="text/css">
        body {background-color : black; color : white;
              font-family : helvetica}
      </style>
    </head>
    <body>
      <h2>Places I've Traveled</h2>
        <table>
          <xsl:apply-templates/>
        </table>
    </body>
  </html>
</xsl:template>

<xsl:template match="country">
  <tr>
    <xsl:apply-templates/>
  </tr>
</xsl:template>

<xsl:template match="name">
  <td style="text-align : center">
    <xsl:apply-templates/><br/>
      <img src="{@flag}"  alt="Country Flag"/>
  </td>
</xsl:template>

<xsl:template match="tour">
  <td>
    <xsl:apply-templates/>
  </td>
</xsl:template>

<xsl:template match="sight">
  <br/><xsl:apply-templates/>
</xsl:template>

</xsl:stylesheet>
```

Figure 16.5 The contents of the **travelSS.xsl** file that produced Figure 16.2.

There are five different tags used in the XML tree, and five templates in the XSL file, one for each. Notice that the templates have a standard form, which specifies how to display the tags in HTML:

```
<xsl:template match="tag name">
. . .
</xsl:template>
```

The match tag attribute tells which XML tag the template is for. Between the start and end tags is the specification in HTML (and possibly other XSL tags) for how to display the XML.

Next, we explain how each of the templates works.

Tags of All Sorts. Because there are tags everywhere, it's important to understand how the computer tells them apart—it's a good way for us to tell them apart, too! The tag at the start—<?xml . . . ?>—is the standard XML tag, although it looks a little odd. The tags beginning with <xsl: . . . > are XSL tags. The rest of the tags are XHTML tags. So, when the transformer is using this file to look up how to display the XML, it can keep everything straight.

Creating the Travelogue Display. Consider the templates of travelSS.xsl. The first template, which matches the <travels> XML tag, has the form in Figure 16.6.

Notice that between the <xsl:template . . . > tags are HTML tags, which you might recognize as the start of a Web page and the end of that same Web page. (We explain the <xsl:apply . . . > momentarily.) This template says that whenever the transformer encounters a <travels> tag in the XML content file, for example, it should include this HTML text as a description of how to display the <travels> tag. Of course, there is only one <travels> tag in the XML file, because it is the root element tag of the XML tree. So, the way to display this one tag is to set up the entire Web page for the display. Then, as the other tags are processed, they will fill in other parts of the page.

You can see that the template includes the necessary heading and body tags to make the image shown in Figure 16.2. At the "deepest point" in these tags are <table> tags,

```
<xsl:template match="travels">
  <html >
    <head><title>Travelogue</title>
        <meta http-equiv="Content-Type"
                content="text/html; charset=utf-8"/>
      <style type="text/css">
        body {background-color : black; color : white;
              font-family : helvetica}
      </style>
    </head>
    <body>
      <h2>Places I've Traveled</h2>
        <table>
          <xsl:apply-templates/>
        </table>
    </body>
  </html>
</xsl:template>
```

Starting HTML text

Ending HTML text

Figure 16.6 The XSL **travels** template, with the start and end of the HTML text marked.

because the content of the travels.xml file is going to be displayed as a two column table. Each <country> will be a row in this table, with the general structure

Info for <name> tag	<sight> entry
Flag display here	. . .
	<sight> entry

This structure calls for two items in the first cell of the table—the name and the flag image—and a list of items in the second cell, depending on how many sights there are in a tour.

We know that a row of the table will correspond to each <country> tag, because the template matching "country" places the <tr> tags for the table rows. Also, the <name> tag and the <tour> tags place the table data tags <td>. Each XML tag has a stylistic role to play in the overall creation of the Web page, which is implemented by the corresponding XSL template (see Table 16.1).

How does the data get inside the table data tags? As the transformer is processing the XML file, it is always looking for tags and trying to match them to the templates of the XSL file. Anything it finds that is not a tag—that is, the actual content—it puts directly into the HTML definition. So, to get the content of the file displayed requires no effort at all.

The apply Operation. A curious aspect of the XSL specification in Figure 16.5 is the

```
<xsl:apply-templates/>
```

tag. We know from the /> that this is a stand-alone tag, like <br/>, with no mate. Also, notice that the tag is included once in each of the templates. The <xsl:apply-templates/> tag means, "now process whatever is inside this tag." For example, the template matching <tour>:

```
<xsl:template match="tour">
  <td>
    <xsl:apply-templates/>
  </td>
</xsl:template>
```

can be expressed in English as: "When encountering a <tour> tag, place a <td> tag in the accumulating HTML definition; then process the items found within the <tour> tag, which as we know will be a bunch of <sight> tags; finally, when that processing is over, place the </td> tag to complete the table data specification."

Table 16.1 A summary of the style roles of the XML tags we have as implemented by XSL.

XML Tag	XSL Template Task for Displaying the Tag's Data
<travels>	Set up the page, start and finish, including the tags for a table.
<country>	Set up a table row.
<name>	Set up the table data tags for the first cell of a row, place the name, skip to the next line, and place the image of the flag.
<tour>	Set up the table data tags for the second cell.
<sight>	Break to a new line and display the sight.

Although the tag is called apply-templates, it really means, "now process whatever is inside this tag," even though it may not have any more tagged items, but only content. As you now know, when actual content is encountered, the transformer simply puts that content into the accumulating HTML definition, which is what we want.

16.1 Emphasize Paragraphs. Write an XSL template that styles text enclosed in the XML tag <emph> as a paragraph in which all text is both bold and italic.

Tag Attributes. Of special interest is the template matching the <name> tag, whose definition is

```
<xsl:template match="name">
  <td style="text-align : center">
    <xsl:apply-templates/><br/>
      <img src="{@flag}" alt="Country Flag"/>
  </td>
</xsl:template>
```

The template obviously places <td> tags for the left cell of the table row, but it is also responsible for including in its cell the image of the flag. To display an image requires the <img src . . . /> tag, of course, as can be seen on the fourth line. It has the usual form except for {@flag}. The @flag refers to the value of the flag tag attribute of the <name> tag, which gives the file name of the *flag*.gif; see the XML in Figure 16.3. By placing a tag attribute reference in braces in the XSL, we cause the tag attribute's value from the XML to be placed inside the quotes specifying the file source name, as shown next.

XML <name flag="fr-flag.gif">France</name>

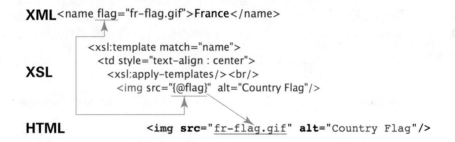

XSL

```
<xsl:template match="name">
  <td style="text-align : center">
    <xsl:apply-templates/><br/>
      <img src="{@flag}" alt="Country Flag"/>
```

HTML

```
<img src="fr-flag.gif" alt="Country Flag"/>
```

This is a standard technique for placing attribute information into the HTML, and we will have several opportunities to use it.

Summary of XSL. When we open our travels.xml file with Firefox, it looks to see what style information is provided. It finds that we specifed the travelSS.xsl file. After opening the style file, the browser's transformer begins to process the XML tree. Finding the <travels> tag first, it checks for a template in the .xsl file. Finding one, it does what the template says: Place the starting HTML commands in the HTML definition up to a <table> tag, then process the other information within the <travels> tag—that is, the rest of the file. When that's done, it appends the remaining HTML tags to the HTML definition, and, when finished, displays the resulting Web page.

While processing "the other information within the <travels> tag," the transformer encounters more tags, which it matches with templates and follows their style specifications. Somewhere within each of those templates, there is a <xsl:apply-templates/>

tag, which requests processing of the information that that tag encloses. The process continues: match a template, do what needs to be done before processing the enclosed information, process the enclosed information, do what needs to be done after processing the enclosed information, and consider that tag processed. It's a very elegant scheme.

That's all you need to know about XSL, although it is a rich, complex language that gives much more power than we need to manage our iDiary.

16.2 Be a Transformer. Say in words what this XSL template accomplishes.

```
<xsl:template match="poem">
   <span style="font-family : century gothic">
     <xsl:apply-templates/>
   </span>
</xsl:template>
```

The iDiary Database

We are now ready to create the iDiary displayed in Figure 16.1. As explained earlier, we solve the problem incrementally, beginning small and adding more information and greater ability to process it as a Web page. It's a good strategy when creating something significant.

Computer Tutor. Read the following sections at a computer, and build the database along with the text; this is an extremely effective way to learn these concepts. Moreover, when finished you will have a database into which you can place your own curious information. Find all the necessary files at pearsonhighered.com/snyder.

The incremental approach will naturally lead us to follow these steps:

1. Getting started
2. Creating a first entry (August 11)
3. Thinking about the nature of things
4. Developing tags and templates

These four steps are the section headings for the following explanations.

Getting Started

Our first concern is building the XML database that will be the physical repository of our iDiary. Because XML allows us to think up the tags, and therefore enables us to have any structure we want, we have a design task: We must figure out our needs and design a structure that meets those needs. In the present case, we need an XML tree in which we can store information about the interesting and curious things that we encounter in our daily lives. This naturally suggests a *sequence* of entries, perhaps one per day, which have a date entry and then the information that we are storing.

Creating the XML Database. With only this small amount of thinking, we can make two decisions about our XML database: First, we decide on <entry> as the Affinity tags to enclose the information we add each day, and second, because we need a root element to enclose the <entry> tags, we choose <idiary> as our Collection tag. So, with these two tags decided upon, we can create a database that contains no data. We create a file with our text editor called iDiary.xml

```
<?xml version = "1.0" encoding="UTF-8" ?>
<!-- <?xml-stylesheet type="text/xsl" href="iDiarySS.xsl"?> -->

<idiary>
  <entry> This is the first entry </entry>
</idiary>
```

and display it with the Firefox browser

```
This XML file does not appear to have any style information
associated with it. The document tree is shown below.

- <!--
     <?xml-stylesheet type="text/xsl" href="iDiarySS.xsl"?>
  -->
- <idiary>
    <entry> This is the first entry </entry>
  </idiary>
```

Notice that the stylesheet specification has been commented out (see the green text in the browser window), because we do not have a style file defined. We know we will need it, and have decided to call it iDiarySS.xsl. We can begin building it, now, too.

Creating the XSL Stylesheet. The XSL stylesheet will need to recognize the two kinds of tags. Using our earlier Travels database as a guideline, we decide to set up the page with the root element <idiary>, and have the <entry> tags produce successive entries of a list. Using a text editor, we enter the lines shown in Figure 16.7 in the iDiarySS .xsl file.

This contains the setup for the Web page, with the title, heading, and italicized comment at the start of the page. (A separate list is used for the italicized comment so its form can be controlled separately from the entries.) Both lists are specified to have a maximum width, so that the page's text is compact. Analogous to <table> in the Travels database, the list containing the entries is also specified as part of the <idiary> template. The template for <entry> tags simply processes the entry itself. This stylesheet produces

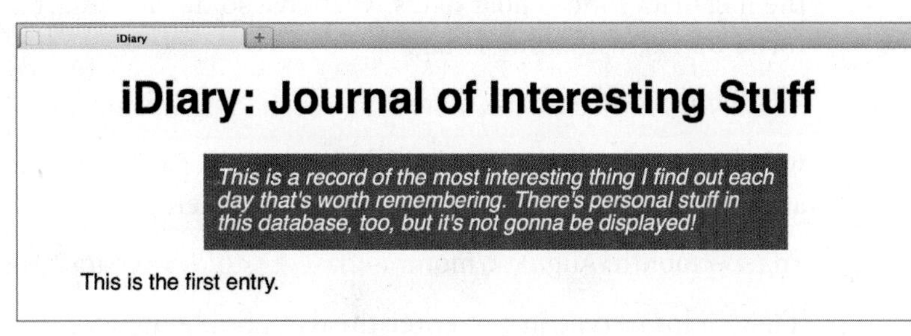

```
<?xml version="1.0" encoding="UTF-8"?>
<xsl:stylesheet version="1.0"
  xmlns:xsl="http://www.w3.org/1999/XSL/Transform">

<xsl:template match="idiary">
  <html><head><title>iDiary</title>
      <style>
        body {background-color : white; font-family : helvetica}
        h1     {text-align : center}
        h2     {text-align : center; color : #993400;}
        ul      {margin-left : auto; margin-right : auto; list-style-type : none}
      </style>
    </head>
    <body>
      <h1>iDiary: Journal of Interesting Stuff</h1>
        <ul style="max-width:435px">
           <li style="background-color : sienna; color:white; padding:10px">
               <i>This is a record of the most interesting
               thing I find out each day that's worth
               remembering. There's personal stuff in this
               database, too, but it's not gonna be displayed! </i>
           </li>
        </ul>
        <ul style="max-width:700px;">
            <xsl:apply-templates/>
        </ul>
    </body>
  </html>
</xsl:template>

<xsl:template match="entry">
       <xsl:apply-templates/>
</xsl:template>

</xsl:stylesheet>
```

Figure 16.7 First XSL styling entries for iDiarySS.xsl.

when we uncomment the stylesheet tag (the second line) of the XML file, and open the XML file with Firefox. With the XML and the XSL files started, the iDiary project is well underway.

Creating a First Entry (August 11)

Continuing our design planning, we consider what goes inside of each <entry> tag by thinking about the August 11 entry. Since the entry is the entity that we're putting in the database, what items should be enclosed by it? Obviously, the date is one part and, of course, there must be some cool content as the other part. This motivates us to create two more tags, <date> and <cool>.

Date Tagging. This sounds like a party game, but it refers to the decisions surrounding the metadata for calendar dates. We have some choices. If we write the date in an atomic form, that is, with a single tag,

```
<date>August 11, 2013</date>
```

we cannot refer to the day, month, and year separately. But, do we want to? The alternative would be to fully tag each component, as in

```
<date><month>August</month><day>11</day><year>2013</year></date>
```

That's a lot to type just to enter the date. So, being lazy, we decide to let it be atomic, and promise to learn more XSL to fix it if we ever change our mind.

16.3 It's a Date. Assuming the fully tagged form of the date just shown, write the XSL templates to produce *August* 11, 2013, that is, the month is italic, the day is large, and the year is small.

Revising the opening entry. With the two new tags decided upon, we can revise the temporary content of the <entry> tag in the iDiary.xml file. It's still the beginning text rather than an official August 11 entry, so we decide to leave it undated, and just use the <cool> tag alone:

```
<entry>
  <cool><title>The Digital Diary</title>
    This will be fun! I start my digital journal today.
    ...
    said. Great minds ... !
  </cool>
</entry>
```

Having added tags, we need to add templates to the iDiary.xsl file. The two new tags will both be displayed as list items with <li> tags, although they will have different "looks." We might have used definitional list <dl> tags to keep the two roles separate, but it's easier to change the looks using the CSS properties, as we see below. To use CSS, we only need to identify which use of the <li> tag we intend, using the class attribute (see Chapter 4) . The appropriate templates are

```
<xsl:template match="cool">
      <li class="entry">
        <xsl:apply-templates/>
      </li>
</xsl:template>

<xsl:template match="date">
      <li class="date">
        <xsl:apply-templates/>
      </li>
</xsl:template>
```

which produces this result.

iDiary

iDiary: Journal of Interesting Stuff

This is a record of the most interesting thing I find out each day that's worth remembering. There's personal stuff in this database, too, but it's not gonna be displayed!

The Digital Diary This will be fun! I start my digital journal today. So, to launch it with the right sentiment, I looked up what Henry David Thoreau wrote on the first day of his famous Journal. He wrote, "'What are you doing now?' he asked. 'Do you keep a journal?' So I make my first entry today." Which, I guess, is pretty much what I just said. Great minds ... !

The text that we entered shows no styling. Why? Because, when the transformer looked for the template for the <li class="entry">, for example, it didn't find anything. So it just ignored the formatting request and used its default information about how to format a list item. That happened with the <title> and <quote> tags, too. So, our next step is to define the CSS for the tags we used in the entry.

```
li.entry { color : black;                    set text color
         padding : 10px;                     add space around item
         border-bottom-style : solid;        define item's bottom side
         border-bottom-width : 0.5px;        set bottom's thickness
         border-right-style : solid;         define item's right side
         border-right-width : 0.5px;         define side line's thickness
         margin-bottom : 20px }              seperate from next entry

li.date { color : white;                     set text color
         position:relative; left : -50px;    move date left to mark item
         background-color : sienna;          color the date item
         padding : 8px}                      put some space around it
```

Figure 16.8 CSS styling for the two classes of list items: entry and date.

Class Styling. The necessary styling for the <li> tags uses mostly familiar CSS, and builds on the concept of styling classes from Chapter 4 (see www.w3schools.com/sitemap/sitemap_references.asp). Check the CSS reference for how to position the date to the left. The styling for the two classes are shown in Figure 16.8.

Once we enter the data for the first day, we see (Figure 16.9) that the <date> and <cool> tags are properly styled. The styling of the content comes next.

Thinking About the Nature of Things

When we create an entry, we want to capture all of the information digitally, and as Figure 16.1 shows, that data can take many forms. These affect both the XML and the XSL definitions.

Recognizing the Need for Specific Tags. When considering the design of the XML, notice that we must specify different data for each type of content. The list on the following page shows some examples.

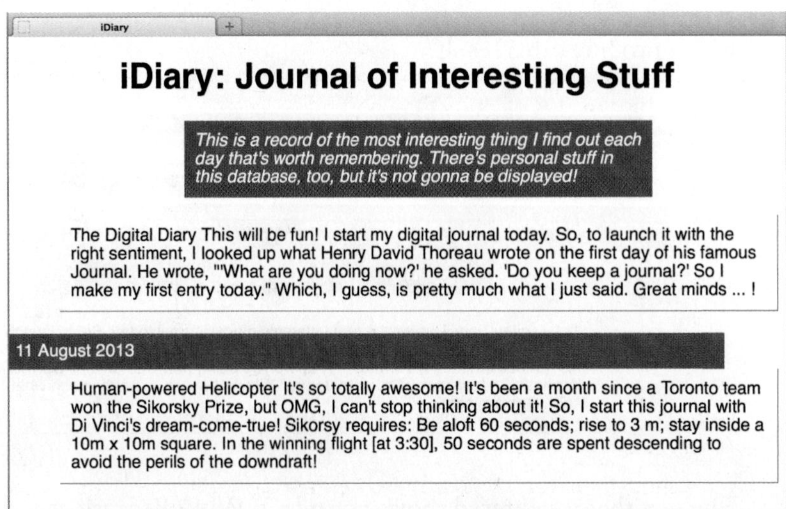

Figure 16.9 Opening information and the first day's entry showing the "class" styling of list items for <date> and <cool> tags. XSL styling for all Identity tags such as <title> are still missing.

Type	Specification
Link	URL and anchor
Image	Source file URL, and possibly width
Text	Written directly into the file, possibly with italic or bold
Video	URL, player dimensions, other parameters

Each of these requires that we specify different information. They also require different formatting. Additionally, the text can take several different forms, including:

Type	Style
Titles	Centered with enlarged size
Quotes	Intended with colored background
Poems	Title, author, and line breaks at specific points

Obviously, to recognize these differences, we need several additional tags.

Choosing Specific Tags. Knowing that different kinds of data need different tags—or, stating it in database terms, each database entity requires its own tag—we assign a new tag to each kind of data we store in the iDiary database. So, we propose to develop the tags in Table 16.2.

The table's tags are Identity tags, except for the <poem> tag, which is an Affinity tag grouping three more Identity tags that give the title of the poem, the author, and the lines. Notice that in addition to <title> we include a <p_title> for the poems. The difference is that <title> will be centered and larger than the normal text, abstracting the idea of a heading; the <p_title> captures the idea of the title for a literary work, which will not be centered and has smaller text. Such distinctions are small, but if we recognize differences among the properties of an object or we are fussy about how we want our iDiary to look, we add tags to recognize such differences. And why not? Tags are free, and templates take 30 seconds to write.

Developing Tags and Templates

Having worked out that we need several new tags, we take a moment to think about each of them, because some have characteristics that need discussing. With each, we give its companion stylesheet template.

Table 16.2 The principal Identity tags used for the iDiary database.

Tag	Encloses
<title>	Text to be centered; font is enlarged
<link>	Anchor text; the URL is a tag attribute
<pic>	Stand-alone tag with file name and width tag attributes
<quote>	Text to be indented and given background color
<poem>	Groups <p_title>, <poet>,and <lines> tags
<ytvid>	Stand-alone tag with URL of video

The Title Tag. The <title> tag announces the most interesting thing entry, when appropriate.

```
<title> The Digital Diary </title>
```

The text should be centered and can use the HTML heading tags to enlarge the font.

```
<xsl:template match="title">
  <h2>
    <xsl:apply-templates/>
  </h2>
</xsl:template>
```

The Link Tag. The <link> tag specifies a Web link. As usual, the Web link has two parts: The tag encloses the anchor text—the highlighted text of the link—and the URL is specified using the tag attribute of that name. For example,

```
<link url="http://apod.nasa.gov/apod/ap130812.html">Here's...</link>
```

illustrates the structure. The stylesheet must place an <a href...> tag and enclose the tag attribute value in quotes. A template to do that is

```
<xsl:template match="link">
  <a href="{@url}">
    <b><xsl:apply-templates/></b>
  </a>
</xsl:template>
```

As explained earlier with the French flag example, the @ symbol is the XSL reference to the tag attribute of the XML tag. By enclosing the reference in curly braces and referring to its tag attribute name, we can place the tag attribute's value in the HTML text.

The Picture Tag. The <pic> tag is a stand-alone tag because all of its information is expressed as tag attributes. The tag encodes the file name of the image and its desired display width, as shown in the following example:

```
<pic file="im/APODpicOfTheDay.jpg" width="350"/>
```

Note that as a stand-alone tag, <pic.../> is terminated by the />, and that the image is stored in a folder called im.

```
<xsl:template match="pic">
      <img src="{@file}" width="{@width}"
            alt="Picture of Interesting Thing"/>
</xsl:template>
```

Of course, being a stand-alone tag, it does not enclose anything. Accordingly, there is no need for the <xsl:apply-templates/> tag that would normally request continued processing of the enclosed tags or content. This makes the <pic /> tag slightly different from those we've seen.

The Quote Tag. Quotes are an example of text that should be set off so it will be noticeable. We can use the <blockquote> HTML tag and simply style it as we like. For example:

```
<quote>"'What are you doing ... today."</quote>
```

We can style the implementing <blockquote> tag in the <head> section of the page, but it is just as easy to style it inline. Thus, the template is

```
<xsl:template match="quote">
  <blockquote style="background-color : #c89848;
     color:white; padding:10px; font-size:small">
    <xsl:apply-templates/>
  </blockquote>
</xsl:template>
```

By classifying different types of text, we keep tight control on the format of the page.

The Poetry Tags. We identify several attributes of poetry—title, author, and lines—and assign tags to each.

They will be enclosed in the Affinity tag <poem>. As noted earlier, we do not use the <title> tag to title a poem. Rather, we invent another, <p_title> tag, which will also allow for different formatting. For example,

```
<poem>
  <p_title>Vespertina Cognitio</p_title>
  <poet>Natasha Trethewey</poet>
  <line>Overhead, pelicans glide in threes—</line>
     ...
</poem>
```

The templates for these new tags are, by now, straightforward. The template for <poem> is given in Try It 16.2, which selects a fancier font for the poetry, which it deserves. The <p_title> and <poet> tags are self-explanatory, as is the basic <line> tag.

```
<xsl:template match="p_title">
  <h3>
     <xsl:apply-templates/>
  </h3>
</xsl:template>

<xsl:template match="poet">
  <h4><i>
    <xsl:apply-templates/>
  </i></h4>
</xsl:template>

<xsl:template match="line">
      <xsl:apply-templates/>
    <br/>
</xsl:template>
```

With this formatting, the poem appears as shown in Figure 16.10(a).

Attribute for Padding. To achieve the styling the poet chose, we create a tag <skip> inserting a blank line with <br/> to separate the stanzas. For the indenting, we have several options. We could create a separate tag for each line customized to the amount to indent; or perhaps we could make a tag that inserts 5 spaces, and use 0, 1 or 2 of them per line. The way to do it with a single <line> tag – and probably the best of these choices – is to add an attribute.

The revised line template looks like this

```
<xsl:template match="line">
    <span style="padding-left:{@amt}0px">
       <xsl:apply-templates/>
    <br/></span>
</xsl:template>
```

and would be used in one of three forms:

```
<line>Overhead, pelicans glide in threes—</line>
<line amt="2"> their shadows across the sand</line>
<line amt="4"> dark thoughts crossing the mind. </line>
```

to produce

Overhead, pelicans glide in threes—
    their shadows across the sand
        dark thoughts crossing the mind.

The first line of the stanza doesn't need any padding, so the amt tag attribute isn't given; that would be the normal case for most poems. The next two lines get padding of 20px or 40px, because when the value of amt—either 2 or 4—replaces {@amt} in the template's text {@amt}0px, the digit completes the padding specification to produce 20px or 40px. Only the leading digit is supplied because in the cases where no amt tag attribute is specified, the value is empty, making the first line's left padding specification 0px. It now looks like Figure 16.10(b).

This approach gives flexibility when styling poems, because amounts other than 2 and 4 are fine. This formatting will not be sufficient for poets like e. e. cummings, but we put that problem off for another day.

Human-Powered Helicopter

The Video Tag. The best way to include videos in the iDiary is to embed a connection to the player using HTML's <iframe> tag. Most sites that stream videos have an "embed" button near the video, and clicking it gives you all of the HTML you need to display the video on your page; see Figure 16.11, where the code was revealed with *Share > Embed*. Packaging this information into an XSL template accesses the video.

The first point to realize is that every video streaming site is different, so the safest thing is to set up a tag for each streamer.

The second point is that the <iframe> content usually needs a bit of surgery to work well for the purposes of XML/XSL. The <iframe> from YouTube is

```
<iframe width="560" height="315"
src="//www.youtube.com/embed/syJq10EQkog"
frameborder="0" allowfullscreen></iframe>
```

and it is a case in point. The main thing is the https: is missing from the URL given in the src attribute, but we fix that when we give the URL in the XML tag attribute.

Vespertina Cognitio
Natasha Trethewey
Overhead, pelicans glide in threes—
their shadows across the sand
dark thoughts crossing the mind.
Beyond the fringe of coast, shrimpers
hoist their nets, weighing the harvest
against the day's losses. Light waning,
concentration is a lone gull
circling what's thrown back. Debris
weights the trawl like stones.
All day, this dredging—beneath the tug
of waves—rhythm of what goes out,
comes back, comes back, comes back.

(a)

Vespertina Cognitio
Natasha Trethewey
Overhead, pelicans glide in threes—
    their shadows across the sand
        dark thoughts crossing the mind.

Beyond the fringe of coast, shrimpers
    hoist their nets, weighing the harvest
        against the day's losses. Light waning,

concentration is a lone gull
    circling what's thrown back. Debris
        weights the trawl like stones.

All day, this dredging—beneath the tug
    of waves—rhythm of what goes out,
        comes back, comes back, comes back.

(b)

Figure 16.10 Poetry styling: (a) Styled with the basic <line> tag; (b) the style in which the poet wrote it.

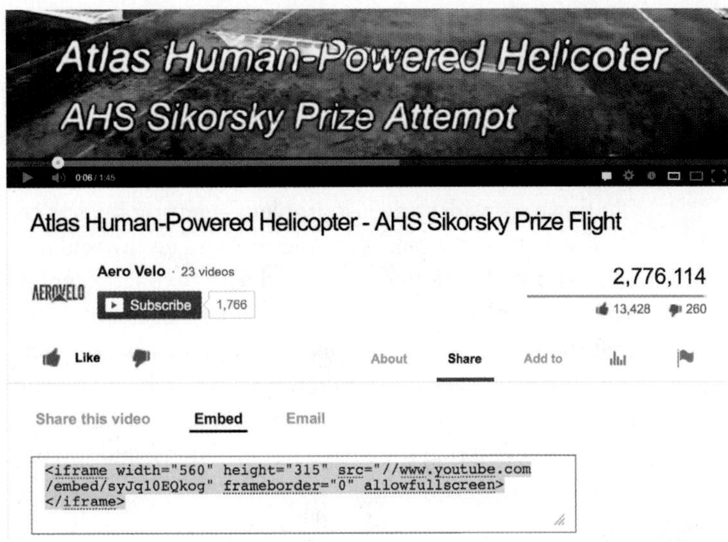

Figure 16.11 Accessing embedding information at YouTube: Navigate *Share* > *Embed* to reveal the **<iframe>** tags for embedding.

The XML is the obvious

```
<ytvid file="https://www.youtube.com/embed/syJq10EQkog">
```

The file tag attribute will be the value of src in the styled <iframe> text. To accommodate it, the XSL template is

```
<xsl:template match="ytvid">
   <br/><br/><iframe width="560" height="315"
     src="{@file}" frameborder="0" allowfullscreen="1">
   </iframe><br/><br/>
</xsl:template>
```

The template begins (and ends) with two <br/> tags to make space around the video; the src value becomes the tag attribute from the <ytvid> tag, giving almost the exact same text as imported from YouTube. The only difference is that we've changed the allowfullscreen that they sent us with allowfullscreen="1". The reason is this. HTML, which YouTube assumes we're using, permits certain attribute specifications like allowfullscreen without any value being given. XHTML, the variant of HTML used for XML/XSL, is stricter. Every tag attribute needs to be given a value. So, for all stand-alone tag attributes like allowfullscreen, we give them the value "1".

Ampersand Alert. The embedding code we grab is usually "ready to go." There is one caution, however. Occasionally, an ampersand (&) is used in a URL or other imported HTML text. They cause a problem with the XML/XSL processing because the ampersand is the escape symbol for special characters. Replace them with: **&** which is the "escaped" version of ampersand. Or the browser will remind you!

16.4 Movie Producer. Give the XML and the XSL to play a Vimeo video as part of the iDiary page. Choose any Vimeo video or use this one: **http://player.vimeo.com/video/29200097**.

Wrap-Up Tags. We have discussed most of the tags and templates used in Figure 16.1. We have skipped simple tags like <skip/> for the blank line between stanzas. We also skipped some of the CSS styling needed to make the design and layout "just right." That's personal taste, of course. The styling used for Figure 16.1 is shown in Appendix C, and doesn't require further comment.

To finish, consider one last problem—getting images centered—and a "trick" to resolve it. The <pic /> tag places the picture, and (as advised in Chapter 4) it can be centered by placing it inside of <p> tags, styled with text-align:center. But, if we include <p> tags in the <pic /> template, say, to center the image of the planets, then when we have two pictures that should be side by side, like Henrietta Lacks and her famous cells, the <p> tags will force the photos one above the other, because each will be enclosed in a <p> tag. So, we don't include <p> in <pic />. Instead, we just make a separate <para> tag that centers its text; it works for centering the image of the planets, and it works for Henrietta and her cells, too.

Using the iDiary Daily

Building the iDiary database has taken some time, which we can't afford to do everyday. But, we don't need to. The database is now set up. We just use it. As long as the only things we want to record are text, quotes, pictures, videos from YouTube or Vimeo, or poetry, we're done. We simply tag the date and the most interesting thing we've learned. But, our database has the flexibility to record any digital data and to display it in an attractive way. All we need to do is add the right tags to identify and display the information. We will do that only occasionally. Possibly less than once a year, once we have handled our "usual" data types.

There are ways we can make our database easier to use each day.

Archiving Photos

As we've built the page, the iDiary.xml and iDiarySS.xsl files and the photos have all been on the desktop. They need to be placed in a permanent location. Because the page will likely include many photos, we should store them in a separate folder within the folder containing the two database files. The folder im has been used here, and is adequate, but it is possible to have separate folders in it, perhaps one for public and one for personal use.

Hiding Information

So far, we have displayed all of the information in the database, but we don't have to. We *do* have to tag everything, and we *must* provide a template to process each tag. But, we don't have to display it.

Suppose we have a tag, <personal>, that encloses our personal thoughts. Though the information can go anywhere in the database, we should consider where we want it placed when we do display it. Assume the <personal> tag is included inside of the <cool> tag, as part of the most interesting thing for the day. Then, the template to display the <personal> content is

```
<xsl:template match="personal">
    <!--Display Personal Information -->
    <xsl:apply-templates/>
</xsl:template>
```

which processes that text and tags as usual; it's wise to include a comment to remind ourselves that we're displaying *personal* information.

Because the <xsl:apply-templates/> tag tells the transformer to "process the information enclosed in the matched tag," all we need to do is leave that tag out of the template. That is, we write

```
<xsl:template match="personal">
   <!--Don't Display Personal Information -->
</xsl:template>
```

When the transformer gets to a <personal> tag, it will check to see what to do, and with no instructions to apply templates to the enclosed information, it will just skip the information inside the tags, as if it were not there. The result is that our personal content is not displayed, though it is part of the database.

Note that including personal information in the file without enclosing it in tags, or tagging it but not providing a template for the tag, *both result in the information being displayed*. In both cases, the transformer doesn't know what to do with the information, so the transformer just adds the information to the HTML file, causing it to display on the page. Hiding information requires that we treat it properly, including saying how not to display it.

Entering Data into the Database

Because we have built our own database system without using commercial database software, we will be adding new data using our trusty text editor, and we'll be tagging everything ourselves. (Once you've learned JavaScript—starting in Chapter 17—you can create "an app for that.") We can simplify the task so that it is not an annoyance by setting up our own template in the comments.

In the XML database, we include a comment in the form shown in Figure 16.12. Then, by copying and pasting the interior portion of the comment—the <entry> tags and the lines they contain—we have all of the tags we need. We delete tags we don't need and edit those we do. This ensures that we remember the tags, match tags, and don't make typos in the tags.

```
<!--The following tags are available for adding a new entry.
  Change the places containing black letters or dashes
<entry>
<date> dd mm yyyy</date>
<cool>
   <para>  <ital>  <bold>
   <link url="http:// - ">anchor text</link>
   <title> title text </title>
   <pic file="-.jpg" width="-" />
   <quote> blockquote text </quote>
   <poem>
     <p_title> poem title</p_title>
     <poet> poet's name </poet>
     <line amt="d"> set d to digit for d tabs </line>
     <skip/>
   </poem>
   <ytvid url=" - "/>
</cool>
</entry>
-->
```

Figure 16.12 A tag list comment as a reminder of available tags.

SUMMARY

In this chapter, we have applied the database ideas from Chapter 15 to a personally relevant task of making a digital diary capable of recording and displaying the many types of media we encounter online. From this case study you now understand the following:

- XML databases can record irregular data that relational databases cannot.
- An XML database can be directly displayed by opening it in a browser.
- Adding a stylesheet line to XML and building templates in XSL allows the XML file to be attractively formatted using HTML so that it can be displayed by a browser.
- A complex database can be set up incrementally, adding tags and templates one at a time, and checking that they work as planned.
- An XML database can optionally hide some of its information, allowing for the selective display of its contents.

TRY IT SOLUTIONS

16.1

```
<xsl:template match="emph">
<b><i>
     <xsl:apply-templates/>
</i></b>
</xsl:template>
```

Enclosing bold tags with italic tags is also correct.

16.2 It changes the font to display poems to Century Gothic by surrounding the text with <span> tags.

16.3

```
<xsl:template match="date">
    <xsl:apply-templates/>
</xsl:template>

<xsl:template match="month">
     <i><xsl:apply-templates/></i>
</xsl:template>

<xsl:template match="day">
    <big><xsl:apply-templates/></big>,
</xsl:template>

<xsl:template match="year">
    <small><xsl:apply-templates/></small>
</xsl:template>
```

Did you remember to include the comma after the day?

16.4 The XML reads

```
<vimeostd url = "http://player.vimeo.com/video/29200097?
   title=0&amp;byline=0&amp;portrait=0" />
```

and the XSL reads

```
<xsl:template match="vimeostd">
    <br/><br/><iframe src="{@url}" width="400" height="225"
        frameborder="0" webkitAllowFullScreen = "1"
        allowFullScreen = "1">
        </iframe><br/><br/>
</xsl:template>
```

Multiple Choice

1. The <idiary> tag is a
   a. Collection tag
   b. Affinity tag
   c. Identification tag
   d. none of the above
2. The <country> tag is a
   a. Collection tag
   b. Affinity tag
   c. Identification tag
   d. none of the above
3. The root element <xsl:stylesheet ... > tag is a
   a. Collection tag
   b. Affinity tag
   c. Identification tag
   d. none of the above
4. What tag should you use when adding a video?
   a. <ivideo>
   b. <frame>
   c. </iframe>
   d. none of the above
5. An incremental approach to development has the advantage of
   a. shortening development time
   b. making the final product smaller
   c. limiting errors to recently developed materials
   d. all of the above
6. When you open an XML file without a stylesheet in a browser, it
   a. won't display and returns an error
   b. displays the text of the file
   c. displays a tree showing the structure of your file
   d. brings up a dialog box to find the stylesheet
7. XSL tag rules are called
   a. licenses
   b. structures
   c. policies
   d. templates
8. The second line of an XML file that uses an XSL template begins with
   a. <?xml-stylesheet
   b. <html>
   c. <!--xsl
   d. <?xsl-stylesheet
9. iDiary is ordered by
   a. event
   b. date
   c. friend
   d. class

10. What tag should you leave out if you want certain information hidden?
    a. <xsl: template>
    b. <xsl: apply/>
    c. <xsl:hide-templates/>
    d. <xsl:apply-templates/>
11. To add entries to iDiary you would
    a. modify the XML file
    b. modify the XSL file
    c. make changes to both files
    d. once created, the file cannot be changed

Short Answer

1. XSL stands for _______.
2. XSL templates describe how the information should be displayed by using _______.
3. XML and XSL files are combined in a(n) _______, where they're converted to HTML for display in a browser.
4. In Firefox, to open the Web console go to: _______ > _______ >_______
5. The root element tag of a stylesheet is a _______ tag.
6. In order for the XSL code <img src = "{@dog}" /> to be valid, the _______ line of HTML must be present.
7. A stand-alone tag does not _______ anything.
8. An XML database can be displayed by opening a _______.
9. _______ can be used to format and style an XML file.
10. XSL files contain a series of _______ to format the information.
11. To cause the content of certain XML tags to be omitted from the transformed HTML, remove the _______ tag from the templates for those tags.

Exercises

1. Use XML to define your class schedule.
2. Create a list of other content that could be added to the iDiary database.
3. Design a database similar to iDiary with details for a vacation.
4. Explain in words what the following XSL template accomplishes

```
<xsl: template match="face">
   <p style="color: blue">
      <xsl: apply-templates/>
   </p>
</xsl: template>
```

5. Create a family history using XML and XSL.
6. Create an iStore database to display items for sale.
7. Create the XML and XSL to play a YouTube video of your choice.
8. A used car dealer wants you to develop a Web site to display his vehicles. The inventory changes daily. Explain what you would include on the site and how you would update it daily.

INTERVIEW

with

Alan Kay

Alan Kay is one of the earliest pioneers of personal computing: In the late 1960s he designed one of the first desktop computers (the FLEX machine), and tablet computers (the Dynabook), and in the early 1970s he invented an early object-oriented programming language, development, and operating system (Smalltalk). Alan also developed the now ubiquitous overlapping window interface. More recently, he helped found the Viewpoints Research Institute, a nonprofit organization dedicated to improving education through new computing technologies for the benefit of the world's children. Alan has been a Xerox Fellow, Chief Scientist of Atari, an Apple Fellow, a Disney Fellow, and a Senior Fellow at Hewlett-Packard.

Alan received his B.A. in Mathematics and Molecular Biology with minor concentrations in English and Anthropology from the University of Colorado in 1966, and his M.S. and Ph.D. degrees in Computer Science from the University of Utah in 1968 and 1969. He is the recipient of numerous awards, including the NAE's Charles Stark Draper Prize, the Inamori Foundation Kyoto Prize, and the Turing Award, widely recognized as the highest distinction in Computer Science, for his work on object-oriented programming.

You started out in show business. What led you to become a computer scientist?

I was a professional jazz musician of modest abilities for about 10 years and did some teaching of guitar in that period. My general background included an artistic and musical mother, a scientific and mathematical father, and a grandfather who wrote and illustrated many books. So I grew up interested in many things and didn't make much distinction between what are called the Arts and the Sciences. I came across a number of books about computers and how to build them as a teenager in the 1950s, and when taking a computer aptitude test in the Air Force was an option, I took it, got a good score on it, and starting programming in the early 1960s.

In college I carried full majors in mathematics and biology and supported this by being a programmer at the National Center for Atmospheric Research in Boulder. I was also still playing jazz in clubs at this time.

I wound up at the University of Utah ARPA (Advanced Research Projects Agency) project for grad school in 1966 as a complete fluke without any planning or knowledge about ARPA. From the moment I got there and met (Professor) Dave Evans (later, my advisor) I "got" what ARPA was trying to do and it was a huge stroke of "romance" that I responded to.

How does the musician in you continue to influence the computer scientist?

Analogies can often be misleading, but there are some interesting ones to be made between music and computing (and mathematics and biology). The big ones for me have been the large aesthetic content of music and math and a wish for computing to always be that beautiful, the textures of different kinds of things interacting over time, the incredible ratio of parsimony to effect, etc.

You often talk about education and the art of teaching. Did someone in particular inspire your concept of the ideal teacher?

The initial ideas about "teaching people to think better—even qualitatively better" came from a number of science fiction novels, one of which led me to the General

Semantics movement started by Alfred Korzybski. I also had one truly fantastic teacher in the fourth grade. She knew how to reach and realize the potential in the many different kinds of children in her classroom "without teaching," and she has been one of the main models for me for how to go about helping people learn.

You have said that "literacy is not just about being able to read street signs or medicine labels. It means being able to deal in the world of ideas." What does it mean to you for someone to be computer literate?

I like Frank Smith's general definition of literacy as something that starts with important ideas, finds ways to write them down in some kind of language, and helps develop more "readers and writers." The computer has ways of "writing" down representation systems of all kinds—it is a simulator and a metamedium. By metamedium, I mean that it is a holder of all the media you can think of, as well as ones you haven't thought of yet. Computer literacy is all about important ideas written and read as simulations. And the writing and reading are actually some kind of programming, where the programs—like mathematics or a musical score or an essay—are a means for expressing a powerful idea.

What many consider to be the prototype for the laptop computer is a machine you designed about 40 years ago, the Dynabook, yet, you often contend that the Dynabook is still a dream...

It is indeed now possible to not just make a physical Dynabook, but one with many more capabilities than my original conception. However, the physical part of the Dynabook is about 5 percent of the dream. In musical terms, we can now make the body of the violin but we are still struggling with the strings, fingerboard, and bow (the user interface that includes authoring) and we still only have a few instances of what the musical expression will be like (the content of the Dynabook). The other difficult part of the design is that we somehow want the early parts of the Dynabook experience to be a lot more value-laden and fun than learning to play the violin usually is. More importantly, we want users to keep experimenting, move on, and not get complacent as many do, for example, after learning to play three chords on the guitar.

What is Squeak?

Squeak is free and open source software, originally created by my research team, for getting to better places in all the areas we've been discussing. It is derived from one of the last Xerox PARC Smalltalks and has been brought forward to twenty-first-century graphics, etc. It contains models of itself, which make it easy to port, and now exists on more than 25 platforms running "bit-identically" (exactly the same). From the computer science standpoint it is a little more interesting than most of the other stuff that is around, but pretty much all of its ideas date from the 1970s, so its interesting features are more of a commentary on what didn't happen in computer science in the last 20 years.

We have now done and tested a child's environment that is working out pretty well, and contains a number of new language and structuring ideas. This has been used to implement a much more comprehensive adult/media authoring environment (a kind of super-duper Hypercard) that contains the child's environment as a subset. This is essentially what we think the Dynabook should be like, plus, you can now download it and use it for free.

You have said, "The best way to predict the future is to invent it." What advice do you have for students who are planning a career in the field of technology?

Gain wide perspective by majoring in something else while an undergraduate. Try to find partial answers to Jerome Bruner's questions: What makes humans human? How did we get that way? How can we become more so? In other words, try to understand human beings and the role that representation systems for ideas have played in this journey called "civilization."

PART 4

Problem Solving

CHAPTER

PART 4

INTRODUCTION

OUR STUDY of computing has already covered problem solving in several different forms. We have solved problems related to writing HTML, finding accurate information sources, debugging and designing an XML database, and more. In all cases, our main tool was logical reasoning applied to a specific situation. In Part 4 we'll become even more effective problem solvers.

Problem solving requires a problem and some medium or mechanism in which to produce a solution. For us, Web pages and familiar applications provide the problems, and JavaScript is our solution medium. The important part of our study—the part that transfers to other aspects of our lives—is neither the problems nor the solutions, but the process by which we find them.

Though problem solving is the "high-order bit" (i.e., most significant information), JavaScript is a programming language. Once you see how programs are written, you will have an understanding of computing which will make you more operationally attuned—and thus a better user. And, the practical bonus from learning JavaScript is that it allows you to create much fancier Web pages.

CHAPTER 17

Fundamental Concepts Expressed in JavaScript

Get with the Program

learning objectives

- Tell the difference between name, value, and variable
- List three basic data types and the rules for specifying them in a program
- Explain the way in which the assignment statement changes a variable's value
- Write expressions using arithmetic, relational, and logical operators
- Write conditional and compound statements

CHAPTER 17

Everything is vague to a degree you do not realize till you have tried to make it precise.

—BERTRAND RUSSELL

PROGRAMMING is a profession, yet we all need to know something about it to be effective computer users. This is analogous to medicine. Doctors and nurses are professionals, but we need to know something about their specialties—our bodies, disease symptoms, nutrition, first aid, and so forth—to care for ourselves and benefit fully from their care. In neither case do we need an expert's knowledge, and in both cases we could probably survive with near total ignorance. But knowing some of what the professionals know is unquestionably beneficial and worth learning, despite its technical nature. What do we need to know?

What we need to know about programming is a fuller elaboration of the concepts already discussed in Chapter 10 on algorithms. These concepts are deep and subtle; Chapter 10 was our introduction. Indeed, our goal is to change our thinking habits to be more "abstract." Just as we need experience writing, reading, and speaking a foreign language in order to acquire it, so too do we need experience writing, reading, and executing algorithms and programs to acquire the thought processes of computation.

After preliminary remarks, we present a sample program. Though it might look like gibberish at the start, the plan is to introduce all of the concepts used in the program. We begin by explaining names, variables, and declarations, giving ourselves the ability to refer to the program's data. Then, we cover the types of data values: numbers, character strings, and Booleans. Next, we introduce assignment statements and expressions, so we can compute new values. A lab practice exercise then illustrates how to try the concepts in Firefox. The last concepts are compound statements for grouping and conditional statements for testing. With this list of concepts, we return to the program and work through its execution. By the end of the chapter, we'll be programming!

Overview: Programming Concepts

Programming is the act of formulating an algorithm or program. It entails developing a systematic means of solving a problem so that an agent—someone other than the programmer and usually a computer—can follow the instructions and produce the intended result for every input, every time. The agent must also be able to perform or execute the program without any intervention from the programmer. This means that all steps must be spelled out precisely and effectively, and all contingencies must be planned for.

This summary of programming—that everything must be explained clearly and all contingencies planned for—is perhaps best expressed by Adele Mildred Koss, in the accompanying quote from the *Annals of the History of Computing*.

In a Programmer's Words. Adele Koss, one of the first professional programmers, summarized programming the Univac I in 1950. It's still a pretty good description:

[Computers] couldn't think in the way a human thinks, but had to be given a set of step-by-step machine instructions to be executed before they could provide answers to a specific problem. Before the computer could solve a problem, a human would have to solve it first, using mathematics, physics, or a business process. The human would have to segment the solution into little building blocks that the machine could handle, and use the machine code to write a program that would execute that process correctly, at high speed and for many iterations without human intervention. Problems could be solved in many different ways, but to devise a correct and elegant solution—and I stress elegant—was the challenge.

Programming has become much, much easier in the years since Ms. Koss programmed, but the principles are the same. Programming actually requires thinking. But relying on thinking alone makes programming too difficult. Instead, in this and following chapters, we introduce basic programming concepts developed over the years that simplify the task. These are the tools you will need to formulate any computation. And, trying to program an algorithm precisely using English is hopeless. Natural languages are too ambiguous for directing anything as clueless as a computer. So, programming languages have been developed to help programmers in two ways: they are precise, and they are specialized in using the concepts mentioned in the previous paragraphs. Using a programming language is actually easier than writing in English. We will use **JavaScript**, a modern programming language that is especially effective for Web applications. You won't become a JavaScript expert from reading this chapter, but you might learn enough to make a glitzy personal Web page.

This chapter introduces the following programming concepts:

- Names, values, and variables
- Declarations
- Data types, numbers, string literals, and Booleans
- Assignment
- Expressions
- Conditionals

With just these few concepts, you will be able to write actual programs. The program shown in Figure 17.1 is an example. It probably looks like gibberish now, but by the end of this chapter you'll be able to read and understand it. (We show it now to make it clear where we are headed, but skip it if it appears intimidating.)

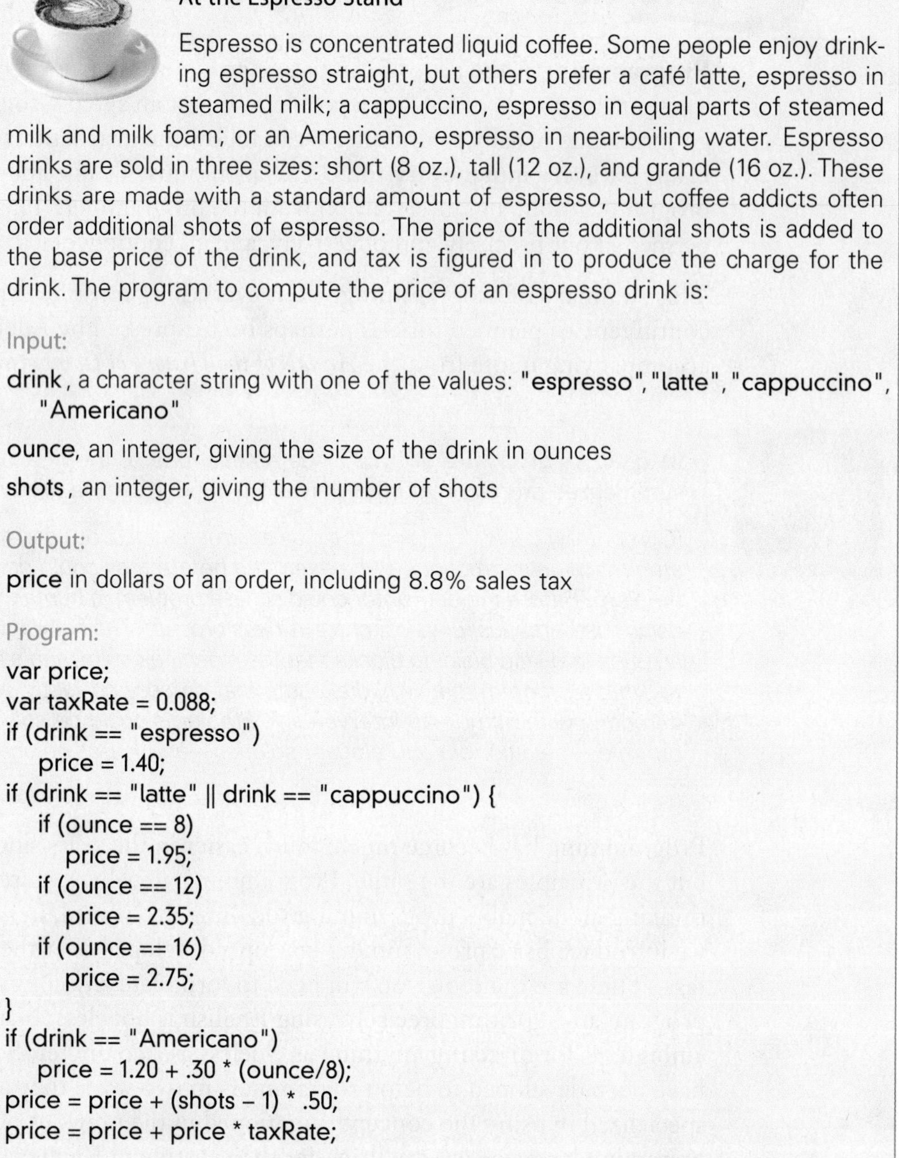

At the Espresso Stand

Espresso is concentrated liquid coffee. Some people enjoy drinking espresso straight, but others prefer a café latte, espresso in steamed milk; a cappuccino, espresso in equal parts of steamed milk and milk foam; or an Americano, espresso in near-boiling water. Espresso drinks are sold in three sizes: short (8 oz.), tall (12 oz.), and grande (16 oz.). These drinks are made with a standard amount of espresso, but coffee addicts often order additional shots of espresso. The price of the additional shots is added to the base price of the drink, and tax is figured in to produce the charge for the drink. The program to compute the price of an espresso drink is:

Input:

drink, a character string with one of the values: "espresso", "latte", "cappuccino", "Americano"

ounce, an integer, giving the size of the drink in ounces

shots, an integer, giving the number of shots

Output:

price in dollars of an order, including 8.8% sales tax

Program:

```
var price;
var taxRate = 0.088;
if (drink == "espresso")
    price = 1.40;
if (drink == "latte" || drink == "cappuccino") {
   if (ounce == 8)
      price = 1.95;
   if (ounce == 12)
      price = 2.35;
   if (ounce == 16)
      price = 2.75;
}
if (drink == "Americano")
    price = 1.20 + .30 * (ounce/8);
price = price + (shots – 1) * .50;
price = price + price * taxRate;
```

Figure 17.1 Sample JavaScript computation to figure the cost of espresso drinks.

Finally, in introducing the deep ideas of the chapter, we must set down the practical details of programming. These rules can be as burdensome as a chapter-long list of dos and don'ts. So, we skip the more obvious rules here—the ones you would guess intuitively—to emphasize the few rules that you cannot guess on your own. When in doubt, refer to Appendix D, where all the requirements are listed.

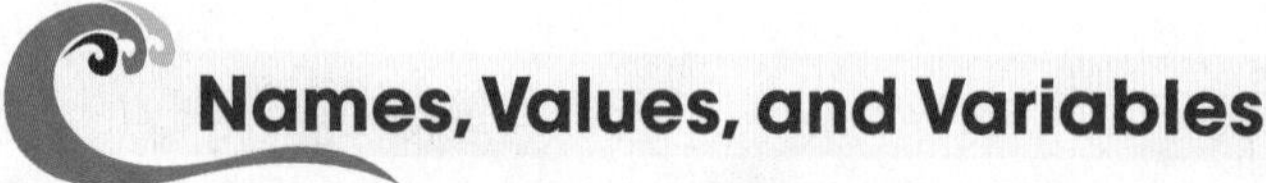

Names, Values, and Variables

Though we are familiar with the concepts of a name (the letter sequence used to refer to something), and a value (the thing itself), in normal conversation we tend not to distinguish carefully between the two. Thus, when we use the letter sequences "Jennifer Lopez" or "Harrison Ford," we mean those specific movie stars. There are many people with those names, of course, and if your friend from geology class is also named Harrison Ford, that name has one value for you in the context of that class and another in the context of the movies. People understand this distinction in everyday conversation. In everyday life we treat names as "bound to" their values.

Names Have Changing Values

Names and values are separable in programming. The best way to think of names and values in programming is to think of names as if they were offices or titles, or other designations purposely selected to have changing values. There are plenty of examples:

Name	Current Value (1/20/14)	Previous Values
U.S. President	Barack Obama	Bill Clinton, George H. W. Bush
Chief Justice U.S. Supreme Court	John Roberts	Warren Burger, Earl Warren
James Bond	Daniel Craig	Sean Connery, Roger Moore
Queen of England	Elizabeth II	Victoria I, Elizabeth I
U.N. Secretary General	Ban Ki-moon	Boutros Boutros-Ghali, Kofi Annan

The names used in the middle and right columns are, of course, the informal usage of names from everyday conversation.

The reason we focus on the case where the values associated with a name can change is that they change in programs. A program is a fixed description of a process. As the process evolves and the program transforms data to produce new values, the old names must refer to these new values, that is, the names change values. This is a natural result of the fixed description of the process. So, for example, the U.S. Constitution contains this specification of a process: "The President-elect will be sworn into office by the Chief Justice on the January 20 following the election." The intent of this command is to describe a process that applies no matter who wins the presidential election, that is, the value of "President-elect," and who is the senior justice of the Supreme Court on that date, that is, the value of "Chief Justice." We naturally interpret the U.S. Constitution this way. The names "President-elect" and "Chief Justice" have changing values.

Names used in this way—a single letter sequence with a varying value—are a familiar concept to you from your previous computing experience. For example, the file named EnglishPaper.doc changes its value every time you save a version of your composition. In computing, the name is always separable from the value, and the value can be changed. It's a basic idea worth thinking about because it enables change.

17.1 What's in a Name? Explain the difference between the names "Best Picture" and the name "Argo."

Names in a Program Are Called Variables

In programming terminology, the names just discussed are called **variables**, a term that reminds us that their values *vary*. The most commonly used programming language operation is the command to change the value of a variable. That command is called **assignment**, and we discuss it shortly.

Names and Values. We've seen one other example of names having multiple values over time. Memory locations—their names are called *addresses*—have different values at different times. This is not a coincidence. Variables *are* memory locations in the computer. Variables are simply a more readable and convenient way to refer to computer memory than the actual binary addresses. The value of the address is the current contents of the memory location, and it is the value of the corresponding variable.

Identifiers and Their Rules

The letter sequence that makes up a variable's name is called the **identifier**. In every programming language, identifiers must have a particular form, although the form is somewhat different from language to language. Generally, identifiers must begin with a letter, followed by any sequence of letters, numerals (the digits 0 through 9), or the underscore symbol (_). (JavaScript permits slightly more general identifiers than suggested here, but throughout this book tiny limitations are implied to make it easier to learn and to help avoid errors. Nothing is lost.)

Identifiers are not allowed to contain spaces. The following are eight identifiers:

```
X
x
ru4it
nineteen_eighty_four
Time_O_Day
Identifiers_can_B_long_but_if_so_typing_them_can_be_a_pain
oO000o
elizaBETH
```

Notice two features of identifiers: The underscore symbol can be used as a word separator to make identifiers more readable while observing the "no spaces" rule, and identifiers in most programming languages, including JavaScript, are case sensitive, meaning that uppercase and lowercase letters are different.

Form Rules. User IDs, logins, and email names follow similar rules, but with a few important differences. For example, login and email names often allow a dash (–), but identifier names do not, because a dash could be confused with a minus sign between variables. Finally, JavaScript reserves a few words for itself (see Appendix D), which cannot be identifiers.

A Variable Declaration Statement

Programs are usually written "starting from scratch." That is, when you begin to program, you can think of the computer as if it were newly manufactured; it knows nothing except how to understand the programming language. So the first thing to do when writing any program is to state what variables will be used. This is called **declaring variables**, and we do it using a command called a declaration. In JavaScript, the declaration command is the word var, short for *variable*, followed by a list of the identifiers for the variables to be declared, separated by commas. For example, to write a computation that computes the area of a circle given its radius, we need variables area and radius. So we declare,

```
var area, radius;
```

This command *declares* that in the program we will use these two identifiers as variables. Notice that the first command in the espresso computation in Figure 17.1

```
var price;
```

is a variable declaration of this type. (The program uses other variables that will be explained momentarily.)

17.2 A Variable Number. How many different variables are possible from a combination of no more than three lowercase and/or uppercase b's?

The declaration was just called a *command*, because it is commanding the computer to record which identifiers will be used as variables. But everything we tell a computer to do is a command, so we should call the declaration by its proper term, declaration **statement**.

The Statement Terminator

A program is simply a list of statements. Because we can't always write one statement per line as in a normal list, the statements are often run together, which means that each must be terminated by some punctuation symbol. The **statement terminator** in JavaScript is the semicolon (;). It's the same idea as terminating sentences in English with periods, question marks, or exclamation points. The main difference is this If I forget to terminate an English sentence, like I just did, you still understand—both from the meaning and from the capital letter beginning the next sentence—that the sentence is over, that is, terminated. The computer isn't that clever. It needs the semicolon. So, the rule is: Terminate every statement with a semicolon.

First Mistake. Everyone makes mistakes when programming. Everyone. One of the most common mistakes for beginners is to forget the semicolon. When the semicolon is missing, the computer becomes confused and debugging is necessary. Remembering semicolons makes programming easier.

Rules for Declaring Variables

Every variable used in a program must be declared. JavaScript allows declaration statements anywhere in the list of program statements. But because variable declarations announce what variables *will* be used in the program, programmers like to place them first in the program. It's like saying, "Here's the list of variables I'll be using in the program that follows." We will declare variables first.

Undefined Values. The declaration states that the identifier is the name of a variable. But what is the name's value? It has no value at first! The value of a declared variable is not defined. It's a name that doesn't yet name anything. Similarly, when a group of people forms an intramural basketball team, say, Crunch, the intramural sports office can refer to the Crunch captain, even if the person who will be captain hasn't been chosen. The name is declared—it will be meaningful when the season is under way—but there is no value assigned yet. The value is **undefined**.

Initializing a Declaration. Often we know an *initial value* for the identifiers we declare. So JavaScript allows us to set the initial value as part of the declaration, that is, to **initialize** the variable. To declare that taxRate and balanceDue will be variables in the program, and that their initial values are .088 and 0, respectively, we write

```
var taxRate = .088;
var balanceDue = 0;
```

We don't have to declare and initialize just one variable at a time in the var statement. We can declare and initialize any number of variables by separating them with commas:

```
var taxRate = .088, balanceDue = 0;
```

The computer doesn't care which style is used. They're equivalent. Typically, programmers include several variables in a single declaration statement when the variables are logically related. This serves as a reminder that the variables are related. For example, variables describing a person's features might be declared

```
var height, weight, hairColor, eyeColor, astrological_sign;
```

If the variables are not related, they are usually specified in separate statements. All approaches are equivalent; there is no "proper" way.

17.3 Make a Declaration. When the founders wrote the U.S. Declaration of Independence, they declared theseTruths to be "self evident." How do you do that in JavaScript?

IN CONGRESS, JULY 4, 1776.

The unanimous Declaration of the thirteen united States of America,

Three Basic Data Types of JavaScript

We will use three types of data in our JavaScript programs: numbers, strings, and Booleans.

Rules for Writing Numbers

The values assigned to the variables taxRate and balanceDue are **numbers**. Like everything in programming, there are rules for writing numbers, but basically numbers are written in the "usual way." (Details are provided in Appendix D.)

One "unusual" aspect of numbers in programming is that there are no "units." We can't write 33% and $10.89; we must write 0.33 and 10.89. This explains why there are no dollar signs in the program in Figure 17.1 even though it is a computation to figure the price of a coffee drink in dollars. Standard computer numbers can have about 10 significant digits and range from as small as 10^{-324} to as large as 10^{308}. (Numbers and computer arithmetic are unexpectedly subtle. Our uses of numbers will be trivial so that we avoid any difficulties. As a general rule, the "safe zone" is the range from 2 billionths to 2 billion plus or minus. Outside that range, we must learn a little more about computer arithmetic.)

Though computers frequently compute on numbers, they compute on other kinds of data as well.

Strings

For us, strings will be the most common kind of data. **Strings** are sequences of keyboard characters. For example, here are nine strings:

```
"abcdefghijklmnopqrstuvwxyz" "May" '!@#$%^&*( )_+|}{:][''
"strings are surrounded by quotes" "" "M&M's"
'strings can contain blanks' " " '"No," she said.'
```

Notice that a string is always surrounded by single (') or double (") quotes.

Strings Can Initialize a Declaration. Like numbers, strings can be used to initialize variables in a declaration. For example,

```
var hairColor = "black", eyeColor = "brown", astrological_sign = "Leo";
```

We need strings when manipulating text, as when we're building Web pages, for example. The program in Figure 17.1 uses several string constants: `"espresso"`, `"latte"`, `"cappuccino"`, and `"Americano"`.

Rules for Writing Strings in JavaScript. The rules for writing strings in JavaScript, most of which can be seen in the preceding examples, are as follows:

1. Strings must be surrounded by quotes, either single (') or double ("), *which are not curly*.
2. Most characters are allowed within quotes except the return character (Enter), backspace character, tab character, \, and two others (little used).
3. Double quoted strings can contain single quotes, and vice versa.
4. The apostrophe (') is the same as the single quote.
5. Any number of characters is allowed in a string.
6. The minimum number of characters in a string is zero (""), which is called the **empty string**.

Rule 3 lets us include quotes in a string. To use double quotes in a string, for example, we enclose the string in single quotes, as in `'He said, "No!"'`. If our string contains single quotes, we enclose it in double quotes, as in `"Guide to B&B's"`. Because the apostrophe is commonly used in English's possessives and contractions, it's a good idea to use double quotes as the default. This allows the free use of apostrophes. We change to single quotes only when the string contains double quotes. Both methods work, and the computer doesn't care which one we use.

Notice that by rule 6 the empty string is a legitimate value. That is, writing

```
var exValDef = "";
var exValUndef;
```

Table 17.1 Escape sequences for characters prohibited from string literals.

Sequence	Character	Sequence	Character
\b	Backspace	\f	Form feed
\n	New line	\r	Carriage return
\t	Tab	\'	Apostrophe or single quote
\"	Double quote	\\	Backslash

results in two quite different situations. After these two statements run, if we ask the computer what kind of value exValDef has, the answer would be "a string," but the answer for exValUndef would be "an undefined value."

Literals. The numbers and strings discussed are known as **literals**. The term *literal* conveys the idea that the characters are typed literally in the program. So there are rules about how to write these values explicitly in a computation. However, when literals become the values of variables and are stored in the computer, the representation changes slightly, especially for strings.

String Literals Stored in the Computer. First, because the surrounding quotes or double quotes are used only to delimit the string literal, they are removed when the literal is stored in the computer. That's why the empty string "" has a length of 0, rather than 2.

Second, any character can be stored in the computer's memory. Specifically, although a prohibited character such as a tab character cannot be *typed* in as a literal, it can be the value of a string in the computer. To do this we use the "escape" mechanism, as follows.

For JavaScript, the escape symbol is the backslash (\) and the escape sequences are shown in Table 17.1. Thus, we can write declarations such as

```
var fourTabs = "\t\t\t\t", backUp = "\b",
    bothQuotesInOne = " '\" ";
```

which give values to the variables that cannot be typed literally. The escape sequences are converted to the single characters they represent when they are stored in the computer's memory. So, the lengths of the values of these three string variables are 4, 1, and 2, respectively.

Boolean Values

Another kind of value is the **Boolean value (Booleans)**. Unlike numbers and strings, there are only two Boolean values: true and false. Boolean values have their obvious logical meaning. We should emphasize that although true and false are written as letter sequences, they are *values*—like 1 is a value—not identifiers or strings. Although Booleans are used implicitly throughout the programming process, as you'll see, they are used only occasionally for initializing variables. Examples might be

```
var foreignLanguageReq = false, mathReq = true, totalCredits = 0;
```

This last declaration illustrates that variables appearing in the same declaration can be initialized with different kinds of values.

It's True. Boolean values get their name from George Boole. True. Boole was an English mathematician who invented true and false. False. True and false have been around since humans began to reason. Boole invented an algebra based on these two values that is basic to computer engineering and other fields.

The different kinds of values of a programming language are called its **data types** or its **value types** or simply its types. (We mentioned data types in Chapter 2, when discussing "new.") We have introduced three types for JavaScript: numbers, strings, and Booleans. There are several other types, but these are sufficient for most of what we will do in JavaScript. JavaScript is very kind to programmers with respect to types, as you will see later in the chapter.

17.4 Literary Work. Declare variables (of your choosing) to describe literary personalities, and initialize them to values appropriate for Mark Twain: his real name, the century in which he wrote *Tom Sawyer*, whether he was a humorist, and a famous quotation in quotation marks: *Nothing so needs reforming as other people's habits.*

Meta-Brackets. In discussing programming languages, we often need to describe syntactic structures, such as declaration statements. To separate the language being defined from the language doing the defining, we enclose terms of the defining language in "angle brackets," (< >), known as **meta-brackets**. Thus, the general form of the earlier initializing variable declaration would be var <*variable name*> = <*initial value*>, where the symbols not in meta-brackets are written literally, and symbols or words in the meta-brackets represent things of the sort indicated, as a kind of placeholder. Notice that these are not tags.

The Assignment Statement

If variables are to change values in an algorithm or program, there should be a command to do so. The **assignment statement** changes a variable's value; it is the workhorse of programming.

An assignment statement has three parts that always occur in this order:

<*variable*> <*assignment symbol*> <*expression*>;

as in

```
week = days / 7;
```

Here <*variable*> is any declared variable in the program, <*assignment symbol*> is the language's notation for the assignment operation (discussed next), and <*expression*> is a kind of formula telling the computer how to compute the new value. Like any other statement, an assignment statement is terminated by a semicolon. JavaScript's <*assignment symbol*> is the equal sign (=), and you've already seen the assignment operation as the initializer for variable declarations.

Assignment Symbol

Different programming languages use different symbols for indicating assignment. The three most widely used symbols are the equal sign (=); the colon, equal sign pair (:=); and the left pointing arrow ←). There are others, but these are the most common. The := is considered a single symbol even though it is formed from two keyboard characters. Like JavaScript, most languages use =. Pascal uses := and more mathematical languages like APL use ←. Regardless of which symbol the language uses, assignment is a standard and commonly used operation in every programming language.

Analyzing our sample assignment statement, we have

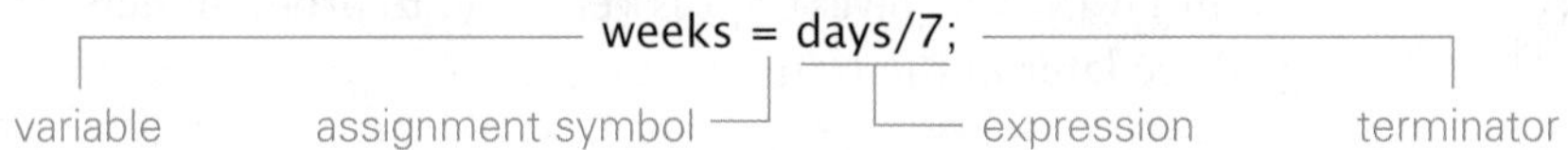

where weeks is the variable whose value is being changed, = is the assignment symbol, and days/7 is the expression. Therefore, this assignment statement illustrates the standard form.

Interpreting an Assignment Statement

To understand how assignment works, you *must* think of a value flowing from the right side (expression side) of the assignment symbol to the left side (variable side). (This view makes the left arrow, ←, perhaps the most intuitive assignment symbol.) The *assignment symbol* should be read as "*is assigned*" or "*becomes*" or "*gets*." Therefore, our example can be read in any of these ways:

- "the variable weeks *is assigned* the value resulting from dividing the value of the variable days by 7"
- "the value of weeks *becomes* the value resulting from dividing the value of the variable days by 7"
- "the variable weeks *gets* the value resulting from dividing the value of the variable days by 7"

Get with the Program. Many programmers prefer *gets* when reading assignments. It conveys the idea of filling a container, as in a "mailbox *gets* a letter" or a "flour tin *gets* flour." The variable is the container.

Terms like *is assigned*, *becomes*, and *gets* emphasize the role that the assignment symbol plays, namely, to change the value of the variable named on the left side.

Definitely Not Equal. If assignment seems like the equal sign of algebra, reread the last paragraph. Assignment is not stating equality; it is moving data from the right to the left.

In an assignment statement, the expression (that is, everything to the right of the assignment symbol) is computed or evaluated first. If there are any variables used in the expression, their current values are used. This evaluation produces a value that then becomes the new value of the variable named on the left side. So, the effect of executing the sample assignment statement

```
weeks = days/7;
```

is that the current value of the variable days is determined by looking in the memory (suppose it is 77), and that value is divided by 7, producing a new value, 11. This new value then becomes the new value of the variable weeks, that is, weeks is assigned 11.

Assignment to Memory. In the computer, an assignment statement causes the value in the memory location(s) corresponding to the variable to be *replaced* by the new value resulting from the expression.

Three Key Points About Assignment

There are three key points to remember about assignment statements. First, all three of the components must be given; if anything is missing, the statement is meaningless. Second, the flow of the value to the name is always right to left. Thus the two variable names in the assignment statement

```
variable_receiving_new_value = newly_computed_value;
```

correctly show the motion of information. Notice that the expression can simply be some other variable; it doesn't have to be a complicated formula. Third, the values of any variables used in the expression are their values before the start of execution of the assignment. This point is extremely important, because the variable being changed in the assignment statement might also be used in the expression.

For example, a program simulating a basketball game would probably use the assignment statement

```
totalScore = totalScore + 3;
```

for a basket from outside the three-point circle. When the expression on the right side of the assignment statement, totalScore + 3, is evaluated, the value of totalScore used in the computation is its value before starting this statement, that is, the score before the shot. When the assignment statement is completed, totalScore is the updated value reflecting the three-point shot.

Similarly, the program might contain the code

```
shotClock = shotClock - 1;
```

to implement the "tick" of the shot clock. Again, when evaluating the right side expression, the values used for variables are those *before* the statement is executed.

Repeating, because this is the most important of all of the ideas in this chapter: The role of = is to *assign* the value computed on the right side to be the new value of the variable named on the left side.

Programming Is Not Algebra. Like algebra, many programming languages use an equal sign in assignments. In programming "=" is read "becomes," which suggests the dynamic meaning of the right-to-left value flow. In algebra "=" is read "equals," which emphasizes the static meaning that both sides are the same. In programming, the statement "*x* = *x* + 1" means the value of *x* becomes one larger; in algebra, the equation "*x* = *x* + 1" is meaningless because there is no number that is identical to itself plus one. The unknowns in algebra are names whose values do not change.

17.5 An Assignment. Declare a variable bestPicture and then write an assignment statement to give it the value *12 Years a Slave*.

Lab Practice

We have learned about variables, declarations, and assignment. Though we can't compute much with only that much knowledge, we can get started writing JavaScript and running it. Our purpose in doing so is simple: From now on in our JavaScript study, everything we learn, we can try in the Firefox browser. This is undoubtedly the fastest and most painless way to learn programming, because nothing proves you know what you're doing like doing it!

Scratchpad "Hello, World"

The development system we will use is called the Firefox Scratchpad (see Figure 17.2). Scratchpad is a Firefox Web page that allows us to type in JavaScript and run it. It is perfect for learning the language and for developing programs. Once we have everything worked out in this *sandbox*—that's what such testing tools for programming systems are called—we will transfer the JavaScript to other Web pages.

To display Firefox's Scratchpad page, navigate Tools > Web Developer > Scratchpad. A Scratchpad window opens (Figure 17.2). It has the first few lines already filled in, explaining how to run programs in Scratchpad. By the way, these lines are a JavaScript comment, so you can leave them there as a reminder. (Comments in JavaScript have two forms: *multiline comments* begin with /* characters and end with */ characters; any characters can be in between except */, of course; *end of line comments* use // and automatically terminate at the end of the line.)

Check It Out. In Scratchpad, type in the declarations for the two variables used in the weeks assignment statement that we discussed earlier, and the assignment statement itself:

```
var days = 77;
var weeks;
weeks = days / 7;
```

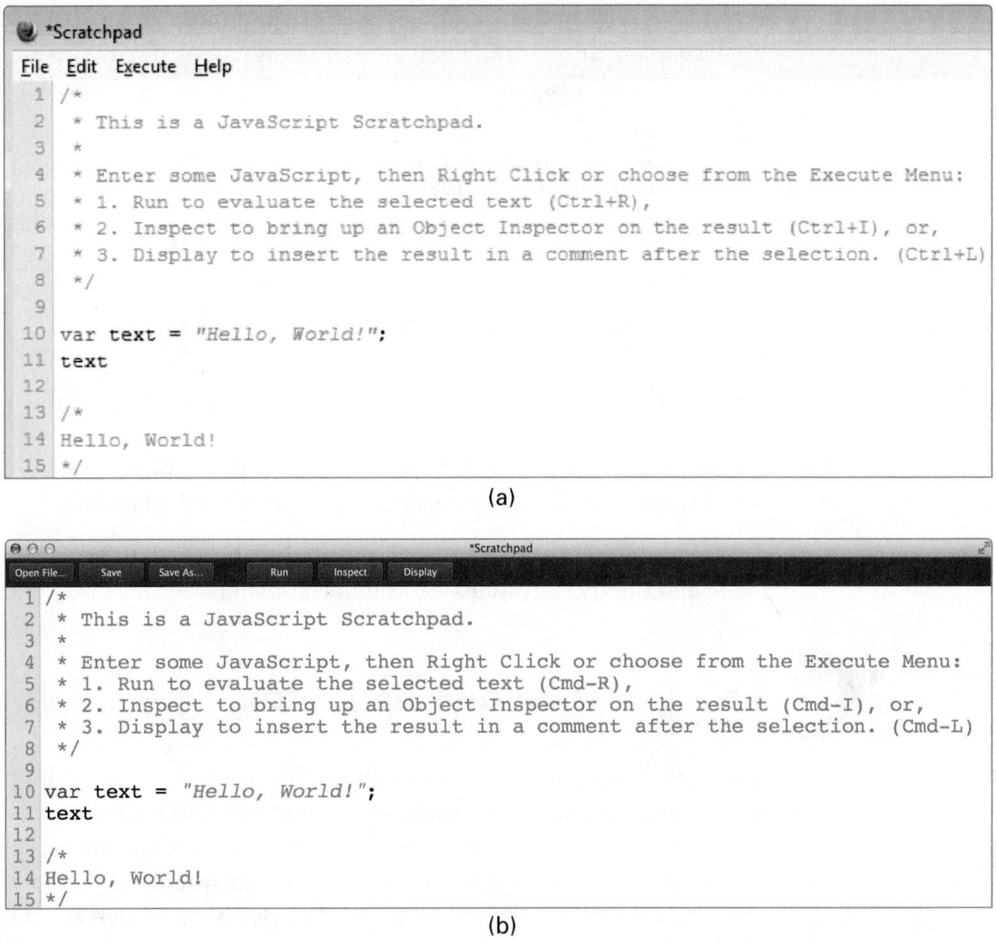

```
*Scratchpad
File Edit Execute Help
/*
 * This is a JavaScript Scratchpad.
 *
 * Enter some JavaScript, then Right Click or choose from the Execute Menu:
 * 1. Run to evaluate the selected text (Ctrl+R),
 * 2. Inspect to bring up an Object Inspector on the result (Ctrl+I), or,
 * 3. Display to insert the result in a comment after the selection. (Ctrl+L)
 */

var text = "Hello, World!";
text

/*
Hello, World!
*/
```

(a)

```
*Scratchpad
Open File... Save Save As... Run Inspect Display
/*
 * This is a JavaScript Scratchpad.
 *
 * Enter some JavaScript, then Right Click or choose from the Execute Menu:
 * 1. Run to evaluate the selected text (Cmd-R),
 * 2. Inspect to bring up an Object Inspector on the result (Cmd-I), or,
 * 3. Display to insert the result in a comment after the selection. (Cmd-L)
 */

var text = "Hello, World!";
text

/*
Hello, World!
*/
```

(b)

Figure 17.2 Firefox's Scratchpad development page: (a) for Windows OS, and (b) for MacOS.

To see the result of the computation, use the *Display* command (^L). Scracthpad displays the result:

```
var days = 77;          //Declare and initialize
var weeks;              //Declare

weeks = days/7;

weeks

/*
11
*/
```

Next, change days to be initialized to some other number besides 77, perhaps 50, and display the new result. The value of weeks is replaced with the new value derived from dividing a new number by 7.

Two More Assignments. Finally, declare and initialize (to 10) two more variables: totalScore and shotClock. Then give the assignment statements that (a) add 3 to the totalScore, and (b) subtract 1 from the shotClock, as shown earlier.

```
var totalScore = 10;
var shotClock = 10;

totalScore = totalScore + 3;   //now typing ^L
/*
13
*/
shotClock = shotClock - 1;     //now typing ^L
/*
9
*/
```

Notice that when using the *Display* (^L) command, the last variable you assign will be the one displayed; to see other variables, put them on the last line.

To save a Scratchpad content for future use, click *Save* or type ^S, and give the file a name and the .js file extension, as in basketball.js.

An Expression and Its Syntax

Although programming is not mathematics, it has its roots in higher math. So, it is not surprising that one of the concepts in programming is an algebra-like formula called an **expression**. Expressions describe the means of performing the actual computation. As you've already seen in earlier spreadsheet chapters and in the expression days/7, expressions are built out of variables and **operators**, which are standard arithmetic operations—such as addition (+), subtraction (–), multiplication (*), and division (/)—that one finds on a calculator.

The symbols of basic arithmetic are called the **arithmetic operators**. The actual symbols used for some operators may be different, depending on the programming language, so we limit ourselves here to JavaScript operators. Examples of expressions include

```
a * (b + c)
height * width / 2
pi * diameter
(((days * 24) + hours) * 60 + minutes) * 60 + seconds
```

As an exercise to learn expressions, declare and initialize all of these variables, and then perform the computations using Scratchpad. (You should initialize pi to 3.1415962.)

Arithmetic Operators

Expressions usually follow rules similar to algebraic formulas, but not quite. Multiplication must be given explicitly with the asterisk (*) multiply operator, so we write a * b rather than ab or a · b or a × b. As with algebra, multiplication and division are performed before addition and subtraction—multiplication and division have *higher precedence* than addition and subtraction—unless parentheses group the operations differently. Therefore, a*b + a*c is equivalent to (a*b) + (a*c) because multiplication is automatically performed before addition. Also, because expressions must be typed on a single line, superscripts, as in x^2, are prohibited. Some languages have an operator for exponents or powers, but JavaScript does not. If we want to compute the area of a circle, we must multiply R times itself because we can't square it. So

```
pi * R * R
```

is the expression for computing the area of a circle (πr^2), assuming that the variable pi has the value 3.1415962.

Operators like + and * are called **binary operators** because they operate on two values. The values they operate on are called **operands**. There are also **unary operators**, like negate (–), which have only one operand. (Language parsers—the part of a compiler that "diagrams" programs so a computer can understand them—can easily figure out whether the minus means negate or subtract.)

One very useful operator applied in future chapters is mod. The **modulus (mod) operation (%)** divides two integers and returns the remainder. So, the result of a%b for integers a and b is the remainder of the division a/b as integers. In particular, the result of 4%2 is 0 because 2 evenly divides 4, whereas 5%2 is 1 because 2 into 5 leaves a remainder of 1. Try these computations in Scratchpad.

Relational Operators

Expressions involving addition, subtraction, and so on are similar to algebra, but programmers use other kinds of expressions. **Relational operators** are used to make comparisons between numerical values—that is, to test the relationship between two numbers. The outcome of the comparison is a Boolean value, either true or false. The operators are illustrated here with sample operands a and b that should be replaced with variables or expressions:

a < b	Is a less than b?
a <= b	Is a less than or equal to b?
a == b	Is a equal to b?
a != b	Is a not equal to b?
a >= b	Is a greater than or equal to b?
a > b	Is a greater than b?

Notice that the "equal to" relational operator (==) is a double equal sign, making it different from assignment. And if we compute 7 > 5 in Scratchpad, true is displayed, demonstrating that relational operators create Boolean values.

Examples of relational expressions include

```
bondRate > certificateDeposit
temperature <= 212
drink == "espresso"
```

Notice that relational tests can apply to string variables, as in the last example, which is taken from the program in Figure 17.1. Both equal (==) and not equal (!=) can be applied to string variables as well as to numeric variables.

One Character or Two? Several operators, such as <=, >=, and !=, are composed of two keyboard characters. They cannot contain a space and are considered a single character. They were invented years ago to make up for the limited number of characters on a standard keyboard. If programming language research started today, compounds would not be necessary because it's now easy to introduce new symbols that are not on the keyboard, such as ≤, ≥, and ≠.

Logical Operators

The relational test like a < b results in a true or false outcome; that is, either the two values are related to each other as the relational operator asks (a is less than b), making the test outcome true, or they are not, making the test outcome false. It is common to test two or more relationships together, requiring that relational expression results be combined. For example, teenagers are older than 12 and younger than 20. In programming, "teenagerness" is determined by establishing that the relational tests age > 12 and age < 20 are both true. In JavaScript, the "teenage" expression is

```
age > 12 && age < 20
```

Logical and. The && is the **logical and** operator, playing the same role that AND plays in query expressions (Chapters 5 and 15). The outcome of *a* && *b* is true if both *a* and *b* are true; otherwise, it is false. (The operands *a* and *b* can be variables, in which case they have Boolean values, or expressions, or a mixture.)

Thus, in the teenager expression, the current value of age is compared to 12, which yields a true or a false outcome. Then the current value of age is compared to 20, yielding another true or false outcome. Finally, these two outcomes, the operands of &&, are tested, and if they are both true, the entire expression has a true outcome; otherwise, it is false. For example,

Value of age	age > 12	age < 20	age > 12 && age < 20
4	false	true	false
16	true	true	true
50	true	false	false

Notice that the operands for relational expressions must be numeric, but the operands for logical expressions must be Boolean (that is, true or false). To try this operator, declare and initialize an age variable and check the results in the teenager expression.

Programming Is Still Not Algebra. In algebra, the notation *12 < age < 20* would be used to assert "teenagerness," the static condition of an age within the indicated limits. In programming, both tests must be specified and the two results "anded" (combined using &&) to produce the final answer. The difference, again, is that in algebra we are just stating a fact, whereas in programming we are *commanding* the computer to perform the operation of testing the two conditions.

Logical or. Not surprisingly, there is also a **logical or** operator, ||. The outcome of *a* || *b* is true if either *a* is true or *b* is true, and it is also true if they are both true; it is false only if both are false. A "preteen" test expression

```
age == 11 || age == 12
```

illustrates the use of the logical operator ||. Because && and || have lower precedence than the relational operators, the relationals are always tested first. To include 10-year-olds as preteens, we write an expression that states that either the person is age 10 or their age satisfies the previous preteen definition:

```
age == 10 || (age == 11 || age == 12)
```

Notice that the subexpression in parentheses produces a true or false value when evaluated, just like a relational test does. It doesn't matter how the operands of || are produced; it only matters that they are true or false values. Another way to achieve the same result is

```
(age == 10 || age == 11) || age == 12
```

Of course, it is also possible to test this definition of preteen with the expression

```
age >= 10 && age <= 12
```

which takes a bit less typing, and is like the teenager test. All of these expressions seem equally clear to a person, and the computer doesn't care which is used.

Logical not. The **logical not (!)** is a unary operator—it takes only a single operand—and its outcome is the opposite of the value of its operand. To command the computer to check if the age is not that of a teenager, write

```
!(age > 12 && age < 20)
```

It works as follows. The subexpression in parentheses tests whether the age qualifies as a teenager, that is, more than 12 and less than 20. The outcome of the test is either true, the age qualifies as a teenager, or false, it does not. By placing the logical not operator in front of the parenthesized expression, we have a new expression, which has the opposite outcome: The whole expression is false if the age is that of a teenager, and it is true if the age is not that of a teenager.

17.6 In the Tropics. The Tropic of Cancer is 23.5° North latitude and the Tropic of Capricorn is 23.5° South latitude; the Arctic Circle is 66.5° North latitude and the Antarctic Circle is 66.5° South latitude. Assume lat is a variable giving the latitude of a location on the globe. Write a relational expression that is true if the location is hot or cold; that is, either tropical or polar.

Operator Overload. Finally, we've reached **operator overload.** That might sound like the description of someone trying to learn too many new operators at a time—a state you have no doubt achieved!—but it is a technical term meaning the "use of an operator with different data types." The case of interest is +. Operators usually apply to a single data type, like numbers. So, we expect 4 + 5 to produce the numerical result of 9. And it does because the operands are numbers. But if the operands are the strings "four" + "five", the result is the string "fourfive". Try these two interpretations in Scratchpad. (What happens if plus gets one number and one string?)

Concatenation. When we use + with strings, it joins the strings by the operation of **concatenation**. In everyday writing, we simply place two strings together if we want them joined, but in programming, we command the computer to do the work, so we need the operator concatenation to tell the computer to put two strings together. We have "overloaded" the meaning of + to mean addition when operands are numeric and concatenation when the operands are strings. Though overloading is common in some programming languages, + is the only example you'll see here with our use of JavaScript.

Quote Note. When manipulating strings, as in the statement

```
fullName = firstName + " " + middleName + " " + lastName;
```

which creates a name from its parts using blanks as separators, it's easy to understand + as concatenation. But for a statement like

```
colt = "4" + "5";
```

the variable colt will be assigned the string "45", not 9, because the operands are (length 1) strings. Thus, you must be alert for quotes that tell you the operand is a string rather than a numerical value. (Using Scratchpad, find out what happens if plus gets one number and one string.)

A Conditional Statement

A specific statement type, called a **conditional statement** or a **conditional**, has been invented to make testing numbers and strings simpler. The conditional statement of JavaScript, which differs from the IF( ) function of spreadsheets, has the form

if (<*Boolean expression* >)
<*then-statement*>;

Here the <*Boolean expression*> is any expression evaluating to a Boolean true or false outcome, such as relational expressions, and the <*then-statement*> is any JavaScript statement, such as an assignment statement.

if Statements and Their Flow of Control

For example, an if statement that checks waterTemp in Fahrenheit

```
if (waterTemp < 32)
    waterState = "Frozen";
```

is a typical conditional statement. In a conditional the <*Boolean expression*>, called a **predicate**, is evaluated, producing a true or false outcome. If the outcome is true, the <*then-statement*> is performed. If the outcome is false, the <*then-statement*> is skipped. Therefore, in the example the value of the variable waterTemp is determined and compared to 32. If it is less than 32, the value of the variable waterState is set to "Frozen". Otherwise, the statement is passed over, and waterState remains unchanged. The following conditional

```
if (waterTemp >= 32 && waterTemp <= 212)
    waterState = "Liquid";
```

tests a range of values using relational operators and the and operator.

Some programming languages use the word *then* to separate the predicate from the *<then-statement>*, but JavaScript does not, because it is unnecessary. Writing the *<then-statement>* indented on the following line is actually only common practice, not a rule; the *<then-statement>* could be on the same line as the predicate,

```
if (waterTempC >= 0 && waterTempC <= 100) waterState = "Liquid";
```

It has the same meaning because white space is ignored in JavaScript. But programmers write the *<then-statement>* indented on the following line to set it off and emphasize its conditional nature for anyone reading the program. By the way, when you read a conditional statement you *say* "then" after the predicate.

Sometimes we need to perform more than one statement on a `true` outcome of the predicate test. We could just repeat the test for each statement, as in

```
if (waterTemp < 32) waterState = "Frozen";
if (waterTemp < 32) description = "Ice";
```

Repeating statements can become tedious, though it is okay.

Compound Statements

Programming languages allow for a sequence of statements in the *<then-statement>*. The problem is that if there are several statements, how will the computer know how many to skip in case the predicate has a `false` outcome? The solution is easy: We group the statements by surrounding them with "curly braces," {}, which collects them to become a single statement known as a **compound statement**. Then they fulfill the requirements of the earlier definition because now the *<then-statement>* refers to the single (compound) statement; it is skipped when the predicate outcome is `false`. For example,

```
if (waterTempC < 0) {
   waterState = "Frozen";
   description = "Ice";
}
```

Notice the location of the curly braces. One immediately follows the predicate to signal that a compound statement is next, and the other is placed conspicuously on its own line below the *i* of `if`. Programmers do this so that compound statement grouping symbols are easy to see, because they are easily overlooked if they are in an unexpected place in a program. As always, the computer doesn't care where the curly braces are placed.

The "exception proving the rule" that every statement must be terminated by a semicolon is the compound statement. The closing curly brace, }, should not be followed by a semicolon.

Show Your Braces. Since compound statement braces have a huge impact on program behavior, always put them in the standard place, where they will be noticed.

Another example of the use of the compound statement is from the espresso computation of Figure 17.1:

```
var drink = "latte";
var ounce = 12;
var price;

if (drink == "latte" || drink == "cappuccino") {
  if (ounce == 8)
     price = 1.95;
  if (ounce == 12)
     price = 2.35;
  if (ounce == 16)
     price = 2.75;
}

price
/*
2.35
*/
```

This code illustrates an if with a compound statement containing three simple if statements. If drink is neither a "latte" nor a "cappuccino", the three statements will be skipped. Otherwise, if drink equals "latte" or drink equals "cappuccino", the three statements will be performed. Notice that at most one predicate of the three statements of the compound statement can be true, because ounce can have only one value at a time: 8, 12, 16, or something else. So, price will be changed at most once.

if/else Statements

Of course, performing statements when a condition is true is handy, but how can statements be executed when the condition's outcome is false? There is another form of the if statement known as the if/else **statement**. It has the form

```
if (<Boolean expression>)
   <then-statement>;
else
   <else-statement>;
```

The *<Boolean expression>* is evaluated first. If the outcome is true, the *<then-statement>* is executed and the *<else-statement>* is skipped. If the *<Boolean expression>*'s outcome is false, the *<then-statement>* is skipped and the *<else-statement>* is executed. For example,

```
var day = "Tuesday";
var calendarEntry;

if (day == 'Friday' || day == 'Saturday')

      calendarEntry = "Party!";

else

      calendarEntry = "Study";

calendarEntry
/*
Study
*/
```

The *<then-statement>* and *<else-statement>* are single statements, but several statements can be grouped into a compound statement with curly braces when necessary. For example,

```
var year = 2015;
var leapYear = false;
var febDays = 28;

if ((year % 4) == 0) {
      leapYear = true;
      febDays = febDays + 1;
}
else
      leapYear = false;

febDays
/*
28
*/
```

This example uses the mod operator %, so the outcome of (year%4) is the remainder of year/4; that is, the result is 0, 1, 2, or 3.

A typical example sets the same variables in both parts of the conditional. Consider a coin toss at the start of a soccer game, which can be expressed as

```
if (sideUp == sideCalled) {
      coinTossWinner = visitorTeam;
      firstHalfOffensive = visitorTeam;
      secondHalfOffensive = hostTeam;
}
else {
      coinTossWinner = hostTeam;
      firstHalfOffensive = hostTeam;
      secondHalfOffensive = visitorTeam;
}
```

Notice that the opening curly brace for the *<else-statement>* is placed right after the else, and the closing curly brace is placed conspicuously on its own line directly below the first *e* of else.

17.7 Even or Odd? After executing the conditional statement

```
if (monthDays < 31 && monthNumber < 8)
   evenOrOdd = "even";
else
   evenOrOdd = "odd";
```

what is the value of evenOrOdd for May, the fifth month, which has 31 days?

Nested if/else Statements

The *<then-statement>* and the *<else-statement>* can contain an if/else, but you have to be careful, because it can be ambiguous which if an else goes with. The rule in JavaScript and most other programming languages is that the else associates with the (immediately) preceding if. For example, the code

```
var description = "muggle";
var ref = "literary";
var report = "?";

if (description == "muggle")
   if (ref == "music")
      report = "Louis Armstrong jazz hit [1928]";
else
   report = "Wizard sighting";
```

Caution: This code is descriptive

has been *deceptively* indented so that it *appears* that the else associates with the first if. But white space is ignored. Running the code in Scratchpad proves that it's deceptive

```
var description = "muggle";
var ref = "literary";
var report = "?";

if (description == "muggle")
   if (ref == "music")
      report = "Louis Armstrong jazz hit [1928]";
else
   report = "Wizard sighting";

report
/*
Wizard sighting
*/
```

In fact, the case where the description is not a muggle isn't even considered in this code. The best policy—the one successful programmers follow—is to enclose the *<then-statement>* or *<else-statement>* in compound curly braces whenever they contain an if/else. Thus, the right way to express the statement is

```
var description = "muggle";
var ref = "literary";
var report = "?";

if (description == "muggle") {
   if (ref == "music")
      report = "Louis Armstrong jazz hit [1928]";
   }
else
   report = "Wizard sighting";

report

/*
?
*/
```

The braces ensure that the else matches with its if, making the only way to have a wizard sighting be when description is not a muggle. The "braces policy" saves a lot of grief.

As one final example of **nested conditionals**, consider the four outcomes from flipping two coins expressed by nested conditionals:

```
if (flip1 == guess1) {
    if (flip2 == guess2)
        score = "win win";
    else
        score = "win lose";
}
else {
    if (flip2 == guess2)
        score = "lose win";
    else
        score = "lose lose";
}
```

Inner if

Outer if

Inner if

This example shows clearly the logic of the true and false outcomes of the predicates.

The Espresso Program

We now return to the program shown in Figure 17.1. The program (shown in Figure 17.3) computes the price of four kinds of espresso drinks based on the type of drink, the size of the drink, and the number of additional shots, plus tax. The input variables are listed at the start of the program, as is the output.

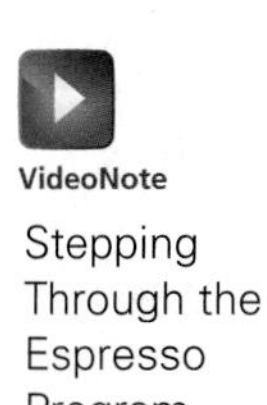

VideoNote

Stepping Through the Espresso Program

The input variables are given here (lines 10–12) as constants. Eventually, this code will be part of a Web page written in HTML. HTML <input> tags are available, see Chapter 18, to specify user data, and they will act as the UI for setting these variables. Because the program will create the output, we declare the output to be a variable in line 13 of the program.

Lines 16 through 27 determine the kind of drink and establish the base price. These statements have been written to show different programming techniques:

- **Lines 16–17:** If the order is straight espresso, the first shot is priced at $1.40. This is an example of a basic conditional statement.
- **Lines 18–25:** These statements establish the base prices for lattes and cappuccinos using an `if` statement with conditionals in the *<then-statement>* compound statement.
- **Lines 26–27:** This statement uses a basic `if` statement to compute the base price for Americanos.
- **Lines 29–30:** Finally, the total `price` is computed in lines 29 and 30. In line 29 the cost of additional shots is added to the base price. In line 30 the tax is added in. This is accomplished by multiplying the total price by the `taxRate`, then adding the result to the total price.
- **Lines 32–34:** These lines display the result of the computation after the user has typed ^L.

```
1  /* Espresso Pricing Program
2  Inputs:
3     drink can be "espresso", "latte",
4                  "cappuccino" or "Americano"
5     ounce can be 8, 12, 16
6     shots can be 1, 2, 3, 4, ...
7  Output:
8     price in dollars                          */
9
10 var drink = "latte";
11 var ounce = 12;
12 var shots = 2;
13 var price;
14 var taxRate = 0.088;
15
16 if (drink == "espresso")
17   price = 1.40;
18 if (drink == "latte" || drink == "cappuccino") {
19   if (ounce == 8)
20      price = 1.95;
21   if (ounce == 12)
22      price = 2.35;
23   if (ounce == 16)
24      price = 2.75;
25 }
26 if (drink == "Americano")
27   price = 1.20 + 0.30*(ounce/8);
28
29 price = price + (shots - 1)*.50;
30 price = price + price*taxRate;
31
32 /*
33 3.1008
34 */
```

Figure 17.3 The Espresso Pricing Program run using Scratchpad.

Notice that the if statements in lines 19–24 will always be executed, but because they apply to different drinks, the statement(s) of their *<then-statement>* will be executed in at most one of the cases.

The Logic of a Double Tall Latte

To see the espresso program in action, compute the price of a double tall latte, the second most common phrase used in Seattle after "it's still raining." A "double" means a total of two shots in the drink, that is, one extra shot. Thus, the input variables to the program are

```
drink ⇔ "latte"
ounce ⇔ 12
shots ⇔ 2
```

where ⇔ means "has the value of" or "contains." This notation allows us to give the value of a variable without using the equal sign, which would look like an assignment statement.

The first statements are declarations, which are like definitions. In particular, we should treat price as not yet having any value. The following lines are executed:

- **Lines 16–17** are executed first. The test drink == "espresso" fails, because the variable drink has the value "latte". As a result, its then statement is skipped.
- **Line 18** is executed next. The test drink == "latte" || drink == "cappuccino" has a true outcome because the subexpression drink == "latte" is true; the relational test drink == "cappuccino" is false, of course, but because one of the operands of the || is true, the whole expression is true. This means that the then statement containing the conditionals in lines 19–25 will be executed.
- **Lines 19–20** are executed next. The test ounce == 8 has a false outcome, so its then statement is skipped.
- **Lines 21–22** are nexecuted. (I made up *nexecuted* for "next executed." Isn't it a great word?) The ounce == 12 test is true, so the then statement is executed, giving price its initial value, price ⇔ 2.35.
- **Lines 23–24** are nexecuted. The ounce == 16 test fails, so its then statement is skipped.
- **Lines 26–27** are nexecuted. The drink == "Americano" test fails, so its then statement is skipped.
- **Line 29** is nexecuted. This causes the value of shots minus 1 to be multiplied by .50, resulting in the value .50, which is added to price, yielding price ⇔ 2.85.
- **Line 30** is nexecuted. The current value of price is multiplied by taxRate, whose value was initialized on line 14 (taxRate ⇔ 0.088), resulting in 0.25, which is added to price to compute the final value of 3.10, which is assigned to price.

Thus, price ⇔ 3.10, so a "double tall latte" costs $3.10. (The extra 0.0008 is dropped as explained in the next chapter.)

SUMMARY

In this chapter, we introduced enough programming concepts—and their JavaScript syntax—for you to read and understand basic programs. The chapter began by introducing the idea that a name can be separated from its value. Captain is a name for a team leader, but its value, that is, the person who is the captain, can change. In fact, the name exists, though with an undefined value, as soon as a team is formed. Names-with-changing-values is a familiar idea. File names work this way as we progressively update a file with, say, a word processor. Variables in programming languages have changing values, too. The reason is simple. A program is a fixed, finite description for a computation written out in a few pages of code. Yet, when the computation is executed, many values may be created to produce the final answer. In the espresso computation, for example, the variable `price`, which is initially undefined, has three different values: the base price, the total price before tax, and the final price. At any point, the value of `price` is the price as computed so far, but the process of computing `price` continues until the program is finished.

In basic programming, you now understand the following:

- Name–value separation is an important concept. It's one of the ways that programming differs from algebra.
- Letter sequences that make up a variable's name (identifiers) must be declared. Variables can be initialized when they are declared. Changing the value of a variable is possible by using assignment.
- An assignment statement has a variable on the left side of the symbol and an expression on the right side. The operation is to compute the value of the expression and make the result the new value of the variable. This makes information flow from right to left in an assignment statement. Statements like `x = x + 1;` make sense in programming, but not in algebra. This statement is a command to the computer to find the current value of the variable `x`, add 1 to it, and make the result of the addition the new value of `x`.
- There are three JavaScript data types of interest to us—numbers, strings, and Booleans—and we can build expressions to compute values of these types.
- Standard arithmetic operators and relationals compute on numbers, and logical operations on Booleans. (See Appendix D for complete details.) In defining concatenation, you learned about "operator overload." Expressions "do the computing" in programs and are generally a familiar idea.
- As a rule, all programming statements are executed one after another, starting at the beginning. The conditional statements are the exception. JavaScript's two conditional forms are `if` and `if/else`. These allow statements to be executed depending on the outcome of a Boolean expression called a predicate. Using conditionals, we can organize our computations so that operations are performed when "the conditions are right."
- We must be careful to group statements within a compound statement to make it clear which statements are skipped or executed. We also must be careful when using `if/else` in a conditional so that the `if` and `else` associate correctly.

- The espresso program in Figure 17.1 illustrates most of the ideas in this chapter. The program uses both numeric and string data types, as well as the declaration, assignment, and conditional statement forms.
- All that keeps us from running the program and demonstrating our knowledge is setting up the input to acquire the values for drink, ounce, and shots, and outputting the price. This requires a UI written in HTML (the topic of Chapter 18).

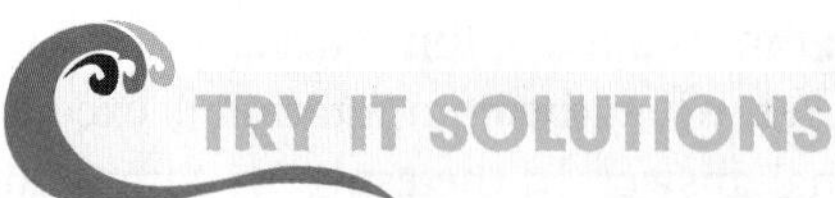

TRY IT SOLUTIONS

17.1 "Argo" is a name bound to a specific movie that will always be the movie's name; "Best Picture" is a variable that changes value each year.

17.2 13: b, bb, bB, Bb, BB, bbb, bbB, bBb, bBB, Bbb, BbB, BBb, BBB

17.3 var theseTruths = "self evident";

17.4 var real_first_name = 'Samuel', real_last_name = "Clemens";

var humorist = true;

var century = 19;

var famous_quote = '"Nothing so needs reforming as other people\'s habits."'

Notice the use of escape apostrophe (\') in famous_quote. It is required because the entire quotation is enclosed in single quotes to allow the text to include double quotes. In the computer's memory the value of famous_quote is the 54-character string:

"Nothing so needs reforming as other people's habits."

That is, the enclosing single quotes and the backslash are gone.

17.5 var bestPicture;

bestPicture = "12 Years a Slave";

Did you remember the semicolon terminators?

17.6 lat <= 23.5 || lat >= 66.5

17.7

```
var monthDays = 31;
var monthNumber = 5;
var evenOrOdd;

if (monthDays < 31 && monthNumber < 8)
   evenOrOdd = "even";
else
   evenOrOdd = "odd";

evenOrOdd
/*
odd
*/
```

Multiple Choice

1. This symbol is often used to describe syntactic structures.
   a. #
   b. < >
   c. ( )
   d. { }
2. What will be stored in the computer's memory after completing the following line of code?
   `var symbol = "/\\'\"'\"//\\";`
   a. "/\\'\"'\"//\\";
   b. /\\""//\\
   c. /\\'\"'\"//\\
   d. /\""//\";
3. On the computer, variables are
   a. memory locations
   b. programs
   c. files
   d. all of the above
4. Which of the following can be used as part of a variable name?
   a. - hyphen
   b. ƀ (space)
   c. _ underscore
   d. ( ) parentheses
5. The symbol to terminate a statement in JavaScript is
   a. : colon
   b. Enter
   c. ! exclamation
   d. ; semicolon
6. When declared, JavaScript variables are
   a. automatically assigned a 0
   b. automatically assigned a blank
   c. undefined
   d. assigned a random number
7. grade = num_right * 2.5 is a(n)
   a. variable
   b. operator
   c. assignment statement
   d. relational operator
8. Following the rules of precedence
   a. addition is done before subtraction
   b. multiplication is done after division
   c. multiplication is done before subtraction
   d. everything is done left to right

9. In JavaScript, the relational test, birth_year > 1944 && birth_year < 1965, is
   a. true if birth_year is 1952
   b. true if birth_year is less than 1965
   c. false if birth_year is greater than 1944
   d. none of the above
10. For a logical AND operator to work
   a. one of the conditions must be true
   b. neither condition can be false
   c. either one but not both conditions must be true
   d. none of the above
11. A typical computer program follows the pattern of
   a. output, processing, input
   b. input, output, processing
   c. input, processing, output
   d. processing, input, output
12. How many characters are in the empty string?
   a. –1
   b. 1
   c. undefined
   d. 0
13. Who makes mistakes when programming?
   a. people who are new to programming or have not been trained successfully
   b. developers who are working on very large programs
   c. everyone
   d. students under the age of 18

Short Answer

1. A(n) ________ terminates every statement in a program.
2. The ________ symbol cannot be used to name identifiers.
3. A(n) ________ is a systematic way of solving a problem so that an agent can follow the instructions and get the correct result.
4. A(n) ________ is the letter sequence of a variable's name.
5. Variables are created using a(n) ________ statement.
6. To ________ a variable is to assign a value to a variable.
7. +, –, *, and / are called ________.
8. A(n) ________ operator has only one operand.
9. ________ are used to make comparisons.
10. The ________ command changes the value of a variable.
11. Joining two strings together using the + is called ________.
12. In programming, the if statement is called a ________.
13. When an else statement follows an if statement and the if statement is false, the ________ statement will execute.
14. ________ are used to group several statements into a compound statement.
15. Natural languages are too ________ for directing a computer.

Exercises

1. A programming statement similar to first_name = " Fred " ; should never be read as first_name equals Fred in programming. Explain two correct ways to state the above statement.
2. Fill in the empty cells in the table below with the appropriate information.

Name	Current Value	Previous Value
Batman		
Top Chef		
	Joe Biden	

3. Why are true and false not strings?
4. For the following, fill in the math operator and the JavaScript relational operator.

Name	Math Operator	JavaScript Operator
less than	________	________
less than or equal to	________	________
greater than	________	________
greater than or equal to	________	________
equal to	________	________
not equal to	________	________

5. Step through each line of the following JavaScript program. (This is the program from Figure 17.1.) Write down the value of each variable as you walk through it. Use an order of a 16 oz. latte with two shots.

```
var price;
var taxRate = 0.088;
if (drink == "espresso")
  price = 1.40;
if (drink == "latte" || drink == "cappuccino") {
  if (ounce == 8)
    price = 1.95;
  if (ounce == 12)
    price = 2.35;
  if (ounce == 16)
    price = 2.75;
}
if (drink == "Americano")
  price = 1.20 + .30 * (ounce/8);
price = price + (shots - 1) * .50;
price = price + price * taxRate;
```

6. After executing the following code, what is the value of posOrNeg (assume the number currently has the value of –2)?

```
if (number >= 1)
    posOrNeg = "pos";
if (number == 0)
```

```
        posOrNeg = "zero";
    else
        posOrNeg = "neg";
```

7. Modify the espresso program to include brewed coffee. It comes in a 12 oz. size only and costs $1.00 plus tax.
8. Explain when you would use quotes and apostrophes for strings.
9. Give the JavaScript expression for determining how many overtime hours an employee has worked.
10. Explain why the following statements won't work.
```
wont_work = "five" * 5 + "5" - '5'
3 * 7 = wont_work
"wont_work" = m * n
```
11. What are the answers for the following?
```
answer = (9 + 7) / 4 * 2 - 5
answer = 6 * 3 / 9 - (17%5)
answer = (4 + 5) - (2 + 3) * 4
```
12. Explain why the following statement works in programming but not math.
```
count = count + 1
```
13. Explain how the following statement works.
```
left = right
```

CHAPTER 18

A JavaScript Program

The Bean Counter

learning objectives

- Use the Bean Counter application as a model to do the following:
  - Write input elements
  - Create a button table
  - Write an event handler in JavaScript
  - Produce a UI similar to that of the Bean Counter
- Trace the execution of the Bean Counter, saying what output is produced by a given input
- Explain event-based programming in JavaScript and the use of event handlers

CHAPTER 18

Programming today is a race between software engineers striving to build bigger and better idiot-proof programs, and the Universe trying to produce bigger and better idiots. So far the Universe is winning.

—RICH COOK

MUCH OF MODERN programming requires two activities. The first is creating the algorithm that directs the computer to solve a problem. The second is creating a user interface (UI) to assist with the human/computer interaction; specifically, a way to enter the input and a way to display the computed output. JavaScript (JS) is designed for Web applications, which means that JavaScript code can be included in Web page source code written in HTML. The Web page is the graphical user interface; the JavaScript does the computing.

In Chapter 17 we wrote a program in JavaScript to charge for espresso drinks. That program is the computational part of our solution in this chapter, as we focus here on creating a user interface and connecting it to the espresso program. So, our main goal is to produce a user-friendly UI for the program.

We will create the Bean Counter application. The first step is to make sure that the computation from Chapter 17 is correct. Then, after covering two preliminaries, we will follow five steps:

1. Review Web page programming, recalling some HTML basics, and introduce the idea of HTML input elements.
2. Build the UI for the Bean Counter program, so that the graphic looks right. Only the picture will be complete; the buttons will not work yet.
3. Introduce the idea of event programming and connect the buttons to the program logic.
4. Test the Web page, evaluating it for its usefulness.
5. Revise the Web page and the logic to improve the solution to the problem.

When the Web page is finished, we will have created our first complete JavaScript program.

Preliminaries

Recall from Chapter 4 that HTML files are simple ASCII text. The fancy formatting of word processors like Pages and Microsoft Word confuses Web browsers and must be avoided. Instead we'll use a basic text editor such as Notepad++ or TextWrangler discussed in Lab Practice I of Chapter 4. The file format must be text or txt, and the file name's extension (the characters following the last dot) must be html. So, bean.html is an appropriate file name. The operating system knows that the file will be processed by a Web browser, and the browser will be able to understand everything in the file without becoming confused.

Build as You Go. The best way to learn the ideas and the practical skills in this chapter is to build the program yourself as you read along. Find relevant files at pearsonhighered .com/snyder.

To create your program, start by opening your starterPage.html in your text editor, and save it with the file name, bean.html. To include JavaScript in an HTML file, enclose the JavaScript text in <script> tags. The information that you include between these tags is the subject of this chapter. When it's time to test your program, save it. Then find the file on your computer and open the file with Firefox. Your JavaScript will run with your HTML. It's that simple.

To work through the mechanics of running a JavaScript program in a Web page, we will ignore the user interface for the moment and simply run the computational part of the program from Chapter 17. This is mostly an exercise, because we will not be able to interact with the result, and all that we will see is one number printed out. We begin this way to make sure the Bean Counter code of the last chapter is working. We'll use this code later in this chapter, so typing it in now is a good way to become familiar with the code. The program structure needed to run just the computation part is shown in Figure 18.1(a). You should *accurately* type it into a file, save it as beanV0.html, and run it.

Because we have not yet built the user interface, we have no way to give inputs. So we fake the input. We declare and initialize three new variables—drink, shots, and ounce—as the first three statements of the JavaScript code. We'll take these out later, when we add the buttons. These initializers are for a "double tall latte," that is, a 12-ounce latte made with two shots of espresso. After you type in and run the program with Firefox, you should see the result shown in Figure 18.1(b).

At the end of the JavaScript code, the alert(price) command prints out the amount that the program computed for the price. This is the same price for a "double tall latte" that we computed in Chapter 17. Our next step is to construct the graphical user interface.

```
<!doctype html>
<html>
 <head>
  <meta charset="UTF-8">
  <title>Bean Counter</title>
 </head>
 <body>
  <h2> Confirming that bean.html works </h2>
  <script>
   var drink = "latte";
   var ounce = 12;
   var shots = 2;
   var taxRate = 0.088;
   var price;
   if (drink == "espresso")
      price = 1.40;
   if (drink == "latte" || drink == "cappuccino") {
      if (ounce == 8)
         price = 1.95;
      if (ounce == 12)
         price = 2.35;
      if (ounce == 16)
         price = 2.75;
   }
   if (drink == "Americano")
      price = 1.20 + 0.30*(ounce/8);
   price = price + (shots - 1)*.50;
   price = price + price*taxRate;
   alert(price);
  </script>
 </body>
</html>
```

(a)

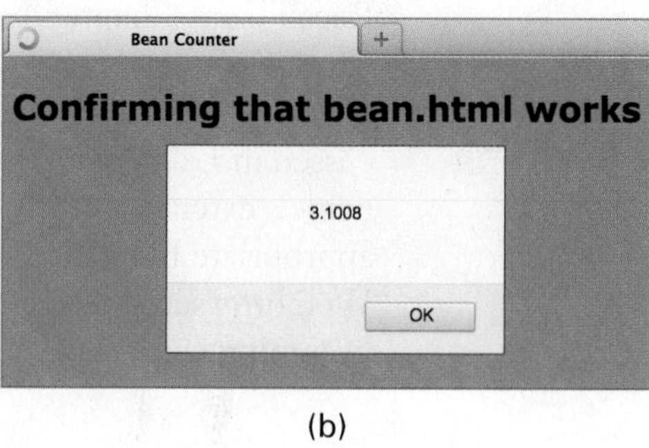

(b)

Figure 18.1 Version 0 of the Bean Counter program without the user interface, and with fixed inputs: (a) the HTML and JavaScript code, and (b) running in the Firefox browser.

Background for the UI

This section covers two introductory topics that you need to understand to create the JavaScript graphical user interface. First we present a quick review of HTML. If you need more information, consult Chapter 4. Next we explain a new HTML tag, the <input.../> tag. This allows us to create buttons and display output.

The Bean Counter Graphical User Interface (see Figure 18.2) presents to the user rows and columns of buttons, and a window in the lower right corner to display the total price

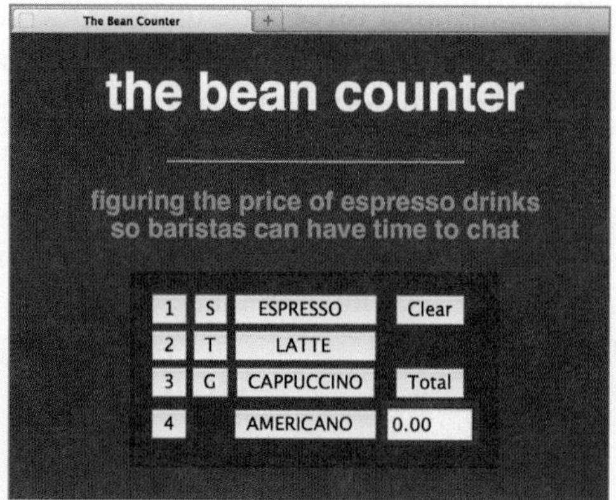

Figure 18.2 The Web interface for the Bean Counter program as it will appear when it is complete.

of the espresso drink. The first column of buttons specifies the number of shots. The second column specifies the size of the drink, where **S**, **T**, and **G** stand for short, tall, and grande. The next column specifies the type of espresso drink. The meanings of the last two buttons in the rightmost column are obvious: click **Clear** to begin a new price computation, and click **Total** to calculate the cost.

Review of HTML Basics

Our review of HTML (covered thoroughly in Chapter 4) entails a quick development of the starting HTML for the bean.html page.

Beginning with the starterPage.html, change the title to <title>The Bean Counter</title>. We will need a global <style> section in the head, so this is a good time to place those tags. And in the body, we replace "Hello, World" with an <h1> heading that reads "the bean counter," an <hr/> for a horizontal line, and a paragraph with the text "figuring the price of espresso drinks so baristas can have time to chat." A <br/> is needed to display the short slogan on two lines. Now all that remains is to format the text.

We will follow the color and font choices of Figure 18.2. We choose saddlebrown as the background color, darkorange for the font color, and helvetica for the font family. The heading, however, will be white, and the horizontal line must be styled, too, to be shorter than the full window. So, check the styling components in Figure 18.3 to recall how these are specified. Notice that we chose a color for the line, changing it from its default gray.

If this discussion reminds you what you've forgotten a lot of HTML, review Chapter 4 or check Appendix A for more information.

Interacting with a UI

Curiously, the input facilities like **buttons** and **check boxes** are known as elements of **forms**. They were introduced into HTML to assist with activities like ordering products or answering survey questions. As you know, users fill out a form by clicking buttons or entering data in text windows. When a form is complete, it is sent to the computer for processing. Although our application doesn't involve questionnaires, we use the input elements, and so we must use the form tags.

```
<!doctype html>
<html>
  <head>
   <meta charset="UTF-8"/>
   <title>The Bean Counter</title>
   <style type="text/css">
         body {background-color : saddlebrown; color : darkorange;
                  font-family : helvetica; text-align : center}
         hr     {width:50%; color: darkorange}
         h1     {color : white;}
   </style>
  </head>
  <body>
    <h1> the bean counter</h1>
    <hr/>
    <p><b>figuring the price of espresso drinks<br />
            so baristas can have time to chat</b></p>
  </body>
</html>
```

Figure 18.3 The Bean Counter interface to this point, and the HTML that produced it.

Forms. The form tags <form> and </form> surround the input elements. Though <form> has several attributes, the only one that matters to us is the name,

```
<form name="unique_name">
```

which identifies this specific form. We'll have more to say about using the name after we introduce the input tags.

Events and Event Handlers. When the UI inputs are used, such as clicking a button, they cause an event to occur. In the case of a button, the event is called a "click event." An **event** is an indication from the computer (operating system) that something just happened (for example, a mouse click).

We want our JavaScript program to respond to that click—that is, perform the operation corresponding to the button command. When JavaScript finds out about the event, it runs a piece of program called the *event handler* for that event. An **event handler** is the program that performs the operation that responds to an event. We will explain this concept further in a moment.

Three Input Elements

Although HTML has several input elements, we will only use three input tags in this book: text boxes, radio buttons, and (command) buttons.

Initial Entry

- **Text Box.** The text box can be used to input or output numbers or words. Its general form is

```
<input type="text" id="ref_name" value="displayed_text" size="n"
   onchange="event_handler" />
```

where type indicates that this is a text box, *ref_name* is the unique name used to refer to this text box, value is the text to be displayed in the box, such as the "Initial Entry" in the figure, and size is the width of the box in characters; the default is 20. Finally, onchange gives the event handler's JavaScript instructions. After the user has changed the contents in the text window, the JavaScript program instructions are performed. This text produced the above figure

```
<input type="text" id="eg" value="Initial Entry" size = "10"
   onchange=" ... "/>
```

The box for the text input is placed where it occurs in the HTML program.

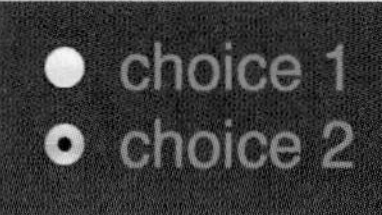

- **Radio Button.** Radio buttons give a selection of preprogrammed settings. Their general form is

```
<input type="radio" name="identifier" onclick="event_handler" />label text
```

where type indicates that this is a (single) radio button, *identifier* is the name of the element, and onclick gives the event handler. (Notice that the *label text*, such as choice 1, is not inside the tag's brackets.) When the user clicks on a radio button, the center darkens to indicate that it is set, and the event handler's JavaScript instructions are performed. If there are other radio buttons with the *same* name, they are also cleared. These tags produced the above figure:

```
<input type="radio" name="pick" onclick=" ... "/> choice 1<br/>
<input type="radio" name="pick" onclick=" ... "/> choice 2
```

The radio button is placed in the HTML text where it occurs.

- **Button.** The form of the button input is

  <input type="button" value="*label*" onclick="*event_handler*" />

  where type indicates this is a button input, value gives the text to be printed on the button, such as Click Me in the figure, and onclick gives the event handler's JavaScript instructions. When the user clicks the button, the JavaScript code of the event handler is executed. This tag produced the figure:

  <input type="button" value="Click Me" onclick=" ... "/>

  The image for the button is placed in the next position in the text of the HTML program.

  The button—technically it's a *command* button—has an alternative form, so, for example, an image could be a button. This tag is convenient, and surrounds the object that is to be the button:

  <button onclick="*event_handler*">*text or other object*</button>

  where onclick gives the event handler's JavaScript instructions. Notice that the label is given *between* the start and end tags.

For the Bean Counter application, we need only the text and button inputs. We will use radio buttons later.

Forms and Their Inputs. In order for the <input/> tags to be associated with the proper form, forms are named. We call ours esp,

<form name="esp">

Then, all input tags that are to be considered part of this form (and thus processed together) simply use the form attribute to connect to it, as in

<input form="esp" ... />

This technique will be illustrated momentarily.

18.1 Give Your Input.

a. Give the HTML text for a button with PANIC written on it; use the string " " for the event handler.

b. Give the HTML text for a 10-letter text box named **author**, containing the initial text **Pen Name** and having the empty string for the event handler.

Creating the Graphical User Interface

We are well on our way to creating the Bean Counter interface, as shown in Figure 18.2. The HTML in Figure 18.3 has the heading information, the horizontal line, and the slogan. "All" we have left to do is create a table and fill in the entries.

Focus Point. When faced with a task, it's a good idea to "think it through" before starting. List the required steps in the order you will do them. Then you can focus your attention on one step at a time. This process, which is a main topic of Chapter 21, is illustrated here by writing down our plan before starting.

Notice that the table in Figure 18.2 is a four-row, four-column table with two empty cells. (The columns are not all the same size, but the browser will take care of making them the right size.) Buttons appear in all of the occupied cells but one, so our table is mostly a table of buttons. This suggests the following algorithm for building the UI:

1. **Create a button table.** Program the HTML for a four-row, four-column table with a generic button in each cell. That is, 16 buttons. This is a good strategy because we can build such a table quickly using *Copy/Paste*.
2. **Delete two buttons.** Two of the cells in the table should be empty. Delete the buttons, but not the cells, leaving 14 buttons.
3. **Insert text box.** Replace the button of the last cell making it a text box, leaving 13 buttons as required.
4. **Label the buttons.** Pass through the table and set the label for the button as needed.
5. **Primp the interface.** Check the interface and adjust the specification where it is necessary.

Once these five steps are complete, the *image* for the Bean Counter interface will be finished. Consider each step in detail.

Table Trick. A fast way to build a table in HTML is to create a skeleton first, then fill it in. This is easy because the skeleton can be constructed "inside out" using copy and paste. Begin with a generic cell such as <td> and </td> tags; copy and paste these as many times as needed to build a row, and enclose the result in <tr> and </tr> tags; copy and paste that for as many rows as needed, and surround the result with <table> and </table> tags. Finally, fill in the entries.

1. Create a Button Table

We use the "inside out" scheme to build the table. Given the information about the button input, we decide that the generic cell can have the form

```
<td><button form="esp" onclick = ''> b </button></td>
```

Here "b" is a placeholder for the button label that we'll fix in Step 4, and '' is a placeholder for the JavaScript text of the event handler that we'll write later.

We type this HTML into the file from Figure 18.3. We copy/paste it to get four copies and surround them by row tags. Then we make four copies of the row and surround them with table tags. We save the page and review it, and immediately notice that the table is left justified. We want it centered. This is more complicated than it ought to be using CSS, but the proper solution is to add a global styling definition for the table element, specifying that the left and right margins should be automatically positioned—this will balance and center the table:

```
table {margin-left : auto; margin-right : auto}
```

(Because older versions of Internet Explorer did not follow widely accepted Web standards, text-align : center must also be included if we want IE users to see the table centered, which we do.) The result is shown in Figure 18.4(a).

18.2 Table Build. When using the "inside out" table building trick to create a six-column table with four rows, you will need to type <td>, </td>, <tr>, </tr>, <table>, </table>, and use copy/paste. How many times will you use copy and how many times will you use paste to build the table?

2. Delete Two Buttons

In row 2, cell 4, and row 4, cell 2, we remove the <button> tags because these cells must be empty. Of course, we can leave a cell empty, but we still need to surround it with the <td> and </td> tags for it to be a cell.

3. Insert Text Box

From the last section, we know we need a text box in the lower right corner, so the next step is to replace the button tag with a text input tag. We decide to name the text box "disp" because we want to *display* the total prices. The window can be five characters wide because no combination of drink inputs will result in a price of more than four digits plus the decimal point. We specify an onchange event handler. And finally, because this is where we display the computation's output, we enclose this input with the form tags. So the button in row 4, cell 4 should be replaced by

```
<form name="esp">
   <input type="text" id="disp" value="0.00" size="5" onchange=' '/>
</form>
```

which produces the result shown in Figure 18.4(b). This looks a little lopsided, but we haven't labeled the buttons yet.

4. Label the Buttons

The next task is to pass through the table cells and correct the label of each button from "b" to its proper button value. The first column is the number of shots (1, 2, 3, 4), the

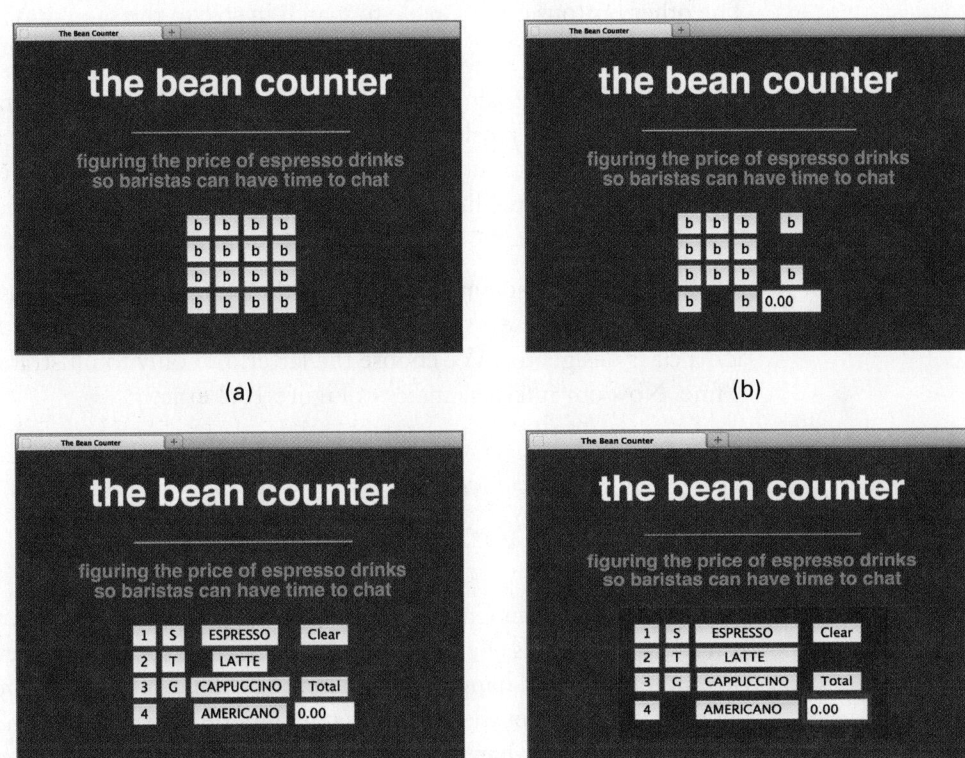

Figure 18.4 Intermediate stages in the construction of the Bean Counter interface: (a) after Step 1, (b) after Step 3, (c) after Step 4, and (d) final form.

second column is the sizes (S, T, G), and the third column is the drinks (espresso, latte, cappuccino, Americano), which will be given in all uppercase letters. The two items in the last column are the controls (Clear, Total).

Because of the row formulation of HTML tables, it is easiest to work row-wise through the table rather than column-wise. The result of our work is shown in Figure 18.4(c). We're close to achieving what we want, but we still need to fix the buttons a bit.

5. Primp the Interface

Our guess that the form of the form wouldn't be quite right was right. Looking at the design in Figure 18.4(c), we notice that the buttons, though centered, look ragged; the appearance would look more polished if they were all about the same width. Because the button is as wide as its value text, we simply add spaces before and after the drink name to make the button wider and to balance the position of the text.

As explained in Chapter 4, HTML reduces all white space to one space before processing the Web page, so adding more space characters between the <button> tags won't work. We need to tell HTML that we really want extra space. And for that we use the escaped symbol   which stands for *non-breaking space*. So, to make the espresso button appear as wide as the cappuccino button, we need two spaces before the word, and three following it,

```
<td><button form="esp" onclick='drink = "espresso"; '>
      ESPRESSO    </button></td>
```

The other buttons can be made to match in size in the same way.

The only remaining difference is that the table in Figure 18.2 has borders and colors. Giving the table a background color requires that we add to the table's global style specification. As we recall from Chapter 8, colors can be numeric; a good choice for this table might be background-color : #993300. In addition, we add a border to the table styling, making it a medium solid line colored firebrick. Also, because the buttons seem crowded in the table, we add 8 pixels of padding.

Finally, we add a medium red border to the price text box. Because it applies only to one cell, we can either use a style attribute on its <td> tag, or style <td> cells globally, but add a class designator. We choose the latter, but only to illustrate the case; either choice is fine. Now our interface matches Figure 18.2 exactly.

Event-Based Programming

How should the Bean Counter program work? Like a calculator, something should happen as each button is clicked, that is, in response to user-caused events. The rest of the time nothing should happen. Programming the Bean Counter application amounts to defining in JavaScript the actions that should be performed when each button is clicked. This is called **event-based programming** and it's pretty intuitive. In this section we'll write the event-handling code.

The onclick Event Handler

The greatest part of the programming task is already done, because the action for the Total button is to compute the final price, and that computation, shown between the <script> and </script> tags in Figure 18.1, is already programmed. Because this code defines the action we want the computer to perform when the Total button is clicked, we make it the onclick event handler for the Total button. Our HTML input element for the Total button is presently

```
<td><button form="esp" onclick =' '/> Total </button></td>
```

where onclick is the **event-handling attribute** for the Total button. To use JavaScript to calculate the price, we insert the price computation code *inside the quotes* for the onclick attribute (red arrow) as shown in Figure 18.5, and it becomes the onclick event handler. Notice that we do not need <script> tags because the browser assumes that the event handler is written in JavaScript.

Click Event

VideoNote

What a Click Event Does

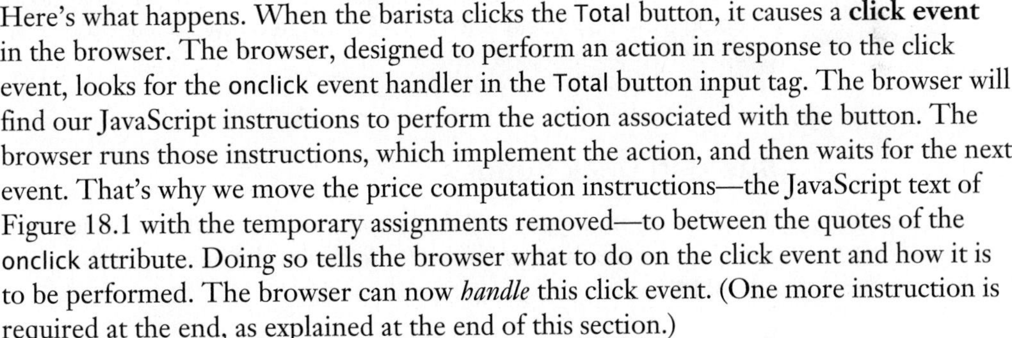

Here's what happens. When the barista clicks the Total button, it causes a **click event** in the browser. The browser, designed to perform an action in response to the click event, looks for the onclick event handler in the Total button input tag. The browser will find our JavaScript instructions to perform the action associated with the button. The browser runs those instructions, which implement the action, and then waits for the next event. That's why we move the price computation instructions—the JavaScript text of Figure 18.1 with the temporary assignments removed—to between the quotes of the onclick attribute. Doing so tells the browser what to do on the click event and how it is to be performed. The browser can now *handle* this click event. (One more instruction is required at the end, as explained at the end of this section.)

```
<td><button form="esp"
   onclick='
      var price = -10;
      var taxRate = 0.087;
      if (drink == "espresso")
          price = 1.40;
      if (drink == "latte" || drink == "cappuccino") {
      if (ounce == 8)
         price = 1.95;
      if (ounce == 12)
         price = 2.35;
      if (ounce == 16)
         price = 2.75;
      }
      if (drink == "Americano")
         price = 1.20 + .30 * (ounce/8);
      price = price + (shots - 1) * .50;
      price = price + price * taxRate;
      /* One more assignment statement needed here */
   '> Total </button></td>
```

Figure 18.5 The **Total** button tag with the price computation inserted as the event handler. (Notice that the three temporary declarations of Figure 18.1 have been removed, as has the temporary **alert( )** command at the end.)

Shots Button

Handling the click events for the other buttons is easier. In each case, we ask what action should be performed when a particular button is clicked. For the first column of buttons—the shots buttons—the answer is to specify the number of shots the customer requests. For example, clicking the 1 button should cause the shots variable to get the value 1. (Recall that "get" is how we pronounce the assignment operator =, suggesting how we will write this handler.) To handle the click event for the 1 button input, we need to assign shots as follows:

```
<td><button form = "esp" onclick = 'shots = 1' > 1 </td>
```

Notice that the 2 button assigns shots the value 2, and so on. Thus, the event handlers for the shots buttons require only one JavaScript command each: an assignment of the right number to shots.

Extra Assignment. The text onclick = 'shots = 1' is unusual because it uses two equal signs in an assignment. Actually, there are two assignments defined: The immediate assignment is to onclick, giving it the *text* value 'shots = 1'. That text will be interpreted as a program, and it assigns to shots. So, we need two equal signs, one for now, and one for later when the button is clicked.

Size and Drink Buttons

The buttons in the size and drink columns are similar. The action to be performed on a click event for the size buttons is to assign the ounce variable the appropriate value, 8, 12, or 16, as in

```
<td><button form = "esp" onclick = 'ounce = 8' > S </button></td>
```

For the drink column, the drink variable gets the name of the drink quoted:

```
<td><button form = "esp" onclick = 'drink = "espresso"'>
       ESPRESSO    </button></td>
```

Notice that single quotes surround the assignment statement, which uses double quotes. To plan for the use of double-quoted string literals, we chose single quotes for the event handler placeholder in the generic button of the last section.

Also, notice that drink was assigned the string "espresso", not "ESPRESSO", as written on the button. The reason is that when the JavaScript code computes the price, the if statement compares the value of the drink with the string literal "espresso", and since the comparison is case sensitive, the two strings have to be the same case to match.

18.3 Second Row. The second row of the table has the form

```
<tr>
  <td><button form="esp" onclick=" "> 2 </button></td>
  <td><button form="esp" onclick=" "> T </button></td>
  <td><button form="esp" onclick=" "> LATTE </button></td>
  <td></td></tr>
```

Give the onclick event handler code for each of the three button elements.

Match Point. You need to be careful when typing string literals like "espresso", because when the computer compares this value with the string literal in the Total button's event handler (Figure 18.5, fifth line), they must match exactly. Misspellings ("expresso"), case differences ("Espresso"), or even unintentional blanks ("espresso") will fail to match.

Clear Button and Initializations

Clicking the Clear button should reset all of the variables (drink, ounce, and shots) to their initial values. When we think about what those initial values are, we realize that we haven't initialized them yet. That means they would still be undefined, except we haven't even declared the variables yet. As is common in programming, working on the solution to one task—setting up the Clear event handler—reminds us that we have another task to do: declare the variables. So, we first handle the declaration with initialization, and then return to the Clear event handler.

The declarations should be placed at the beginning of the program, but we don't really have a single program. Rather, we have many little program pieces in the form of event handlers. So, referring to Figure 18.1, we place the declarations for the three variables in the head just before the <style> tag. As usual, the declarations must be enclosed in <script> tags. (Recall that <script> tags are not needed for the event handlers, because the browser *expects* JavaScript.) The declarations are

```
<script>
   var shots = 1;
   var drink = "none";
   var ounce = 0;
</script>
```

The initial value for shots is 1 because every espresso drink will have at least one shot. The initial values for drink and ounce are chosen to be illegal values, so that if the barista forgets to specify either one, he or she will receive an error message, indicating that an input has been forgotten. Finally, the Clear button should make these same assignments, resulting in its onclick event handler being

```
<td><button form="esp" onclick='
 shots = 1;
 drink = "none";
 ounce = 0;
 disp.value = "0.00"
  '> Clear </button></td>
```

completing both the initialization and Clear event handler specifications.

The last assignment statement of the Clear event handler

```
disp.value = "0.00"
```

is important. It places 0.00 in the price window, reinitializing it. The next section explains how the assignment statement works.

18.4 More Assignments. Like all onclick event handlers, the Clear event handler is assigned a text string. How many assignment statements make up the Clear event handler?

Referencing Data Across Inputs

In Step 3 above we created the text box for the lower right corner of our UI. When we defined it,

```
<input type="text" id="disp" value="0.00" size="5" onchange=' '/>
```

we gave the window the identification disp and set its initial value to 0.00. The id is a global name, and it allows statements from other event handlers to refer to the window and make assignments to it. That's what the Clear button event handler is doing in its last statement:

```
disp.value = "0.00"
```

It is setting the value—the displayed content—in the disp window to 0.00. Although there are no other windows in the form (at the moment), if there were, prefixing this window by the id makes it clear which one we mean. So, we always include the prefix.

The key point is that event handlers can refer to values in other tags by using the id.

Changing the Window. Notice that when the value is reassigned, the window displays the 0.00 and thus acts as an output. The idea that something called an *input* is used to output information may seem strange. But the window can be seen from both the user's and the computer's point of view. If one side gets information (input) from it, the other must have put (output) the information. And vice versa. Input elements are for both input and output.

Displaying the Total. The other case where the event handler of one element must refer to the value attribute of disp is in the Total event handler, the one we built first. It must output the price. It does so in the same way the Clear button event handler clears the disp window—by assigning the computed price to disp.value. Thus, the final line of the Total event handler—the one that is a comment in Figure 18.5 promising one more assignment statement—should be replaced by

```
disp.value = price;
```

in order to display the final price. That change completes the Total event handler, which means we've finished the Bean Counter application. Run it!

18.5 Double-Click. Using the fact that the value of the price window can be tested using an expression such as disp.value == "0.00", change the Clear button event handler using an if/else statement so that if Clear is clicked and the price window already contains "0.00", then it is filled with "No Sale".

Critiquing the Bean Counter

Every design must be critiqued to ensure that it meets the requirements of solving the problem and to determine if it can be improved. Therefore, the next task is to experiment with the Bean Counter application, trying a dozen or more sample values to see how well it works.

Be a Reviewer. This critique is most valuable if you have taken a moment to try the application. If you didn't program it as you read through the chapter, you can find it at pearsonhighered.com/snyder. Try it!

Does our design fulfill the barista's needs? We'll organize our analysis by topic.

Numbers Versus Money

The most obvious and annoying problem with the Bean Counter application is that the final price is shown as a decimal number with several digits of precision rather than as currency with only two digits to the right of the decimal point. This problem can be almost completely fixed by changing the last line of the Total button event handler to

```
disp.value = Math.round(price*100)/100;
```

The computation works as follows: The price is first multiplied by 100. This changes the price from a "dollars amount" to a "cents amount," that is, the price is expressed as the total number of pennies. That result is then rounded by using the built-in JavaScript function Math.round( ) to eliminate any digits to the right of the decimal point that now represent less than a penny. Finally, that result is divided by 100 again to convert back to a "dollars amount." The computation is a standard way to remove unwanted digits.

The solution doesn't quite solve the problem, because trailing zeros are dropped; that is, the price of $3.10 for a double tall latte would print as 3.1. Although this is a small problem that doesn't come up much, we can fix it, too, by asking for two digits of precision:

```
disp.value = (Math.round(price*100)/100).toFixed(2);
```

Organization

The organization of the buttons is generally consistent with how the application will be used. Because espresso drinks are typically named with syntax of the form

<shots> <size> <kind>

as in "double tall latte," the buttons are in a good order for the left-to-right cursor flow. It might make sense to put the Clear button on the left side to start the process, but because there is no obvious place for it and because the cursor will generally be positioned on the Total button at the end of the previous purchase—that is, on the right side of the table below the Clear button—the design is not inconvenient. We will leave the page organized as it is.

Feedback

One problem with the design is that it doesn't give the barista any feedback about the current settings of the variables. One principle of user interfaces from Chapter 2 is that there should always be feedback for every operation. For some browsers there is *a bit of* feedback because buttons are automatically highlighted when they are clicked. But once another button is clicked, the automatic highlighting moves to that button. (It's called *focus*.) Adding feedback—for example, a window above each column of buttons that gives the current setting—might be better (see Figure 18.6).

Application

Assuming for a moment that the Bean Counter is to be used in a business, then it needs features other than just computing the price of espressos. For example, it might be helpful to know which barista is working. (Because this is a different kind of information

```
<tr>
  <td class="echo"><input type="text" form="esp"
      id="shotpic" value=" " size="1"/></td>
  <td class="echo"><input type="text" form="esp"
      id="sizepic" value=" " size="1"/></td>
  <td class="echo"><input type="text" form="esp"
      id="coffee" value=" " size="10"/></td>
  <td> </td>
</tr>
```

(a)

```
<tr>
  <td><button form="esp" onclick='shots = 1;
      shotpic.value=" 1"' > 1 </button></td>
  <td><button form="esp" onclick='ounce = 8;
      sizepic.value=" S"'> S </button></td>
  <td><button form="esp" onclick='drink = "espresso";
      coffee.value=" Espresso "'>
        ESPRESSO    </button></td>
  <td><button form="esp" onclick='
   shots = 1;
   drink = "none";
   ounce = 0;
   disp.value = "0.00"
   shotpic.value= " "; sizepic.value=" "; coffee.value=" ";
   '> Clear </button></td></tr>
```

(b)

Figure 18.6 The Bean Counter application improved to give the barista feedback: (a) the <button> tags for the first row, and (b) showing how the revised button event handlers assign the barista's choice to the proper text window.

to be used in a different way, it would be in a different form.) So, to illustrate one more input, we add a pull-down menu of employee names.

Making Space. We need somewhere in the design to place the menu, and for that we add extra space at the top. Because we want the information inside the table window, we need to make this space as a table row. Recalling from Chapter 4 that colspan is the way to merge cells, we add a new row at the top

<tr><td colspan="4"> *menu tags go here* </td></tr>

with all of its cells merged. This gives ample space to display a menu.

Menus. The <select> tag is the input tag that implements menu options. It surrounds a series of <option> tags, each of which gives an item of the menu. The first option is shown in the window at the time the page is loaded. So, the menu information for our six baristas is

```
<select id="employee" >
<option value="-">-Sign In-</option>
<option value="C"> Charlie </option>
<option value="J"> Juliette </option>
<option value="M"> Mike </option>
<option value="O"> Oscar </option>
<option value="R"> Romeo </option>
<option value="V"> Victor </option>
 </select> Is Pulling For Us
```

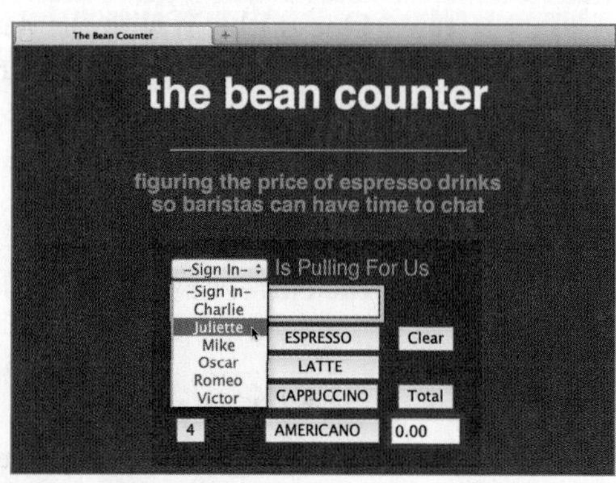

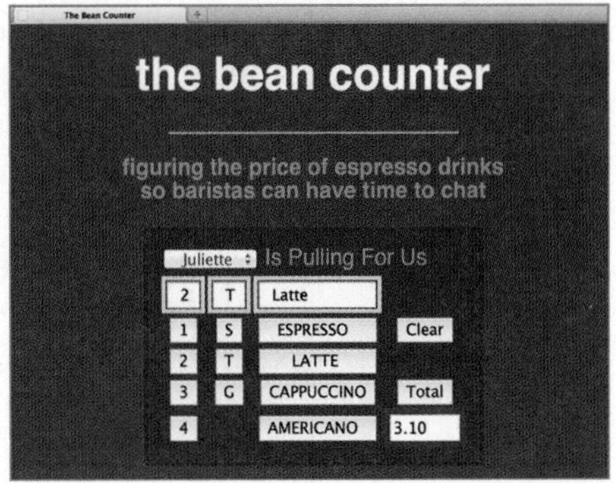

Figure 18.7 Final Bean Counter page with improvements: (a) as it loads, and (b) in use.

The value attribute gives the value of the select input if the user picks this item. The value is referenced just like we've seen with the price earlier. So after the barista has selected his or her name, the value can be referenced by employee.value. Such a change will make a more useful application.

The final design, incorporating all of these improvements, is shown in Figure 18.7. The final code is given in Appendix E.

18.6 Hello? The feedback-windows solution is appropriate for a desktop, laptop and possibly a tablet. Say why it is not a desirable solution for a phone?

Bean Counter Recap

The sample program of Chapter 17 is now a "useful" application. In the process, we learned the basics of event-based programming using JavaScript. Because this chapter focused on building the application, we didn't spend much time discussing the ideas generally. So, let's review the major ideas now.

We created a user interface for the Bean Counter application by first creating the HTML text to produce the image of the interface, and then adding JavaScript—mostly in event handlers for inputs—to make the application work. Though we discussed programs in Chapter 17 as if they were single, monolithic sequences of statements, the Bean Counter application is actually many tiny code segments that are mostly one or two statements long. This is typical of event-based programming. Other, less interactive forms of computing are more monolithic.

Program and Test

The programming process for the Bean Counter application was incremental. We began by producing a minimal 19-line HTML program (see Figure 18.3), and then we tested it. We added a skeleton table and tested it. We improved the table one feature at a time, testing as we went. We wrote JavaScript to solve one event handler at a time. And, recognizing similarities among the various events, we developed their event handlers together. Finally, we critiqued the result.

The result is a 111-line program of 3,900 characters. Compared to other first programs, it's huge! This strategy—the result of breaking the task into tiny pieces and testing the program after each small milestone—had two advantages: At no point did we have to solve a complex task that taxed our brains, and the continual testing meant that we immediately knew where any errors were located, namely, in the part we just added. Though the program in Appendix E looks impressive, it is not hard to produce by the program-and-test method. Obviously the approach works generally, as you'll see again in Chapter 21.

Assess the Program Design

When the initial design was completed, we critiqued the result. We were not critiquing the programming. Rather, we were critiquing how well our solution fulfilled the baristas' needs. This is an important part of any design effort, but it is especially critical for software. Since software can do anything, it should perfectly match the solution requirements. We found that our design did not give the barista feedback, and therefore violated one of the principles listed in Chapter 2. This shortcoming could be remedied by adding feedback windows.

SUMMARY

We created the Bean Counter application using the price computation program of Chapter 17 and a UI developed in this chapter. The result is a substantial program that performs a useful computation, at least if you are a barista. The application is analogous to using a calculator: the user uses the application by clicking. The requested computation is performed immediately in response to the input events. In the process of creating this application we did the following:

- Used HTML to set up a context in which event handlers perform the actual work. The setup involved placing buttons and other input elements on a Web page, so a user could enter data and receive results. This is the input/output part of the application and it is principally written in HTML.
- Wrote JavaScript code for the event handlers. This is the processing part of the application. We used the event-based programming style and the basic instructions discussed in Chapter 17. The style, which is ideal for interactive applications, is used widely in Web applications. Though HTML and JavaScript are separate languages, that won't matter much. Generally, HTML will simply be the input/output part of a program written in JavaScript.

TRY IT SOLUTIONS

18.1 The HTML is:

a.
```
<input type = "button" value = "PANIC" onclick = " " />
```
or
```
<button onclick = " ">PANIC</button>
```

b.
```
<input type = "text" name = "author" size = "10" value = "Pen Name"
onchange = " " />
```

18.2 *Copy* is needed twice: once for a cell and once for a row; *paste* is needed eight times: five times to create additional cells and three times to create additional rows.

18.3 The onclick assignments for the three "Row 2" items are:

```
onclick = 'shots = 2' ; onclick = 'ounce = 12' ; onclick = 'drink = "latte" '
```

18.4 The text inside of the single quotes—the event handler—has four assignment statements.

18.5 Replace the assignment for the price window (last line) of the Clear button event handler to

```
if (disp.value == "0.00")
   disp.value = "No Sale";
else
   disp.value = "0.00";
```

18.6 The problem is that our feedback windows take up valuable screen space, which is okay for a laptop. A better solution for phones is to indicate the choice by changing the button somehow—change its color, change its background, draw a colored box around it, and so forth. These solutions do not take up additional space.

Multiple Choice

1. Which tag can be used to create menus?
   a. <select>
   b. <form>
   c. <text>
   d. <checkbox>
2. The first tag of a Web page is
   a. <script>
   b. <!doctype html>
   c. <top>
   d. <html>
3. When creating the espresso button, which is the correct way to write espresso in the form code?
   a. Espresso
   b. espresso
   c. ESPRESSO
   d. the capitalization does not matter
4. All of the following are input elements except
   a. print
   b. radio button
   c. text box
   d. command button
5. In JavaScript, onclick is a(n)
   a. variable
   b. event
   c. event handler
   d. button

6. The operating system signals that a mouse click has occurred. This is called a(n)
   a. handler
   b. event
   c. trigger
   d. action
7. When a button is clicked, the browser
   a. looks for an `onclick` event handler
   b. looks for the JavaScript program to download
   c. creates the button for the program
   d. none of the above
8. The UI for a Web-based application is built with
   a. HTML
   b. JavaScript
   c. both of the above
   d. none of the above

Short Answer

1. _______ are the tags that should enclose JavaScript text.
2. The _______ tags surround the input elements.
3. A(n) _______ occurs when a button is clicked on a UI.
4. The _______ needs to be named in order for the input tags to be associated with the correct form.
5. A(n) event _______ responds to an event.
6. The _______ is being changed by the assignment statement `disp.value = "0.00"`.
7. _______ elements are used for both input and output.
8. Event handlers can refer to values in other tags by using the _______.
9. Automatic highlighting as you move from button to button in a form is called _______.
10. HTML replaces all white space with one _______.

Exercises

1. Explain the difference between an event and an event handler. Provide at least two examples of an event.
2. How many inputs are needed for the Bean Counter program (Figure 18.1) to run correctly?
3. How many outputs does the Bean Counter program have?
4. Explain how variables are initialized. Why do variables need to be initialized?
5. Could radio buttons be used for this application? What would they be like?
6. What could the variable for storing a person's age be called? Create an input element that asks for a person's age.
7. The tax rate for the Bean Counter program is 8.8 percent. What needs to be changed if the tax rate drops to 7 percent?

8. What events are coded into the Bean Counter program?
9. Why won't you know how much your coffee costs until you click the *Total* button?
10. Explain for each why 'Espresso' does not match: 'espresso', 'ESPRESSO', 'Expresso', 'Espresso'.
11. In layman's terms, explain what happens when the user clicks the *Tall* button.
12. Why is an ID attribute needed when referencing some variables and not others?
13. Write the HTML code that produces the following form (check boxes have the same format as radio buttons, except that you should use check box for the type).

Name:
Sex: Male Female
Age: Under 20 20-30 Over 30

CHAPTER 19

Programming Functions

Thinking Big

learning objectives

- Apply JavaScript rules for functions, declarations, return values, function calls, and local/global variable references
- Apply your knowledge of functions in the context of publicly available software
- Design Web applications for mobile use
- Write JavaScript functions with the proper structure
- Build a UI that contains functions
- Explain what a computer-generated random number is

CHAPTER 19

Civilization advances by extending the number of important operations which we can perform without thinking about them.

—ALFRED NORTH WHITEHEAD, 1911

AS YOU KNOW, an algorithm is a precise and systematic method for producing a specific outcome. If we want an algorithm that we can "carry around" and use in different settings—say while we're programming JavaScript—we put it into a function. A *function* is simply the standard package into which we place algorithms so they are useful in practice.

We have two motives for packaging algorithms into functions. The first benefit of functions is *reuse*; once we work out the details of how an algorithm produces its result, we'd rather not think about it again. Functions allow us to reuse our thinking over and over without repeating the actual thinking. That's a great advantage. The second benefit is to *reduce complexity*, that is, to simplify our thinking. Many times—you'll see a specific case in Chapter 21—problems get so complicated that we experience "brain fry" trying to figure out how to solve them. Functions allow us to set aside parts of the solution (hide them) so they no longer confuse us. That's a great advantage, too.

In this chapter you learn how to create functions in JavaScript. While discussing the syntax and operation of functions, we will show many simple examples. The task of learning about functions is not too difficult, so there is time at the end of the chapter to create several apps that we can use from a smartphone.

Anatomy of a Function

Functions are packages for algorithms, which implies they have three parts:

1. Name
2. Parameters
3. Definition

Together these parts form the *function declaration*; they are present in functions of all sorts, including JavaScript and other programming languages, spreadsheets, databases, mathematics, and so forth. As we consider each, we'll use the process of converting from the Celsius to Fahrenheit temperature scales as a running example, since it's a computation many Americans struggle with. (We'll do the Fahrenheit to Celsius conversion, the one the rest of the world struggles with, in Try It 19.1.) Recall that the relationship between Celsius and Fahrenheit is

$$Fahrenheit = \frac{9}{5}\ Celsius + 32$$

This is an equation, not an assignment statement. It is this simple computation that we want to package into a function.

Alternate Function. Functions are also known as *procedures* in both informal and computing languages. *Subroutine* is an antiquated computing term for the same idea. Another technical term for them is *method.*

Converting Some Temperatures

The three parts of a function must be explained, of course. But first, let's write the Celsius to Fahrenheit conversion function in JavaScript using Scratchpad. (Recall that the Scratchpad development system is available in Firefox: *Tools > Web Developer > Scratchpad.*) Figure 19.1 shows the function—lines 1–3—followed by the application of the function (line 5) to convert 0° Celsius into Fahrenheit. The answer (line 8) displays as a comment.

```
1 function convertC2F ( tempInC ) {
2     return 9/5 * tempInC +32;
3 }
4
5 convertC2F(0);
6
7 /*
8 32
9 */
```

Figure 19.1 Running the convertC2F( ) function in Scratchpad: the function is in lines 1–3, its call, that is, its application (on the input value 0), in line 5, and its result in line 8 in a JavaScript comment.

We can try other values, too. For example, if we type convertC2F(38), select it, and choose *Execute > Display* or click ^L,

```
convertC2F(38);
/*
100.4
*/
```

we convert 38° Celsius to Fahrenheit.

Isn't that hot? If your browser is handy, type in the function and try some other values.

Standard Form. Naturally, JavaScript requires a standard form for writing function declarations:

```
function <name> ( <parameter list> ) {
    <statement list>
}
```

Compare the general form with the example in Figure 19.1: The *<name>* is convertC2F, the only parameter in the *<parameter list>* is tempInC, and the only statement in the *<statement list>* is a return statement.

Notice the punctuation. Parentheses *always* follow a function name, even if there is no *<parameter list>*. And the curly braces, although they can be positioned anywhere to enclose the *<statement list>*, should always be placed where they are obvious. Like the curly braces used with if statements, they are easy to miss, which is why programmers get in the habit of placing them as shown here so that everyone knows where to look for them.

Picking A Name. We picked convertC2F as the name for our conversion function. Obviously, the *name* is the identifier for the function, and it is common to use it to describe what the function does. Although computers would be happy with any unique name, it's best to try to pick a name that will be meaningful to humans. A suggestive name reminds us what the function does when we rediscover it weeks or years later.

In JavaScript, function names follow the usual rules for identifiers, that is, they begin with a letter, use any mix of letters, numbers, and underscores (_), avoid reserved words (see Table D.2 in Appendix D), and are case sensitive.

Parameters. The **parameters** are the values that the function will compute on, the *input* to the function. For our example, the input is the Celsius temperature. In order for the statements of the algorithm to refer to the input values, the inputs are given names. The *<parameter list>* is simply the list of names for all of the function's inputs separated by commas.

Parameter names follow the usual rules for identifiers in all programming languages. They can be anything, and like function names, we choose names so that they remind us what they name. Our tempInC parameter name reminds us that this is the Celsius temperature we want to convert to Fahrenheit.

When writing the function's statements, the parameters are like normal variables. The only differences are that (1) they begin with a defined value, the function's input, (2) they don't have to be declared; that is, no var is needed, and (3) they can only be used "inside" the function, that is, only in the statements of the *<statement list>*. Because they're parameters, JavaScript automatically declares them for us.

Definition. The **function definition** is the algorithm, written in the programming language, to compute the function's result. The function definition follows the language's general rules for program statements, so for JavaScript, the rules that apply are those covered in Chapters 17 through 20 and Appendix D.

Because the function definition is computing an algorithm—a precise and systematic method for producing a specified result—there must be some way to say what the result is, that is, some way to give the answer. Different languages do this differently, but JavaScript uses the statement

```
return <expression>
```

where the answer is whatever value the *<expression>* produces. We call the answer the function's *value* or *result*. For example, the function

```
function greeting ( ) {
    return "Hello, World!";
}

greeting( )

/*
Hello, World!
*/
```

is a function that returns the letter string Hello, World! when we run it. It is also a function with no parameters.

The algorithm for converting Celsius to Fahrenheit is so easy—we just program the right side of the earlier equation, $\frac{9}{5}$ *Celsius* + 32—that our entire function definition is a single line:

```
return 9/5 * tempInC + 32;
```

We use our parameter tempInC as the variable in the conversion computation, because it provides the data we are computing with. Also, notice that unlike the math given above, we must write the multiplication operation (*) explicitly, as is normal in programming.

That's it! We never have to think about how to convert Celsius to Fahrenheit again. This function will do it for us, saving our brainpower for more important stuff, like movies.

19.1 Fahrenheit to Celsius. Write a JavaScript function to convert from Fahrenheit to Celsius. (If Scratchpad is handy, use it.) The equation for the relationship given earlier implies that *Celsius* = $\frac{5}{9}$ (*Fahrenheit* – 32).

Making the Call

The convertC2F( ) function (lines 1–3) *defines* the algorithm for converting from Celsius to Fahrenheit; that is, the declaration says how it works. But how will we get the answers? We must *call* the function.

To **call** a function is to ask the computer to run or execute the statements of the function to produce the answer. That's what we did on line 5 of Figure 19.1. We simply write the function's name and give the input value(s), known as **arguments**, in parentheses after it, as in convertC2F(0). The computer follows the definition of the function and returns the answer, 32. Getting answers couldn't be easier.

Definition Versus Call

Figure 19.1 illustrates an important point about functions: A function's declaration (specification) is different from its call (use). To emphasize the distinction, let's review what we just did.

We *declared* the function by writing down its three parts in the form required by JavaScript, lines 1–3. Functions are only declared once, because it's unnecessary to tell the computer more than once how the function works.

We *called* the function convertC2F( ) twice, once on line 5 and again on line 11, to convert two numbers. Functions are typically called many times because the answers they give are needed many times. For example, we expect to call convertC2F( ) every time someone mentions a Celsius temperature we don't understand. *One declaration, many calls.*

Although we could open our JavaScript file in the Scratchpad sandbox whenever we needed to convert a number, it is more convenient to set up a user interface as a Web page and make our function into a legitimate Web application. This allows us to apply our algorithm in a more user-friendly way.

19.2 Which Is Which? In Try It 19.1 you wrote a function to convert Fahrenheit to Celsius. In giving that answer, did you write a declaration or a call?

Arguments Versus Parameters. Notice that parameters and arguments are two different ways to refer to the same thing. In a function *declaration*, where we say how the function works, we write `function convertC2F(tempInC)` and use the term *parameter* for `tempInC`. In the function *call*, when we ask the computer to run the function, we write `convertC2F(0)` and use the term *argument* for 0. These correspond, so `tempInC`'s value is `0`. It's a parameter when the function's input is viewed from "inside" the function, that is, looking at the definition; it's an argument when the function's input is viewed from "outside" the function, that is, when we run it. They are opposite sides of the same thing.

Forms and Functions

In this section we will create the following page:

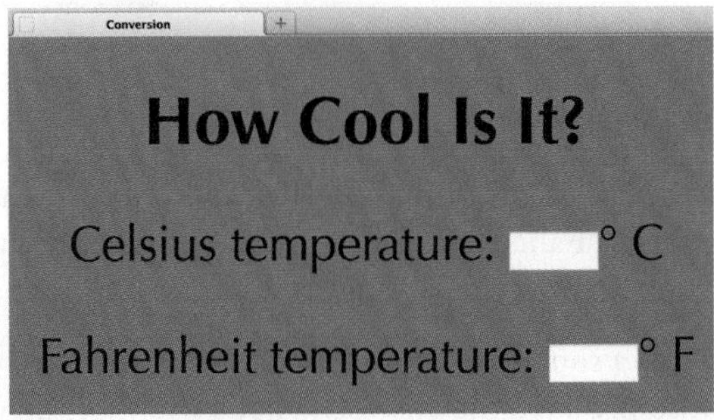

The user enters a temperature in one of the windows, and the temperature is displayed in the other window in the other scale. Most of the work has been thought out already. All that remains is to set up the page.

Recall the following from Chapter 18:

- Forms are defined by <form> tags.
- Text boxes are specified by an `<input type="text" . . . />` tag.
- Text boxes have an `id`, `value`, `size`, and other attributes.
- To refer to the value or contents of a text box with `id="tb"`, we write `tb.value`.
- The main event handler of interest for text boxes is `onchange`.

The `onchange` event handler recognizes when a value is entered into the Celsius window (by the cursor moving out of the window and clicking) and handles it as we direct in the event handler. Of course, the operation is pretty easy—we call the `convertC2F( )` function with the number typed into the window as the argument. More specifically, let's set up the form as follows:

```
<form id="cool">
  <p> Celsius temperature:
    <input type="text" id="textTempC" size="4"
      onchange="textTempF.value=Math.round(
      convertC2F(textTempC.value))"/>&#176; C</p>
  <p> Fahrenheit temperature:
    <input type="text" id="textTempF" size="4"
      onchange="textTempC.value=Math.round(
      convertF2C(textTempF.value))"/>&#176; F</p>
</form>
```

Our form has two inputs: the textTempC window for Celsius temperatures—either user entered or program produced—and textTempF for Fahrenheit temperatures, also either entered by the user or produced by the computer. (Recall that even though we use it as an output in this case, JavaScript uses the <input . . . /> tag for both input and output text boxes.) The logic to convert to Fahrenheit is accomplished by the onchange event handler with the function call

```
onchange = "textTempF.value = convertC2F(textTempC.value)"
```

In English, this line says when the input window (textTempC) is changed, use the value in that window textTempC.value as an argument to convertC2F( ) and assign the result to display as the value textTempF.value of the Fahrenheit window.

If we enclose the JavaScript definitions for convertC2F( ) and convertF2C in <script> tags, and place them in the head section of the Web page, before the <style> tags, we only need a bit of HTML to produce the page shown in Figure 19.2.

```
<!doctype html>
<html>
  <head> <meta charset="UTF-8"/><title>Conversion</title>
    <style>
      body {background-color : dodgerblue; font-family : optima;
             color: midnightblue; text-align : center}
      p     {font-size : x-large}
    </style>
  </head>
  <body>
    <h1>How Cool Is It? </h1>
    <script>
      function convertC2F (tempInC) {
        return 9/5*tempInC + 32;
      }
      function convertF2C (tempInF) {
        return 5/9*(tempInF - 32);
      }
    </script>
    <form id="cool">
      <p> Celsius temperature:
        <input type="text" id="textTempC" size="4"
          onchange="textTempF.value=Math.round(
          convertC2F(textTempC.value))"/>&#176; C</p>
      <p> Fahrenheit temperature:
        <input type="text" id="textTempF" size="4"
          onchange="textTempC.value=Math.round(
          convertF2C(textTempF.value))"/>&#176; F</p>
    </form>
  </body>
</html>
```

Figure 19.2 The HTML/JavaScript source for the temperature conversion page.

Writing Functions, Using Functions

VideoNote

A Function for Calculating Wages

Though our knowledge of functions is not quite complete, it is good enough to write some functions for interesting computations. In this section we try flipping electronic "coins," and we compute the Body Mass Index, a combined measure of height and weight. Both computations give further practice with functions.

Flipping Electronic Coins

How can a computer flip a coin? It seems impossible, except for robots, because computers have no moving parts. The answer is not to focus on the act of flipping, but on the fact that a coin flip is an unpredictable event whose two outcomes are "equally probable." That is, heads and tails will each turn up about half the time. We might guess that a computer could generate a random number between 0 and 1, and round to the nearest whole number; 0 could represent tails and 1 could represent heads. About half the time the outcome would be tails (the random number was less than 0.5) and the rest of the time it would be heads. The only problem is that computers are completely deterministic, as we learned in Chapter 9: Given a program and its input, the outcome is perfectly predictable. It's not random in any way. It would be possible to create truly random numbers based on an unpredictable physical process such as counting the particle emissions from a radioactive material like U_{238}, but computers don't have to be radioactive to generate random numbers. They can generate pseudo-random numbers.

Flipping Out. The mathematician John von Neumann, one of the computing pioneers, once said, "Anyone who attempts to generate random numbers by deterministic means is, of course, living in a state of sin."

Pseudo-random numbers are an invention of computer science in which an algorithm produces a sequence of numbers that passes the statistical tests for randomness. For example, a sequence of pseudo-random numbers between 0 and 1 has the property that about half are closer to 0 and the others are closer to 1; that is, the sequence of items, when rounded to the nearest whole number, behave like a coin flip. (It's still deterministic: If you know the algorithm and the starting point, you can perfectly predict the sequence; but you don't!) Because pseudo-random numbers are so believable, we'll drop the "pseudo" part from here on.

Random numbers are important in many applications, so programming languages come with a built-in function for generating them. In JavaScript the random number generator is called Math.random( ). It's part of a library of handy mathematical functions, which includes Math.round( ). Each time Math.random( ) is called, it generates a random number between 0 (inclusive) and 1 (exclusive); that is, it could be 0, but never 1. So, a function to flip electronic coins—that is, to generate a 0 or a 1 with roughly equal probability—has the form

```
function coinFlip( ) {
    return Math.round( Math.random( ));
}

coinFlip( )

/*
0
*/
```

When coinFlip( ) is called, it returns with equal probability a 0 or a 1, which can represent tails and heads. Because we got a 0 back (line 8), we conclude that the number was less than 0.5.

The obvious improvement to the coinFlip( ) function is to return the text Heads and Tails rather than numbers. So, we create another function

```
1 function coinFlip( ) {
2     return Math.round( Math.random( ));
3 }
4
5 function flipOut( ) {
6     if (coinFlip( ) == 0)
7         return "Tails";
8     else
9         return "Heads";
10 }
11
12 flipOut( )
13
14 /*
15 Tails
16 */
```

Notice that we have called the previous coinFlip( ) function in the if statement test of the flipOut( ) function. Because we got a "Tails" (on line 15) when we called flipOut( ) on line 12, we conclude that the call to Math.random( ) must have resulted in a random number that was *less* than 0.5. Calling functions from inside other functions is the most common way to use functions because it allows us to build more complex programs progressively.

19.3 Heads or Tails? If, when calling flipOut( ), the Math.random( ) function returns 0.514093540772, what prints on our Web page? Heads or Tails?

Our flipping function would be even more useful if it gave the outcome in response to clicking a button on a Web page. As you learned in Chapter 18, buttons are inputs just like text boxes, so creating such a Web page is not too difficult. We will need a form, which we call flipper, and the functions we've just finished programming. Figure 19.3 shows the image and source for this program.

Bug Report. When you cannot figure out why a JavaScript program is not working, you can often find helpful information from Firefox's Web Console, where the browser informs us what it doesn't like about a JavaScript program: *Tools > Web Developer > Web Console.*

19.4 Rock-Paper-Scissors. The coinFlip( ) function produces one of two outcomes, but it would be better to choose integer outcomes from a range, say 0 to *n*–1. The function randNum( ) does that by multiplying the random number by its parameter, range, and then dropping digits right of the decimal point with Math.floor( ).

(Continued)

```
function randNum( range ) {
    return Math.floor( range * Math.random( ));
}

randNum(2)
/*
1
*/
randNum(3)
/*
0
*/
randNum(3)
/*
1
*/
```

Write a function using randNum( ) to play Rock-Paper-Scissors and that randomly gives "Rock," "Paper," or "Scissors" as the result.

The Body Mass Index Computation

The Body Mass Index (BMI) is a standard measure of a person's weight in proportion to his or her height. (An "acceptable" BMI is generally in the range of 18.5 to 25, but as usual, experts disagree.) What is your BMI? The formula for determining BMI, using metric units, that is, height in meters and weight in kilograms, is

$$Index = weight/height^2$$

In the same way that it was easy to translate the Celsius conversion into a function, it is easy to translate the metric BMI into a function, though this time we need two

```
<!doctype html>
<html>
  <head>
   <meta charset="UTF-8"/><title>eCoin Flipping</title>
    <script>
      function coinFlip( ) {
         return Math.round(Math.random());
      }
      function flipOut( ) {
         if (coinFlip( )==0)
             return 'Tails';
         else
             return 'Heads';
      }
    </script>
    <style>
       body {background-color : #ccffcc; color : green;
               font-family : verdana; text-align : center}
    </style>
  </head>
  <body>
    <form id="flipper">
      <h2>Heads or Tails? </h2>
         <input type="button" value="Flip" onclick='ans.value=flipOut( );'/>
         <input  type="text" id="ans" size="5" onchange=" "/>
    </form>
  </body>
</html>
```


Figure 19.3 The JavaScript and image for the eCoin Flipping page.

parameters, one for weight and one for height. Also, let's take the height in centimeters and convert:

```
function bmiM( weightKg, heightCm ) {
   var heightM = heightCm / 100;
   return weightKg / (heightM * heightM);
}

bmiM(75, 180)
/*
23.148148148148145
*/
```

We have used var to declare an extra variable (heightM) for use in converting from centimeters to meters. In fact, the conversion is part of the initialization for the variable. Also, there's no "square" in JavaScript, so we must multiply heightM times itself.

For weight and height in English units, the formula is

$Index = 703\ weight/height^2$

where weight is given in pounds and height is given in inches. (The constant 703 corrects for using English units in a quantity defined in metric units.) Of course, Americans give their height in feet and inches—that is, a person says, "I'm 5 feet, 6 inches" rather than "I'm 66 inches"—but working with feet and inches is a little messy. So, we use inches. The solution parallels the function for metric units

```
function bmiE( weightLbs, heightIn ) {
    return 703 * weightLbs / (heightIn * heightIn);
}

bmiE(165, 70.5)
/*
23.33786026859816
*/
```

The two functions are quite similar.

It would be more universal if the function could compute the BMI in whatever units the user preferred. That would require a new function with three inputs, one for the kind of units and the other two for weight and height. Such a function could use our previous functions—another example of calling a function within a function. The definition for the universal BMI is (with its two companion functions)

```
function bmiM( weightKg, heightCm ) {
   var heightM = heightCm / 100;
   return weightKg / (heightM * heightM);
}
function bmiE( weightLbs, heightIn ) {
    return 703 * weightLbs / (heightIn * heightIn);
}
function BMI( units, weight, height) {
    if (units == "E")
       return bmiE( weight, height);   // English
    else
       return bmiM( weight, height);   // Metric
}

BMI( "E", 165, 70.5)
/*
23.33786026859816
*/

BMI( "M", 75, 180)
/*
23.148148148148145
*/
```

Notice that first we check the units parameter to call the correct function. Second, we have simply passed the weight and height parameters as arguments to our previously programmed BMI functions. Third, slight errors creep in the computation when we quote our height and weight in "round" numbers.

Counting Arguments. A function must be given as many arguments as it has parameters, because they correspond one-to-one. For this reason, for multiparameter functions, it is also important that the arguments are given in the right order.

19.5 That's Heavy! Suppose a person is six feet tall (72 inches) and weighs 200 pounds. Give the call to compute this person's BMI using BMI( ).

How should the BMI function be used? Perhaps the most convenient way would be to have a Web page similar to the Coin Flipping page. For that, we need to define the functions, set up the forms and inputs, and define the event handlers, as we've done before. The final result is shown in Figure 19.4.

Code Breaking. Notice the structure of the Figure BMI page in Figure 19.4. Besides the HTML tags at the beginning and end, the program has two main parts: A section enclosed in script tags, where functions and other JavaScript computations are given, and a section enclosed in form tags, where input, output, and other text of the page are given. Most programs in this chapter (and this book) have that structure; recognizing it helps with understanding long sequences of text.

We have used radio buttons to select the units as English or metric. Recall from Chapter 18 that radio buttons, like command buttons, are specified with <input /> tags, and so must be connected to <form> tags.

- All related radio buttons share the same name; that is, if when clicking one of them, any other radio button that is on should click off, then they must have the same name.
- Radio buttons can be preset by writing checked.

The button has been preset to English units, but can easily be preset to metric.

In addition to presetting a radio button, we must also write the onclick event handlers for them. What should happen when the user clicks the radio button? Obviously, we need to remember the type of units chosen. But we are not quite ready to call the BMI( ) function—the other inputs are not yet available—so we need to store the values in a variable that we will pass to BMI( ). At the start of the JavaScript code we declare and initialize

```
var scale = "E";
```

Thus, scale starts with the value that was preset in the radio button. When the Metric button is clicked, we want

```
scale = "M";
```

```
<!doctype html>
<html>
  <head><meta charset="UTF-8"/><title>Figure BMI</title>
    <script>
      var scale='E';
      function bmiM( weightKg, heightCm ) {
        var heightM = heightCm / 100;
        return weightKg / (heightM * heightM);
      }
      function bmiE( weightLbs, heightIn ) {
        return 703 * weightLbs / (heightIn * heightIn);
      }
      function BMI( units, weight, height) {
        if (units == "E")
          return bmiE( weight, height); // lbs
        else
          return bmiM( weight, height) // kgs
      }
    </script>
    <style>
      body {background-color : indigo;
      color : white; font-family : verdana}
      p  {text-align : right}
    </style>
  </head>
  <body>
    <form name="mass">
      <p> What units do you use:
        <input type="radio" name="unit" onclick='scale="E"'
          checked/> English
        <input type="radio" name="unit" onclick='scale="M"'/>
          Metric</p>
      <p>Enter your weight (<i>lbs</i> or <i>kg</i>):
        <input type="text" id="wgt" size="4"/></p>
      <p> Enter your height (<i>in</i> or <i>cm</i>):
        <input type="text" id="hgt" size="4"/> </p>
      <p> Your
        <input type="button" value="Body Mass Index" id="figure"
          onclick="ans.value= BMI( scale, wgt.value, hgt.value)"/> is:
        <input type="text" id="ans" size="4"/></p>
    </form>
  </body>
</html>
```

Figure 19.4 The image and source for the Figure BMI page.

as the response to the click-event. So, that becomes the onclick event handler for Metric. Similarly, when the English button is clicked we should assign scale the value "E" again. (It might be that scale, which was initialized to "E", could have changed.)

Finally, notice that we call the BMI( ) function from the onclick event handler for the Body Mass Index button. Since we assume the values will be filled in sequentially, all of the inputs will be available after the height has been entered. So, the computation can be performed. The arguments to the call

```
onclick = "ans.value= BMI( scale, wgt.value, hgt.value)"
```

require some explanation. The scale variable, having been declared outside of any function or form, is a **global variable**. That is, scale can be referenced in any function, unlike parameters, which can only be referenced in the function in which they are in the parameter list. So, no id reference is needed. The wgt.value and hgt.value are the numbers in the two windows.

Customizing Pages

One of the powerful features of JavaScript is the ability to create pages on-the-fly. In this section we illustrate this idea with functions we have already created. First, though, let's discuss how a browser builds a page.

Creating Page Content

A browser begins to create a page by reading through the HTML file, figuring out all of the tags, and preparing to build the page. As it's reading the file, it finds our JavaScript tags. The browser removes those tags and all of the text between them, that is, our JavaScript. Then it does whatever the JavaScript tells it to do. One thing that the JavaScript could tell the browser to do is to put some text back into the file, where the JavaScript just came from. There is a built-in function, document.write( ), that does just that: It inserts the text of its argument into the Web page at the point of the JavaScript tags, as shown in Figure 19.5.

So, to create a custom page, simply write a JavaScript function to create the HTML tags and put them in the file using the document.write( ) function. Let's see how it works by improving our coin flipping program.

Customizing the Coin Flip

Although the coin flipping page in Figure 19.3 illustrated how to use functions in an onchange event handler, the UI is very primitive. Wouldn't it be better to show an actual coin—either heads or tails, depending on the outcome of the coinFlip( ) function? So, let's create a new coin flipping page that uses document.write( ) to display on-the-fly the proper heads or tails image.

We begin by locating two photos of some coin. Ours is the U.S. Sacajawea one dollar coin, and the two file names are us1heads.jpg and us1tails.jpg.

Source File As Submitted

```
<body><p> The browser reads the
  HTML before it creates the page.
  When it comes to a script tag, it
  processes it immediately. If it
  has document.write( ) calls, the
  browser writes the argument</p>
  <script>
    document.write("into the file");
  </script>
  <p>at the point of the script .</p>
</body>
```

Text Used To Build Page

```
<body><p> The browser reads the
  HTML before it creates the page.
  When it comes to a script tag, it
  processes it immediately. If it
  has document.write( ) calls, the
  browser writes the argument</p>

  into the file

  <p>at the point of the script .</p>
</body>
```

Figure 19.5 An HTML source file containing a JavaScript document.write( ), and the HTML text used by the browser to create the page.

Next, we change the flipOut( ) function (see Figure 19.3) from giving Heads or Tails output, and instead give as a text string the name of the image file we want to display. The logic is as follows:

```
function coinFlip( ) {
  return Math.round(Math.random( ));
  }
function flipOut( ) {
  if (coinFlip( ) == 0)
    return "us1tails.jpg";
  else
    return "us1heads.jpg";
}
```

Now, all that is necessary is to create a page that places the right image based on the flipOut( ) function. The final application is shown in Figure 19.6, and we see that it flips the coin on loading; if another flip is desired, the page is simply reloaded.

19.6 Rock-Paper-Scissors with Style. Revise your Rock-Paper-Scissors program from Try It 19.4 so that when it loads, it randomly displays one of three images: rock.gif, paper.gif, or scissors.gif.

```
<!doctype html>
<html>
  <head>
    <meta charset="UTF-8"/><title>eCoin Flipping</title>
     <script>
       function coinFlip( ) {
          return Math.round(Math.random());
       }
       function flipOut( ) {
          if (coinFlip( )==0)
              return "us1tails.jpg";
          else
              return "us1heads.jpg";
       }
     </script>
      <style>
        body {background-color : black; color : goldenrod;
                font-family : verdana; text-align : center}
      </style>
  </head>
  <body>
       <h2>Heads or Tails? </h2>
       <script>document.write('<img src=" ' +
            flipOut( ) + ' " alt="coin" width="150"/>');
       </script>
  </body>
</html>
```

Figure 19.6 A revised eCoin flipping program, which flips the coin on loading using document.write( ).

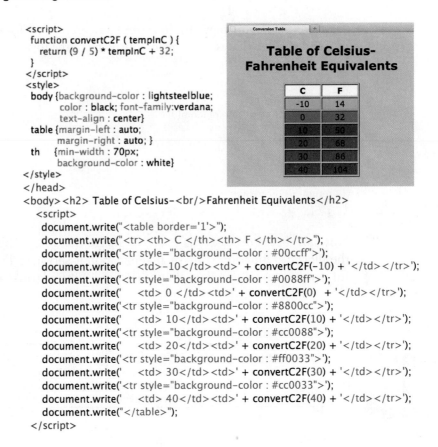

```
<script>
 function convertC2F ( tempInC ) {
   return (9 / 5) * tempInC + 32;
 }
</script>
<style>
 body {background-color : lightsteelblue;
        color : black; font-family:verdana;
        text-align : center}
 table {margin-left : auto;
        margin-right : auto; }
 th    {min-width : 70px;
        background-color : white}
</style>
</head>
<body><h2> Table of Celsius-<br/>Fahrenheit Equivalents</h2>
   <script>
    document.write("<table border='1'>");
    document.write("<tr><th> C </th><th> F </th></tr>");
    document.write('<tr style="background-color : #00ccff">');
    document.write('    <td>-10</td><td>' + convertC2F(-10) + '</td></tr>');
    document.write('<tr style="background-color : #0088ff">');
    document.write('    <td> 0 </td><td>' + convertC2F(0)  + '</td></tr>');
    document.write('<tr style="background-color : #8800cc">');
    document.write('    <td> 10</td><td>' + convertC2F(10) + '</td></tr>');
    document.write('<tr style="background-color : #cc0088">');
    document.write('    <td> 20</td><td>' + convertC2F(20) + '</td></tr>');
    document.write('<tr style="background-color : #ff0033">');
    document.write('    <td> 30</td><td>' + convertC2F(30) + '</td></tr>');
    document.write('<tr style="background-color : #cc0033">');
    document.write('    <td> 40</td><td>' + convertC2F(40) + '</td></tr>');
    document.write("</table>");
  </script>
```

Conversion Table

Table of Celsius-Fahrenheit Equivalents

C	F
-10	14
0	32
10	50
20	68
30	86
40	104

Figure 19.7 Source text and image for the Conversion Table computation.

Table of Equivalents. We can use the customize-on-the-fly idea to build a conversion page. Suppose we want a table of temperature conversions for a Web page with a column for Celsius and a column for Fahrenheit (see Figure 19.7).

It is easy to set up the page and specify the heading tags using normal HTML. Place <script> tags where the table will go. Then, using document.write( ) within the JavaScript tags, create the table on-the-fly. A row will be composed of several components joined (concatenated) together. (Recall that concatenation—the joining of two letter sequences—uses the + sign.) For example, the first row is built from

`<tr style="background-color : #00ccff">`	*Table row tag and attribute*
`<td>-10</td>`	*Table data tags for first cell*
`<td>convertC2F(-10)`	*Call to conversion function*
`</td></tr>`	*Closing tags for data and row*

Compare this text and the "minus 10" row in Figure 19.7, and study how it was created. The content of the left cell was specified as the text "–10", but the right cell was computed with convertC2F(–10).

When the components are combined into document.write( ) calls with the proper quotes and concatenations, it has the form

```
document.write( '<tr style="background-color:#00ccff">');
document.write( '<td>-10</td><td>'
                    + convertC2F(—10) + '</td></tr>');
```

All of the rows have a similar structure.

Automatically Created Rows. As the browser is setting up the page, it encounters the script tags. It does what our JavaScript program says and calls the document.write( ) functions. To call those functions, the browser must construct the functions' arguments using concatenation. As the browser begins to build the argument string, it encounters our convertC2F(–10) function call with its argument (–10), and runs it. The Fahrenheit value is returned (14); it is included with the other parts of the argument string, and the document.write( ) function places the newly constructed row tags into the document. When the browser builds the page, the table is formed from our created on-the-fly rows that use our conversion function to calculate the Fahrenheit temperature.

Making a Web-Based Phone App

Although software is available to program smartphone applications, we will show off our knowledge of JavaScript by creating a Web-based phone app to access our functions. This is simpler than creating commercial apps because it uses what we already know.

The plan is to build an interface as shown in Figure 19.8. The page, which we load with the browser on our smartphone or tablet, gives us convenient access to the pages we have written in this chapter.

Design for Mobility

Phones and tablets present a different set of constraints on the design of a Web page than do "normal" pages used on a laptop. For example, the Bean Counter program of Chapter 18, which though small enough to fit nicely on a phone display, had small buttons and a drop-down menu. Such programs are less convenient on devices that emphasize the touch metaphor. The touch metaphor benefits from larger blocks and a more "open" organization. Consequently, rather than, say, using a bulleted list to enumerate our apps, we create a two-dimensional grid—a table, actually—of blocks that the user taps.

Figure 19.8 Navigation Web page for executing user-created functions from this book, organized for use on a mobile device.

```
<!doctype html>
<html>
 <head>
  <meta charset="UTF-8"><title>myApps</title>
  <style>
    body  {background-color:black; color:cyan;font-family:helvetica}
    h2    {color:white;text-align:center;}
    table {margin-left:auto;margin-right:auto;}
    td    {background-color:orangered; color:white;min-width:100px;
            text-align:center; padding:20px;}
    td.alta {background-color:deeppink;}
    td.altb {background-color:fuchsia;}
    a     {text-decoration:none;color:white;}
  </style>
 </head>
 <body>
  <h2>myApps</h2>
  <table border="0">
   <tr><td><a href="bmi.html"> bmi </a></td>
        <td><a href="temperature.html"> C° ≈ F°</a></td></tr>
   <tr><td class="alta"><a href="counter.html"> counter </a></td>
        <td class="alta"><a href="rps.html"> RPS</a></td></tr>
   <tr><td class="altb"><a href="flipOut.html">coin flip</a></td>
        <td class="altb"><a href="itsMagic.html"> magic 8</a></td></tr>
  </table>
   <script type="text/javascript">
    var today = new Date( );   // Get today's date
    var myBdate = new Date( );  // Get a date object to modify
    var difference;  // Declare a temporary variable
    myBdate.setFullYear(1995);  // Set my birth year to 1995
    myBdate.setMonth(6);  // Set my birth mo to July (mos start at 0)
    myBdate.setDate(4); // Set my birth day to 4th
    myBdate.setHours(12); // Set my hour of birth to noon
    myBdate.setMinutes(0);// Set my minute of birth to o'clock
    myBdate.setSeconds(0);   // Set my second of birth on the hour
    difference = today.getTime( ) - myBdate.getTime( );
    difference = Math.floor(difference/1000);
    document.write(" <p style='text-align:center'> my age: " + difference +
       " seconds </p>");
   </script>
 </body>
</html>
```

Figure 19.9 The HTML for the navigation Web page. (To include the "age" text at the bottom, see the companion Fluency Byte).

Of course, this UI works just fine on a laptop or desktop, too.

The by-now-familiar code defining the navigation page is shown in Figure 19.9. Almost all of the formatting for this 3 × 2 table is done in the <td> tags. These tags get their size from the min-width and padding properties. Further, two classes are defined to fill each row with a different color. Notice that this solution assumes that if additional rows are added in the future, they will follow this same color scheme. That is, they will cycle through no associated class, alta, and altb. If instead additional rows are to get a separate color, then styling cells explicitly with the style attribute would be a better approach.

Time of Your Life. Computers can easily work with dates because they usually keep track of dates and time with "UNIX dates." The UNIX operating system began recording dates as the number of milliseconds since 1 January 1970 at 00:00:00 Universal Time, that is, New Year's Day 1970 in Greenwich, England. Thus, the number of milliseconds between any two dates after New Year's Day 1970 can be found by subtracting the two UNIX dates, making it much easier to compute than if time were recorded in years, days, and hours.

JavaScript uses UNIX dates. It also provides functions to refer to time as if it were recorded in days and hours, when that is convenient for us. We use these features to compute your age in seconds. (Of course, your age in milliseconds is just 1,000 times more.)

This JavaScript code should be placed inside of <script> tags:

```
var today = new Date( );      // Get today's date
var myBdate = new Date( );    // Get a date object to modify
var difference;               // Declare a temporary variable
myBdate.setFullYear(1995);    // Set my birth year to 1995
myBdate.setMonth(6);          // Set my birth mo to July (mos start at 0)
myBdate.setDate(4);           // Set my birth day to 4th
myBdate.setHours(12);         // Set my hour of birth to noon
myBdate.setMinutes(0);        // Set my minute of birth to o'clock
myBdate.setSeconds(0);        // Set my second of birth on the hour
difference = today.getTime( ) - myBdate.getTime( );
difference = Math.floor(difference/1000);
document.write( " <p style='text-align:center'> my age: " + difference +
     " seconds </p>");
```

The code creates two date objects, one for today and one for your birthday. (Objects are complex and will not be covered here.) In the six statements after the declarations, we set your birthday as if it were exactly noon, July 4, 1995 (as noted in the code comment for setMonth, months start counting at 0, not 1 in UNIX dates—and a good example of why it's important to both write and read comments). To do this, we use JavaScript functions that allow us to refer to the time using months and hours. Once your birthday has been set, we compute difference, the difference between the present time and that date. This computation uses UNIX dates. Then we divide the result by 1,000 to convert it to seconds and display it at the bottom of the myApps page, which only requires <script> tags and the line

```
document.write(' <p style="text-align:center"> my age: ' + difference +
   ' seconds </p>');
```

Referencing Functions

As can be seen in Figure 19.9, each table entry references Web pages, some of which we have created or will create in this chapter. A sampling of some of the apps is shown in Figure 19.10.

Every Little Bit Counts. When searching for things or watching sports, it's common to keep track of counts. It's easy enough to get a scrap of paper and tally the number, and it's equally easy to tap or click on a counter. So, we create the Counter Assistant page (see Figure 19.11).

Its operation is obvious: Clicking the Count button increments the Total field; the Meaning field can be filled with any text to remind us which counter is which among several; and the C button clears the fields.

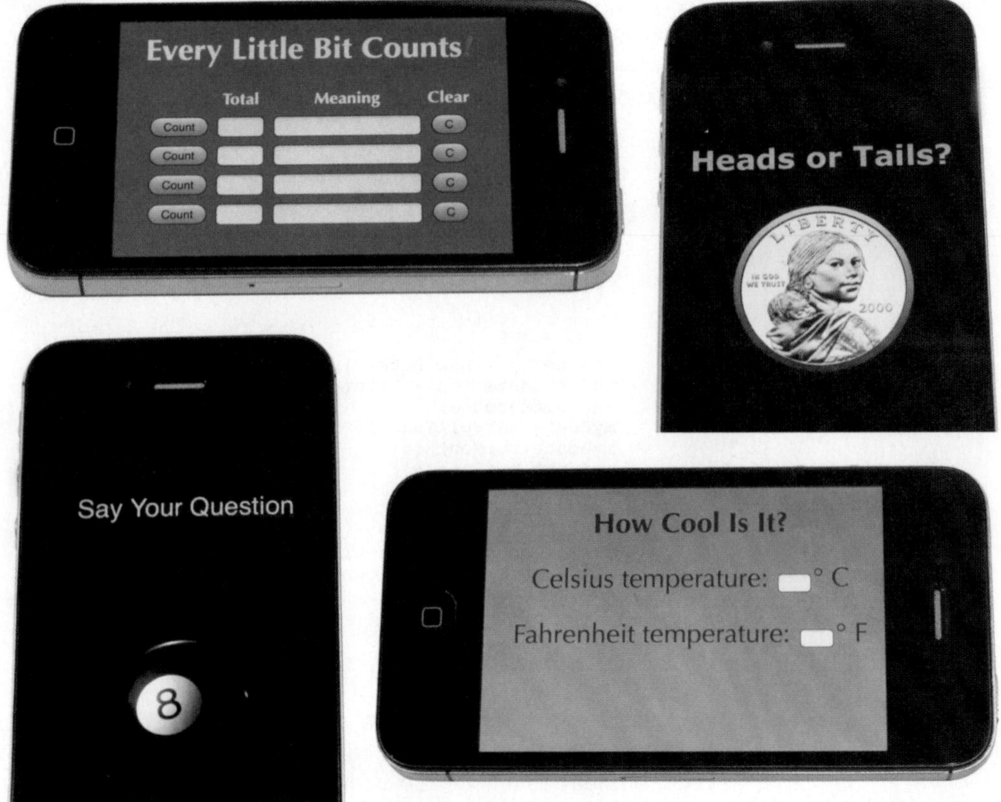

Figure 19.10 Examples of pages connecting to functions written in this chapter (the Magic Decider app is written in Chapter 20).

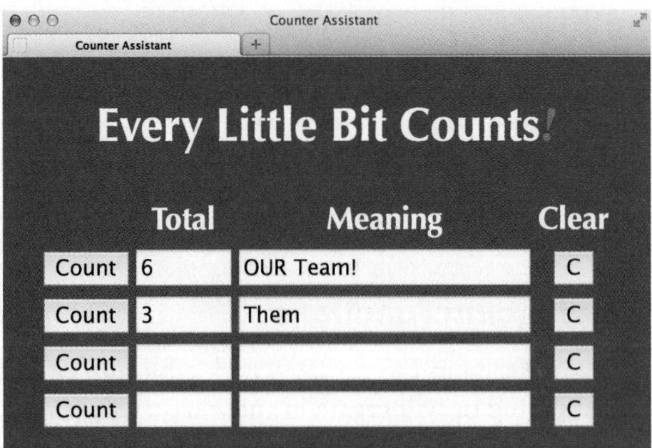

Figure 19.11 The Counter Assistant page to track four items.

The Counter Assistant's Structure

The Counter Assistant page uses an interesting approach: We write a function to create a row of the table, placing the entire HTML text in the function. The strategy requires us to use a sequence of document.write( ) functions. The program is shown in Figure 19.12.

Checking the code, we see that it relies on four global variables to keep track of the counts, count1 through count4. After declaring these variables, the makeTable( )

```
<!doctype html>
<html>
  <head>
   <meta charset="UTF-8"/><title>Counter Assistant</title>
    <style type="text/css">
      body {background-color : blueviolet; color : white; font-family : optima;
               text-align : center}
      table {margin-left : auto; margin-right : auto}
    </style>
   <script>
     var count1=0, count2=0, count3=0, count4=0;
     function row(num) {
       document.write('<tr><td><input type="button" value="Count"' );
       document.write(' onclick="count'+num+'=count'+num+'+1;' );
       document.write('arch'+num+'.value=count'+num+'"/></td>' );
       document.write('<td><input type="text" size="5" id="arch'+num+'"/></td>' );
       document.write('<td><input type="text" size="20" id="what'+num+'"/></td>' );
       document.write('<td><input type="button" value="C" ' );
       document.write( ' onclick="arch'+num+'.value='+"' ';" );
       document.write("what"+num+".value=' ';" );
       document.write('count'+num+'=0"/></td></tr>' );
     }
   </script>
  </head>
  <body>
   <h2>Every Little Bit Counts<i style="color : hotpink">!</i></h2>
   <form>
     <table>
       <tr><th> </th><th> Total </th><th> Meaning </th><th>Clear</th></tr>
       <script>
         row(1); row(2); row(3); row(4);
       </script>
     </table>
   </form>
  </body>
</html>
```

Figure 19.12 The makeTable( ) and row( ) functions, which generate the Counter Assistant application.

function is defined. It sets up the structure of the table, and then calls a row( ) function, which constructs the rows and their input controls. The row( ) function has a single parameter that is the number of the row being specified. Then comes a series of document.write( ) calls in which the value of the parameter is concatenated with other text to produce the required code. The HTML is familiar by now. The onclick event handlers for the two buttons perform the obvious operations: The Count button increments the correct counter, and the C button overwrites the two text boxes with a space and reinitializes the proper counter to 0. The table is easily constructed by writing four calls to row( ). A Counter Assistant with more rows could be constructed by editing the counter.html file so that more counter variables are declared and more calls to row( ) are placed.

Better Applications

The functions written in this and the next chapter are useful, but the functionality provided has been chosen for educational reasons. It is possible to think up more interesting applications and program them. With a little imagination, it is possible to think of apps that are personally useful; writing them in JavaScript and replacing those shown above is an easy way to make computers and smartphones more useful.

Recap: Two Reasons to Write Functions

Most of our functions—convertC2F( ), BMI( ), randNum( ), and so on—are general. We wrote them for our application, but we hope that we will have a chance to use them again. Think of them as building blocks for programs that we may write in the future. They are like the programs in the software stack mentioned in Chapter 1—programs that use other programs, and that are used by other programs. To a small extent, we illustrated this point with the myApps page.

But remember that the makeTable( ) and row( ) functions are *not* building blocks. Because makeTable( ) and row( ) contain explicit references like what.value, they must run within a document with a form, and that form must have within it input tags *with specific names*. We do not expect this situation ever to happen again. Instead, we wrote these two functions to encapsulate the complexity of building the Counter Assistant program. Packaging the event-handling operation and the row construction processes allowed us to get them out of the way. Managing complexity is the other reason to write functions.

So, we have had an opportunity to write functions that reflect the two main reasons for packaging algorithms into functions: reuse and complexity management. The former are the building blocks of future programming; the latter help us keep our sanity while we're solving problems. Both are extremely important.

Social Functions

We have studied the structure of functions and how to write them. That knowledge is handy, but perhaps more important is the ability to recognize and use them to your own advantage. In this section we demonstrate how to "boldly go" after software that you may not fully understand, but which you can still make work for your goal simply by trying it out and noticing what happens.

Using Other People's Code

There is a strong tradition in computing to share code. Examples of this tradition range from the Open Source Movement to the fact that all browsers display the Page Source code, that is, the code that produces the page you're looking at. It's a great tradition, and we can benefit from it!

A Scenario. Suppose one day you are poking around online tutorials on JavaScript and HTML5 when you come across a page from Mozilla.org—the team that gave us Firefox—on how to use the <canvas> tag. This tag—new in HTML5—provides the ability to draw images in your browser, and there are many interesting things that you can do with it. Before you even learn much about <canvas>, you find an example of its basic use in HTML (Figure 19.13): both the code and the image it produces.

The example isn't too intimidating, and some of it actually makes sense when you look at it. In the draw( ) function, for example, there are familiar statement forms, and you notice the use of the rgb(200,0,0) function, which obviously is setting the fill

```
<html>
 <head><title>Sample Canvas Code</title>
  <script type="application/javascript">
   function draw() {
     var canvas = document.getElementById("canvas");
     if (canvas.getContext) {
       var ctx = canvas.getContext("2d");

       ctx.fillStyle = "rgb(200,0,0)";
       ctx.fillRect (10, 10, 55, 50);

       ctx.fillStyle = "rgba(0, 0, 200, 0.5)";
       ctx.fillRect (30, 30, 55, 50);
     }
   }
  </script>
  <style>canvas {border-style:solid;border-color:lightgray}</style>
 </head>
 <body onload="draw();">
  <canvas id="canvas" width="150" height="150"></canvas>
 </body>
</html>
```

Sample Canvas Code

Added to show canvas shape

Figure 19.13 Example of the basic use of the <canvas> tag, (a) code, and (b) display.

color to red. . . for the red rectangle, probably. And there are two functions that seem to be drawing rectangles. Can you figure out what the (green) arguments mean based on the picture? Sure. The first two must specify the (upper left) corner of the rectangle, because they are offset by the same amount in each direction like the squares (remember, 0,0 is in the upper left corner of Web pages), and the other pair must be the shape, width × height. The units are probably pixels judging from where they are on the screen.

Also, we notice that the draw( ) function is called after the Web page is loaded (that's what the onload event handler does), and we see that there is a <canvas> tag used. This must make a 150 × 150 canvas with the rectangles in it. It doesn't seem so hard.

When looking at other people's code, a good way to verify that your guesses are correct about the meaning of the text is to drop the code into a file, run it, check it, make a few changes, and then run it again to see what happens. If the changes match your expectations, your guesses are probably right.

Another Discovery. So, with almost no understanding of <canvas>, you've already tried it. It would be helpful to learn more, but we're all impatient. And soon, you spot a function that makes word balloons using something called "quadratic Bézier curves," definitely a topic of interest only to specialists. But it has an example, too (see Figure 19.14), and it looks like fun!

This time only a draw( ) function is given, so we guess (correctly!) that we need to replace the draw( ) function from the basic usage program to get the word balloon drawn on the canvas. And it works.

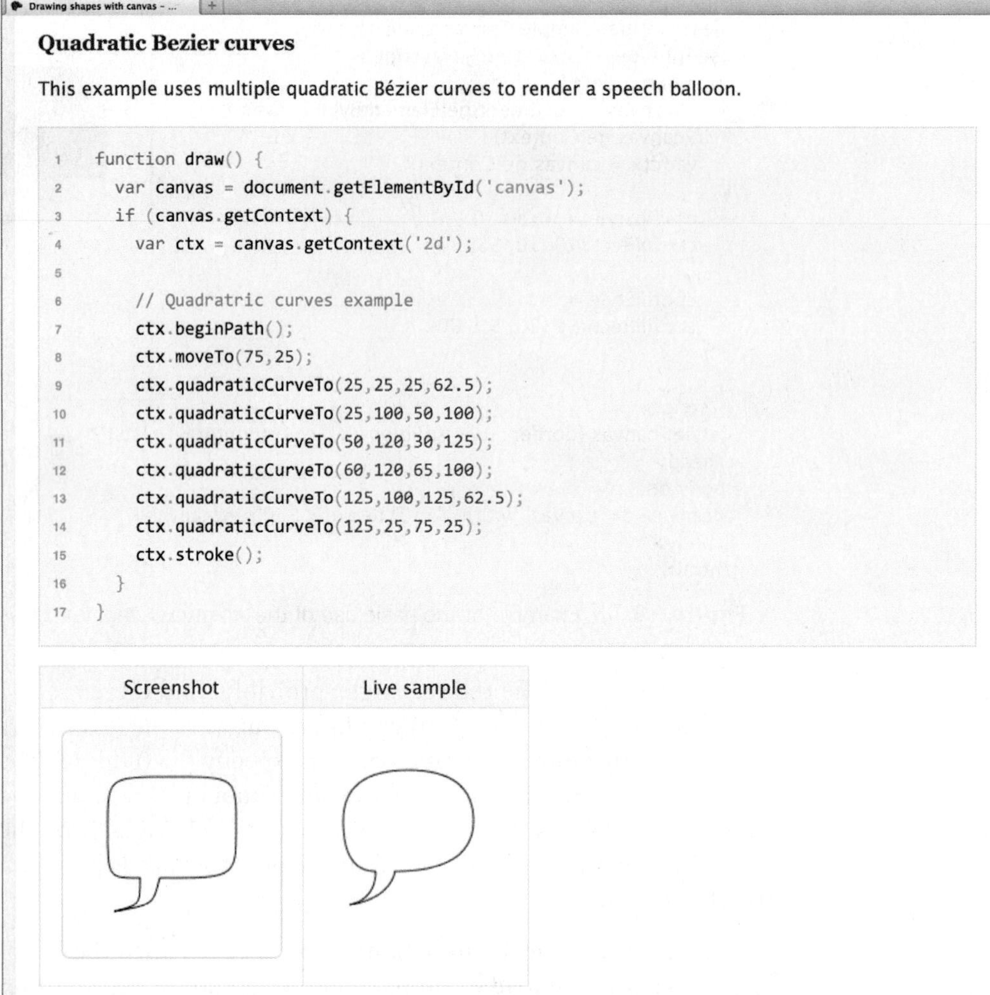

Figure 19.14 Mozilla tutorial on quadratic Bézier functions to make word balloons (from https://developer.mozilla.org/en-US/docs/Web/Guide/HTML/Canvas_tutorial/Drawing_shapes).

Making a Comment

Knowing how to draw word balloons is handy, and so far we haven't even needed to learn how to pronounce Bézier's (*BEZZ-ee-aye*) name, much less find out what a quadratic curve is. Let's try to create a page that has an image and a word balloon on it, as in Figure 19.15.

The steps needed to make the page are:

1. Include text in the word balloon.
2. Move the balloon and text around.
3. Place an image on the page.
4. Make the final page by positioning the comment in the right place.

All of these operations involve working with functions and parameters, and they are explained in the following sections.

Add Text to a Balloon. The HTML/JavaScript we are working with is shown in Figure 19.16. To add text, suppose we add a paragraph tag right after the <canvas> tag,

Figure 19.15 A planned page combining an image and a word balloon comment.

```
<!doctype html>
<html>
 <head><title>Word Balloons</title>
  <script type="application/javascript">
function draw() {
  var canvas = document.getElementById('canvas');
  if (canvas.getContext) {
    var ctx = canvas.getContext('2d');
    // Quadratric curves example
    ctx.beginPath();
    ctx.moveTo(75,25);
    ctx.quadraticCurveTo(25,25,25,62.5);
    ctx.quadraticCurveTo(25,100,50,100);
    ctx.quadraticCurveTo(50,120,30,125);
    ctx.quadraticCurveTo(60,120,65,100);
    ctx.quadraticCurveTo(125,100,125,62.5);
    ctx.quadraticCurveTo(125,25,75,25);
    ctx.stroke();
  }
}
  </script>
 </head>
 <body onload="draw();">
   <canvas id="canvas" width="150" height="150"></canvas>
 </body>
</html>
```

Sample Canvas Code

Figure 19.16 Initial word balloon program, which combines two Mozilla tutorial programs.

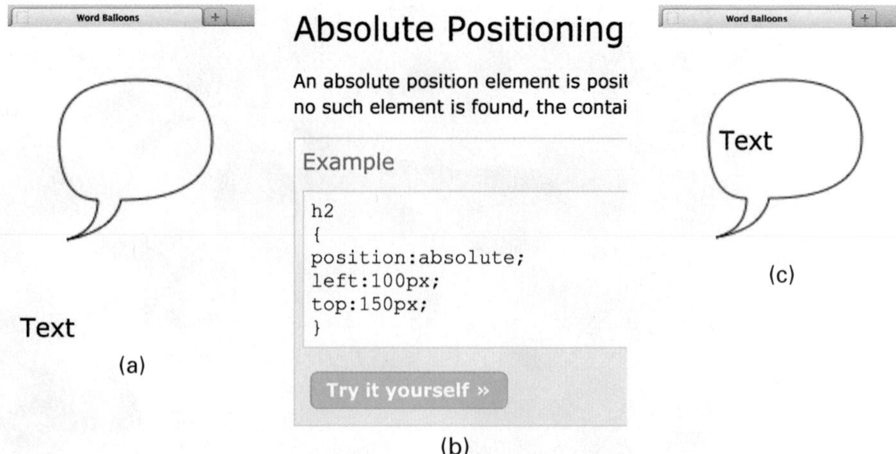

Figure 19.17 Trying to place text on a page: (a) placing a paragraph, (b) CSS's absolute positioning reference, and (c) the text placed in the balloon.

as in `<p>Text</p>`. What happens? We get the balloon in Figure 19.17(a). The text has obviously printed after the canvas. So, we need to figure out how to position the text on the canvas.

Recalling (from Chapter 4) that Cascading Style Sheets (CSS) have many properties for positioning, we begin by checking the CSS site for specific information. We find that absolute positioning is possible for elements, and Figure 19.17(b) shows the absolute positioning for a heading. So, applying this idea to the paragraph element, maybe we can move the text to the correct position in the balloon and get it to work. So we revise our paragraph tag to

```
<p style="position:absolute;left:40px;top:45px">Text</p>
```

because the canvas starts in the corner, implying that 40,45 is probably close. We get the result in Figure 19.17(c), which is pretty close to where the text needs to start. We may fiddle with this later.

Move the Balloon Around. The canvas only covers the upper left 150 × 150 corner of the page right now—we know this because the area of the 150 × 150 canvas was outlined in gray in Figure 19.13 so that its position would be visible. To have a word balloon anywhere on the screen we need to expand the canvas. JavaScript gives us the window's size with `window.innerWidth` and `window.innerHeight`, a fact we can find with a Google search. So, let's just cover the whole window with the canvas. To modify the <canvas> tag to use these two values, we'll need this `document.write` function

```
document.write('<canvas id="canvas" width="' + window.innerWidth
  + '" height="' + window.innerHeight + '"></canvas>');
```

so we can place a customized <canvas> tag in the file on-the-fly. Notice that this code only replaces the two instances of "150" of the Figure 19.16 code.

Expanding the canvas to cover the whole window makes sure the balloon can move to the right place, but it doesn't move the balloon. To do that, we need to change where the Bézier curves are drawn. Commands such as `ctx.quadraticCurveTo(25,25,25,62.5)` of Figure 19.14 specify a (curved) line. They do this by giving the positions *x* and *y* for its two endpoints; thus, this curve starts at `x=25` and `y=25`, and ends at point `x=25` and `y=62.5`.

The new position for the balloon should be specified by parameters—the position is an input, after all. So, we revise the draw( ) function to have x and y as parameters, and add these values to all of the endpoints. The result is

```
function draw(x, y) {
  var canvas = document.getElementById('canvas');
  if (canvas.getContext) {
    var ctx = canvas.getContext('2d');
    // Quadratric curves example
    ctx.beginPath();
    ctx.moveTo(75+x,25+y);
    ctx.quadraticCurveTo(25+x,25+y,25+x,62.5+y);
    ctx.quadraticCurveTo(25+x,100+y,50+x,100+y);
    ctx.quadraticCurveTo(50+x,120+y,30+x,125+y);
    ctx.quadraticCurveTo(60+x,120+y,65+x,100+y);
    ctx.quadraticCurveTo(125+x,100+y,125+x,62.5+y);
    ctx.quadraticCurveTo(125+x,25+y,75+x,25+y);
    ctx.stroke();
  }
}
```

The x and y parameters will translate all of the endpoints to new positions, which just moves the word balloon.

Finally, the balloon's text needs to move, too. Obviously, we want it to use the same x, y values as the balloon, but we'd like to change the text easily. So, for that we write a little function that uses document.write( ) to place the paragraph tag in the file. The proper form is

```
function comment(x, y, remark) {
  document.write('<p style="position:absolute; left:' + (40+x)
    + 'px; top:' + (45+y) + 'px;">' + remark + '</p>');
}
```

Notice that we've offset the position just as we did in draw( ). We also left the text absolutely positioned.

Place an Image. Perhaps the easiest way to cover the window with an image is to make it the background. Recall from Chapter 4 that to make emperor.jpg be the background image, we style the body tag as

```
body {background-image:url('emperor.jpg');background-repeat:no-repeat; }
```

With the travel page in Chapter 4, we wanted it to repeat, but this time we do not.

Position the Balloon. We are ready to place the balloon on the picture. We estimate that it should be about 700 pixels from the left side, and 10 pixels down from the top. We use 700, 10 as the arguments for the draw( ) and comment( ) functions, and we get this

It's close, but we need to fill in the background of the word balloon with white, and then we need to adjust the position.

Recalling how RGB for red was specified in Figure 19.13, and noticing how the line was drawn with ctx.stroke( ) in Figure 19.14, we guess that the two lines

```
ctx.fillStyle = "rgb(255, 255, 255)";
ctx.fill();
```

added to the end of draw( ) will make the balloon white, which it does. Adjusting the positioning to realign the balloon to be closer to the penguin results in the image in Figure 19.15. We're done!

Summary of the Word Balloon App. Although we have created a page using HTML5's new <canvas> tag, we did not actually study the tag itself. We only checked out some working code in Mozilla's online tutorials and made a series of "best guesses" as to how it worked. We checked the guesses, and they were good enough to create the page. If this is the last time we ever need <canvas>, then we've had fun. If we need to know it, then we need to learn it, which will take working through the tutorials and understanding the concepts.

There have been two points to this exercise. The first one is that we should try to figure out technical material, assuming we can understand it, at least at a superficial level. We will fail a lot, and it's easy to make mistakes. So, it takes some courage. And some persistence. But there is rarely any harm in trying. And who knows? "Boldly going. . . " could succeed.

The second point is that functions are our friends when it comes to creating interesting Web pages. We adjusted the sample Bézier draw( ) code so it could be moved around. It was already a function; we just added some parameters—inputs—so it was a more useful function. We also made a custom comment( ) function to apply the same adjustments for positioning the text. Packaging up code into functions, or modifying functions to be more general, are common ways to apply other people's code.

SUMMARY

This chapter began by introducing the concept of a function as a package for an algorithm. Two motivations led us to study functions: They are a means of reusing our thinking and a tool for managing complexity. Both benefits were demonstrated in the chapter. The following were the main topics:

- The three parts of a function—name, parameter list, and definition—are specified in a function declaration using a standard form. We illustrated their use in defining convertC2F( ), bmiE( ), randNum( ), and many others.
- The function declaration specifies to the computer how the function works, so we give it only once. To use the function—-something we will likely do many times—requires that we give the function name and its input values, known as arguments. The arguments correspond one-to-one with the parameters of the function definition's parameter list.
- Writing functions packages algorithms, but to get their benefit in JavaScript and HTML requires that we develop Web pages with which we give the inputs to the functions and get their answers displayed.
- There are three different ways to display the results of a function in HTML: using alert( ), interacting with a page that has text boxes, and using document.write( ) to include the results of a function while the page is being constructed. The chapter refined our understanding of all three.

- We put all of our knowledge about functions into a small Web Apps page; the source code is shown in Appendix F. It gave us the ability to apply functions directly using our smartphones. The next thing is to think up and implement some apps of personal interest.
- Finally, we "boldly went" online to find tutorial examples that we could put to use simply by trying them out and noticing what happened. We quickly figured them out and put them to use.

19.1 The solution is completely analogous to the convertC2F( ) function:

```
function convertF2C (tempInF) {
   return 5/9*(tempInF - 32);
}

convertF2C(32)

/*
0
*/
```

19.2 Declaration. A call might be: convertF2C(104).

19.3 Tails

19.4

```
function randNum( range ) {
   return Math.floor( range * Math.random( ));
}
function RPS( ) {
   var guess = randNum(3);
   if (guess == 0)
      return "Rock";
   if (guess == 1)
      return "Paper";
   if (guess == 2)
      return "Scissors";
}

RPS( )
/*
Scissors
*/
```

19.5 BMI('E', 200, 72)

19.6

```
<!doctype html>
<html>
 <head><meta charset="UTF-8"/><title>RPS</title>
 <script>
   function randNum( range ) {
     return Math.floor( range * Math.random( ));
   }
   function RPS( ) {
     var guess = randNum(3);
     if (guess == 0)
       return "rock.gif";
     if (guess == 1)
       return "paper.gif";
     if (guess == 2)
       return "scissors.gif";
   }
  </script>
  </head>
  <body style="color:firebrick">
    <h4> Rock-Paper-Scissors</h4>
    <script> document.write('<img src=" ' + RPS( ) +
          ' " alt="Throw" height="100"/>');   </script>
  </body>
</html>
```

Multiple Choice

1. How many arguments must a function be given?
   a. it does not matter
   b. 1 argument for every variable used in the function
   c. 1 argument for every parameter in the function definition
   d. 2 arguments for every parameter in the function definition
2. Radio buttons will work together when
   a. the checked attribute is set to checked
   b. they are on the same form
   c. when all of them are selected
   d. when all of them have the same name
3. In JavaScript random numbers are generated by using
   a. `Math.random( )`
   b. `Rnd`
   c. `Math.rnd`
   d. `Random.Math( )`
4. What two properties allowed the buttons on the navigation page to be large?
   a. `max-width` and `padding`
   b. `min-width` and `margin`
   c. `min-width` and `padding`
   d. `max-width` and `margin`
5. What must be in the <form> tag in order for a radio button to be already checked?
   a. `checked`
   b. `radio`
   c. `filled-in`
   d. `onclick`
6. When choosing variable and function names, we should
   a. pick names meaningful to computers
   b. pick names no one has ever used before
   c. pick any random name
   d. pick names meaningful to humans
7. Curly braces are needed in the body of a function when
   a. there is more than one line of code
   b. always
   c. never; they are optional
   d. only when there are parameters
8. Variables declared outside any function are called
   a. local variables
   b. global variables
   c. function variables
   d. legal variables

Short Answer

1. _______ are variables in a function that do not need to be declared with a var statement.
2. The two major benefits of using functions are _______ and _______.
3. From the perspective of the function body, input values for a function are called _______.
4. JavaScript uses _______ dates.
5. A random number generated in JavaScript is always between _______ and _______.
6. There is a strong tradition in coding to _______ code.
7. A _______ is a request to the computer to execute the statements inside the function.
8. The minimum number of parameters when writing a function is _______.

Exercises

1. Name at least three mistakes you can imagine programmers making when writing functions.
2. Explain the two major benefits of creating functions for algorithms.
3. Explain the difference between a declaration and a call?
4. In a 300 × 150 canvas, write a piece of code that will draw a yellow rectangle in the bottom right corner.
5. Describe how random numbers can be used to simulate the roll of a die. How can two dice be simulated using this function?
6. Identify the three parts of a function.
7. There is a variation of the Rock, Paper, Scissors game that is played with the addition of Spock and lizard. Lizard poisons Spock and eats paper. Scissors decapitates lizard and rock crushes lizard. Spock smashes scissors and vaporizes rock. Paper disproves Spock, probably because it's a scientific paper. Change your RPS program to also have lizard and Spock, and make sure to include images for these options as well.
8. Adjust your temperature conversion code to also contain a column for the Kelvin temperature.
9. Write a function to calculate your wages for a part-time job. (Don't worry about calculating overtime.)

CHAPTER 20

Iteration Principles

Once Is Not Enough

learning objectives

- Trace the execution of a given **for** loop
- Write a World-Famous Iteration **for** loop
- Discuss the structure of nested loops
- Explain the use of indexes
- List the rules for arrays; describe the syntax of an array reference
- Explain the main programming tasks for online animations

CHAPTER 20

There are three kinds of programmers: those who make off-by-one errors, and those who don't.

—ANONYMOUS

THE TOPIC of this chapter is iteration—the process of repetition. You are familiar with the English word *reiterate*, which means to repeat something, as in "The attorney reiterated her client's position." Because *iterate* means to repeat, *reiterate* sounds redundant. But repetition is redundant; that's what it's about. So, English has both words, and maybe it needs a third, *rereiterate*, meaning, perhaps, "repeated endlessly," as in "Beer commercials are rereiterated." Repetition is usually tiresome, but learning about it is not. And, iteration is the source of considerable computational power, making it a very important topic. By learning how to use iteration, you can make the computer perform the tiresome parts of programming.

In this chapter, you complete your study of programming concepts by learning about iteration and applying it to computational problems. We begin by explaining the for statement, one of JavaScript's iteration statements and the key to iterative computation. The key to understanding iteration is to focus on how the iteration variable changes values. We mention the fundamental principle of iteration and then we return to the topic of random numbers. After that, we consider the companion topics of indexing and arrays. Together, indexing and arrays can be used with iteration to perform almost unlimited amounts of computation, making them a major source of computing power. Finally, to bring all of these topics together, we study online animation, which allows us to add action to our Web pages. We work through the animation of a familiar icon to prepare us for more interesting animations.

Iteration: *Play It Again, Sam*

There is a slight difference between the meanings of *iterate* and *repeat*. When your mother said, "I've repeated myself four times," she meant, strictly speaking, she'd said the same thing five times. Usually, the first time isn't considered a "repeat." Only the second through the last are "repeats." If she'd actually said the sentence exactly four times, she should have used *iterate*. (Pointing this out to her would *not* have been smart.) We often ignore this difference in terminology in common speech. For example, "reps" (for *repetitions*) in weight training count the total number. In this book, we follow common usage and use *repeat* and *iterate* interchangeably, except where precision is essential, in which case we use *iterate*. When something is iterated five times, there are five instances; you can't be off by one.

The for Loop Basic Syntax

Iteration—probably the fourth most important programming idea after assignment, conditionals, and functions—means looping through a series of statements to repeat them. In JavaScript, the main **iteration statement** is the **for loop**, which has the following syntax:

```
for ( <initialization>; <continuation>; <next iteration> ) {
    <statement list>
}
```

The four items shown in meta-brackets will be explained momentarily. The remaining text—for and all of the punctuation—must be given literally. (Notice the prominent position of the curly braces.)

The statement sequence to be repeated is in the *<statement list>*, and the constructs in parentheses control how many times the *<statement list>* is iterated. The whole statement sequence is performed for each iteration. So, if the for loop

```
for ( <initialization>; <continuation>; <next iteration> ) {
   document.write('First');
   document.write('Second');
   document.write('Third');
   document.write('Home');
}
```

iterates three times, it will produce the sequence →

```
First
Second
Third
Home
First
Second
Third
Home
First
Second
Third
Home
```

That is, the computer completes the whole statement sequence of the *<statement list>* *before* beginning the next iteration.

The Iteration Variable. The three items in the parentheses of the for loop—*<initialization>*, *<continuation>*, and *<next iteration>*—control the number of times the loop iterates. They are called the *control specification*. They control the loop by using an **iteration variable**. Iteration variables are normal variables, so they must be declared, but we typically declare them at the start of the loop. They are called iteration variables only while they are serving to control the loop. Here's a typical example in which the iteration variable is j:

```
for ( var j=0 ; j < 3 ; j=j + 1 ) {
   <statement list>
}
```

To see how these statements work, imagine that the for loop has been replaced with the schematic form:

General Form

```
<initialization>;
if (<continuation>) {
    <statement list>;
    <next iteration>;
}
```

Specific Example with j

```
j = 0;
if ( j < 3 ) {
    <statement list>;
    j = j + 1;
}
```

The arrow means to go back to do the if statement again.

Here's what happens. The first operation of a for loop is the *<initialization>*. The **initialization** sets the iteration variable's value for the first (if any) iteration of the loop. Next, the **continuation** has the same form as the predicate in a conditional statement. If the *<continuation>* test has a false outcome, the loop terminates, the *<statement list>* is skipped, and it is as if nothing happened except that the iteration variable got assigned its initial value.

However, if the *<continuation>* test has a true outcome, the *<statement list>* is performed. The statement list can be any sequence of statements, including other for statements. When the statements are completed, the *<next iteration>* operation is performed. The **next iteration** expression changes the iteration variable. That completes the first iteration. The next iteration starts with the *<continuation>* test, performing the same sequence of operations. All following iterations proceed as this one until the *<continuation>* test has a false outcome, terminating the loop. In this way, the statement sequence can be performed many times without having to write each of the statements to be performed.

Following the Iteration Variable. In the for loop with iteration variable j—and in all for loops—we can understand what's happening by following the iteration variable. Consider the sequence of operations on j shown in Table 20.1.

Table 20.1 The sequence of operations on j from the for loop with control specification (j=0; j<3; j=j+1)

Operation	Operation Result	Role
j = 0	j's value is 0	Initialize iteration variable
j < 3	true, j is *less than* 3	First *<continuation>* test, do statements, continue
j = j + 1	j's value is 1	First *<next iteration>* operation
j < 3	true, j *is less than* 3	Second *<continuation>* test, do statements, continue
j = j + 1	j's value is 2	Second *<next iteration>* operation
j < 3	true, j *is less than* 3	Third *<continuation<* test, do statements, continue
j = j + 1	j's value is 3	Third *<next iteration>* operation
j < 3	false, j *is equal to* 3	Fourth *<continuation>* test, terminate

The loop iterates three times by beginning at 0 and, after assigning a new value to j, testing to see if it should continue. The statements of the *<statement list>* are executed between the *<continuation>* test and the *<next iteration>* operation. Notice that j counts from 0 to 2, but at 3, the test determines that j has counted too far, so it quits before performing the *<statement list>* again. Thus, the *<statement list>* is performed the right number of times.

Terminator, Too. The second item among the control specifications is called the *continuation* test here, because if its outcome is true, the iteration continues, and if its outcome is false, it ends. But the proper programming term for this test is **termination test** because it checks to see if the loop should terminate. However, as a termination test, the outcomes are backward: true means continue, false means terminate! Both terms are useful. To remember the meanings of the outcomes, think of the test as asking "Continue?"

How a for Loop Works

To get a little experience programming with for loops, check this computation written with Firefox's Scratchpad, which uses the declared variable text.

```
var text = "She said, ";                 //Declare/initialize text

for (var j = 0; j < 3; j = j + 1) {     //Specify a 3 iteration loop
     text = text + "Never! ";           //Concatenate on more text
}                                        //... end of loop

text
/*
She said, Never! Never! Never!
*/
```

This for loop, which iterates three times, used an assignment statement to concatenate a copy of the string "Never! " to the value of text, resulting in three copies total. To follow the code's operation, notice that through the four continuation tests, text has the following values:

"She said " *Before the loop is entered, first test*
"She said Never! " *After one iteration, second test*
"She said Never! Never! " *After two iterations, third test*
"She said Never! Never! Never! " *After three iterations, fourth test*

So the for loop allowed us to build the phrase one word at a time. Of course, this phrase could have been typed, "She said Never! Never! Never! ". But the more emphatic phrase in which she says "Never! " 1,000 times would be much harder to type. Using a for loop, we can simply change the 3 to 1,000. It's easy to be emphatic with for loops.

20.1 Apologetic by Analogy. Guided by the "Never!" example, write a very apologetic JavaScript program. Construct the variable text with the string value "I am so so so sorry." **Hint:** You will need one additional assignment statement *after* the loop is over.

JavaScript Rules for for Loops

Loops are powerful because computers are good at doing the same thing over and over again. Loops quickly become your friend. In this section we set out the rules for writing them.

The World-Famous Iteration

Because JavaScript has the same for loop statement structure as other popular programming languages (e.g., C, C++, and Java), thousands of for loops of the form we describe are written every day—millions have been written in the past decade. With so many loops, programmers have gotten in the habit of using one standard form most of the time:

```
for (var j=0; j<n; j++) {. . . }
```

Without a doubt this is the most frequently written for loop of all time, so we will call it the **World-Famous Iteration (WFI)**. The following sections outline the rules for the WFI.

Iteration Variable. The iteration variable (j in the example) can be any identifier, and follows the usual rules. Programmers tend to choose short or even single-letter identifiers for iteration variables because they are usually typed frequently. By far, i, j, and k are the most common. Notice that it is alright to declare the iteration variable in the for loop, which many programmers prefer, but you can use any declared variable, too.

Starting Point. The WFI starts at 0, so the first item in the control section of a for loop is

```
for ( j = 0;
```

or

```
for ( var j = 0;
```

Starting the count at 0, which computer people always do anyway, simplifies using loops, as we'll see.

Continuation Test. The *<continuation>* test for the World Famous Iteration is the less-than relational operator <, as in j < n. Of course, n can be replaced by any number, variable or expression, as long as it results in a numeric value.

Step Size. Step size is the amount the iteration variable changes after each iteration. For the WFI the step size should be 1, so the *<next iteration>* statement should increment by one, as in j = j + 1. But, adding by 1 is so common in programming, JavaScript and other languages have a "post increment" operation, written as j++. It is equivalent to j = j +1, and takes a little less typing. Either choice is good for defining the step size. By the way, x-- is equivalent to x = x – 1.

Reference to the Iteration Variable. As you will soon see, the iteration variable is often used in the computations of the *<statement list>*, which is why we have focused on the values of the iteration variable. The WFI's iteration variable gets the values 0, 1, 2, . . . , n –1 because the continuation test is j < n.

We care what these values are because we compute with them. So, for example, the iteration variable i is used in the statement that computes 5 factorial (5!):

```
var fact = 1;
for (var i = 0; i < 5; i=i+1) {
    fact = fact * (i + 1);
}

fact
/*
120
*/
```

0 + 1 on
1st iteration
↓

That is, the iteration variable gets the values 0, 1, 2, 3, 4, the loop computes ((((1 * 1) * 2) * 3) * 4) * 5 ⇔ 120. Using the iteration variable in the computation is necessary and useful.

No Planning. The for loop *might have been* designed to figure the number of iterations to perform before starting out, and then doing them. But iteration doesn't work that way. Instead, the computer just plods along, testing to see if it should continue before starting an iteration, doing the statement sequence, changing the iteration variable, and repeating. Plodding is more powerful, because it's not always possible to predict the number of iterations.

Why So Famous?

JavaScript permits a much, much wider range of for loops than the WFI loops just described. In JavaScript it is legal for loops to start anywhere, end by any *<continuation>* test a programmer can dream up, step by any amount, either positive or negative, and much more. But, as noted above, programmers have settled into the WFI style. Why?

Know the Number of Iterations Easily. The WFI iteration counts up from 0 in steps of 1 because the post-increment j++ is used. And the iteration ends when the iteration variable is no longer strictly less than n—that is, the loop's last iteration is when j ⇔ n - 1. Thus, the for loop *<statement list>* is performed n times with an iteration variable of 0, 1, 2, . . . , n - 1. When used in this stylized form, the variable or expression following the < symbol—the n in this case—is *exactly the number of times through the loop*. That fact is so important it should be repeated:

The value following < is exactly the number of times through the loop.

So, we know the number of times the loop iterates in an instant without thinking about it.

Knowing the number of iterations is a fact programmers always need to know, and the WFI makes it easy to figure it out. That's why it's so famous.

A Small Price to Pay. Notice that in the factorial example above, 1 had to be added to the iteration variable, i, for the computation to work out. If the loop began counting at 1 rather than 0, this would not have been necessary. But, it is so common to "correct" the iteration variables in this way, programmers are used to it.

Off Again. An extremely common error in computing—you've probably made it several times in *this* section—is to miscount by one. It's so common it has a name, the *Off-by-One Error*. "Exam week is from the 3rd to the 10th," so how many days is it? We tend to subtract to get seven, but it's eight because it includes the end points. Figuring the number of iterations is similarly error prone. Happily, the World-Famous Iteration helps. The n following < in the WFI form is the *exact* iteration count.

20.2 Geek Love. Declare a variable n initialized to some value, say 2. Using a for loop, write code to give the variable love the string value: "If I've said it once, I've said it *n* times: " followed by the text " I love you." repeated *n* times. For example, love ⇔ "If I've said it once, I've said it 2 times: I love you. I love you." Don't forget to declare your love.

Avoiding Infinite Loops

Especially when we follow the WFI form, for loops are relatively error free, but it's still possible to create infinite loops; that is, loops that do not stop. To avoid this, think about what could go wrong.

Every loop in a program must have a continuation test or it will never terminate. As you learned in Chapter 10, the fifth property of algorithms is that they must be finite, that is, stop and report an answer, or stop and report that no answer is possible. for loops have a *<continuation>* test, so they meet the requirement of testing in each iteration. But just because there is a test doesn't mean that it will stop the loop. It must test a condition based on a value that is changing during the loop, such as the value changed by the *<next iteration>* operation. If the test is based on values that don't change in the loop, the outcome of the test will never change, and the loop will never complete. Again, if we follow the rules, things will work out.

Nevertheless, it's not too difficult to make a mistake and create an infinite loop. For example,

```
for (var j = 0 ; j < 3; i = i + 1) {. . .}
```

looks almost like our earlier "emphatic" for loop, but it is broken and will loop forever. (Very emphatic, indeed!) The problem is that the variable being compared in the *<continuation>* test, j, is not the one incremented in the *<next iteration>* operation (i). Unless the iteration variable is changed somewhere else in the loop—iteration variables should never be changed by statements in the *<statement list>*—the iteration will loop forever. Anyone carefully analyzing this for statement will spot the problem, but it's easy to miss. It's also easy enough to create, say, by making incomplete edits. (Imagine that the statement had previously used i as an iteration variable and was incompletely revised.)

Infinite Loops. Infinite loops happen. It's a fact of programming. Luckily, JavaScript is kind to programmers who make this mistake. Firefox and Internet Explorer warn you that the script is running slowly ("unresponsive," as in the figure) and ask if you want to terminate it; other browsers can simply be forced to close. In the past, you had to turn off the computer to stop an infinite loop.

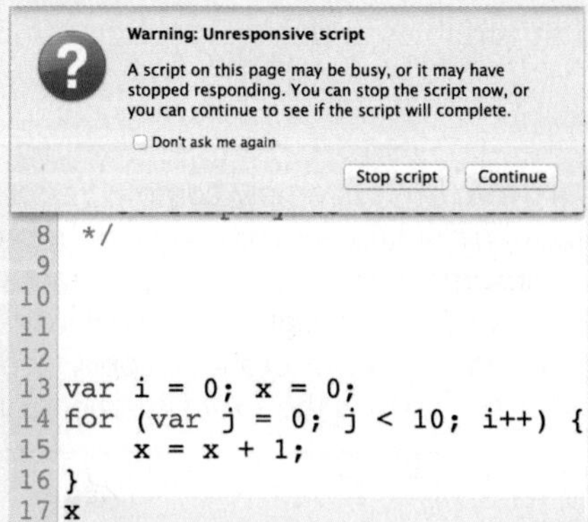

Experiments with Flipping Coins

To practice for loops, we experiment with flipping electronic coins. Recall that in Chapter 19 we wrote a function randNum( ); its parameter is the range of integers from which the random choice is made.

```
function randNum( range ) {
    return Math.floor( range* Math.random( ));
}
randNum(3)
/*
0
*/
```

The reasoning is that multiplying an integer range—say, r—times a random real number between [0, 1) produces a random real number between [0, r); dropping the digits to the right of the decimal point, which is the task for Math.floor( ), produces a random integer in the list: 0, 1, . . . , r – 1.

Obviously, randNum(2) returns either 0 (tails) or 1 (heads), which is perfect for our experiments.

One Trial of 100 Flips

The first experiment is to find out how many heads and tails we get in 100 flips. We expect the numbers to be roughly equal. To run the experiment, we must set up an iteration in which our randNum( ) function is performed 100 times and counts are gathered along the way. The code is:

```
var heads=0, tails=0;                //Counters
function randNum(range) {
     return Math.floor(range*Math.random());
}
for (var i=0; i<100; i++ ) {         //WFI
   if (randNum(2) == 1)              //Is pick 1?
          heads++;                   //Yes, count heads
      else
         tails++;                    //No, count tails
}

"Heads: " + heads + " Tails: " + tails

/*
Heads: 53 Tails: 47
*/
```

The for loop iterates 100 times—the iteration variable i ranges from 0 through 99—and uses a conditional statement to check and record the outcomes of the random number generation. The post-increment (++) notation has been used three times, allowing us to replace statements like heads=heads + 1 with the briefer heads++. Notice that the run shown gave 53 heads and 47 tails, but other runs will produce different numbers. (If you have Scratchpad handy, try it!) In five runs my results ranged from a 50–50 outcome to a 57–43 outcome. This motivates us to experiment with our program.

Notice how we printed out both counts of heads and tails by constructing an output string.

20.3 Rock On. Rewrite this Coin Flips example to count three possible outcomes as would be needed for Rock-Paper-Scissors and have it iterate 300 times. (See Try It 19.6 in Chapter 19 for a related problem.)

Our trial will be the 100-sample iteration just described. To run several trials, it will be convenient to put the sampling into a function, as explained in Chapter 19. Packaging the loop in a function makes it a unit that we can conveniently use in different situations; the code is shown in Figure 20.1. Notice that thinking of a trial as a unit is an *abstraction*, as discussed in Chapters 1 and 10.

```
function randNum(range) {
     return Math.floor(range*Math.random());
}
function trial (count) {
  var heads=0, tails=0;
  for (var i=0; i<count; i++ ) {
      if (randNum(2) == 1)
         heads++;
      else
         tails++;
  }
  return heads ;
}

trial(100)

/*
52
*/
```

Figure 20.1 The trial( ) declaration, and the results of a 100-flip trial.

The function has a parameter, count, that says how many times we want to sample, which has been 100 up to now, but it is convenient to allow the user to change that. Naturally, count is used in the continuation test of our iteration.

Finally, notice that trial( ) returns the heads count. Given that there are only two choices, the tails count must be count—heads.

Apple's Outside Inside Joke. Apple Corporation's Cupertino, California, campus is at 1 Infinite Loop. Perhaps that means the company will continue forever—or perhaps be considered "unresponsive."

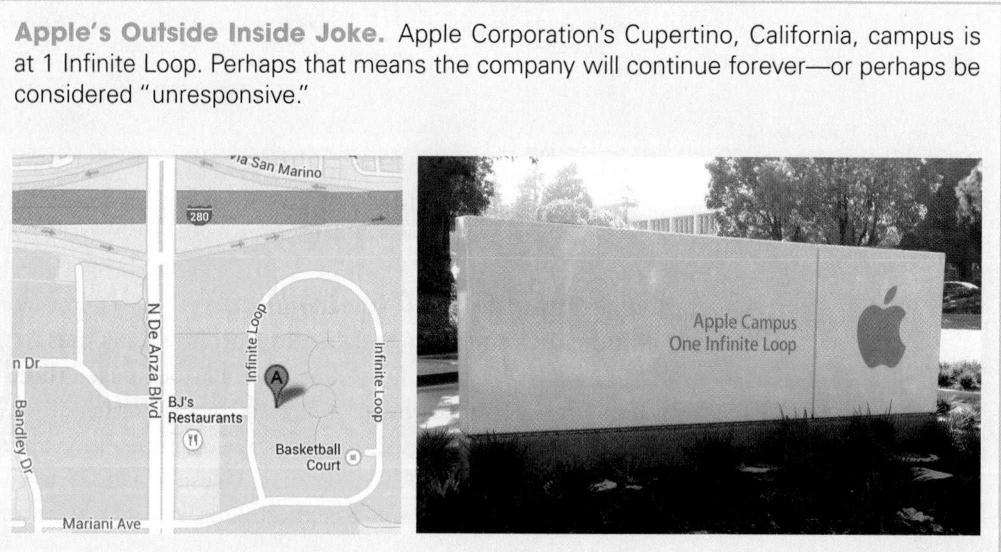

Multiple Trials

To run five trials, we write a new JavaScript program in which we include the declarations for the functions trial( ) and randNum( ), because we will use both of them, and we write new code to call trial( ) five times. Naturally, we repeat the call using a second loop. The logic of the two loops and a sample run are shown in Figure 20.2.

The three variables used in forming the answer are:

headCount	a temporary variable to save the number of heads from a trial(100) call
outAns	a string variable to be used to form the answer
j	the iteration variable

```
function randNum(range) {
     return Math.floor(range*Math.random());
}
function trial (count) {
  var heads=0, tails=0;
  for (var i=0; i<count; i++ ) {
      if (randNum(2) == 1)
         heads++;
      else
         tails++;
  }
  return heads ;
}
var headCount, outAns = "";          //Output text is empty
for (var j=0; j < 5; j++) {
    headCount = trial(100);          //Compute a trial
    outAns = outAns + "Trial " + j  //Build answer string
       + ": " + headCount + ":" +
       (100-headCount) + '\n';
}

outAns
/*
Trial 0: 45:55
Trial 1: 43:57
Trial 2: 63:37
Trial 3: 52:48
Trial 4: 48:52

*/
```

Figure 20.2 The JavaScript program to run five trials of 100 flips each.

After the declaration, we enter the loop. The loop runs the trial( ) function, sampling 100 times, and saves the answer in headCount. Then, using outAns, it constructs a line to describe the trial outcome, giving the heads first followed by a colon, and then the tails followed by a colon. At the end, there is a new line symbol (recall from Table 17.1). This operation works like other cases where we have built up a string to form an answer.

20.4 Odd Counting. Why are the trials listed 0 through 4 instead of 1 through 5?

We've produced a handy computation, but it can be improved.

A Diagram of Results

Suppose we are interested in how far off from a perfect 50–50 score a trial is. Such information is easily displayed with a diagram. We compute the difference of the coin flip from 50–50 and show that number using asterisks. For example, the fourth trial, 52–48, can be represented by two asterisks because it differs from perfect by two coin flips. Either of the quantities heads – 50 or tails – 50 gives us the right number of asterisks, but one expression is positive and the other one is negative. JavaScript has the function Math.abs( ) for the absolute value; that is, it makes all numbers—positive or negative—positive, implying that Math.abs(headCount–50) is the number of asterisks to display.

As with the original output, the line of asterisks is added to text at the end of the trials( ) call. But how do we include a variable number of asterisks? With another loop, of course.

```
14 var headCount, outAns = "", aster;                      //Output text is empty
15 for (var j=0; j < 5; j++) {
16
17     headCount = trial(100);                             //Compute a trial
18     outAns = outAns + "Trial " + (j+1) + ': ';          //Build answer string
19     aster = "";                                         //Initialize
20     for (var k=0; k < Math.abs(headCount-50); k++) {    //Loop by difference
21        aster = aster + "*";                             //Add * for each one
22     }
23     outAns = outAns + aster + "\n";                     //Include in output
24 }
25
26 outAns
27
28 /*
29 Trial 1: **
30 Trial 2: ****
31 Trial 3: ***
32 Trial 4: **
33 Trial 5: *
34
35 */
```

Figure 20.3 JavaScript for a program using three iterations (one not shown) to display the results for five trials using asterisk diagram.

After declaring another text variable, aster, and initializing it to the empty string, we replace the previous outAns assignment statement with this statement sequence

The result when I first ran it is shown in Figure 20.3.

Line 18 marks display of the *j*th trial result with the text "Trial " followed by j+1 to correct for the iteration variable counting from zero as mentioned in Try It 20.4.

```
                                    ↓
18    outAns = outAns + "Trial " + (j+1) + ': ';          //Build answer string
```

This is a very unusual statement because the + has two different meanings. The third + is addition (arrow), while the other three are concatenation. How does the computer know which one we mean? It looks to see if we are combining numbers (in which case it adds) or strings (in which case it concatenates). The special rule is that if there is one number and one string, it concatenates. So, we need the parentheses around j + 1 to cause the addition.

Continuing with the listing of asterisks (the highlighted loop), an iteration—lines 20–22—adds asterisks one at a time, up to a total of Math.abs(headCount–50). We need a new iteration variable, k, because the iteration variable j is already in use for the "trials loop," which the asterisks loop is a part of. Using j again would create a collision between the two loops. Notice that it is okay to put the math function in the *<continuation>* test. (Because this is a WFI form, we know immediately that we have the right number of iterations.) Finally, after the iteration, the asterisks and a new line character are added, so each experiment starts on a new line.

20.5 Shorter Program. Will the program in Figure 20.3 continue to work if we remove the text **+ '\n'** in the last statement of the Trials loop?

outAns=outAns + aster + '\n' ;

Nested Loops

A final curiosity about the program in Figure 20.3 is that it contains a **nested loop,** which is simply a loop within another loop. It is no surprise that when computing an iteration, it might be necessary to use another loop for part of the *<statement list>*

```
<script>
 function randNum( range) {
   return Math.floor( range * Math.random( ));
 }
 function coinFlip ( ) {
   if (randNum(2) == 1)
     return "us1heads.jpg";
   else
     return "us1tails.jpg";
 }
   document.write("<div style='margin:50px'>")
   for (var j=0; j<5; j++) {
     for (var i=0; i<7; i++) {
     document.write('<img src=" ' + coinFlip( )
         + ' " width="50" />');
     }
     document.write('<br/>');
   }
   document.write('<div>');
</script>
```

Figure 20.4 Nested loops, with the inner loop iterating seven times and the outer loop iterating five times.

computation. Figure 20.3 is a clear example of this: As we are computing each of the five trials, that is, as we are looping through the outer loop, we need to construct a results-diagram, so we simply use a second loop, the nested loop that is highlighted, to construct the results row.

The inner loop completes all of its iterations during each iteration of the outer loop, as can be verified in Figure 20.3.

Programming languages all allow loops to nest, just like they allow if statements to nest, and there is no limit—programs often use triply nested loops, or more. The only trick is to remember that in nested for loops, all loops in the nest must use *different* iteration variables or else they will interfere with each other.

Figure 20.4 shows another simple example of a doubly nested loop.

Indexing

If you're familiar with Elizabeth II, Super Bowl XXV, *Rocky 3*, and Apollo 13, you are acquainted with indexing. **Indexing** is the process of creating a sequence of names by associating a base name ("Apollo") with a number ("13"). When a new name is needed, the next number in sequence is used ("Apollo 14"). Each indexed item is called an **element** of the base-named sequence.

Index Syntax

Naturally, in programming, indexing has a special syntax. An index is enclosed in square brackets in JavaScript, for example, Apollo[13]. The index can be a constant, variable, or expression. It must evaluate to a non-negative integer, the index value. (See the section Array Reference Syntax for more information.) Indexing is important in computing because of its close link to iteration: Iterations can be used to refer to all elements of a name; that is, a notation like A[j] can, on successive iterations over j, refer to different elements of A.

Index Terms. The terms *indexes* and *indices* are both commonly used to refer to more than one index.

20.6 Loop-the-Loop. Answer the following questions about Figure 20.4.

(a) What is the index variable for the inner loop?

(b) How many image tags do the two loops generate by working together?

(c) Between the time j gets assigned the value 3 and the time it changes to 4, how many times does i change?

(d) If the line document.write('<br/>') is moved inside the bracket above it, how would the page change, if at all?

Index Origin

When indexing queens, Super Bowls, popes, and so on, we usually start counting at 1, though often the first item doesn't initially get an index; for example, Queen Elizabeth I was just called Queen Elizabeth until Elizabeth II came along. Yard lines in football begin indexing with 0 (goal is 0). Movie sequels start at 2 because there can't be a *sequel* to nothing. The point at which indexing begins, that is, the least index, is known as the **index origin**. The index origin of JavaScript is 0.

Arrays

In programming, an indexed base name is called an **array**. Arrays must be declared; in JavaScript, arrays are declared with the syntax

var <*identifier*> = new Array(<*number of elements*>)

Notice that the word Array starts with an uppercase A. And, in the declaration the <*number of elements*> is surrounded by parentheses; we reserve square brackets for array *references*. Also, unlike queens, variables either are or are not arrays; they don't change. In the sample declaration

```
var week = new Array(7);
```

week is the identifier being declared, and new Array(7) specifies that the identifier will be an array variable. The number in parentheses gives the number of **array elements**. *JavaScript uses index origin 0*, meaning that the least index of any array element is always 0, and the greatest index is the number of elements minus 1. Thus, the array just declared has elements week[0], week[1], . . . , week[6], that is, seven elements. The term **array length** also refers to the number of elements in an array. To refer to an array's length in a program, we use <*variable*>.length. For example, week.length ⇔ 7.

20.7 Watch for Disaster. If Apollo is an array of length 17, what element does Apollo[13] refer to?

Rules for Arrays

To summarize, here are the rules for arrays in JavaScript:

- Arrays are normal variables initialized by new Array(*<number of elements>*).
- *<number of elements>* in the declaration is just that—the number of array elements.
- Array indexing begins at 0.
- The number of elements in an array is its *length*.
- The greatest index of an array is *<number of elements>* – 1 because of the 0 origin.

Array Reference Syntax

An **array reference**—that is, what to write when you want the value of an array element—consists of the array name together with an index—a constant, variable, or expression—enclosed in brackets and evaluating to a non-negative integer, the **index value**. The value to which the index evaluates must be less than the array's length. Thus, the statements

```
var dwarf = new Array(7);     //Declarations use parens
var deux = 2;                 //Create a value for examples
dwarf[0] = "Happy";           //References use brackets
dwarf[1] = "Sleepy";          //Index by a constant
dwarf[deux] = "Dopey";        //Index by a variable
dwarf[deux + 1] = "Sneezy"; //Index by an expression
dwarf[2*deux] = "Bashful";
dwarf[3*deux - 1] = "Grumpy";
dwarf[10-(2*deux)] = "Doc";

dwarf

/*
Happy,Sleepy,Dopey,Sneezy,Bashful,Grumpy,Doc
*/
```

assign values to the array elements using a variety of indexing alternatives.

Sub Standard. The index is also known as a *subscript.* In mathematics, indexes, written below the line as in x_1 and y_1, are called subscripts. Programming inherits the same term but writes them in brackets, for example, x[1] and y[1].

When introducing the World-Famous Iteration, we said that the reason for indexing from 0 to n–1 would soon be evident. Now you can see that 0-origin iteration is perfect for 0-origin indexing. Study the following version of the WFI:

```
for(var i = 0; i < week.length; i++) {
    week[i] = dwarf[i] + " & " + dwarf[(i+1)%7] + " do dishes";
}
```

The variable i ranges over all of the elements of the array week, that is, 0 through 6. By using <*array name*>.length in the <*continuation*> clause of the control, we set up to enumerate all of the array's elements. This iteration creates the values

```
for(var i = 0; i < week.length; i++) {
    week[i] = dwarf[i] + " & " + dwarf[(i+1)%7] + " do dishes";
}

week

/*
Happy & Sleepy do dishes,
Sleepy & Dopey do dishes,
Dopey & Sneezy do dishes,
Sneezy & Bashful do dishes,
Bashful & Grumpy do dishes,
Grumpy & Doc do dishes,
Doc & Happy do dishes
*/
```

Looping from 1 to 100

for the array week by referring to a consecutive pair of elements from dwarf. The final pair—Doc & Happy—which must "wraparound," uses (i+1) *mod* 7 to index the dwarf array in the second reference. That is, (i+1)%7 results in an index value of 0 because (6+1) divided by 7 has a 0 remainder, which is Happy.

Why So Famous? Our focus on computing the index with an expression provides another reason why the WFI is so popular. Because it's common to have to program *some* expression for the index values, it doesn't matter much whether the iteration variable counts starting at 0 or at 1 or at 14. The index expression can adjust the value as long as the *total* number of values is correct. The WFI does this, and does it better than other iterations.

20.8 Indexes Simplified. Revise your Rock-Paper-Scissors code from Try It 20.3 to save the counts in a three-element array. By using indexing you should be able to solve the problem without an if statement.

It's Magic

We postponed programming one of the mobile apps of Chapter 19 until now. The Magic Decider question answerer is an example of an app that is most easily programmed using an array to store the responses.

Setting Up the Array

Earlier, when we assigned the names to the dwarf array, we wrote assignment statements to fill in the elements. But we can also initialize an array when we declare it, like other variables. The technique is to list the items inside of the parentheses, separated by commas, as in

```
var respond = new Array(
  "It is certain", "It is decidedly so", "Without a doubt",
  "Yes, definitely", "You may rely on it", "As I see it, yes",
  "Most likely", "Outlook good", "Yes", "Signs point to yes",
  "Reply hazy, try again", "Concentrate, and ask again",
  "Better not tell you now", "Cannot predict now",
  "Concentrate and ask again", "Don't count on it",
  "My reply is, no", "My sources say, no", "Outlook not so good",
  "Very doubtful");
```

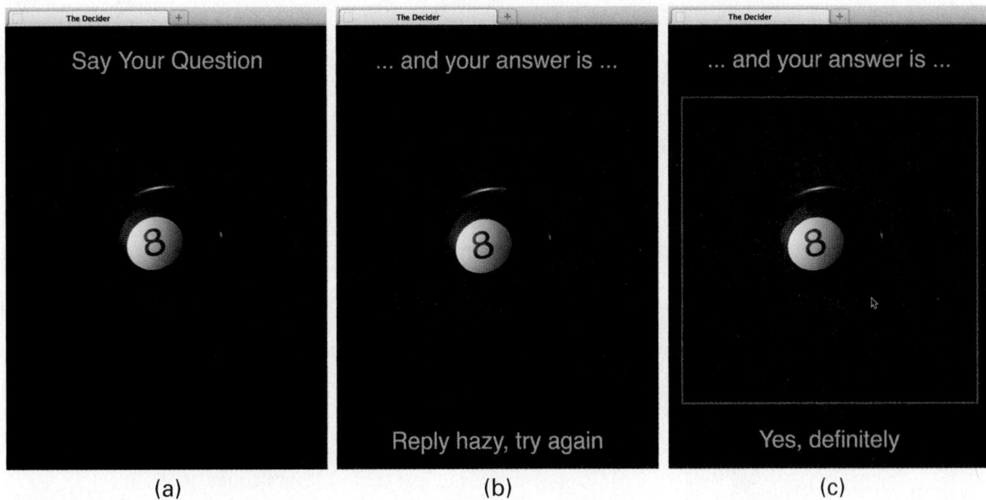

Figure 20.5 Magic Decider displays (a) the initial question request, (b) the UI after tapping or clicking on the image, and (c) the image with a visible border to show its extent.

The array `respond` is loaded with twenty text sequences. Notice that we don't have to say how many elements the array has—the number of initial values is the number of elements.

Now, to "magically" answer a question, we simply write `respond[randNum(20)]`. The `randNum( )` function call generates a random integer in the range 0 to 19. This reference is the index of one of the strings, which is the element of the array we will select.

Structuring the Page

The Magic Decider page is structured around three paragraphs (see Figure 20.5). The first paragraph asks for a question; the middle paragraph is an image, which is a "button" that the user can tap or click; and the last paragraph displays the answer to the question. For the image, we use an 8-ball, because of its well-known magical powers.

Notice that when the user taps the image, the text in the top paragraph changes, and the text in the bottom paragraph appears. Both of these are implemented by an `onclick` event handler.

Changing the DOM. The button's `onclick` event hander will change the **Document Object Model (DOM)**, which is the browser's representation (data structure) for the page. The browser reads our HTML and sets up its own description of the page; that's the DOM. JavaScript gives us handy methods to make changes to it, which results in changes to the page. So, all we need to do when the `onclick` event happens is to change the text in the two paragraphs. The body of the code for the Magic Decider is shown in Figure 20.6.

In Figure 20.6 we notice that the first paragraph has `ask` as its `id`, and the last paragraph has `tell` as its `id`. These identifiers allow us to reference the two paragraphs to make changes. In the `onclick` event handler of the middle paragraph's button, we make two assignments that are similar to operations we've seen, but not quite the same.

In the assignment

```
document.getElementById('ask').innerHTML = '. . . and your answer
is . . . '
```

```
<!doctype html>
<html>
  <head>
   <meta charset="UTF-8"><title>The Decider</title>
   <style>
     body {background-color:black; color:orange;
            text-align:center; font-family:helvetica}
      button {margin:0; padding:0; background-color:black;
             border-style:none}
     p      {font-size:x-large; }
   </style>
   <script>
     var respond = new Array(
       "It is certain", "It is decidedly so", "Without a doubt",
       "Yes, definitely", "You may rely on it", "As I see it, yes",
       "Most likely", "Outlook good", "Yes", "Signs point to yes",
       "Reply hazy, try again", "Concentrate, and ask again",
       "Better not tell you now", "Cannot predict now",
       "Concentrate and ask again", "Don't count on it",
       "My reply is, no", "My sources say, no", "Outlook not so good",
       "Very doubtful");
      function randNum( range ) {
            return Math.floor( range * Math.random( ));
     }
   </script>
  </head>
  <body>
   <p id="ask"> Say Your Question</p>
   <p><button
      onclick="document.getElementById('ask').innerHTML='... and your answer is ... ';
                  document.getElementById('tell').innerHTML=respond[randNum(20)]">
      <img src="8-ball.jpg" alt="8 Ball" width="300"/></button></p>
    <p id="tell" > </p>
  </body>
</html>
```

Figure 20.6 The HTML for the Magic Decider highlighting its three-paragraph structure.

the reference on the left side identifies the text of the ask paragraph in the DOM, and the assignment replaces it with new text. The other assignment does the same thing for the tell paragraph, but it replaces the existing text (blank) with a randomly chosen answer from the respond list. That's it. It's magic!

Concluding Remarks. Working directly to modify the DOM is the next step in learning Web programming. We have shown a glimpse here, and one more example comes later. Generally, these JavaScript facilities are powerful and fun to use. And they're not too hard to learn.

The Busy Animation

As you know, movies, cartoons, and flipbooks animate by the rapid display of many still pictures known as **frames**. Human visual perception is relatively slow—presumably because of the amazingly complicated tasks it performs—so it is fooled into observing smooth motion when the **display rate** is about 30 frames per second, that is, 30 Hz. In this section, we discuss one way to animate online; it gives us practice using iteration, arrays, and indexing.

The animation we plan to construct is a familiar "busy" indicator. In Figure 20.7 the 12 frames contributing to the animation are shown with their names. The rapid

Figure 20.7 The .gif images for the Busy Animation. These files are available at pearsonhighered.com/snyder.

display of these frames makes the black bar appear to revolve. Creating this Busy Animation is the goal of this section.

Fast Forward. The quickest way to learn both the ideas and the practical skills of animation is to build the animation program yourself as you read along.

Before you can successfully program an animation in JavaScript, you must understand three concepts:

1. Using a timer to initiate animation events
2. Prefetching the frames of the animation
3. Redrawing a Web page image

As the ideas are introduced, we program the Busy Animation.

A Story, But Not A Flipbook. The Busy Animation is very basic. Commercial animations like *Toy Story* use much more sophisticated techniques to create characters. (A simple introduction is www.youtube.com/watch?v=LDogpuChe94&feature=share, the *Despicable Me 2* trailer.) In both movies and the Busy Animation, the animation is created one frame at a time.

Using a Timer to Initiate Animation

The animation we produce will be displayed by a Web browser. As you know, Web browsers are *event driven*. That is, they are told to perform a task, they do it, and then they sit idle waiting for an event, which will cause them to do the next task. If browsers are idle when they are not working on a task, how can they animate something?

Animations require action every 30 milliseconds (ms). The obvious solution is to turn the activity of drawing the next frame into an event. The event will be the regular "ticking" of a clock. We'll use a timer analogy.

We set a timer to wake up the browser to tell it to display the next frame, and then set it again for 30 ms into the future. In 30 ms, we repeat the process. In this way, we draw the frames at regular intervals and create an animation. We use such a scheme for *online animations*. Not surprisingly, JavaScript comes equipped with all of the features, for example, timers needed to implement online animation.

Setting a Timer. Computers have extremely fast internal clocks, which are too fast for most programming purposes. Instead, the timers programmers use typically "tick" once per millisecond. Timers are intuitive. In JavaScript, the command to set a timer is

setTimeout("*<event handler>*", *<duration>*)

where *<event handler>* is a string giving the JavaScript computation that will run when the timer goes off, and *<duration>* is any positive number of milliseconds, saying how far into the future the timer should go off.

For example, to display a frame in 30 ms using the function animate( ) as an event handler, we write setTimeout("animate( )", 30). Thirty milliseconds later, the computer runs the animate( ) function and displays the frame. Of course, the last step for the animate( ) function must be to set the timer so that it "wakes up" again. Otherwise, the animation stops. ("Every 30 ms" is different from 30 times a second, of course, because 1,000/30 = 33.333 ms. We can set the timer to 33 ms, but animation is not an exact science and 30 is close enough.)

Using a Handle to Refer to a Timer. Unlike mechanical timers, computer timers can keep track of many different times at once. How does the computer keep the settings straight? When we perform setTimeout( ), we get back a special code—it's called a **handle**—that the computer uses to identify our timer. We can use the handle to refer to our timer, say, to cancel it. For example, if we declare a variable, timerID, with which to save the handle, and write

```
timerID=setTimeout("animate( )", 30);
```

we can cancel the timer by writing

```
clearTimeout(timerID);
```

and the computer will know which of the timers it's tracking should be canceled.

Using Buttons to Start/Stop the Animation. Because timers can be set and canceled, we will include two buttons to start and stop our animation. Their definitions are

```
<form>
  <input type="button" value="Start"
     onclick='setTimeout("animate( )",100);'/>
  <input type="button" value="Stop"
     onclick='clearTimeout(timerID);'/>
</form>
```

The **Start** button sets the timer for the first time. The animation keeps going on its own thereafter. Each time animate( ) sets the timer, the handle is stored in timerID. Then, when the **Stop** button is clicked, its event handler clears the timer and stops the animation.

Prefetching Images

Next, we'll consider displaying images. Recall from Chapter 3 that to keep our Web pages tidy, we keep the .gif and .jpg images in a separate directory or folder. So, assume that the graphics files shown in Figure 20.7 are in a folder gifpix. The first of the images would be displayed on a Web page with the HTML

```
<img src="gifpix/Busy0.gif" alt="spinner"/>
```

We begin with this skeleton HTML page that includes the <form> tags and the two buttons.

```
<!doctype html>
<html>
  <head>
   <meta charset="UTF-8"/><title>Spinner</title>
   <style>
     body {text-align:center}
   </style>
  </head>
 <body>
    <img src="gifpix/Busy0.gif" alt="spinner"/>
    <form>
      <input type="button" value="Start"
         onclick='setTimeout("animate( )",100);'/>
      <input type="button" value="Stop"
        onclick='clearTimeout(timerID);'/>
    </form>
  </body>
</html>
```

We would like to overwrite that single image with all of the other .gif files in gifpix in sequence, one every 30 ms. But we can't do so directly. The problem is that loading the images is generally too slow to allow us to show a new image so quickly. Web images must be transferred from the Web server across the Internet, where they encounter all sorts of delays. (We don't notice this while we're developing a Web application on our computers because all of the files are already stored locally.) Consequently, the strategy is to get the images first, store them locally so they are available in the computer's memory, and then display them. The process of loading the images ahead of time is called **prefetching**.

Where will the 12 images (Busy0.gif through Busy11.gif) of the gifpix folder be put? Because they are indexed already, it's logical to use an array. We'll name the array pics and declare it

```
var pics = new Array (12);
```

indicating that it will have 12 elements.

Initializing to an Image Object. In order for the elements of the array to store an image, they must be initialized to an **image object**. An image object is a blank instance of an image (introduced in Chapter 2). Think of an image object as a skeleton that provides places for all the information needed to store an image, such as its name, size of its two dimensions, and its actual pixels. To initialize the 12 array elements to image objects requires an iteration and the new Image( ) operation:

```
for (var i = 0; i < pics.length; i++) {
  pics[i] = new Image( );
}
```

Notice that Image( ) begins with a capital I.

Using the src Component. Among the places in the image object is a field called src where the image's source name is stored—that is, the file name of the file containing the image. This is the string that we give in the <img src=". . . "/> tag in HTML. When we assign to the src field, the browser saves the name and gets the file, storing it in memory, just as we require. Thus,

```
pics[0].src="gifpix/Busy0.gif"
```

parallels our earlier explicit fetch of the initial frame. Because there are 12 images in total, we use a loop,

```
for (var i = 0; i < pics.length; i++) {
  pics[i].src = "gifpix/Busy" + i + ".gif";
}
```

which constructs the file names on-the-fly. That is, we build up the file name gifpix/Busy*i*.gif using the iteration variable and concatenation.

There is an important difference between the prefetching by assigning to the .src field of an image variable, and using <img src=". . . "/> in HTML. The former is not visible on the screen, whereas the latter is. This works to our advantage both ways. The image variable, which is just a part of our JavaScript program, is not visible because it hasn't been placed on the page. But that's fine, because we don't want the user to see the prefetch happening anyway. The <img src=". . . "/> tag places an image on the page, and so is visible. We need both.

Redrawing an Image

To animate the initial frame that we placed earlier with <img src=". . . "/>, we need to overwrite it with the images that we just prefetched at a rate of one every 30 ms. How do we refer to the initial frame in order to overwrite it? As with forms (recall Chapter 18), Web browsers keep an array of the images used on the page in their data structure, the *DOM*, mentioned above; it is just like our pics array. As the <img src=". . . "/> commands are encountered, the browser fills its images array just like we filled pics. So, document.images[0] is the name of the first image—that is, our initial frame Busy0.gif. Any additional <img src=". . . "/> images are indexed with higher numbers in sequence. The browser's images array elements each have the src property too, and assigning to it overwrites the image. Thus, to change the initial frame, we write the assignment

```
document.images[0].src=pics[i].src;
```

which replaces the existing frame with the *i*th element of the pics array, causing it to be displayed. All that needs to happen to animate the **Busy** icon is to sweep through all of the i values, cyclically. We display a new one every 100 ms rather than 30 ms because this regular figure looks better at the slightly slower rate.

Defining the animate( ) Event Handler. The animate( ) event handler overwrites the image, sets up for the next frame, and sets the timer to call itself again:

```
function animate( ) {
  document.images[0].src = pics[frame].src;
  frame = (frame+1)%12;
  timerID = setTimeout("animate( )", 100);
}
```

```
<!doctype html>
<html>
 <head>
  <meta charset="UTF-8"/><title>Spinner</title>
  <style>
    body {text-align:center}
  </style>
  <script>
   var frame = 0;                        //Frame counter
   var timerID;                          //Timer handle var
   var pics = new Array(12);             //Array for prefetched gifs
   function animate( ) {
   document.images[0].src = pics[frame].src;
   frame = (frame+1)%12;
   timerID = setTimeout("animate( )", 100);
}
   for (var i = 0; i < pics.length; i++) {
     pics[i] = new Image( );
   }
   for (var i = 0; i < pics.length; i++) {
     pics[i].src = "gifpix/Busy" + i + ".gif";
   }
  </script>
 </head>
 <body>
   <img src="gifpix/Busy0.gif" alt="spinner"/>
   <form>
     <input type="button" value="Start"
        onclick='setTimeout("animate( )",100);'/>
     <input type="button" value="Stop"
       onclick='clearTimeout(timerID);'/>
   </form>
  </body>
</html>
```

Figure 20.8 The Busy Animation program, assuming that the 12 .gif files are stored in a folder called gifpix.

We set the timer for 100 ms rather than 30 ms because it makes the bar appear to revolve at a nice pace.

The whole Busy Animation program, including the familiar Start and Stop buttons, is shown in Figure 20.8, with the concepts explained. As a postscript to the Busy Animation, try clicking Start several times, followed by an equal number of Stop clicks. Can you explain what happens?

Not So Busy Animation

RPS

The concepts in the last section are important because they are used so often, not just in a Busy Animation exercise. So, we summarize three of them in a quick tour of the final Rock-Paper-Scissors app. We have used RPS at different stages of our study; this time it will illustrate saving state, prefetching, and updating the document.images array in the browser's DOM representation of the Web page. The final RPS app's operation is shown in Figure 20.9. Here's what it does.

The page opens with the RPS splash page. When the user clicks/taps the image, it randomly selects one of three images of hands, displaying one of the three choices.

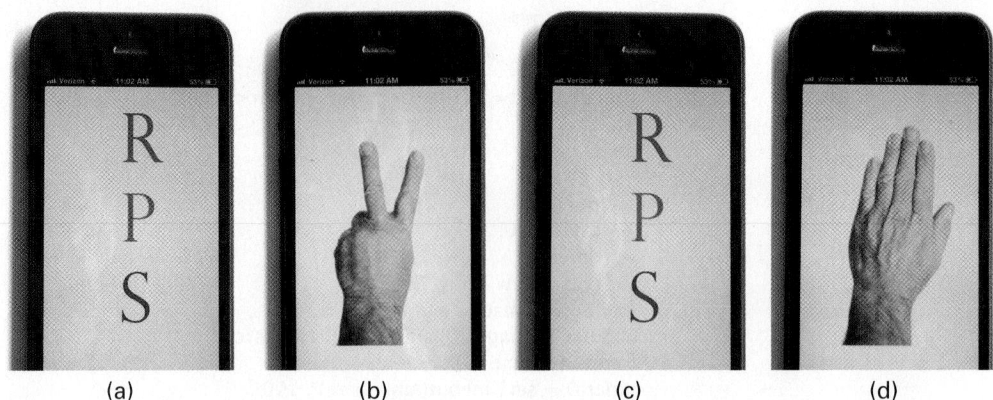

Figure 20.9 The Rock-Paper-Scissors app's operation: (a) splash image, (b) random choice, (c) return to splash for next throw, and (d) random choice. All transitions are caused by click/tap on image.

Click/tap the image again, and it returns to the splash page. And so on. Try it at media.pearsoncmg.com/aw/ecs_snyder_fluency_6/rps.html.

Three Key Ideas

Figure 20.10 shows the code implementing the RPS app. The code is commented, and illustrates these three standard ideas.

- **Saving state.** The app needs to remember which picture to display next, so it keeps a variable, `thro`, to serve that purpose. (`throw` is a reserved word in JavaScript; see Appendix D.) `thro` starts out with the value 1, meaning that on the next change of image, it should be the random choice, because the app opens with the splash image. The bit is "flipped" at the end of the `RPS ( )` function by the code `thro = 1 – thro`.
- **Prefetching.** Just as the Busy Animation prefetched images and stored them locally so they could be displayed rapidly, the RPS app does the same. This involves declaring an array, `pix`, of four elements—the splash and three hand images—setting the elements so they can store images, and loading them. Notice that this is performed explicitly rather than in a loop since the pictures have different names.
- **Changing `document.images`.** As we learned, the browser stores the page's pictures in an array known as `document.images`. The splash image will be the only one stored there, so it must be stored in `document.images[0]`. The `RPS( )` function simply calls `randNum(3)`, getting a 0, 1 or 2 back. It adds 1 so it refers to indexes 1, 2, or 3 of `pix`, and stores the image's `src` value in `document.images[0].src`. Or, if it just did that (`thro ⇔ 0`), it restores the splash page. Either way, a new image is displayed.

It's a simple app, and it nicely illustrates these three ideas. We will use them in the next chapter.

```
<!doctype html>
<html>
 <head><meta charset="UTF-8"/><title>RPS</title>
 <style> button {margin:0; padding:0; background-color:white;
                  border-style:none; border-width:0}
         p {text-align:center}      <!--above styling centers pic-->
 </style>
 <script>   //this code prefetches, randomizes and flips a picture
  var thro = 1;                        //alternates betw 0 and 1
  var pix = new Array(4);              //array to hold 4 pictures
  for (var i=0; i<4; i++){
    pix[i] = new Image( );             //set up element for pics
  }
  pix[0].src = "im/splash.gif";        //prefetch the 4 pics
  pix[1].src = "im/rock.gif";
  pix[2].src = "im/paper.gif";
  pix[3].src = "im/scissors.gif";
  function randNum( range ) {          //old randomizing friend
    return Math.floor( range * Math.random( ));
  }
  function rps( ) {                    //display a new image
    if (thro == 1)                     //is this a throw or reset?
       document.images[0].src          //throw, change picture
           =pix[1+randNum(3)].src;     //its random from pix 1-3
    else
       document.images[0].src          //reset, change picture
           =pix[0].src;                //to splash picture
    thro = 1-thro;                     //flip thro for next time
  }
 </script>
 </head>
 <body><p>
   <!--The program is just a picture that acts as a button
        flipping between the splash page and a random throw-->
   <button onclick="rps( )">
     <img src="im/splash.gif"
        alt="R-P-S Throw" height="300"/>
   </button></p>
 </body>
</html>
```

Figure 20.10 The JavaScript for the Rock-Paper-Scissors app, summarizing the ideas of the last two sections.

SUMMARY

We studied the fundamentals of programming to understand the sources of power in computation. The concepts of this chapter—iteration, indexing, and arrays—account for much of it. There is much more to say about programming, but we'll leave the rest of it to the experts. In this chapter we discussed the following:

- The basics of for loop iteration. The control part of a for statement is written in parentheses and the *<statement list>* is enclosed in curly braces. With each iteration, the entire statement list is performed. The number of iterations is determined by assignments to, and tests of, the iteration variable as specified in the control part.

- In the JavaScript for statement, the *<initialization>* component is executed first. Then, prior to each iteration, including the first, the *<continuation>* predicate is tested. If it is true, the *<statement list>* is performed; otherwise, it is skipped, and the for statement terminates. After each iteration, the *<next iteration>* operation is performed.
- The principles of iteration ensure that every iteration contains a test and that the test is dependent on variables that change in the loop.
- The for statement is very flexible. The *<initialization>* can begin with any number, the *<continuation>* test can stop the loop at any number, and the *<next iteration>* operation can increment by various amounts and count upward or downward.
- Programmers routinely use the World-Famous Iteration (WFI)—a stylized iteration that begins at 0, tests that the iteration variable is strictly less than some limit, and increments by 1. There is no obligation to use the WFI, but it allows us to determine the number of times around the loop quickly—it's the limit to the right of <. Because it is common to make errors figuring out the number of iterations, programmers use the WFI to recognize the number of iterations quickly.
- In indexing, we create a series of names by associating a number with a base name. If we need more names, we count more numbers. Indexed variables are known as arrays in programming. Like ordinary variables, arrays must be declared, but they use the new Array(*<length>*) syntax, in which *<length>* is the number of elements of the array.
- Array elements—referenced by giving the name and a non-negative index in brackets—can be used like ordinary variables. Arrays and iterations can be effectively used together.
- The basic concepts of online animation. All animations achieve the appearance of motion by rapidly displaying a series of still frames.
- When animating information displayed by a Web browser, we should prefetch the images so that they are readily accessible for rapid display. The key idea is to use a timer to create events, and then use the timer-event handler to redraw an image that has been placed on the Web page by the <img src=". . . "/> tag. These are referenced as the elements of the document's images array.

TRY IT SOLUTIONS

20.1

```
var text = "I am ";                         //Declare/initialize text

for (var j = 0; j < 3; j = j + 1) {         //Specify a 3 iteration loop
    text = text + "so ";                    //Concatenate on more text
}                                           //... end of loop

text = text + "sorry."                      //Complete sentence

text
/*
I am so so so sorry.
*/
```

20.2 Obviously, a more passionate statement results when n is increased.

```
var n = 2;
var love;
love = "If I've said it once, I've said it ";
love = love + n;
love = love + " times:"
for (var i = 0; i < n; i++) {
  love = love + " I love you.";
}
love
/*
If I've said it once, I've said it 2 times: I love you. I love you.
*/
```

20.3

```
var rock = 0, paper = 0, scissors = 0, temp;
function randNum( range ) {
    return Math.floor( range * Math.random( ));
}
for (var i=0; i<300; i++ ) {                  //WFI
     temp = randNum(3);                       //Make random choice
    if (temp == 0)
       rock++;
    if (temp == 1)
       paper++;
    if (temp == 2)
       scissors++;
}
"R: " + rock + " P: " + paper + " S: " + scissors

/*
R: 92 P: 107 S: 101
*/
```

20.4 Because the iteration variable, j, counts from 0 rather than from 1.

20.5 Yes, the program will work, but the results will print out in a line.

20.6 (a) i. (b) 35. (c) 7. Starting at 0 →1→2→3→4→5→6→7, and when it gets to 7 it is too large, halting the iteration. (d) Placing the <br/> inside the inner loop after each <img /> tag makes the 35 coins print out in a column.

20.7 Apollo[13] refers to the 14th item of the Apollo array, because array indexing always starts at 0, unlike the Apollo missions.

20.8

```
function randNum( range ) {
    return Math.floor( range * Math.random( ));
}
var rps = new Array(3);                       //Counters
var pick;                                     //Loop variable
rps[0] = 0; rps[1] = 0; rps[2] = 0;           //Initialize counters
for (var i=0; i<300; i++ ) {                  //WFI
     pick = randNum(3);                       //Make random choice
     rps[pick]++;                             //Index array by pick
}

rps
/*
101,83,116
*/
```

Notice that the array has three elements, numbered 0, 1, and 2; by indexing with the number, we don't have to handle the separate cases. The right element is incremented.

Multiple Choice

1. A false outcome for the continuation test means
   a. terminate the loop
   b. terminate the program
   c. continue the loop
   d. restart the program
2. The minimum number of times a loop can iterate is
   a. 1
   b. 5
   c. 0
   d. –1
3. Regarding, the following for statement, which statement is true?

   `for (var j = 0; j < n; j++) { . . . }`

   a. the loop starts at 0
   b. the loop increments by 1
   c. the loop stops after *n* iterations
   d. all of the above
4. When wanting to use a timer in JavaScript you should use
   a. `setTimeout`
   b. `Math.Timer`
   c. `Timer`
   d. `setTick`
5. Given the following line, which is a valid array reference?

   `var cols=new Array(9);`

   a. `cols[0]`
   b. `cols[4.5]`
   c. `cols[9]`
   d. `cols[10]`
6. Loading an image in advance is known as
   a. buffering
   b. prefetching
   c. caching
   d. backlogging
7. What is the first operation of a for loop?
   a. continuation test
   b. incrementation
   c. completing the statements inside of the for loop
   d. initialization
8. m++; is equivalent to
   a. `m = m + 1;`
   b. `m = m - 1;`
   c. `m = 1 - m;`
   d. `m + m;`

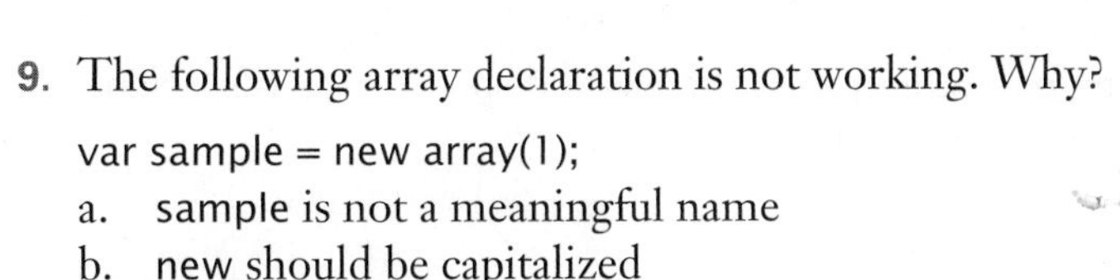

9. The following array declaration is not working. Why?

```
var sample = new array(1);
```

   a. sample is not a meaningful name
   b. new should be capitalized
   c. array should be capitalized
   d. an array must have at least two elements; change 1 to 2

10. When writing code, what can be nested?
   a. if statements
   b. for statements
   c. both if and for statements
   d. neither if nor for statements; only functions

Short Answer

1. The ________ is the browser's data structure for the page.
2. The first step of the second iteration of a loop is the ________ test.
3. The shortcut to add 1 to i and store it back into i is ________.
4. A loop that never ends is known as a(n) ________.
5. A loop inside a loop is called a(n) ________.
6. Math.abs() is used in JavaScript to find ________.
7. The elements of an array are accessed by their ________.
8. The number of elements in an array is its ________.
9. The ________ is the number of frames per second that are displayed in an animation.
10. The highest valid index in an array is its ________.

Exercises

1. You're making cookies (the real ones) and the directions say to stir until thoroughly mixed. Explain how such a loop works.
2. What property of a loop ensures it will terminate?
3. Write the code for a loop that starts at 0 and iterates seven times.
4. Create an array that holds the names of all the cities you have visited.
5. Referencing the array you created in Exercise 4, write a for loop that iterates through the array displaying "I have visited" followed by the name of each city.
6. Write a loop that finds the sum of the numbers from 0 to 100, and display the sum in an alert box.
7. Write code that displays a die, and when the user clicks the die it then displays a random number between 1 and 6 (use the Magic Decider code as a reference).
8. Young lovers often use a daisy to determine their true feelings. With each petal they count, they alternate "She loves me" and "She loves me, not." Generate a random number up to 25 and then use that to determine if your girlfriend (or boyfriend) loves you. Even numbers mean love. Odd numbers mean not. Display the process.

9. Using nested loops write code to display (using document.write) a set of asterisks to create a set of “stairs.”

```
*
**
***
****
*****
******
*******
```

10. Write a for loop that prints all the even numbers from 1 to 101.
11. Write code which randomly chooses a number from 1 to 10. It should then display low if the number is 5 or less, otherwise it should display high.
12. Explain why it is better to start at 0 rather than 1 when writing code.
13. What are off-by-one errors? How common are they? Are they avoidable?
14. Write an infinite loop, then explain in detail why it is an infinite loop and how to fix it so it becomes finite.
15. Write a piece of code that creates a “Warning: unresponsive script” error. Then explain in detail what caused the error and how you can fix it.

CHAPTER 21

A Case Study in Algorithmic Problem Solving

The Smooth Motion Application

learning objectives

- State and apply the Decomposition Principle
- Explain the problem-solving strategy used in creating the Smooth Motion application
- Discuss the use of the JavaScript operations for iteration, indexing, arrays, functions, animation controls, and event handlers in Smooth Motion
- Describe how mouse events are handled in Smooth Motion

CHAPTER 21

If it keeps up, man will atrophy all his limbs but the push-button finger.

—FRANK LLOYD WRIGHT

THE PROGRAMMING that you've learned shows how computers solve problems and demonstrates the source of their speed and versatility. You've learned enough programming to be able to embellish Web pages, making them more adaptive and dynamic. But the great value of the knowledge you've learned is neither insight nor embellishment. Rather, you can apply the programming ideas to general problem-solving situations. Processes, procedures, instructions and directions, decision-making, and so forth are phenomena we meet in daily life beyond the sphere of computers. Your knowledge applies in all of those cases, making you more effective at learning, performing, and planning tasks. In this chapter we apply this knowledge by solving a more substantial task.

Though the ideas have broad application, our interest and preparation are still Web related. Accordingly, the task at hand is a Web application, Smooth Motion, that tests a user's coordination at manipulating a mouse. How smooth are you? The application will use event programming, including "mouse events," animation, controls, somewhat more sophisticated HTML, functions, iteration, indexing, and arrays. Smooth Motion is a generic application that allows us to focus on the problem-solving activity. By patiently following this fully explained case study, there will be opportunities to discuss when and how to apply the ideas you have learned.

The Smooth Motion Application

Step 0 in solving any problem is to understand what must be accomplished. (Almost everything in this chapter is 0-origin!) The Smooth Motion application is a coordination test. (Try Smooth Motion at pearsonhighered.com/snyder.) The graphical user interface is shown in Figure 21.1. Naming the components from top to bottom we have these parts:

- **Heading:** The text "Smooth Motion"
- **Grid:** The 7 × 20 grid of squares
- **Keys:** The row of seven orange/yellow boxes
- **Controls:** The buttons and radio settings
- **Instructions:** The text at the bottom

Further, the components are enclosed in a one-column, five-row table with a border and a colored background.

How the Smooth Motion Application Should Work

Smooth Motion works as follows. The application starts up automatically five seconds after it is loaded. It begins filling the grid from the right with stacks of blocks of random height. The blocks move steadily to the left at a rate determined by the controls.

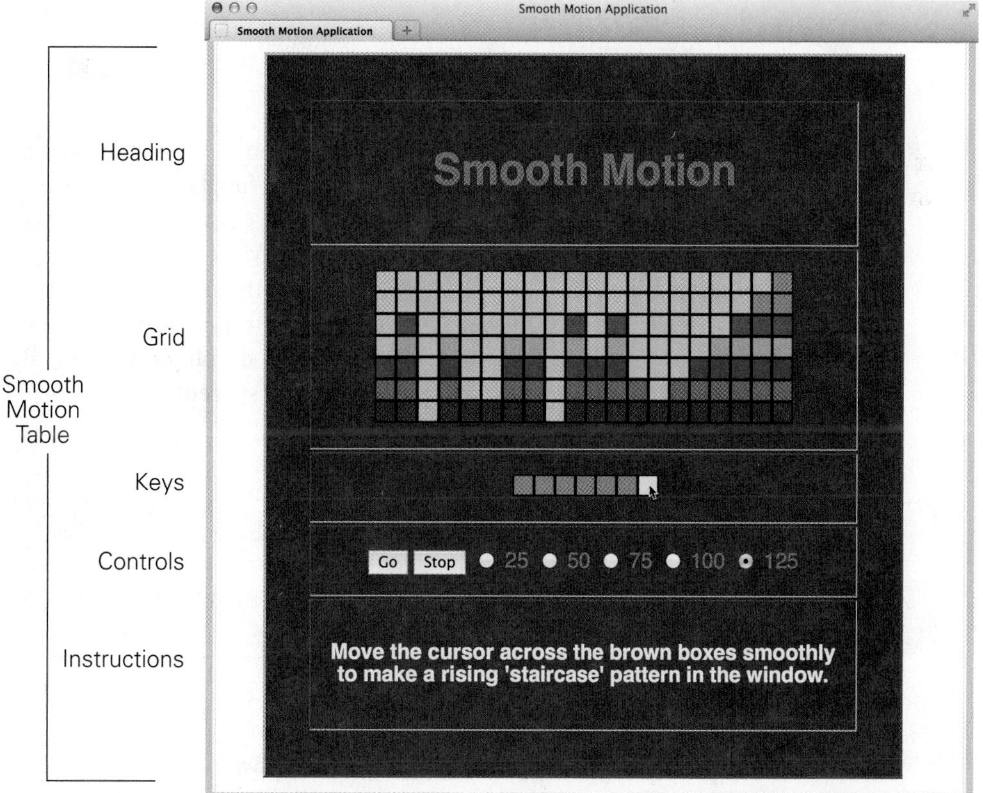

Figure 21.1 The Smooth Motion application user interface. Try it at pearsonhighered .com/snyder.

Examples of the random stacks of blocks are shown in the left side of the grid in Figure 21.1.

The random stack generation continues until the user places the mouse cursor over one of the orange keys. At that point, the user is in control of the stacks of blocks displayed in the grid. If we call the leftmost key, key 1, and the rightmost key, key 7, then when the mouse hovers over key *n*, a stack of *n* blocks appears in the grid. Figure 21.1 shows the mouse hovering over key 7.

The user's goal is to move the mouse across the orange keys as smoothly as possible. When the user has moved the mouse smoothly enough to create a perfect staircase rising to the right in the grid, the action stops. The process can be started or stopped at any point using the Go and Stop buttons. The speed selections are given in milliseconds (ms) and describe the rate at which the blocks move left. The test requires a smooth mouse motion across the keys from left to right at a rate corresponding to the frame rate of the grid animation.

Programming the Smooth Motion application is a substantial project, but surprisingly it requires only a modest amount of HTML and JavaScript.

Totally Immobile. Although the Web pages we've developed to this point work on both a laptop and a phone, Smooth Motion is an exception. It relies on hovering, and hovering needs a pointing device like a mouse or touchpad. So, we play with Smooth Motion when there's a mouse around. Like a cat.

Planning Smooth Motion

The goal is to design and construct the Smooth Motion application. Achieving such a goal entails a substantial design with several functions and some intricate logic. A complicating factor is that we have both timer events for the animation and mouse events for the controls happening simultaneously. Most of us would never succeed with such an effort by trying to "brain it out." The complications of the project would overwhelm us. Instead, we will succeed by approaching it in a methodical step-by-step way, applying a standard divide-and-conquer technique to simplify our work. By breaking the project into convenient, manageable pieces, we will succeed.

Smooth Move. How would you program Smooth Motion? Before reading about problem solving in this chapter, spend two minutes thinking about how you would create the Smooth Motion application. Truly, thinking about your own solution first will help you to understand the chapter more readily.

Apply the Decomposition Principle

A fundamental strategy for solving complex problems is the following principle.

Decomposition Principle: *Divide a large task into smaller subtasks that can be solved separately and then combine their solutions to produce the overall solution.*

Of course, the subtasks may not be small enough to be worked out easily, so the Decomposition Principle can be applied again to each of the subtasks, producing even smaller subtasks. Eventually the components become small enough that it is possible to figure out how to solve them directly. When the subtasks are all solved, we begin the assembly process, combining the most primitive components to produce the more complex components, and so on until the overall problem is solved. The Decomposition Principle is little more than common sense, but when applied judiciously, it is a powerful technique for achieving significant results.

List the Tasks

The Smooth Motion application has several parts that provide an obvious beginning point for applying the Decomposition Principle.

Task	Description
Build UI	Create a Web page with the table and its five parts: heading, grid, keys, controls, and instructions
Animate Grid	Move the block stacks to the left
Sense Keys	Handle the mouse events and transfer the control information to the grid animator
Detect Staircase	Recognize, when among a stream of events, the user has "met the test"
Build Controls	Implement the actions to control the application
Assemble Overall Design	Build the automatic random start-up, handle the starting and stopping, set the speeds, and interconnect the other components
Primp Design	Make the page attractive and functional

Only the Build UI task is simple enough to be solved directly, and even it is fancier than the other Web pages we've constructed so far. All of the other tasks will require further decomposition when we start to solve them.

Decide on a Problem-Solving Strategy

Decomposing the problem into tasks is step one in solving it. Step two is to strategize how to solve each of the parts. The strategy is concerned mostly with the order in which we'll solve the parts.

Build a Basic Web Page First. First, because JavaScript programming usually needs a Web page to host the computation, it makes sense to begin with the Build UI task rather than any of the others. This approach gives us a place to test and save the solutions to the other tasks. The page becomes an organizing structure, a location where we record our progress by adding our JavaScript code to it.

Total Waste. One pitfall to avoid in any JavaScript design is spending hours constructing a splashy Web page only to discover that it doesn't fit well with the solutions to the other tasks. Such a mistake won't happen here—this is a "textbook example," after all—but it is an error to avoid on your other projects.

So, we begin by building the host page, but to avoid wasting time on a splashy, but inappropriate page, we will build only the basic primitive page, and wait to embellish the design until after the parts are all working. Thus, we're splitting the UI construction into two parts.

Though our problem is too small to illustrate it, there is a problem-solving strategy that creates a working prototype first before completing the whole design. This strategy is smart because it is easier to add to an already-working primitive design. Our plan to focus on the basic Web page and leave the cosmetic features to the end is in the spirit of this approach.

Solve Independent Tasks Before Dependent Tasks. Deciding the order in which to solve the other tasks requires us to consider the **task dependencies**. That is, some tasks—for example, Detect Staircase—*rely on* or *depend on* the solution of other tasks, such as Sense Keys. Tasks that do not rely on the solution of any other tasks are *independent*, and should be done first. Tasks that depend on the independent tasks are done next, tasks that depend on them follow, and so on. Plan to schedule the tasks based on the rule: *Perform any task when all of the tasks it depends on are solved.* All of the tasks could be mutually dependent, though this is rare. In that case, the dependent tasks are started, pushed as far as possible until they absolutely need the results of another task, and then are interrupted to work on the other task. For us, Build UI is the independent task, and the Animate Grid task is dependent only on it. So, we'll schedule it second. Sense Keys is also dependent only on the UI, but it is easier to test when the Animate Grid task is completed. It will be our third task.

PERT Chart. Keeping track of many dependencies can be confusing, so systems engineers and managers draw a **task dependency graph**, or **PERT chart**. Standing for Program Evaluation and Review Technique, PERT charts were developed by the U.S. Navy in the 1950s.

There are several ways to draw them; we place tasks in circles and use arrows to show dependencies. In Figure 21.2 we have placed an arrow between two circles so that the task at the head of the arrow depends on the task at the tail of the arrow. In this (very common) form of a PERT chart, we begin with circles that have no incoming arrows. From any circle, the arrows show which tasks can be done next when the task in the circle is completed.

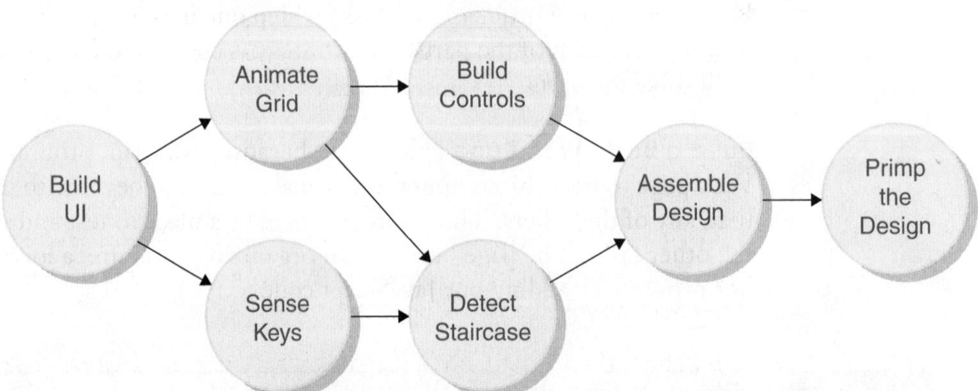

Figure 21.2 A task dependency diagram, also known as a PERT chart. Tasks are in circles and arrows are read as "task at head of arrow depends on task at tail of arrow."

Our strategy is to solve the tasks in this order:

1. *Build UI, to give us the basic Web page*
2. *Animate Grid, which is dependent only on the Build UI task*
3. *Sense Keys, which is dependent only on the Build UI task*
4. *Detect Staircase, which is dependent on Animate Grid and Sense Keys*
5. *Build Controls, which is dependent on Animate Grid*
6. *Assemble Overall Design, wrapping up those parts not yet complete*
7. *Primp Design, embellishing the Web page*

Usually each of these tasks would be further simplified using the Decomposition Principle until all of its subtasks were simple enough to solve directly. Doing so ensures that the decomposition has produced a practical solution. For our purposes, we will use a slightly different strategy, choosing instead to assign a section of this chapter to each task and to apply the Decomposition Principle at the start of the section.

Build the Basic Web Page UI

The full UI for Smooth Motion will have a table with constituent parts: heading, grid, keys, controls, and instructions. For now, we'll create the basic structure. We'll call this the *structural page*. The "basic" features include the table, heading, and instructions as well as the background color, font style and color, and the centering of the application on the page. We'll improve it later when the application is completely working.

The Structural Page

The structural page contains a five-row, one-column table; the text for the Smooth Motion heading and instructions are placed in the first and last rows. As you learned from making the Bean Counter application page in Chapter 18, it is easiest to build tables "inside out" using *Copy/Paste*. That is, we construct a generic table cell with <td> tags, replicate it to make a row that we enclose in <tr> tags, and then replicate the row to make the whole table, which we enclose in <table> tags. Then we fill it in. Because the present table has only one column, it's not necessary to replicate the cells to make a row for this situation. For us, the "generic" table cell is centered and contains a single blank character, that is, <td> </td>. The "basic" table has a border.

The Structural Page Heading

For the heading text, we use an <h1> heading, and for the instructions, we use a paragraph tag. Because the instructions text has a different text color than the other text on the page, we must set its font color.

The graphic and the HTML for the structural page definition are shown in Figure 21.3. Notice that the middle three rows of Figure 21.1 are empty in Figure 21.3 because they are white space. However, they are defined in the HTML, providing a site for our next programming step, the Animate Grid task.

```
<!doctype html>
<html>
  <head>
   <meta charset="UTF-8"/>
    <title>Smooth Motion Application</title>
    <style>
      body {background-color : white; color : #ff6600; font-family : helvetica;
            text-align : center}
      table {margin-left : auto; margin-right : auto; background-color : #a80000}
      p     {color:black;}
    </style>
  </head>
  <body>
    <table border="1">
      <tr><td>
        <h1>Smooth Motion</h1>
        </td></tr>
      <tr><td>
        </td></tr>
      <tr><td>
        </td></tr>
      <tr><td>
        </td></tr>
      <tr><td>
        <p><b>
        Move the cursor across the brown boxes smoothly <br/>
        to make a rising 'staircase' pattern in the window.</b>
        </p></td></tr>
    </table>
  </body>
</html>
```

Figure 21.3 Image and HTML for the structural page. The table appears compressed because rows 2–4 contain nothing. Remember, your browser image may be slightly different.

Animate the Grid

The Animate Grid task must animate the 7 × 20 = 140 grid of blocks moving from right to left. This task is much too complicated to solve directly, so we apply the Decomposition Principle again.

First Analysis

The Busy Animation of Chapter 20 illustrated the three basic steps of animation:

1. Define and place the initial image.
2. Prefetch the frames for updating the image.
3. Set a timer and build a timer event handler, which updates the image.

These are the starting decomposition steps for the Animate Grid task. But they don't fully solve the problem. We need to think and strategize further.

Frames for the Columns of Blocks. How will we organize the rapid redrawing of 140 images, keeping track of each block's trajectory? Reviewing how the application is supposed to work, we first notice that it only discusses "stacks" of blocks. This implies that there is no "motion" of images vertically, only horizontally. (This is obvious by the color scheme, too.) And, the horizontal motion is limited only to moving from right to left. From these observations, we can conclude that we don't have to animate individual squares at all. The images can be whole columns. That simplification reduces the total

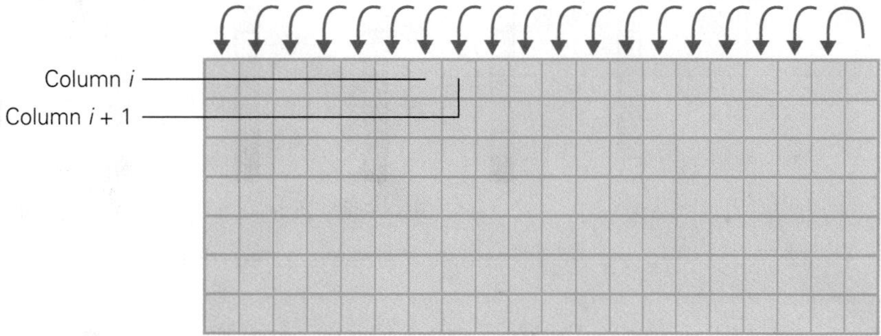

Figure 21.4 With column 0 at the left, the image in column i should be replaced by the image in column $i + 1$ to implement the left-moving motion for the Grid Animation event handler.

number of images in the grid to 20, that is, the number of columns. Of course, we will need a frame image for each stack of blocks: a 0-stack, a 1-stack, . . . , and a 7-stack, resulting in a total of eight frames. So, a new subtask to add to our list of three is to define and organize the column frames.

Indexing Columns Left to Right. Next we consider the "motion of an image." On each time step, a given column is replaced by the column to its right. If the 20 columns are indexed left to right, then the image in column i of the grid at a time step is replaced on the next time step by the image in column $i + 1$ (see Figure 21.4). The columns will be indexed from 0, left to right, because, as was mentioned in Chapter 20, when browsers place images on a page, they record them in the array `document.images` in the order encountered; that order is the construction sequence of an HTML page, left to right, top to bottom. So, the leftmost column of the grid is `document.images[0]`. The action replaces the contents of `document.images[i]` with the contents of `document.images[i+1]`. Shifting each column to the left is quite easy, and it leaves only the last column to be handled differently.

Handling column 19 (the last column) is also easy because we only need to assign a new image—that is, one of the eight frames. Which frame do we assign? If we are in the random start-up phase, it should be a random frame. If we are in the user-controlled phase, it should be whichever frame the user has specified by the mouse position, if any. We will leave this choice of the frame open for the time being, because the Assemble Overall Design task will set the frame selection properly.

Second Analysis

From our first analysis, it seems that we should add subtasks for defining an image-shifting process and for defining a column-19 fill process, but it's not necessary. Both activities will be part of the timer event handler, which is already on our list. So, our subtask list for the Animate Grid task has increased by only one item:

1. Define and organize the eight columnar frames.
2. Define and place the initial images, 0 through 19.
3. Prefetch the eight frames for updating the image.
4. Set a timer with an event handler that shifts the images in columns 1 through 19 to columns 0 through 18, respectively, and introduce a new frame into column 19.

We'll assign a subsection to each subtask.

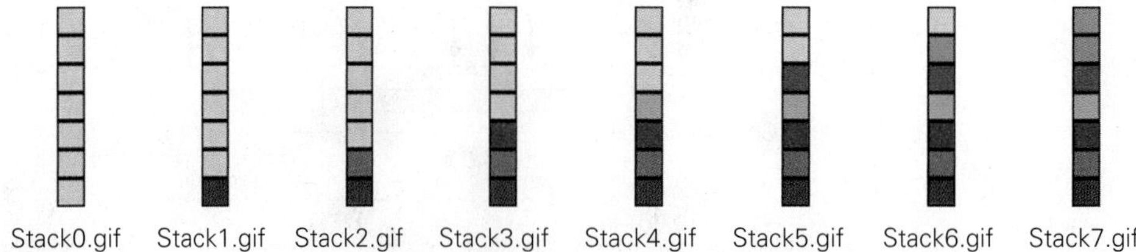

Figure 21.5 The eight frames required for the Smooth Motion application.

Subtask: Define and Organize the Frames

The eight frames for the Smooth Motion application are shown in Figure 21.5. The files are available online (pearsonhighered.com/snyder) so we don't need to create them here. Notice that they have names indexed in accordance with the block height. Also, the images have the necessary colors and lines that will be placed densely side-by-side to construct the grid.

If the gif frames had not been available, we would have had to create them. Numerous tools are available for this purpose, from simple paint programs to sophisticated image editing facilities. Though the tools vary in capabilities, convenience, and sophistication, there are only two guidelines to follow when creating frame images for JavaScript animations:

1. Ensure that all images overwriting one another have the same dimensions in pixels. An easy way to meet this constraint is to create an initial "blank" frame instance, save it, and use it as the base for creating all of the other frame instances.
2. Ensure that all files are saved using either the .gif or .jpg formats, and that they are used consistently; that is, only overwrite .gifs with .gifs.

To use images in HTML, it is recommended that they be placed in a separate folder, simply as an organizing technique (see the discussion in Chapter 3). Following that advice, the stack gifs in Figure 21.5 are saved in a folder called gifpix, meaning that their names relative to the HTML file are gifpix/Stack0.gif, gifpix/Stack1.gif, and so on.

Subtask: Define and Place Initial Images

This subtask constructs the grid in the second row of the structural page (see Figure 21.3). The initial state of the grid is created from 20 copies of Stack0.gif. As usual, to place an image on a page, we use the <img src=". . . "/> tag. But the 20 images will require 20 such tags, which calls for a loop. To use JavaScript's for statement, we place the <script> tags inside of the second row's <td> tags, and within them we write the necessary JavaScript. To have the images appear on the structural page, we must place them using the document.write() function.

The iteration can use the World-Famous Iteration form and must declare an iteration variable. The necessary code to implement these objectives is

```
<tr><td>
  <script>
      for (var j = 0; j < 20; j++){                    //Place grid imgs
         document.write('<img src="gifpix/Stack0.gif" alt=" "/>');
      }
  </script>
  </td></tr>
```

which completes the image initialization. (Notice that the alt tag is left blank because these images will be overwritten.)

Subtask: Prefetch the Frame Images

As explained in Chapter 20, animating with images fetched from across the Internet is not likely to work well because of delays that the .gif files might encounter during transfer. So, prefetching is necessary, and it is the goal of this subtask. (Review prefetching from the Busy Animation of Chapter 20, if necessary.)

Relative to the creation of the Web page, the prefetching activity can be performed at any time prior to the start of the animation. Because the prefetching also requires JavaScript code, we decide to place it with the code from the initialization subtask just completed, say, after the declaration. This is a good location because to prefetch the frames, we need an eight-element image array to prefetch into, and so we need another declaration for that array.

The three steps of prefetching are as follows:

1. Declare the array into which the images will be fetched.
2. Initialize the array elements to be image objects; that is, define the image structure for each array element using the new Image( ) specification.
3. Assign the names of the files to the src fields of the image objects, causing the browser to record the names and get the files, thus implementing the prefetch.

The file names are those given in Figure 21.5. We call the array pics, and use a separate iteration for the second and third tasks, though combining the two operations into a single iteration is equivalent. The resulting code is inserted in <script> tags in the head section of the page. Notice that the file names are constructed on-the-fly to save us from typing separate statements.

```
var pics = new Array(8);                //Prefetch array
for (var j = 0; j < 8; j++) {           //Initial img array
  pics[j] = new Image();
}
for (var j = 0; j < 8; j++) {           //Prefetch images
  pics[j].src = "gifpix/Stack" + j + ".gif";
}
```

21.1 Pharaoh's Pyramid. Using the idea of "building the name" for a file using concatenation, write two for loops that together would display the files of Figure 21.5 as the pyramid shown.

Subtask: Set Timer and Build Timer Event Handler

This subtask is mostly concerned with writing the event handler to move each of the grid's images one position left, obliterating the 0 image and assigning a new image to position 19. So we begin by constructing that event handler, called animate( ). As we work on it, several additional details arise that require our attention.

The timer event handler animate( ) has three operations:

1. To move all images but the first, one position left
2. To assign a new frame to image 19
3. To schedule itself for some time in the future

The mechanism for choosing the new frame is not yet worked out, but the Assemble Overall Design task will resolve it. For the moment, we simply assign a random frame as an easy way to have something different happening on each tick. And, assigning random frames is the way the application is to begin anyway.

Recall that browsers store the details of the images they display in an array called images in the DOM, that the array is referenced as document.images, and that the source field, src, is the relevant one to change if we want to display a new image. We use document .images and we program the three steps of the animate( ) function as

```
function animate() {                                      //Animate
   for (j = 0; j < 19; j++) {                             //Shift images L
      document.images[j].src = document.images[j+1].src;
   }
   document.images[19].src = pics[randNum(8)].src;  //Place random img
   timerId = setTimeout("animate()", duration);           //Set timer for next
}
function randNum (range) {                                //Rand No. picks
   return Math.floor( range * Math.random( ));            // nums from range
}
```

We have used the randNum( ) function developed in Chapter 19, so we must include its declaration in order to reuse it. Also, we added a variable duration to the accumulating list of declarations:

```
var duration = 125;
```

To get the process started automatically after five seconds, we include the additional statement before the function definitions

```
timerId = setTimeout("animate( )", 5000);
```

which sets the animate() function to be run 5,000 ms after the browser starts. As with the Busy Animation, we save the handle received from the setTimeout function in a variable timerId (it must be declared!) so that the animation can be stopped. And, with that code, the Set Timer subtask is finished, completing the Animate Grid task. Figure 21.6 shows the state of the structural page at this point.

The Best Laid Plans . . .

The next step in our task decomposition strategy is to solve key sensing. However, now that we have the grid animation worked out, we find it cumbersome not to be able to start and stop the animation on demand. It would be very helpful to have the controls available to stop the animation so that we don't have to kill the browser window each time to do so. But the Build Controls task is planned for later. Perhaps it makes more sense to solve it now to simplify our work. As Robert Burns noted, plans don't always work out, no matter how hard we try. (Burns put it more poetically: *The best laid schemes o' mice and men gang aft agley.*) Adjusting the order of tasks is very typical of large

```
  <script>
   var duration = 125, timerId;                  //vars
   timerId = setTimeout("animate()", 5000); //Initial timer
   var pics = new Array(8);                      //Prefetch array
   for (var j = 0; j < 8; j++){                  //Initial img array
     pics[j] = new Image();
   }
   for (var j = 0; j < 8; j++){                 //Prefetch images
     pics[j].src = "gifpix/Stack" + j + ".gif";
   }
   function animate() {                                      //Animate
     for (j = 0; j < 19; j++){                               //Shift images L
       document.images[j].src = document.images[j+1].src;
     }
     document.images[19].src = pics[randNum(8)].src;  //Place random img
     timerId = setTimeout("animate()", duration);        //Set timer for next
   }
   function randNum (range) {                               //Rand No. picks
     return Math.floor( range * Math.random( ));           // nums from range
   }
  </script>
 </head>
 <body>
  <table border="1">
   <tr><td><h1>Smooth Motion</h1></td></tr>
   <tr><td>
     <script>
          for (var j = 0; j < 20; j++){                 //Place grid imgs
            document.write('<img src="gifpix/Stack0.gif" alt=" "/>');
          }
     </script>
     </td></tr>
   <tr><td></td></tr>
   <tr><td></td></tr>
   <tr><td>
     <p style="color : black"><b>
     Move the cursor across the brown boxes smoothly <br/>
     to make a rising 'staircase' pattern in the window.</b>
     </p></td></tr>
  </table>
 </body>
</html>
```

Figure 21.6 HTML, JavaScript, and image for the table of the Smooth Motion implementation after the completion of the Animate Grid task.

projects because it isn't always possible to determine ahead of time all of the relevant interactions. So, we proceed to the Build Controls task.

Build Controls

Inspecting the UI in Figure 21.1, we see that the controls entry of the table contains seven input controls. Thus, the fourth row of the table must contain <form> tags so that we can specify the controls. (Chapters 19 and 20 covered <form> tags.) The only challenge is how to handle the click-events. As always, we ask, "What should happen when the control is clicked?" There are three scenarios:

1. **Go button click-event.** Start the animation with setTimeout( ), keeping track of the handle.
2. **Stop button click-event.** End the animation by clearing the timer using the handle.
3. **Radio button click-event.** Set the timer interval by assigning to duration.

None of these activities is more than a single statement, so rather than creating functions for the event handlers, we simply place the code as the input control onclick value.

```
<tr> <td>
  <form>
    <input type="button" value="Go"
      onclick='timerId=setTimeout("animate()",duration)'/>
    <input type="button" value="Stop"
      onclick="clearTimeout(timerId)"/>
    <input type="radio" name="speed" onclick="duration=25"/> 25
    <input type="radio" name="speed" onclick="duration=50"/> 50
    <input type="radio" name="speed" onclick="duration=75"/> 75
    <input type="radio" name="speed" onclick="duration=100"/> 100
    <input type="radio" name="speed"
      onclick="duration=125" checked="checked"/> 125
  </form>
</td></tr>
```

Notice that the last button is checked to indicate that duration ⇔ 125 is the default. We place the code in the fourth row of the structural page table.

Easily Repeated. We could have used a for loop to place the radio buttons, though only the first four have the consistent structure suitable for a loop. Looping would require <script> tags, document.write, and so on. With so few repetitions, it's simpler to use *Copy/Paste/Edit* rather than a loop.

Having completed the Build Controls task, we can start and stop the animation. "We now return to our originally scheduled program."

Sense the Keys

The Sense Keys task implements the ability to recognize when the mouse hovers over a given key. The task requires us to understand how mouse motions are sensed, a topic that has not yet been introduced. But, it's typical when solving a large problem not to know the details of every activity and to have to learn a new concept, system, or operation to solve the task. That's our situation with respect to sensing mouse motions. So, before attempting the task decomposition, we learn about mouse motions.

Actually, sensing mouse motions is very easy. Browsers recognize events on the objects of a Web page, such as images, just as they recognize events caused by controls. For example, if we click an image, we cause a click-event, which we can process with an event handler. We specify the event handler by using the onclick attribute of the image tag, as in <img src=". . . " onclick= "doSomething( )"/>. This enables a mouse click on an image of a Web page to be recognized.

The browser, with the help of the operating system, keeps track of where the mouse pointer is at any moment. (After all, it's the operating system that is drawing the mouse pointer in the first place.) When the mouse pointer moves over an image or other Web page object, a *mouseover* event is recognized. When the mouse pointer moves off of the object, a *mouseout* event is recognized. We need these two events to follow the mouse cursor across the Smooth Motion keys. The keys are images, so we write an event handler for each of the two mouse events. We specify them to the browser with the onmouseover and onmouseout event handler specifications in the <img src=". . . "/> tag placing the key's image.

With that information, we can decompose the Sense Keys task by asking, "How should key sensing work?" First, we notice that there are no keys yet (see Figure 21.6), so we have to define them. Second, after thinking about their operation—they change their color from orange to yellow on *mouseover* and then change back to orange on *mouseout*—it's clear that the keys are effectively another animation. The difference between other animations we've written and the keys' animation is that the former are updated by a timer, whereas the latter are updated by mouse motions. This observation is a tremendous help in our planning, because we have solved animation problems before. So, we begin our problem decomposition with the standard animation decomposition used for the Animate Grid task:

1. Define and organize the necessary frames.
2. Place the initial images and create the keys.
3. Prefetch the frames.
4. Build the event handlers.

This is a sufficient strategy to solve the problem.

Subtask: Define and Organize the Frames

The first subtask involves only two images, ■ and □. They are named OrangeBox.gif and YellowBox.gif and are stored in the gifpix directory with the Stack images. Moving the files to that directory completes the first subtask.

Subtask: Place the Initial Images

Placing the images creates the keys. Seven images will be placed in the center of the third row of the structural page's table. They are all OrangeBox.gif. As before, we write a JavaScript loop to iterate the document.write of the <img src=". . . "/> tags. The resulting code, which is still incomplete—but will be fixed momentarily—is

```
for (var j = 0; j < 7; j++) {
   document.write('<img src="gifpix/OrangeBox.gif" alt=" "/>'); //Incomplete
}
```

This completes the placement subtask for the time being.

Subtask: Prefetch the Frames

Prefetching the frames is also completely analogous to our earlier animations, and by now its three-subtask sequence is becoming familiar. There are only two frames to prefetch, leading to the declaration of a small array, code for image initialization, and prefetching, because it isn't worth writing loops. These lines complete the prefetch subtask.

```
var keypix = new Array(2);
keypix[0] = new Image();
keypix[1] = new Image();
keypix[0].src = "gifpix/OrangeBox.gif";
keypix[1].src = "gifpix/YellowBox.gif";
```

Subtask: Build the Event Handlers

Finally, we build the two event handlers, here( ) for mouseover and gone( ) for mouseout. They're not difficult to build.

As with any event handler, we ask, "What should happen when the mouse moves over a key?" First, the key must change color to give feedback to the user that the mouse is on or off the key. This involves simply updating the key's image with the YellowBox.gif or the OrangeBox.gif image. But how do we refer to the key's image? We know that it is listed in the images array that the browser keeps of the images on the page. Because the keys come *after* the grid, the key images are obviously stored in the array *after* the grid images. The grid images are images[0], . . . , images[19], so by the preceding loop, the keys must be images[20], . . . , images[26]. Of course, if we know the position of the key, say, pos, we can refer to the image as images[20+pos]. We conclude that we need to record the position of each key in the sequence.

Next, the mouse-sensing event handlers must tell the Grid Animation event handler which new Stack image to draw in the last position of the grid. All that event handler needs is the key's position, so if we assign it to a global variable, say, frame, we've done the job. These observations lead us to declare a variable frame and to define the two mouse event handlers.

```
function here (pos) {
   document.images[20+pos].src = "gifpix/YellowBox.gif";
   frame = pos + 1;
}
function gone (pos) {
   document.images[20+pos].src = "gifpix/OrangeBox.gif";
   frame = 0;
}
```

We have made the key's position a parameter.

Notice how here( ) solves a problem of mismatched indices. The keys are 0-origin indexed (that is, 0, 1, . . . , 6); pos will have one of these values. The stacks of blocks are 1-origin indexed (that is, Stack1.gif, Stack2.gif, . . . , Stack7.gif); frame should have one of these values. Thus, the mouse over key[0] means draw Stack1.gif. The here( ) function makes up for this mismatch with the assignment

```
frame = pos + 1;
```

Also, notice that for gone( ), we don't know where the mouse is moving to. It could be moving to another key, or it could be moving off the keys entirely, which should draw the Stack0.gif. The safe thing is to set frame = 0. If the mouse moves to another key, its mouseover event handler will be called immediately, setting frame to the right number.

21.2 Quick Mouse. When the mouse moves over the rightmost sense key image, the function here() will be called. (a) What is the value of pos for that call? (b) What is the index of the element in the document.images array that is changed? (c) What is the name of the image that should be displayed in document.images[19] as a result of the call?

```
<script>
  var keypix = new Array(2);
  keypix[0] = new Image();
  keypix[1] = new Image();
  keypix[0].src = "gifpix/OrangeBox.gif";
  keypix[1].src = "gifpix/YellowBox.gif";
  for (var j = 0; j < 7; j++) {
    document.write('<img src="gifpix/OrangeBox.gif" ' +
    'onmouseover = "here(' + j + ')" ' +
    'onmouseout = "gone(' + j + ')" alt=" "/>');
  }
</script>
```

Figure 21.7 JavaScript for the Sense Keys task (the two declarations and the two event handlers are not shown).

Combine the Subtasks

With the two mouse event handlers defined, we return to the image initialization subtask to add the event handler specifications to the <img src=". . . "/> tags. The revised and final form of the initialization is

```
for (var j = 0; j < 7; j++) {
  document.write('<img src="gifpix/OrangeBox.gif" ' +
  'onmouseover = "here(' + j + ')" ' +
  'onmouseout = "gone(' + j + ')" alt=" "/>');
}
```

The two mouse event handler functions have their position parameters specified by the for loop's iteration variable j. To test the Sense Keys task solution, we make one tiny change in the Grid Animation event handler, animate( ), namely, to change the frame assigned to the last column from the random choice to the frame variable. The new line has the form

```
document.images[19].src = pics[frame].src;
```

allowing us to test the code.

Having completed the Sense Keys task, Figure 21.7 shows the code entered into the structural page in the third row. (The two declarations—keypix and frame—are included with the earlier declarations, and the event handling functions are included with the previously defined functions.)

Staircase Detection

When the user has manipulated the mouse in such a way as to create a rising "staircase" of blocks in the grid, the animation should stop. How do we recognize the "staircase"? It's not possible to look at the grid, of course, so we must identify it by other characteristics. Observe that the user will have created a staircase when the frame values for seven consecutive animate( ) calls are 1, 2, 3, 4, 5, 6, 7.

This is true because the value of frame tells the animate( ) event handler which Stack frame to display, and if it is directed to display the seven frames in order on seven consecutive ticks, there will be a staircase in the grid.

Subtask: Recognizing the Staircase

How do we recognize the seven consecutive frame values? There are many techniques. Some involve keeping an array of the seven most recent frame values and checking each time to see if the desired sequence occurs. Another involves looking at the src fields in the last seven images of the grid—it's almost like looking at the picture—to see if they have the right sequence of file names. But the technique we will employ requires slightly less programming and seems cleverer. The idea is to keep predicting the next frame value.

Subtask: Recognizing Continuity

Notice that we are trying to recognize continuity across a sequence of events, that is, seven events in which the value for frame is 1, 2, 3, 4, 5, 6, 7. By analogy, imagine you are sitting at a bus stop trying to determine if seven consecutive buses ever pass by with the last digit of their license numbers making the sequence 1 through 7. But you have no paper to write down the data and your memory isn't so good. You have exactly seven coins—your bus fare—so you put one coin in your left pocket. That's a prediction that the next bus has a license ending in 1.

As a bus arrives, you check to see if the last digit of its license plate is equal to the number of coins in your left pocket. If so, and you still have coins, you add another coin to your left pocket. This is the next prediction. If not, you put all the coins but one back in your right pocket. If you ever try to add a coin but have run out, it happened! What you are doing with the coins in your left pocket is predicting the number on the next bus's license plate. If the prediction is right, you make the next prediction by adding another coin; but if not, you start back with 1. It's an easy way to keep track of the continuity of a series of events.

Implementing the bus analogy, we modify the animate( ) function at the point where it is about to set the timer for the next tick, because if the staircase is found, there should be no next tick. Additionally, we'll declare another variable, next1, that corresponds to the coins in your left pocket, that is, as if predicting an event. The following code implements the steps of this process.

```
if (frame == next1)                                  //Correct prediction?
   next1 = next1 + 1;                                //Yes, make another
else                                                 //No
   next1 = 1;                                        //Go back to start
if (next1 != 8)                                      //Are we still looking?
   timerId = setTimeout("animate( )",duration); //Yes, set timer
```

Notice that the test in the last if statement compares to 8 rather than 7 because next1 was incremented previously, and so the condition of "no more coins left" is equivalent to next1 ⇔ 8. With that addition to animate( ) we have completed the Detect Staircase task.

Assemble Overall Design

With the Build Controls task performed out of order and parts of the Assemble Overall Design task performed ahead of time, there is not much left to do to complete the programming of the Smooth Motion application. Nevertheless, this is the point at which we make sure that the whole application works as planned.

Reviewing the description at the start of the chapter, we notice that the display of randomly selected stacks of blocks isn't presently working. Originally we generated random stacks when we solved the Animate Grid task. But we took that feature out to test the keys. Now we want to put it back in.

Basically we should set image 19 to frame or randNum(8), depending on whether or not the user has ever passed the mouse over a key. How will we know? The mouseover event handlers will recognize the situation, but at the moment they are programmed only to return a frame value from 1 through 7. So, if we started out with frame initialized to some erroneous number, say, –1, and test it in the animate( ) event handler before using the frame value, we could recognize the two situations: –1 means the mouse has not yet passed over the keys the first time; anything else means the mouse has passed over the keys the first time. Thus, we must change frame in its declaration to initialize it to –1 and rewrite the assignment to the last column of the grid one more time:

```
if (frame == -1)
   document.images[19].src = pics[randNum(8)].src;
else
   document.images[19].src = pics[frame].src;
```

This last change to animate( ) makes it quite cluttered with if statements. The clutter obscures the simple two-part logic of shifting the grid and checking for the staircase. So, we relegate both operations to functions. The resulting solution, as shown in Figure 21.8, is no shorter—in fact, it is longer by four lines—but it makes the important animate( ) event handler clearer, making the exercise worthwhile.

After checking the operation of the Smooth Motion application, it seems that we've taken care of all of the design elements, except the fancy UI, which is the last remaining task.

```
function animate() {
   shiftGrid ()
   checkStairAndContinue ();
}
function shiftGrid() {
   for (var j = 0; j < 19; j++) {
      document.images[j].src = document.images[j+1].src;
   }
   if (frame == -1)
      document.images[19].src = pics[randNum(8)].src;
   else
      document.images[19].src = pics[frame].src;
}
function checkStairAndContinue() {
   if (frame == next1)                          //Correct prediction?
      next1 = next1 + 1;                        //Yes, make another
   else                                         //No
      next1 = 1;                                //Go back to start
   if (next1 != 8)                              //Are we still looking?
      timerId = setTimeout("animate( )",duration); //Yes, set timer
}
```

Figure 21.8 Revision of the function animate() to encapsulate portions of the computation into functions.

Primp the Design

The structural page we've built our application around can be made more attractive. In fact, the task of improving the aesthetics of a Web page is probably an unending task. We recognize the following improvements that will produce the page shown in Figure 21.1:

- Cell padding
- Revised instruction colors

Cell padding seems essential because the design is very dense. It would be more inviting with more space. To get the space we need, we need to add styling to both the table element and the table data element td. The two enhancements are:

```
table {margin-left : auto; margin-right : auto; background-color : #a80000;
       padding : 5%}
td    {padding : 15px}
```

Notice that we specify the amount of the padding in two different ways.

Changing the instruction colors so they are somewhat more easily read, but not "in your face" requires mostly that we decide what that color is. Changing it is a one-word modification; the color used in Figure 21.1 is tan.

Assessment and Retrospective

When we are asked to design a solution to someone else's problem, we are usually finished when we verify that we've done what we've been asked to do. If the design is to achieve a goal of our own choice, however, an assessment step remains. When we pick a goal, we usually do not have a fixed target like Figure 21.1 to work toward. Rather, we design a solution to our original "best guess"; then we consider whether the result is the best possible solution. (We have used such an assessment in Chapter 18.) Generally, having a working solution suggests many worthwhile improvements.

In this chapter, the first case applies, and so we are finished. Instead of an assessment, let's consider the ideas from earlier chapters applied in this chapter. There are three primary topics:

1. Loops
2. Parameterizing functions for reuse
3. Managing complexity with functions

Applying these ideas has produced a better program. Consider how.

Loops. The Smooth Motion application used several for loops. These saved us from tedious activities like writing 20 <img src=". . . "/> statements in a row. Such loops simplified the programming. But at times, when we might have used loops, we chose not to. For example, we explicitly wrote the instructions for defining the radio buttons and for prefetching the key images. We used *Copy*, *Paste*, and *Edit* commands rather than a loop, because it was easier to program. Had there been more iterations, or had the specification been slightly simpler, we might have used a loop. The computer does the same work either way; we decide which method is more convenient.

Parameterizing Functions for Reuse. The here( ) and gone( ) functions each use a single parameter that is the position of the key in sequence. The argument is passed to the functions in the event handler specifications. For example, the third key from the left was defined by a document.write that produces

```
<img src="gifpix/OrangeBox.gif"
      onmouseover="here(2)" onmouseout="gone(2)" alt=" "/>
```

where the "2" indicates the key's 0-origin number. The parameter customizes the event handler for each key. We could have written separate functions in which the key's position is used explicitly everywhere pos occurs, but this would create a proliferation of almost-identical functions. The parameter says where and how the event handlers differ from each other, and their use produces a more abstract—and easier to understand—solution.

Managing Complexity with Functions. The functions shiftGrid( ) and checkStairAndContinue( ) shown in Figure 21.8 are examples of creating functions to manage complexity. Both functions "package" program logic allowing us to *name them* and *move them* out of the way, revealing the simple two-part logic of the animate( ) function.

```
function animate() {
   shiftGrid ()
   checkStairAndContinue ();
}
```

As with loops and parameters, functions clarify to humans how the animation function works; it's all the same to the computer. Humans will see our choice of function names—for example, shiftGrid()—and correctly interpret them as describing what the function does. If people need to know how the program shifts the grid, they can check the function; otherwise, it's out of the way, replaced by a succinct statement of what it does (its name). This role of shifting the grid might have been expressed as a comment at the start of the code sequence, but comments are often overlooked. The abstraction—naming the function and giving its definition—creates a new concept in our minds, raising our level of understanding of Smooth Motion's animation process. Though these two functions will never be used again, the goal of simplifying the program justifies our effort to define them. See Appendix G for a complete listing of the Smooth Motion application.

Thus, we see that programming is as much about teaching viewers of our program how we solved the problem as it is about instructing the computer. Even for programs that are not "textbook" examples, helping humans understand programs is essential. It helps with debugging—an important concern for us—and by organizing the solution in an understandable way, and instills confidence in others about the correctness of our solution.

SUMMARY

We have programmed a substantial application that would have been too complicated to achieve directly. To succeed, we applied the Decomposition Principle, first to create the high-level tasks that guided our overall solution, and then again, when it came time to solve the tasks that were still too complicated. Though it is mostly common sense, the Decomposition Principle provides a strategy that works to solve all difficult programming problems. To solve the problem at hand we did the following:

- Defined the tasks and strategized about the order in which to solve them. Because there were dependencies among the tasks, we defined a feasible plan to solve them.
- Used a dependency diagram to show which tasks depended on others and to assist us in strategizing. We planned an order consistent with the diagram—that is, no task was scheduled ahead of the tasks it depended on—and produced a workable plan.
- Considered other features, such as ease of testing, and adjusted the schedule to address these aspects.
- Developed the actual solution of the Smooth Motion program directly. We decomposed each task into several subtasks. There was similarity among these subtasks. For example, the timer-driven animation and the key-driven animation used a similar set of subtasks.
- Decided to solve the tasks out of order from our original schedule, to give ourselves the ability to start and stop the animation. Convenience motivated us to depart from our original schedule. Originally it was not possible to predict the benefits of the alternative plan.
- Learned about mouse events, a topic we had not previously encountered. This was not a difficult concept to grasp, but it illustrated a common feature of any large task—that it is often necessary to learn new information to solve a complex problem.
- Used the programming facilities covered in earlier chapters—loops, functions, parameters, and so on—as tools to instruct both the computer and humans looking at the program. Those facilities clarified the program, making it plain how the problem was solved.
- Developed an IT application with techniques that have wide application. You can expect to use decomposition in other problem solving, to abstract the components of a solution by giving them names and precise definitions, and to reduce the complexity of a solution to an understandable level.
- Learned powerful problem-solving techniques.

TRY IT SOLUTIONS

21.1

```
for (var i = 0; i < 8; i++) {
  document.write('<img src="gifpix/Stack' + i + '.gif"/>');
}
for (var i = 0; i < 7; i++) {
  document.write('<img src="gifpix/Stack' + (6-i) + '.gif"/>');
}
```

21.2 (a) The value of `pos` for that call is 6, because the 7 sense keys are indexed 0 to 6, and the rightmost key is the last one. (b) The element in `document.images` that is changed is 26, because 20 + 6 = 26. (c) The image displayed—the frame—is `Stack7.gif`, because the images containing more than 0 blocks are indexed 1 through 7.

Multiple Choice

1. Solving subtasks of a large task and then combining subtasks into an overall solution is known as
   a. Problem-Solving Strategy
   b. Decomposition Principle
   c. JavaScript Operations
   d. Smooth Motion
2. You should make sure all the parts of your app are working before
   a. using the Decomposition Principle
   b. writing the JavaScript part of the app
   c. making the design look better
   d. building the functions
3. The Build Controls task is dependent on
   a. Assemble Overall Design
   b. Detect Staircase
   c. Sense Keys
   d. Animate Grid
4. Before the Animate Grid task can be completed, the
   a. Build Controls task must be completed
   b. Detect Staircase task must be completed
   c. Build UI task must be completed
   d. Sense Keys task must be completed
5. The Detect Staircase task is not dependent on
   a. Build Controls
   b. Sense Keys
   c. Animate Grid
   d. Build UI
6. Prefetching images requires what kind of code?
   a. HTML
   b. JavaScript
   c. DOM
   d. special
7. To use a graphic that has been prefetched
   a. the `href` command must be used
   b. the `src` command must be used
   c. a specific image must be placed in a specific location
   d. none of the above
8. To get the browser to delay 5 seconds, you need to set the `setTimeout` function to
   a. `5`
   b. `500`
   c. `5000`
   d. `.5`

9. It is worthwhile to write a loop to do a repetitive task when there are
   a. 2 or more tasks
   b. more than 3–5 tasks
   c. more than 8–10 tasks
   d. 20 or more tasks
10. A meaningful name for a function
   a. makes the code easier to read
   b. raises the level of understanding for those who read the code
   c. means as much to the computer as a meaningless name
   d. all of the above

Short Answer

1. The _______ is used to break a task into smaller, easy-to-solve tasks.
2. _______ are the relationships between tasks that determine the order in which the tasks in a program are solved.
3. When solving a problem, the _______ should be solved first.
4. A(n) _______ can be used to visually keep track of which tasks depend on another.
5. The _______ task must be completed before the Sense Keys task can be completed.
6. An array called _______ is where a browser stores information about the images on a page.
7. In the Smooth Motion app both _______ and _______ are happening simultaneously.
8. The function used for timing JavaScript events on the computer is called _______.
9. State one function that was reused in the Smooth Motion app from a previous chapter: _______.

Exercises

1. Describe the Decomposition Principle.
2. Apply the Decomposition Principle to cooking a meal.
3. Create a PERT chart for Exercise 2.
4. List the dependent tasks and the independent tasks for cooking a meal.
5. Write code that places 6 images of size 20px × 20px in a 3 × 2 table.
6. Explain why it's a good idea to create the UI early in the process, and finalize it at the end of the process.
7. What is the advantage of prefetching images for an animation?
8. How would you modify the Smooth Motion code to keep track of how long the user took to solve the problem, and display it at the end?
9. Explain how the onmouseover and onmouseout events work.

CHAPTER 22

Limits to Computation

Computers Can Do Almost {❑ Everything, ❑ Nothing}

learning objectives

- Explain what the Turing test was designed to show
- Discuss the issue of a computer being intelligent and able to think; refer to Deep Blue and Watson
- Discuss the issue of computer creativity; refer to computer-generated music and art
- State the meaning of the Universality Principle
- Describe the way in which the amount of work in a program is related to the speed of the program

CHAPTER 22

The real danger is not that computers will begin to think like men, but that men will begin to think like computers.

—SYDNEY J HARRIS

Artificial Intelligence is no match for natural stupidity.

—ANONYMOUS

Some people worry that artificial intelligence will make us feel inferior, but then, anybody in his right mind should have an inferiority complex every time he looks at a flower.

—ALAN KAY

COMPUTERS have achieved sustained speeds of well over 1,000 trillion additions per second. On a pocket calculator, at one operation per second, it takes 1,000 lifetimes (assuming 60 years of daily calculating for 14 hours each day) to perform 1 trillion operations. But so what? Everyone knows computers are amazingly fast at arithmetic. Shouldn't we be more impressed if a computer ever had an original thought, no matter how trivial? Absolutely! But it probably won't happen. As you have learned, for a computer to do anything, it must be programmed to do it, and so far "thought" in the sense we usually mean the term has eluded researchers. So, we have a curious situation. Computers can be truly awesome at some tasks and completely hopeless at others. Because they're so different from humans, it's reasonable to wonder what computers can and cannot do.

This chapter addresses philosophical issues. First, we ask whether a computer can think. Thinking about thinking leads us to the famous Turing test. Chess—a game requiring smarts—became a *de facto* goal of artificial intelligence (AI) research. We explore how computers play chess, summarize the advancements, and report the victory of Deep Blue. In 2011, the AI program Watson won *Jeopardy!* against the best players of all time, and we'll discuss that achievement. We also speculate on how creative computers can be. Next, we consider the easy-to-understand but significant idea—the Universality Principle—that asks how different computers can be. Any "new and improved" computer will be faster or larger, but not more capable. How important is more speed? We explore how fast computers can solve various problems by revisiting algorithms from Chapter 10. Finally, there are problems that cannot be solved by a computer even in principle, not because they are too nebulous to specify for a computer, but because to do so would be a contradiction.

Can Computers Think?

The inventors of electronic computers thought that they were discovering how to "think with electricity." And to the extent that operations like addition and multiplication require humans to think, it's easy to see their point. Previously, electricity had been used directly as an energy source for driving motors and powering light bulbs. With the digital computer, electricity switched complex circuits, implementing logical operations. The power was applied to manipulate information. The phenomenon was truly new.

Today, electronic devices that manipulate information are so common, we are less impressed by them. It is difficult to regard a calculator as "thinking." But our view of what constitutes thinking has changed over time, too. In the Middle Ages, when very few people could read or reckon, as performing arithmetic was called, anyone who could add and multiply was thought to have special powers, divinely or perhaps mystically conferred. Reckoning was a uniquely human activity. It took centuries for addition and multiplication to be codified into the algorithms that we all learn in elementary school. Is a capability, once classified as thinking and believed to be a divine gift, no longer thinking when it turns out to be algorithmic? It required thinking when we learned it. Maybe all thought is algorithmic. Maybe it's thinking only as long as no one understands how it's done.

Sub Text. Computer scientist Edsger Dijkstra is quoted as saying, "The question of whether a computer can think is no more interesting than the question of whether a submarine can swim." But he seems to be in the minority.

The Turing Test

The problem of defining thinking for the purposes of deciding whether a computer thinks concerned Alan M. Turing, one of the pioneers of computing. Turing was aware of definitions like "thinking is what people do," and the tendency for people to call an activity "thinking" until it turns out to be algorithmic. So, he decided to forget trying to define what thinking is, and proposed a simple experiment that would demonstrate intelligence. Turing proposed the following experimental setting, which has since become known as the **Turing test**.

Turing test: *Two identical rooms labeled A and B are connected electronically to a judge who can type questions directed to the occupant of either room. A human being occupies one room, and the other contains a computer. The judge's goal is to decide, based on the questions asked and the answers received, which room contains the computer. If after a reasonable period the judge cannot decide for certain, the computer can be said to be intelligent.*

Thus, the computer is intelligent if it acts enough like a human to deceive the judge.

In his paper "Computing Machinery and Intelligence" (published in 1950), which proposed the test, Turing offered an idea of how he thought the dialog would go:

(*Continued*)

Judge:	In the first line of your sonnet which reads 'Shall I compare thee to a summer's day', would not 'a spring day' do as well or better?
Computer:	It wouldn't scan.
Judge:	How about 'a winter's day'? That would scan all right.
Computer:	Yes, but nobody wants to be compared to a winter's day.
Judge:	Would you say Mr. Pickwick reminded you of Christmas?
Computer:	In a way.
Judge:	Yet Christmas is a winter's day, and I do not think Mr. Pickwick would mind the comparison.
Computer:	I don't think you're serious. By a winter's day one means a typical winter's day, rather than a special one like Christmas.

Passing the Test

Turing's experiment not only sidestepped the problem of defining thinking or intelligence, but also it got away from focusing on any specific ability such as performing arithmetic. The judge can ask any questions, so as to explore the entire range of thought processes. Apparent stumpers for the computer like

In Hamlet's famous soliloquy, what metaphors does Shakespeare use for "death"?

might not be so hard if the computer has access to online sources of Shakespearean criticism. Perhaps IBM's Watson could get this one right (see below) since Shakespearean criticism might be in its huge database. Apparent "gimmes" for the computer like

What are the prime factors of 72,914,426?

might be answered in more human-like ways such as being slow or refusing to answer such questions at all. When Turing proposed the test in 1950, there was little prospect that a computer could deceive the judge. Nevertheless, it emphasized the important point that thinking is a process; how it is accomplished—with synapses or transistors—shouldn't matter.

Speaking of Robots. The word *robot* was first used by the Czech author Karel Čapek in his 1921 play *R.U.R. (Rossum's Universal Robots)*. According to Čapek, the word was created by his brother, Josef, from the Czech word "robota," meaning servitude.

Advances in the past 60 years have definitely improved the computer's chances of "passing" the Turing test, though perhaps they are still not very good. Researchers reading Turing's paper in 1950 might have conceded that computers could be better than people at arithmetic, but probably all of them would have believed that "natural language"—a true human invention—was beyond the abilities of computers. For example, when Turing conceived the test, no algorithmic process was known for parsing (analyzing) English into its grammatical structure, as word processors's grammar checkers do today. Nor was "machine translation"—converting text from one language into its semantic equivalent in another language, as Google does today—anything more than science fiction. And neither was recognizing semantically meaningful information something a computer could perform, as Watson does today.

22.1 Well Versed. In Turing's sample dialog, the Judge asks, "In the first line of your sonnet which reads 'Shall I compare thee to a summer's day', would not 'a spring day' do as well or better?" Give at least five facts about the content of this sentence that a computer would need to know to answer it.

Admittedly, computers are still a long way from being perfect at any of these tasks, but they are pretty good at all three—at least good enough to be the basis for useful applications. More important, they are good enough at these language tasks that we can imagine a day when computers are better than most humans. And then, like reckoning, the tasks of parsing, translation, and semantic searching in natural language will have been reduced to algorithmic form. Does it add to our admiration of computers that they are closer to passing the Turing test? Or does it detract from our opinion of ourselves, suggesting that instead of computers being more like people, perhaps people are just computers? The questions are truly profound.

Grand Turing. Englishman Alan Mathison Turing (1912–1954) was probably the most brilliant of all of the computer pioneers. In addition to the Turing test, he invented the first theoretical computer, now known as the Turing Machine, and discovered the Universality Principle (explained later in this chapter). During World War II he worked at the British Government's Code and Cypher School at Bletchley Park breaking Germany's Enigma Code. The Cambridge-educated mathematician and marathon runner was awarded the Order of the British Empire (OBE) and was a member of the Royal Society. He died in 1954 of potassium cyanide poisoning under suspicious circumstances.

Acting Intelligently?

Anyone with even passing experience with grammar or spell checkers knows that these programs don't "understand" the sentences. They know the parts of speech such as prepositions and verbs, concepts like subject/object agreement, passive voice, and so on, but they don't understand complete sentences. Such concepts are not trivialities. It takes tremendously complex software and substantial dictionary resources to implement grammar and spell checking, and they're occasionally good enough to be helpful. But they definitely do not "understand" English.

The distinction between being intelligent and being programmed to seem intelligent concerned researchers in the 1950s and 1960s. The Doctor program (also known as

Eliza) developed by MIT researcher Joseph Weizenbaum demonstrated this difference clearly. Doctor was programmed to ask questions in a dialog, as if between a psychotherapist and a patient:

> **User:** I'm depressed.
>
> **Doctor:** Why are you depressed?
>
> **User:** My mother is not speaking to me.
>
> **Doctor:** Tell me about your mother.
>
> **User:** She doesn't want me to major in engineering.
>
> **Doctor:** No?
>
> **User:** No, she wants me to go into medicine.

Doctor was programmed to keep the dialog going by asking questions and requesting more information. It would take cues from words like *mother*, including a reference to them in its next response. It would also notice the use of negative sentences and respond appropriately, but the dialog was essentially preplanned. It may have appeared to be intelligent, but it definitely was not. What would a computer have to do to be intelligent or to demonstrate that it "understands" something?

As the research field of artificial intelligence came into existence, a consensus grew that to exhibit intelligence, a computer would have to "understand" a complex situation and reason well enough to act on its "understanding." Moreover, the actions could not be scripted or predetermined. Most complex situations require the ability to understand natural language and/or require much real-world knowledge. Both properties badly handicapped computers of the day. Now in the twenty-first century, AI researchers have made tremendous progress; we study two landmark accomplishments.

It's Therapeutic. There are Web-based programs that conduct Doctor-type dialogs. Search for "eliza" to find one.

Playing Chess

Playing chess does not require natural language or much real-world knowledge. It offered a challenging task that humans were both good at and interested in. The rules were clear, and success could be easily defined: beat a grand master in a tournament. Indeed, in the initial exuberance over computing, it was predicted as early as 1952 that a computer would beat a grand master "sometime in the next decade." Though it took more than a decade before computers could do much more than know the legal chess moves, the problem was well established as a litmus test for AI.

A Modest Proposal. Claude Shannon, a pioneer in information theory, was the first to propose how a computer might play chess in 1949.

A Game Tree

How does a computer play chess? First, like all computational problems, the information must be represented in bits. The chess "world" is especially easy to represent because it is completely defined by an 8×8 checkered board, 32 pieces of two colors and

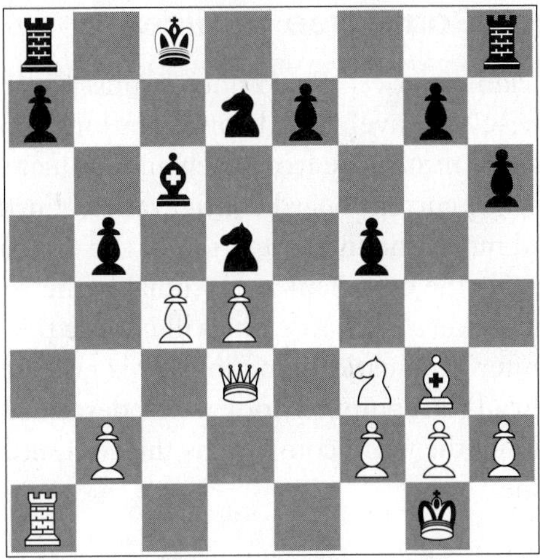

Figure 22.1 A chessboard configuration.

six different types, and a single bit indicating whose turn it is to move. Because details are unimportant, think of the graphic of a chessboard as shown in game books or chess sites (see Figure 22.1). Call it a board configuration, or simply a board.

Next, the computer must decide on a move. It does this in roughly the same way people do, by exploring possible moves to determine,

"Will a move of this piece to that position make me better off or worse off?"

"Better off or worse off" are determined with respect to winning, of course, but it is very difficult to "compute" such information. Humans use intuition and experience. A computer uses an **evaluation function**, a procedure that assigns a numerical value to each piece and, taking into account things like captures and board position, computes a score for the move. If the score is positive, it's better; if it's negative, it's worse. Then, starting from the current board configuration, the computer checks the evaluation function on the result of every possible single legal move, as shown in the **game tree** in Figure 22.2. One of these moves—suppose there are 28 legal moves—will give the highest score, which might be the one that the computer should pick.

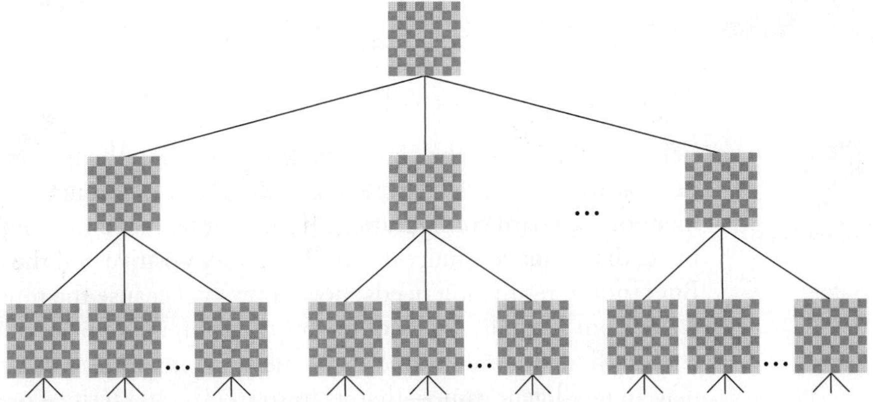

Figure 22.2 A schematic diagram of a game tree for chess. The current board position is at the top (root). The boards produced in a single move are on the layer below, those reachable in two moves are on the layer below that, and so forth.

Using the Game Tree Tactically

Before picking a move, the computer must consider what the opponent might do. So for each of these "1-move" board configurations considered so far, the computer considers every possible next move from each and evaluates them. These boards are two moves away from the current board configuration. Furthermore, because the opponent makes the second move, the interpretation of the evaluation function is reversed. That is, the best move for the opponent is presumably the worst move for the computer, so the computer assumes the opponent will choose the move with the most negative score in the computer's evaluation function. This process is known as "look ahead." Clearly, the further ahead the computer looks—it's described as *deeper* in chess because of the tree formulation—the more complete is the computer's knowledge about possible outcomes of the game.

AI and the Fruit Fly. Artificial Intelligence pioneer John McCarthy once commented that "Chess is the Drosophila of artificial intelligence."

It would seem that the computer, being very fast, could look all the way to the end of the game, find a winning path, and follow that. But checking the whole game tree is generally impossible because of the geometric increase in the number of boards that must be considered. For example, if there are 28 moves possible from the current position, and an average of 28 from each of those, and each of their descendants, and so on, then considering only six moves deep (that is, three for each side) generates

$$28 + 28^2 + 28^3 + 28^4 + 28^5 + 28^6 = 499{,}738{,}092$$

which is a half billion boards. It's infeasible for a computer to look 50 moves into the future.

22.2 Look Forward. Compute the size of the three-move tic-tac-toe (naughts and crosses) game tree beginning from an empty board. The size is the number of game boards required to draw the three-move tree; the boards at the bottom of the tree will have three marks—two x's and one o.

VideoNote

Game Trees

Which move should the computer select? Picking the best move at the first level is not necessarily the best strategy, because the evaluation function is generally a static assessment of the board configuration. If in that one move the computer could reach a checkmate, the evaluation function would be very positive and the computer should pick it. But if not, the situation needs more strategy, because the most positive evaluation might come from a capture that would give the computer a piece advantage, whereas another choice, though less desirable at the moment, might lead in a few moves to a win. To play an intelligent game—that is, to strategize, to sacrifice pieces, to force the opponent into specific behaviors—requires the computer to analyze the game tree much more carefully.

Using Database Knowledge

Finally, in addition to representing the game and making moves, the computer needs some knowledge. In chess, this takes the form of a database of openings and endgames. Because chess is interesting and has been studied for so long, much is known about how to start and finish the game. Providing this database is like giving the computer chess experience. Because learning is probably even harder than being intelligent, loading the database saves the computer the need to "learn from experience." It's analogous to aspiring chess players reading books by grand masters.

Using Parallel Computation

Slowly, as the basic logic just discussed got worked out, chess programs got better and better. Eventually they were beating duffers, then serious players, and then masters. Progress came as a combination of faster computers, more complete databases, and better evaluation and "strategizing" functions. In time, **parallel computation**—the application of several computers to one task—and custom hardware allowed computer researchers to entertain the possibility of beating a grand master in tournament conditions.

The Deep Blue Matches

In 1996, reigning grand master Garry Kasparov trounced an IBM computer dubbed Deep Blue. Deep Blue was a parallel computer composed of 32 general-purpose computers (IBM RS/6000 SP) and 256 custom chess processors, enabling it to consider on average 200 million board positions per second. In one of the six games of the match, the computer played very well and won. Kasparov saw himself as victorious in defending the human race, but AI researchers were also euphoric. At last a computer had played world-class chess in tournament conditions. A rematch was inevitable. On May 11, 1997, Kasparov lost 3.5–2.5 to an improved Deep Blue, achieving the "in the next decade" goal of the 1950s in a mere 45 years.

Motto. IBM, the dominant computer manufacturer of the 1950s–1970s, used "Think" as its corporate motto. It was common to see the command in computer rooms and on programmers' desks. Perhaps one of the best signs employed "negative space" to get the reader's brain working.

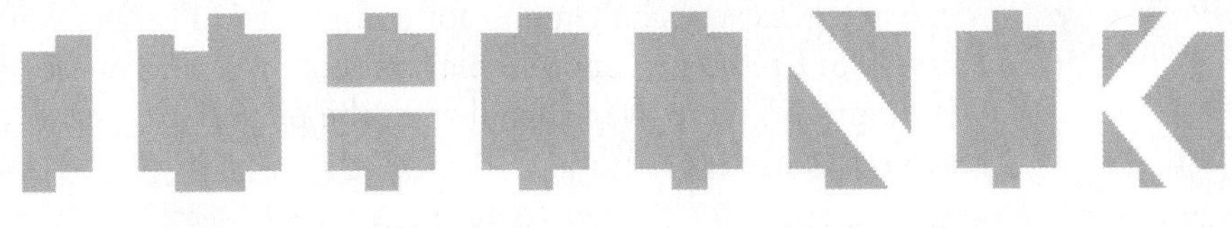

Interpreting the Outcome of the Matches

Did Deep Blue settle the question of whether computers can be intelligent? Not to everyone's satisfaction. To its credit, it answered one of the greatest technical challenges of the century. To do so required a large database of prior knowledge on openings and endgames, but that's analogous to reading books and playing chess. It also required special-purpose hardware that allowed rapid evaluation of board positions, but that's probably analogous to synaptic development in the brains of chess experts, giving them the ability over time to encapsulate whole board configurations as single mental units. But disappointingly—at least to some observers, and probably the AI pioneers who made the predictions in the first place—the problem was basically solved by speed. Deep Blue simply looked deeper. It did so *intelligently*, of course, because the geometric explosion of boards prevents success based simply on raw power. And that may be the strongest message from the Deep Blue/Kasparov matches. Intelligence may be the ability to consider many alternatives in an informed and directed way. Deep Blue surely demonstrated that.

The Deep Blue experience may have demonstrated that computers can be intelligent, or it may have demonstrated that IBM's team of chess experts and computer programmers is very intelligent. In the final analysis, the hardware was simply following the instructions that the programmers and engineers gave it. Such an objection has been raised in the "intelligence" debate since the beginning. It is a weak criticism because we can imagine intelligence, or creativity, or any other intellectual process being encoded in a general form, so that once started on a body of information, the program operates autonomously, responding to new inputs and realizing states not planned by its designers. Deep Blue operates autonomously in this sense and thus transcends its designers.

The main cautionary note regarding Deep Blue is that it is completely specialized to chess. That is, the 256 chess processors only evaluate board positions and are not useful for any other purpose. The 32 general-purpose processors can run other programs, of course, but none of Deep Blue's "intelligence" is transferable to another computation unless a programmer abstracts the ideas from Deep Blue and incorporates them into that computation. The "intelligence" isn't formulated in any general-purpose way. Thus, Deep Blue speaks only indirectly to the subject of general-purpose intelligence. Watson is different.

Watson

Playing chess is obviously a challenging intellectual activity. How difficult is it to "answer" *Jeopardy!* questions? Many of us don't think it's hard at all, because when watching the program we play along and do well enough to impress ourselves. (If we were actually good at it, we would apply to be a contestant.) As we will see, playing *Jeopardy!* is very challenging for computers. (The game actually "asks" the answer, "First U.S. President," and the players reply with the question, "Who was George Washington?" Here, we will call what the players are asked "questions" and their responses "answers.")

Computer Versus Humans

Computer scientists were ecstatic in February 2011 when an IBM semantic analysis system competed in and won a special edition of *Jeopardy!* (see Figure 22.3). In the three-night event, *Jeopardy!* champions Ken Jennings and Brad Rutter played against the Watson AI program developed by IBM researchers. When it was over, the game winnings were $77,147 for Watson, $24,000 for Jennings, and $21,000 for Rutter. Perhaps the cleverest summary of the event was Jenning's remark, "I, for one, welcome our new computer overlords," a parody of the *The Simpsons* episode "Deep Space Homer."

Figure 22.3 Thinking through the first day's Final Jeopardy! question are *Jeopardy!* champions Ken Jennings and Brad Rutter, and an artificial intelligence system developed by IBM, known as Watson.

Watson is a program with many specialized functions and a huge database (see Figure 22.4). The program, which is self-contained (not on the Internet), parses English, formulates queries to its database, filters the results it receives, evaluates the relevance to the question, selects an answer, and gives its answer in the form of spoken English. The database is built from 200 million pages of unstructured input, like encyclopedias, dictionaries, blogs, magazines, and so forth. See "Building Watson" (www.youtube.com/watch?v=3G2H3DZ8rNc) for an informal explanation of the system.

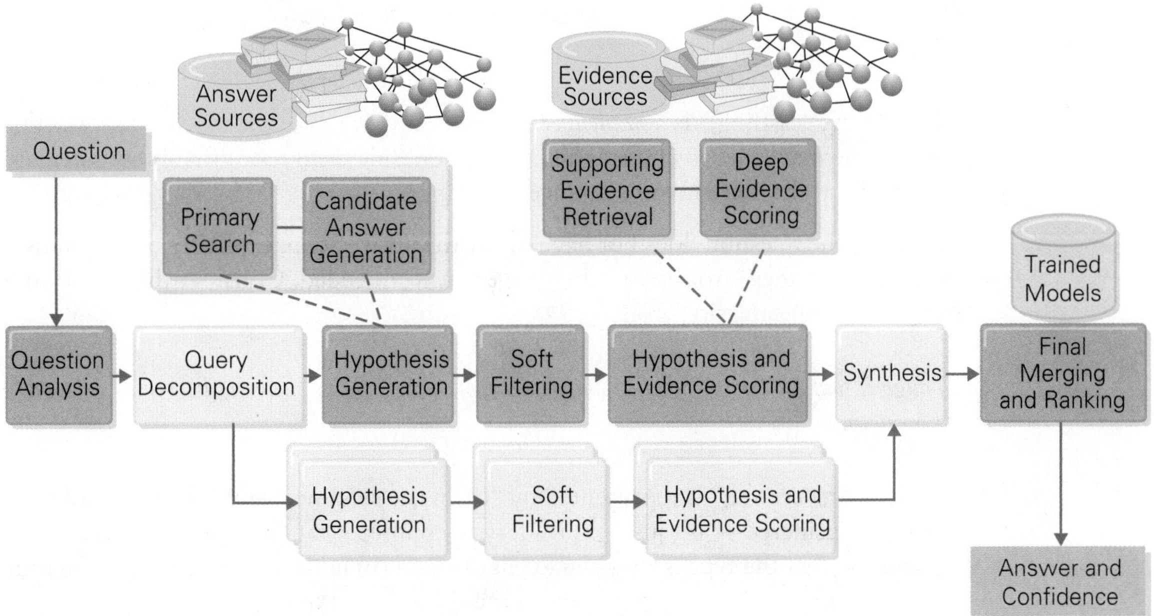

Figure 22.4 The logic of Watson from David Ferrucci et al., "Building Watson: An Overview of the DeepQA Project," *AI Magazine*, Vol. 31 No. 3. See www.aaai.org/ojs/index.php/aimagazine/article/view/2303.

When a standard desktop computer runs the Watson program, it takes two hours to answer a *Jeopardy!* question. To compete, Watson had to answer in 2–6 seconds, which required 2,880 computers with 16 terabytes of memory.

Technical Challenge

So, what have the IBM researchers done? They have produced a general Q&A system based on information gathered as it occurs "in the wild," that is, as we see it in a natural language form without any special processing. One result is that unlike Deep Blue, Watson's techniques and software can be applied to other problems.

What's so hard? David Ferrucci, the Watson project leader, pointed out that the *questions*, the *database*, and the *answers* were all represented in English. He notes that natural language is

- Implicit—often refers to things without "saying it in so many words,"
- Highly contextual—the meaning depends on the topic being discussed,
- Ambiguous—can often be "taken in two different ways," and
- Imprecise—doesn't use words "by their dictionary definitions."

Considering these difficulties, being able to figure out the question, make a query into the database, get information back, and put it together into an answer is amazing!

Watson used a range of techniques to solve several very difficult problems, so we'll discuss just one representative problem: Figure out what *type of answer* is needed to answer a question. For example, "name of a baseball player" is the type of answer to "Who's on first?" Once Watson knows the type, it can launch searches for information answering questions of that type.

Humans are so good at determining the answer type, you probably didn't know it could be a problem. But consider this *Jeopardy!* question from the Chess category:

Invented in the 1500s to speed up the game, this maneuver involves two pieces of the same color.

The answer, "castling," is a *maneuver*. Watson must analyze the clue to discover that it needs some maneuver in chess. The problem doesn't seem too difficult considering that the word is right there in the sentence.

However, the question does not have to say the answer type explicitly; we often use pronouns—it, they—to refer to the type of answer needed. Consider this question from the Decorating category:

Though it sounds "harsh," it's just embroidery, often in a floral pattern, done with yarn on cotton cloth.

The answer, "crewel," is represented by "it" in the sentence, and other parts of the clue must be considered—"it's just embroidery"—to infer what "it" refers to. Watson must (a) find out that the type isn't given explicitly, and (b) use the rest of the information in the clue to make an inference to determine the answer type.

To understand how a computer could figure out answer types, researchers considered 20,000 previous *Jeopardy!* questions. Each was analyzed for its "lexical answer type" or LAT (see Figure 22.5). There were more than 2,500 different explicit LATs, and more

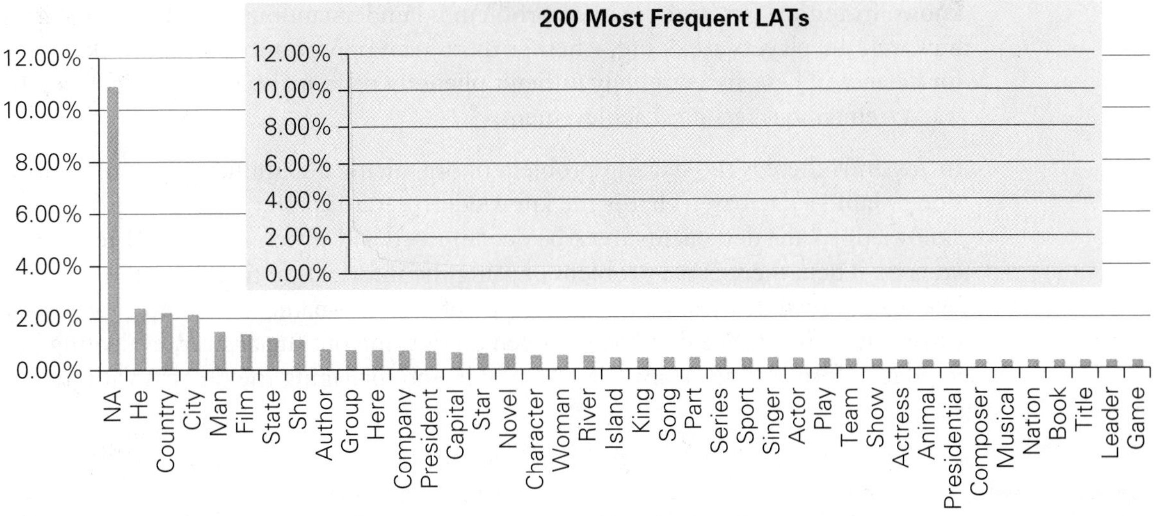

Figure 22.5 Frequency (in 20,000 questions) of the top 40 "lexical answer types," and (inset) the plot of the 200 most frequent. Notice that the top 200 account for fewer than half of the questions.

than 10 percent of the questions didn't have an explicit LAT. That is, even if Watson were perfect at figuring out the LAT, one time in 10 it wouldn't even know what *kind* of answer to produce. General Q&A could be considerably worse, because *Jeopardy!* has carefully formulated questions.

In the end the researchers figured out how to work with the LATs it discovered and use them to guide the search. To help further narrow the answer type, they programmed Watson to learn as the game progressed, using answers early in a category as a guide to the type of answers needed later in the category. So, Watson has a small amount of adaptivity.

No Longer in Jeopardy! Because Watson's database is built from documents expressed in natural language, it's possible to apply its software to other, more useful domains by creating a new database. Medicine is one area where Watson will be applied in the future.

Summary on Watson

Watson was a major technical accomplishment by a large team building on decades of research in topics from natural language processing to risk analysis. It did amazingly well, and took a large step toward passing the Turing test. Even so, it was not too hard to stump. Here is the question in the U.S. Cities category of "Final Jeopardy!":

Its largest airport is named for a World War II hero, its second largest for a World War II battle.

The answer, "Chicago," whose airports are O'Hare (a famous pilot) and Midway (a Pacific battle), was among Watson's list of choices, but it was below its confidence threshold. So it guessed "Toronto." Notice that this could have been a LAT problem. The question doesn't say the answer must be a U.S. city, though the category, which Watson tends to ignore, does.

Watson solves a tougher problem than Deep Blue did. In tournament chess, the goal is known from the start, and the main problem is "understanding" the flow of the game, how well the players are doing, whether there is an opportunity for an attack, or a need for defense. These are extremely difficult phenomena to make algorithmic; Deep Blue was a tremendous technical achievement.

In *Jeopardy!* there is the starting problem of organizing 200 million pages of information to build a database. That is the knowledge used to answer the questions, but to be "knowledge," the documents must be decomposed and structured; ASCII text isn't good enough. Then, there is the problem of using the information to answer the question. We have argued that just knowing the type of answer—name of a baseball player—is extremely difficult. We didn't even touch on figuring out the answer, evaluating how good it is, formulating an answer based on it, and managing the process within a game setting.

22.3 LAT Workout. Watson missed the question, "Its largest airport is named for a World War II hero, its second largest for a World War II battle" despite being told that the category is U.S. Cities, which implies the answer type is "city in United States." Because it is not explicit in the clue, how do you think Watson figured out a city is needed?

Acting Creatively?

An alternative approach to understanding the limitation and potential of computers is to consider whether they can be "creative." For example, can a computer create art? It's not a question of whether a computer can be the art medium—artists have manipulated computers to produce art for decades. Rather the question is whether a computer can prevail in, perhaps, a "graphic version" of the Turing test: A judge visits an art gallery and decides whether a person or a computer produced the art. Could a computer be successful at fooling the judge? The task may be more daunting even than the original Turing test because creativity is by definition a process of breaking the rules, and computers only follow rules. How could they ever succeed at being creative? Perhaps there are rules—**metarules**—that describe how to break the rules or, perhaps, transcend existing rules. A computer could follow those. To see how this might be, let's first look at a program to create fine art.

There are several clever Web applications to create graphic designs after artists such as the famed cubist Piet Mondrian (1872–1944) and abstract expressionist Jackson Pollock (1912–1956), whose paintings are exhibited in the great art collections of the world (see Figure 22.6).

One program displays a new Mondrian-like picture with each mouse click. Inspecting the code, we find that the programs use random numbers to steer a deterministic process for placing lines and filling regions with color. That is, the program encodes a set of rules for creating graphics in the style of Mondrian, using what looks to the casual observer like the same design elements, same colors, and so on. The graphics are new in the sense that they have never before existed, but as art critics love to say, "The work is derivative."

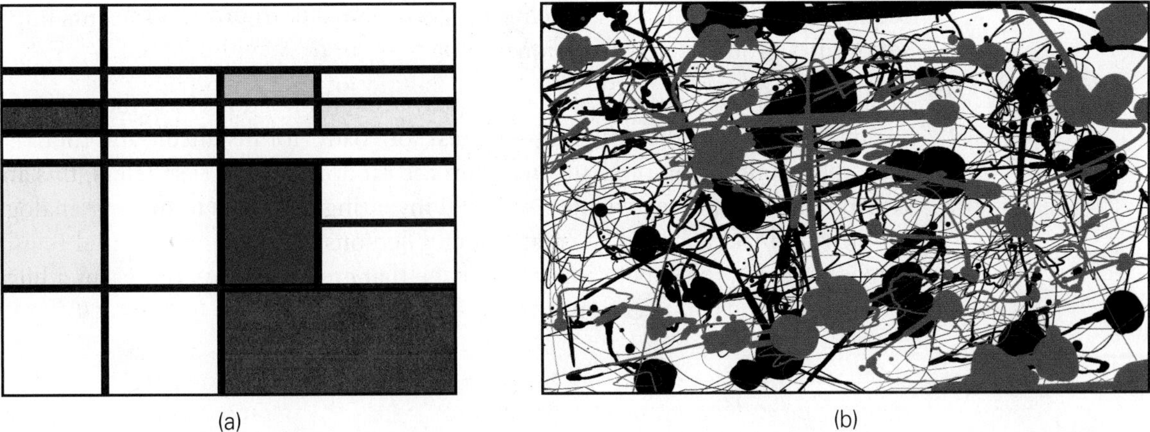

Figure 22.6 Examples of artist-free art. (a) Graphic design suggestive of the style of Piet Mondrian (search for programs on the Web such as **www.stratigery.com/automondrian.php**). (b) Graphic design suggestive of the style of Jackson Pollock (go to **www.jacksonpollock.org**, and move and click the mouse).

In the Pollock case, we provide the randomization by the timing and motions of the mouse. As with Mondrian, the program translates this random data into form and color suggestive of Pollock's work.

Mondrian and Pollock are famous not because they created pleasing pictures with distinctive elements, but because they had something to say about their experiences that they expressed through art. That is, they're famous for a body of work from which the program's rules have been (reasonably faithfully) abstracted. The program only produces variations on the application of the rules using random numbers. But to many, creativity means inventing the rules in the first place.

Creativity as a Spectrum

Computer scientist Bruce Jacob distinguishes between the form of creativity that comes from inspiration—"a flash out of the blue"—and the form that comes from hard work—"incremental revision." Inspiration remains a mystery; in Jacob's view the hard work is algorithmic. (This is reminiscent of Thomas Edison's famous description of genius: 1 percent inspiration, 99 percent perspiration.)

To organize our discussion, think of creativity as a spectrum ranging from "flash out of the blue" to "Mondrian in a click." To be creative in fine art at the "flash out of the blue" end, the computer would have to step outside of the "established order," inventing its own rules, whereas at the Mondrian-in-a-click end of the spectrum, the computer just randomly assembles parts by the rules some programmer gave it, never extending or modifying them. Between those two extremes, there are many options.

The Hard Work Forms. Jacob illustrates the hard work form of creativity using canons (musical compositions that have the incremental-variation-on-a-theme property).

Jacob has developed a music composition system, Variations, which attempts to create canons by extending a repertoire of base themes by (randomly) generating new themes, assessing them as "good" or "bad," and discarding the "bad" ones. Interestingly, Jacob points out that because the program must work within the underlying characteristics of the base themes, getting a random variation to "fit" within those constraints "sometimes requires creativity!" That is, forcing a random variation on the constraints imposed by a set of rules produces new techniques.

Calling Jacob's work *computer creativity* may seem difficult, because the program appears to embody much of the designer—the test for "bad," for instance—and there is a certain "stumbling onto a solution" quality from the randomness. Nevertheless, this and similar efforts, which span creative pursuits from inventing typefaces to making analogies, focus on the rule-making aspect of creativity and demonstrate that incremental revision is algorithmic. So, the conclusion seems to be that creativity does represent a huge range of different kinds of invention.

Classical Question. In an interesting demonstration at the University of Oregon, three pianists played three different pieces of music in the style of Bach: one composed by Bach, one composed by Steven Larson (a UO professor), and one composed by EMI, a computer program. The audience voted on who they thought wrote which piece.

	Audience Guess	True Composer
Composition 1	EMI	Larson
Composition 2	Larson	Bach
Composition 3	Bach	EMI

What Part of Creativity Is Algorithmic?

When the Turing test was invented, "Draw a picture in the style of Mondrian" would have been a request that a computer would have utterly failed at. Today it is a three-page Java program.

AI researchers have demonstrated in various contexts that the "hard work" form of creativity is algorithmic. If the matter of whether a computer can be creative is not taken to be a yes/no question, but rather is seen as an expedition into the process of creativity, we find our answer. The more deeply we understand creativity, the more we find ways in which it is algorithmic. Will it be found to be entirely algorithmic at some point in the future? Will there be rules for breaking the rules? Will it become like reckoning? Or will there necessarily be a nonalgorithmic part at the inspirational end? No matter how it turns out, aspects of creativity are algorithmic. To the extent that creativity is algorithmic, a computer can be creative. But who needs a computer? If creativity is algorithmic, we can all be creative by following the same rules. Progress in understanding creativity can benefit us, too. And how it is accomplished—with synapses or transistors—shouldn't matter.

Fill in the Blank. In an essay on creativity published in *Science*, Jacob Goldenberg, David Mazursky, and Sorin Solomon report that, in one study, 89 percent of award-winning advertisements use one of six "creativity templates," that is, follow-the-rules techniques, and that one simple template, *Replacement*, accounts for 25 percent of all award-winning ads.

The Universality Principle

Another problem that concerned Turing and other computer pioneers was to determine what makes one computer more powerful than another. Their amazing discovery was that any computer using only very simple instructions could simulate any other computer. This fact—known as the **Universality Principle**—means, for example, that all computers have the same power!

All Computers Are Created Equal. Though computer scientists have found different fundamental instruction sets, the six instructions `Add` (as described in Chapter 9), `Subtract`, `Set_To_One`, `Load`, `Store`, and `Branch_On_Zero` are sufficient to program any computation.

It goes without saying that every computer has these primitive instructions and much more. From the commercial point of view, the Universality Principle means that Intel and AMD cannot compete with each other to build a processor that can compute more computations. Every processor the two companies have ever made is equivalent to all other processors in terms of what they can compute. The Universality Principle says that all processors compute the same set of computations. It's surprising.

The Universality Principle has deep theoretical implications, but there are important practical consequences, too.

Getting Down to Basics. Another startling consequence of the Universality Principle is that programs, in effect, reduce *all* computation—playing chess or checking grammar or figuring income tax—to the point where it is expressible with only a half dozen different operations.

Universal Information Processor

Perhaps the most important aspect of the Universality Principle is that if we want to do some new information-processing task, we don't need to buy a new computer. The computer we have is sufficient if we can write or buy the software for the task.

This is quite different, say, from wanting to perform a new task in the kitchen or the shop, where we would have to buy a new gadget. Machines that transform material must be specialized to each activity, requiring us—or enabling us, if you like to get new gadgets!—to buy a specialized device. By contrast, there is only one information-processing machine, the computer.

Because computers are general purpose, people play a greater role in setting them up and configuring them for a specific task—installing software, for example—than they do for single-purpose machines like food processors or table saws. This greater role in customizing the general-purpose device to our needs is one reason why it is important to become fluent with computing.

Competing Machines and the Universality Principle. To understand why all computers are equivalent, imagine two computers, the ZAP^2 and the BXLE, and suppose they have the same hardwired instructions, except that the ZAP^2 has one additional instruction. Its manufacturer claims, contrary to the Universality Principle, that the new instruction enables new computations on the ZAP^2 that are not possible on the BXLE. "Baloney," says BXLE's CEO. "Using the instructions already in the BXLE, we will program a function that performs the operation of ZAP^2's special hardwired instruction. Then, in any program, we will replace every use of their special instruction with a call to our function. Anything ZAP^2 can do, BXLE can do, too." For a schematic diagram, see Figure 22.7.

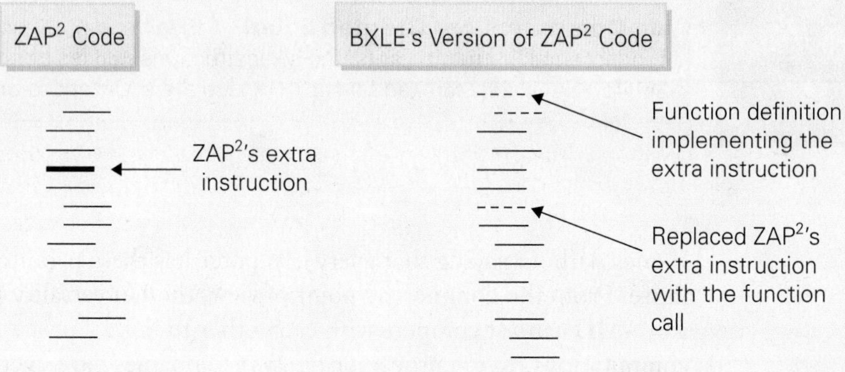

Figure 22.7 Schematic diagram showing a revision of ZAP^2's program to run on the BXLE, in which the special instruction has been replaced by a function call.

In effect, the ZAP^2 performs the instruction in hardware while the BXLE performs the instruction in software, that is, by using a function. The argument holds up as long as the special instruction can be programmed with the basic instructions of the BXLE, which we can be confident, will be possible. But the skeptic needn't accept that on faith. Rather, it's possible to write a program for the BXLE to simulate circuits and to simulate the entire circuitry of the ZAP^2. Simulating the ZAP^2 by the BXLE is possible because the ZAP^2 is built from (zillions of) two-input logic gates. There are only 16 different gates, and they can be trivially simulated with the six basic instructions, which the BXLE surely has. Because the BXLE can exactly duplicate the ZAP^2 operation in the simulator, it's possible to do all of the same computations, too. Notice that this solution also solves the problem in software.

Because all computers do the same computations, the main basis for technical competition among manufacturers is speed.

Practical Consequences of the Universality Principle

The Universality Principle says that all computers compute the same way, and their speed is the only difference. Unfortunately, the Universality Principle's claim that any computer can simulate any other computer has the disadvantage that simulation does the work much more slowly.

In the first solution of the ZAP^2/BXLE example, the BXLE was only slower on the special instruction, which presumably takes several basic instructions to implement. The second case was much slower because each instruction of the ZAP^2 might take thousands of logical operations, and the BXLE must simulate each of them. So, although both computers can realize the same computations, they perform them at different rates. For that reason, manufacturers *do* include special instructions for tasks such as digital signal processing, graphics, and encryption, hoping that their frequent use will speed up their computer.

The Universality Principle seems to conflict with our everyday experience, however. Two obvious objections arise:

1. I have to buy apps for my PC and phone separately; why can't I run one copy on both machines?
2. People say old machines become outmoded; how so, if they're all the same?

Despite these apparent problems, the Universality Principle is a practical fact. Consider each query in turn.

Separate Software. Your PC (Intel processor) and phone (ARM processor) require separate copies of the same app, though if all computers are the same, shouldn't it be possible to buy just one copy of the app and run it on each platform? It's true that all computers have equal power in that they can figure the same computations, but they don't all use the exact same instructions. The Intel and ARM processors have different instructions, different encodings, and a lot of other important internal variation. None of these expand the computations they can do, but they prevent them from sharing programs. In the same way, the last two cars you drove were very different, but they both reached your destination.

Also, consumer software relies heavily on operating system (OS) facilities and a lot of other software. (Recall the software stack from Chapter 1.) OS software extends the basic instruction set of the computer—as you learned in Chapter 9—so it can perform useful operations like firing up apps and allocating memory to them. This is the most profound difference between the PCs and phones: The operating systems do things very differently. None of the differences is fundamental, and it's possible in principle to simulate each OS on the other platform. Business considerations keep the two separate.

The solution, which software companies like Adobe, Microsoft, and Oracle use, is to translate their programs to each computer family, as explained in Chapter 9. That's how the browsers can be the same on the PC and phone. The program, written in a language like C, C#, or Java, and then translated (compiled) to each machine language allows the processor/OS combinations to run the code. The result is that rather than simulating the software of one computer on another computer, there is a separate custom version of the software for each vendor's computer. So, the Universality Principle is applied daily, but not along the lines of our original discussion.

Outmoded Computers. As noted, speed is the main difference among computers. Often, the reason why people buy a new computer is that they own new software, doubtless loaded with slick new features, that runs slowly on their old machine. With the new software doing more, it is not surprising that a faster computer would help. But, for those who are patient, there is no need to upgrade.

People usually give two reasons in support of their claim that older computers become "outmoded." The first reason is that hardware and/or software products are often incompatible with older machines. For example, input/output devices, such as printers, are often incompatible with older computers because of other internal parts, such as the system bus. (See the computer components diagram, Figure 9.4, in Chapter 9.) As a result, it's not possible to connect the new devices. However, these parts are not closely connected with instruction execution.

The second reason is that software vendors simply don't support old machines. As explained, software vendors compile their programs to each platform—-usually a processor/OS combination—to sell to customers. But, if there are too few customers running an old processor/OS combination, the vendor may decide that it isn't profitable to sell and maintain a version for that machine. Thus, new software is often not available for old computers. This is a business decision; there is no technical impediment.

So, the Universality Principle is not only a theoretical fact, but also a practical fact.

More Work, Slower Speed

When we use computers, they are simply idling most of the time, waiting for us to give them something to do. Tasks like word processing, even including continuous grammar and spell checking, doesn't keep them busy. So we listen to MP3 tunes too, which still doesn't stress them. And watch videos. Eventually, we notice that some tasks take a lot of time, such as video editing. What determines how fast a program runs?

Several features affect how much time a computation takes. Obviously, larger problems (more data) take more time because there is more to do. But it also matters how clever the algorithm is that solves it. Recall that we saw this in Chapter 10, where J-DB's nurses used a frequency ordered alphabet to help him spell faster than using the straight alphabetical order. It was cleverer. Most good algorithms are clever in this sense.

Comparing *IAL* with *NAL*

Also in Chapter 10 we discussed two algorithms, Intersecting Alphabetized Lists (IAL) and No Alphabetized Lists (NAL). As their names suggest, they solve the problem of finding hits in lists of URLs by different means: The IAL exploited alphabetization, the NAL did not; it worked like an odometer. From our earlier analysis, we noticed the following properties of the computations:

- IAL visits one new URL (in some list) each time it checks for a match.
- NAL, working like an odometer, checks the same URL repeatedly with many wasted checks for a match.

We gave an example of five lists (key words in our search) each with 10 URLs in the list. We computed

$\text{Steps}_{IAL} = 10 + 10 + 10 + 10 + 10 = 50$
$\text{Steps}_{NAL} = 10 * 10 * 10 * 10 * 10 = 100{,}000$

That's a huge difference in the number of steps to solve the problem. Clearly, exploiting the alphabetization produces a very fast solution, while using unordered data is very slow.

But the situation is actually worse than it appears, because of how the time increases when the data increases. Suppose we add one more search term, and therefore one more list, also with 10 URLs, then the new numbers would be

$\text{Steps}_{IAL} = 10 + 10 + 10 + 10 + 10 + 10 = 60$
$\text{Steps}_{NAL} = 10 * 10 * 10 * 10 * 10 * 10 = 1{,}000{,}000$

That is, adding a 10-item list increased the IAL's time by 10 steps, but adding a 10-item list increased the NAL's time by 900,000.

A computer scientist would summarize these observations by saying,

Finding hits for k *lists, the longest of which has* n *URLs, will take at most* kn *steps using IAL, but will take* n^k *steps using NAL.*

In this example, $k = 6$ and $n = 10$.

22.4 Different Query. Suppose there are three keywords in the search, and 100 URLs in each list. How many steps do IAL and NAL require?

Summarizing, more data implies that algorithms must do more work. But how an algorithm operates determines how much more work it will take. IAL is a fast algorithm, and with a "linear" growth rate. So, adding n more URLs only increases the work by n additional steps.

Are "Best" Algorithms All Fast?

Obviously, a programmer's choice of algorithm can matter a lot. So, one question of importance to programmers and users alike is, "Is there a fast algorithm for every problem?" If there is, we all want it, and the programmers may have to stay up nights trying to figure it out. Surprisingly, they'll probably get their sleep.

NP-Complete Problems

There are very difficult computations, many of which are important to business, science, and engineering, with no known fast algorithm. In fact, one of the most significant discoveries of the 1970s was that many problems of interest—for example, finding the cheapest set of airplane tickets for touring n cities—don't have any known "practical" algorithmic solutions. Such problems are known by the rather curious name of **NP-complete problems**. In essence, the best-known algorithms work pretty much like NAL, doing little more than trying all possible solutions, and then picking the best. It seems that there should be cleverer algorithms than that. If there are, the person who discovers one will enjoy tremendous fame. In the meantime, such problems are said to be **intractable**—the best way to solve them is so difficult that large data sets cannot be solved with a realistic amount of computer time on any computer. Computers can solve them in principle, but not in practice.

Hard Problems. Steve Cook of the University of Toronto and Richard Karp of UC Berkeley discovered NP-completeness. They also discovered the amazing fact that if anyone finds a better algorithm for just one NP-complete problem, their algorithm will improve *every* NP-complete problem.

Unsolvable Problems

Perhaps more surprisingly, there are problems computers cannot solve at all. It's not that the algorithms take too long, but that there are no algorithms, period! These are not problems like being intelligent or creative, but precisely defined problems with a clear quantifiable objective. For example, it's impossible for an algorithm to determine if a program has a bug in it, like looping forever. Such an algorithm would have been quite handy in Chapter 20 in our study of looping, when we messed up the *<next iteration>* step, causing infinite loops. We'd simply give our program to this imagined Loop-Checker algorithm, and it would tell us whether or not our program loops forever. Notice that the Loop-Checker would be especially useful for computations like NAL that take a long time for the results. While we're waiting, we'd like to be sure we're going to get a result eventually, rather than have the program caught in an infinite loop, forcing us to wait forever.

The Nonexistent Loop Checker. But the Loop-Checker can't exist. Suppose it did. That is, suppose there is a program LC(P, x) that takes as its input any program P and input data x, analyzes P working on x, and answers back "Yes" or "No" as to whether P will loop forever on input x. This actually seems plausible, because LC could look through P, checking every loop to see if the *<next iteration>* and *<continuation>* tests are set right. And then it could follow the execution of P on x, looking to see if anything could go wrong. It seems plausible, but it's not. Here's why.

Create another program, CD(P), that also takes as input a program P. CD is an abbreviation for "contradiction." The program works according to the flowchart shown in Figure 22.8. What does CD(CD) compute? We're not sure what the assumed LC(CD,CD) will answer back, but suppose it says "No," CD does not loop forever when the CD program is its input. In that case, the left arrow out of the diamond is taken and CD loops forever. So, LC would be wrong. Perhaps LC answers "Yes," that CD will loop forever when CD is its input. In that case, the right arrow out of the diamond is taken and the program doesn't loop forever, but just stops. Wrong again. The Loop-Checker cannot answer correctly—neither "Yes" nor "No" is the right answer. This problem cannot be algorithmically solved.

Does this sound like Russell's Paradox from Chapter 4? It should, they're related.

The Halting Problem. The Loop-Checker is trying to solve a famous computation known as the **Halting Problem**. Alan M. Turing was the first to recognize the impossibility of creating the perfect debugger, like the theoretical Loop-Checker. It's too bad, because having such a debugger would be handy. Interestingly, debugging (the topic

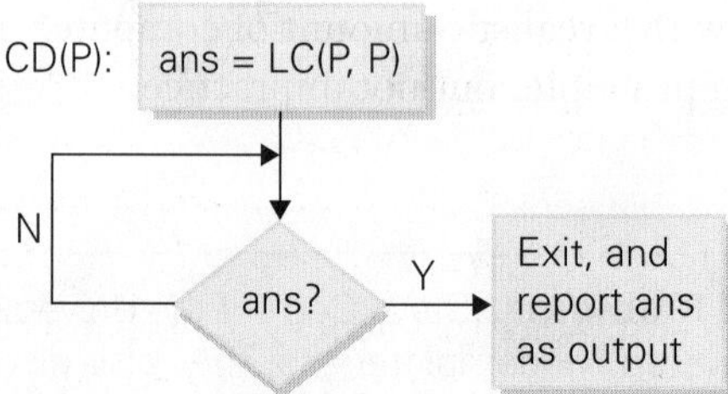

Figure 22.8 The logic of the CD program, given the assumed program LC.

of Chapter 6) is something that humans can do, admittedly with great difficulty sometimes. In fact, it requires considerable intelligence to figure out what has gone wrong when a computing task doesn't work. It's something that computers won't ever be able to do in any general way. So, maybe we were looking in the wrong place for capabilities that are uniquely human. Making computers solve our problems *properly* is something only humans can do!

SUMMARY

We have explored the limits of computation. We began by asking a question that has puzzled people since computers were invented—can computers think? The question challenged us to define what thinking is. In this chapter we did the following:

- Identified a tendency for people to decide that an intellectual activity isn't considered thinking if it is algorithmic. Thinking is probably best defined as what humans do, and therefore something computers can't do *by definition*.
- Discussed the Turing test, an experimental setting in which we can compare the capabilities of humans with those of computers.
- Studied the question of computer chess and learned that computers use a game tree formulation, an evaluation function to assess board positions, and a database of openings and endgames. Deep Blue became the chess champion of the world in 1997, a monumental achievement, but not one that closed the book on the algorithmic nature of intelligence.
- Studied the problem of semantic analysis as implemented in the Watson program. We learned that it is even difficult to figure out *what type of answer* is required. Watson solved this and many other difficult problems, and its algorithms can be applied to other domains like medicine.
- Studied creativity, deciding it occurs on a spectrum: from algorithmic variation (Mondrian and Pollock graphics-in-a-click) through incremental revision to a flash of inspiration. The degree to which the activities along the spectrum are algorithmic has advanced over the years.
- Presumed that there will be further advancement, but we do not know where the "algorithmic frontier" will be drawn. It's too early to tell if creativity, like reckoning, is entirely algorithmic. Computers will be creative insofar as creativity is algorithmic. And so will we all.
- Considered the Universality Principle, which implies that computers are equal in terms of what they can compute. This is not only a theoretical statement; we benefit from its practical consequences daily.
- Learned that important problems—the so-called NP-complete problems—require much more computational work than the computations we do daily. Many of the problems we would like to solve are NP-complete problems, but unfortunately the NP-complete problems are intractable—large instances are solvable by computer only in principle, not in practice.
- Learned the amazing fact that some computations—for example, general-purpose debugging—cannot be solved by computers, even in principle. If it were possible, we could solve the Halting Problem, and that's not logically possible. We should remember this when it seems computers can do anything!

22.1 There is no one correct answer to this question. One possible answer is: (a) a sonnet is a poem, (b) poems are composed of lines, (c) lines in English poems have meter based on syllables, (d) summer has two syllables, and (e) spring has one syllable. Other needed facts include (f) the clause "which reads . . . " is quoting the first line, (g) having appropriate meter is called "scanning," and so on.

22.2 By level, $1 + 9 + (9 \times 8) + (9 \times 8 \times 7) = 586$

22.3 Watson might have inferred that "its airport" applies to the answer, and things that "have" airports are cities.

22.4 IAL: kn for $k = 3$ and $n = 100$ is 300. NAL: n^k is 100^3 or 1,000,000.

Multiple Choice

1. Computers can
   a. think
   b. manipulate information
   c. be creative
   d. all of the above
2. The top of a game tree is called the
   a. base
   b. top
   c. root
   d. solution
3. The ability of any computer to imitate another computer is known as
   a. mimicry
   b. the Imitation Principle
   c. the Universality Principle
   d. the Turing test
4. They programmed Watson to do this as the game progressed
   a. think
   b. learn
   c. determine the category
   d. ask intelligent questions
5. NP-complete problems
   a. have no known solution
   b. have too many possibilities to solve
   c. must consider every possible solution to find the best one
   d. can be solved with a work-proportional-to-n algorithm
6. One thing that humans can do that computers can't is
   a. play games of chance
   b. perform sort algorithms
   c. make computers work properly
   d. solve the Halting Problem

7. How many instructions are sufficient to program any computation?
   a. one
   b. six
   c. 1,024
   d. millions
8. Putting several computers to work on the same problem is called
   a. algorithmic thinking
   b. parallel computation
   c. universality
   d. none of the above
9. Calculating every possible move in a chess game generates a(n)
   a. game tree
   b. Turing test
   c. algorithm
   d. none of the above
10. In a game, looking ahead for potential moves is called
    a. deepening
    b. drilling down
    c. variation
    d. none of the above

Short Answer

1. _______ is the name of the IBM computer designed for chess.
2. A computer is intelligent if it acts enough like a _______ to deceive a _______.
3. When playing chess, humans use intuition and _______. A computer uses a(n) _______.
4. For computer chess, a(n) _______ shows the result of every possible legal move for the computer along with a numeric evaluation of each move.
5. When playing Jeopardy, Watson was not connected to _______.
6. _______ are rules about rules.
7. The _______ maintains that any computer can be made to imitate any other computer.
8. To the extent that creativity is _______, a computer can be creative.
9. The main basis for technical competition among manufacturers is _______.
10. Any hardwired computer instructions can be simulated in _______.
11. _______ is something that computers cannot do.
12. _______ is a problem that a computer cannot solve.
13. Programs do not understand _______.
14. _______ are problems with no practical algorithmic solutions.

Exercises

1. What other domains (besides Jeopardy and medicine) could Watson's database be applied to (be creative)?
2. Explain how computer art is derivative and not creative.

3. Explain NP-complete problems in your own words.
4. Explain how a game tree could be used for card games.
5. Describe why the argument on whether computers can think has little impact on our daily lives. Use your word processor to answer this.
6. What does a computer have to do to pass the Turing test?
7. What is the Halting Problem? Can it be solved by a computer, and if so how?
8. Suppose there are four keywords in the search, and 84 URLs in each list. How many steps do the IAL and NAL algorithms require?

CHAPTER 23

A Fluency Summary

Click to Close

learning objectives

- Discuss how being *Fluent* affects your ability to remember IT details and ideas
- Discuss lifelong IT learning through finding new uses, asking for help, and noticing new technology
- Discuss the benefits of achieving *Fluency* now and in the future

CHAPTER 23

When you wish to instruct, be brief; that men's minds take in quickly what you say, learn its lesson, and retain it faithfully. Every word that is unnecessary only pours over the side of a brimming mind.

—CICERO

WE HAVE COME to the final chapter. There has been no miracle revealed. The parts of computing we've discussed make sense. It has been a substantive and, at times, challenging tour. But your ability to apply computing ideas has dramatically improved. You have acquired basic information about a broad spectrum of topics. Though you may not be an expert, you know enough to know when you need to learn more. As your study proceeded, you integrated the basic information into a powerful intuitive computing model. As you acquire new knowledge, this model gives it a place to "fit into."

In this chapter we wrap up our *Fluency* study by summarizing two of several repeating ideas. Then we consider the two most pressing matters: How much of the information in this book do you have to remember, and how do you learn the technology that hasn't yet been invented? Both topics have unexpected outcomes. Finally, we reflect on the fact that in the world of computing, we can shift for ourselves.

Two Big Computing Ideas

Recalling the chapter summaries, several ideas have recurred in our study—for example, information structuring and strategies for nonalgorithmic tasks. We consider each in turn.

Information Structuring

In Chapter 5 we learned that collections of information are structured hierarchically—that is, organized by descriptive metadata into groups and subgroups—in order to assist us in locating specific items. In Chapter 7 we found that the *Oxford English Dictionary*'s digitization includes metadata structural tags that enclose the constituents of each definition. Knowing the purpose of each part of the *OED*'s content (headword, citation, etc.) allows the computer to perform complex searches and analysis. In Chapters 13 through 16, specifying the structure of the information gave the same powerful advantage when we built spreadsheets and databases. Specifying the characteristics of the data stored in a table—its type, whether it is a key, and so on—allowed for sophisticated queries and prevented erroneous uses that would have produced garbage.

The idea is that *specifying structure is as essential as specifying content*. This idea comes up again and again because the value of information depends on how effectively we can use it, and all of the powerful applications rely on the computer's knowing the structure. The truth of this observation is clear from our studies. But we can learn more from it!

As we become increasingly more effective users, we will acquire a growing collection of personally important digital information. Years of old email correspondence, digital photos, MP3 collections, and other items will fill our hard disks. As our collections grow, eventually we may decide to move certain information into databases or other structured archives in order to manipulate them efficiently. But as we accumulate the information as independent files, it's smart to keep it structured—simply by the way we arrange it in folders and subfolders. We should assign our MP3s and JPEGs to their own folders—substructured perhaps into folders based on content—so that we can find files when we want them; the details of the organization could be a private part of our iDiary. This simple directory hierarchy organization is not as effective as the examples cited earlier because the computer does not know the structure. But *we* know it and it will assist us in a manual navigation of our collections.

Strategies for Nonalgorithmic Tasks

Algorithms have been an important topic in our *Fluency* study. We learned the placeholder technique for reformatting text (Chapter 2), the *Intersecting Alphabetized Lists* algorithm for finding multiword query matches (Chapter 10), an effective query construction to build a supertable with joins and then trim it down using `Select` and `Project` (Chapter 15), and many other algorithms.

But perhaps the most significant content of our study concerned capabilities that are not algorithmic. Finding accurate information and satisfying our curiosity through search (Chapter 5), debugging (Chapter 6), formulating a password (Chapter 11), designing a database (Chapter 16), testing and assessing a user interface (Chapter 18), and programming a complex Web application (Chapter 21) are all examples in which there are no deterministic, guaranteed-to-yield-a-solution rules. In each case, we could only give guidelines. For example, debugging is facilitated by the following guidelines:

Debugging Guidelines

- *Make sure that you can reproduce the error.*
- *Determine exactly what the problem is.*
- *Eliminate the "obvious" causes.*
- *Divide the process, separating the parts that work from the parts that don't.*
- *When you reach a dead end, reassess your information, ask where you may be making wrong assumptions or conclusions, and then step through the process again.*
- *As you work through the process from start to finish, predict what should happen and verify that your predictions are fulfilled.*

The steps prescribe a rational approach to the task, but they don't form an algorithm.

Exit Conditions

The nonalgorithmic capabilities have been presented as though they form a separate knowledge base, and they do, in the sense that each entails a separate list of guidelines. But generally, the capabilities are all applications of logical reasoning in the service of achieving some higher goal—true information, correct program, convenient application, and so on. Reasoning is the key. It is applied in small ways on nearly every page of the book. Indeed, an overarching theme of this text is that *precision and the directed application of logical reasoning can solve problems great and small, algorithmic and nonalgorithmic*. The more we apply such thinking, the better we become at it!

Fluency: Less Is More

In reviewing the material discussed in this book, it is sobering to realize the enormous amount of detailed information covered. You've learned about anchor tags in HTML, the `if/else` statement in JavaScript, the Vacation Message, the Nyquist rule, `Select` operations, and on and on. How can anyone remember it all?

Recall that *Fluency* knowledge is compartmentalized into three components:

1. **Skills**—competency with contemporary computing applications like word processing
2. **Concepts**—understanding the foundations on which computing is built, like the Fetch/Execute Cycle
3. **Capabilities**—facility with higher-level thinking processes like reasoning

These three kinds of knowledge are co-equal and interdependent. But when we analyze them from the point of view of how much we have to remember, we realize that they are very much *unequal*.

- The skills all require much detailed knowledge. For example, is the property of line length in the HTML `<hr/>` tag `size` or `length`? It is impossible to have short lines in HTML without knowing which is correct. Furthermore, an annoying property of this detail is that the computer demands that we are *exactly right*; it is unforgiving. We can't use computers without knowing such facts, or, more likely, researching them.

- The concepts might be quite detailed, but the "basic ideas" are not. We know a computer's Fetch/Execute Cycle is an infinite process for interpreting instructions, but now that we understand the core idea, we don't really need to remember that the third of the five steps is called Data Fetch. It's the concept of an instruction execution engine that is important. Computing concepts are like other scientific information: Ideas must be explained in full to be understood, but after they're learned, only the ideas themselves, not the particulars, are important for the nonspecialist.
- The capabilities are the least detailed of all. Capabilities are mainly approaches to thinking. For example, problem decomposition, in which a complex task is broken into smaller tasks that are either solved directly or are themselves broken into smaller pieces still, is simply a rational way to tackle complex problems. Debugging—thinking objectively about a faulty IT application—is mostly a matter of being a good detective. Yes, there are guidelines on how to proceed, but debugging mainly comes down to forcing yourself to look at a situation the way it is rather than the way it seems. The capabilities require you to remember almost no detail whatsoever.

So, there is a spectrum of detail from skills through concepts to capabilities.

Curiously, our *Fluency* study allows us to remember less, rather than requiring us to remember more. How can this be? We remember less *detail* because we remember the *basic ideas* instead.

The clearest example—much of our *Fluency* study works this way—was our discussion in Chapter 2. The chapter seemed to cover necessary skill-level information about user interfaces, how to exploit *Find* and *Replace*, and so on. But the chapter is really about the capability of *thinking abstractly about technology*, and how we learn to think abstractly. We asked sweeping questions such as the following:

- How do we learn technology?
- How do software designers, indeed any tool designers, expect users to learn to use their new creations?
- When we're confronted with a task that requires technology, how do we figure out what to do?

The answers to these questions were not "Memorize thick, boring manuals." Rather, we pointed out that thinking abstractly about technology implies an adaptive approach to learning. Tool creators exploit consistent interfaces—every music player uses the same icons—so we should look for the consistency. Look for metaphors. When presented with a tool, explore it by "clicking around" to see what the inventor provided. Wonder what you're expected to do. And finally, simply "blaze away," trying things and watching what happens, knowing that the garbage created when mistakes are made must be thrown away (at no cost) before starting over. In other words, don't memorize the tool's details. Rather, learn the details as you need them. If you use software frequently, you will become adept at the specifics, memorizing the details through use. If you use software rarely, you will forget the specifics. But even that's fine, because you will know abstractly what to do and how to figure out the details again.

Thus, the higher-level capabilities make us rational people, approaching computing tasks thoughtfully, enabling us to proceed in a directed and disciplined way toward the goal, solving problems as they arise, figuring out what to do as required, logically figuring out what's wrong when a bug has us blocked. You've learned how to learn IT. *Fluency* doesn't require that you use your head to memorize details. It only requires that you use your head.

23.1 Remembering. Capabilities require little recall—the debugging guidelines list has only six items. Similarly, the problem decomposition idea used to design the Web page in Chapter 21 had only one rule for building a plan from the task dependency graph. Do you remember it?

Lifelong IT Learning

Information technology learning is a process of lifelong learning, but that doesn't mean you have to read 20 pages of *C++ GUI Programmer's Guide* every night before bed. In fact, it doesn't mean that you have to do much at all. To learn computing throughout life requires only that you engage in three activities:

1. Pursue new computing uses that fulfill your personal needs.
2. Be rational about asking for help.
3. Notice new ideas and technology as they arise.

There's no course of study to attend.

Pursuing New Uses

While studying *Fluency*, you have had to learn many new and unfamiliar applications. Though learning new skills may initially have been daunting, the process should have become steadily easier as your experience broadened and your facility with "clicking around" and "blazing away" developed. This success, and the fact that learning becomes easier the more you know, should give you confidence that you can learn IT on your own. Expanding your use of computing is the best way to continue to learn.

If you think objectively when you ask the question, "Can IT help in this situation?" the answer will not always be "yes." Your grandparents like to chat with you on the phone; should you encourage them to get a camera and Skype? You could help them set it up, but would they adopt this new-for-them technology? Perhaps not. Should you Skype with your lab partner, who lives in the next building? Probably not. In the first case, the technology presents a barrier that might be difficult for your grandparents to adjust to; in the second case, the technology's advantage—face-to-face interaction over distance—is no real benefit; it's more fun to get together. Should you Skype with close friends in other cities? Of course. In summary, apply IT only if it can help, and if it can help, apply it.

Asking for Help

One goal of our study is to convert you into a self-reliant computer and information user. Does that mean that you should solve all of your problems yourself? Of course not. In fact, it's certain that there are problems beyond your knowledge now, and there always will be. We always need experts. So, eventually we need assistance from someone more knowledgeable than we are.

But acknowledging that we need help doesn't mean that the moment things go awry we throw up our hands in desperation. *Fluency* has taught you how to troubleshoot your problems, and this experience has given you some perspective. We should assess whether the problem is probably due to our own stupidity—and eagerly fix it on our own to save the embarrassment of revealing that stupidity to someone else—or something more fundamental that requires greater expertise. Only after we've applied reasonable efforts to solving the problem ourselves will we need to ask for help. But when we do need assistance, we should ask. Of course, one reason we may hesitate to ask for professional help is that it usually takes longer to solve the problem than we are willing to wait.

As a contributor to lifelong learning, trying to solve our own problems and asking for help when we're truly stuck can contribute to greater understanding. If we figure it out ourselves, we're at least more experienced at troubleshooting. If someone else helps us, we may learn some facts we didn't know. Either way, we win.

Noticing New Technology

If the technological changes of the last half-century are any guide to the changes to come, IT will be quite different at the end of the next half-century. To learn about and apply the upcoming advances requires attention. Is the "advance" being touted in the press a fundamental leap forward that's potentially beneficial to you, or is it just hype about an old product in a different package? The latter is far more common. You must be attentive and skeptical.

When there is a fundamental advancement—it happens, perhaps, every few years rather than once a month—we need to be willing to learn about it. The media often covers the "science" of new technologies; following these technologies should be easy now that you've learned the concepts taught in this book. Using the technology might require taking a class, but more likely it won't. After all, thinking about technology abstractly, we know that those eager to deploy a new technology will prepare a "migration path" for those of us who are competent, daily users of the current technology. Innovations will likely be harder to use than the mature technologies with which we are familiar, of course. But if, as *Fluent* users, we don't have the background and experience to overcome those difficulties—that is, if we can't succeed with a new technology—then it isn't ready.

It often happens that technologies—small advances as well as large ones—are rushed to market before they're ready, so there is considerable risk in being an early adopter. But waiting involves risks too. One of technology's defining characteristics is that it steadily improves. Inventing technology is a difficult creative activity, and engineering it to perfection the first time never happens. So, there are steady improvements—automobiles improved throughout the entire twentieth century and enhancements continue and will probably always continue. There will always be a next-generation technology that is more convenient, more functional, and more versatile with better price performance, and so on. But waiting for perfection might take 100 years, and during that time you won't benefit from the technology. The lesson: Adopt a technology as soon as there's a high probability that it will assist you, but expect it to continue to improve.

Shifting for Yourself

Ted Nelson, the inventor of hypertext, tells a story of his first meeting with a software development team for a project he was to direct. He was depressed to find that everyone on the team drove a car with a standard transmission (a car requiring the driver to shift gears manually). Nelson's point in telling the story is that software should be as easy for people to use as automatic transmissions are, and that programmers who enjoy shifting their own gears may not produce such software. Whether his point is correct or not, his story gives us a valuable—if different—perspective.

Fluency enables *us*, the users, to shift gears. It doesn't give us the ability to build a car, to repair it, or to modify it. But, we can control computing devices to extract their full power, to be in command, and to reach our destination. Nelson may be right regarding developers, but for users, the ability to manipulate the levers of computation is not an ability to deplore.

Whatever the computing equivalent of the automatic transmission is, it is still on the drawing board. It took 60 years for cars to come equipped with automatic transmissions. With personal computing's 60th birthday still years away, we can't wait. We'll shift for ourselves.

TRY IT SOLUTIONS

23.1 Perform any task when all of the tasks it depends on are solved.

REVIEW QUESTIONS

Multiple Choice

1. Examples of nonalgorithmic tasks include all of the following except
   a. finding information
   b. using placeholders to reformat text
   c. designing a database
   d. creating a password
2. The first step in debugging is to
   a. determine the problem
   b. reproduce the error
   c. eliminate obvious causes
   d. divide the problem into smaller parts
3. Thinking *Fluently* involves
   a. memorization
   b. repetition and practice
   c. abstract thinking
   d. attention to detail

4. You should adopt technology when
   a. the price/performance ratio is in your favor
   b. as soon as you can get your hands on it
   c. only after most of the rest of the public has adopted it
   d. when there is a high probability that it will be beneficial to you
5. Fundamental advances in IT come along
   a. daily
   b. monthly
   c. yearly
   d. less often than yearly

Short Answer

1. _______ should be given when there is no deterministic, unfailing method to solve a problem.
2. A(n) _______ is a series of steps that, when taken, guarantees the successful completion of a task.
3. Debugging is not algorithmic, but, rather, it is _______.
4. Of the three *Fluency* components, the ability to use email is considered a _______.
5. Of the three *Fluency* components, the understanding of networking principles is considered a *Fluency* _______.
6. Of the three *Fluency* components, the understanding of algorithmic thinking is considered a _______.
7. Content is just as important as _______.
8. We remember less _______ because we remember the basic _______ instead.
9. With *Fluency*, _______ are to details what _______ are to the "big picture."
10. One of technology's defining characteristics is that it _______ improves.

Exercises

1. Explain how much of the information in this book you have to remember.
2. What are three things you should do when you encounter a new piece of software?
3. Explain what "be rational" means in relation to asking for help.
4. Name at least three ways to stay on top of new ideas and technology as they arise.
5. Explain how knowledge of program debugging can be used to solve other problems.
6. Describe the debugging process as a loop. What condition allows you to end the loop?
7. When should you apply IT? Explain your answer in detail.
8. At what point should you be satisfied with your knowledge of IT?

INTERVIEW

with

David Ferrucci

David Ferrucci worked at the IBM Thomas J. Watson Research Center for nearly 20 years, where he built and led the Semantic Analysis and Integration Department, a team of over 40 researchers and software engineers specializing in a wide application of artificial intelligence (AI).

In 2007, David took on the Jeopardy Challenge—to create an intelligent computer system that could rival human champions at the game of *Jeopardy!* David led his team to create a single, extensible intelligent systems architecture, dubbed DeepQA. Built on a software framework for integrating text and multimodal analytics, DeepQA combined many independently developed neuro-linguistic programming (NLP) algorithms. David took bold research, engineering, and management steps to lead his team to adapt the architecture to integrate many search, NLP, and semantic technologies into a single system that could meet the challenging language-processing demands of *Jeopardy!* Watson, the computer system Ferrucci and his team built using DeepQA, outperformed all expectations and ultimately performed a task considered well beyond any known technology: Watson beat the highest ranked Jeopardy champions of all time on national television in February of 2011.

After Watson's successful appearance on *Jeopardy!*, David and his team applied Watson's ability to commercial ventures in the healthcare field. In particular, he launched a project with Cleveland Clinic that uses Watson to teach—and learn from interactions with—medical students.

For David, Watson was an incredible high point in his 30-year journey in artificial intelligence. David graduated from Manhattan College with a B.S. in Biology, and from Rensselaer Polytechnic Institute in 1994 with a Ph.D. in Computer Science. He has over 25 patents and has published papers in the areas of AI, knowledge representation and reasoning (KR&R), NLP, and automatic story generation and question answering. David was awarded the title of IBM Fellow in 2011 and has won numerous awards, including the Chicago Mercantile Exchange's Innovation Award. David attributes much of his success to his commitment to innovation and his ability to strike a critical balance between software architecture, engineering, and the science of AI, and he is determined to continue to leverage what he has learned to drive rapid innovation in the advancement of AI.

Would you briefly describe Watson in layman's terms?

Watson is a software program capable of parsing an arbitrary English question about almost anything, figuring out what it is asking for, and then finding the most likely answer by searching and analyzing millions of documents in just a few seconds. Watson provides not just an answer, but a confidence [level] indicating its certainty that it was able to parse, match, and triangulate enough information to provide a good answer. Determining an accurate confidence is a key element for providing effective decision support systems. Given that interpreting questions and language content is ambiguous and uncertain, providing an estimation of certainty becomes critical for the user to weigh the system's output. Imagine if you interacted with a consultant who provided good answers 70 percent of the time but could not tell when the answers were right or wrong. You'd prefer the consultant who could tell you if there was uncertainty in an answer and how much uncertainty, and even why the evidence seemed to fall short.

For Watson to find a confident answer, however, there must be a chain of evidence in the body of documents it has searched. Think of the chain of evidence as a series of sentences which together would justify the answer to a person. This does not mean that Watson understands the sentences and builds a mental picture of what they mean to a person; rather it finds, weighs, and combines a series of cues based on the words used, the contexts of other words in which they are used, and their relationships.

One way to think about it is to pretend you had to answer your friend's test question about a topic you knew very little about. For example, pretend you knew nothing at all about molecular biology, but you know English and you can use dictionaries, books, and encyclopedias to trace a path of shallow cues and find an answer. You may, in fact, stitch together some good evidence for the right answer (and for a few wrong ones as well). But you still may not be able to make sense out of the content since you lack the background to form a deep logical understanding of what you read. Nonetheless, you have done the work to narrow it down to just a few answers with good candidate evidence for each. After you rank the answers based on your confidence, you can present them to your friend. Your friend would then be able to consume the information and judge the answers quickly based on a deep understanding.

What were your goals in building Watson?

No one who understood the current limits of search, AI, and natural language processing thought it could be done. The community had failed at much simpler question-answering challenges. My goal was to advance the science of AI—to learn what was possible in AI/natural language processing; if the seemingly impossible could be done; and if so, then how, and if not, then, why not.

My goal was to ask and try to answer a hard enough question—a grand challenge—sufficient to either dramatically advance the field *or* to learn where we should invest more research to tackle the hard problems. Simply stated, my goal was to learn the limits of AI in the automatic question-answering space by trying our absolute best at solving a problem everyone believed was really hard, if not impossible.

As the project evolved, an architecture emerged that motivated more specific goals ranging from how can we accurately answer general factoid questions, to how can we accelerate the AI research process to tackle a broader range of grand challenges at a faster pace than ever before?

In your view, what did Watson's *Jeopardy!* win demonstrate?

In the *science* of artificial intelligence, it demonstrated that a loosely coupled diversity of many independent methods can be efficiently combined using machine learning techniques to solve a more holistic problem—one that none of the individual methods were designed to solve. Watson's success provides support for Marvin Minsky's view of intelligence discussed in *The Society of Mind.* It provokes a deconstructive view of cognition.

In the *engineering* of AI research, it demonstrated that carefully engineered frameworks and integrated architectures are essential for leveraging and quickly integrating the work of many scientists into an end-to-end system enabling robust and rapid progress.

From a *management* perspective, it demonstrated that clear, crisp measurable goals, end-to-end metrics, and tight collaboration can provide key motivators fundamental to success.

What were the biggest obstacles in Watson's development?

From a purely scientific perspective, attaining the level of question-answering accuracy—the number of questions the system had to get exactly right—and confidence—the accurate self-assessment of the system's own internal algorithms to correctly determine the likelihood an answer is right—over such an unconstrained space/broad domain of possible questions required to beat humans at the game was unheard of when we started. The vast majority of experts thought it simply could not be done.

There was no one algorithm that stumped us. The challenge, given our approach, was how to quickly create, advance, and combine many algorithms that all nibbled at the goal from many different perspectives—to entertain an open flow of algorithm ideas and have them all contribute to the end-to-end goal.

Why did Watson give Toronto as an answer in the U.S. Cities category? [The question was "Its largest airport is named for a World War II hero; its second largest for a World War II battle."]

Watson, after training over many prior games, had learned that the name of the category was not a clear indicator of the type of the answer. Other cues may lead to a different determination. Consider these *Jeopardy!* category clues and answers also under a U.S. Cities category:

Clue: St. Petersburg is home to Florida's annual tournament in this game popular on shipdecks.

Answer: Shuffleboard

Clue: Rochester, New York grew because of its location on this.

Answer: The Erie Canal

So Watson was not 100 percent sure what the answer type should be. Moreover, it found other nongeographical evidence that linked Toronto to World War II heroes and battles, and some that linked Toronto to the U.S. Watson had alternative parses for the question that left additional doubt.

Watson knew it was on weak ground and only gave Toronto 14 percent confidence. The right answer, Chicago, was a close second but also an uncertain answer at 11 percent confidence. Watson knew it was not sure and could not pull together a confident view; normally it would not even try to answer without greater than 50 percent confidence, but this was a Final Jeopardy question and it had no choice.

All considering . . . not bad . . . at least it knew what it didn't know.

How would you like to see the technology behind Watson applied in the future?

I would love for future developers and users of Watson to recognize that its strength is its ability to use many shallow text-based and semantic features to find, navigate, and weigh paths through a large body of documents to connect questions to possible answers.

This can help people search for, find, connect, and weigh text-based evidence more quickly and more effectively than ever before, providing the foundation for decision support products that can quickly and more efficiently exploit the vast amount of natural language content we have available in areas ranging from medicine to economics, from scientific research to politics.

Watson, on the other hand, does not deeply understand and reason about the content it "reads." The expectation for machines to demonstrate deep human-like comprehension of natural language content is still unrealized. This is a much harder nut to crack and will require more sophisticated learning strategies and I believe a different fundamental model for human-machine interactions.

Setting the right expectation for the Watson technology will ensure it gets applied more effectively and that future research in AI is better directed.

How do you envision the future of artificial intelligence?

I think AI got a slow start during its first 50 years or so, but its second 50 years will be absolutely startling. It will change everything about how we work, how we interact and how we relate to each other, and how we understand and define ourselves.

In the long run AI will become an integral part of how we work, learn, and play. AI will help diagnose and treat diseases, pilot our planes, trains, and automobiles, help us design and visualize new ideas, extend our mental and physical talents and abilities, manage the global economy, and accelerate scientific research. In short, there is no question that our love affair with intelligent machines has only just begun.

What advice do you have for students studying IT?

Think in terms of what is different about human and machine cognition and think in terms of creating computer applications that will accelerate and improve human performance and creativity. We are past the stage of computers doing the payroll, and moving into an era where computers will be our creative companions.

APPENDIX A

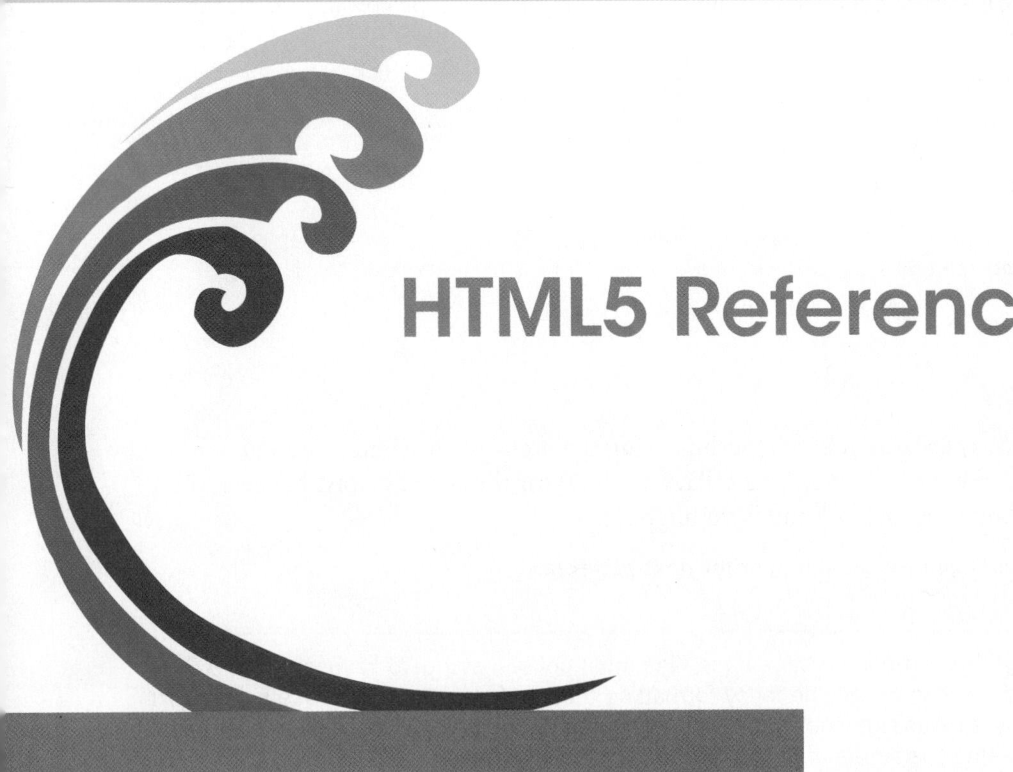

HTML5 Reference

THE FIRST PART of this appendix includes brief descriptions that form an alphabetical list of the HTML tags used in this book. Check Chapter 4 for further explanation or consult

www.w3schools.com/tags/default.asp.

The solution for the Washington, D.C., Trip Page is at the end of this appendix. Other useful links from W3C are:

Box model	www.w3schools.com/css/css_boxmodel.asp
Color names	www.w3schools.com/cssref/css_colornames.asp
CSS tutorial	www.w3schools.com/css/default.asp
HTML lists	www.w3schools.com/html/html_lists.asp
List styles	www.w3schools.com/cssref/pr_list-style-type.asp
Special characters like Ö	www.w3schools.com/tags/ref_entities.asp
Tags	http://www.w3schools.com/tags/tag_html.asp
Validation	validator.w3.org/#validate_by_upload

Required HTML Tags

Every HTML source file must contain the following tags except <p> ... </p> in the given order:

```
<!doctype html>
<html>
 <head>
  <meta charset="UTF-8"/>
  <title>Required Tags</title>
 </head>
 <body>
  <p>Content</p>
 </body>
</html>
```

HTML Tags

Anchor (<a> </a>): Defines a hyperlink using the href="*fn*" attribute, where *fn* is a pathname to the file (relative), or a URL (absolute) for the file. The text between the two tags is known as the *link* and is highlighted.

```
<a href="nextPage.html">Click here for next page</a>
```

Text Only! Remember, HTML source files must contain standard keyboard text (ASCII) only. Word processors include fancy formatting that confuses browsers. Use simple text editors only, such as Notepad++ for Windows or TextWrangler for Macs. Also, the file name extension—the characters after the last dot in the file name—must be html.

Body (<body> </body>): Specifies the extent of the body of the HTML document (see the Required HTML Tags section above). Useful style attributes include:

- "background-color: *color*" paints the background the specified *color*
- "color: *color*" displays text in the specified *color*
- "font-family: *face*" displays the text in the specified font *face*

Bold (<b> </b>): Specifies that the style of the enclosed text is to be a bold font.

```
<b>This text prints as bold</b>
```

Caption (<caption> </caption>): Specifies a table caption, and must be enclosed by table tags (see the entry for "Table" for an example).

Comment (<!-- *comment goes here* -->): The comment text is enclosed within angle brackets; avoid using angle brackets or "double minuses" in the comments.

```
<!-- This text will not appear on the finished Web page -->
```

Definitional List (<dl> </dl>): Defines a definitional list, which is composed of two-part entries, called the definitional-list term (<dt> </dt>) and the definitional-list definition (<dd> </dd>). Terms are on separate lines and the definitions are on the following lines.

```
<dl>
  <dt>First term</dt>
  <dd>First definition goes here</dd>
  <dt>Second term</dt>
  <dd>Second definition goes here</dd>
</dl>
```

Header (<head> </head>): Defines the extent of the head section of the HTML document, which must include a title (see the Required HTML Tags section above).

Headings (<h1> </h1> . . . <h6> </h6>): Specifies that the enclosed text is to be one of six heading levels.

```
<h1> Heading level 1 </h1>
<h2> Heading level 2 </h2>
...
<h6> Heading level 6 </h6>
```

The smaller the number, the larger and more prominent the text.

Horizontal Rule (<hr/>): Defines a line that spans the window; should appear outside of paragraph tags. Reduce the span using the styling property width="*p*%", as in

```
<hr style="width:75%"/>
```

The (point) thickness of the line is styled by the property size="*n*".

HTML (<html> </html>): Defines the beginning and end of the document (see the Required HTML Tags section above).

Image (<img . . . />): Causes an image—specified by the src="*fn*" attribute—to be placed in the document at the current position. In addition to the src attribute, the alt="*text*" attribute is required to give the image a text interpretation. Position styling information uses the float property. Also, one of height or width attributes (but not both at once) can specify the displayed image's size in pixels.

```
<img src="prettyPic.jpg" style='float:left' alt='Sunset' width='140'/>
```

Italics (<i> </i>): Specifies that the style of the enclosed text is to be italic.

```
<i>This text is emphasized by italics</i>
```

Line Break (<br/>): Ends the current line and continues the text on the next line.

This text is on one line.
 This text is on the next line.

List Item (<li> </li>): Specifies an entry in either an ordered or an unordered list (see the entries for "Ordered List" and "Unordered List" for examples).

Ordered List (<ol> </ol>): Specifies the extent of an ordered list, whose entries are list items. The list items are automatically prefixed with a number.

```
<ol>
  <li>First list item</li>
  <li>Second list item</li>
</ol>
```

Paragraph (<p> </p>): Specifies the extent of a paragraph. Paragraphs begin on a new line.

```
<p> This text forms a one-line paragraph.</p>
```

Table (<table> </table>): Defines a table of table rows; the rows contain table data. Optionally, the first row of the definition can be formed with table heading tags. The attribute border gives the table a border.

```
<table border="1">
  <caption>Description</caption>
  <tr>
    <th>Head Col 1</th>
    <th>Head Col 2</th>
    <th>Head Col 3</th>
  </tr>
  <tr>
    <td>Row 1, Cell 1</td>
    <td>Row 1, Cell 2</td>
    <td>Row 1, Cell 3</td>
  </tr>
  <tr>
    <td>Row 2, Cell 1</td>
    <td>Row 2, Cell 2</td>
    <td>Row 2, Cell 3</td>
  </tr>
  <tr>
    <td>Row 3, Cell 1</td>
    <td>Row 3, Cell 2</td>
    <td>Row 3, Cell 3</td>
  </tr>
</table>
```

Table Data (<td> </td>): Specifies a cell in a table, and must be enclosed by table row tags. A useful styling property is "background-color= *color*".

Table Heading (<th> </th>): Specifies a cell in the heading row of a table, and must be enclosed by table row tags. A useful styling property is "background-color:*color*".

Table Row (<tr> </tr>): Specifies a row in a table, and must be enclosed by table tags. See the entry for "Table" for an example.

Title (<title> </title>): Defines the page title; it must be given in the header section of the HTML source.

```
<title> Title displays at the top of the browser window</title>
```

Unordered List (<ul> </ul>): Specifies the extent of an unordered list, whose entries are list items. The list items are automatically preceded by a bullet. A list item can enclose another list.

```
<ul>
  <li>First list item</li>
  <li>Second list item</li>
</ul>
```

Worked Example: D.C. Trip Page

```
<!doctype html>
<html>
 <head>
  <meta charset="UTF-8">
  <title>Travel Page</title>
  <style>
   body {background-image:url('background1.jpg');
         background-repeat:repeat-x;
          color:white;
          font-family:Helvetica Neue Light;
          }
```

```
    p   {color:white; margin-left:160px; margin-right:120px}
    ul  {list-style-type:none; margin:0; margin-left:140px; padding:0;}
    li  {text-align:center; font-size:20px;}
    li.top   {display:inline;}
    a.top   {text-decoration:none; width:140px; height:40px; background-color:none;
            float:left; padding:10px;padding-top:20px; margin-left:3px; color:white;
            border-bottom-color:white; border-bottom-width:1px; border-bottom-style:solid}
    a.top:hover  {background-color:blueviolet;}
    a.side  {text-decoration:none;display:block; width:100px; color:white; background-color:none; }
    a.side:hover {background-color:magenta;}
  </style>
 </head>
 <body>
     <ul>
     <li class="top"><a class="top" href=" ">HOME</a></li>
     <li class="top"><a class="top" href=" ">ABOUT</a></li>
     <li class="top"><a class="top" href=" ">TRIPS</a></li>
     <li class="top"><a class="top" href=" ">CONTACT</a></li>
   </ul><br/><br/>
   <h1 style="margin:50px; text-align:center;font-weight:lighter">Welcome To My Travel Page</h1>
   <h2 style="margin:30px; text-align:center">Washington DC</h2>
   <ul style="float:left; margin-right:35px; margin-left:25px">
     <li class="side">Past Trips</li>
     <li class="side"><a class="side" href=" ">2014</a></li>
     <li class="side"><a class="side" href=" ">2013</a></li>
     <li class="side"><a class="side" href=" ">2012</a></li>
     <li class="side"><a class="side" href=" ">2011</a></li>
     <li class="side"><a class="side" href=" ">2010</a></li>
     <li class="side"><a class="side" href=" ">2009</a></li>
     <li class="side"><a class="side" href=" ">2008</a></li>
     <li class="side"><a class="side" href=" ">2007</a></li>
     <li class="side"><a class="side" href=" ">2006</a></li>
   </ul>
   <img src="dcFLAT.jpg" alt="Telephoto of DC Monuments" width="600"/>
   <p> My trip to Washington DC was a total wipe out. People never
       sleep there, and I didn't either. We visited monuments,
       statues and museums all day, and then partied all night.
  </body>
</html>
```

APPENDIX B

RSA Public Key Cryptosystem

THE RSA public key cryptosystem is the best known of the PKC systems. Named for its inventors, Ron Rivest, Adi Shamir, and Len Adleman, the RSA scheme is basically the same as the PKC scheme we described in Chapter 12. We need to learn enough about how it works to retrieve the original cleartext. *Why* it works relies on very deep mathematics and computer science that are not described here. But it does work. It has withstood formidable attacks and will continue to do so as computers get faster. We'll describe the assaults on RSA after we give it a try.

Secret Prize. Rivest, Shamir, and Adleman were awarded the 2003 Turing Award by the Association for Computing Machinery, computing's Nobel Prize, for their creation of the RSA cryptosystem.

The RSA scheme relies on prime numbers. Recall from middle school that **prime numbers** can only be divided evenly—that is, without a remainder—by 1 and themselves. So, the first few prime numbers are 2, 3, 5, 7, 11, 13, 17, 19, 23, 29, 31, ...

Mathematicians adore prime numbers because they have amazing properties. The rest of us only know that prime numbers are the basic "atoms" of a whole number: Any number can be **factored** into primes in only one way. The factors of a number x are just whole numbers that when multiplied together give x. So, factors of 30 are

$1 \times 30 = 30$
$2 \times 15 = 30$
$3 \times 10 = 30$
$5 \times 6 = 30$
$2 \times 3 \times 5 = 30$

but only {2,3,5} are the prime factors of 30.

Choosing a Key

The secret of the RSA scheme, of course, is that the receiver didn't publish any random 129-digit sequence as the public key, K_R. The key has some special properties. Specifically, the public key must be the product of two different prime numbers, p and q,

$K_R = pq$

Because multiplying two numbers of roughly equal size produces a number twice as long, p and q must be about 64 or 65 digits long to produce the 129-digit public key of the example. Additionally, p and q, besides being long enough and prime, must also be 2 greater than a multiple of 3. It's a rather strange requirement, but essential, as you'll see in a moment. Many primes have this property. For example, 5 and 11 are 2 larger than multiples of 3, namely, 3 and 9. As a running example, take

$p = 5$
$q = 11$
$K_R = pq = 55.$

Encrypting a Message

To encrypt a cleartext, divide it into blocks—we'll use 6-bit blocks of the ASCII encoding for the running example, but they're usually many bytes long—cube the blocks, divide them by the public key, and transmit the remainders from the divisions. (We use 6-bit blocks just to keep the numbers small.)

Thus, to encrypt the amount of a credit card transaction,

****$0.02

the ASCII characters are expressed in their byte representation

0010 1010 0010 1010 0010 1010 0010 1010 0010 0100 0011 0000
0010 1110 0011 0000 0011 0010

and grouped into 6-bit blocks,

0010 1010 0010 1010 0010 1010 0010 1010 0010 0100 0011 0000
0010 1110 0011 0000 0011 0010

shown in white and blue.

Recalling from Chapter 8 that bits can be interpreted in any way that is convenient, our groups are interpreted as numbers

T = 10, 34, 40, 42, 10, 34, 16, 48, 11, 35, 0, 50

Cubed, they are

T^3 = 1000, 39304, 64000, 74088, 1000, 39304, 4096, 110592, 1331, 42875, 0, 125000

and divided by the key $K_R = 55$ and expressed in quotient-remainder form they are as follows:

1000	$= 55 \cdot 18 + 10$
39304	$= 55 \cdot 714 + 34$
64000	$= 55 \cdot 1163 + 35$
74088	$= 55 \cdot 1347 + 3$
1000	$= 55 \cdot 18 + 10$
39304	$= 55 \cdot 714 + 34$
4096	$= 55 \cdot 74 + 26$
110592	$= 55 \cdot 2010 + 42$
1331	$= 55 \cdot 24 + 11$
42875	$= 55 \cdot 779 + 30$
0	$= 55 \cdot 0 + 0$
125000	$= 55 \cdot 2272 + 40$

And finally, only the remainders are kept to yield the cipher text:

C = 10, 34, 35, 3, 10, 34, 26, 42, 11, 30, 0, 40

These numbers are the encrypted message to be sent. (The apparent coincidence that some of the cipher text numbers happened to be the same as their corresponding cleartext occurs because our sample numbers (55) are so small. The result is still incomprehensibly scrambled.)

The Decryption Method

How does the receiver reconstruct the cleartext? First, we must compute the quantity

$$s = (1/3)[2(p - 1)(q - 1) + 1]$$

For our running example, this curious number is

$$s = (1/3)\ (2 \cdot 4 \cdot 10 + 1) = 81/3 = 27$$

To make s come out right, we added the requirement of "2 greater than a multiple of 3" when choosing p and q.

The amazing fact is that if the cipher text numbers C are each raised to the s power, C^s—that's right, C^{27} in our example—and divided by the key K_R, the remainders are the cleartext! That is, for some quotient c that we don't care about,

$$C^s = K_R \cdot c + T$$

which is *truly* the key to the RSA scheme.

Decrypting: $C = 10$. To demonstrate this amazing fact, take the first number of our cipher text

$$C = 10$$

and compute

$C^s = C^{27} = 10^{27} = 1{,}000{,}000{,}000{,}000{,}000{,}000{,}000{,}000{,}000$

which is not a binary number, but the huge decimal number of 1 followed by 27 zeros. Divide by $K_R = 55$ and express the result in the quotient-remainder form

$1{,}000{,}000{,}000{,}000{,}000{,}000{,}000{,}000{,}000$
$= 55 \cdot 18{,}181{,}818{,}181{,}818{,}181{,}818{,}181{,}818 + 10$

Thus, $T = 10$, so the first 6 bits of the cleartext must be 10 in binary, 001010, as can be checked.

Decrypting: $C = 3$. The numbers can get very large for us—encryption algorithms actually use several techniques, such as modular arithmetic, to avoid the large intermediate numbers—but let's try another example. The fourth term of the cipher text is

$C = 3$

which we can raise to the 27th power with a calculator to get

$3^s = 3^{27} = 7{,}625{,}597{,}484{,}987$

Dividing by the public key K_R and expressing the result in the quotient-remainder form yields

$7{,}625{,}597{,}484{,}987 = 55 \cdot 138{,}647{,}226{,}999 + 42$

implying that the fourth block of the text is binary for 42, or 101010, as can be verified. As a third example, we notice that everything works out right for the cipher text $C = 0$.

Why does the RSA work? Euler proved the following theorem in 1736. (This is the only occurrence of higher mathematics in this book. It isn't necessary to understand it; simply accept that Euler's formula makes the RSA scheme work.)

Theorem: Let p and q be distinct primes, $K = pq$, $0 < T < K$, and $r > 0$.

If $T^{r(p-1)(q-1)+1}$ is divided by K, the remainder is T.

For our use of Euler's formula, $r = 2$, because

$$(T^3)^s = (T^3)^{(1/3)[2(p-1)(q-1)+1]}$$
$$= T^{2(p-1)(q-1)+1}$$

Thus, when the cipher text—that is, the remainders—is raised to the s power and divided by the key, the cleartext is recovered.

Summarizing the RSA System

To summarize, (our sample version of) the RSA public key crypto scheme follows these steps:

1. **Publishing.** Select two different prime numbers, p and q, which are 2 larger than a multiple of 3, and define $K_R = pq$, the public key. Compute $s = (1/3)[2(p-1)(q-1) + 1]$. Keep p, q, and s secret. Publish K_R where senders can find it.
2. **Encrypting.** Get the public key from the receiver, and break the cleartext bit sequence into blocks according to the receiver's instructions, but less than K_R. Cube each block, divide each of the cubes by K_R, and send the remainders to the receiver as the cipher text.

3. **Decrypting.** Using the secret value *s*, raise each number in the cipher text to the *s* power, divide each result by K_R, and assemble the remainders into the blocks of the bit sequence of the cleartext.

Of course, humans don't do these calculations. Software does. And though the software is extremely sophisticated to perform these operations fast, the principles that the programs implement are embodied in these three steps.

RSA Security Challenge. Can RSA withstand attacks? Can anyone actually break the code? As far as is known, scientifically, a code cracker would have to figure out what *s* is to break the code. Constructing *s* is easy if the two primes *p* and *q* are known.

Factoring the Key. The problem of finding *s* reduces to factoring the public key K_R to discover *p* and *q*. But factoring large numbers is a computationally difficult problem, even for the world's fastest computers. It is the fact that factoring large numbers is so difficult that keeps the public key encryption schemes secure. Put another way, if the key is large enough, it can be published because there is no known way to factor it into its two prime components in any reasonable amount of time.

APPENDIX C

iDiary: Tags and Templates

THIS APPENDIX contains the XML database and the XSL template style information for the iDiary in Chapter 16. The content shown here produced Figure 16.1. All tags used in the chapter are illustrated here.

XML Database File iDiary.xml

```
<?xml version = "1.0" encoding="UTF-8" ?>
<?xml-stylesheet type="text/xsl" href="iDiarySS.xsl"?>

<idiary>
  <entry>
    <cool><title>The Digital Diary</title>
      This will be fun! I start my digital journal today. So, to launch it with the right sentiment,
      I looked up what Henry David Thoreau wrote on the first day of his famous <ital>Journal.
      </ital> He wrote, <quote>"'What are you doing now?' he asked. 'Do you keep a journal?'
      So I make my first entry today."</quote>
      Which, I guess, is pretty much what I just said. Great minds ... !
    </cool>
  </entry>

  <entry>
   <date> 11 August 2013 </date>
   <cool><title>Human-powered Helicopter</title>
     It's so totally awesome! It's been a month
     since a Toronto team won the Sikorsky Prize, but OMG, I can't stop thinking about it!
     So, I start this journal with Di Vinci's dream-come-true!
     <ytvid file="https://www.youtube.com/embed/syJq10EQkog"/>
     Sikorsy requires: Be aloft 60 seconds; rise to 3 m; stay inside a 10m x 10m square. In the
     <link url="http://youtu.be/U7ZOqYpLWJY">winning flight </link>[at 3:30], 50 seconds are
     spent descending to avoid the perils of the downdraft!
   </cool>
  </entry>

  <entry>
   <date> 12 August 2013</date>
    <cool>I ran across this today, and am saving it here so I don't lose track of it. It needs
    more reading.
```

```
    <poem>
      <p_title>Vespertina Cognitio</p_title>
      <poet>Natasha Trethewey</poet>
      <line>Overhead, pelicans glide in threes—</line>
      <line amt="2"> their shadows across the sand</line>
      <line amt="4"> dark thoughts crossing the mind. </line>
      <skip/>
      <line>Beyond the fringe of coast, shrimpers</line>
      <line amt="2"> hoist their nets, weighing the harvest</line>
      <line amt="4"> against the day's losses. Light waning, </line>
      <skip/>
      <line>concentration is a lone gull</line>
      <line amt="2">circling what's thrown back. Debris</line>
      <line amt="4">weights the trawl like stones. </line>
      <skip/>
      <line>All day, this dredging—beneath the tug</line>
      <line amt="2"> of waves—rhythm of what goes out,</line>
      <line amt="4"> comes back, comes back, comes back.</line>
    </poem>
   </cool>
 </entry>

 <entry>
  <date>13 August 2013</date>
  <cool>
    <title>Potentially Hazardous Astroids</title>
     Wow! I read so much poetry, I missed yesterday's APOD!
     NASA has plotted the orbits of the inner planets, and potentially hazardous astroids.
     Hmm ... don't a lot of 'em cross Earth's orbit?<para>
     <pic file="im/APODpicOfTheDay.jpg" width="350"/></para>
     <link url="http://apod.nasa.gov/apod/ap130812.html">Here's the high resolution
     image.</link> The Astronomy PIcture of The Day has to be about the BEST science
     site on the Internet. Thanks APOD! (<ital>Sun not shown actual size.</ital>)
  </cool>
 </entry>

 <entry>
  <date> 14 August 2013</date>
  <cool>
    <title>Science Finally Asks Permission</title>
      Last year I read<ital>The Immortal Life of Henrietta Lacks</ital> by Rebecca Skloot.
      Lacks was a poor African American tobacco farmer and mother of five, who died of
      cervical cancer in 1951 at age 31. Doctors at Johns Hopkins took cancer cells from
      her without permission. Because her cells continue to grow in the lab, they're key to
      medical research. Skloot profiles her and her family, stressing their confusion and
      hurt because her cells cured diseases; scientists got fame, she got nothing. HeLa cells,
      cited in 70,000 scientific papers, are <ital>still </ital>growing 60 years later. <bold>
      Immortal!</bold>
      <para>
      <pic file="im/lacks.jpg" width = "100"/> <pic file="im/hela.jpg" width="390"/></para>
      Her genome has now been sequenced. Today the National Institutes of Health set up a
      board to approve research with her genome; 2 family members sit on the board. Finally!
      <link url="http://www.npr.org/player/v2/mediaPlayer.html?action=1&amp;t=1&amp;islist=false&amp;id=209807857&amp;m=210062375">
      Hear NPR Here</link>
    </cool>
  </entry>
  <!--The following tags are available for adding a new entry.
    Change the places containing black letters or dashes
  <entry>
   <date> dd mm yyyy</date>
   <cool>
     <para>  <ital>  <bold>
     <link url="http:// - ">anchor text</link>
     <title> title text </title>
     <pic file="-.jpg" width="-" />
     <quote> blockquote text </quote>
     <poem>
       <p_title> poem title</p_title>
       <poet> poet's name </poet>
       <line amt="d"> set d to digit for d tabs </line>
       <skip/>
     </poem>
     <ytvidd url=" - "/>
   </cool>
  </entry>
-->
</idiary>
```

XSL file iDiarySS.xsl

```
<?xml version="1.0" encoding="UTF-8"?>
<xsl:stylesheet version="1.0"
  xmlns:xsl="http://www.w3.org/1999/XSL/Transform">

<xsl:template match="idiary">
  <html><head><title>iDiary</title>
      <style>
        body  {background-color : white; font-family : helvetica}
        h1    {text-align : center}
        h2    {text-align : center; color : #993400; margin-bottom:5px;
               margin-top:8px}
        h3    {margin-bottom:5px; margin-top:8px}
        h4    {margin-bottom:5px; margin-top:8px}
        ul    {margin-left : auto; margin-right : auto; list-style-type : none}
        li.entry { color : black; padding : 10px; border-bottom-style:solid;
              border-bottom-width: 0.5px; border-right-style:solid;
              border-right-width: 0.5px; margin-bottom : 20px }
        li.date {color : white; position:relative; left : -50px;
               background-color : sienna; padding : 8px}
        p     {text-align:center ;}
        a:link {text-decoration: none; color : #993400 }
        a:visited {color :  #993400}
        a:hover {color : #c3bc9a }
      </style>
    </head>
    <body>
      <h1>iDiary: Journal of Interesting Stuff</h1>
        <ul style="max-width:435px">
            <li style="background-color : sienna; color:white; padding:10px">
              <i>This is a record of the most interesting
              thing I find out each day that's worth
              remembering. There's personal stuff in this
              database, too, but it's not gonna be displayed! </i>
          </li>
        </ul>
        <ul style="max-width:700px;">
            <xsl:apply-templates/>
        </ul>
    </body>
  </html>
</xsl:template>

<xsl:template match="entry">
        <xsl:apply-templates/>
</xsl:template>
<xsl:template match="cool">
      <li class="entry">
        <xsl:apply-templates/>
      </li>
</xsl:template>

<xsl:template match="date">
      <li class="date">
       <xsl:apply-templates/>
      </li>
</xsl:template>

<xsl:template match="title">
  <h2>
    <xsl:apply-templates/>
  </h2>
</xsl:template>
```

```
<xsl:template match="quote">
  <blockquote style="background-color : #c89848;
     color:white; padding:10px; font-size:small">
    <xsl:apply-templates/>
  </blockquote>
</xsl:template>
<xsl:template match="link">
  <a href="{@url}">
    <b><xsl:apply-templates/></b>
  </a>
</xsl:template>

<xsl:template match="pic">
      <img src="{@file}" width="{@width}"
            alt="Picture of Interesting Thing"/>
</xsl:template>

<xsl:template match="ytvid">
    <br/><br/><iframe width="560" height="315"
      src="{@file}" frameborder="0" allowfullscreen="1">
    </iframe><br/><br/>
</xsl:template>

<xsl:template match="poem">
    <span style="font-family : century gothic">
      <xsl:apply-templates/>
    </span>
 </xsl:template>

<xsl:template match="p_title">
  <h3>
     <xsl:apply-templates/>
  </h3>
</xsl:template>

<xsl:template match="poet">
  <h4><i>
     <xsl:apply-templates/>
  </i></h4>
</xsl:template>

<xsl:template match="line">
    <span style="padding-left:{@amt}0px">
      <xsl:apply-templates/>
    <br/></span>
</xsl:template>

<xsl:template match="skip">
    <br/>
</xsl:template>

<xsl:template match="bold">
  <b><xsl:apply-templates/></b>
</xsl:template>

<xsl:template match="ital">
    <i><xsl:apply-templates/></i>
</xsl:template>

<xsl:template match="para">
    <p><xsl:apply-templates/></p>
</xsl:template>
```

```
<xsl:template match="personal">
    <!--Display Personal Information -->
    <xsl:apply-templates/>
</xsl:template>

</xsl:stylesheet>
```

APPENDIX D

JavaScript Programming Rules

THIS APPENDIX summarizes in brief statements the "rules" for writing JavaScript and the rules that JavaScript follows when executing programs. The chapter in which each rule was introduced is given in brackets. Notice Tables D.1, escape sequences; D.2, reserved words; and D.3, JavaScript operators.

Program Structure

White space is ignored [17]. Any number of spaces, tabs, or new line characters can generally separate the components of a program. Avoid breaking up identifiers and literals such as numbers and strings.

Place declarations first [17]. Declarations should appear before other statements. If there are multiple blocks of JavaScript code, place global declarations at the beginning of the first block.

First-to-last execution [17]. Program statements are all executed from first to last, unless specifically commanded to skip using conditional `if` statements or told to repeat using `for` statements.

Terminate statements with semicolons [17]. Every statement, including those on their own line, must be terminated with a semicolon (;), except the compound statement (i.e., the curly brace (}) is *not* followed by a semicolon).

Slash slash comment [17]. Text from // to the end of the line is treated as a comment. For example,

```
x = 3.1; //Set rate
```

Slash star–star slash comment [17]. All text enclosed by the symbols /* and */ is treated as a comment, and so can span several lines. For example,

```
/* The text in a Slash Star-Star Slash comment can spill across lines of a program, but the
Slash Slash comment is limited to the end of one line. */
```

Data Types

Four rules for numbers [17]. Numerical constants:

1. Keep the digits together without spaces, so `3.141 596` is wrong, whereas `3.141596` is right.
2. Don't use digit grouping symbols of any type, so `1,000,000` is wrong, whereas `1000000` is right.
3. Use a period as the decimal point, so `0,221` is wrong, whereas `0.221` is right.
4. Use no units, so `33%` and `$10.89` are wrong, whereas `0.33` and `10.89` are right.

Six rules for strings [17]. When typing string literals:

1. The characters must be surrounded by quotes, either single (') or double (").
2. Most characters are allowed within quotes except new line, backspace, tab, \, form feed, and return (Enter).
3. Double-quoted strings can contain single quotes and vice versa.
4. The apostrophe (') is the same as the single quote.
5. Any number of characters is allowed in a string.
6. The minimum number of characters in a string is zero (""), which is called the empty string.

String literal escape characters [17]. Table D.1 gives the escape sequences for the special characters of string literals that cannot be typed directly. For example, "\b\b" is a string of two backspaces.

Boolean data type [17]. There are two Boolean values: `true` and `false`.

Table D.1 Escape sequences for characters prohibited from string literals

Sequence	Character	Sequence	Character
\b	Backspace	\f	Form feed
\n	New line	\r	Carriage return
\t	Tab	\'	Apostrophe or single quote
\"	Double quote	\\	Backslash

Variables and Declarations

Identifier structure [17]. Identifiers must begin with a letter and may contain any combination of letters, numerals, or underscores (_). Identifiers cannot contain white space. For example, green, eGGs, and ham_and_2_eggs are three identifiers.

Case sensitivity [17]. JavaScript identifiers are case sensitive, so y and Y are different.

Reserved words [17]. Some words, such as var and true, are reserved by JavaScript and cannot be identifiers. Table D.2 lists these words. To use a word in the list as an identifier, prefix it with an underscore (for example, _true), but it's safer (and smarter) to think up a different identifier.

Table D.2 Reserved words and property terms in JavaScript. These words cannot or should not be used as identifiers.

abstract	eval	moveBy	scrollbars
alert	export	moveTo	scrollBy
arguments	extends	name	scrollTo
Array	false	NaN	self
blur	final	native	setInterval
boolean	finally	netscape	setTimeout
Boolean	find	new	short
break	float	null	static
byte	focus	number	status
callee	for	Object	statusbar
caller	frames	open	stop
captureEvents	function	opener	String
case	Function	outerHeight	super
catch	goto	outerWidth	switch
char	history	package	synchronized
class	home	Packages	this
clearInterval	if	pageXOffset	throw
clearTimeout	implements	pageYOffset	throws
close	import	parent	toolbar
closed	in	parseFloat	top
confirm	infinity	parseInt	toString
const	innerHeight	personalbar	transient
constructor	innerWidth	print	true
continue	instanceof	private	try
Date	int	prompt	typeof
debugger	interface	protected	unescape
default	isFinite	prototype	unwatch
defaultStatus	isNaN	public	valueOf
delete	java	RegExp	var
do	length	releaseEvents	void
document	location	resizeBy	watch
double	locationbar	resizeTo	while
else	long	return	window
enum	Math	routeEvent	with
escape	menubar	scroll	

Declare variables [17]. All variables must be declared using var. Do not declare any variable more than once.

Variable declaration list separated by commas [17]. For example,

```
var prices, hemlines, interestRates;
```

Variable declaration initializers can be expressions [18]. For example,

```
var minutesInDay = 60 * 24;
```

Expressions

Operators [17]. A selection of JavaScript operators is given in Table D.3.

Table D.3 JavaScript operators used in this book

Name	Symbol	# of Operands and Data Type	Example	Comment	Result of Example
Addition	+	2 Numeric	4 + 5		9
Concatenation	+	2 String	"four"+"five" 6 + "pack"	1 numeric operand implies concatenate	"fourfive" "6 pack"
Subtraction	–	2 Numeric	9 – 5		4
Multiplication	*	2 Numeric	–2 * 4		–8
Division	/	2 Numeric	10/3		0.33333...
Modulus	%	2 Numeric	10%3	Remainder	1
Increment	++	1 Numeric	3++	See Chapter 20	4
Decrement	--	1 Numeric	3--	See Chapter 20	2
Less Than	<	2 Numeric	4 < 4		false
Less Than or Equal	<=	2 Numeric	4 <= 4		true
Equal	==	2 Numeric 2 String	4 == 4 "a" == "A"		true false
Not Equal	!=	2 Numeric 2 String	4 != 4 "a" != " a"		false true
Greater Than or Equal	>=	2 Numeric	4 >= 4		true
Greater Than	>	2 Numeric	4 > 4		false
Negation	–	1 Numeric	– 4		–4
Logical Not	!	1 Boolean	! true		false
Logical And	&&	2 Boolean	true && true		true
Logical Or	||	2 Boolean	false || true		true

Note: The examples use literal data (actual numbers) to show the operation; in practice the operands are variables.

Use parentheses [17]. Though JavaScript uses precedence to determine the order in which to perform operators when no parentheses are given, that feature is for professionals. To be safe, parenthesize all complex expressions.

Operator overloading [17]. Plus (+) means addition for numerical operands; it means concatenation for string operands. If + has an operand of each type (e.g., 4 + "5"), the number converts to a string and returns a string (e.g., "45").

Arrays and Indexes

Array declarations [20]. Arrays are declared using the var statement and the new Array (<*elements*>) designation, where <*elements*> is the number of array elements. For example,

```
var zodiacSigns = new Array (12);
```

Arrays are 0-origin, meaning the least index value is 0, and the largest index is <*elements*> – 1.

Array references [20]. Array elements can be referenced by the syntax

<*array_name*>[<*index*>]

where <*array_name*> is a declared array and <*index*> is any integer value from 0 to <*elements*> – 1. An array reference, for example, A[i], is a variable and can be used wherever variables can be used.

Index values [20]. An index value can be any expression, including a constant (e.g., 3), a variable (e.g., i), or an expression involving operators (e.g., (i + 12)%5) that evaluates to an integer in the range from 0 to the highest index of the array, <*elements*> – 1.

Statements

Assignment statement [17]. The assignment statement (e.g., lap = lap + 1) updates the value of a variable on the left side of the = (e.g., lap) by computing the value of the expression on the right side of the = (e.g., lap + 1) and making it the new value of the variable. The value flow is from the right side to the left side.

Compound statements [17]. A sequence of statements enclosed by { } is a compound statement and is treated as one statement, say, for purposes of the <*statement*> in if, if/else, iteration statements, and function declarations. The compound statement is not terminated by a semicolon, though statements it contains must be.

if statement [17]. The if statement, or conditional statement, has the form

if(<*Boolean expression*>)
  <*then-statement*>;

If the value of the Boolean expression is true, the <*then-statement*> is performed; if the Boolean expression is false, the <*then-statement*> is skipped.

if/else statement [17]. The if/else statement, or conditional statement, has the form

```
if( <Boolean expression> )
   <then-statement>;
else
   <else-statement>;
```

If the result of the Boolean expression is true, the *<then-statement>* is performed and the *<else-statement>* is skipped. If the Boolean expression is false, the *<then-statement>* is skipped and the *<else-statement>* is performed.

Conditional within a conditional [17]. If a conditional's *<then-statement>* or *<else-statement>* contains another conditional, make it a compound statement (enclose it in { }) to avoid ambiguity as to which if statement the else associates with.

for loops[20]. The for statement has the syntax

```
for( <initialization>; <continuation>; <next iteration> ) {
   <statement list>
}
```

The *<initialization>* is an assignment to the iteration variable, the *<continuation>* is a Boolean expression like those used in if statements, and the *<next iteration>* is an assignment to the iteration variable.

for loop operation [20]. A for loop works as follows: The initialization assignment is performed first, followed by the continuation test. If the test result is false, the *<statement list>* is skipped and the for loop ends. If the test result is true, the *<statement list>* is performed followed by the next iteration assignment. That completes one iteration. At the completion of an iteration, the process repeats with the continuation test.

World-Famous Iteration [20]. The World-Famous Iteration (WFI) is a for statement that has the following standard form:

```
for( <iteration var> = 0; <iteration var> < <limit> ; <iteration var>++ ) {
   <statement list>
}
```

The *<iteration var>* is any declared variable, and the *<limit>* is any expression or variable. An example is

```
for( j = 0; j < n ; j++ ) {
   <statement list>
}
```

The number of iterations—the number of times the loop loops—is n.

Functions

Function declaration [19]. Functions are declared using the following syntax:

```
function <name> ( <parameter list> ) {
   <statement list>
}
```

Notice the conspicuous position of the closed brace on its own line, below the *f* in function. The brace is not followed by a semicolon. An example is

```
function prefixTitle ( familyName, mORf ) {
   if (mORf = "M")
       return "Mr.  " + familyName;
   else
       return "Ms  " + familyName;
}
```

Function names are identifiers [19]. Function names, for example, prefixTitle, follow the rules for identifiers. It is best if the chosen name says what the function does.

Parameters are identifiers [19]. Function parameters, for example, familyName, follow the rules for identifiers.

Parameters are not declared [19]. Function parameters should not be declared because the JavaScript interpreter automatically declares them.

Return statement [19]. A function completes when it reaches a return statement:

return <*expression*>

The result of the function is the result of <*expression*>, which could simply be a variable.

Guidelines

Programmer's rules: Professional programmers have a set of good programming practices, including:

- Choose meaningful identifiers for variables. For example, interestRate is better than, say, p.
- Insert white space liberally to improve code readability. For example,

  ```
  if(input!="")name=first+last;
  ```

  is poor, while

  ```
  if( input != "" )
     name = first + last;
  ```

  is preferred.
- Comment programs liberally, saying what the variables mean and what the logic is doing.
- Align code—especially when the statements are logically related—and be consistent; it helps to locate errors.

Wrong:	Right:
`   able="a;`	`able    = "a";`
`baker = 'b';`	`baker   = "b";`
`   charlie = "c";`	`charlie = "c";`

APPENDIX E

The Bean Counter Program

THE FINAL HTML and JavaScript code for the Bean Counter application in Chapter 18 appears on the following pages. Note that variations in Web browsers will affect how closely it matches the sample output in the figure.

```
<!doctype html>
<html>
  <head>
   <meta charset="UTF-8"/>
   <title>The Bean Counter</title>
   <script>
      var shots = 1;
      var drink = "none";
      var ounce = 0;
   </script>
   <style>
       body {background-color : saddlebrown; color : darkorange;
              font-family : helvetica; text-align : center}
       hr     {width:50%; color: darkorange}
       h1    {color : white;}
       table {margin-left : auto; margin-right : auto; text-align : center;
              background-color : #993300; border-style : solid;
              border-color : firebrick; border-width : medium; padding : 8px }
       td.tot, td.echo {border-style : solid; border-width : medium; }
       td.tot {border-color : red;}
       td.echo {border-color:gold;}
       select {color:saddlebrown; text-align:center;   }
   </style>
  </head>
  <body>
    <h1> the bean counter</h1>
    <hr/>
    <p><b>figuring the price of espresso drinks<br />
           so baristas can have time to chat</b></p>

     <table>
      <tr><td colspan="4" style="text-align:left;">
       <form name="emp">
       <select id="employee" >
       <option value="-">-Sign In-</option>
       <option value="C"> Charlie </option>
       <option value="J"> Juliette </option>
       <option value="M"> Mike </option>
       <option value="O"> Oscar </option>
       <option value="R"> Romeo </option>
       <option value="V"> Victor </option>
        </select> Is Pulling For Us
        </form>
        </td>
     </tr>

     <tr>
      <td class="echo"><input type="text" form="esp" id="shotpic" value=" " size="1"/></td>
      <td class="echo"><input type="text" form="esp" id="sizepic" value=" " size="1"/></td>
      <td class="echo"><input type="text" form="esp" id="coffee" value=" " size="10"/></td>
      <td> </td>
    </tr>

     <tr>
       <td><button form="esp" onclick='shots = 1; shotpic.value="  1"' > 1 </button></td>
       <td><button form="esp" onclick='ounce = 8; sizepic.value="  S"'> S </button></td>
       <td><button form="esp" onclick='drink = "espresso"; coffee.value="  Espresso  "'>
                ESPRESSO     </button></td>
       <td><button form="esp" onclick='
         shots = 1;
         drink = "none";
         ounce = 0;
         disp.value = "0.00"
         shotpic.value= " "; sizepic.value=" "; coffee.value=" ";
          '> Clear </button></td>
      </tr>
```

```
<tr>
 <td><button form="esp"  onclick='shots = 2; shotpic.value="  2" '> 2 </button></td>
 <td><button form="esp" onclick='ounce = 12; sizepic.value="  T"  '> T </button></td>
 <td><button form="esp" onclick='drink = "latte"; coffee.value="  Latte     " '>
            LATTE        </button></td>
 <td></td>
</tr>

<tr>
 <td><button form='esp' onclick='shots = 3; shotpic.value = "  3" '> 3 </button></td>
 <td><button form="esp" onclick='ounce = 16; sizepic.value= "  G"'> G </button></td>
 <td><button form="esp" onclick='drink = "cappuccino";  coffee.value=" Cappucino "'>
       CAPPUCCINO  </button>
 </td>
 <td><button form="esp"
     onclick='
       var price = -10;
       var taxRate = 0.087;
       if (drink == "espresso")
          price = 1.40;
       if (drink == "latte" || drink == "cappuccino") {
       if (ounce == 8)
          price = 1.95;
       if (ounce == 12)
          price = 2.35;
       if (ounce == 16)
          price = 2.75;
       }
       if (drink == "Americano")
          price = 1.20 + .30 * (ounce/8);
       price = price + (shots - 1) * .50;
       price = price + price * taxRate;
       disp.value = (Math.round(100*price)/100).toFixed(2);
     '> Total  </button></td>
</tr>

<tr>
 <td><button form="esp"  onclick='shots = 4; shotpic.value = "  4"'> 4 </button></td>
 <td></td>
 <td><button form="esp" onclick='drink = "Americano"; coffee.value = "  Americano"'>
       AMERICANO  </button>
 </td>
 <td class="tot">
  <form name="esp">
  <input type="text" id="disp" value="0.00" size="5" />
  </form>
 </td>
</tr>
</table>

</body>
</html>
```

APPENDIX F

myApps Page

THE FOLLOWING HTML and JavaScript code produces the Web-based myApps page from Chapter 19 (and 20).

myApps

myApps

bmi | C° ≈ F°

counter | RPS

coin flip | magic 8

my age: 573449015 seconds

myApps Page

```
<!doctype html>
<html>
 <head>
  <meta charset="UTF-8"><title>myApps</title>
  <style>
    body  {background-color:black; color:cyan;font-family:helvetica}
    h2    {color:white;text-align:center;}
    table {margin-left:auto;margin-right:auto;}
    td     {background-color:orangered; color:white;min-width:100px;
             text-align:center; padding:20px;}
    td.alta {background-color:deeppink;}
    td.altb {background-color:fuchsia;}
    a      {text-decoration:none;color:white;}
  </style>
 </head>
 <body>
  <h2>myApps</h2>
  <table border="0">
    <tr><td><a href="bmi.html"> bmi </a></td>
         <td><a href="temperature.html"> C° ≈ F°</a></td></tr>
    <tr><td class="alta"><a href="counter.html"> counter </a></td>
         <td class="alta"><a href="rps.html"> RPS</a></td></tr>
    <tr><td class="altb"><a href="flipOut.html">coin flip</a></td>
         <td class="altb"><a href="itsMagic.html"> magic 8</a></td></tr>
  </table>
   <script type="text/javascript">
    var today = new Date( );   // Get today's date
    var myBdate = new Date( );  // Get a date object to modify
    var difference;  // Declare a temporary variable
    myBdate.setFullYear(1995);  // Set my birth year to 1993
    myBdate.setMonth(6);  // Set my birth mo to July (mos start at 0)
    myBdate.setDate(4); // Set my birth day to 4th
    myBdate.setHours(12); // Set my hour of birth to noon
    myBdate.setMinutes(0);// Set my minute of birth to o'clock
    myBdate.setSeconds(0);   // Set my second of birth on the hour
    difference = today.getTime( ) - myBdate.getTime( );
    difference = Math.floor(difference/1000);
    document.write(" <p style='text-align:center'> my age: " + difference +
       " seconds </p>");
   </script>
 </body>
</html>
```

Body Mass Index

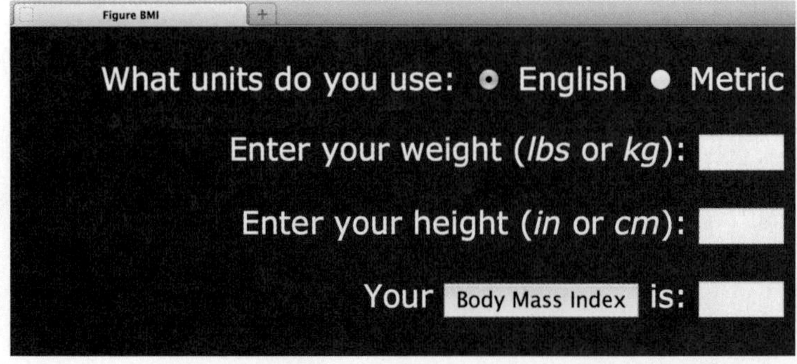

```
<!doctype html>
<html>
  <head>
   <meta charset="UTF-8"/>
    <title>Figure BMI</title><style>
      body {background-color : indigo; color : white; font-family : verdana}
      p   {text-align : right}</style>
  </head>
  <body>
   <script>
     var scale='E';
     function bmiM( weightKg, heightCm ) {
       var heightM = heightCm / 100;
       return weightKg / (heightM * heightM);
     }
     function bmiE( weightLbs, heightIn ) {
       return 703 * weightLbs / (heightIn * heightIn);
     }
     function BMI( units, weight, height) {
       if (units == "E")
         return bmiE( weight, height);  // English
       else
         return bmiM( weight, height);  // Metric
     }
   </script>
   <form name="mass">
     <p> What units do you use:
       <input type="radio" id="unit" onclick='scale="E"'
         checked/> English
       <input type="radio" id="unit" onclick='scale="M"'/>
         Metric</p>
     <p>Enter your weight (<i>lbs</i> or <i>kg</i>):
       <input type="text" id="wgt" size="4"/></p>
     <p> Enter your height (<i>in</i> or <i>cm</i>):
       <input type="text" id="hgt" size="4"/> </p>
     <p> Your
       <input type="button" value="Body Mass Index" id="figure"
         onclick="ans.value= BMI( scale, wgt.value, hgt.value)"/> is:
       <input type="text" id="ans" size="4"/></p>
   </form>
  </body>
</html>
```

Temperature Conversion

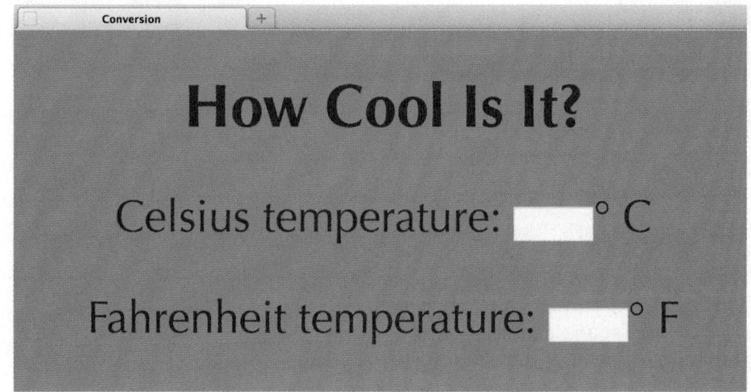

```
<!doctype html>
<html>
  <head> <meta charset="UTF-8"/><title>Conversion</title>
     <style>
       body {background-color : dodgerblue; font-family : optima;
             color: midnightblue; text-align : center}
       p      {font-size : x-large}
     </style>
   </head>
  <body>
    <h1>How Cool Is It? </h1>
    <script>
      function convertC2F (tempInC) {
        return 9/5*tempInC + 32;
      }
      function convertF2C (tempInF) {
        return 5/9*(tempInF - 32);
      }
    </script>
    <form id="cool">
      <p> Celsius temperature:
        <input type="text" id="textTempC" size="4"
          onchange="textTempF.value=Math.round(
          convertC2F(textTempC.value))"/>&#176; C</p>
      <p> Fahrenheit temperature:
        <input type="text" id="textTempF" size="4"
          onchange="textTempC.value=Math.round(
          convertF2C(textTempF.value))"/>&#176; F</p>
    </form>
  </body>
</html>
```

Count and Score

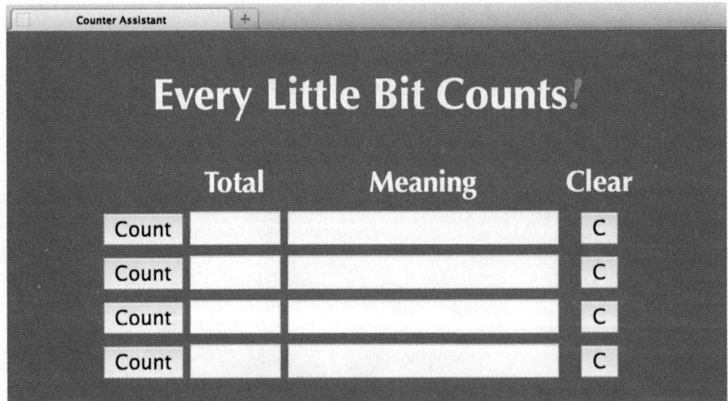


```
<!doctype html>
<html>
  <head>
    <meta charset="UTF-8"/><title>Counter Assistant</title>
     <style type="text/css">
       body  {background-color : blueviolet; color : white; font-family : optima;
              text-align : center}
       table {margin-left : auto; margin-right : auto}
     </style>
```

```
<script>
  var count1=0, count2=0, count3=0, count4=0;
  function makeTable ( ) {
    document.write('<table> <tr><th> </th><th> Total </th>');
    document.write('<th> Meaning </th> <th>Clear</th></tr>');
    row(1); row(2); row(3); row(4);
    document.write('</table>');
  }
  function row(num) {
    document.write('<tr><td><input type="button" value="Count"' );
    document.write(' onclick="count'+num+'=count'+num+'+1;' );
    document.write('arch'+num+'.value=count'+num+'"/></td>' );
    document.write('<td><input type="text" size="5" id="arch'+num+'"/></td>' );
    document.write('<td><input type="text" size="20" id="what'+num+'"/></td>' );
    document.write('<td><input type="button" value="C" ' );
    document.write( ' onclick="arch'+num+'.value='+"' ';" );
    document.write("what"+num+".value=' ';" );
    document.write('count'+num+'=0"/></td></tr>' );
  }
</script>
</head>
<body>
  <h2>Every Little Bit Counts<i style="color : hotpink">!</i></h2>
  <form>
      <script>
       makeTable( );
      </script>
  </form>
</body>
</html>
```

Coin Flip

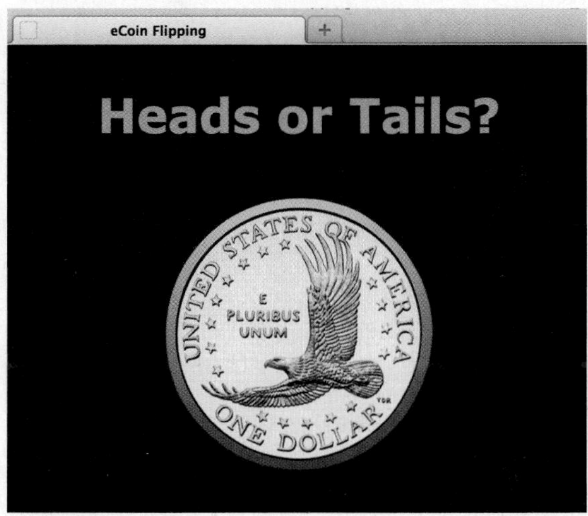


```
<!doctype html>
<html>
  <head>
   <meta charset="UTF-8"/><title>eCoin Flipping</title>
   <script>
     function coinFlip( ) {
       return Math.round(Math.random());
     }
```

```
      function flipOut( ) {
        if (coinFlip( )==0)
          return "us1tails.jpg";
        else
          return "us1heads.jpg";
      }
    </script>
    <style>
      body {background-color : black; color : goldenrod;
            font-family : verdana; text-align : center}
    </style>
  </head>
  <body>
    <h2>Heads or Tails? </h2>
    <script>document.write('<img src=" ' +
      flipOut( ) + ' " alt="coin" width="150"/>');
    </script>
  </body>
</html>
```

us1heads.jpg

us1tails.jpg

Rock-Paper-Scissors

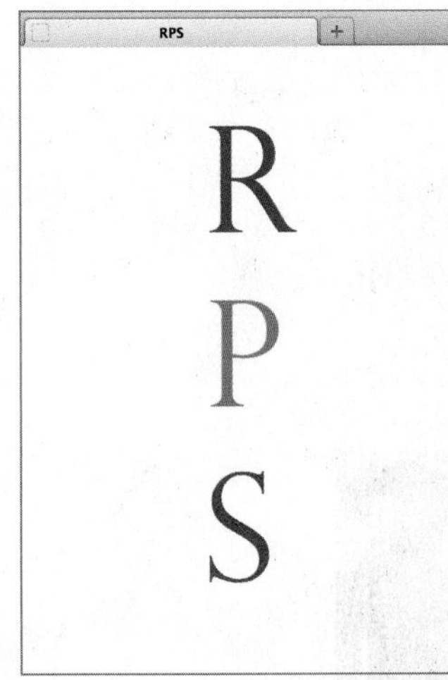

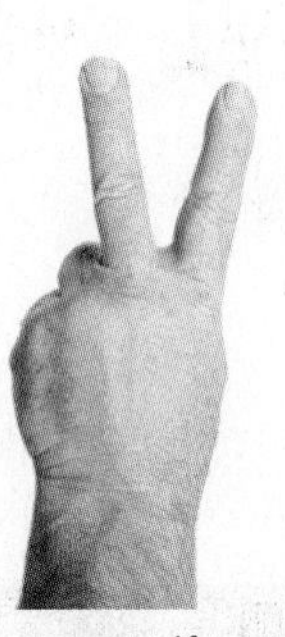
paper.gif

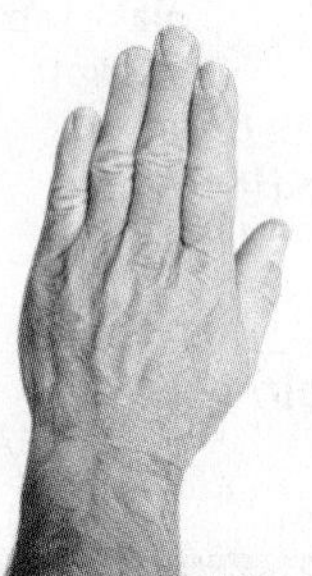
rock.gif

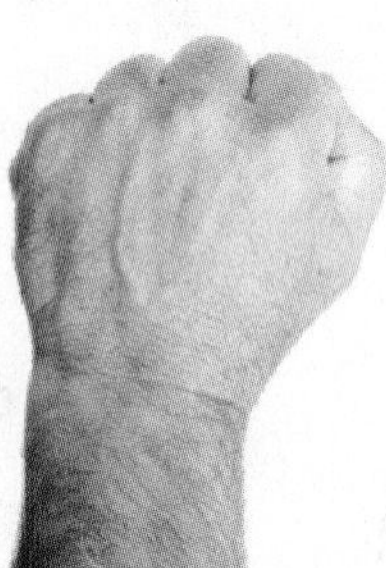
scissors.gif

```
<!doctype html>
<html>
  <head><meta charset="UTF-8"/><title>RPS</title>
  <style> button {margin:0; padding:0; background-color:white;
                  border-style:none; border-width:0}
          p {text-align:center}      <!--above styling centers pic-->
  </style>
  <script>   //this code prefetches, randomizes and flips a picture
    var thro = 1;                       //alternates betw 0 and 1
    var pix = new Array(4);             //array to hold 4 pictures
    for (var i=0; i<4; i++){
      pix[i] = new Image( );            //set up element for pics
    }
    pix[0].src = "imRPS/splash.gif";       //prefetch the 4 pics
    pix[1].src = "imRPS/rock.gif";
    pix[2].src = "imRPS/paper.gif";
    pix[3].src = "imRPS/scissors.gif";
    function randNum( range ) {         //old randomizing friend
      return Math.floor( range * Math.random( ));
    }
```

```
  function rps( ) {                    //display a new image
    if (thro == 1)                     //is this a throw or reset?
      document.images[0].src           //throw, change picture
          =pix[1+randNum(3)].src;      //its random from pix 1-3
    else
      document.images[0].src           //reset, change picture
          =pix[0].src;                 //to splash picture
    thro = 1-thro;                     //flip thro for next time
  }
 </script>
 </head>
 <body><p>
  <!--The program is just a picture that acts as a button
       flipping between the splash page and a random throw-->
  <button onclick="rps( )">
    <img src="imRPS/splash.gif"
       alt="R-P-S Throw" height="300"/>
  </button></p>
 </body>
</html>
```

Magic Decider

```
<!doctype html>
<html>
 <head>
  <meta charset="UTF-8"><title>The Decider</title>
  <style>
    body {background-color:black; color:orange;
          text-align:center; font-family:helvetica}
    button {margin:0; padding:0; background-color:black;
          border-style:none}
    p      {font-size:x-large; }
  </style>
```

```
  <script>
    var respond = new Array(
      "It is certain", "It is decidedly so", "Without a doubt",
      "Yes, definitely", "You may rely on it", "As I see it, yes",
      "Most likely", "Outlook good", "Yes", "Signs point to yes",
      "Reply hazy, try again", "Concentrate, and ask again",
      "Better not tell you now", "Cannot predict now",
      "Concentrate and ask again", "Don't count on it",
      "My reply is, no", "My sources say, no", "Outlook not so good",
      "Very doubtful");
    function randNum( range ) {
          return Math.floor( range * Math.random( ));
    }
  </script>
 </head>
 <body>
  <p id="ask"> Say Your Question</p>
  <p><button
     onclick="document.getElementById('ask').innerHTML='... and your answer is ... ';
                 document.getElementById('tell').innerHTML=respond[randNum(20)]">
     <img src="8_ball.jpg" alt="8 Ball" width="300"/></button></p>
  <p id="tell" > </p>
 </body>
</html>
```

8_ball.jpg

APPENDIX G

Smooth Motion Program

THE FOLLOWING HTML and JavaScript code produces the Smooth Motion program in Chapter 21.

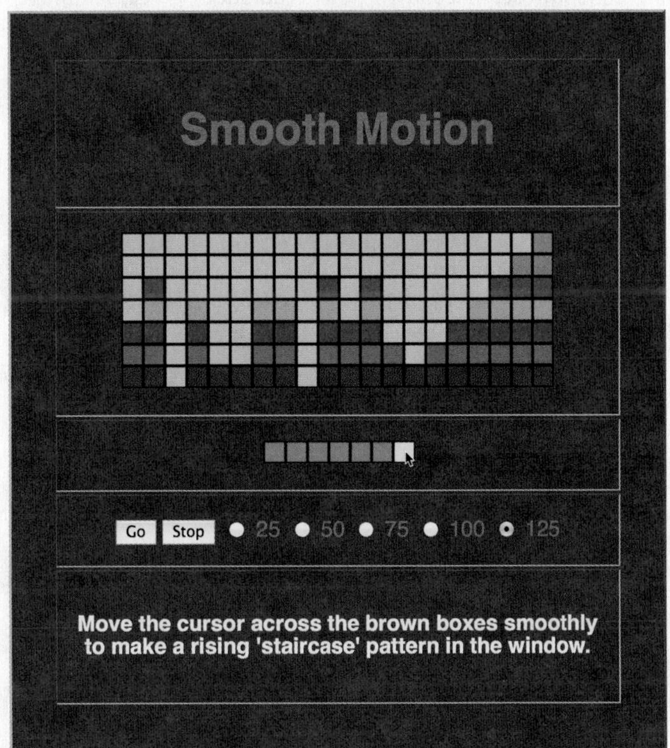

```
<!doctype html>
<html>
  <head>
   <meta charset="UTF-8"/> <title>Smooth Motion Application</title>
    <style>
      body {background-color : white; color : #ff6600; font-family : helvetica;
              text-align : center}
      table {margin-left : auto; margin-right : auto; background-color : #a80000;
             padding : 5%}
      td    {padding : 15px}
    </style>
    <script>
       var duration = 125, timerId;          // vars
       var pics = new Array(8);              // array
       var keypix = new Array(2);
       var next1 = 0, frame = -1;
       timerId = setTimeout("animate()", 5000);      //Initial timer
       function animate() {
          shiftGrid ()
          checkStairAndContinue ();
       }
       function shiftGrid() {
          for (var j = 0; j < 19; j++) {
             document.images[j].src = document.images[j+1].src;
          }
          if (frame == -1)
             document.images[19].src = pics[randNum(8)].src;
          else
             document.images[19].src = pics[frame].src;
       }
       function checkStairAndContinue() {
          if (frame == next1)                          //Correct prediction?
             next1 = next1 + 1;                        //Yes, make another
          else                                         //No
             next1 = 1;                                //Go back to start
          if (next1 != 8)                              //Are we still looking?
             timerId = setTimeout("animate( )",duration); //Yes, set timer
       }
          function here (pos) {
             document.images[20+pos].src = "gifpix/YellowBox.gif";
             frame = pos + 1;
          }
          function gone (pos) {
             document.images[20+pos].src = "gifpix/OrangeBox.gif";
             frame = 0;
          }
          function randNum (range) {                   //Rand No. fcn from
             return Math.floor(range * Math.random());  // Chapter 20
       }
     </script>
   </head>
   <body>
   <table border="1">
      <tr> <td>
         <h1>Smooth Motion</h1>
      </td></tr>
      <tr> <td>
         <script>
            for (var j = 0; j < 8; j++) {            //Initial img array
               pics[j] = new Image();
            }
            for (var j = 0; j < 8; j++) {            //Prefetch images
               pics[j].src = "gifpix/Stack" + j + ".gif";
            }
```

```
        for (var j = 0; j < 20; j++) {          //Place grid imgs
          document.write('<img src="gifpix/Stack0.gif" alt=" "/>');
        }
      </script>
    </td></tr>
    <tr> <td>
      <script>
        keypix[0] = new Image();
        keypix[1] = new Image();
        keypix[0].src = "gifpix/OrangeBox.gif";
        keypix[1].src = "gifpix/YellowBox.gif";
        for (var j = 0; j < 7; j++) {
          document.write('<img src="gifpix/OrangeBox.gif" ' +
          'onmouseover = "here(' + j + ')" ' +
          'onmouseout = "gone(' + j + ')"  alt=" "/>');
        }
      </script>
    </td></tr>
    <tr> <td>
      <form>
        <input type="button" value="Go"
          onclick='timerId=setTimeout("animate()",duration)'/>
        <input type="button" value="Stop"
          onclick="clearTimeout(timerId)"/>
        <input type="radio" name="speed" onclick="duration=25"/> 25
        <input type="radio" name="speed" onclick="duration=50"/> 50
        <input type="radio" name="speed" onclick="duration=75"/> 75
        <input type="radio" name="speed" onclick="duration=100"/> 100
        <input type="radio" name="speed"
          onclick="duration=125" checked="checked"/> 125
      </form>
    </td></tr>
    <tr> <td>
      <p style="color : cornsilk"><b>
      Move the cursor across the brown boxes smoothly <br/>
      to make a rising 'staircase' pattern in the
      window.</b></p>
    </td></tr>
  </table>
  </body>
</html>
```

GLOSSARY

1-way cipher, *see* one-way cipher
419 fraud, the name for advance-fee fraud derived from the applicable section number of the Nigerian Criminal Code
802.11 (eight-oh-two eleven), wireless communications protocol

A

absolute cell reference, an address or pointer that does not change; in a spreadsheet, a cell with an absolute reference does not change even if copied
absolute reference, an href value given as a complete URL
abstract, to remove an idea, concept, or process from a specific situation
abstraction, the central idea or concept removed from a situation
ADC, *see* analog-to-digital converter
advance-fee fraud, an online scam often called the *Nigerian Widow scam* or the *419 fraud*
agent, the person or thing (usually a computer) following an algorithm's instructions
algorithm, a precise and systematic method for producing a specified result
ALU, *see* arithmetic logic unit
American Standard Code for Information Interchange (ASCII), a standard for assigning numerical values to the letters in the Roman alphabet and to typographical characters; pronounced *AS·key*
analog, information that comes from or is stored as a continuously varying medium
analog signal, a continuously varying representation of a phenomenon, e.g., a sound wave
analog-to-digital converter (ADC), in digitizing sound, takes the continuous sound wave and samples it at regular intervals, outputting binary numbers that are written to memory for each sample
anchor tag, the HTML tag that specifies a link, or the text associated with the reference that is highlighted in the document
anchor text, the highlighted (often blue) text indicating the presence of a hyperlink
AND-query, a search request for items in which all keywords must apply
apps, computer applications
arguments, the values given for a function's parameters in a function call
arithmetic/logic unit (ALU), a subsystem of a computer that performs the operations of an instruction
arithmetic operators, the functions of basic arithmetic
array, a multi-element variable in a programming language, formed from a base name indexed by one or more integers
array element, an indexed item; also called an *element*
array length, the number of elements of an array; also the array size
array reference, the specification of an element of an array by giving the array name and index or index expression
ASCII, *see* American Standard Code for Information Interchange
assembler, software that converts assembly code into binary code
assembly code, computer instructions written in an assembly language
assembly language, a symbolic form of a binary machine language
assignment, the act of setting a variable to have a new value
assignment statement, a programming command expressed with a variable on the left and a variable or expression on the right of an assignment symbol, usually =
asynchronous communication, indicates that the actions of senders and receivers occur at separate times, as in the exchange of email
attribute, in HTML, a parameter used within the tags to specify additional information; in a database, a property of an entity; also called a *field*
attribute name, in relational databases, a column heading or field name
authoritative, reliably correct; what experts say
authoritative name server, a computer of the Domain Name System that knows for its domain the IP address of all computers and authoritative name servers in it

automated reply, a function of mail servers that allows a user to set up a message saying that he or she is temporarily away and unable to reply to emails; also called a *vacation message*

B

backdoor, a modification to a software system allowing security procedures to be by-passed
bandwidth, the bit-transmission capacity of a channel, usually measured in bits per second
base, the number that is raised to various powers to generate the counting units of a number system; e.g., the base of the decimal system is 10 and the base of the binary system is 2; also called *radix*
binary, having two related components; also, a program expressed in binary code
binary code, computer instructions expressed in bits, and suitable for direct interpretation by the hardware
binary number, a quantity expressed in radix 2 number representation
binary operator, an operator such as addition (+) having two operands
binary system, any information encoding using symbols formed from two patterns; also called *PandA representation* in this book
bit, basic unit of information representation having two states, usually denoted as 0 and 1
body, that part of an HTML file surrounded by <body> and </body> tags, and containing the page's content
Boolean, having the property of being either true or false
Boolean value, true or false
boot, to start a computer and load its operating system
Box Model of CSS, an abstraction describing the spacing properties of HTML elements
broadcast communication, a type of transmission of information from one sender to all receivers
button, in HTML, a form input type
byte, a sequence of eight bits treated as a unit

C

cache, to keep information, typically acquired at some effort, in the expectation of its reuse in the near future
call, to use or apply a function
candidate key, a relational database field that could potentially be chosen as the table's key
captcha, an acronym for **Completely Automated Public Turing test to tell Computers and Humans Apart**
Cascading Style Sheets (CSS), a system for globally styling Web pages written in HTML
cell, in a spreadsheet, the intersection of a row and a column
cell phone tracking, the process of determining a person's movements based on the proximity of their phone to cell phone towers
cell range, in a spreadsheet, a naming scheme that allows the user to refer to a group of cells by naming the first cell and the last cell and placing a colon (:) in between
central processor, the ALU and control components of a computer, typically including cache memory
channel, the physical medium, e.g., wires, over which signals are sent; in silicon technology, the area under the gate of a transistor
checkbox, in HTML, a form input type
chrominance, the difference between an area of color and a (gray) reference of the same brightness
ciphertext, in a cryptosystem, an encrypted form of the cleartext
classifier, a component of an optical character recognition system that ranks characters by the probability that they match a given set of features
cleartext, information before encryption or after decryption
click event, the result caused by a user clicking a command button
client/server interaction, the protocol for information exchange by computers in the client/server structure
cloud, an online storage resource
CMOS (Complementary Metal Oxide Semiconductor), the most widely used integrated circuit technology; pronounced *SEE·moss*
collating sequence, an ordering for a set of symbols used to sort them; for example, alphabetical ordering
columns, in relational databases, an attribute of a relation
compiling, translating a programming language into another language, usually machine language
complement, in binary representations, an encoding that switches 0's to 1's, and 1's to 0's
Compose and Check, a code development cycle of programming and testing
compound statement, in programming, a group of statements surrounded by curly braces to become a single statement
compression, encoding information with fewer bits than a given representation by exploiting properties of regularity or unimportance
compression ratio, the factor by which compression reduces an encoding from its uncompressed size
computer, a device that deterministically follows instructions to process information
concatenate, in programming, to join strings
conditional or **conditional statement,** a programming statement, usually identified by `if`, that optionally executes statements depending on the outcome of a Boolean test
conditional formatting, controlling the display of text in spreadsheet cells based on the values stored in the cell
conditional formulas, spreadsheet formulas that use the `IF()` function
continuation, a control component of a `for` loop specifying when the loop ends
continuation test, a Boolean expression to determine whether an iteration statement will execute its statement sequence again; also called a *termination test*
control unit, a subsystem of a computer that is the hardware implementation of the Fetch/Execute Cycle
cookie, information stored on a Web client computer by an HTTP server computer

copyright, the legal protection of many forms of intellectual property
core, one of several processors on a chip sharing resources
CPU, central processing unit
crawler, a program that navigates the Internet, cataloging and indexing Web pages by the words they contain for use by a query processor
crowdsourcing, information or computation resulting from the aggregated behavior of many Web users
CSS, *see* Cascading Style Sheets

D

DAC, *see* digital-to-analog converter
data controller, in Fair Information Practices, the person who sets policies, responds to individuals regarding information, and is accountable for those policies and actions
data types, the different kinds of values of a programming language; also called *value types*
database scheme or **schema,** the declaration of entities and relationships of a database
database table, a relation
debugging, the act of discovering why a system does not work properly
declaring variables, stating what variables will be used in a program
definiteness, a property of algorithms requiring that a specific sequence of steps is defined
definitional data, that part of a definitional list item inside of <dd> and </dd> tags, and containing the definition
definitional list, in HTML, a list form usually comprising a sequence of terms and their definitions
definitional term, that part of a definitional list item inside <dt> and </dt>, tags containing the word being defined
delimited or **delimited by,** ends with
device driver, software that enables a computer to communicate with a peripheral device
DHCP, *see* Dynamic Host Configuration Protocol
digital-to-analog converter (DAC), in playing sound, creates an electrical wave by interpolation between the digital values; the signal is input to a speaker, which converts it to a sound wave
digitize, originally to encode with decimal numerals, now to encode in bits
directory, a named collection of files, other directories, or both; also called a *folder*
directory hierarchy, the complete file structure of a computer
display rate, in animation, the frequency with which images are changed
DNS, *see* Domain Name System
DNS name server, a computer of the Domain Name System that finds IP addresses for a network domain
Document Object Model (DOM), the browser's representation (data structure) for the components of a Web page
DOM, *see* Document Object Model
Domain Name System (DNS), the collection of Internet-connected computers that translate domain addresses into IP addresses
domain name, the name by which a computer is known in the Domain Name System
dot-dot-slash, a notation (../) specifying a relative path reference one level higher in a directory hierarchy
downloading, transferring information from a server to a client
Dynamic Host Configuration Protocol (DHCP), a networking protocol in which an IP address is assigned to a computer at startup and returned at shutdown

E

effectiveness, a property of algorithms requiring that all instructions can be performed mechanically within the capabilities of the executing agent
element, an indexed item; also called an *array element*
element name, in HTML the word inside of angle brackets of an element's tag, e.g., body from <body>
emoticon, a character sequence that is common in email and that expresses an emotion by its physical form, e.g., the "smiley face" :) or ☺ to express happiness or humor
empty string, a character sequence of zero length
encrypt, to transform a digital representation so that the information cannot be readily discerned; also called *digitally encrypt*
end tag, the second of a pair of tags, such as </i>
entity, something that can be identified by a fixed number of its characteristics
entity instance, a specific data value for an entity
escape symbol, a character, often & or \, that is a prefix to another character or word used to enlarge a character's encoding, e.g., &infinity to encode ∞
evaluation function, in computer games, e.g., in chess, a procedure that assigns a numerical value to each piece, accounts for captures and board position, and computes a score for the move
even parity, a property of binary numbers in which the number of 1-bits is even
event, an indication from the operating system that a mouse click or other action has occurred
event-based programming, a programming style that responds to events, such as mouse clicks
event handler, the program that performs the task that responds to an event
event-handling attribute, in JavaScript, tells the browser how to respond to an event like onclick
execution, the performance of a program's instructions, usually by a computer; to run a program
exploit, a programming error used by malware as a means to compromise a system
expression, in programming, a formula-like description of how to compute a value
Extensible Hypertext Markup Language (XHTML), a W3C standard dialect of HTML compatible with XML
Extensible Markup Language (XML), a W3C standard for structured information encoding

Extensible Stylesheet Language (XSL), a Web standard language for specifying formatting information for XML

F

factor, to find the prime numbers whose product equals a given number

fail-safe, in software, a program that stops operating to avoid harm

fail-soft, in software, a program that continues to operate but with possibly degraded functionality

fair use, a concept in copyright law in which copyright limitations are waived for explicitly listed, socially valuable purposes

feature, a component of a character in an optical character recognition system

feedback, in a user interface, an indication that the computer is working or has completed a request

Fetch/Execute Cycle, the basic instruction execution process of a computer

field, in a database, a property of an entity; also called an *attribute*

field effect, the use of an electric field to control current in a semiconductor

field effect transistor, in semiconductors, a device used to control conductivity

file structure, the organization of a computer's directories and files

File Transfer Protocol (FTP), the rules governing the way Internet-connected computers send and receive files

fill handle or **tab,** in a spreadsheet, used to drag a selection to extend a series or fill a selection

filling, in a spreadsheet, automated copying and pasting; allows the user to replicate the contents of a cell

filtering, a process (used in spreadsheets, databases and Web search) for selecting items based on one or more criteria

finiteness, a property of algorithms requiring that they terminate with the intended result or an indication that no solution is possible

flame war, nasty email exchanges in which many uninvolved users are copied

folder, a named collection of files, other directories, or both; also called a *directory*

for loop, a common programming structure for iterating a sequence of instructions over a regular range of index values

foreign data, data from another application that one wants to import into a spreadsheet

form, in HTML, used to collect user input, e.g., when ordering a product on the Web

frame, in animation, one of many images rapidly redrawn to create the illusion of motion

frequency, in sound, the number of waves per second

frequency order, an arrangement of items, e.g., letters, based on how often they occur in a domain

FTP, *see* File Transfer Protocol

full backup, a complete copy of a body of information usually performed at a specific point in time

function, a programming structure with a name, optional parameter list, and a definition that encapsulates an algorithm

function definition, a function body, the program implementing the function; one of three parts of a function declaration

G

game tree, a conceptualization of the possible future configurations of a game

gate, a part of a transistor that controls the flow of charge

generalization, statement of a rule deduced by generalizing

generalize, to formulate an idea, concept, or process so that it abstracts multiple situations

H

Halting Problem, determining if a computation halts for a given input; a problem that cannot be solved by a computer

handle, in programming, an identifying value returned by a function or server and used for subsequent references

head, that part of an HTML file surrounded by `<head>` and `</head>` tags

heuristic, a guideline used to solve a problem that can, but may not, result in a solution; for example, "when looking for a lost item check the last place you had it"

hexadecimal numbering system, radix 16 number representation

hierarchy, an organizing structure composed of a sequence of levels that partition all items so that those of one level are partitioned into smaller groups at the next level

hop, in networking, the transfer of a packet or message to an adjacent router

HTML, *see* Hypertext Markup Language

HTTP, *see* Hypertext Transfer Protocol

hyperlink, a mechanism that allows the linear sequence of text to be interrupted to visit another location, and return to the point of interruption

hyperlink reference, the destination Web address of a hyperlink

Hypertext Markup Language (HTML), a notation for specifying the form of a Web page to a browser

Hypertext Transfer Protocol (HTTP), the rules governing the interaction between client and server on the Web

I

IC, *see* integrated circuit

identifier, a legal sequence of letters, numerals, or punctuation marks forming the name of a variable, file, directory, etc.

identity theft, the crime of posing as someone else for fraudulent purposes

if/else statement, a programming structure that allows the conditional execution of statements based on the outcome of a Boolean test

image object, a (data) structure in a computer containing an image

image tag, a singleton HTML tag used to place an image in a document, e.g., `<img . . . />`
index, in information structures, an organizing mechanism used to find information in a large collection; in programming, the number that together with an identifier forms an array reference
index origin, the number at which indexing begins; the least index
index value, the result of evaluating an index expression; the number of an array element
indexing, in programming, the mechanism of associating a number and an identifier to locate an element
indirect reference, specifying values such as operands by specifying where to find them such as giving a memory address
information, the presence or absence of a phenomenon at a specific place and time
initialization, one of the control specification parts of a `for` loop giving the starting value of the loop variable
initialize, to give a variable or other name its starting value
input, data put into a communication system for transmission or into a computer system for processing
input device, hardware that senses or detects information in the real world, and transfers it to the memory of a computer
instance, one of whatever type of information the application processes; the current values of an entity, table, or database
integrated circuit (IC), a complex set of electronic components and their interconnections that are etched or imprinted on a computer chip
integration, in silicon technology, the ability to fabricate both active and connective parts of a circuit using a family of compatible materials in a single complexity-independent process
intellectual property, creations of the human mind that have value to others
intensity, the brightness of the light of a subpixel of an LCD display, typically ranging from 0 (off) to 255
Internet Protocol address (IP address), a unique address given to each computer connected to the Internet composed of (usually) four numbers in the range 0–255
interpretation, to follow a computer program's instruction
intersect, to determine if two data objects have members in common
intractable, a description for computations solvable by a computer in principle, but not in practice
intranet, a local network that supports communication within an organization and connects to the Internet by a gateway
IP address, *see* Internet Protocol address
IP packet, a fixed quantum of information packaged together with an IP address and other data for sending information over the Internet
ISO-8859-1, an international standard for encoding into binary alphabets used in North American and Western European languages
iteration, in programming, looping through a series of statements to repeat them
iteration statement, in programming, a loop that repeatedly executes a statement
iteration variable, any variable controlling an iteration statement, e.g., a `for` statement

J

JavaScript, a programming language

K

key, in a database, field(s) that make the rows of an entity (table) unique; in cryptography, a value used to encrypt and subsequently decrypt information

L

LAN, *see* local area network
latency, the time required to deliver or generate information
literals, values explicitly given in a computer program
local area network (LAN), a network connecting computers within a small physical space such as a building; acronym usually pronounced
logical and, in programming, the operator && that represents "and"
logical database, the database constructed using one or more queries
logical not, in programming, the operator ! that changes its operand to the opposite logical value
logical operator, a connective (*and*, *or*, or *not*)
logical or, in programming, the operator | | that represents "or"
lossless compression, the process of reducing the number of bits required to represent information in which the original form can be exactly reconstructed
lossy compression, the process of reducing the number of bits required to represent information in which the original cannot be exactly reconstructed
luminance, the brightness of a given area

M

malware, collective term for software intended to compromise or do harm to a computer
memory address, a whole number that designates a specific location in a computer's memory
meta-brackets, angle brackets, < and >, used to enclose syntactically defined terms
metadata, information describing the properties of other information
metaphor, an object or an idea used as an analogy in computing, e.g., a desktop
metarules, in programming, rules that describe how to operate on other rules
microprocessor, component of a computer that computes or performs instructions; also called a *processor*
mnemonic, an aid for remembering something
modulus operation, in JavaScript (%), divides two integers and returns the remainder

MOS (metal oxide semiconductor), a transistor made of metal, oxide, and semiconductors (cross sections, top to bottom)
MPEG (Motion Picture Experts Group), a committee of the ISO; pronounced *EM·peg*
multicast, a type of transmission of information from one sender to many receivers
multimedia, information such as images, audio, and video

N

nested conditionals, in JavaScript, an `if` statement as the `then` or `else` statement of another conditional
nested loop, the condition of a loop (inner loop) appearing in the statement sequence of another loop (outer loop)
netiquette, Internet etiquette
next iteration, code in a `for` loop's control specification saying how to compute the loop variable's next value
NP-complete problems, a measure of difficulty of problems believed to be intractable for computers
number, a base data type in JavaScript
Nyquist rule, a digitization guideline stating that the sampling frequency should exceed the signal frequency by at least two times

O

object code, the binary code produced by a programming language compiler
OCR, *see* optical character recognition
one-way cipher, a form of encryption that cannot easily be reversed, i.e., decrypted, often used for passwords
online tracking, a process, typically using third-party cookies, to follow a user's click behavior on the WWW
open source, software for which the source code is publically available
operand, the data used in computer instructions; the value(s) that operators operate on
operating system (OS), software that performs tasks for the computer; it controls input and output, keeps track of files and directories, and controls peripheral devices such as disk drives and printers
operationally attuned, thinking about how a device, tool or application works to simplify its use
operator, in programming, a symbol used to perform an operation on some value(s)
operator overload, a property of some programming languages in which operators like + have different meanings depending on their operand data types, e.g., + is used for both addition and concatenation in JavaScript
optical character recognition (OCR), a computer application in which printed text is converted to the ASCII letters that represent it
opt-in/opt-out, the choice of approving or objecting to a use of information
OR-queries, a search request for items in which one or more of the keywords apply
OS, *see* operating system
output, the information produced by a program or process from a specific input

P

PageRank, in Google, computing the importance of a Web page based on its relevancy, determined by links to that page
PandA, *see* Presence and Absence
parallel computation, the use of multiple computers to solve a single problem
parameter, an input to a function
parity, refers to whether a number is even or odd
partial backup, new information copied to another medium that has been added to a system since the last full or partial backup
password, a sequence of characters that one must input to gain access to a file, application, or computer system
payload, user content in an IP-packet
PC, acronym for program counter, printed circuit (board), or personal computer
perfect reproduction, a quality of digital information that allows exact copies to be made
peripherals, devices connected to a computer, usually for I/O purposes
PERT (Program Evaluation and Review Technique) chart, a task-dependency graph used by systems engineers and managers in project management; acronym pronounced
phishing, a social engineering technique to trick people into voluntarily giving up personal (security) information; short for password harvesting fishing
photolithography, a process of transferring a pattern by means of light shown through a mask or negative
photoresist, a material used in a silicon chip fabrication process that is chemically changed by light, allowing it to be patterned by a mask
physical database, in a database, the tables stored on the disk drive
picture element or **pixel,** the smallest displayable unit of a video monitor
pipeline, to execute multiple machine instructions at once, each at a different stage of completion
pixel, contraction for picture element
place value, in decimal numbers, positions representing the next higher power of 10, starting from the right
placeholder technique, a searching algorithm in which strings are temporarily replaced with a special character to protect them from change by other substitution commands
point-to-point communication, a type of transmission of information from one sender to one receiver
predicate, the Boolean expression in a conditional statement that is evaluated to produce a true or false outcome
prefetching, in online animation, the process of loading the images prior to beginning an animation
preformatted, in HTML, text that is enclosed between `<pre>` and `</pre>` tags
Presence and Absence (PandA), in this book, a term for the fundamental physical representation of a bit of information; also binary encoding
primary key, the chosen column(s) in a database table that always has a unique value for every row

primary source, a person who provides information based on direct knowledge or experience
prime number, a number that can only be divided evenly by itself and one
print queue, an operating system's list of in-process or waiting printing jobs
privacy, the right to choose freely the circumstances under which and the extent to which people will reveal themselves, their attitudes, and their behaviors
private key encryption, a system where parties use a common key to encrypt and decrypt messages
processor, the component of a computer that computes, i.e., performs the instructions
program, an algorithm encoded for a specific situation
program counter, a register in a computer that stores the address of the next instruction to be executed
programming, the act of encoding an algorithm that is to be executed by a computer
property value, content following the colon symbol in HTML/CSS styling
pseudo-random numbers, a series of algorithmically generated numbers passing statistical tests for randomness
public domain, the status of a work in which the copyright owner has explicitly given up all rights
public key cryptosystem, software that uses a public key
public key, a key published by the receiver and used by the sender to encrypt messages

Q

query, database command defining a table expressed using the five database operators
query processor, the part of a search engine that uses the crawler's index to report Web pages associated with keywords provided by a user

R

radix, the number that is raised to various powers to generate the counting units of a number system; e.g., the radix of the decimal system is 10 and the radix of the binary system is 2; also called *base*
RAM, *see* random access memory
random access memory (RAM), a subsystem of a computer used for storing programs and data while they execute; acronym pronounced
reachable configurations, in software, the possible configurations that a program can define
reboot, to restart a computer by clearing its memory and reloading its operating system
reCaptcha, a captcha successor that tests users with text that fails optical character recognition
records, antiquated term for table rows in a database system
redundancy, used to resolve hardware failures by having computers perform computations of a safety critical system and make decisions based on majority vote; in databases, duplicated information
relational database, a table-based organization for a database in which queries can be specified using relational database operators
relational operator, one of six operators (< ≤ = ≠ ≥ >) that compare two values; in JavaScript, one of the six operators (< <= == != >= >)
relations, in relational databases, tables
relationship, a correspondence between two tables of a database
relative cell reference, in a spreadsheet, a cell with a relative reference changes its formula when copied
relative references, an `href` value given as a path in the local directory hierarchy
RGB, acronym for red, green, blue; name for a color encoding method
root element, in XML, the tag that encloses all content in a file
root name server, one of several Internet DNS servers that contain the IP addresses of the top-level domain registry organizations that maintain global domains (`.com`, `.net`, `.org`, `.gov`, `.edu`, etc.)
rootkit, malware that directly manipulates operating system tables to hide its presence
router, a computer in a network with several wired connections or a wireless connection to other computers in the network, which forwards arriving traffic to destination computers
RSA public key cryptosystem, an encryption method invented by Rivest, Shamir, and Adelman
run-length encoding, a representation in which numbers are used to give the lengths of consecutive sequences of 0's or 1's

S

safe harbor, minimum privacy protections agreed to by U.S. companies to handle data from EU countries
safe software, the goal of software programs to be reliable in safety-critical situations, such as life support
sample, to take measurements at regular intervals, as in sound digitization
sampling rate, the number of samples per second
scenario, in spreadsheets, a collection of revised cell values used collectively for "what if" analysis
search engine, a software system composed of a crawler and a query processor that helps users locate specific information on the Web or on a specific Web site
secondary source, a person providing information without direct knowledge of or experience with the topic
secure communication, message exchange in which the content is encrypted to keep it private
secure socket layer (SSL), a security protocol used in Web communication, and denoted by "s" in `https`
semiconductor, matter such as silicon capable of conducting, or not conducting, electrons
series, in a spreadsheet, results from the automatic incrementing of data by adding one to a cell's value to produce the next cell's value
series fill, in a spreadsheet, allows the user to enter a series of numbers or dates into a range of cells
shareware, software available on the Web, paid for on the honor system
singleton tag, a tag such as the image tag `<img . . . />` that has no end tag

site search, a search restricted to a single domain
software, a collective term for programs
software license, generally allows use of the software; the ownership remains with the party who markets the program
source, on the Web, the HTML or other text description of how a Web page should be displayed
source code, program text written in a programming language
spam filter, email screening software that checks pre-delivery for content typical of unsolicited commercial email
specification, in programming, a precise definition of the input; how the system should behave and what the output should be
SQL, *see* Structured Query Language
start tag, the first of a pair of tags, such as <i>
statement, in JavaScript, a program instruction
statement terminator, in JavaScript, the semicolon (;) used to end each statement
string, in searching, a sequence of characters; in programming, a data type for a sequence of characters
Structured Query Language (SQL), a standard notation for defining tables from tables in a database; sometimes pronounced *SEE·quel*
superuser, having the capability to access all functions of a computer or software system, including overriding passwords; also called *administrative authority*
symmetric key encryption, private key encryption systems where parties exchange keys before communicating
synchronous communication, requires that both the sender and the receiver are simultaneously active, e.g., a telephone conversation

T

tab-delimited text, in a spreadsheet, how foreign data is imported; each cell's entry ends with a tab and each row ends with a return
table instance, a relational database table containing specific data values
tag, a word or abbreviation enclosed in angle brackets, usually paired with a companion starting with a slash, which describes a property of data or expresses a command to be performed; e.g., <italic>You're it!</italic>
task dependencies, when solving tasks, the fact that some tasks rely or depend on the resolution of other tasks
task-dependency graph, used by systems engineers and managers in project management; also called a *PERT chart*
TCP/IP, acronym for Transmission Control Protocol/Internet Protocol
template, the structural information of a document with placeholders for content that is later filled in to produce a complete document
termination test, a Boolean expression to determine whether an iteration statement will execute its statement sequence again; also called a *continuation test*
tertiary source, someone whose information comes from secondary sources
text editor, document preparation software for code with no formatting capabilities
third-party cookie, in a browser, a cookie from a site the user didn't explicitly request
TLD, *see* top-level domain
token, a symbol sequence treated as a single unit in searching or in languages
top-level domain (TLD), is a domain, such as .com or .edu, that is not a member of any higher level domain (except root)
tracking, one of several forms of electronic surveillance; *see* phone tracking, Web tracking
Transmission Control Protocol/Internet Protocol (TCP/IP), the structures, representations, and algorithms used in the Internet's physical data transmission
Trojan, malware that quietly records user activity and information such as passwords
troubleshoot, in computing, determining why something does not work due to malfunctioning hardware or buggy or outdated software
tuple, a set of values for the attributes of an entity; also called a *row*
Turing test, an experimental setting to determine if a computer and a person can be distinguished by their answers to a judge's questions
type, a kind of information, such as number, text, or image

U

unary operator, an operator, such as negation (–), with a single operand
undefined, in JavaScript, the value of declared variables before they are assigned
Universal Resource Locator (URL), a two-part name for a Web page composed of an IP address followed by the file name, which can default to index.html
Universality Principle, a property of computation that all computers with a minimal set of instructions can compute the same set of computations
unmediated, not requiring permission; no barrier between creating information and publishing it
uploading, transferring information from a client to a server
URL, *see* Universal Resource Locator
URL parameters, a mechanism for recording information to implement Web-session continuity
UTF-8, Unicode Translation Format for bytes

V

vacation message, a function of mail servers that allows a user to set up a message saying that he or she is temporarily away and unable to reply to email; also called an *automated reply*
value types, the different kinds of values of a programming language; also called *data types*
variable, a named quantity in a programming language

W

W3C, *see* World Wide Web Consortium
WAN, *see* wide area network
Web client, a computer requesting services from a Web server; a computer running a Web browser
Web server, a computer providing pages to Web clients; a computer hosting a Web page
WFI, *see* World-Famous Iteration
"what if" analysis, a spreadsheet tool that temporarily recomputes entries based on alternative cell values
white space, in HTML, space inserted for readability
wide area network (WAN), a network connecting computers over a wider area than a few kilometers
wireless networking, a network connecting computers using radio frequency (RF) signals; network connections using the 802.11 standard
workaround, the process of achieving a goal by avoiding buggy or failing parts of a system
World-Famous Iteration (WFI), in JavaScript, the most frequently written `for` loop used by programmers
World Wide Web (WWW), the collection of all HTML servers connected by the Internet and their information resources
World Wide Web Consortium (W3C), a standards body composed mainly of companies that produce Web software
worm, an independent program that replicates itself from machine to machine across network connections
WYSIWYG (what you see is what you get), pronounced *WHIZ·ee·wig*

X

XHTML, *see* Extensible Hypertext Markup Language
XML, *see* Extensible Markup Language
XSL, *see* Extensible Stylesheet Language

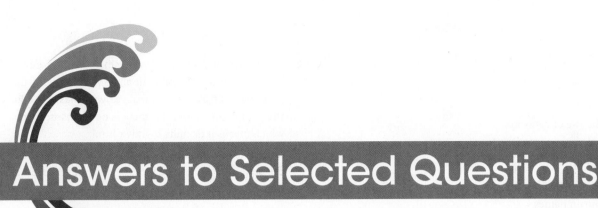

Answers to Selected Questions

Chapter 1

Multiple Choice

1. b
3. d
5. d

Short Answer

1. ENIAC, Philadelphia
3. Integrated Circuits
5. cheap; expensive
7. relevant; irrelevant

Exercises

1. Many possible answers; include items like cell phones, game consoles, etc.
3. Hard instructions are expressed by wiring; soft instructions are expressed with digital memory
5. The tech support staff knows the right terms, and they will explain the solution using the right terms, so you need to know them to communicate.
7. Many possible answers

Chapter 2

Multiple Choice

1. c
3. d
5. d
7. a
9. d

Short Answer

1. exact copy
3. File
5. Edit
7. Avoid placeholder collisions, and replace before final proofreading
9. Alto computer

Exercises

1. The desktop metaphor became the universal way most people thought of using a computer. The computer became a virtual desktop on which one could store, view, and edit documents. Most people were familiar with desks, but fewer understood command line programs. So the metaphor made the basic computer operations simpler for people to understand and use.
3. Inform the user that the computer is still working, and giving an estimate of how much work remains.
5. The user needs to know whether the thing he asked a computer to do was understood, whether it has completed, and whether it was successful. Otherwise, he will not know whether it is safe or worthwhile to proceed. A classic example is a progress bar displayed while a page loads: users will quickly become impatient and upset if they don't know whether the machine is working or if it has stalled. The progress bar is a simple way to reassure them.
7. *Copy* makes a duplicate entry of the selection in memory; *Paste* duplicates the contents of the memory to the selection. Both are copies of digital information.
9. The touch metaphor refers to an illusion that the user is touching the content of the display; the change was required because it is inconvenient for mobile devices to use a pointing device like a mouse.
11. Blazing away is a way to experiment with the software and discover what it does and how to use it.

Chapter 3

Multiple Choice

1. a
3. c (256*256*256*256)
5. b
7. d

Short Answer

1. root name
3. domain
5. The use of gateways
7. Web servers
9. FTP
11. client; server
13. domain names
15. higher; lower

Exercises

1. Answers should focus on the common languages used for the Internet and Web communication.
3. It then asks the authoritative name server, which keeps the complete list of the IP addresses of all computers in its domain.
5. namerica.htm; the traffic report navigation page
7. Many possible answers, including software companies that benefitted, and newspapers that were harmed.
9. The client/server interaction is brief, so a server can move quickly from one to another
11. TCP/IP: Transmission Control Protocol/Internet Protocol; LAN: local area network; WAN: wide area network; DSL: digital subscriber line; WWW: World Wide Web; URL: Universal (or Uniform) Resource Locator; HTML: Hypertext Markup Language; ISP: Internet service provider
13. Network reliability (broken links) and congestion relief (busy links)

Chapter 4

Multiple Choice

1. b
3. c
5. b
7. b
9. c

Short Answer

1. do; learn
3. Nested
5. source
7. HTML
9. ignores

Exercises

1. Although there are calculators, you should learn basic arithmetic, for example.
3. The hyperlink is http://www.nasm.si.edu/museum/, the anchor text is National Air and Space Museum, the protocol is http://, the domain is www.nasm.si.edu, the path is /museum, and there is no file name given, which means it defaults to index.html.
5. The style information closest to the text will be used; the style of a page overrides the style of an external file.
7. Large blocks of untested coding usually contain many errors that are hard to find.
9. An activity with many possible answers.
11. An activity with many possible answers.

Chapter 5

Multiple Choice

1. d
3. a
5. d
7. b
9. c

Short Answer

1. page rank
3. crawler
5. ^F, that is, Ctrl+F or Command+F
7. no one
9. half

Exercises

1. Many possible answers that touch on the fact that Web content is not organized and search engines look around and organize what they find.
3. Physical books went through a detailed process involving many experts. Anyone can post any information (fake or real) on a Web page.
5. When using AND all terms must be on the page; when using OR at least one or more terms can be on the page. Many possible answers.
7. Many possible answers, possibly including book titles, quotations, music lyrics.
9. Many answers including the fact that you know where to find the information, or you know that the organization is an educational institution.
11. For Google, the page title is *Quick HTML Reference*, snippet is *A tag list with explanations covering the HTML 3.2 version*; the URL is www.htmlgoodies.com/.../reference/article.../Quick-HTML-Reference..., and one of the site links is *Top*.

Chapter 6

Multiple Choice

1. b
3. a
5. a
7. d
9. d

Short Answer

1. feedback
3. fail-soft
5. mean, say
7. deterministic
9. fix, locate

Exercises

1. Errors can be in any layer of the software implementing an app; but users are in context of the top layer only.
3. Possible answers should emphasize getting this one document printed.
5. Possible answers should say how to apply the debugging heuristics.
7. Debugging is purposeful and goal directed, and so is more likely to solve the problem.
9. Once that bug is fixed it could result in more bugs being revealed.

Chapter 7

Multiple Choice

1. c
3. d
5. c
7. b

Short Answer

1. Present and absent
3. 16
5. PandA
7. base; radix
9. Digitizing

Exercises

1. Many possible answers.
3. 0010 1000 0011 1000 0011 0000 0011 0000 0010 1001 0011 0101 0011 0101 0011 0101 0010 1101 0011 0000 0011 0000 0011 0001 0011 0010
5. 01101000 01100101 01111000 01100001 01100100 01100101 01100011 01101001 01101101 01100001 01101100; hexadecimal
7. Way to go!
9. Improves the chances letters will be recognized when spoken under less-than-ideal conditions.
11. "It seemed that after 'bit' comes 'bite.' But we changed the 'i' to a 'y' so that a typist couldn't accidentally change 'byte' into 'bit' by the single error of dropping the 'e'."

Chapter 8

Multiple Choice

1. d
3. b
5. c
7. a
9. d

Short Answer

1. bytes
3. black; white
5. MP3
7. dark
9. optical character recognition
11. more
13. Bias-Free Universal Medium Principle

Exercises

1. Bits can represent all discrete information (e.g., numbers, colors, sounds, etc.); there is no way to determine what a bit sequence represents without more information.
3. 1492 = 10111010100

   1776 = 11011110000

   10111010100 + 11011110000 =

   110011000100
5. 168 = 10101000

   123 = 1111011

   10101000 + 1111011

   = 100100011

   Each number can be represented in a byte; their sum requires more than one byte.
7. Many potential solutions (e.g., having 1 pixel represent the average of a 3x3 group of colored pixels).
9. After the sounds from the recording equipment are digitized by an analog-to-digital converter, they are compressed to MP3 format; they are then read off of the CD, decompressed, and sent to the digital-to-analog converter for the earphones.
11. 9 seconds; each second transmits 25 Kb, and 225/25 = 9.

13. Colored light is direct and pure; colored paint reflects some colors and absorbs others.
15. 8 0's, 2 1's, 6 0's
    8 1's, 2 0's, 6 1's
    2 0's, 6 1's, 8 0's
    2 1's, 10 0's
17. Remove all of the vowels.

Chapter 9

Multiple Choice

1. a
3. d
5. b
7. c
9. b

Short Answer

1. Computers
3. RAM
5. the data
7. keyboard
9. address
11. semiconductor
13. A binary object file
15. An operating system

Exercises

1. Many possible answers.
3. When a computer finishes its work, it enters an idle loop, just checking to see if there are any external inputs.
5. Light is used to "burn" an image into a light-sensitive film, which can be chemically treated to act like a mold to produce a copy of the image out of some other material. This technique allows cheap mass production of integrated circuits.
7. It means to add the value in memory word 1050 to the value of the memory word 1900 and store the result in memory word 3000.
9. Every byte must have an address; one million addresses requires 20 bits, but 2^{20} totals 1,048,576, so extra bytes are included to match the number of addresses.

Chapter 10

Multiple Choice

1. c
3. b
5. b
7. b

Short Answer

1. repeated instructions such as loops
3. finite
5. unambiguous

Exercises

1. Nurses presented letters — the phenomenon; usually he didn't wink; when they got to the right letter he did, indicating that was the phenomenon he was detecting.
3. All properties hold; the text is the input, the three-step placeholder technique is definite and effective; and the revised text is the output.
5. The agent can compare all of the URLs on the first letter, selecting the alphabetically earliest; if several are earliest, find those with the earliest second letter, and so forth until only one is left.
7. Many answers, depending on mailer.
9. Many answers, though basically it begins with a sequence of steps to prepare the toothbrush, followed by one or more iterations, followed by a sequence of put everything away.

Chapter 11

Multiple Choice

1. a
3. d
5. a
7. b
9. c

Short Answer

1. Netiquette
3. system administrator/superuser
5. derivative work
7. Phishing
9. sleep on it

Exercises

1. Crowd sourcing is solving a problem by combing the contributions of a large, unconstrained volunteer population. Examples include FoldIt, a game that helps understand protein structures; NASA's Martian mapping program; and Wikipedia. Crowd sourcing is beneficial because it massively parallelizes large workloads, captures a wide variety of skill sets, and is self-correcting as volunteers contribute and peer-review others' contributions.
3. People you communicate with over the Internet may have very different backgrounds, and behave in ways

that might offend you; rather than criticizing them for their different experiences, be tolerant.

5. Many possible answers, which should use the process described in this chapter.
7. For many people, the Internet is a poorly understood realm because it is so new. Physical safety is well understood, though, so sometimes people can trust naively online even while they are prudent about trust in person.
9. a. probably legal if it doesn't look like Mickey Mouse
   b. legal if you created all of the content
   c. probably illegal unless you have the right to create a derivative work
   d. legal
   e. probably legal because of the Fair Use principle
   f. charging would probably violate the rights available, but given money as a gratuity might be okay
   g. probably legal
   h. probably legal
   i. legal
   j. illegal
11. Many possible answers.
13. Donations play a key role, but some companies also charge for the service of packaging and distributing software for users who lack the expertise to compile the software themselves.

Chapter 12

Multiple Choice

1. d
3. d
5. b
7. b
9. c
11. c

Short Answer

1. Privacy
3. Cash
5. Fair Information Practices
7. businesses; governments
9. 2-way cipher
11. RSA
13. Spyware
15. increases

Exercises

1. It means data on EU citizens must be protected by the same standards; in the U.S. that means companies must have a "safe harbor" commitment to privacy. Example countries: Germany, Australia, Hong Kong, etc.
3. Many possible answers. They can sell the transaction data to other companies and they can use it to target individuals for advertising, promotions, and other potentially undesirable contact without individual consent.
5. Businesses
7. No. In the U.S., for example, the hope is that businesses will self-regulate due to self-interest and market pressure. Given the relative power of businesses over individuals and a sober review of history, it is unlikely that this market pressure actually exists. Laws and government agencies must exist in order to ensure that businesses actually respect individual privacy.

Chapter 13

True/False

1. b
3. a
5. a
7. b
9. b

Multiple Choice

1. c
3. a
5. d
7. b
9. d
11. b

Short Answer

1. data
3. =MAX(J3:J7)
5. range
7. relative
9. tab-delimited ASCII
11. Functions
13. MAX
15. negative number
17. Concatenate

Exercises

1. Data to store, or a formula on how to compute the information for that cell. If a cell starts with an equal sign it is a formula, otherwise it is data.
3. Many possible answers.

5. Many possible answers.
7. Many possible answers. Use formulas to store values in the computation and store intermediate results as needed.
9. Many possible answers.
11. It's faster to check a cheat sheet than to load a Web page.

Chapter 14

Multiple Choice

1. d
3. a
5. c
7. b
9. a
11. d

Short Answer

1. "what if ?"
3. Conditional formatting
5. range
7. name a range
9. scenario manager

Exercises

1. Many possible answers; consult text for an example.
3. Each shot is worth a point; one column will be number of attempts, another can be various points scored using random numbers. Use IF to exclude nonsensical entries and highlight those which have 75 percent or better averages.
5. Many possible answers.
7. Many possible answers.
9. Many possible answers.
11. Many possible answers.
13. Many possible answers.
15. Many possible answers.

Chapter 15

Multiple Choice

1. d
3. d
5. c
7. a
9. a
11. d

Short Answer

1. Metadata
3. Numbers or underscore
5. Metadata; content
7. Candidate key
9. database scheme
11. spreadsheets
13. relational database
15. affinity

Exercises

1. Many possible answers.
3. Many possible answers.
5. Many possible answers.
7. Many possible answers.
9. Many possible answers.
11. Many possible answers.

Chapter 16

Multiple Choice

1. a
3. b
5. d
7. d
9. b
11. a

Short Answer

1. Extensible Stylesheet Language
3. transformer
5. <?xml-stylesheet>
7. surround or enclose
9. XSL
11. <xsl:apply-templates/>

Exercises

1. Many possible answers; something like a class tag with a title/subject attribute that contains date and/or time tags.
3. Many possible answers.
5. Many possible answers.
7. Many possible answers; create XML tags for each kind of question, and an XSL template for each tag.

Chapter 17

Multiple Choice

1. b
3. a
5. d
7. c
9. a

11. c
13. c

Short Answer

1. semicolon
3. program
5. declaration
7. binary operators/arithmetic operators
9. Relational operators
11. concatenation
13. else
15. ambiguous

Exercises

1. “Fred” is assigned to first_name; first_name gets “Fred”.
3. It is true that they contain characters but are not surrounded by quotes, and in programming they are Boolean values.
5.

variable	value
price	undefined
taxRate	0.088
price	2.75
price	3.25
price	3.54

7.

```
var price;
var taxRate = 0.088;
if (drink == "espresso")
      price = 1.40;
if (drink == "latte" || drink == "cappuccino") {
      if (ounce == 8)
            price = 1.95;
      if (ounce == 12)
            price = 2.35;
      if (ounce == 16)
            price = 2.75;
}
if (drink == "Americano")
      price = 1.20 + .30 * (ounce/8);
if (drink == "brewed") {
      price = 1.00;
} else {
      price = price + (shots - 1) * .50;
}
price = price + price * taxRate;
```

9.

```
if (hours <= 40)
      overtime = 0;
else
      overtime = hours - 40;
```

11. 3; 0; –11
13. It assigns the value in right to the variable left.

Chapter 18

Multiple Choice

1. b
3. b
5. c
7. a

Short Answer

1. <script type="text/javascript"></script>
3. event
5. handler
7. Input
9. focus

Exercises

1. An event is an indication that something just happened; a mouse click or a key press. An event handler is a program that responds to the event.
3. One
5. Yes, there are many ways to use them.
7. The value of the tax rate at the beginning of the program.
   var tax_rate = .07;
9. There will be no output to the user until the Total button is clicked.
11. A memory location (variable) that records the size of the drink is set to “T” by the event handler, the program that responds to clicking this button.
13.

```
<form id="exercise">
Name: <input type="text" id="disp" size="30" onchange= " "/><br/>
Sex:  <input type="checkbox" name="pick1" onchange=" "/>Male
      <input type="checkbox" name="pick2" onchange=" "/>Female <br/>
Age:  <input type="radio" name="pick3" onchange=" "/>Under 20
      <input type="radio" name="pick3" onchange=" "/>20-30
      <input type="radio" name="pick3" onchange=" "/>Over 30
</form>
```

Chapter 19

Multiple Choice

1. b
3. a
5. c
7. b

Short Answer

1. Parameters
3. arguments
5. 0; 1
7. call

Exercises

1. Forgetting semicolons, not having matching curly braces, and forgetting parentheses after the function name.
3. A declaration defines the function; a call executes the code inside of a function.
5. Math.floor(7*Math.random( )). Calling the function twice could simulate two dice.
7. Many different answers.
9.
```
function calculate_wages(pay_rate,
    hours_worked){
      return pay_rate*hours_worked;
}
```

Chapter 20

Multiple Choice

1. a
3. d
5. a
7. d
9. c

Short Answer

1. Document Object Model
3. i++;
5. nested loop
7. index (or indices)
9. frame rate

Exercises

1. Combine ingredients in a bowl.

   Then, begin the loop: Check to see if thoroughly mixed. If so, stop. If not, stir. Repeat.
3. for(i=0; i<7; i++){...} *Please note: Any variable may be used.*
5.
```
for (var i=0; i < cities.length; i++) {
    myList = myList + "I have visited " + cities[i] + "\n";
    }
```
7. Multiple solutions based on the Decider.
9.
```
for(var i=0; i<7; i++){
    for( j=0; j<=i; j++){
        document.write("*");
        }
    document.write("\n");
    }
```
11.
```
if (Math.round(Math.random( )) > 0.5) {
        document.write("Low");
} else {
        document.write("High");
}
```
13. Off-by-one errors happen when code is correct except that the beginning or ending index of computation is one more or one less than the correct solution. They happen very frequently since the beginning or end of a sequential computation is a special case that is often difficult to see even when the general solution is clear. They can be avoided through testing and a rigorous consideration of the correct end points of a loop process.
15. for(var i=0; i < 10; j++) { } The loop never terminates because it tests and increments different variables.

Chapter 21

Multiple Choice

1. b
3. d
5. a
7. b
9. b

Short Answer

1. Decomposition Principle
3. subtasks
5. Animate Grid
7. animation; mouse events
9. setTimeout()

Exercises

1. The Decomposition Principle is a method for solving complex problems. The idea is to break tasks down into subtasks, and subtasks down into even more subtasks, and then complete each subtask one at a time. Then combine all the subtasks into a finished task.
3. Many possible answers.
5. The images can be specified using <img . . . width ="20px" /> tags, with a <br/> after the third.

7. The animation might hang or freeze if you have to wait to fetch the next image while the animation is in progress. Loading images can take time, something that you might not have when needing to change quickly among images.
9. onmouseover is raised by the browser when the browser detects the mouse has moved over a specific part of the page.

   onmouseout is the same in reverse: the browser raises it when the mouse leaves the specific part of the page, raising the event. If a function has been set as the handler for either of these events, code can be executed in response to the events.

Chapter 22

Multiple Choice

1. b
3. c
5. c
7. b
9. a

Short Answer

1. Deep Blue
3. experience; evaluation function
5. the Internet
7. Universality Principle
9. speed
11. Debugging themselves
13. human language

Exercises

1. Explaining about government services and humanities research, but there are many other answers.
3. Problems for which there is no algorithmic solution that can run in a reasonable time; NP-complete solutions are characterized by "brute force" approaches that search all possible solutions for the correct one.
5. Many possible answers; computers are still useful even if the semantic description for what they are really doing can be debated.
7. The Halting Problem is determining whether a program will terminate or whether it will be caught in an infinite loop on a given input. It cannot be solved in general by a computer, because an algorithm to answer the Halting Problem for any arbitrary program and input would be self-contradictory and therefore cannot exist.

Chapter 23

Multiple Choice

1. b
3. c
5. d

Short Answer

1. A heuristic method
3. heuristic
5. concept
7. Metadata
9. skills; capabilities

Exercises

1. You do not have to remember any of the information. You should use the information you learned that is relevant to your life, and through the use remembering will come easily.
3. Be rational means don't ask for help every time something goes wrong or you can't figure something out. It also means you should be open to asking for help after you have tried other ways to figure out the problem on your own. In other words, be prudent.
5. A rational, orderly approach of the sort required to find errors in code can be applied to a host of other real-world problems. Framing and testing hypotheses, questioning assumptions, and a general curiosity can help in anything from solving a math problem to choosing the best candidate for public office.
7. Apply technology when it is preferable to other solutions, evaluated broadly. Is it convenient, secure, correct, economical in a cost/benefit way, etc.?

INDEX

B

C

D

E

J

N

O

P

Q

R

S

T

U

V

W

X

Y

CREDITS

Cover

Surf Graphic illustration, without gradient fill. Photochatree / fotolia.

Chapter 1

Page 4 (top): "I have always wished for . . . " (33 words). Bjarne Stroustrup, 2011, Inventor of C++; (bottom): "It would appear that we . . . " (40 words). John von Neumann, 1947, Computer Pioneer.
Page 6 (Figure 1.2): Herman Hollerith (1860–1929), American inventor of a punch card tabulating machine for automating the 1890 U.S. Census. Everett Collection Inc / Alamy.
Page 7: Plug Board. Chris Shrigley.
Page 8 (Figure 1.4): J. Presper Eckert, foreground left, and John W. Mauchly, leaning against pole, are pictured with the Electronic Numerical Integrator and Computer (ENIAC) in this undated photo from the University of Pennsylvania Archives. UNIVERSITY OF PENNSYLVANIA / ASSOCIATED PRESS.
Page 8 (Figure 1.5a): Memory Cell Alongside Vacuum Tube, Corbis; (Figure 1.5b): Replacing a Bad Tube on the ENIAC Computer, U.S. Army / Science Source.
Page 9: Alan Turing, English Mathematician. Sherborne School / AFP.
Page 9 (Figure 1.6a): First working transistor, 1947. Science and Society / SuperStock; (Figure 1.6b): Transistor next to a vacuum tube. Corbis / SuperStock; (Figure 1.6c): Old circuit board with transistors. Ronald Sumners / Shutterstock.
Page 10 (photo labeled "Top View"): SEM of integrated circuit from Computer's. PASIEKA / SCIENCE PHOTO LIBRARY; (photo at bottom of page): Microelectronics concept, female hand, LeoSad/Fotolia.
Page 11: "There is no reason for . . . " (14 words). Ken Olsen, president of Digital Equipment Corporation.
Page 12 (Figure 1.7a): Tim Berners-Lee at CERN in Geneva, Picture Alliance / Photoshot; (Figure 1.7b) W3C (World Wide Web Consortium)
Page 16 (Figure 1.9a): the circuit board. Image courtesy of iFixit.com; (Figure 1.9b): the open case. Image courtesy of iFixit.com; (Figure 1.9c): detail of the A6. Image courtesy of Chipworks.com.

Chapter 2

Page 27: Time Machine Backup. By permission of Apple, Inc.
Page 29 (left): Abstract binary code background. Leszek Glasner / Shutterstock; (right): Illustration with zeros and ones and a flare at the center. nexus 7 / Shutterstock.
Page 30: Scanning Electron Micrograph (SEM) of the surface of a long-playing record (L.P.) showing a plan view of 10 grooves. DR. TONY BRAIN / Science Source.
Page 32 (Figure 2.2): June 15, 2012—Oslo, Norway: Aung San Suu Kyi arrives at Grand Hotel in Oslo during the first day of her visit to Oslo. Alexander Widding / Alamy.
Page 35 (Figure 2.5a): Prototype of the 1st computer mouse presented in 1968 (invented in 1963 by Douglas C. Engelbart). Apic / Contributor / Hulton Archive / Getty Images; (Figure 2.5b) Alto's 3-button mouse. Courtesy of Marcin Wichary. (Figure 2.5c): Vintage Mac Style Mouse. Aeromass / Shutterstock.
Page 36 (Figure 2.6 left to right): ARGO, Warner Bros. Pictures / Courtesy Everett Collection; DJANGO UNCHAINED, U.S. poster art. Weinstein Company / Courtesy Everett Collection; LINCOLN, U.S. poster art, Daniel Day-Lewis, as Abraham Lincoln, 2012. Touchstone Pictures / Courtesy Everett Collection; LES MISERABLES, clockwise, from top left: Russell Crowe, Hugh Jackman, Amanda Seyfried, Eddie Redmayne, Anne Hathaway, 2012. Universal Pictures / Courtesy Everett Collection; LIFE OF PI, British poster art, top and bottom: Suraj Sharma, 2012, 20th Century Fox Film Corp. All rights reserved / Courtesy Everett Collection; SKYFALL, U.S. advance poster art, Daniel Craig as James Bond, 2012. Columbia Pictures / Courtesy Everett Collection; FLIGHT, U.S. poster art, Denzel Washington, 2012. Paramount Pictures / Courtesy Everett Collection; FRANKENWEENIE, Movie poster art. Everett Collection; WAR WITCH (aka REBELLE), International poster art, from left: Serge Kanyinda, Rachel Mwanza, 2012. Metropole Films Distribution / Courtesy Everett Collection.

Chapter 3

Page 44 (top): "We've all heard that a . . . " (31 words). Robert Wilensky; (middle): "Describing the Internet as the . . . " (18 words). John Lester; (bottom): "While modern technology has given . . . " (27 words). Lee Gomes, San Jose Mercury News.
Page 46: "Country's computers linked here first." © Daily Bruin.
Page 52 (Figure 3.5): "multipoint data communication channel with collision detection." Robert Metcalfe.
Page 60 (Figure 3.10): The map of Root Name Servers and their "mirrors;" for example, there is a copy of Root K in Reykjavik, Iceland. © Google Maps. Reproduced by permission.
Page 61: 404 page. magnt, LLC.
Page 62 (Figure 3.11): Alto 2 Workstation, Core Memory Project.
Page 65 (Figure 3.13): Yellowstone Geyser Live! National Park Service.
Page 66 (Figure 3.15): Yellowstone National Park. National Park Service.

Chapter 4

Page 73: Browser tab. By permission of Apple, Inc.
Page 75: Google homepage. Courtesy of Google, Inc.
Page 76 (top): Firefox homepage. Mozilla; (margin): HTML highlighted in Notepad++. Notepad++.
Page 84 (Figure 4.5): Young woman using notebook computer. All on white background. kaarsten / Shutterstock.
Page 85 (Figure 4.6): The W3C Markup Validation Service page. W3C.
Page 87 (Figure 4.7) and page 90: Ceci n'est pas une pipe. Digital Image © 2009 Museum Associates / LACMA. Licensed by Art Resource, NY.
Page 93: W3C Validation Service. W3C.

Pages 97 (Figure 4.10), 98 (Figure 4.11), 99, 101 (Figure 4.12), 102 (Figure 4.13): "Only two things are infinite . . . " (17 words). Albert Einstein.

Pages 98 (Figure 4.11) and 102 (Figure 4.13): "The surest sign that intelligent life . . . " (20 words). Calvin and Hobbes © Watterson. Reprinted with permission of Universal Uclick. All rights reserved; "Don't worry about the world coming . . . " (16 words). Charles Shultz; "The universe started in 1970. Anyone . . . " (16 words). Randall Munroe, xkcd, http://www.xkcd.com/376/.

Page 106 (Figure 4.18): Washington skyline photo. J. Scott Applewhite / ASSOCIATED PRESS.

Chapter 5

Page 114: "With Google I'm starting to . . . " (29 words). Doug Coupland.

Page 115: "According to some accounts, they . . . " (13 words), Google; Photo: Google co-founders Larry Page (left) and Sergey Brin. MGP, Inc. / RGB Ventures LLC dba SuperStock / Alamy.

Page 116 (Figure 5.1): Green-eyed cat. Justin Black / Shutterstock.

Pages 118, 121 (Figure 5.4), 123, 124, 125: Google search results. Google.

Page 119 (Figure 5.3): Google technician working on some of the computers in The Dalles, Oregon, data center. Connie Zhou / Google / ASSOCIATED PRESS.

Page 125: Manifest art festival. Columbia College Chicago.

Page 127: Gettysburg Address. Courtesy of Chris Taylor Courtenay B.C.

Page 128: Vector colour card (paper) with various colors. Micha Klootwijk / Shutterstock.

Page 133: "Last week, Sarah Palin told . . . " (156 words). Slate.

Page 134: Car crashed against tree. Sapsiwai / Shutterstock.

Page 136 (Figure 5.7) and photo at bottom: Centre NAD, École des arts númeriques, de l'animation et du design (NAD).

Page 137: "some students still insisted vehemently . . . " (13 words). Don Leu; Figure 5.8: Manhattan Airport. Audrey Cortlandt, The Manhattan Airport Foundation.

Page 138: "... high-density areas the . . . " (24 words). The Manhattan Airport Foundation; Margin image: Contact Us. The Manhattan Airport Foundation.

Chapter 6

Page 144 (top): "One item could not be . . . " (10 words). By permission of Apple, Inc.; (bottom): "The most overlooked advantage of . . . " (23 words). Eric Porterfield.

Page 147: Computer Pioneer Grace Hopper, US Navy Permissions Dept. Academx Publishing; The Harvard Mark II logbook noting "First actual case of bug being found." U.S. Navy Permissions Dept. Academx Publishing.

Page 150 (Figure 6.2): Diagnostic message from Chrome. Google.

Page 152 (Figure 6.3): Hachette Book Group USA.

Page 152 (Figure 6.3), 153 (Figure 6.4), 157 (Figure 6.9), 159 (Figure 6.10), and 160 (Figure 6.11): Firefox. Mozilla.

Pages 152–154 (Figures 6.3–6.7), 157 (Figure 6.9), 159 (Figure 6.10), and 160 (Figure 6.11): Jackie Joyner-Kersee. Mike Powell / Hulton Archive / Getty Images, Inc.

Page 153 (Figure 6.5): The buggy page displayed with Safari 6.0. By permission of Apple, Inc.

Page 154 (Figure 6.6): The buggy page displayed with Chrome 29.0, Google; (Figure 6.7): The buggy page displayed with Internet Explorer 9.0. Microsoft.

Page 171 (photo): Vinton G. Cerf.

Pages 171–173 (interview): Vinton G. Cerf.

Chapter 7

Page 178 (top): "Most of the fundamental ideas . . . " (23 words). Albert Einstein; (bottom): "Omnibus Ex Nihilo Ducendis Sufficit . . . " (14 words). Gottfried Wilhelm Leibniz; (end first paragraph): "the dog didn't bark in the night." Sir Arthur Conan Doyle.

Page 181 (left): Coffee. Tamara Kulikova / fotolia; (right): Cola with ice cubes close up. saddako / Shutterstock.

Page 182: Comparison of cross-sections from a CD and a DVD. Encyclopaedia Britannica / UIG via Getty Images.

Page 184 (Figure 7.2a): Images of cola with ice isolated on white. Africa Studio / Shutterstock; (Figure 7.2b): Images of mugs. Pearson Higher Education.

Page 184 (bottom): Images of glasses isolated on white background. artcasta / Shutterstock; Aaron Amat / Shutterstock; Evgeny Karandaev / Shutterstock; Kesu / Shutterstock; serg_dibrova / Shutterstock.

Page 188: Postage stamp Germany 1980 Gottfried Wilhelm Leibniz. laufer/fotolia.

Page 189: Concept for struggle sign made with hands isolated on white. Lusoimages / Shutterstock.

Page 200: "We needed a word for . . . " (48 words). Quotation from conversation between author and Werner Buchholz.

Page 202: Four glasses with orange juice isolated on white. Pavel Vakhrushev / Shutterstock.

Chapter 8

Page 204 (top): "Blue color is everlastingly appointed . . . " (14 words). John Ruskin. (bottom): "Science will never be able . . . " (14 words). Dr Louis Orr speech to the American Medical Association, 6/6/1960.

Page 206: White "a" on a blue background. Jackob Riskin.

Page 207 (Figure 8.2): Pointer detail. Jackob Riskin; (margin photo): RGB triple lights that make pixels. Jackob Riskin.

Pages 212, 214 (Figure 8.7), 216, and 217 (Figure 8.11): Antique photo of a woman. Lawrence Snyder.

Pages 213 (Figure 8.6), 214 (Figure 8.8), 217 (Figure 8.10): By permission of Apple, Inc.

Page 222: Suzanne Vega. Keely Jade Dakin.

Page 223: "The Oxford English Dictionary accepts . . . " (20 words). Steve Wilhite, *New York Times* interview.

Page 224 (Figure 8.16): Lifesavers images. Lawrence Snyder.

Page 226 (Figure 8.18): Letters "a." Peter Carey West Photography.

Page 227 (top): Kurzweil with Personal Reader. Courtesy of Kurzweil Technologies, Inc.; (bottom): Kurzwail reading machine—the phone set. Courtesy of K-NFB Reading Technology, Inc.

Page 227: "It gave blind people the . . . " (15 words). Stevie Wonder.

Chapter 9

Page 236 (top): "Don't worry about people stealing . . . " (19 words). Howard Aiken; (bottom): "In their capacity as a . . . " (34 words). Edsgar Dijkstra 1972 ACM Turing Award lecture. Transcript: Dijkstra, E. W. (Aug. 1972), "The Humble Programmer," *Communications of the ACM* 15(10): 859–866. doi:10.1145/355604.361591. (EWD340).

Page 241 (central photo): Elizabeth Jean Jennings and Frances Bilas preparing for the public unveiling of ENIAC. U.S. Army Photo.

Page 247 (clockwise from top left) J. Presper Eckert and John Mauchly. John W. Mauchly Papers, Rare Book & Manuscript Library, University of Pennsylvania; John V. Atanasoff. Courtesy University Archives, Iowa State University Library; Clifford E. Berry. Iowa State University, Special Collections Department; Alan M. Turing. Science Source; Tommy Flowers. UPPA / Photoshot; Konrad Zuse. Gerten / DPA / Landov.

Page 259 (top): Jack Kilby with lab journal. Courtesy Texas Instruments; (bottom): Kilby's first integrated circuit. Courtesy Texas Instruments.

Page 239 (Figure 9.1): Program in C#. Microsoft.

Page 257: "a seminal event of postwar . . . " (14 words). T. R. Reid, *The Chip*.

Chapter 10

Page 270 (top): "The most beautiful thing we . . . " (20 words). Albert Einstein, 1930, as quoted from Introduction to Philosophy (1935) by George Thomas White Patrick and Frank Miller Chapman; (bottom): "We are faced with insurmountable opportunity." Walt Kelly (Pogo), 1970.

Page 271 (Figure 10.1): Photo of Jean-Dominique Bauby and nurse. Estate of Jeanloup Sieff.

Page 272 (Figure 10.2): MARIE-JOSEE CROZE THE DIVING BELL AND THE BUTTERFLY; LE SCAPHANDRE ET LE PAPILLON (2007). AF archive / Alamy.
Page 276: Vintage soviet stamp, "Muhammad ibn Musa al-Khwarizmi." Juulijs/fotolia.
Page 279 (Figure 10.4): Figure 4. Google Query Evaluation. Sergey Brin and Lawrence Page, The Anatomy of a Large-Scale Hypertextual Web Search Engine.
Page 284: Marching Band. *LA Times*.
Page 288 (photo): Ray Kurzweil.
Pages 288–291 (interview): Ray Kurzweil.

Chapter 11

Page 296 (top): "I hear that a new . . . " (22 words). Admiral John Fisher to Churchill, 1917, The earliest use of OMG; (bottom): "No matter how well you . . . " (17 words), Don Rittner.
Page 297 (Figure 11.1): Cockpit image from NASA's Be a Martian welcome page, beamartian.jpl.nasa.gov/welcome. NASA Jet Propulsion Laboratory, NASA.
Page 298 (Figure 11.2): Foldit video game. Firas Khatib, Frank DiMaio, Foldit Contenders Group, Foldit Void Crushers Group, Seth Cooper, Maciej Kazmierczyk, *Nature Structural and Molecular Biology* Vol. 18, Issue 10, Nature Publishing Group, Sept. 18, 2011; (quote middle of page): "Following the failure of a . . . " (68 words). *Nature Structural and Molecular Biology* Vol. 18, Issue 10, Nature Publishing Group, Sept. 18, 2011; (margin image bottom of page): Freerice.com.
Page 299 (Figure 11.3): Kickstarter screenshots. Kickstarter. Out of Nothing, LLC. Courtesy of Megan Rose Gedris.
Page 302 (top): Typographical Art image. Puck Magazine, 1881; (bottom): E-mail. Scott Fahlman.
Page 303 (Figure 11.4): Portion of the policies page at www.css-discuss.org/policies.html. CSS-Discuss.org.
Page 310 (Figure 11.5): Beginning of a typical "Nigerian Widow" scam email. Anonymous.
Page 312 (Figure 11.6): Recent variation of the "Advanced Fee Fraud" claiming the recipient is a lottery winner. Anonymous.
Page 313 (Figure 11.7): Request for personal identification to complete a shipment from Ghana. Anonymous.
Page 314 (Figure 11.8): Phishing scam claiming to be validating email accounts against a phishing scam. Anonymous; (Figure 11.9): Example of a fraudulent email phishing attempt claiming to be from the U.S. Internal Revenue Service. Anonymous.
Page 318: "Open the pod bay doors, HAL." *2001: A Space Odyssey*.
Pages 320 and 321: Creative Commons symbology.

Chapter 12

Page 328 (top): "I've never looked through a . . . " (12 words). Judy Garland, commenting on her lack of privacy, 1967 Interview, NBC TV (16 March 1961).
Page 329: "The [original] narrower doctrine may . . . " (144 words). Warren and Brandeis, Harvard Law Review, 1890.
Page 333 (Figure 12.1): Comparison of privacy and data protections by country. © 2013 Forrester Research. All rights reserved.
Page 337: Firefox, Mozilla.
Page 344: Mythos Troja at Glyptothek Museum Konigsplatz Munich Germany. Pat Behnke / Alamy.
Page 353 (left): Switzerland 10 Franc Bank Note. Glyn Thomas / Alamy; (right): Leonhard Euler, rook76 / Deposit Photo.
Page 339 (Figure 12.2): Retention periods for information held by cellular phone providers. Data gathered by the Computer Crime and Intellectual Property Section, U.S. Department of Justice.
Page 341: "ChoicePoint, which recently admitted it . . . " (28 words). Electronic Privacy Information Center.
Page 345: "Adware such as iLivid wreaked . . . " (53 words). Electronic Privacy Information Center.

Chapter 13

Page 364 (top): "The purpose of computing is insight, not numbers." (1961) and "The purpose of computing numbers is not yet in sight." (1997). Richard W. Hamming, From the author's 1997 book, "The Art of Doing Science and Engineering: Learning to Learn"? (ISBN 90-5699-501-4), p.22.
Pages 365–377, 379–384, 386–389: Microsoft Excel screenshots. Microsoft.
Page 381: A Pepperoni pizza on a white background. Mike Flippo / Shutterstock.
Page 386 (Figure 13.8): Bus schedule. Screenshot copyright © 2007 by King County Metro Transit. Reprinted with permission of King County Metro Transit.

Chapter 14

Page 396 (top): "Informed decision-making comes from a . . . " (16 words). Scott Adams. http://www.ocsea.net/2010/11/good-decision-making/.
Page 397: Welcome to Saskatchewan, Canada sign. Dennis Macdonald / Photolibrary / Getty Images, Inc.
Page 398 (Figure 14.1): Google map directions for a trip from Chicago, Illinois (A pin) to Fort McPherson, Northwest Territories (B pin). Google.
Pages 399–403, 405–408, and 410–418: Microsoft Excel screenshots. Microsoft.
Page 400: Welcome to Alberta, Canada sign. Dennis Macdonald / Photolibrary / Getty Images, Inc.
Page 405: Welcome to the Yukon Territory, Canada sign. Mark Herreid / Shutterstock.
Page 408: Welcome to the Northwest Territories, Canada sign. Cliff LeSergent / Alamy.
Page 411: Dempster Highway sign, Yukon, Canada. Gary Cook / Alamy.
Page 412: Snowy Arctic Circle sign. Mike Theiss / National Geographic / Getty Images, Inc.
Page 415: A sign at the beginning of the Arctic Circle on the Dempster Highway. Mike Theiss / National Geographic / Getty Images, Inc.
Page 419 (Figure 14.16 top left): Polarkreis. osnapicture / fotolia; (top right): Sunset at midnight over the Yukon River, near Dawson City, Yukon, Canada. John E Marriott / All Canada Photos / Getty Images, Etc.; (bottom left): A sow and cub grizzly bear. Ron Niebrugge / Alamy; (bottom right): Houses on Front Street, Dawson City, Yukon, Yves Marcoux / First Light / Getty Images, Etc.

Chapter 15

Page 424 (top): "Computers are useless. They only give answers." Pablo Picasso, http://quoteinvestigator.com/2011/11/05/computers-useless/; (bottom): "Now that we have all . . . " (43 words). Unix Programmer's Manual, http://plan9.bell-labs.com/7thEdMan/index.html.
Pages 425 and 426: Microsoft Excel screenshots. Microsoft.
Page 427: Moorea. Kristine T. Pham Photography / Flickr / Getty Images, Inc.
Pages 433 (Figure 15.4), 435–445 (including Figures 15.5–15.14), and 448 (Figures 15.15 and 15.16): Microsoft Access screenshots. Microsoft.
Page 435: Pod of orcas. Michael Nolan / AGE Fotostock.
Page 430: Firefox error message. Mozilla.

Chapter 16

Page 456: "For a list of all . . . " (19 words). Alice Kahn.
Page 459 (Figure 16.1a top): Atlas Human-Powered Helicopter—AHS Sikorsky Prize Flight (AeroVelo). By permission of AeroVelo Inc.; (bottom): Natasha Trethewey, "Vespertina Cognitio" from Thrall, Houghton Mifflin Harcourt, 2012.
Page 460 (Figure 16.1b top): NASA image. NASA; (bottom left): Henrietta Lacks (1920–1951). NYPL / Science Source / Getty Images, Etc.; (bottom right): HeLa cells, light micrograph. Thomas Deerinck, NCMIR / Science Source.
Pages 461 (Figure 16.2), 462 (Figure 16.3), 469, 471, and 472 (Figure 16.9): Firefox screenshots. Mozilla.

Page 477 (Figure 16.11): Accessing embedding information at YouTube, Google; Atlas Human-Powered Helicopter—AHS Sikorsky Prize Flight (AeroVelo). By permission of AeroVelo Inc.
Page 483 (photo): Alan Kay.
Pages 483–485 (interview): Alan Kay.

Chapter 17

Page 490: "Everything is vague to a . . . " (18 words). Bertrand Russell, from "The Philosophy of Logical Atomism" lectures of 1918.
Page 491: "[Computers] couldn't think in the . . . " (119 words), Bertrand Russell.
Page 492: Cup of cappuccino. PhotoBarmaley / Shutterstock.
Page 496: Declaration of Independence 1776. National Archives.
Pages 503 (Figure 17.2), 504, and 510–512 (including Figure 17.3): Firefox screenshots. Mozilla.

Chapter 18

Page 522: "Programming today is a race . . . " (32 words). Rich Cook from "The Philosophy of Logical Atomism" lectures of 1918.
Pages 524 (Figures 18.1b and 18.2), 536 (including Figure 18.6), and 537 (Figure 18.7): Firefox screenshots. Mozilla.

Chapter 19

Page 544: "Civilization advances by extending the . . . " (17 words). Alfred North Whitehead.
Pages 545, 547–553 (including Figures 19.2 and 19.3), 555 (Figure 19.4), 557 (Figure 19.6), 558 (Figure 19.7), 560–562 (including Figures 19.9 and 19.11), 565 (Figure 19.13), 566–568 (including Figures 19.14–19.17), and 571: Firefox screenshots. Mozilla.
Page 550: "Anyone who attempts to generate . . . " (19 words). John von Neumann.
Pages 556, 557 (Figure 19.6), and 562 (Figure 19.10 upper right): New Golden Dollar Coin, Thursday, Nov. 18, 1999, in Philadelphia, Pa. Designed by American sculptor Glenna Goodacre. U.S. Mint / ASSOCIATED PRESS.
Page 559 (Figure 19.8): Phone app. Lawrence Snyder.
Page 562 (Figure 19.10): Phone apps. Lawrence Snyder; (Figure 19.10 lower left): 8-ball. Pearson Higher Education.
Pages 567 (Figure 19.15) and 569: Trio of emperor penguins surrounded by chicks on the frozen Ross Sea. Paul Nicklen / Getty Images.
Page 571: Closeup of hand isolated on white. Jeff Banke / Shutterstock.

Chapter 20

Pages 579, 580, 582–587 (including Figures 20.1–20.4), 589–592 (including Figure 20.5), 597 (Figure 20.8), and 600–601: Firefox screenshots. Mozilla.
Page 584 (left): Google Maps. Google; (right): Apple sign photo. Lawrence Snyder.
Page 587 (Figure 20.4 right): New Golden Dollar Coin, Thursday, Nov. 18, 1999, in Philadelphia, Pa. Designed by American sculptor Glenna Goodacre. U.S. Mint / ASSOCIATED PRESS.
Page 591 (Figure 20.5): 8-ball. Pearson Higher Education.
Page 598 (Figure 20.9): Phone images. Lawence Snyder; Closeup of hand isolated on white. Jeff Banke / Shutterstock.

Chapter 21

Page 606: "If it keeps up, man . . . " (14 words). Frank Lloyd Wright.
Pages 607 (Figure 21.1), 612 (Figure 21.3), 617 (Figure 21.6), and 621 (Figure 21.7): Firefox screenshots. Mozilla.

Chapter 22

Page 630 (top): "The real danger is not . . . " (22 words). Sydney J. Harris; (bottom): "Some people worry that artificial . . . " (30 words). Alan Kay.
Page 632: "Judge: In the first line . . . " (117 words). Vol. LIX (236): 433–460, (1950) A. M. TURING. I.—COMPUTING MACHINERY AND INTELLIGENCE. Reproduced by permission.
Page 633: Alan M. Turing. Science Source.
Page 639 (Figure 22.3): IBM's Watson made television history on February 16, 2011, by winning the first-ever "Jeopardy!" man vs. machine competition. "Jeopardy!" Courtesy Sony Pictures Television; (Figure 22.4): The logic of Watson, David Ferrucci et al. [2011], "Building Watson: An Overview of the DeepQA Project," AI Magazine, 31:3, www.aaai.org/ojs/index.php/aimagazine/article/view/2303.
Page 641 (Figure 22.5): Frequency (in 20,000 questions) of the top 40 "lexical answer types," and (inset) the plot of the 200 most frequent. Notice that the top 200 account for fewer than half of the questions. Association for the Advancement of Artificial Intelligence.
Page 642: "The question of whether a . . . " (21 words). Edsger Dijkstra.
Page 643 (Figure 22.6a): Graphic design suggestive of the style of Piet Mondrian (find programs on the Web by searching mondrian AND java). Lawrence Snyder; (Figure 22.6b): Graphic design suggestive of the style of Jackson Pollock (go to www.jacksonpollock.org, and move and click the mouse). Based on http://www.openprocessing.org/sketch/38979. Lawrence Snyder.

Chapter 23

Page 664 (photo): David Ferrucci.
Pages 664–667 (interview): David Ferrucci.

Appendix F

Pages 699–705: Firefox screenshots. Mozilla.
Pages 703 and 704: New Golden Dollar Coin, Thursday, Nov. 18, 1999, in Philadelphia, Pa. Designed by American sculptor Glenna Goodacre. U.S. Mint / ASSOCIATED PRESS.
Page 704: Closeup of hands isolated on white. Jeff Banke / Shutterstock.
Pages 705 and 706: 8-ball. Pearson Higher Education.

Bookwide